济南统计年鉴

JINAN STATISTICAL YEARBOOK

2019

（总第37期 NO.37）

济 南 市 统 计 局
国家统计局济南调查队 编

Jinan Municipal Bureau of Statistics
NBS Survey Office In Jinan

图书在版编目（CIP）数据

济南统计年鉴. 2019/ 济南市统计局，国家统计局济南调查队编.
——北京：中国统计出版社，2019.9
ISBN 978-7-5037-8947-2
Ⅰ. ①济…
Ⅱ. ①济… ②国…
Ⅲ. ①统计资料－济南市－2019－年鉴
Ⅳ. ①C832.521-54

中国版本图书馆CIP 数据核字（2019）第183087号

济南统计年鉴—2019

作　　者/ 济南市统计局　国家统计局济南调查队
责任编辑/ 钟　钰　朱立峰
装帧设计/ 济南市政府机关文印中心
出版发行/ 中国统计出版社有限公司
地　　址/ 北京市丰台区西三环南路甲6号
邮政编码/ 100073
电　　话/ 邮购（010）63376909　书店（010）68783171
网　　址/ http://www.zgtjcbs.com
印　　刷/ 济南市政府机关文印中心
经　　销/ 新华书店
开　　本/ 890mm×1240mm　1/16
字　　数/ 259千字
印　　张/ 35
版　　别/ 2019年9月第1版
版　　次/ 2019年9月第1次印刷
定　　价/ 320.00元

如有印装差错，由本社发行部调换。

《济南统计年鉴－2019》
编辑委员会及编辑工作人员

编辑委员会

编辑工作人员

Jinan Statistical Yearbook-2019
Editorial Board and Editorial Staff

编 辑 说 明

一、《济南统计年鉴－2019》是一部全面反映济南市国民经济和社会发展情况的资料性统计年刊。本书收录了济南市及所辖县、区2018年经济和社会发展各方面大量的统计数据，以及历史重要年份的主要统计数据，是认识和研究济南市情、经济和社会发展，制定宏观政策、指导工作的重要工具书。

二、本年鉴以丰富、翔实的统计资料为主，辅以直观的统计图、特载，全面反映了济南市国民经济和社会发展状况。全书统计资料共分为二十三个部分，即：1. 行政区划；2. 人口；3. 综合；4. 国民经济核算；5. 劳动就业；6. 固定资产投资；7. 城市公用事业和环境保护；8. 财政和金融保险；9. 物价；10. 人民生活；11. 农业；12. 工业；13. 建筑业；14. 运输与邮电；15. 国内贸易；16. 对外贸易与国际旅游；17. 科技；18. 教育与文化；19. 体育与卫生；20. 民政、司法和其它；21. 原莱芜市主要经济指标；特载和附录。各篇末附有《主要统计指标解释》，对主要统计指标的含义、统计范围、统计方法以及历史变动情况作了简要说明。

三、本年鉴中使用的度量衡均采用国际统一标准计量单位，统计口径除特别注明外，均包括济南市区、平阴县、商河县。资料取自济南市统计局、国家统计局济南调查队及有关部门的统计报表。

四、本年鉴中部分数据合计数或相对数由于计量单位取舍不同而产生的计算误差，均未做机械调整。

五、本年鉴表中的符号使用说明：

“空格”表示该项统计指标数据不足本表最小单位数、数据不详或无该项数据；

“–”表示无此项事实；

“#”表示其中的主要项；

“*”或“①”表示本表下有注解。

《济南统计年鉴》自出版以来，受到了社会各界的关心和支持，对此我们深表感谢。同时，欢迎使用《济南统计年鉴－2019》，敬请广大读者提出宝贵意见，帮助我们进一步提高统计年鉴编辑工作，更好的为社会各界服务，谢谢!（网址：http://jntj.jinan.gov.cn/）

编 者

2019 年 9 月

EDITOR'S NOTES

Ⅰ. *Jinan Statistical Yearbook-2019* is a statistical reference book published yearly that comprehensively reflects the development of Jinan' s national economy and society. With a vast amount of statistical data on various aspects of economic and social development in Jinan and the counties and districts under its jurisdiction in 2018, as well as the main s tatistical data of important historical years, the yearbook is an important reference book for people to understand and study Jinan and its economic and social development, for government to formulate macro policies and guidance work.

Ⅱ. The yearbook is centered on rich and detailed statistical data with intuitive statistical charts and special articles added, comprehensively reflecting Jinan' s economic and social development. Statistical data of the yearbook contains 23 parts, namely:1. Division of Administrative Areas;2. Population;3. General Survey;4. National Accounts;5. Labor and Employment;6. Investment in Fixed Assets;7. Urban Public Utilities and Environmental Protection;8. Government Finance and Financial Insurance;9. Prices;10. People's Livelihood;11.Agriculture;12. Industry;13. Construction;14. Transportation, Post and Telecommunications;15. Domestic Trade;16. Foreign trade and International Tourism;17. Science and Technology;18. Education and Culture;19. Sports and Public Health;20. Social Welfare Civil Administration and Justice; 21. Main Economic Indicators of the Original Laiwu City; Special Published and Appendices. We edit *Exploratory Notes on Main statistical Indicators* at the end of every article, briefly explaining the meaning, statistical scope, methods and historical changes of the main statistical indicators.

Ⅲ. The units of measurement used in this yearbook are internationally unified and standard measurement units. The statistical caliber includes Jinan City, Pingyin County and Shanghe County unless otherwise noted. The data in this yearbook are from the statistical reports of Jinan Municipal Bureau of Statistics, Jinan Investigation Team of National Bureau of Statistics and relevant departments.

Ⅳ. The statistical discrepancies caused by the unit of measurement in the total or relative numbers of some data in this yearbook are not adjusted.

Ⅴ. Notations used in this yearbook:

"Blank Space" indicates that the statistical index data is not large enough to be measured with the smallest unit in this table, or data are unknown or not available;

"–" means that there is no such fact;

"#" indicates the main item;

"*" or "①" means there are annotations in this table.

Since its publication, *Jinan Statistical Yearbook* has received the concern and support of all sectors of society, for which we are deeply grateful. At the same time, welcome to use *Jinan Statistical Yearbook-2019* and offer valuable suggestions, so as to help us further improve the editing of statistical yearbooks and better serve all sectors of society, thank you! (Website: http://jntj.jinan.gov.cn/)

Editor

September 2019

目　录

特载　Special Report

一　行政区划　Divisions of Administrative Areas

二　人　口　Population

三　综　合　General Survey

四 国民经济核算 National Accounts

五 劳动就业 Labor and employment

六 固定资产投资 Investment in Fixed Assets

七　城市公用事业和环境保护

Urban Public Unilities and Environmental Protection

八　财政和金融保险　Government Finance and Financial Insurance

九　物　价　Price

十 人民生活 People's Livelihood

十一 农 业 Agriculture

十二 工 业 Industry

十三 建筑业 Construction

十四 运输与邮电 Transportation Post and Telecommunication

十五 国内贸易 Domestic Trade

十六 对外贸易与国际旅游 Foreign Trade and International Tourism

十七 科技 Science and Technology

十八　教育与文化　Education and Culture

十九　体育与卫生　Sports and Public Health

二十　民政、司法和其它
Social Welfare Civil Administration and Others

二十一　原莱芜市主要经济指标
Main Economic Indicators of The Original Laiwu City

附 录 Appendix

特　载

SPECIAL REPORT

特载-1

济南概况

济南市位于山东省中部，地理位置介于北纬36°01′至37°32′、东经116°11′至117°44′之间，面积7998平方公里。南部为泰山山地，北部为黄河平原，地势南高北低，地形复杂多样。境内河流较多，主要有黄河、小清河两大水系。还有南北大沙河、玉符河等河流。湖泊有大明湖、白云湖等。济南属于暖温带大陆性气候，春季干燥少雨，多西南风；夏季炎热多雨；秋季天高气爽；冬季严寒干燥，多东北风。年平均气温13.5℃−15.5℃，全年无霜期230天左右，降水量600−900毫米。

济南矿产资源丰富，主要有铁、煤、花岗石、耐火粘土以及铜、钾、铂、钴等多种有色金属、稀有金属和非金属。特别是石灰岩品位高、储量大。花岗石中的黑色花岗石，质地纯正，为国内独有。林木资源分乔木、灌木两大类，共有60多科300多种。南部山区盛产苹果、黄梨、柿子、核桃、山楂、板栗等，并产有远志、丹参、野菊、香附等多种药材。北部沿黄河的平原地带，大枣也有很高的产量。济南种植和养殖资源也相当丰富，有多种粮食作物、经济作物以及家禽、家畜、水产品等。这些资源为济南城乡建设和经济发展储备了一定的物质基础。

济南自然景色秀丽，名胜古迹众多，是中国历史文化名城之一。尤以泉水遍布、清冽甘美而闻名于世，有“济南泉水甲天下”和“泉城”之美誉。主要风景名胜有趵突泉、黑虎泉、珍珠泉、五龙潭、百脉泉五大泉群，大明湖、千佛山、龙洞、灵岩寺、五峰山、华山、城子崖龙山文化遗址、孝堂山汉代郭氏祠、隋代四门塔、唐代龙虎塔、九顶塔以及抢救挖掘的洛庄汉墓、新建的野生动物世界、红叶谷生态旅游区等供人们观赏游览。

济南现在共辖历下、市中、槐荫、天桥、历城、长清、章丘、济阳八区和平阴、商河二县。2018年，全市地区生产总值7856.6亿元，比上年增长7.4%。年末全市常住人口746.04万人，户籍总人口655.90万人。济南又是一个多民族聚居的城市，除汉族外，主要有回、满、苗、蒙古、壮、朝鲜等53个少数民族。

济南是一座有着悠久历史的古城。据史学家考证，早在公元前45世纪之前，已有人类在此繁衍、生息。传说东夷族的首领舜，曾躬耕于济南历山（今千佛山）之下。2600多年前，就建有城郭，最早出现史册上的名称为“泺”（《春秋左传》），系因济南诸泉汇为泺水，故名。春秋战国时代，济南为齐国之泺邑。随后，齐国又把泺邑改为历下。2100多年前的汉代改称济南（《史记》），因处于济水之南，故名。公元前164年设立济南国。公元前154年又废国改郡。到了宋代至道三年（公元997年），分全国为15路，济南属京东路，为齐州（《宋史》）。徽宗政和六年（公元1116年），齐州升为济南府，辖历城等五县，治所设历城，为府治之始。自明代以来，一直是山东省的省会。1929年7月设济南市至今。1928年4月至1937年底，日本帝国主义先后二次侵占了济南，济南人民深受暴虐的民族压迫和经济掠夺，致使大部分工厂倒闭，无辜同胞惨遭杀戮。1945年8月，日寇投降后，国民党反动派又进行强盗式的劫收，城市又遭到了摧残蹂躏，民生凋敝，物价飞涨，古城一片萧条。1948年9月24日，济南获得解放，这座古城终于回到了人民的怀抱，开始了她新的历史时期。

新中国建立后，济南市始终是中国东部沿海经济大省—山东省省会。是全国副省级城市之一，环渤海地区南翼的中心城市，是全省的政治、文化、教育、经济、交通和科技中心，是山东半岛城市群和济南都市圈核心城市。2017年；荣膺“全国文明城市”称号，跨入全国文明城市行列。济南是全国区域性金融中心，2018年年末金融机构本外币各项存款余额达17060.1亿元，各项贷款余额16059.9亿元。

济南是山东省铁路、公路、航空的交通枢纽，京沪、胶济铁路在市区交汇，北连北京、天津，南接南京、上海、福州，东达港口城市青岛、烟台。济南为京沪高铁沿线5个始发终到站之 。济南机场是经国家批准的国际空港，有通往香港、北京、哈尔滨、上海、广州、深圳、福州、厦门、西安、武汉、珠海、海口等城市的182条空中航线，通航城市96个。“济青高速”“济聊高速”与“京福高速”在济南交汇，从而形成了辐射全省、连接全国的高速公路系统省内中心、全国区域性枢纽的格局。济南基本形成了铁路、航空、公路立体构造，联结全省、全国和海外的现代交通网络。

Introduction of Jinan

Jinan is located in the middle of Shandong Province with an area of 7998 km^2. The geographic position of it is between 36° 01′ N ~ 37° 32′ N and 116° 11′ E ~ 117° 44′ E with the Mount Tai land in the south and Yellow River plain in the north. The terrain in the south is higher than that in the north and is complex and diverse. Jinan mainly enjoys the Yellow River, Xiaoqinghe River two major river systems. There are also rivers, such as the North-South Dasha River and Yufuhe River, etc. within the border. The lakes here are Daming Lake, Baiyun Lake, etc. Jinan has the warm temperate continental climate. Dry and rainless in spring, and southwest wind is prevailing; hot and rainy in summer; the sky is high and the weather is fine in autumn; cold and dry in winter, the northeast wind is always prevailing. The annual average temperature is 13.5℃-15.5℃, the frost-free period all year round is about 230 days and the amount of precipitation is 600~900mm.

Jinan has abundant mineral resources, mainly including various non-ferrous metals, rare metals and non-metals, such as the iron, coal, granite, fire clay and copper, kalium, platinum and cobalt, etc. In particular, the limestone has large reserves with high grade. The texture of black granite pure and unique in China. The forest resources are divided into the arbor and shrub and there are more than 300 varieties of more than 60 families in total. The apple, yellow pear, persimmon, walnut, hawthorn and Chinese chestnut, etc. are rich and the polygala tenuifolia, Salvia, chrysanthemum indicum and rhizoma cyperi, etc. medicinal materials are produced in the southern mountain area. The output of Chinese-date is very high in the flat-bottomed land along the Yellow River in the north. Jinan has rather abundant planting and breeding resources with various grain crops, economic crops and poultry, livestock and aquatic products, etc. These resources reserve a certain of material basis for the urban and rural development and economic development of Jinan.

As one of China's famous historical and cultural cities, Jinan has beautiful natural scenery and many scenic spots and historical sites. It is especially famous for clear and luscious springs and enjoys good reputations of "Jinan Springs Are the Best in the World" and "Spring City". The main scenic spots are Baotu Spring, Heihu Spring, Pearl Spring, Five Dragon Pool, Five Groups of Baimai Spring, Daming Lake, Qianfo Mountain, Dragon Cave, Lingyan Temple, Five Mountain, Mount Hua, Chengziya Longshan Cultural Site, Stone Memorial Hall at Guos' Temple on Xiaotang Mountain, Sui Dynasty Pagoda of Four Gates, Tang Dynasty Dragon Tiger Tower, Jiuding Tower and Luozhuang Han Tombs through rescue and excavation, newly-built Wildlife World and Red Leaves Canyon, etc. for viewing and sightseeing.

Now, Jinan administers eight districts of Lixia, Shizhong, Huaiyin, Tianqiao, Licheng, Changqing, Zhangqiu and Jiyang and two counties of Pingyin and Shanghe. In 2018, local GDP of Jinan city reached RMB 785.66 billion, with an increase of 7.4 % over that of the previous year; The permanent resident population of the whole city at the end of the year was 7.4604 million and the total registered population was 6.559 million. Jinan is a city inhabited by multiple nationalities which mainly include 53 ethnic minorities, such as Hui, Man, Miao, Mongol, Zhuang and Korean, etc., in addition to Han.

Jinan is a city with a long history. According to the historians textual research, human beings had lived here long before 45th Century B.C. Legend has it that Shun, the leader of Dongyi Tribal Groups, farmed at the foot of Mount Li once(Qianfo Mountain today). More than 2600 years ago, the city walls had been built. It was named as "Luo" first appeared in history annals (*Zuo's Commentary*). Because Jinan springs converge to the Luoshui River, hence the name. Jinan was Luoyi of the State of Qi in the warring state period. Later, it was named as Lixia by the State. Lixia was changed into Jinan (*Records of the Historian*) in Han Dynasty more than 2100 years ago. Because it was located in the south of Ji Shui, hence the name. The State of Jinan was set up in 164 B.C. Then it was changed into the County of Jinan in 154 B.C. The whole state was divided into 15 regions in Emperor Taizong Zhidao Sannian (997 A.D.), Jinan belonged to Jingdong Region, named Qizhou (*History of the Song Dynasty*). Qizhou was promoted to Jinan Palace in Emperor Huizong Zhenghe Liunian (1116 A.D.), governing five countries of Licheng, etc. with the seat in Licheng. It is the provincial capital of Shandong Province all the time since the Ming Dynasty. Jinan City was set up in Jul. 1929 to this day. The Japanese imperialist successively occupied Jinan for two times at the end of Apr. 1928 to 1937. Jinan people are deeply influenced by tyrannical national oppression economic plundering. Most of the factories closed down and innocent compatriots are massacred in cold blood. In Aug. 1945, KMT reactionaries took over the city like bandits upon surrender of Japanese aggressors. The city was destroyed and devastated again. The people live in destitution, the prices are soaring and the city was in the great depression. On Sep. 24, 1948, Jinan was liberated and finally returned to the people's arms, starting her new historical period.

Jinan is still the provincial capital of Shandong Province which is the coastal economic big province of East China after the founding of new China. It is one of sub-provincial cities around the country, central city of Circum-Bohai Sea Region South Wing, the center of the whole Province in politics, culture, education, economics, transportation and science and technology and the core city of Shandong Peninsula Urban Agglomerations and Jinan Metropolitan Circle. In 2017, it was awarded as the title of "National Civilized City" and stepped into the national civilized city list. Jinan is the regional financial center around the country. The outstanding of deposits of local and foreign currencies for the financial institutions at the end of 2018 was RMB 1.70601 trillion and the loan balance was RMB 1.60599 trillion.

It is the transportation junction of Shandong railway, highway and aviation. Beijing-Shanghai Railway and Jiaozhou-Jinan Railway converge at the city, connecting Beijing and Tianjin in the north, Nanjing, Shanghai and Fuzhou in the South and port cities of Qingdao and Yantai in the east. Jinan is one of 5 starting-terminating stations along Beijing-Shanghai High-Speed Railway. Jinan Airport is an international airport which is approved by our country with 182 airways leading to Hong Kong, Beijing, Harbin, Shanghai, Guangzhou, Shenzhen, Fuzhou, Xiamen, Xi'an, Wuhan, Zhuhai and Haikou, etc. and 96 destinations. "Jinan-Qingdao Expressway", "Jinan-Liaocheng-Handan Expressway" and "Beijing-Taibei Expressway" converge at Jinan, thus forming the provincial central and national regional hub pattern of expressway system which radiates the whole province and connects the whole nation. Jinan basically forms the stereometric structure of railway, aviation and highway and modern traffic network that connects the whole province, the whole nation and foreign countries.

2018年济南市 国民经济和社会发展统计公报[1]

济　南　市　统　计　局
国家统计局济南调查队

2018年，在市委市政府坚强领导下，全市上下以习近平新时代中国特色社会主义思想为指导，全面贯彻党的十九大和十九届二中、三中全会精神，坚持稳中求进工作总基调，坚定践行新发展理念，着力推动高质量发展，以供给侧结构性改革为主线，围绕加快打造“四个中心”、建设“大强美富通”现代化国际大都市，砥砺奋进，顽强拼搏，经济综合实力显著增强，产业转型升级加速推进，质量效益持续提升，创新驱动能力持续增强，城市形象持续改善提升，改革开放力度持续加大，民生保障持续加快改善，开创了省会经济社会发展新局面。

一、综　合

经济运行稳中有进。初步核算，全年全市地区生产总值[2]7856.56亿元，比上年增长7.4%。其中，第一产业增加值272.42亿元，增长2.5%；第二产业增加值2829.31亿元，增长7.8%；第三产业增加值4754.83亿元，增长7.5%。三次产业构成为3.5：36.0：60.5。人均地区生产总值[3]106302元，增长5.7%，按年均汇率折算为16064美元。

人口保持平稳增长。年末常住人口746.04万人，比上年末增长1.90%。户籍人口655.90万人，增长1.91%。申报出生率14.57‰，申报死亡率6.98‰，人口自然增长率7.59‰。

就业保持良好态势。全年新增城镇就业18.95万人，年末城镇登记失业率2.06%。

物价水平温和上涨。全年居民消费价格上涨2.6%，其中，食品烟酒类价格上涨3.2%。工业生产者出厂价格上涨4.8%，工业生产者购进价格上涨8.3%。

2018年居民消费价格指数（以上年同期为100）

指　标	全市
居民消费价格指数	102.6
#食品烟酒	103.2
衣着	103.8
居住	103.5
生活用品及服务	100.6
交通和通信	102.1
教育文化和娱乐	99.6
医疗保健	104.7
其他用品和服务	99.6

2018年工业生产者生产价格指数（%）

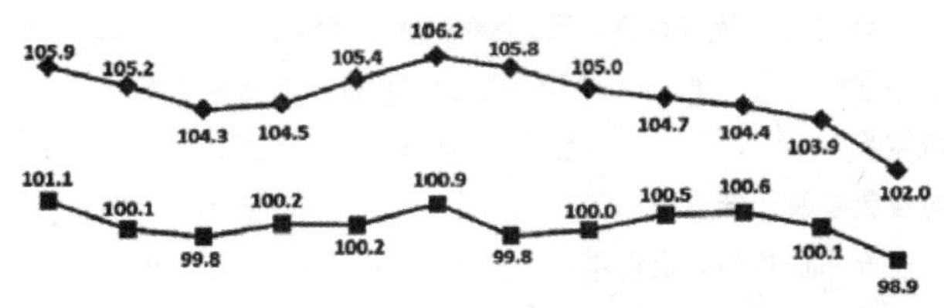

2018年工业生产者购进价格指数（%）

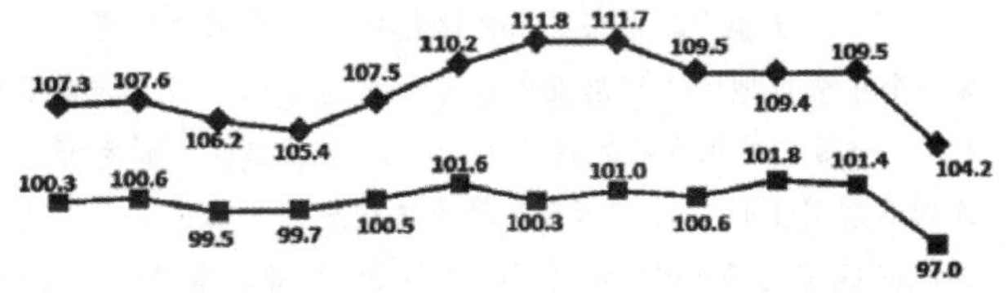

新建住宅销售价格指数环比涨幅基本保持稳定。

2018年新建住宅销售价格指数（%）

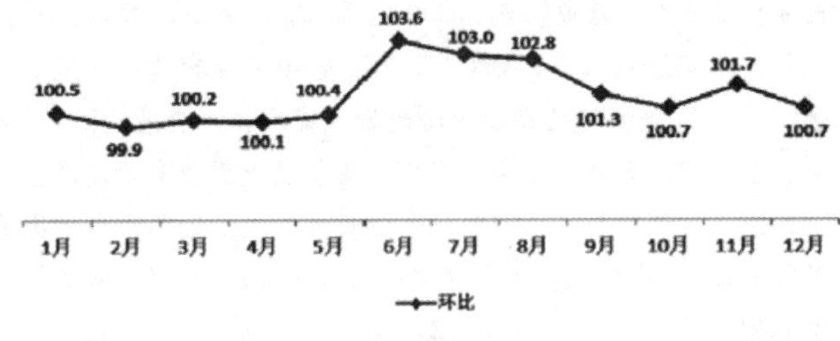

现代服务业[4]增速较快。全年现代服务业实现增加值2767.38亿元，增长12.8%，占服务业比重为58.2%。

非公有经济稳定发展。全年非公有经济增加值3237.50亿元，增长3.6%，占GDP比重为41.2%。其中，民营经济增加值2833.58亿元，增长3.7%，占GDP比重为36.1%。

重点改革成效显著。深入实施“三去一降一补”，加快东部老工业区搬迁改造，新搬迁改造或关停腾退企业10家，累计完成66家。全面实施“一次办成”改革，优化提升营商环境，创造性实施“立体式”监督、“点穴式”察访、“清单式”整改、“靶向式”问责，“拿地即开工”审批模式被国务院在全国复制推广，市场主体总量突破80万户。大力推进“放管服”改革，济南公共数据开放网已开放65个部门1405项数据集，下放市级行政权力事项19项，实现了“四十五证合一”。打造对外开放新高地，构建“双招双引”新格局，先后承办了儒商大会2018、青年企业家创新创业国际峰会、第七届文博会、首届全国工商联主席高端峰会等重大国际性会议。创新创业活力不断释放，省市共建山东省技术成果交易中心挂牌成立，全市科技企业孵化器达47家，众创空间达186家，新增各级知识产权企业178家。在2018年全国文明城市年度测评中居省会（首府）、副省级城市第一位。

新旧动能转换加快推进。全年新经济增加值[5]比重达到26.5%，居全省第3位，提高1.7个百分点。规模以上高技术制造业增加值增长17.8%，累计实现主营业务收入968.8亿元，增长15.3%。高端装备制造产业增加值实现增长11.1%。新兴产品中，生产电子工业专用设备和工业机器人产量分别增长52.0%、38.9%，传统耗能产品中，粗钢、钢材产量分别下降64.4%、45.5%。限额以上单位通过互联网实现商品零售额63.2亿元，增长28.0%，高于限额以上零售额平均增幅20.3个百分点。

二、“四五四”工作

“四个中心”建设实现历史性突破。1、**区域性经济中心建设**。全年全市地区生产总值占全省比重达到10.27%，居全省第2位；一般公共预算收入占比11.61%，居第2位；固定资产投资增速居第1位；社会消费品零售总额居第2位；第三产业增加值占GDP比重60.5%，居第1位。2、**区域性金融中心建设**。金融业增加值831.11亿元，增长3.3%。年末金融机构本外币各项存款余额居全省第1位，金融机构本外币各项贷款余额居全省第2位。新增新三板挂牌公司7家，总数达到163家（其中17家进入创新层），占全省比重22.1%。新三板挂牌公司通过定向发行股票、发行优先股、发行公司债等形式累计融资130.5亿元。3、**区域性物流中心建设**。国家5A级物流企业达到11家、国家级示范物流园区2家，均居全省第1位。重点物流企业256个，营业收入265.3亿元，增长9.6%。成功入选国家物流枢纽承载城市，荣获“改革开放40年城市物流发展成就奖”。4、**区域性科技创新中心建设**。高新技术企业达到1547家，新认定高新技术企业683家。规模以上工业高新技术企业741家，实现产值增长13.4%，占规模以上工业总产值的比重为56.12%。国家级企业技术中心（分中心）27家，省级工程实验室（工程研究中心）77家，省级（示范）工程技术研究中心161家。建成国家、省级企业重点实验室16家。R&D经费投入185.15亿元，占GDP比重为2.59%，比上年提高0.21个百分点。

五项重点工作成果丰硕。1、**招商引资**。引进市外投资增长22.7%，引进世界500强项目23个、大院大所和高端研发机构103家，泰山产业领军人才新入选数量全省第一，城市创新环境竞争力排名全国第九。2、**项目建设**。240个重点项目开工237个，开工率98.8%，完成投资2958.7亿元，占计划投资的105.1%，其中，36个项目已竣工。3、**棚改旧改征收拆迁**。棚改安置房开工71351套，其中，省级棚改开工46673套，提前超额完成省定任务。整治改造老旧住宅小区761.5万平方米，既有住宅加装电梯竣工186部、占全省80%以上。完成农村危房改造3254户、无害化卫生厕所改造13.95万户、村庄街巷硬化209个。4、**拆违拆临建绿透绿**。拆除违法建设3428万平方米，建绿透绿150.3万平方米，建成口袋公园、街头游园103处，开工建设山体公园20处，完成35座山体绿化提升项目。5、**城市更新**。“1+5”特色街区综合更新、“一湖一环”景观照明和“明湖秀”项目点亮泉城，完成31条黑臭水体治理任务，华山人水和谐生态治理模式在全国复制推广。

四大攻坚战不断克难。1、**治霾**。完成农村地区清洁取暖户数7.8万户，城市（县城）清洁取暖项目完工1412万平方米。新能源发电装机总容量75.2万千瓦，占发电总装机容量的18.3%。其中，生物质发电装机7.9万千瓦，太阳能发电装机31.9万千瓦，风力发电装机35.5万千瓦。购置新能源公交车1039辆。报废更新国三老旧柴油车10361辆，兑付补贴资金1.3亿元。2、**治堵**。轨道交通R1、R2、R3线完成投资分别为39.4亿元、37.5亿元、34.0亿元。轨道交通1号线提前建成通车。北园大街西延高架提前开通。当年开工当年打通28条瓶颈路，150公里BRT走廊成网运行，一举退出全国十大拥堵城市行列。3、**脱贫攻坚**。完成了减贫计划，实现脱贫0.16万人，2个贫困村摘帽退出，巩固提升已脱贫贫困人口10.16万人，基本完成现行标准下脱贫任务。分类推进贫困村实施产业项目270个，发放富民生产贷、富民农户贷0.28亿元。转移就业贫困群众3.90万人次。享受到教育资助的贫困学生数达2.46万人次。贫困村饮水安全工程全部完成，贫困户危房改造3254户。4、**新旧动能转换先行区建设**。坚持多规合一，编制完成先行区总体规划和50余项专项规划。450平方公里的新旧动能转换先行区直管区全面启动建设，加快建设“三桥一隧”，总投资约1500亿元的高端装备制造产业园、国际会展中心等八大引领支撑性重点项目全面开工，120余个“高精尖”项目纳入储备项目库。

三、农业

农业综合生产能力保持稳定。全年农林牧渔业增加值286.4亿元，比上年增长2.8%。粮食总产量251.4万吨，减少1.6%；油料产量4.2万吨，增长15.6%；蔬菜产量527.2万吨，减少10.9%；水果产量42.2万吨，减少2.2%。

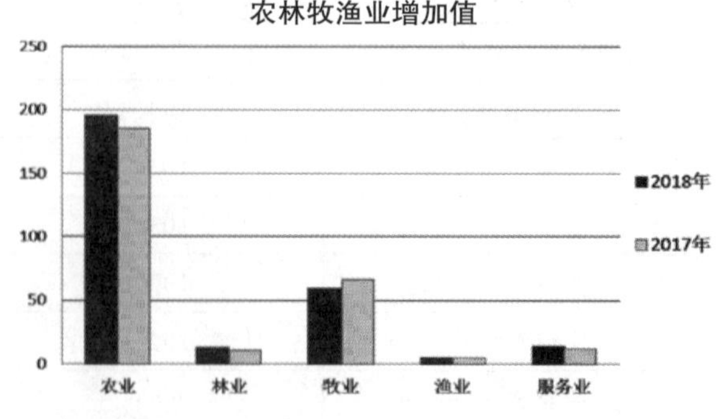

林牧渔“一升两降”，畜牧业产能有所下降。全年新造林面积4902公顷，经济林种植面积65033公顷，植树造林1306万

株。肉类总产量29.8万吨，减少8.3%；禽蛋产量33.2万吨，减少15.7%；奶类产量32.8万吨，增长24.6%。水产品产量3.2万吨，减少22.7%。

农业产业化水平持续提高。市级农业龙头企业402家，新认定31家；农民专业合作社6632家，新登记216家。新创建国家级畜禽养殖标准化示范场1处。农机总动力达到454.6万千瓦，主要农作物综合机械化率达到90%。

四、工业、建筑业

工业生产平稳增长。全年全部工业增加值比上年增长7.0%。规模以上工业增加值增长7.1%，分经济类型看，公有制经济增长9.2%，非公有制经济增长5.3%；分轻重工业看，轻工业增长5.6%，重工业增长7.6%。

全部行业增长面保持稳定。规模以上工业41个大类行业中，有24个行业增加值实现增长，增长面为58.5%。

2018年规模以上工业重点行业增加值增长速度

行业名称	比上年增长（%）
汽车制造业	8.5
计算机、通信和其他电子设备制造业	18.7
医药制造业	17.9
石油、煤炭及其他燃料加工业	22.3
通用设备制造业	6.7
非金属矿物制品业	23.3
金属制品业	−11.2
化学原料和化学制品制造业	7.0
专用设备制造业	0.8
电气机械和器材制造业	−3.1

半数以上工业产品实现增长。全年规模以上工业产品产品销售率为97.5%。所生产的147种大类产品中，有82种产品产量实现增长，增长面为55.8%。其中，增幅超过30%的产品有20种，占比为13.6%，较上年提高0.8个百分点。

2018年规模以上工业企业[6]主要产品产量及增长速度

产品名称		单位	产量	比上年增长（%）
支柱产品	载货汽车	万辆	17.6	−3.8
	服务器	万台	99.6	76.3
	原油加工量	万吨	442.1	21.0
	化学药品原药	吨	9630.3	17.3
	发电量	亿千瓦时	152.8	−5.2
	初级形态塑料	万吨	57.7	6.3
	钢材	万吨	223.3	−45.5
	铁路货车	辆	4998	5.7
	农用氮、磷、钾化学肥料（折纯）	万吨	20.8	−1.0
	矿山专用设备	万吨	4.3	−10.4
	金属切削机床	台	5964	15.9
	变压器	万千伏安	15845	3.9
	石墨及碳素制品	万吨	191.3	3.6
	气动元件	万件	292.1	17.5
	乳制品	万吨	46.9	1.1
	锻件	万吨	71.4	5.6
	水泥	万吨	604.3	0.7
	家用洗衣机	万台	65.0	173.1
	饮料酒	万千升	26.4	−7.7
	鲜、冷藏肉	万吨	8.4	5.0
	发动机	万千瓦	3172.6	−23.6
	化学农药原药（折有效成分100%）	吨	8942.1	8.3
其他新兴产品	电子计算机整机	万台	101.4	27.8
	工业机器人	套	1003	38.9
	电力电缆	万千米	13.4	3.9
	电子元件	亿只	31.7	−13.9

工业经济效益持续改善。全年规模以上工业主营业务收入5171.0亿元，增长6.5%。重点行业中，石油、煤炭及其他燃料加工业增长36.1%，汽车制造业增长22.8%，计算机通信和其他电子设备制造业、化学原料和化学制品业、医药制造业分别增长18.4%、14.8%、11.9%。

建筑业较快发展。全年建筑业增加值688.3亿元，增长11.1%，占GDP比重为8.8%。在建工程总施工面积达到12984.0万平方米。具有资质等级的建筑业企业507家，增加3家。实现建筑业总产值2823.5亿元，增长27.2%，其中，国有及国有控股企业产值2205.9亿元，增长31.7%。签订合同额6820.6亿元，增长17.3%，其中，本年新签合同额3640.2亿元，增长36.1%。

五、固定资产投资

投资结构继续优化。全年固定资产投资比上年增长9.6%。分产业看，第一产业投资增长9.8%；第二产业投资下降10.1%；第三产业投资增长14.3%。年末亿元以上固定资产投资项目872个，增加128个。分项目规模看，五十亿元以上项目19个，增加3个，完成投资增长21.0%；十亿元以上至五十亿元项目147个，增加41个，完成投资下降0.9%；亿元以上至十亿元投资项目706个，增加84个，完成投资增长34.0%。民间投资增长8.5%，基础设施投资增长10.2%，实体经济投资增长8.4%。

服务业投资较快增长。全年服务业投资增长14.4%。其中，高技术服务投资增长7.8%，物流业投资增长2.8%。

房地产投资平稳发展。全年房地产开发完成投资1369.3亿元，增长11.1%，其中，住宅完成投资928.5亿元，增长12.9%。房屋施工面积9112.1万平方米，增长13.8%，其中，住宅施工面积5932.7万平方米，增长11.3%。房屋竣工面积1203.8万平方米，增长90.7%，其中，住宅竣工面积897.4万平方米，增长82.7%。商品房销售面积1234.6万平方米，增长1.6%，其中，住宅销售面积963.6万平方米，下降1.0%。商品房销售额1473.8亿元，增长25.7%，其中，住宅销售额1172.8亿元，增长23.9%。

六、国内贸易

消费品市场平稳运行。全年社会消费品零售总额4404.5

亿元，比上年增长10.0%。其中，商品零售3717.7亿元，增长10.0%；餐饮收入686.8亿元，增长9.9%。分城乡看，城镇社会消费品零售额4003.1亿元，增长10.0%；乡村社会消费品零售额401.4亿元，增长9.4%。限额以上单位[7]实现零售额1334.4亿元，增长7.7%。

主要商品销势良好。在限额以上单位商品零售中，粮油、食品类151.5亿元，增长6.4%；服装、鞋帽、针纺织品类113.2亿元，增长6.0%；金银珠宝类33.0亿元，增长20.4%；家用电器和音像器材类74.6亿元，增长10.4%；通讯器材类67.8亿元，增长22.0%。

2018年限额以上批发和零售业单位商品零售额及增长速度

商品类别	零售额（亿元）	比上年增长(%)
粮油、食品类	151.5	6.4
饮料类	11.9	2.8
烟酒类	22.3	-0.2
服装、鞋帽、针纺织品类	113.2	6.0
化妆品类	20.7	5.0
金银珠宝类	33.0	20.4
日用品类	36.1	-5.7
家用电器和音像器材类	74.6	10.4
中西药品类	46.3	4.9
文化办公用品类	36.2	-1.6
通讯器材类	67.8	22.0
石油及制品类	151.2	6.4
汽车类	390.2	0.7

七、开放型经济

对外贸易增长较快。全年货物进出口总额825.0亿元，比上年增长16.2%。其中，出口519.3亿元，增长14.6%；进口305.7亿元，增长19.0%。出口市场中，对欧洲国家和地区出口增长16.8%，对韩国、日本出口分别下降13.3%和增长7.7%，对美国出口增长39.6%。主要出口商品中，机电产品出口372.2亿元，增长17.5%；高新技术产品出口92.2亿元，增长65.6%。

利用外资水平大幅提高。全年实际使用外资178.2亿元，增长41.0%，其中，制造业使用外资51.5亿元，服务业使用外资123.0亿元。总投资过亿美元的项目41个，合同外资261.3亿元。世界500强企业投资项目23个，实际使用外资99.8亿元。

对外经济合作积极拓展。全年备案设立境外企业（机构）51家，派出各类劳务人员6254人。

经济外向度进一步扩大。全年经济外向度10.5%，提高0.7个百分点。

八、交通、邮电、旅游和会展

交通运输保持稳定。年末公路通车里程12637.7公里，其中，境内高速公路488.5公里。公路客运量完成3149.0万人，下降1.3%；旅客周转量完成52.9亿人公里，增长0.5%。公路货运量完成2.6亿吨，增长6.3%；货运周转量完成474.0亿吨公里，增长3.1%。年末拥有民用机动车230.4万辆，其中，民用汽车216.1万辆。济南机场累计保障起降12.7万架次，增长9.8%；完成旅客吞吐量1661.2万人次，增长16.0%；完成货邮吞吐量11.4万吨，增长19.4%。

邮电通信业快速增长。全年邮政企业和快递服务企业业务收入(不包括邮政储蓄银行直接营业收入)累计完成61.6亿元，增长26.4%；业务总量完成89.8亿元，增长38.7%。快递服务企业业务收入完成48.4亿元，增长27.9%；业务量完成43195.5万件，增长43.0%。年末移动电话用户1013.7万户，其中，4G电话用户725.0万户、增长16.3%。

旅游业稳步发展。全年接待国内外游客8007.7万人次，增长9.9%，其中，接待国内游客7967.8万人次，增长9.9%；接待入境游客39.9万人次，增长6.2%。实现旅游消费总额1129.6亿元，其中，国内游客消费额1054.7亿元，入境游客消费额22285.1万美元。共有A级旅游景区62家，其中，5A级景区1家，4A级景区13家。省级旅游强乡镇30个，省级旅游特色村82个，省级以上旅游度假区1家。

会展业加快发展。全年举办会展196场，其中，国际性展会12场。

九、财政和金融

财政收支健康运行。全年一般公共预算收入752.8亿元，比上年增长11.2%。其中，税收收入619.5亿元，增长14.3%；占一般公共预算收入比重为82.3%，提高2.3个百分点。一般公共预算支出1018.3亿元，增长22.1%。其中，教育支出153.1亿元，增长6.8%；社会保障和就业支出132.9亿元，增长17.2%；城乡社区支出246.4亿元，增长33.8%。

金融机构数量稳步增加。年末金融机构单位数660家，增加88家。其中，银行49家，保险公司91家，证券公司及营业部139家，期货公司及营业部54家，财务公司10家，其他各类机构317家。

金融存贷款规模持续扩大。年末金融机构本外币各项存款余额17060.1亿元，增长3.0%。金融机构本外币各项贷款余额16059.9亿元，增长11.9%。

资本市场相对活跃。全年完成证券交易额2.8万亿元。期货营业部代理交易额7.9万亿元，增长9.0%；新增直接融资1787.6亿元，增长159.8%。年末全市区域内上市公司34家，股票36只；私募投资基金机构新增21家，总数达到163家。

保险业保持稳定增长。全年保费收入415.6亿元，增长9.1%。其中，财产险公司保费收入91.4亿元，增长12.9%；人身险公司保费收入324.1亿元，增长8.0%。各项赔款与给付103.4亿元，增长16.6%。

十、科技、教育、文化、卫生和体育事业

科技发明成果显著。全年万人有效发明专利拥有量29.3件，比上年增长14.5%。技术合同实现交易额130.6亿元，增长54.2%。规模以上工业企业研发人员数量5.47万人。规模以上工业企业办研发机构366个。全市获省科技进步一等奖2项、

二等奖 10 项。专利申请量 36027 件，其中，发明专利申请量 13685 件。专利授权量 20636 件，其中，发明专利授权量 4887 件。

教育事业扎实推进。高等学校 51 所，中等职业学校 34 所，技工学校[8]19 所，普通中学 251 所，小学 575 所，特殊教育学校 12 所。新建、改扩建幼儿园 93 处，新增学位 2 万余个，新建改扩建 129 处学生集中就餐场所。学龄儿童入学率和小学毕业生升学率均为 100%。编制完成《济南市高中阶段教育普及攻坚计划》，全市 26 所学校纳入高中普及攻坚计划。

文化事业稳繁荣发展。年末（国有）艺术表演团体 195 个，文化馆（站）及群众艺术馆 150 个，档案馆 15 个，公共图书馆 14 个。市级以上文物保护单位 374 处，其中，国家级 21 处。城市可统计票房数字影院 54 家，放映 64.0 万场，观众 1180.9 万人次，票房收入 4.6 亿元。年末广播人口混合覆盖率和电视人口混合覆盖率均为 100%。完成文化产业投资增长 18.3%。扶持新建贫困村综合文化服务中心（文化大院）95 家。新创建 40 个基层群众文化示范点，基层群众文化活动示范点达到 240 个。

卫生服务水平持续提升。年末拥有卫生机构 6030 个，增加 259 家，增长 4.5%，其中，医院、卫生院 293 家（三甲医院 21 家、民营医院 154 家）。卫生机构床位 5.8 万张，增长 4.7%。各类卫生技术人员 8.3 万人，增长 8.5%；执业（助理）医师 3.2 万人，增长 10.7%。按常住人口计算，每千人拥有病床 7.7 张，增长 2.8%；每千人拥有执业（助理）医师 4.3 人，增长 8.6%。

全民体育健身深入开展。成立体育社会组织 108 个，培训社会体育指导员 3845 人。组织各类全民健身活动（赛事）59 次，参与人数 20 万人次。建设体育活动点 3347 个。获省级及以上金牌 496 枚，银牌 358 枚，铜牌 332 枚。

十一、城乡建设、环境和安全生产

城市建设[9]水平明显提升。年末城市建成区面积 561.0 平方公里，比上年增加 22.7 平方公里。建成区绿化覆盖率 40.6%，人均公园绿地面积 12.7 平方米。全年天然气供气量 11.4 亿立方米，增长 25.6%；液化石油气供气量 4.1 万吨，减少 17.7%。集中供热面积 19833.8 万平方米，增长 9.1%。自来水供水量 3.9 亿吨，增长 9.8%。垃圾无害化处理率 100%。

新型城镇化进展顺利。年末常住人口城镇化率达到 72.10%，提高 1.57 个百分点。济阳实现撤县设区。

生态环境进一步改善。全年市区空气质量良好以上天数达到 203 天，增加 18 天。城区环境空气中可吸入颗粒物（PM_{10}）年均浓度 112 微克/立方米，下降 13.8%；细颗粒物（$PM_{2.5}$）52 微克/立方米，下降 17.5%；二氧化硫 17 微克/立方米，下降 32.0%；二氧化氮 45 微克/立方米，下降 2.2%。区域环境噪声昼间平均等效声级 53.3 分贝，市区道路交通噪声平均等效声级 69.5 分贝。

平安济南建设深入推进。全年刑事案件立案 18594 件。破获当年刑事案件 7103 件。受理社会治安案件 75393 件。实现 301 天街面“两抢”零发案，打掉涉黑涉恶组织团伙 165 个，抓获涉黑涉恶违法犯罪团伙成员 1125 名。

安全生产形势保持总体稳定。全年发生各类安全生产死亡事故 258 起，死亡 280 人，重伤 50 人。亿元国内生产总值生产安全事故死亡率[10]0.036。

十二、居民生活和社会保障

居民生活持续改善。全年城镇居民人均可支配收入 50146 元，比上年增长 7.5%；城镇居民人均生活消费支出 32977 元，增长 7.3%。农村居民人均可支配收入 17924 元，增长 8.0%；农村居民人均生活消费支出 11172 元，增长 8.2%。城乡居民收入比由上年的 2.81：1 缩小为 2.80:1。城镇居民恩格尔系数[11]23.5%，农村居民恩格尔系数 30.5%。

2018 年城镇、农村居民人均可支配收入及增长速度

指　　标	城镇居民		农村居民	
	2018 年(元)	比上年增长(%)	2018 年(元)	比上年增长(%)
可支配收入	50146	7.5	17924	8.0
工资性收入	28108	6.9	10200	7.6
经营净收入	2758	6.5	6295	8.6
财产净收入	9616	9.9	465	2.4
转移净收入	9664	7.2	965	11.0

2018 年末每百户居民家庭主要耐用消费品拥有量[12]

指　　标	单位	城镇居民	农村居民
家用汽车	辆	53.7	42.2
电冰箱(柜)	台	103.2	97.4
洗衣机	台	99.3	94.6
热水器	台	101.1	87.3
空调	台	172.8	87.2
彩色电视机	台	106.0	114.1
照相机	台	36.4	6.2
计算机	台	80.6	41.5
移动电话	部	219.5	244.9

社会保障更加健全。年末城镇职工基本养老保险参保人数 331.66 万，增加 27.03 万；职工医疗保险参保人数 241.54 万，增加 12.86 万；失业保险参保人数 158.29 万，增加 11.10 万；工伤保险参保人数 220.47 万，增加 32.96 万；生育保险参保人 163.97 万，增加 11.24 万。居民养老保险和医疗保险参保人数分别达到 244.76 万和 408.14 万。

最低生活保障标准进一步提高。城市最低生活保障标准由上年人均每月 596 元提高到 616 元，享受城镇最低生活保障的城镇居民 0.90 万户、1.33 万人，发放最低生活保障金及各类补贴 0.96 亿元。农村最低生活保障标准由年人均不低于 4277

元提高到4928元，享受农村最低生活保障的农村居民4.53万户、6.43万人，发放最低生活保障金及各类补贴2.64亿元。农村特困人员基本生活标准每人每年6406元；照料护理标准按照自理、半自理和完全不能自理人员分三种档次，每人每年分别为1968元、3276元、6552元。

社会救助事业稳定发展。共有救助管理站1处，流浪未成年人保护中心1处，救助0.25万人次。城乡医疗救助资金支出5569.8万元，救助1.59万人次。培训残疾人4802人次，安置残疾人员就业2169人，帮扶救助残疾人投入资金1.4亿元。

十三、原莱芜市国民经济和社会发展情况

初步核算，全年实现地区生产总值1005.65亿元，按可比价格计算，比上年增长7.2%。分产业看，第一产业增加值60.31亿元，增长3.9%；第二产业增加值566.08亿元，增长7.0%；第三产业增加值379.26亿元，增长8.1%。三次产业结构为6.0:56.3:37.7。人均GDP达到73005元，增长7.1%。年末全市常住人口为137.90万人，增加0.30万人。其中，城镇人口为87.87万人，增加1.76万人，城镇人口占总人口比重为63.72%，提高1.14个百分点。规模以上工业实现增加值增长8.3%；实现主营业务收入2093.9亿元，增长11.5%；利润总额90.4亿元，增长39.8%。完成固定资产投资增长7.2%。社会消费品零售额完成373.2亿元，增长8.8%。实现一般公共预算收入62.6亿元，增长11.7%。其中，税收收入50.4亿元，增长16.2%。一般公共预算支出100.4亿元，增长13.1%。城镇居民人均可支配收入37401元，增长7.2%；人均消费支出21304元，增长7.0%。农村居民人均可支配收入17468元，增长8.2%；人均消费支出12263元，增长8.4%。

注释：

[1]2018年统计数据为统计快报数或初步核算数，正式数据以出版的《济南统计年鉴－2019》为准。根据数据发布统一要求，2018年数据按照济南市、莱芜市两个城市分别发布。

[2]全市地区生产总值、各产业增加值绝对数按现价计算，增长速度按不变价格计算。

[3]人均地区生产总值按年均常住人口计算。

[4]现代服务业包括：信息传输、软件和信息技术服务业，金融业，房地产业，租赁和商务服务业，科学研究和技术服务业，水利、环境和公共设施管理业，居民服务、修理和其他服务业，教育，卫生和社会工作，文化、体育和娱乐业。

[5]按照制度要求，涉及新经济增加值指标错年使用2017年数据。

[6]规模以上工业企业指年主营业务收入2000万元及以上的工业法人单位。

[7]限额以上单位是指年主营业务收入2000万元及以上的批发业单位、500万元及以上的零售业单位、200万元及以上的住宿和餐饮业单位。单位包括法人企业、产业活动单位和个体户。

[8]技工学校自2017年起统计口径调整为济南市属技工学校。

[9]城市建设指标口径为包含两县的整个济南地区。

[10]亿元国内生产总值生产安全事故死亡率是指安全生产事故死亡人数与亿元GDP之比。

[11]恩格尔系数是指食品支出在消费支出中的比重。

[12]数据来自于住户收支与生活状况调查。

资料来源：本公报中社会治安数据来自公安部门；财政数据来自财政部门；城镇新增就业、新增农村劳动力转移就业、登记失业率、城镇职工各类保险参保数据、人才数据来自人力资源社会保障部门；安全生产数据来自应急管理部门；淘汰落后产能相关数据来自工业和信息化部门；水产品产量、农业数据来自农业农村部门；林业数据、建绿透绿数据来自园林和林业部门；外资数据来自投资促进部门；进出口、对外承包工程、新设境外企业、外派劳务人员、会展数据来自商务部门；公路里程、公交数据、公路运输数据来自交通运输部门；邮政、快递数据来自邮政管理部门；保险、证券数据来自地方金融管理部门；旅游、文化数据来自文化和旅游部门；教育数据来自教育部门；科技数据来自科技部门；新认定国家级企业技术中心数据、新增省级工程实验室（工程研究中心）数据来自发展改革部门；卫生数据、新型农村合作医疗相关数据来自卫生健康部门；体育数据来自体育部门；棚改旧改、城市更新、城市建设相关数据来自住房城乡建设部门；环境保护相关数据来自生态环境部门；拆违拆临数据来自城管部门；城乡最低生活保障、农村特困人员救助供养相关数据来自民政部门；全面深化改革数据来自市委全面深化改革领导小组办公室、发展改革委；扶贫数据来自市扶贫开发领导小组办公室；残疾人保障数据来自残联；居民收入与支出数据、恩格尔系数、价格指数、粮食产量来自国家统计局济南调查队；新旧动能转换先行区建设数据来自新旧动能转换先行区管委会；其他数据均来自市统计局。

STATISTICAL COMMUNIQUÉ OF JINAN City ON THE 2018 NATIONAL ECONOMIC AND SOCIAL DEVELOPMENT[1]

Jinan Municipal Bureau of Statistics
NBS Survey Office In Jinan

In 2018, the whole city overall carried out the spirit of the 19th National Congress of the Communist Party, the Second and Third Plenary Meetings of the 19th Central Committee of the Communist Party of China, insisted on the total working tone of seeking improvement in stability, determinedly fulfilled the new development philosophy and focused on promoting the high-quality development under the strong leadership of the municipal party committee and municipal government and the guidance of Xi Jinping Thought on Socialism with Chinese Characteristics for a New Era; strived ahead and to succeed by taking the supply-side structural reform as the principal line and centering on speeding up the creation of "Four Centers" and construction of modern international metropolis with "great scale, strong strength, beautiful life, rich people and clear road". The comprehensive economic strength was remarkably strengthened, industry transformation and upgrading was accelerated, quality and benefit were enhanced continuously, innovation driving ability was strengthened continuously, city image was improved and promoted continuously, reform and opening-up force increased continuously, and the people's livelihood security was improved continuously, thus starting a new situation of the socio-economic development of provincial capital.

I. General

Steady progress in the economic operation. Upon preliminary accounting, the whole city's annual gross value of production [2] was RMB 785.656 billion, increased by 7.4% over the previous year. The value added of the primary industry was RMB 27.242 billion, increased by 2.5%; the value added of the secondary industry was RMB 282.931 billion, increased by 7.8%; the value added of the tertiary industry was RMB 475.483 billion, increased by 7.5%. The proportion of the three industries was 3.5: 36.0: 60.5. The gross regional product per capita [3] was RMB 106,302, increased by 5.7%, equivalent to USD 16,064 based on the annual exchange rate.

The population maintained the steady growth. The permanent resident population at the end of the year was 7.4604 million, increased by 1.90% than that at the end of last year. The registered population was 6.559 million, increased by 1.91%. The birth rate declared was 14.57‰, death rate 6.98‰ and natural population growth rate 7.59‰.

The employment kept good situation. The newly increased urban employment quantity all year round was 189,500 and the urban unemployment rate registered at the end of the year was 2.06%.

The price level rose mildly. The annual consumer price increased by 2.6%, of which, the prices of food, tobacco and wine increased by 3.2%. PPI and IPI respectively increased by 4.8% and 8.3%.

Consumer Price Index of 2018 (based on 100 of last year)

Indicator	The whole city
CPI	102.6
Food, tobacco and wine	103.2
Clothing	103.8
Residence	103.5
Daily necessities and services	100.6
Transport and communication	102.1
Education culture and entertainment	99.6
Health care	104.7
Other goods and services	99.6

Industrial Producer Price Index In 2018 (%)

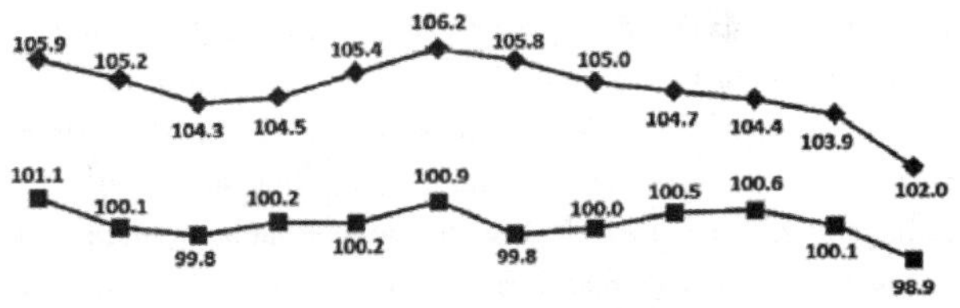

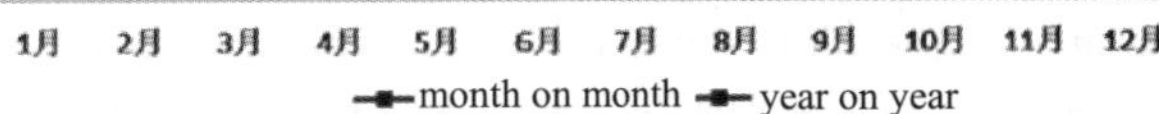

Purchasing Price Index Of Industrial Producers In 2018 (%)

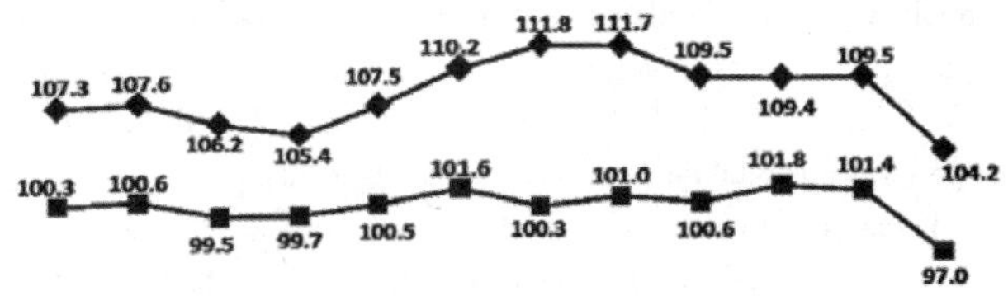

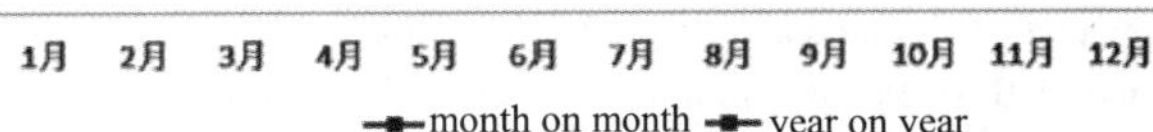

The month-on-month increase of sales price index of newly built houses remained stable basically.

Sales Price Index Of New Houses In 2018 (%)

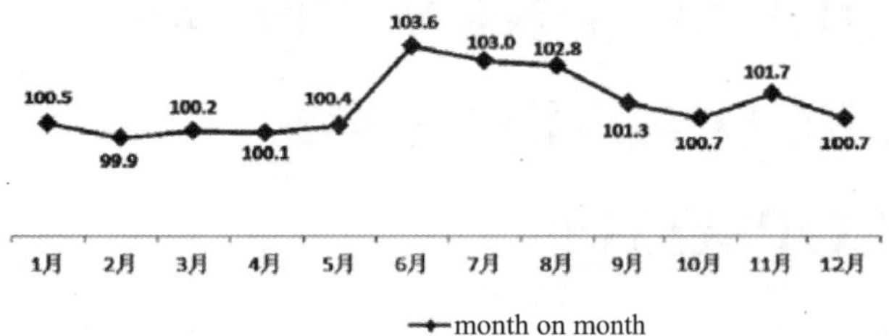

The growth rate of modern service industry [4] was faster. The annual value added of the modern service industry was RMB 276.738 billion, increased by 12.8%, accounting for 58.2% of the service industry.

The non-public economy kept stable development. The annual value added of non-public economy was RMB 323.75 billion, increased by 3.6%, accounting for 41.2% of GDP. The value added of private economy was RMB 283.358 billion, increased by 3.7%, accounting for 36.1% of GDP.

The key reform achieved notable results. Deeply fulfilled "three cuts, one reduction and one improvement", accelerated the moving and transformation of old industrial areas in the east with 10 enterprises moved or closed down, and 66 enterprises completed in total. Overall implemented the reform of "One-time Completion", optimized and improved the business environment, implemented creatively the "Stereometric" supervision, "Pinpoint Style" inspection visit, "List Format" rectification, "Target Type" accountability and "Commencement upon Land Acquisition" pattern were promoted by the State Council around the country. The total quantity of the market subject broke through 800,000. Vigorously promoted the reform of streamlining administration and instituting decentralization, delegating power and strengthening regulation and optimizing service. Jinan public data open network opened 1,405 items of dataset of 65 departments and delegated 19 items of municipal administrative power, realizing "Integration of Forty-five Licenses". Built new heights opening to the outside world, constructed a new pattern of "Investment Promotion and Talent Attraction" and successively held major international conferences, such as Conference of Great Business Partners of 2018, International Summit of Innovation and Development of Young Entrepreneurs, the 7th International Cultural Industries Fair and The 1st High-end Summit of All-China Federation of Industry and Commerce Chairman, etc. Released the innovative and entrepreneurial energy continuously and established Shandong technological achievements trading center jointly set up by province and city. There were 47 technology business incubators, 186 maker spaces and 178 new intellectual property enterprises at all levels in the whole city. Ranked top first in the 2018 review of the national civilized city at the provincial capital and sub-provincial city levels.

Transition to new energy from old was accelerated. The proportion of annual new economic value added [5] reached to 26.5%, improved by 1.7%, ranking top 3 in the whole province. The value added of high technology manufacturing industry above state designated scale increased by 17.8%, realizing a main business income of RMB 96.88 billion accumulatively, increased by 15.3%. The value added of high-end equipment manufacturing industry realized an increase of 11.1%. In the new products, the output of equipment for electronic products manufacturing and industrial robot increased by 52.0% and 38.9%, respectively, and the crude steel and steel in the traditional energy consumption products, reduced by 64.4% and 45.5%, respectively. Units above designated size realized the retail sales of RMB 6.32 billion through the Internet, increased by 28.0%, higher than the average growth of retail sales of 20.3%.

II. "454" Work

The construction of "Four Centers" realized the historical breakthrough. 1. Construction of the regional economic center. The annual gross regional product of the whole city accounted for 10.27% of that of the whole province, ranking top 2 in the province; the general public budget income accounted for 11.61%, ranking top second; the fixed-asset investment growth ranked top 1; the total retail sales of social consumer goods ranked top 2; the value added of the tertiary industry accounted for 60.5% of GDP, ranking top 1. **2. Construction of the regional financial center.** The value added of the financial industry was RMB 83.111 billion, increased by 3.3%. The outstanding of deposits of local and foreign currencies for the financial institutions at the end of the year ranked top 1 the loan balance ranked top 2 in the whole province. There were 7 new OTC listed companies, 163 in total (of which 17 entered into the innovation layer), accounting for 22.1% of that of the whole province. The cumulative financing of the new OTC listed companies was RMB 13.05 billion through issuing shares, preferred shares and corporate bonds directionally. **3. Construction of the regional logistics center.** There were 11 national 5A logistics enterprises and 2 national demonstration logistics parks, ranking top 1 in the whole province. There were 256 key logistics enterprises with the operating income of RMB 26.53 billion, increased by 9.6%. The city was successfully selected into the national logistics hub bearing city and won the "Urban Logistics Development Achievement Award for the 40th Anniversary of China's Reform and Opening Up". **4. Construction of regional science and technology innovation center.** There were 1,547 new high-tech enterprises and 683 new designated high-tech enterprises. There were 741 industrial new high-tech enterprises above state designated scale and the output growth of 13.4% was realized, accounting for 56.12% of the total industrial output value above state designated scale. There were 27 national enterprise technical centers (sub-centers), 77 provincial engineering laboratories (engineering research centers) and 161 provincial (demonstration) engineering technology research centers. Constructed 16 national and provincial key enterprise laboratories. The R&D fund investment was RMB 18.515 billion, improved by 0.21% compared to the last year, accounting for 2.59% of GDP.

The five key working achievements were rich. 1. Attracting business and investment. The investment introduced outside the city increased by 22.7%, the world top 500 projects introduced were 23 and the large institutes and high-end research and development institutions were 103. The new election of mount Tai industry leading talent ranked top 1 in the whole province and the city innovation environment competitiveness ranked top 9 nationwide. **2. Project construction.** Two hundred and thirty-seven key projects (240 in total) were started, with a rate of operation of 98.8%. Completed the investment of RMB 295.87 billion, accounting for 105.1% of planned investment, of which 36 projects had been completed. **3. Renovation of shanty towns and demolition.** A total of 71,351 settlement houses were commenced, of which 46,673 were the provincial renovation, outperformed the provincial tasks in advance. Renovated old residential communities of

7.615 million m^2 and installed 186 elevators for existing apartments, accounting for more than 80% of that of the whole province. Completed the renovation of 3,254 rural dangerous houses, 139,500 non-hazardous sanitary toilets and 209 village street sclerosis. **4. Remove of the illegal/unauthorized/unapproved buildings and temporary buildings and construction of green land.** Removed the illegal construction of 34.28 million m^2, constructed the green land of 1.503 million m^2, 103 pocket parks and street parks, 20 mountain parks under construction, and completed 35 mountain forestation promotion projects. **5. Urban renewal.** Updated "1+5" characteristic urban block comprehensively, lighted up Spring City through "One Lake One Ring" landscape lighting and "Daming Lake Show", completed 31 black and odorous water treatment tasks and promoted Mount Hua man-water harmony ecological governance model around the country.

Difficulties had been overcoming in the four problem solving wars. 1. Haze treatment. Completed 78,000 clean energy heating households in the rural areas and 14.12 million m^2 city (county) clean energy heating projects. The total installed capacity of new energy power generation was 752,000 kW, accounting for 18.3% of the installed gross capacity. The installed capacity of biomass power generation was 79,000 kW, solar power generation 319,000 kW and wind power generation 355,000 kW. Purchased 1,039 new energy buses. Renovated 10,361 China III old diesel vehicles and honored a subsidy of RMB 130 million. **2. Traffic congestion management.** Completed investment in rail transit of Line R1, R2 and R3 of RMB 3.94 billion, 3.75 billion and 3.4 billion, respectively. Line 1 was open to traffic in advance. The Beiyuan street overhead extended westward was open in advance. Got through 28 bottleneck roads in that commencement year, with 150 km BRT corridor network operation, thus dropping out the list of national top ten congested cities. **3. Poverty alleviation.** Completed the poverty reduction plan, realized the poverty alleviation population of 1,600 and made 2 poor villages got out of poverty, consolidated and improved the poverty stricken population who had got rid of poverty of 101,600 and basically completed poverty alleviation missions under the current standard. Promoted 270 industrial projects to be implemented in poor villages by classification and issued production loans and household loans of RMB 28 million for enriching people. Transferred poverty stricken population in employment of 39,000. The poverty students who enjoyed the education aids were 24,600. Completed the whole drinking water safety engineering of poor villages and renovated 3,254 dangerous houses of poverty-stricken families. **4. Construction of the pilot area for the transition to new energy from old.** Insisted on the integration of rules and prepared and completed the overall planning of the pilot area and more than 50 specialized planning. A total of 450 m^2 pilot area and direct management area of transition to new from old economic engines comprehensively started the construction,and "three bridges and one tunnel" was accelerated in construction. Eight leading and supportive key projects, including the high-end equipment manufacturing industrial park and international convention center with the total investment amount of RMB 150 billion, started the construction comprehensively, and more than 120 "high-grade" projects had been included in the reserve project library.

III. Agriculture

The comprehensive production capacity of agriculture kept stable. In the whole year, the value added in the agriculture, forestry, animal husbandry and fishery were RMB 28.64 billion, with an increase of 2.8% than the last year. The output of grain (total), vegetable and fruit were 2.514, 5.272 and 0.422 million tons, respectively, with a decrease of 1.6%, 10.9% and 2.2%, respectively. The oil output was 0.042 million tons, with an increase of 15.6%.

Added value of agriculture, forestry, animal husbandry and fishery

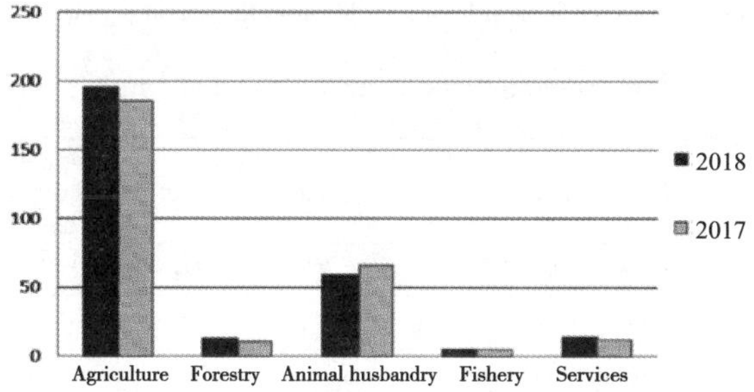

"One increase and two decrease" occurred among the forestry, animal husbandry and fishery, and the animal husbandry capacity decreased. The new afforestation area in the whole year was 4,902 ha., the planting area of economic forest was 65,033 ha. and planting 13.06 million trees. The output of meat (total), poultry eggs and aquatic products were 0.298, 0.332 and 0.032 million tons, respectively, with a decrease of 8.3%, 15.7% and 22.7%, respectively. The dairy product output was 0.328 million tons, with an increase of 24.6%.

The industrial level of agriculture improved continuously. It had 402 city-level leading enterprises of agriculture, with 31 newly-recognized enterprises; 6,632 farmers' professional cooperatives, with 216 newly- registered cooperatives and 1 newly-established state-level livestock and poultry breeding standardization demonstration site. The total power of agricultural machinery reached 4.546 million kW, and the comprehensive mechanization rate of main crops was up to 90%.

IV. Industry and Construction Industry

Industrial production promoted steadily. The annual total value added of the industrial sector was increased by 7.0% than that of the previous year. The large-scale industrial value added was increased by 7.1%. In view of economic types, the public sector and non-public sector of the economy were increased by 9.2% and 5.3%, respectively. From the point of light and heavy industry, the light and heavy industries were increased by 5.6% and 7.6%, respectively.

The growth rates of all industries kept stable. In 41 sectors of large-scale industries, the value added of 24 industries achieved the growth and the growth surface was 58.5%.

The Value Added and Growth Speed of Key Sectors of Large-scale Industries in 2018

Name of industry	Increase over the previous year (%)
Automobile making industry	8.5
Computer, communication and other electronic equipment manufacturing industries	18.7
Pharmaceutical manufacturing industry	17.9
Petroleum, coal and other fuel processing industries	22.3
General equipment manufacturing industry	6.7
Non-metallic mineral products industry	23.3
Metal products industry	-11.2
Chemical raw materials and chemicals manufacturing industry	7.0
Special equipment manufacturing industry	0.8
Electrical machinery and equipment manufacturing industry	-3.1

More than half industrial products achieved the growth. The sales rate of large-scale industrial products in the whole year reached 97.5%. Among 147 kinds of large-scale products, the output of 82 kinds of products reached the growth, and the growth surface was 55.8%. Among them, it had 20 kinds of products with the growth rate over 30%, with the proportion of 13.6%, a growth rate of 0.8% over the previous year.

Main Product Output and Growth Speed of Large-scale Industrial Enterprises [6] in 2018

	Product name	Unit	Output	Increase over the previous year (%)
Pillar product	Goods vehicle	10,000 vehicles	17.6	-3.8
	Server	10,000 units	99.6	76.3
	Crude oil processing volume	10,000 tons	442.1	21.0
	Technical material of chemical medicine	Ton	9,630.3	17.3
	Generated energy	100 million KWH	152.8	-5.2
	Primary form plastics	10,000 tons	57.7	6.3
	Steel	10,000 tons	223.3	-45.5
	Railway goods wagon	Pcs	4,998	5.7
	Agricultural nitrogen, phosphorus and potassium chemical fertilizers (purity)	10,000 tons	20.8	-1.0
	Mine-specific equipment	10,000 tons	4.3	-10.4
	Metal-cutting machine tool	Set	5,964	15.9
	Transformer	10,000 KVA	15,845	3.9
	Graphite and carbon products	10,000 tons	191.3	3.6
	Pneumatic component	10,000 pieces	292.1	17.5
	Dairy products	10,000 tons	46.9	1.1
	Forging	10,000 tons	71.4	5.6
	Cement	10,000 tons	604.3	0.7
	Household washing machine	10,000 units	65.0	173.1
	Food alcohol	10,000 kl	26.4	-7.7
	Fresh and cold meat	10,000 tons	8.4	5.0
	Engine	10,000 KW	3,172.6	-23.6
	Technical material of chemical pesticide (material-effective constituent was 100%)	Ton	8,942.1	8.3
Other new products	Whole electronic computer machine	10,000 units	101.4	27.8
	Industrial robot	Set	1,003	38.9
	Power cable	10,000 km	13.4	3.9
	Electronic component	100 million pieces	31.7	-13.9

Industrial economic benefit kept continuous improvement. Main business in industries above the designated size achieved RMB 517.1 billion in the whole year, increased by 6.5%; In the key industries, the petroleum, coal and other fuel processing were increased by 36.1%, the automobile making industry was increased by 22.8%, computerized communication and other electronic equipment manufacturing, raw chemical material and chemical product industry, and pharmaceutical manufacturing industry were increased by 18.4%, 14.8% and 11.9%, respectively.

The construction industry kept the rapid development. The value added of the construction industry in the whole year reached RMB 68.83 billion, with an increase of 11.1%, which accounts for 8.8% of GDP. The total construction area of the construction in process reached 129.84 million m^2. It had 507 construction enterprises with the qualification level, with an increase of 3 enterprises. The total output value of the construction industry reached RMB 282.35 billion, with an increase of 27.2%, of which, the values of state-owned and state holding enterprises reach RMB 220.59 billion, with an increase of 31.7%. The contract signing amount was RMB 682.06 billion, with an increase of 17.3%, of which, the newly-signed contract amount this year reached RMB 364.02 billion, with an increase of 36.1%.

V. Fixed Asset Investment

The investment structure kept the continuous optimization. The annual fixed asset investment was increased by 9.6% than that of the previous year. In terms of different industries, the primary industry investment was increased by 9.8%; the secondary industry investment was decreased by 10.1%, and the tertiary industry investment was increased by 14.3%. At the end of the year, it had 872 fixed asset investment projects with the amount over RMB 100 million, with an increase of 128 projects. In terms of the project scale, it had 19 projects with the amount over RMB 5 billion, with an increase of 3 projects, which completed the investment increase by 21.0%; it had 147 projects with the amount between RMB 1 billion and 5 billion, with an increase of 41 projects, which completed the investment decrease by 0.9%; it had 706 investment projects with the amount between RMB 100 million and RMB 1 billion, with an increase of 84 projects, which completed the investment increase by 34.0%. The private investment, infrastructure facilities and real economy were increased by 8.5%, 10.2% and 8.4%, respectively.

The service industry investment kept a rapid growth rate. The service industry investment in the whole year was increased by 14.4%. Among them, the high-tech service investment was increased by 7.8%, and the logistics industry was increased by 2.8%.

The real estate investment developed smoothly. The real estate development investment in the whole year reached RMB 136.93 billion, with an increase of 11.1%, of which, the residence investment reached RMB 92.85 billion, with an increase of 12.9%. The construction area of the building was 91.121 million m^2, with an increase of 13.8%, of which, the construction area of the residence was 59.327 million m^2, with an increase of 11.3%. The completion area of the building reached 12.038 million m^2, with an increase of 90.7%, of which, the completion area of the residence reached 8.974 million m^2, with an increase of 82.7%. The sales area of commercial housing reached 12.346 million m^2, with an increase of 1.6%, of which, the sales area of the residence was 9.636 million m^2, with a decrease of 1.0%. The sales amount of commercial housing reached RMB 147.38 billion, with an increase of 25.7%, of which, the sales amount of the residence reached RMB 117.28 billion, with an increase of 23.9%.

VI. Domestic Trade

The consumer market operated steadily. The total annual retail sales of social consumer goods was RMB 440.45 billion, increased by 10.0% over that of last year. The commodity retail sales were RMB 371.77 billion, with growth of 10.0%; the catering revenue was RMB 68.68 billion, an increase of 9.9%. In terms of towns and villages, the retail sales of social consumer goods in urban areas amounted RMB 400.31 billion, with an increase of 10.0%; The rural retail sales were RMB 40.14 billion, with growth of 9.4%. Units [7] above quota realized the retail sales of RMB 133.44 billion, with an increase of 7.7%.

The major goods kept the good sales trend. In the above-quota unit goods retail, the retail amount of grain and oil and food reached RMB 15.15 billion, with an increase of 6.4%; the clothing, shoes and hats and knitwear and textile reached RMB 11.32 billion, with an increase of 6.0%; the gold, silver and jewelry reached RMB 3.3 billion, with an increase of 20.4%; the household appliance and audio and video equipment reached RMB 7.46 billion, with an increase of 10.4%; and the communication equipment reached RMB 6.78 billion, with an increase of 22.0%.

Retail Sale Amount and Growth Rate of Above-quota Wholesale and Retail Unit Goods in 2018

Commodity class	Retail sale amount (RMB 000,000,000)	Increase over the previous year (%)
Grain and oil, food	151.5	6.4
Beverage	11.9	2.8
Tobacco and wine	22.3	-0.2
Clothing, shoes and hats, knitwear and textile	113.2	6.0
Cosmetics	20.7	5.0
Gold, silver and jewelry	33.0	20.4
Daily necessities	36.1	-5.7
Household appliances, audio and video equipment	74.6	10.4
Chinese and western medicine	46.3	4.9
Stationery & office supplies	36.2	-1.6
Communication equipment	67.8	22.0
Oil and products	151.2	6.4
Automobile	390.2	0.7

VII. Open Economy

The foreign trade had a rapid growth rate. Total export-import volume of goods in the whole year reached RMB 82.5 billion, with an increase of 16.2%. Therein, the export amount was RMB 51.93 billion increased by 14.6%; the import amount was RMB 30.57 billion, increased by 19.0%. In the export market, the export to European countries and regions grew by 16.8%, to South Korea and Japan decreased by 13.3% and 7.7%, respectively, and to the United States increased by 39.6%. In the main export goods, the electromechanical product export amount reached RMB 37.22 billion, with an increase of 17.5%; the high-tech product output reached RMB 9.22 billion, with an increase of 65.6%.

Level of utilizing foreign investment was improved dramatically. Actual use of foreign capital in the whole year reached RMB 17.82 billion, with an increase of 41.0%, of which, the foreign capital use of manufacture reached RMB 5.15 billion, and the foreign capital use of service industry reached RMB 12.3 billion. It had 41 projects with an investment over RMB 100 million, and the contractual foreign capital reached RMB 26.13 billion. It included 23 investment projects of top 500 enterprises, and the actual use of foreign capital was RMB 9.98 billion.

Economic cooperation with foreign countries was expanded actively. Fifty-one overseas enterprises (institutions) were set up and 6,254 workers were assigned.

The economic export-oriented degree was expanded further. The economic export-oriented degree was 10.5% in the whole year, with an increase of 0.7%.

VIII. Traffic, Post and Telecommunications, Tourism and Convention and Exhibition

The traffic and transportation kept stable. The length of highways reached 12,637.7 km at the end of the year, of which, the domestic highways reached 488.5 km. The highways passenger capacity reached 31.49 million, with a decrease of 1.3%. The volume of passenger transportation was 5.29 billion person-kilometers, with an increase of 0.5%. The highways freight volume achieved 0.26 billion tons, with an increase of 6.3%; the freight turnover quantity reached 47.4 billion ton-kilometers, with an increase of 3.1%. The number of the civil motor vehicle reached 2.304 million at the end of the year, of which, the number of the civil automobile reached 2.164 million. The bus lines reached 386 lines at the end of the year, with an increase of 54 lines; the total length of lines was 7,388.1 km, with an increase of 1,066.9 km; the volume of passenger traffic was 0.77 billion person-times, which was equivalent with that of the previous year. Jinan Airport guarantees 127,000 sorties, with an increase of 9.8%. It achieved the passenger throughput of 16.612 million person-times, with an increase of 16.0%; the cargo and mail realized a throughput of 114,000 tons, an increase of 19.4%;

The post and telecommunication had a rapid growth rate. The business income of postal enterprises and express service enterprises (excluding the direct business income of postal savings banks) totaled RMB 6.16 billion, with an increase of 26.4%; the total business volume achieved RMB 8.98 billion, with an increase of 38.7%. The business income of express service enterprises achieved RMB 4.84 billion, with an increase of 27.9%; the business volume achieved 431.955 million pieces, with an increase of 43.0%. The number of mobile telephone subscribers reached 10.137 million at the end of the year, of which, the number of 4G telephone subscribers reached 7.25 million, with an increase of 16.3%.

The tourism industry kept the stable development. Over the year, domestic and foreign tourists of 80.077 million person-times were received, with an increase of 9.9%, of which, 79.678 million person-times were received, with an increase of 9.9%; It received entry visitors of 0.399 million person-times, with an increase of 6.2%. It realized the total tourism consumption amount of RMB 112.96 billion, of which, the domestic tourist consumption amount was 105.47 billion, and entry visitor consumption amount was USD 222.851 million. It included 62 A-class tourism scenic areas, including 1 5A-level scenic area and 13 4A-level scenic areas, 30 provincial tourism strong townships, 82 provincial tourism characteristic villages and 1 above-provincial-area resort area.

The exhibition industry accelerated the development. It held 196 convention and exhibition in the whole year, including 12 international exhibitions.

IX. Finance and Banking

The financial revenue and expenditure operate kept the healthy operation. The general public budget income reached RMB 75.28 billion in the whole year, with an increase of 11.2%, of which, the tax revenue reached RMB 61.95 billion, with an increase of 14.3%; it accounted for 82.3% of the general public budget income, with an increase of 2.3%. The general public budget revenue was RMB 101.83 billion, increased by 22.1%; of which, education spending reached RMB 15.31 billion, with an increase of 6.8%; the social security and employment expenditure was RMB 13.29 billion, with an increase of 17.2%; the expenses of urban and rural communities was RMB 24.64 billion, with an increase of 33.8%.

The number of financial institutions kept the stable growth. The number of financial institutions reached 660 at the end of the year, with an increase of 88 units, of which, it included 49 banks, 91 insurance companies, 139 security companies and business departments, 54 futures companies and business department, 10 finance companies and 317 other institutions.

The scale of financial deposits and loans continued to expand. At the end of the year, the balance of deposits in local and foreign currencies in financial institutions reached RMB 1.70601 trillion, with an increase of 3.0%. The balance of loans in local and foreign currencies in financial institutions reached RMB 1.60599 trillion, with an increase of 11.9%.

The capital market was relatively active. The amount of securities trading completed in the whole year was RMB 2.8 trillion. The agency transaction amount of futures business department was RMB 7.9 trillion, with an increase of 9.0%; The newly-added direct financing was RMB 178.76 billion, with an increase of 159.8%. It had 34 listed companies in the whole city area at the end of the year, with 36 stocks; there were 21 new private investment fund institutions, and the total number of institutions reached 163.

The insurance industry kept the stable growth. The premium income was RMB 41.56 billion in the whole year, with an increase of 9.1%. The premium income of property insurance company was RMB 9.14 billion, increased by 12.9%; the premium income of the life insurance company was RMB 32.41 billion, with an increase of 8.0%. Various indemnities and payments was RMB 10.34 billion, with an increase of 16.6%.

X. Science and Technology, Education, Culture, Health and Sports

The scientific and technological inventions had remarkable results. The number of valid invention patents owned per 10,000 people in the whole year was 29.3, with an increase of 14.5% over the previous year. The transaction amount achieved in the technical contract was RMB 13.06 billion, with an increase of 54.2%. The number of research personnel in the large-scale industrial enterprises was up to 54,700. There were 366 research and development institutions of large-scale industrial enterprises. The city won 2 first-class prizes and 10 second-class prizes for provincial scientific and technological progress. The number of patent application quantities was 36,027, of which, the number of patent application quantities for invention was 13,685. The number of patent authorization was 20,636, of which, the number of patent authorization for invention was 4,887.

The education cause was promoted steadily. It included 51 institutes of higher education, 34 secondary vocational schools, 19 technician training schools [8], 251 ordinary secondary schools, 575 primary schools and 12 special education school. It had 93 newly-built and rebuilt and expanded kindergartens, more than 20,000 newly-added positions, 129 newly-rebuilt and expanded places for students to eat together. The enrolment rate of school-age children and the graduation rate of primary school graduates were 100%. *Jinan High School Education Popularization and Problem Solving Plan* was prepared and 26 schools in the city were included in the high school education popularization and problem solving plan.

The public cultural undertakings kept the stable and prosperous development. At the end of the year, the city had 195 (state-owned) art performance groups, 150 cultural centers (stations) and mass art centers, 15 archives and 14 public libraries. There were 374 cultural relics protection units above the municipal level, including 21 national-level units. There are 54 digital cinemas with the countable box office in the city, with 640,000 screenings and 1,189,000 audiences, earning RMB 460,000,000. At the end of the year, both the mixed coverage rate of broadcasting and television are 100%. Investment in cultural industries has increased by 18.3%. A total of 95 Comprehensive Cultural Service Centers (Cultural Compounds) are newly built in poverty-stricken villages. Forty grassroots Cultural Demonstration Sites are newly built, adding up to 240 demonstration sites.

The level of health services continued to improve. At the end of the year, there are 6,030 health institutions, an increase of 259, growth rate of 4.5%. Among them, there are 293 hospitals and health centers (21 are Grade-A Tertiary Hospitals and 154 are private hospitals). The number of beds in health institutions is 58,000, in an increase of 4.7%. There are 83,000 health technicians of various types, in an increase of 8.5%; and the number of practicing (assistant) physicians are 32,000, in an increase of 10.7%. Based on the resident population, there are 7.7 beds per thousand people, an increase of 2.8%; there are 4.3 practicing (assistant) physicians per thousand people, in an increase of 8.6%.

The national physical fitness has been carried out in a deep-going way. A total of 108 social sports organizations have been established, with 3,845 social sports instructors trained. Fifty-nine national fitness activities (competitions) are organized with 200,000 participants. A total of 3,347 sports activities sites are built. We have won 496 gold medals, 358 silver medals and 332 bronze medals at and above the provincial level.

XI. Urban and Rural Development, Environment and Safety Production

Significantly improving urban construction level [9] At the end of the year, the urban built-up area is 561.0 square kilometers, in an increase of 22.7 square kilometers over the previous year. The green coverage rate of the built-up areas is 40.6%, with per capita park green area 12.7 square meters. The annual natural gas supply volume is 1,140,000,000 cubic meters, in an increase of 25.6%; the supply of liquefied petroleum gas is 41,000 tons, a decrease of 17.7%. The area of central heating is 198,338,000 square meters, in an increase of 9.1%. The supply of tap water is 390,000,000 million tons, in an increase of 9.8%. The innocent treatment rate of garbage is 100%.

New urbanization proceeded smoothly. At the end of the year, the urbanization rate of the resident population reached 72.10%, in an increase of 1.57 percentage points. Jiyang realizes the establishment of districts and revocation of counties.

The ecological environment has been further improved. Throughout the whole year, the number of days with good air quality in the urban area is 203, in an increase of 18 days. The average concentration of inhalable particles (PM_{10}) per year in the urban ambient air is 112 micrograms per cubic meter, in a decrease of 13.8%; fine particles ($PM_{2.5}$) are 52 micrograms per cubic meter, in a decrease of 17.5%; sulfur dioxide is 17 micrograms per cubic meter, in a decrease of 32.0%; nitric oxide is 45 micrograms per cubic meter, in a decrease of 2.2%. The daily average equivalent sound level of regional environmental noise is 53.3 decibels, and urban road traffic noise is 69.5 decibels.

The construction of Safe Jinan has been further advanced. There are 18,594 criminal cases filed throughout the year. A total of 7,103 criminal cases are cracked. A total of 75,393 cases of public security are accepted. In 301 days, there are no "robbery or grabbing" on the streets, and 165 gangs of criminal organizations involved in crimes are eliminated, and 1,125 members are arrested.

The safety production situation has maintained stable on the whole. A total of 258 safety production fatalities of all varieties occur throughout the year, with 280 deaths and 50 serious injuries. The death rate of production safety fatalities in RMB 100 million GDP [10] is 0.036.

XII. Living standards of residents and social security

The living standards of residents realized continuous improvement. The per capita disposable income of urban residents is RMB 50,146, rising by 7.5% over last year; the per capita consumption expenditure of urban residents is RMB 32,977, rising by 7.3%. The per capita disposable income of rural residents is RMB 17,924, with an increase of 8.0%; The per capita consumption expenditure of rural residents is RMB 11,172, rising by 8.2%. The income ratio of urban and rural residents decreased from 2.81:1 last year to 2.80:1 now. Engel's Coefficient of urban residents [11] is 23.5%, while that of rural residents is 30.5%.

2018 per capita disposable income and growth rate of urban and rural residents

Indicator	Urban residents		Rural residents	
	In 2018 (RMB)	Increase over the previous year (%)	In 2018 (RMB)	Increase over the previous year (%)
Disposable income	50,146	7.5	17,924	8.0
Wage income	28,108	6.9	10,200	7.6
Net business income	2,758	6.5	6,295	8.6
Net property income	9,616	9.9	465	2.4
Net transfer income	9,664	7.2	965	11.0

The possession of major durable consumer goods per hundred households at the end of 2018 [12]

Indicator	Unit	Urban residents	Rural residents
Auto Life	Pcs	53.7	42.2
Refrigerator (freezer)	Set	103.2	97.4
Washing machine	Set	99.3	94.6
Water heater	Set	101.1	87.3
Air conditioner	Set	172.8	87.2
Color TV sets	Set	106.0	114.1
Camera	Set	36.4	6.2
Computer	Set	80.6	41.5
Mobile phone	Set	219.5	244.9

Social security is further improved. At the end of the year, the number of urban workers participating in the basic endowment insurance reached 3,316,600, an increase of 270,300; the number of employees participating in medical insurance is 2,415,400, an increase of 128,600; the number of people participating in unemployment insurance is 1,582,900, an increase of 111,000; the number of workers participating in employment injury insurance is 2,204,700, an increase of 329,600; the number of people covered by maternity insurance is 1,639,700, an increase of 112,400. The number of residents participating in endowment insurance and medical insurance reached 2,447,600 and 4,081,400 respectively.

The minimum living guarantee standard is further raised. The urban minimum living guarantee standard has been raised from RMB 596 per month per person last year to RMB 616 of this year. A total of 9,000 households cover 13,300 urban residents have access to the minimum living guarantee, and 96,000,000 yuan of minimum living guarantee and other various subsidies have been paid by the government. The per-capita annual minimum living guarantee standard in rural areas has been raised from RMB 4,277 to RMB 4,928. A total of 45,300 households covering 64,300 rural residents are available to the minimum living guarantee, and RMB 264,000,000 of minimum living guarantee and other various subsidies has been paid by the government. The annual basic living standard for the rural underprivileged is RMB 6,406 per person; the serving and nursing standard is divided into three grades according to if a person could self-care, semi-self-care and completely unable-to-care to take care of himself, with RMB 1,968, RMB 3,276 and RMB 6,552 per year per person respectively.

The course of social assistance has developed steadily. There has been 1 relief management station and 1 protection center for homeless juveniles, providing assistance for 2,500 people. Expenditure on urban and rural medical assistance funds is RMB 55,698,000, with 15,900 people being aided. A total of 4,802 people with disabilities are trained, 2,169 people with disabilities are arranged for employment, and RMB 140,000,000 is invested in helping and assisting the disabled.

XIII. National Economic and Social Development of the Original Laiwu City

Upon preliminary accounting, annual gross regional product reached to RMB 100,565,000,000 and increased by 7.2% over the previous year calculating at comparable prices. In terms of different industries, the value added of the primary industry is RMB 6,031,000,000, in an increase of 3.9%; the value added of the secondary industry is RMB 56,608,000,000, in an increase of 7.0%; the value added of the tertiary industry is RMB 37,926,000,000, in an increase of 8.1%. The structure of the three industries is 6.0:56.3:37.7. Per capita GDP reached RMB 73,005, in an increase of 7.1%. By the end of the year, the population of permanent residents is 1,379,000, in an increase of 3,000. Among them, the urban population is 878,700 (an increase of 17,600), accounting for 63.72% of the total population, in an increase of 1.14 percentage points. Growth of industrial value added of above-scale enterprises realizes 8.3%; major business revenue reached RMB 209,390,000,000, in an increase of 11.5%. Total profits are RMB 9,040,000,000, in an increase of 39.8%. The growth of fixed asset investment reached 7.2%. A total retail sales of consumer goods is RMB 37,320,000,000, in an increase of 8.8%. The general public budget revenue is RMB 6,260,000,000, in an increase of 11.7%; Among them, tax revenue is RMB 5,040,000,000, in an increase of 16.2%. The general public budget revenue is RMB 10,040,000,000, in an increase of 13.1%. The per capita disposable income of urban residents is RMB 37,401, in an increase of 7.2%; The per capita consumption expenditure is RMB 21,304, rising by 7.0%. The per capita disposable income of rural residents is RMB 17,468, with an increase of 8.2%; the per capita consumption expenditure is RMB 12,263, in an increase of 8.4%.

Notes:

[1] Statistics 2018 are statistical preview or preliminary accounting data, and the official data are subject to the published *Jinan Statistical Yearbook-2019*. According to the unified requirements for data release, statistics 2018 will be released based on Jinan City and Laiwu City respectively.

[2] The city gross regional product and the absolute amount of the value added of various industries are calculated on current price, while the growth

rate is calculated at a constant price.

[3] Per capita gross regional product is calculated by the average annual permanent resident population.

[4] Modern service industry includes: Information transmission, software and IT, financial industry, real estate, leasing and business services, scientific research and technology services, water conservancy, environment and management of public facility, residential service, repair and other services, education, health and social work, culture, sports and entertainment.

[5] According to the requirements of the system, 2017 data are used for value added indicators of the new economy.

[6] Industrial enterprises above designated size refer to industrial legal entities with annual prime business revenue of RMB 20,000,000 and above.

[7] Units above quota refer to wholesale enterprises with annual prime business revenue of RMB 20,000,000 and above, retail enterprises with annual prime business revenue of RMB 5,000,000 and above, and accommodation and catering enterprises with annual prime business revenue of RMB 2,000,000 and above. Unit includes corporate enterprises, industrial activity units and self–employed business.

[8] Technical schools have been adjusted to Jinan Municipal Technical Schools since 2017.

[9] The index caliber of urban construction is the entire Jinan area including two counties.

[10] The death rate of production safety fatalities to RMB 100 million GDP refers to the ratio of the number of deaths due to production safety fatalities to RMB 100 million of GDP.

[11] Engel's Coefficient refers to the proportion of food expenditure in consumption expenditure.

[12] The data is from the survey of household income and expenditure and living conditions.

Source of data: The social security data in this statement is from the Public Security Department; the data of financial is from the Financial Department; the number of new jobs in cities and towns, new transfer of the rural labor force, registered unemployment rate, all kinds of insurance data for urban workers, and the data of talent is all from Jinan Municipal Human Resources and Social Security Department; the data of safety production is from Department of Emergency Management; the relevant data of eliminating backward capacity is from the Industry and Information Technology Department; the data of the output of aquatic products and agriculture is from the Agriculture and Rural Department; the data of forestry and expansion of green are from the Landscape and Forestry Department; the data of foreign capital is from the Investment Promotion Department; the data of import and export, contract foreign projects, newly established overseas enterprises, employees dispatched abroad and exhibition is from the Commerce Department; the data of highway mileage, public transportation and highway transportation is from the Transportation Department; the data of postal and express delivery data is from the Postal Administration Department; the data of insurance and securities data is from local Financial Management Department; the data of tourism and cultural is from the Cultural & Tourism Department; the data of education is from the Education Department; the data of science and technology data is from the Science and Technology Department; the data of newly recognized national enterprise technology centers and the newly added provincial engineering laboratories (Engineering Research Center) is from the Development and Reform Department; the relevant data of health and the new rural cooperative medical care system is from the Health & Sanitation Department; the data of sports are from Sports Department; the relevant data of the transformation of shanty towns, urban redevelopment, urban renewal and urban construction is from the Housing and Urban–Rural Development Department; the relevant data of environmental protection is from the Ecological Environment Department; the data of demolition of squatter and temporary houses is from the Urban Management Department; the relevant data of the minimum living guarantee in urban and rural areas and the assistance and support for the poor in rural areas is from the Civil Affairs Department; the data of deepening reform in an all–round way is from the Leading Group Office for Deepening Comprehensive Reform and the Development and Development and Reform Commission; The data of Poverty alleviation is from the Municipal Leading Group Office for Poverty Alleviation and Development; the data of the insurance of the disabled is from the China Disabled Persons' Federation; the data of residents' income and expenditure, Engel's Coefficient, the price index and grain output is from the Jinan Investigation Team of the National Bureau of Statistics; the data of the pilot zones for replacing old growth drivers with the new one is from the management committee of the Jinan Prior Zone Committee for Replacing Old Growth Drivers with New Ones; other data is all from the Jinan Municipal Bureau of Statistics.

2018年的济南
Jinan in 2018

7856.56
地区生产总值(亿元)
Gross Domestic Product
(100 million yuan)

60.5
第三产业比重(%)
Proportion of Tertiary Industry(%)

746.04
常住人口(万人)
Permanent Population
(10 000 persons)

752.8
一般公共预算收入(亿元)
General Public Budget Revenue(100 million yuan)

9.6
全社会固定资产投资增长幅度(%)
Growth rate Total Investment in Fixed Assets(%)

131.8
海关进出口总额(亿美元)
Total Value of Imports and Exports(100 million USD)

106302
人均地区生产总值(元)
Per Capita Gross Domestic Product(yuan)

50146
城镇居民人均可支配收入(元)
Per Capita Disposable Income of Urban inhabitant(yuan)

4404.5
社会消费品零售总额 (亿元)
Total Retail Sale of Consumer Goods(100 million yuan)

17924
农村居民人均可支配收入(元)
Per Capita Disposable Income of rural inhabitant(yuan)

102.6
居民消费价格指数(%)
Consumer Price Index(%)

济南一日
A Day in Jinan

每日创造
Daily Production

一般公共预算
收入(万元/天)
General Pubilic Budget
Revenue
(10 000 yuan/day)

一般公共预算
支出(万元/天)
General Public Budget
Expenditure
(10 000 yuan/day)

海关进出口总额
(万美元/天)
Total Value of Imports and
Exports
(10 000 USD/day)

入境游客人数
(人次/天)
Number of Inbound Tourists
(person-time/day)

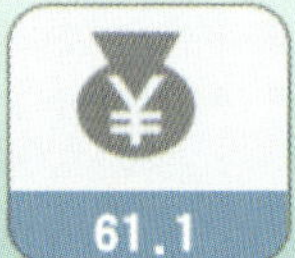

旅游外汇收入
(万美元/天)
Foreign Exchange Income of
Tourism
(10 000 USD/day)

7463.6
第一产业(万元/天)
Primary Industry(10 000 yuan/day)

215248.2
地区生产总值(万元/天)
Gross Domestic Product (10 000 yuan/day)

公路客运量
(人/天)
Highways Passenger
Traffic
(person/day)

77515.3
第二产业(万元/天)
Secondary Industry(10 000 yuan/day)

民航客运量
(人/天)
Civil Aviation Passenger
Traffic
(person/day)

130269.3
第三产业(万元/天)
Tertiary Industry(10 000 yuan/day)

生产汽车
(辆/天)
Automobile Manufacturing
(unit/day)

发电量
(万千瓦时/天)
Power Generating Capacity
(10 000 kwh/day)

蔬菜产量
(吨/天)
Output of Vegetables
(tons/day)

粮食产量
(吨/天)
Output of Grain
Crops(tons/day)

原油加工量
(吨/天)
Crude Processing
Volume(tons/day)

生产服务器
(台/天)
Server manufacturing
(unit/day)

每日生活
Daily Life

259
出生人口
(人/天)
Population of Birth(person/day)

124
死亡人口
(人/天)
Population of Death (person/day)

1828.8
城乡居民生活用电量
(万千瓦时/天)
Household Electricity Consumption of Urban and Rural Residents(10 000 kwh/day)

141
登记结婚
(对/天)
Registered Marriages(couple/day)

195
法人单位在岗职工平均工资
(元/天)
Average Wages of on-post staff in Legal Entities(yuan/day)

87
离婚
(对/天)
Divorces(couple/day)

137
城镇居民人均可支配收入
(元/天)
Per Capita Disposable Income of Urban inhabitant(yuan/day)

107.5
自来水供水量
(万吨/天)
Volume of Water Supply (10 000 tons/day)

101824.1
批发零售业零售额
(万元/天)
Total Retail Sale of Wholesale and Retail Trades(10 000 yuan/day)

732.7
住宿业零售额(万元/天)
Total Retail Sale of Wholesale and Retail Trades(10 000 yuan/day)

18113.4
餐饮业零售额(万元/天)
Total Retail Sale of Accommodation (10 000 yuan/day)

120670.2
社会消费品零售总额 (万元/天)
Total Retail Sale of Consumer Goods (10 000 yuan/day)

312.2
天然气供气量
(万立方米/天)
Total Natural Gas Supply (10 000 cu.m/day)

5551.8
生活垃圾清运量
(吨/天)
Domestic Waste Removed and Transported(tons/day)

31
农村居民人均生活消费支出
(元/天)
Per Capita Consumer Expenditure of rural inhabitant(yuan/day)

90
城镇居民人均生活消费支出
(元/天)
Per Capita Consumer Expenditure of Urban inhabitant(yuan/day)

49
农村居民人均可支配收入
(元/天)
Per Capita Disposable Income of rural inhabitant(yuan/day)

综 合
General Survey

地区生产总值（亿元）
Gross Domestic Product (100 million yuan)

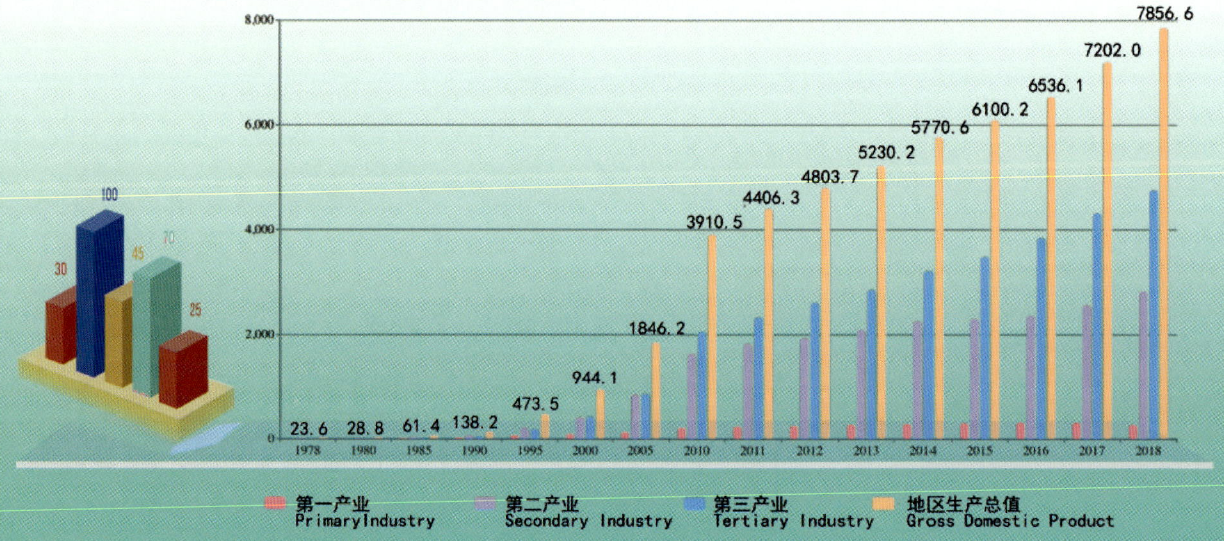

人均地区生产总值（元）
Per Capita Gross Domestic Product (yuan)

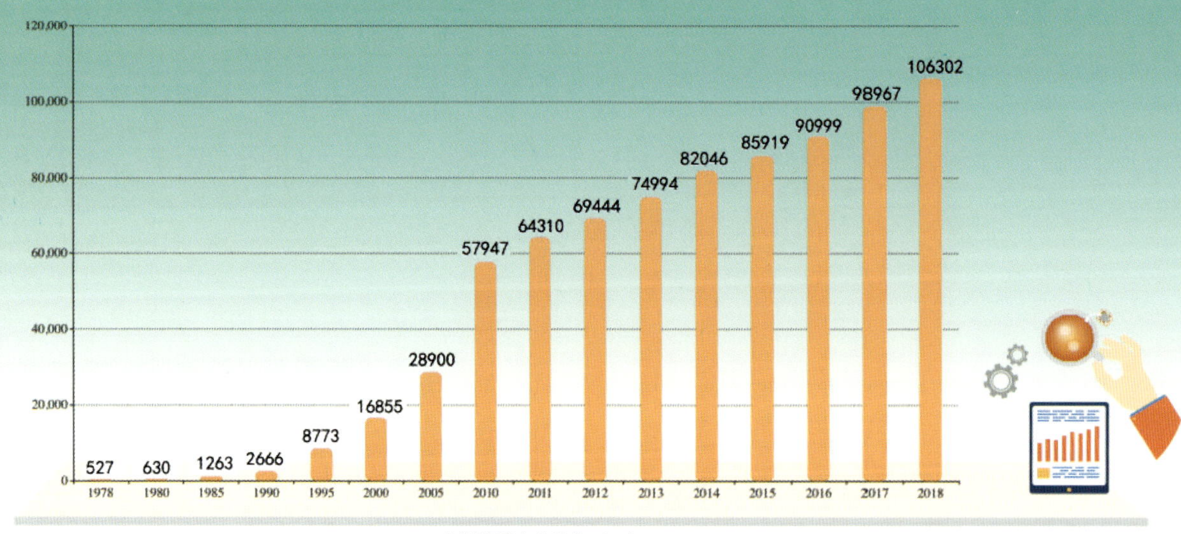

年末户籍总人口（万人）
Registered Population Year-end (10 000 persons)

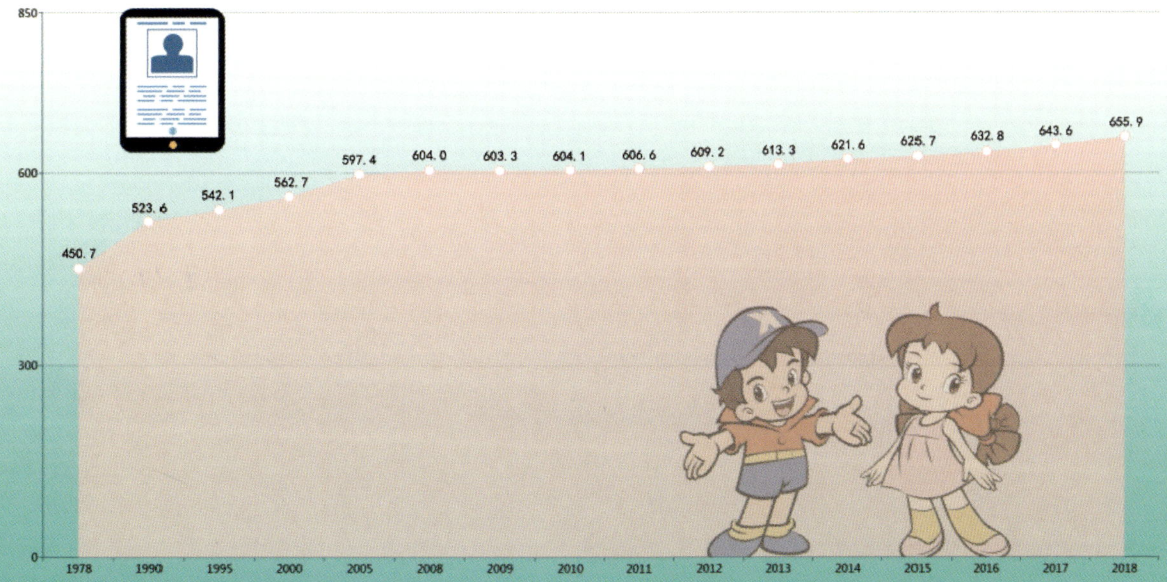

人口自然变动情况（‰）
Natural Changes of Population (‰)

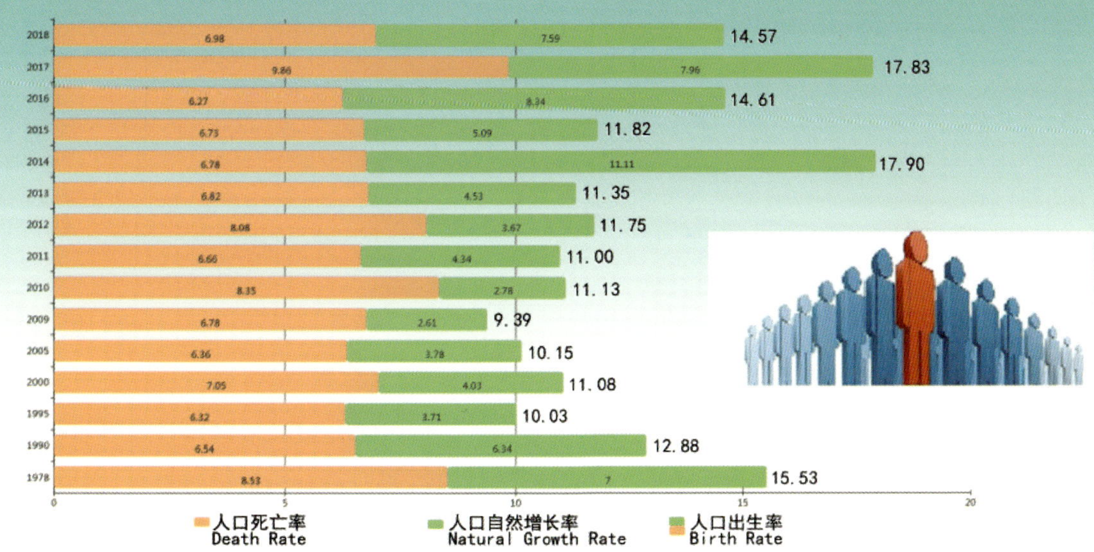

就 业
Employment

全社会从业人员（万人）
Total Employed Persons (10 000 persons)

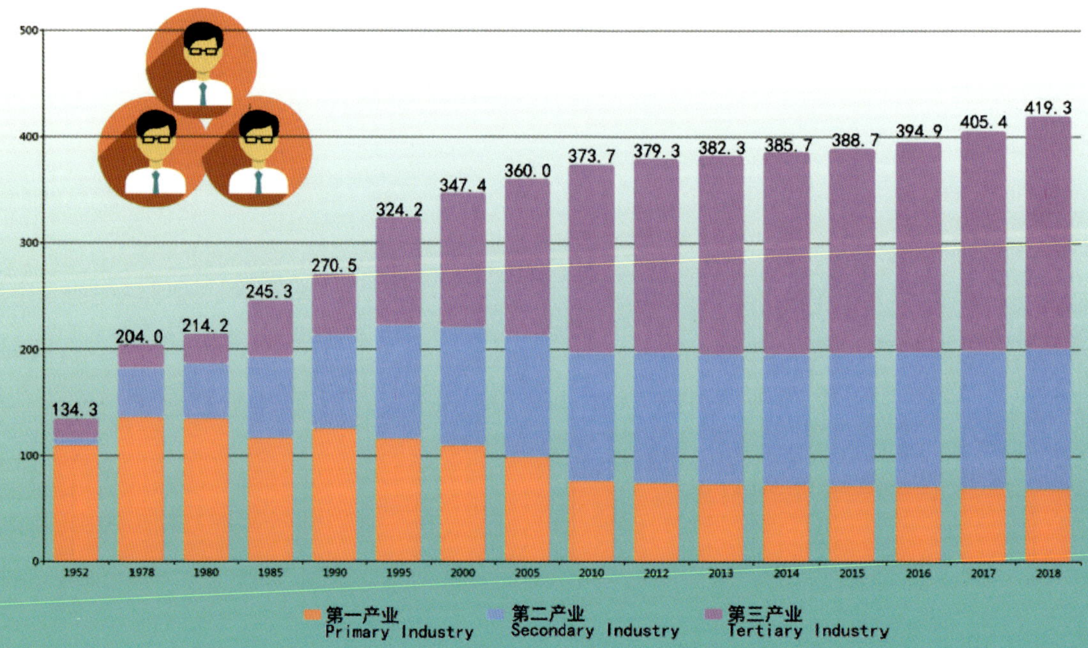

在岗职工平均工资（元）
Average Wage of Staff and Workers (yuan)

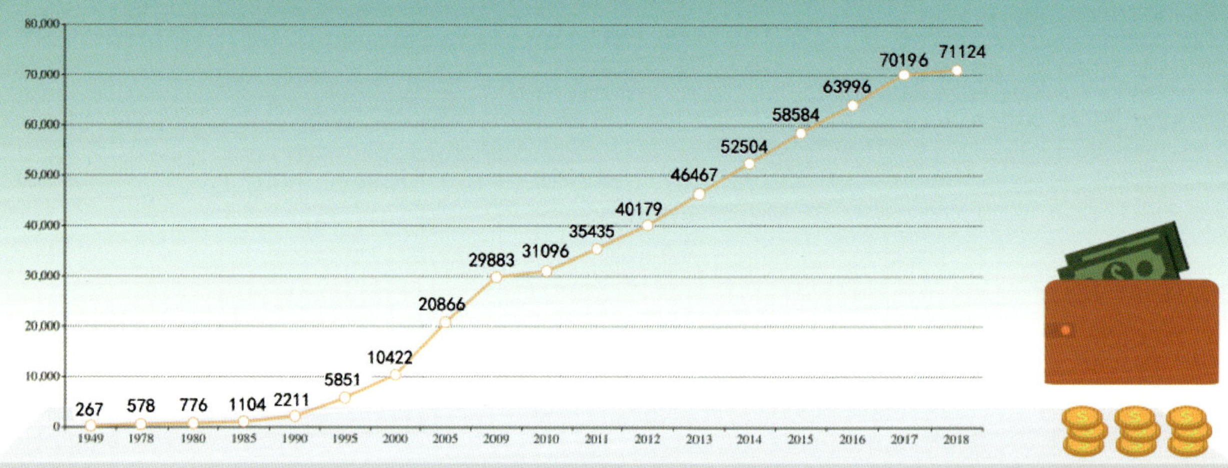

注：2006 年后数据为法人单位在岗职工口径
Notes: The data after 2006 are based on the caliber of on-the-job employees of legal entities.

财政 金融
Government Finance Financial

一般公共预算收入支出（亿元）
General Public Budget Revenue and Expenditure(100 million yuan)

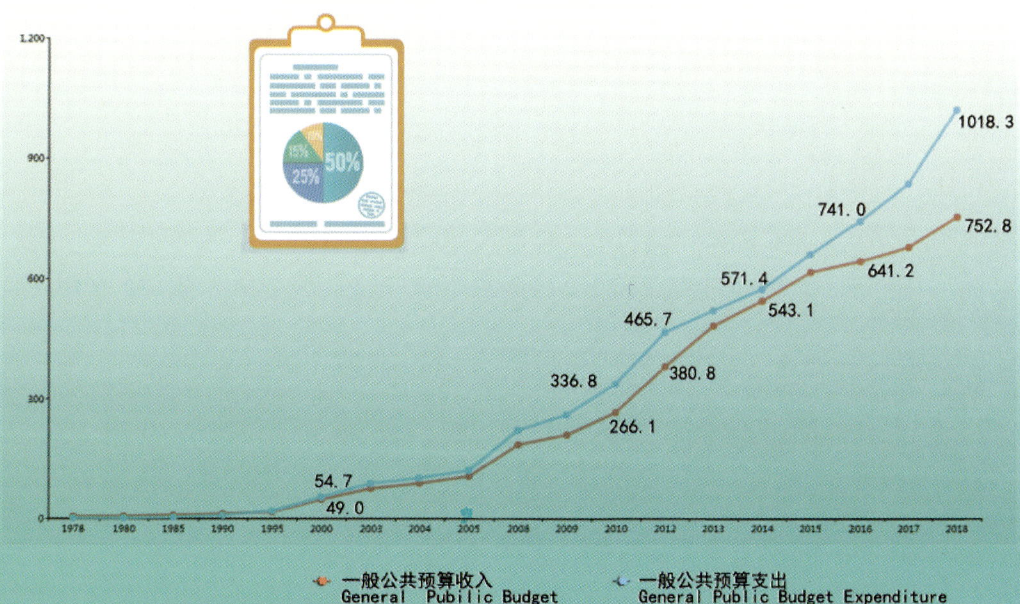

一般公共预算收入 General Public Budget
一般公共预算支出 General Public Budget Expenditure

金融机构人民币存、贷款金额（亿元）
The Ending Balance of all Deposits and Loans in RMB of Financial Institutions(100 million yuan)

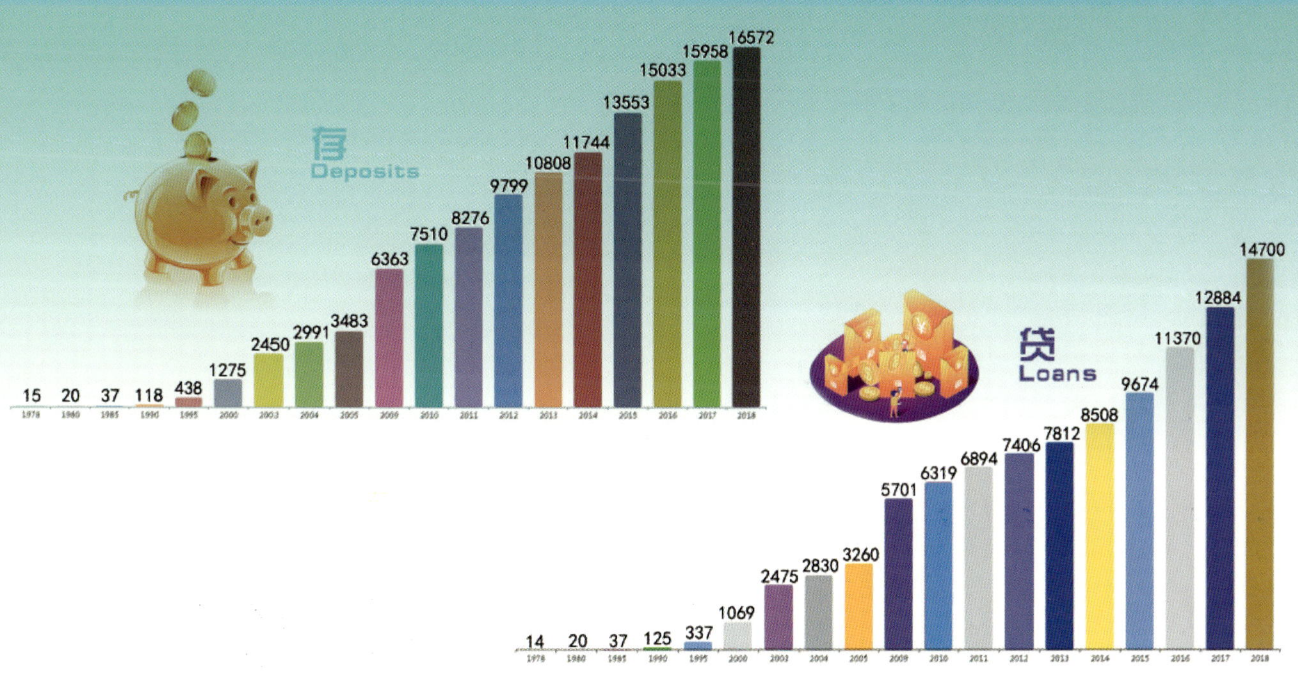

人民生活
People's Livelihood

城镇居民人均可支配收入和农村居民人均可支配收入（元）
Per Capita Disposable Income of Urban and Rural Inhabitant(yuan)

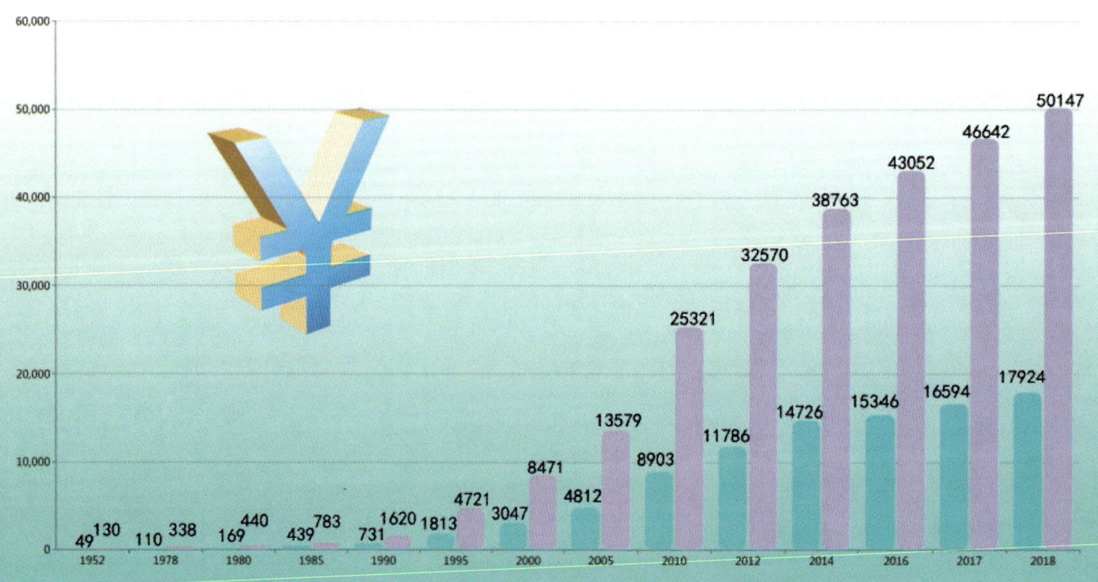

城镇居民人均消费支出和农村居民人均消费支出（元）
Per Capita Consumer Expenditure of Urban and Rural Inhabitant(yuan)

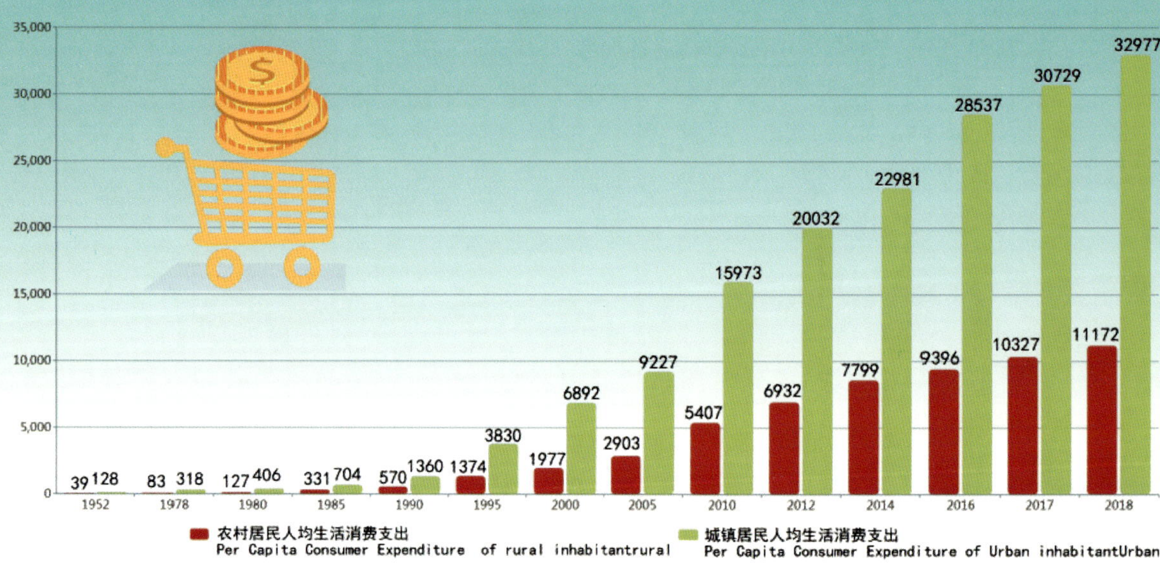

注：城乡一体化改革，2015年起为城镇居民人均支配收入和农村居民人均可支配收入口径；之前年份为城市居民人均可支配收入和农民人均纯收入口径。
Notes: The urban-rural integration reform has been based on the caliber of per capita disposable income of urban residents and rural residents since 2015; the urban-rural integration reform in previous years was based on the caliber of per capita disposable income of city residents and the per capita net income of farmers.

城镇居民与农村居民恩格尔系数（%）
Engel's Coefficient of Urban and Rural Inhabitant(%)

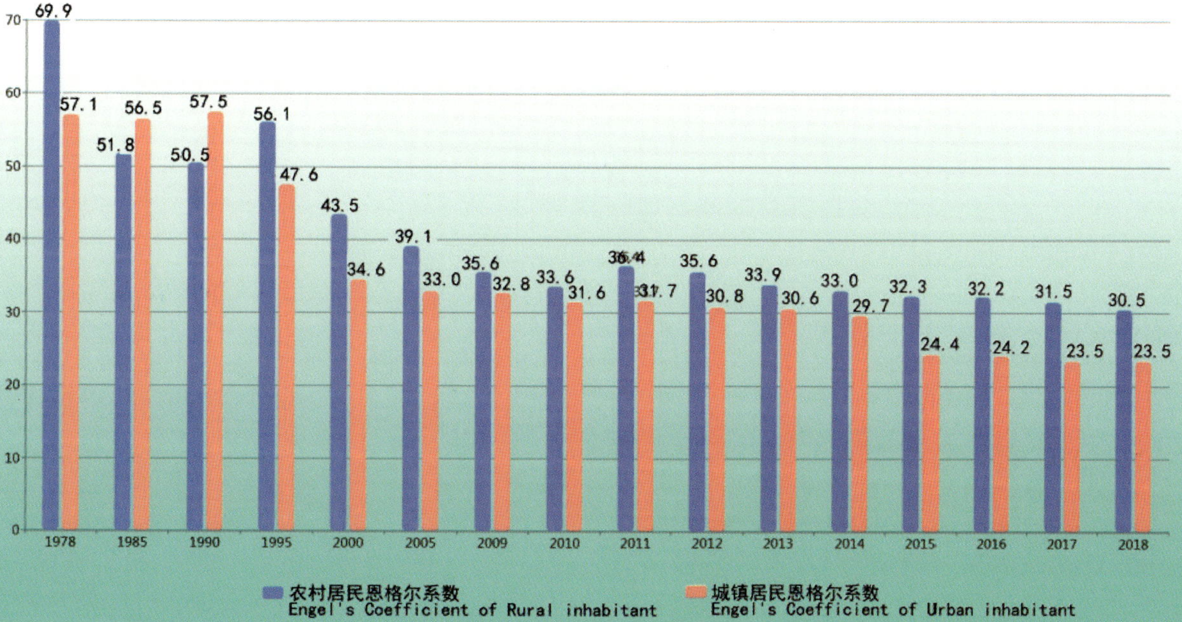

人民币住户存款余额（亿元）
The Balance RMB Household Deposits(100 million yuan)

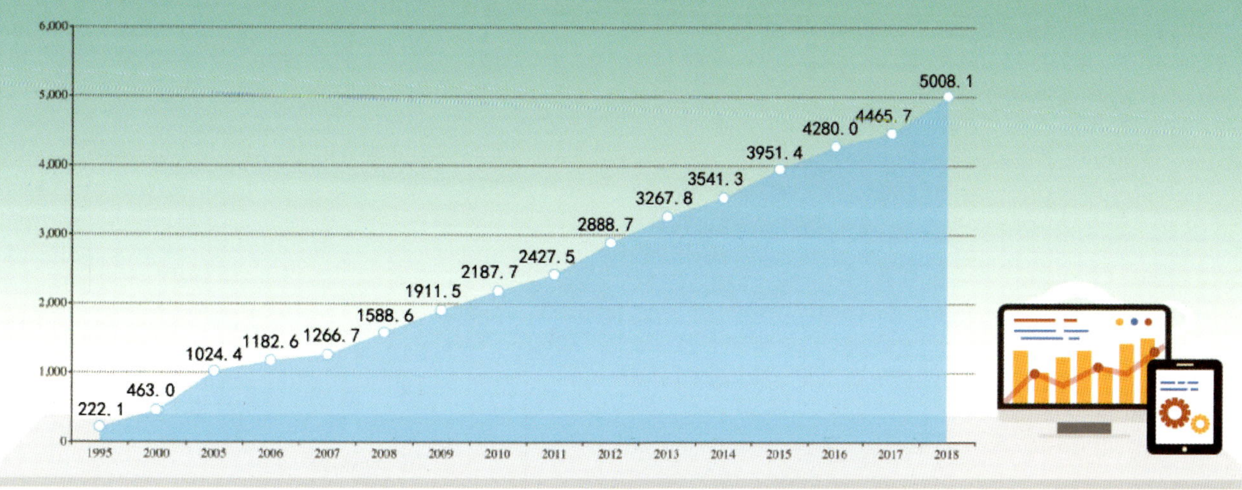

注：从 2015 年年开始，本市居民收支调查指标采用新口径。“农村居民人均生活消费支出”2014 年以前为农民人均生活费支出口径
Notes: Starting from 2015, the city's residents' income and expenditure survey indicators adopt a new caliber. "Per capita consumption expenditure of Rural Residents" was the "per capita living expenses of farmers" before 2014.

物 价
Prices

居民消费价格指数与商品零售价格指数（以上年为 100）
Consumer Price Index and Retail Price Index (Preceding Last Year=100)

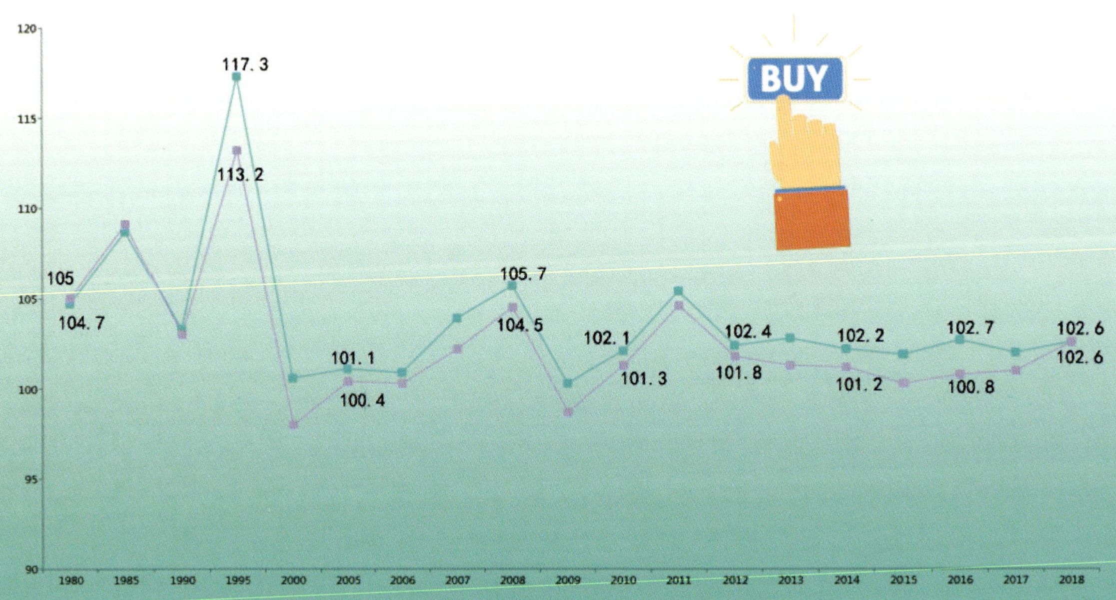

工业生产者出厂价格指数与工业生产者购进价格指数（以上年为 100）
Producer Price Index and Purchasing Price Index for Industrial Products(Preceding Last Year=100)

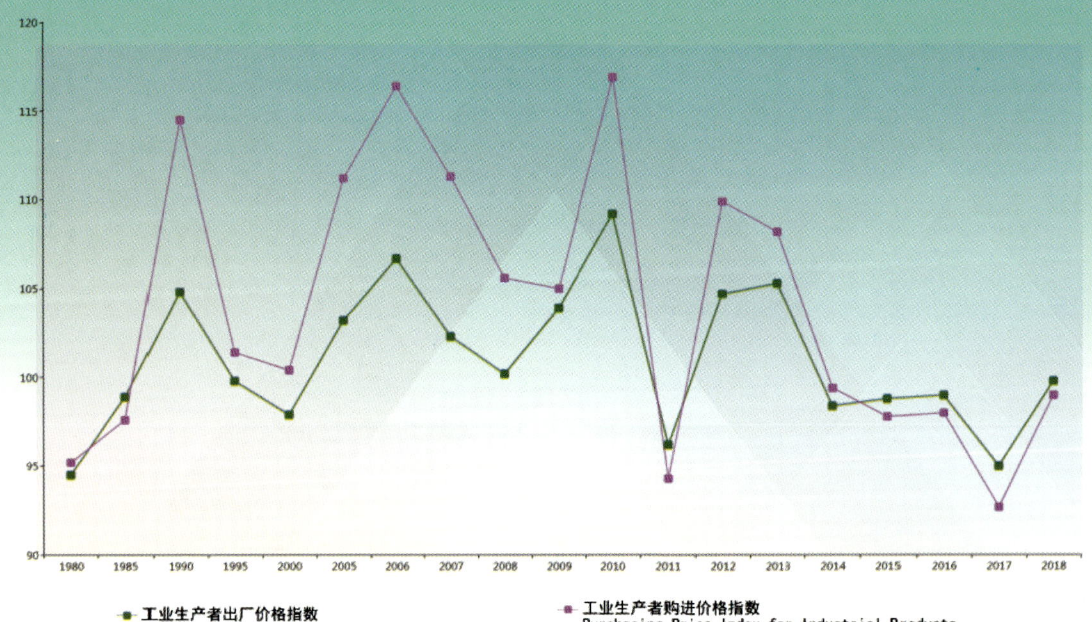

外经外贸
Foreign Trade

实际使用外资（万美元）
Actual Use of Foreign Capital (10 000 USD)

海关进出口总值（万美元）
Total Value of Imports and Exports (10 000 USD)

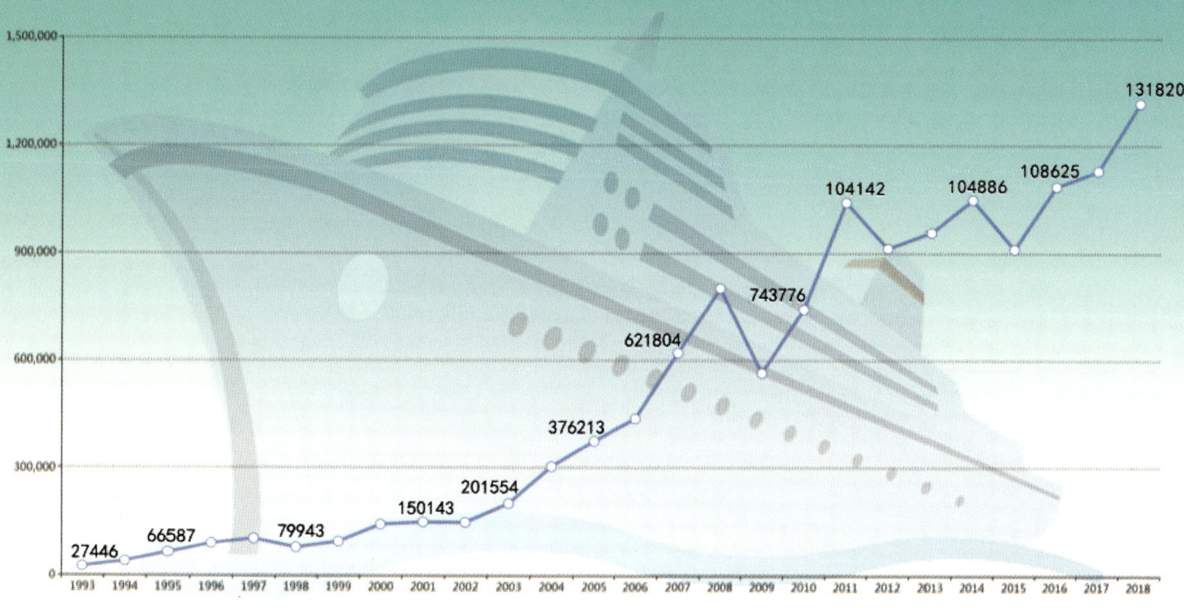

工 业
Industry

规模以上工业主营业务收入（亿元）
Revenue from Principal Business of Industrial Enterprises Above Designated Size (100 million yuan)

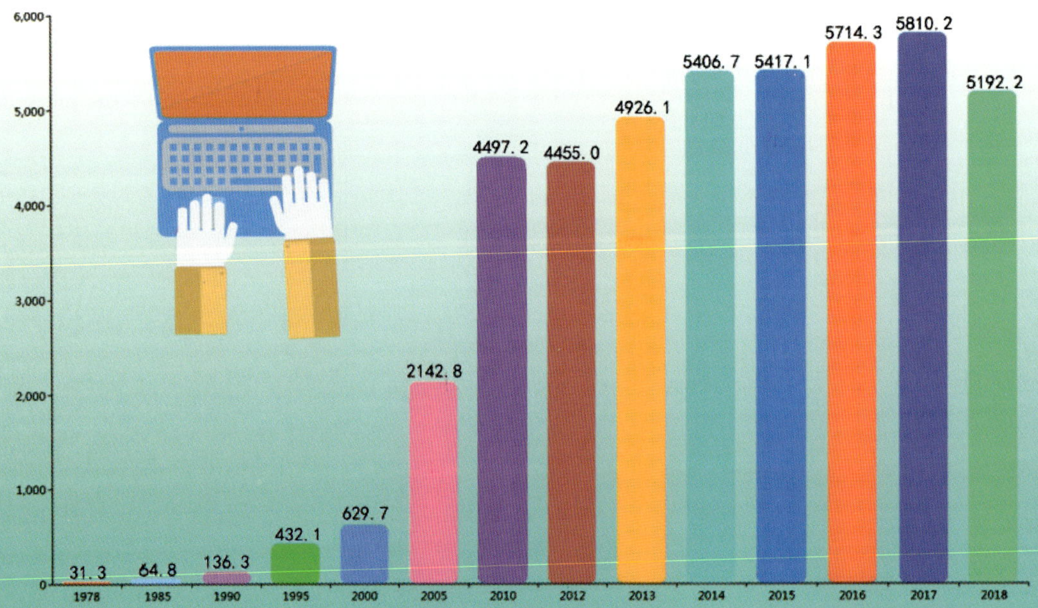

规模以上工业利税总额（亿元）
Total Profits and Taxes of Industrial Enterprises Above Designated Size(100 million yuan)

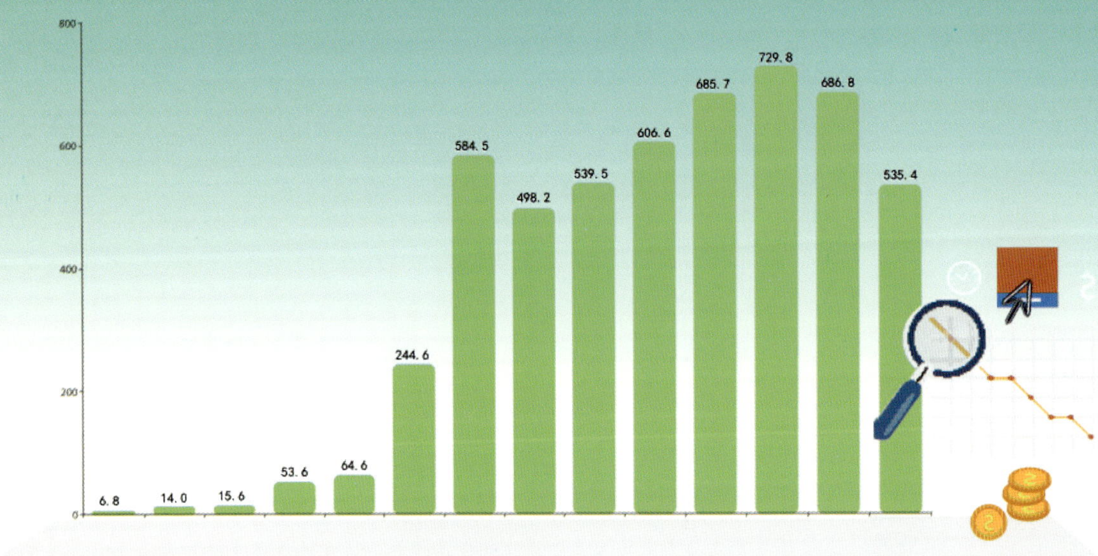

规模以上工业利润总额（亿元）
Total Profits of Industrial Enterprises Above Designated Size(100 million yuan)

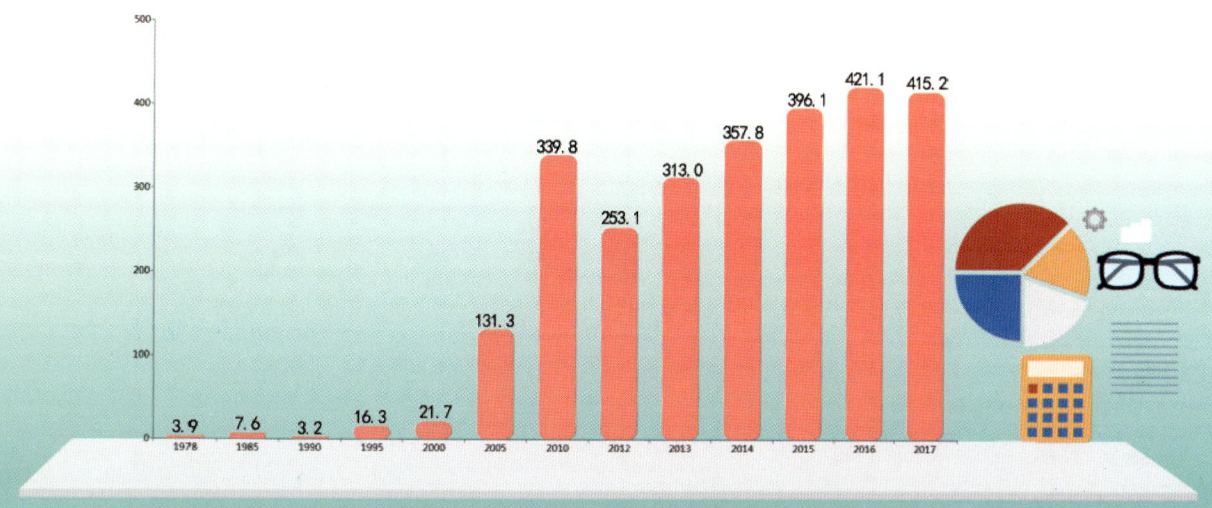

主要工业产品产量
Output of Major Industrial Products

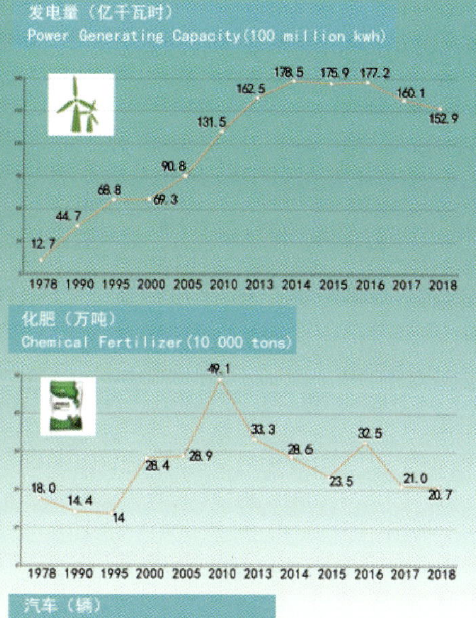

汽车（辆）
Motor Vehicles(unit)

4025 6239 5657 3078 42214 212047 165963 139751 96184 124200 201883 232082

1978 1990 1995 2000 2005 2010 2015 2016 2017 2018

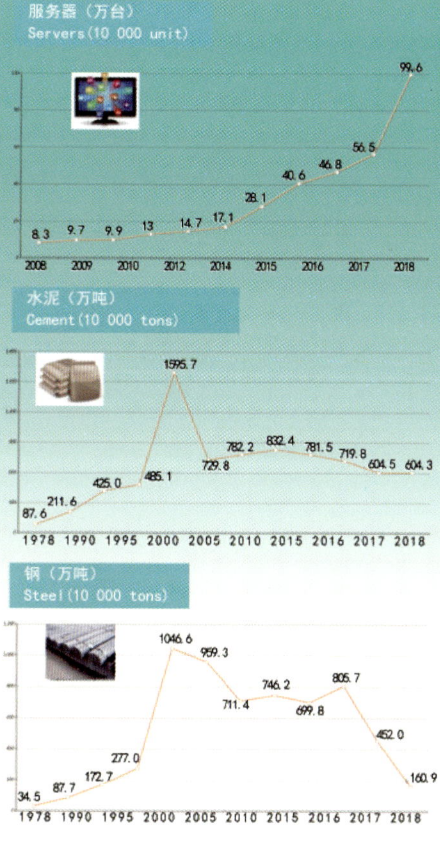

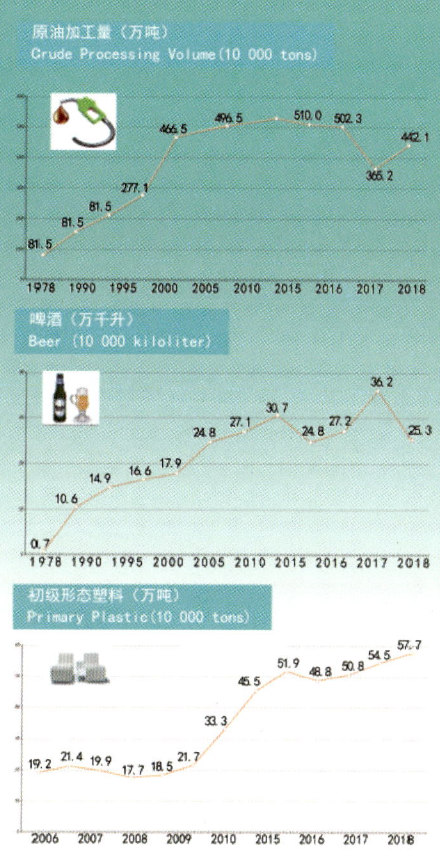

国内贸易 投资
Domestic Trade Investment

社会消费品零售总额及构成（亿元）
Total Retail Sales of Consumer Goods and Composition(100 million yuan)

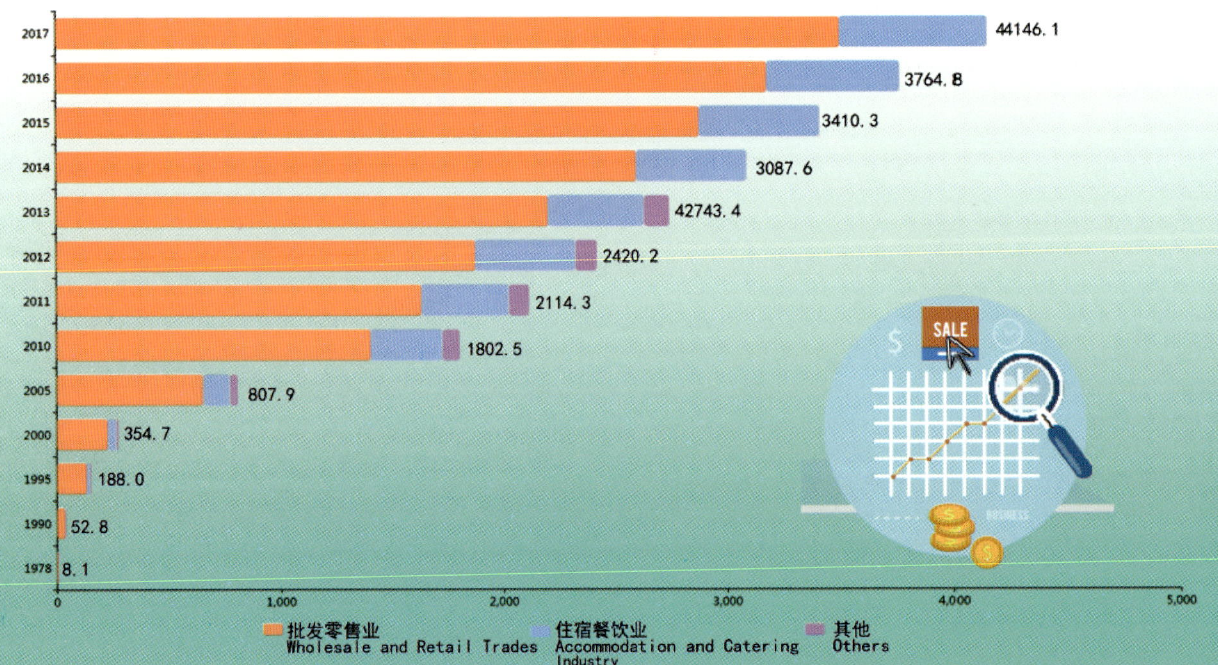

固定资产投资及构成（亿元）
Total Investment in Fixed Assets and Composition(100 million yuan)

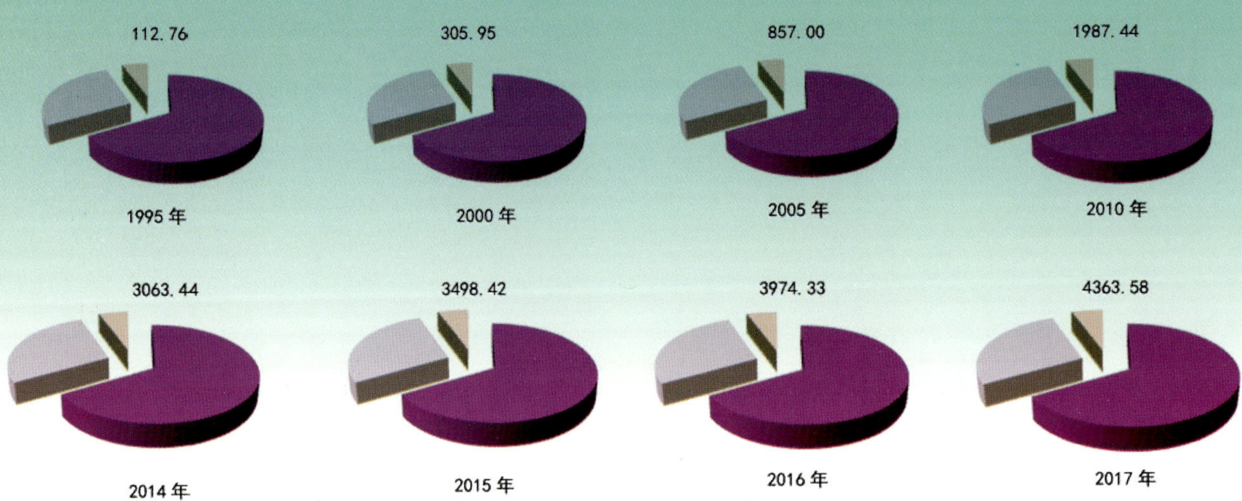

农业
Agriculture

农林牧渔业增加值（亿元）
Added Value of Agriculture, Forestry, Animal Husbandry and Fishery (100 million yuan)

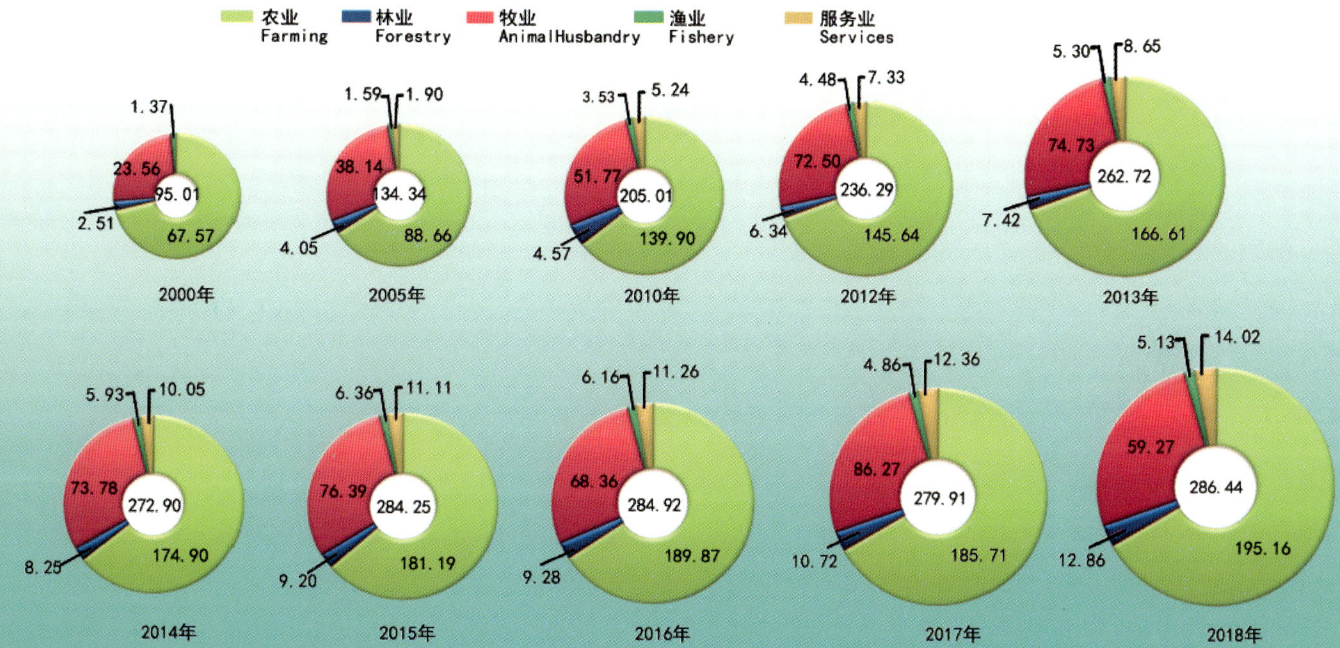

主要农产品产量（万吨）
Output of Main Agricultural Products (10 000 tons)

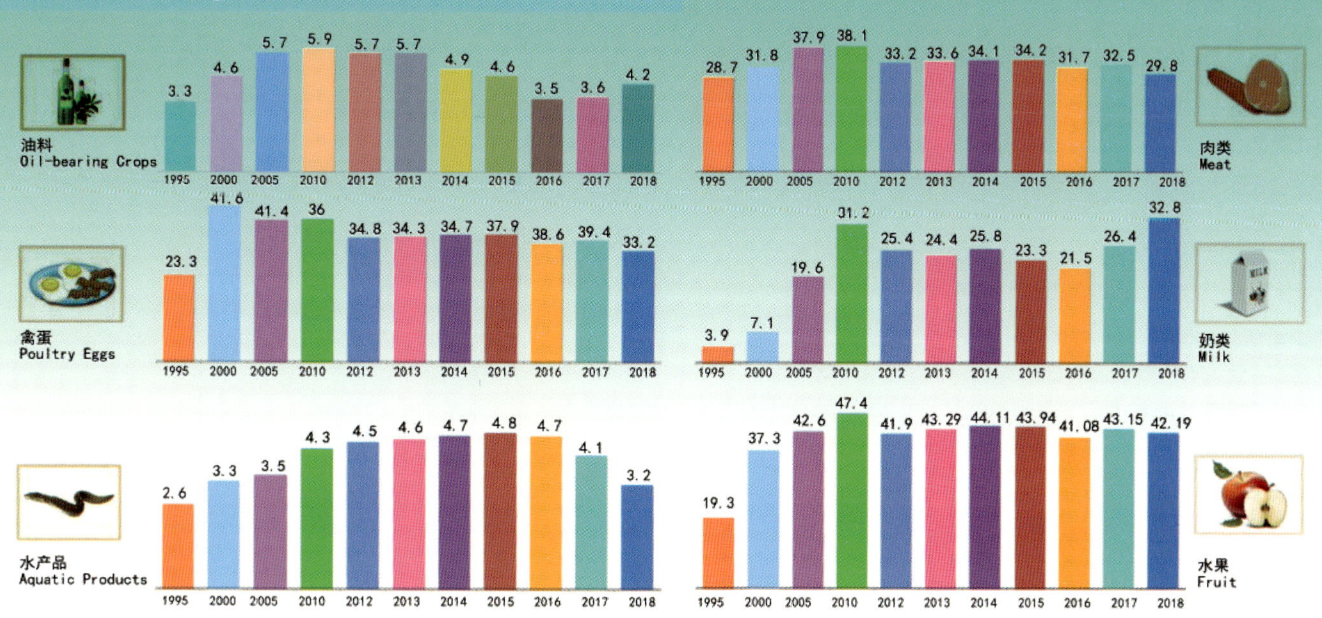

城市建设
Urban Public

供热面积（万平方米）
Area of Central Heating(10 000 sq. m)

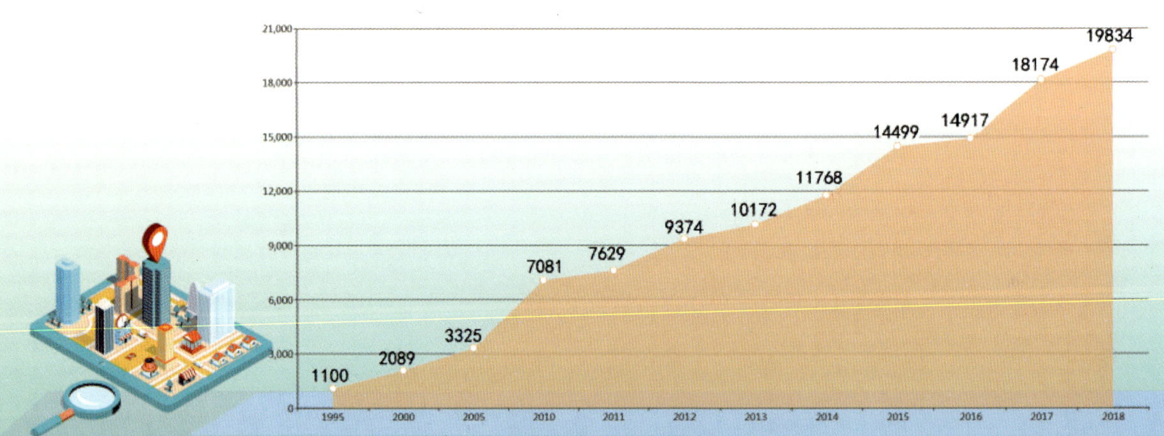

公共交通客运量（万人次）
Public Transportation of Passenger Traffic(10 000 person-times)

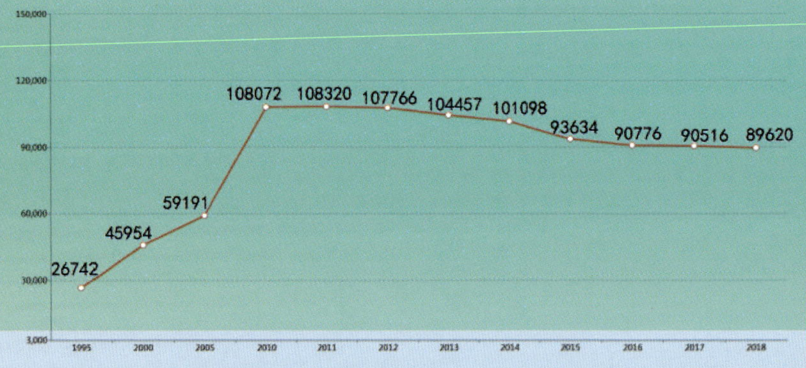

人均公园绿地面积（平方米/人）
Per Capita Public Green Area(sq. m/person)

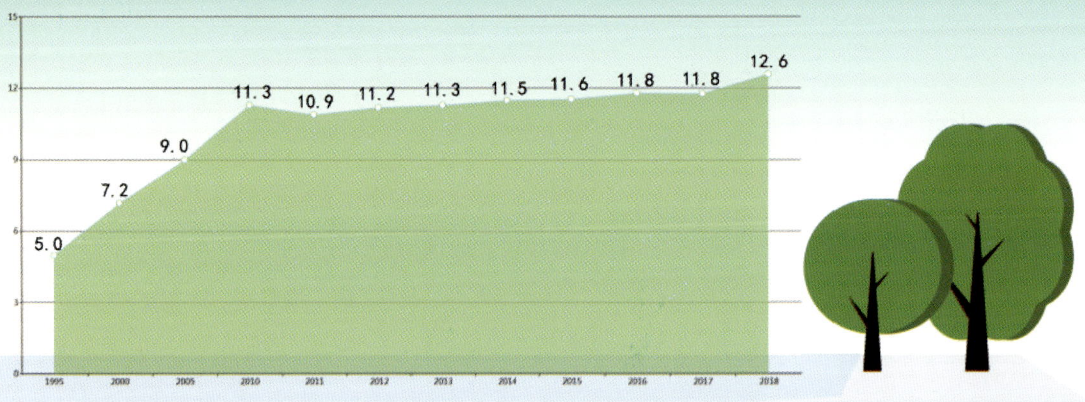

全社会用电量（万千瓦时）
Electricity Consumption(10 000 kwh)

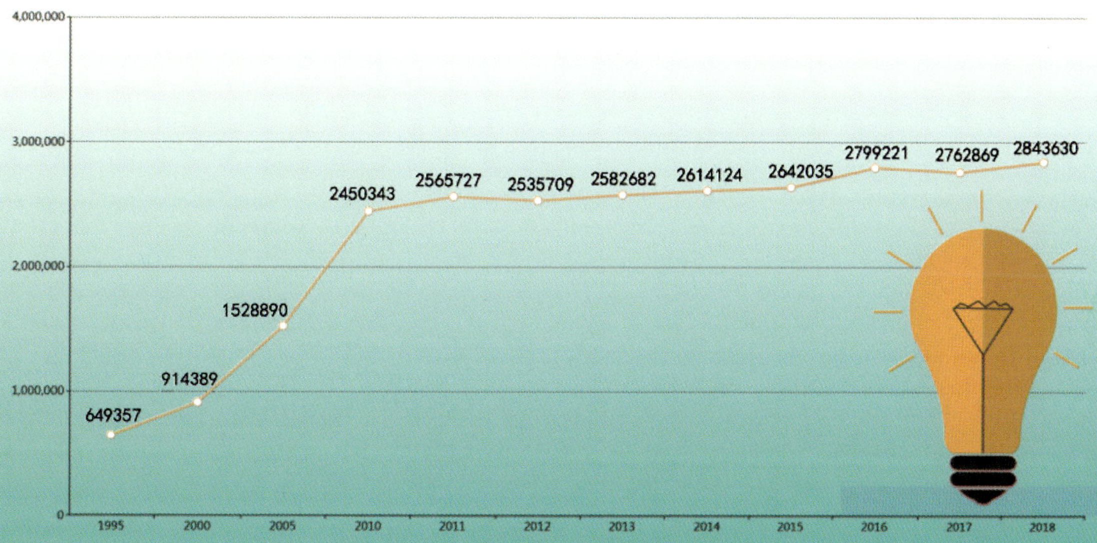

全社会供气量
Total Social Gas Supply

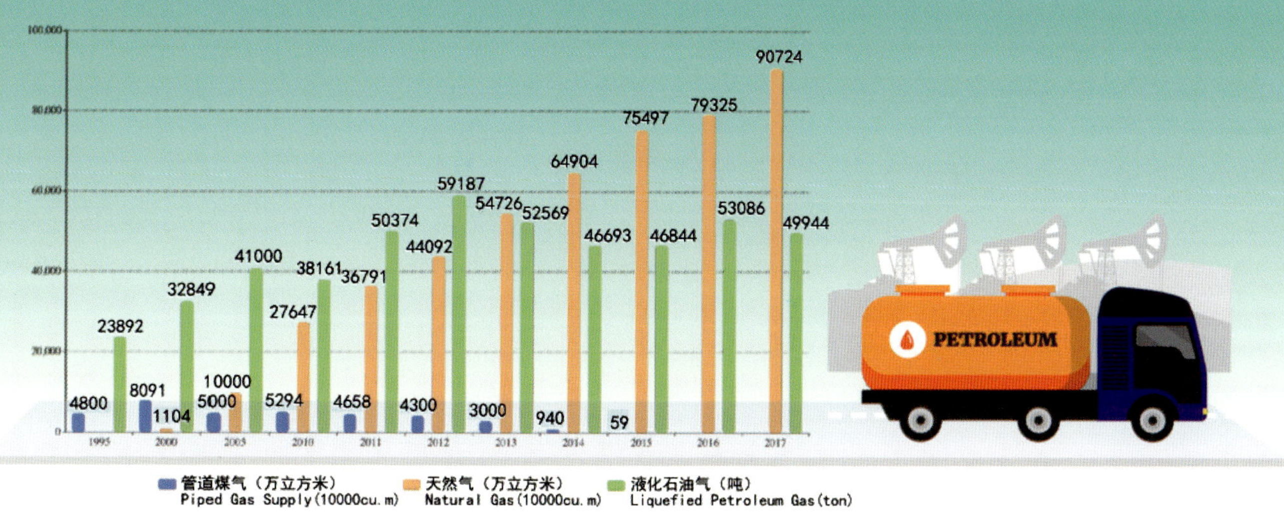

邮电 交通
Transportation Post and Telecommunications

移动电话用户、宽带互联网接入用户数（万户）
Number of Mobile Telephone Subscribers、Subscribers of Broad Band Internet (10 000 subscribers)

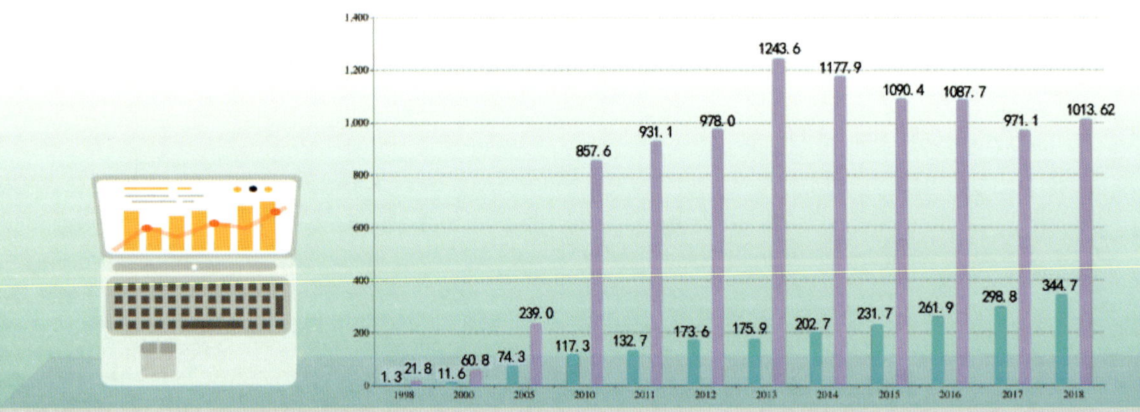

宽带互联网接入用户数（万户）
Subscribers of Broad Band Internet(10 000 subscribers)

移动电话用户（万户）
Number of Mobile Telephone Subscribers(10 000 subscribers)

客运量（万人）
Passenger Traffic(10 000 persons)

货运量（万吨）
Freight Traffic(10 000 tons)

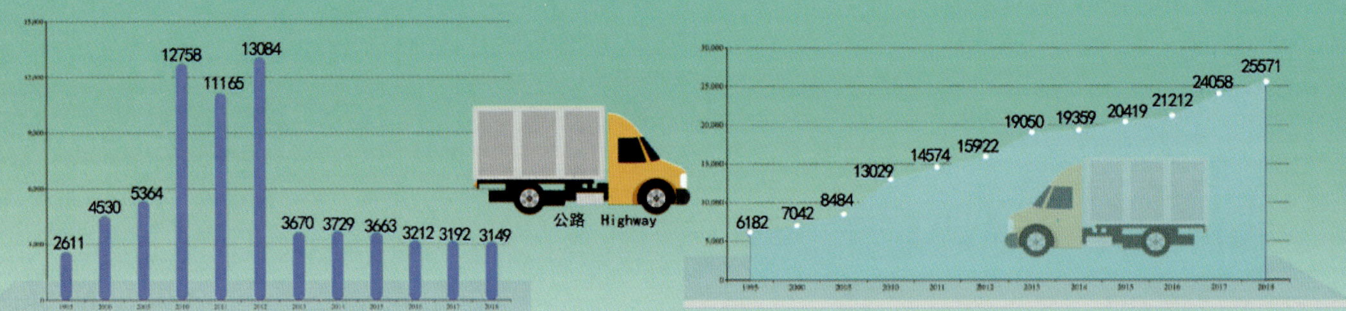

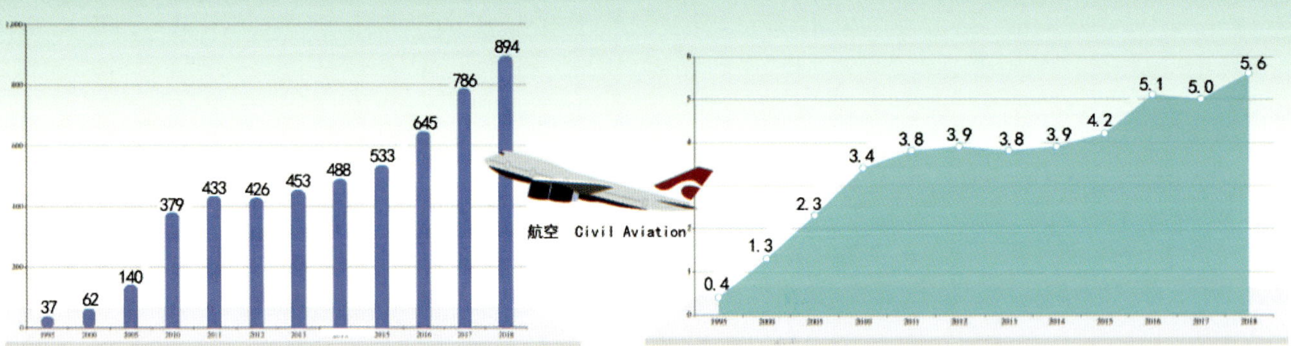

教育 卫生
Education Public Health

各类学校专任教师（人）
Full-time Teachers(person)

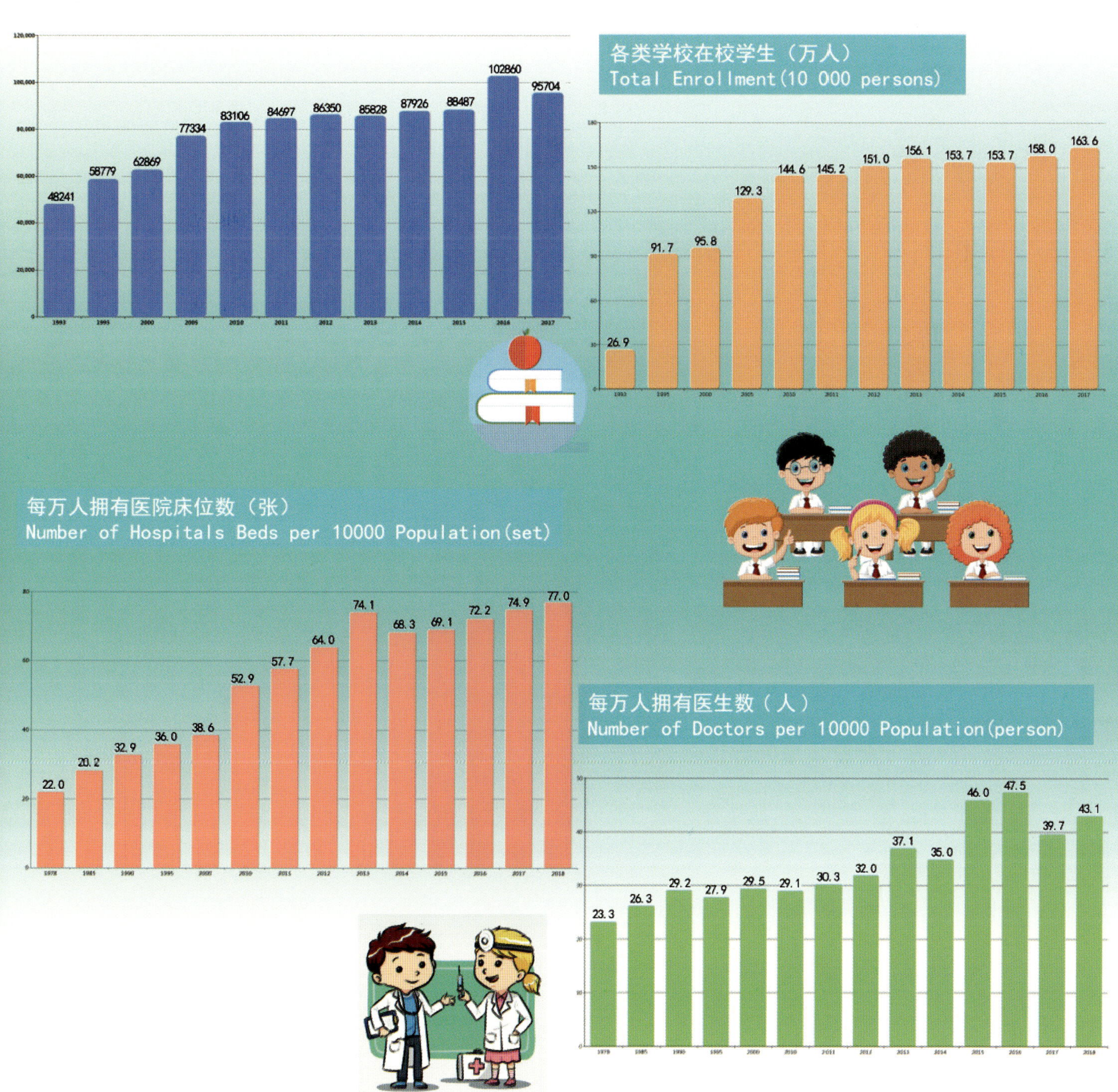

区划调整后的济南—2018

Jinan after Adminstrative Division Adjustment—2018

8862.2
地区生产总值(亿元)
Gross Domestic Product
(100 million yuan)

57.9
第三产业比重(%)
Proportion of Tertiary Industry(%)

883.94
常住人口(万人)
Permanent Population
(10 000 persons)

815.4
一般公共预算收入(亿元)
General Pubilic Budget
Revenue(100 million yuan)

9.3
全社会固定资产投资增长幅度(%)
Growth rate Total Investment
in Fixed Assets(%)

936.4
海关进出口总额(亿美元)
Total Value of Imports and
Exports(100 million yuan)

101071
人均地区生产总值(元)
Per Capita Gross Domestic
Product(yuan)

48364
城镇居民人均可支配收入(元)
Per Capita Disposable Income
of Urban inhabitant(yuan)

17835
农村居民人均可支配收入(元)
Per Capita Disposable Income
of rural inhabitant(yuan)

4777.6
社会消费品零售总额 (亿元)
Total Retail Sale of Consumer
Goods(100 million yuan)

1

行 政 区 划

DIVISIONS OF ADMINISTRATIVE AREAS

1-1 行政区划

Divisions of Administrative Areas

单位：个 （unit）

年份地区	Year and Region	乡 Townships	镇 Towns	街道 Street Communities	村 Village	居委会 Neighborhood committee	土地面积 (平方公里) Land Area (sq.km)
全市主要年份							
1989		57	54	53	4710	702	8227
1990		57	54	48	4752	669	8227
1991		57	54	48	4752	670	8227
1992		57	54	48	4759	670	8227
1993		56	55	48	4756	670	8227
1994		55	56	48	4759	670	8227
1995		48	63	49	4723	721	8227
1996		42	68	49	4704	685	8154
1997		42	68	50	4696	616	8154
1998		42	69	50	4711	505	8154
1999		42	69	50	4714	468	8154
2000		42	69	50	4702	416	8154
2001		28	64	54	4677	417	8177
2002		27	65	54	4657	487	8177
2003		27	61	58	4657	487	8177
2004		27	61	58	4657	487	8177
2005		12	53	64	4628	400	8177
2006		11	53	64	4604	487	8177
2007		11	50	73	4563	500	8177
2008		11	50	73	4551	521	8177
2009		11	50	75	4553	522	8177
2010		6	49	86	4552	532	8177
2011		4	51	86	4538	556	8177
2012		4	51	86	4532	586	8177
2013		2	51	90	4548	597	7998
2014		2	51	90	4547	627	7998
2015		2	46	95	4546	641	7998
2016			39	104	4547	669	7998
2017			29	112	4548	711	7998
2018			29	112	4546	740	7998
2018 年分地区							
市　区	Districts unber City		12	109	3262	702	6121
历下区	Li xia			13	20	99	101
市中区	Shi zhong			17	77	118	281
槐荫区	Huai yin			16	92	94	152
天桥区	Tian qiao			15	120	148	259
历城区	Li cheng		1	13	266	81	1301
长清区	Chang qing		3	7	580	59	1209
章丘区	Zhang qiu		3	15	890	17	1719
济阳区	Ji yang		4	6	811	46	1099
高新区	Gao xin			5	152	40	
南部山区	Nan shan		1	2	254	0	
平阴县	Ping yin		6	2	336	24	715
商河县	Shang he		11	1	948	14	1162

注：指标“土地面积”2013 年起为第二次全市土地调查数据

Note: Indicator–"land area" is the city land survey data for the second time as of 2013.

1-2 县区所辖镇、办事处（2018年末）

Town and Street Communities Under the Jurisdiction（End of 2018）

县区	Region	镇、街道办事处数量（个） Number of Towns and Street Communities (unit)	镇、街道办事处名称 Name of Towns and Street Communities
历下区	Li xia	13	大明湖街道 千佛山街道 燕山街道 泉城路街道 趵突泉街道 东关街道 解放路街道 建筑新村街道 文化东路街道 甸柳新村街道 姚家街道 智远街道 龙洞街道
市中区	Shi zhong	17	泺源街道 杆石桥街道 魏家庄街道 大观园街道 四里村街道 六里山街道 七里山街道 二七新村街道 舜玉路街道 舜耕街道 王官庄街道 七贤街道 白马山街道 十六里河街道 兴隆街道 党家街道 陡沟街道
槐荫区	Huai yin	16	西市场街道 五里沟街道 道德街街道 营市街街道 青年公园街道 中大槐树街道 振兴街街道 南辛庄街道 段店北路街道 匡山街道 张庄路街道 美里湖街道 兴福街道 玉清湖街道 腊山街道 吴家堡街道
天桥区	Tian qiao	15	无影山街道 堤口路街道 宝华街街道 工人新村南村街道 工人新村北村街道 官扎营街道 北坦街道 天桥东街街道 纬北路街道 制锦市街道 北园街道 泺口街道 药山街道 大桥街道 桑梓店街道
历城区	Li cheng	14	洪家楼街道 山大路街道 东风街道 全福街道 华山街道 荷花路街道 王舍人街道 鲍山街道 郭店街道 唐冶街道 港沟街道 董家街道 彩石街道 唐王镇
长清区	Chang qing	10	文昌街道 平安街道 崮云湖街道 五峰山街道 归德街道 张夏街道 万德街道 孝里镇 马山镇 双泉镇
章丘区	Zhang qiu	18	明水街道 双山街道 龙山街道 枣园街道 埠村街道 圣井街道 绣惠街道 相公庄街道 文祖街道 普集街道 官庄街道 高官寨街道 白云湖街道 宁家埠街道 曹范街道 垛庄镇 刁 镇 黄河镇
济阳区	Ji yang	10	济阳街道 济北街道 回河街道 孙耿街道 太平街道 崔寨街道 垛石镇 曲堤镇 仁风镇 新市镇
高新区	Gao xin	5	舜华路街道 孙村街道 巨野河街 临港街道 道遥墙街道
南部山区	Nan shan	3	仲宫街道 柳埠街道 西营镇
平阴县	Ping yin	8	榆山街道 锦水街道 洪范池镇 东阿镇 孔村镇 孝直镇 玫瑰镇 安城镇
商河县	Shang he	12	许商街道 玉皇庙镇 龙桑寺镇 贾庄镇 殷巷镇 郑路镇 怀仁镇 白桥镇 孙集镇 韩庙镇 张坊镇 沙河镇

人 口

POPULATION

2-1 主要年份总户数、总人口（户籍人口）

Total Household and Population in Major Years（registered population）

年份 Year	年末总户数 (万户) Total year-end Households (10 000 households)	年末总人口 (万人) Total year-end Population (10 000 persons)	按性别分 (万人) Grouped by Sex (10 000 persons)		性别比 (女＝100) Sex Ratio (Femal=100)	年平均人口 (万人) Annual Average Population (10 000 persons)	比上年增长 (‰) Growth Rate (‰)	人口密度 (人/平方公里) Density of Population (Person/sq.km)
			男性 Male	女性 Femal				
1952	70.19	318.66	157.68	160.98	97.95	315.94	3.30	387
1957	76.44	346.38	170.30	176.09	96.71	343.25	17.40	421
1962	81.45	351.44	174.55	176.89	98.68	350.18	–4.60	427
1965	83.01	373.22	186.08	187.14	99.43	370.24	19.50	454
1970	89.48	407.50	203.16	204.34	99.42	404.17	16.60	495
1975	96.54	437.73	217.82	219.91	99.05	435.15	9.90	532
1976	98.63	442.09	220.89	221.20	99.86	439.91	10.90	537
1977	100.60	445.05	222.46	222.59	99.94	443.57	8.30	541
1978	102.93	450.67	226.31	224.36	100.87	447.86	9.70	548
1979	105.34	456.37	228.57	227.80	100.34	453.52	12.60	555
1980	106.83	458.61	230.47	228.15	101.02	457.49	8.80	557
1981	110.52	467.93	235.35	232.58	101.19	463.27	12.60	569
1982	112.51	474.23	238.99	235.26	101.59	471.08	16.80	576
1983	114.92	479.38	242.02	237.36	101.54	476.81	12.20	583
1984	116.92	483.85	244.32	239.53	102.00	481.62	10.10	588
1985	120.19	488.39	246.86	241.53	102.21	486.12	9.30	594
1986	122.67	494.06	250.09	243.97	102.51	491.23	10.50	601
1987	125.43	501.03	253.95	247.08	102.78	497.55	12.90	609
1988	130.32	507.18	257.22	249.86	102.95	504.11	13.20	616
1989	134.77	513.39	260.79	252.61	103.24	510.29	12.30	624
1990	140.36	523.60	265.91	257.69	103.19	518.50	16.10	636
1991	143.42	527.43	267.78	259.65	103.13	525.52	13.50	641
1992	147.50	530.70	269.46	261.25	103.14	529.07	6.70	645
1993	149.42	533.53	270.77	262.76	103.05	532.12	5.80	649
1994	153.60	537.31	272.76	264.54	103.11	535.42	6.20	653
1995	156.45	542.12	274.98	267.14	102.93	539.72	8.00	656

2-1 续 1

年份 Year	年末总户数 (万户) Total year-end Households (10 000 households)	年末总人口 (万人) Total year-end Population (10 000 persons)	按性别分 (万人) Grouped by Sex (10 000 persons)		性别比 (女 = 100) Sex Ratio (Femal=100)	年平均人口 (万人) Annual Average Population (10 000 persons)	比上年增长 (‰) Growth Rate (‰)	人口密度 (人/平方公里) Density of Population (Person/sq.km)
			男性 Male	女性 Femal				
1996	156.42	543.45	275.59	267.86	102.89	542.79	5.70	666
1997	157.66	549.20	278.30	270.90	102.73	546.33	6.50	674
1998	160.93	553.54	279.91	273.63	102.30	551.37	9.20	679
1999	163.52	557.63	281.71	275.93	102.09	555.59	7.70	684
2000	166.63	562.65	284.19	278.46	102.06	560.14	8.20	690
2001	168.46	569.00	287.39	281.61	102.06	565.83	10.20	696
2002	170.10	575.01	290.58	284.43	102.16	572.00	10.90	703
2003	172.18	582.56	294.04	288.52	101.91	578.78	11.90	712
2004	173.24	590.08	297.25	292.82	101.51	586.32	13.03	722
2005	177.69	597.44	300.42	297.02	101.15	593.76	12.69	731
2006	179.48	603.35	302.72	300.63	100.70	600.39	11.17	738
2007	181.88	604.85	302.87	301.98	100.29	604.10	6.17	740
2008	184.63	603.99	302.00	301.99	100.00	604.42	0.53	739
2009	187.70	603.27	301.26	302.01	99.75	603.63	-1.30	738
2010	190.65	604.08	301.28	302.80	99.50	603.68	0.08	739
2011	193.61	606.64	302.19	304.44	99.26	605.36	2.78	742
2012	195.79	609.21	303.30	305.91	99.15	607.92	4.23	745
2013	199.67	613.25	304.93	308.32	98.90	611.23	5.44	767
2014	201.93	621.61	309.09	312.52	98.90	617.43	15.64	777
2015	203.59	625.73	310.92	314.80	98.77	623.67	10.11	782
2016	205.45	632.83	314.28	318.55	98.66	629.28	9.00	791
2017	208.08	643.62	319.21	324.41	98.40	638.22	14.21	805
2018	216.64	655.90	324.74	331.15	98.06	649.76	19.08	820

2-2 主要年份市区总户数、总人口(户籍人口)

Total Household and Population of Urban in Major Years（registered population）

年份 Year	年末总户数 (万户) Total year-end Households (10 000 households)	年末总人口 (万人) Total year-end Population (10 000 persons)	按性别分 (万人) Grouped by Sex (10 000 persons)		年平均人口 (万人) Annual Average Population (10 000 persons)
			男性 Male	女性 Femal	
1952	26.46	124.96	63.95	61.01	123.83
1957	29.13	143.17	72.05	71.13	140.11
1962	32.25	153.35	78.52	74.83	154.18
1965	34.03	162.82	83.20	79.62	161.90
1970	37.21	167.82	85.61	82.21	168.51
1975	40.67	178.78	90.83	87.95	177.74
1976	41.59	180.99	91.83	89.16	179.88
1977	42.34	181.49	91.92	89.57	181.24
1978	43.79	186.43	94.70	91.73	183.96
1979	45.33	189.26	96.22	93.04	187.84
1980	46.12	190.01	97.22	92.79	189.63
1981	48.64	194.05	99.37	94.69	192.03
1982	50.60	201.31	101.44	99.87	197.68
1983	52.32	205.48	103.42	102.07	203.39
1984	54.30	209.55	105.57	103.99	207.52
1985	56.88	213.28	107.96	105.33	211.42
1986	58.65	216.98	111.54	105.43	215.13
1987	60.54	221.49	113.79	107.70	219.23
1988	63.03	225.00	115.51	109.39	223.25
1989	65.29	228.88	117.49	111.39	226.94
1990	81.22	283.66	145.29	138.36	
1991	83.30	286.20	146.55	139.65	284.93
1992	85.87	288.52	145.19	143.33	287.36
1993	88.02	291.24	149.07	142.17	289.88
1994	90.10	294.60	150.75	143.85	292.92
1995	92.04	299.20	152.97	146.23	296.90

2-2 续 1

年份 Year	年末总户数 (万户) Total year-end Households (10 000 households)	年末总人口 (万人) Total year-end Population (10 000 persons)	按性别分 (万人) Grouped by Sex (10 000 persons)		年平均人口 (万人) Annual Average Population (10 000 persons)
			男性 Male	女性 Femal	
1996	93.12	302.78	154.58	148.20	300.99
1997	93.90	306.98	156.54	150.44	304.88
1998	96.65	309.90	157.58	152.32	308.44
1999	97.74	313.18	159.19	153.99	311.54
2000	99.25	317.20	161.03	156.17	315.19
2001	100.53	322.45	163.73	158.72	319.83
2002	101.62	327.55	166.43	161.12	325.00
2003	102.71	334.80	169.84	164.96	331.18
2004	102.68	341.73	172.91	168.82	338.27
2005	104.87	347.87	175.41	172.45	344.80
2006	106.19	352.29	177.10	175.19	350.08
2007	107.55	352.71	176.70	176.01	352.50
2008	109.26	350.23	175.08	175.15	351.47
2009	111.07	348.24	173.71	174.53	349.24
2010	112.91	348.02	173.19	174.83	348.13
2011	114.75	349.44	173.51	175.93	348.73
2012	116.49	352.17	174.55	177.62	350.81
2013	118.50	355.38	175.86	179.52	353.78
2014	120.33	360.99	178.55	182.44	358.19
2015	121.96	364.54	180.12	184.42	362.77
2016	154.64	473.33	233.74	239.59	418.94
2017	157.42	483.75	238.48	245.27	478.54
2018	182.76	554.13	273.31	280.82	518.94

注：1990 年以前的数据中不包括长清区。2016 年起数据包括章丘区。2018 年起数据包括济阳区。

Note: The data before 1990 excludes Changqing District. The data as of 2016 includes Zhangqiu District. The data as of 2018 includes Jiyang District.

2-3 主要年份人口自然变动情况

Natural Change of Population in Major Years

年份 Year	申报出生人口 (人) Population of Birth (person)	申报出生率 (‰) Birth Rate (‰)	申报死亡人口 (人) Population of Death (person)	申报死亡率 (‰) Death Rate (‰)	人口自然增长 (人) Population of Natural Growth (person)	人口自然增长率 (‰) Natural Growth Rate (‰)
1952	72861	23.06	29949	9.48	42912	13.58
1957	108432	31.59	38082	11.09	70350	20.50
1962	108029	30.85	44464	12.70	63565	18.15
1965	121364	32.78	39355	10.63	82009	22.15
1970	111861	27.68	29965	7.41	81896	20.27
1975	82939	19.06	33837	7.78	49102	11.28
1976	70065	15.93	34693	7.89	35372	8.04
1977	67413	15.20	33723	7.60	33690	7.60
1978	69541	15.53	31343	7.00	38198	8.53
1979	72596	16.01	30205	6.66	42391	9.35
1980	60336	13.19	32004	7.00	28332	6.19
1981	70327	15.18	31671	6.84	38656	8.34
1982	74147	15.74	28679	6.09	45468	9.65
1983	56454	11.84	30080	6.31	26374	5.53
1984	61156	12.70	32277	6.70	28879	6.00
1985	55386	11.39	31678	6.52	23708	4.87
1986	69901	14.23	30790	6.27	39111	7.96
1987	86752	17.44	30007	6.03	56745	11.41
1988	78922	15.66	32850	6.52	46072	9.14
1989	76380	14.97	30721	6.02	45659	8.95
1990	66806	12.88	33916	6.54	32890	6.34
1991	59374	11.30	32675	6.20	26699	5.10
1992	52825	9.98	34969	6.61	17856	3.37
1993	46007	8.65	35317	6.64	10690	2.01
1994	49940	9.30	35308	6.60	14632	2.70
1995	54132	10.03	34107	6.32	20025	3.71

2-3 续 1

年份 Year	申报出生人口 (人) Population of Birth (person)	申报出生率 (‰) Birth Rate (‰)	申报死亡人口 (人) Population of Death (person)	申报死亡率 (‰) Death Rate (‰)	人口自然增长 (人) Population of Natural Growth (person)	人口自然增长率 (‰) Natural Growth Rate (‰)
1996	58254	10.73	36452	6.71	21802	4.02
1997	62245	11.39	35768	6.55	26477	4.84
1998	62490	11.33	36497	6.64	25893	4.69
1999	55931	10.07	34956	6.29	20975	3.78
2000	62059	11.08	39499	7.05	22560	4.03
2001	55536	9.82	33816	5.98	21720	3.84
2002	57317	10.02	36234	6.33	21083	3.69
2003	54599	9.43	42539	7.35	12060	2.08
2004	60670	10.35	38158	6.51	22512	3.84
2005	60240	10.15	37782	6.36	22458	3.78
2006	57706	9.61	39040	6.50	18666	3.11
2007	58367	9.66	39752	6.58	18615	3.08
2008	59600	9.86	39887	6.60	19713	3.26
2009	56694	9.39	40911	6.78	15783	2.61
2010	67162	11.13	50380	8.35	16782	2.78
2011	66563	11.00	40310	6.66	26253	4.34
2012	71449	11.75	49148	8.08	22301	3.67
2013	69351	11.35	41713	6.82	27638	4.53
2014	110503	17.90	41887	6.78	68616	11.11
2015	73688	11.82	41999	6.73	31689	5.09
2016	91941	14.61	39460	6.27	52481	8.34
2017	113766	17.83	62958	9.86	50808	7.96
2018	94694	14.57	45374	6.98	49320	7.59

2-4 分地区户数、人口数(2018 年)(户籍人口)

Household and Population by Region（2018）（registered population）

地 区	Region	户数 （万户） Households (10 000 households)	人口数 （万人） Population (10 000 persons)	按性别分（万人）Grouped by Sex (10 000 persons)	
				男性 Male	女性 Femal
全 市	Total City	216.64	655.90	324.74	331.15
市 区	Districts unber City	182.76	554.13	273.31	280.82
历下区	Li xia	23.35	68.37	33.51	34.86
市中区	Shi zhong	23.57	64.84	31.66	33.18
槐荫区	Huai yin	15.78	43.60	21.20	22.40
天桥区	Tian qiao	18.96	52.60	25.77	26.83
历城区	Li cheng	34.32	103.47	51.07	52.40
长清区	Chang qing	17.89	56.85	28.31	28.54
章丘区	Zhang qiu	31.54	105.18	52.01	53.18
济阳区	Ji yang	17.35	59.22	29.78	29.45
平阴县	Ping yin	13.52	37.49	18.78	18.71
商河县	Shang he	20.36	64.27	32.65	31.62

2-5 计划生育情况（2018）

Basic Statistics of Family Planning (2018)

地区	Region	合法生育(人) legal Childbearing(person)			出生政策符合率(%) Legitimate Fertility (%)	违法生育(人) Illegal Childbearing(person)			
		一孩 First Child	二孩 SeCond Child	三孩 Third Child		一孩 First Child	二孩 SeCond Child	三孩 Third Child	多孩 Multiple Birth
总　计	**Total**	25589	42171	1110	96.22	373	64	2199	66
市　区	Districts unber City	22537	34787	832	96.99	281	41	1447	37
历下区	Li xia	2974	3295	70	99.98	0	0	1	0
市中区	Shi zhong	2349	3222	67	99.52	2	0	24	1
槐荫区	Huai yin	1572	2538	46	98.91	1	0	41	4
天桥区	Tian qiao	2198	3076	62	96.93	36	5	125	3
历城区	Li cheng	3140	4859	104	97.65	16	5	172	2
长清区	Chang qing	2172	3723	75	96.48	41	7	169	1
章丘区	Zhang qiu	3737	5292	108	96.51	66	8	248	8
济阳区	Ji yang	1950	4896	194	91.00	112	15	552	17
高新区	Gao xin	1664	2236	51	98.43	6	0	56	1
南部山区	Nan shan	781	1650	55	97.61	1	1	59	0
平阴县	Ping yin	1301	2627	79	96.79	22	5	101	5
商河县	Shang he	1751	4757	199	89.79	70	18	651	24

2-6 分地区人口机械变动情况（2018 年）

Un-Natural Changes of Population by Region (2018)

地 区	Region	迁入人口(人) Move Into the Population (person)	迁入率(‰) Move In Rate (‰)	迁出人口(人) Move Out the population (person)	迁出率(‰) Move Out Rate (‰)	人口机械增长(人) Mechanical Growth of Population(person)	人口机械增长率(‰) Mechanical Growth Rates of Population (‰)
全 市	Total	116368	17.91	42831	6.59	73537	11.32
市 区	Districts unber City	98691	18.01	27445	5.01	71246	13.00
历下区	Li xia	20945	31.23	5404	8.06	15541	23.17
市中区	Shi zhong	12992	20.28	3494	5.45	9498	14.83
槐荫区	Huai yin	13825	32.25	2024	4.72	11801	27.53
天桥区	Tian qiao	10438	19.95	2285	4.37	8153	15.58
历城区	Li cheng	22355	21.96	3876	3.81	18479	18.16
长清区	Chang qing	5562	9.83	1605	2.84	3957	6.99
章丘区	Zhang qiu	8687	8.30	2531	2.42	6156	5.88
济阳区	Ji yang	3887	6.61	6226	10.59	–2339	–3.98
平阴县	Ping yin	3447	9.20	5012	13.38	–1565	–4.18
商河县	Shang he	14230	22.17	10374	16.16	3856	6.01

2-7 分地区人口自然变动情况（2018 年）

Natural Changes of Population by Region (2018)

地 区	Region	申报出生人口(人) Population of Birth (person)	申报出生率(‰) Birth Rate (‰)	申报死亡人口(人) Population of Death (person)	申报死亡率(‰) Death Rate (‰)	人口自然增长(人) Population of Natural Growth (person)	人口自然增长率(‰) Natural Growth Rate (‰)
全 市	Total	94694	14.57	45374	6.98	49320	7.59
市 区	Districts unber City	81063	14.79	38357	7.00	42706	7.79
历下区	Li xia	10852	16.18	3211	4.79	7641	11.39
市中区	Shi zhong	9562	14.93	3781	5.90	5781	9.02
槐荫区	Huai yin	6641	15.49	2689	6.27	3952	9.22
天桥区	Tian qiao	6614	12.64	3938	7.53	2676	5.11
历城区	Li cheng	18558	18.23	6729	6.61	11829	11.62
长清区	Chang qing	7145	12.62	4741	8.38	2404	4.25
章丘区	Zhang qiu	12086	11.55	8371	8.00	3715	3.55
济阳区	Ji yang	9605	16.34	4897	8.33	4708	8.01
平阴县	Ping yin	4473	11.94	2136	5.70	2337	6.24
商河县	Shang he	9158	14.27	4881	7.61	4277	6.66

2-8 结婚情况

Number of Marriages

单位：对 (couple)

地区	Region	2010 年	2012 年	2013 年	2014 年	2015 年	2016 年	2017 年	2018 年
总　计	Total	55735	62281	56819	55475	50300	47457	52663	51383
市　直	Departments Directiy Under the Municipal Government	77	92	111	114	88	82	67	90
历下区	Li xia	6481	8401	6212	7139	6594	5742	5830	5763
市中区	Shi zhong	5839	7032	6527	6315	5975	5364	5973	5699
槐荫区	Huai yin	4397	4801	4229	4179	3772	3445	3728	3863
天桥区	Tian qiao	4987	6018	5387	5472	4953	4447	4563	4874
历城区	Li cheng	8288	8529	8123	7816	7163	7296	7551	7419
长清区	Chang qing	4328	4705	4465	4270	3777	3649	4331	4003
章丘区	Zhang qiu	6700	7658	7034	6811	6119	6135	7613	6840
济阳区	Ji yang	5970	5821	4969	4484	3938	3615	4023	4248
高新区	Gao xin			1676	1707	1577	1593	2516	2621
平阴县	Ping yin	3191	3553	3262	2893	2550	2563	2564	2330
商河县	Shang he	5477	5671	4824	4275	3794	3526	3904	3633

2-9 离婚情况

Number of Divorces

单位：对 (couple)

地　区	Region	2010 年	2012 年	2013 年	2014 年	2015 年	2016 年	2017 年	2018 年
总　计	Total	18395	22633	25638	25899	25399	26915	32491	31611
法院数	Divorce Case Handled	6658	7399	6521	6995	7395	6909	6024	6228
民政数	Divorces Handled through Civil	11737	15234	19117	18904	18004	20006	26467	25383
市　直	Departments Directiy Under the Municipal Government	14	15	16	14	12	17	25	19
历下区	Li xia	1999	3083	2736	2517	2382	2800	3474	3322
市中区	Shi zhong	1726	2096	2764	2458	2262	2327	3448	3288
槐荫区	Huai yin	1238	1281	1785	1681	1510	1720	2223	2362
天桥区	Tian qiao	1624	1717	2275	2251	2104	2224	2834	2810
历城区	Li cheng	1802	2395	3068	3110	2666	3177	4337	3664
长清区	Chang qing	646	1022	1280	1319	1301	1422	1549	1801
章丘区	Zhang qiu	1203	1579	1997	1967	2026	2171	3303	2916
济阳区	Ji yang	634	894	1156	1281	1344	1434	1733	1783
高新区	Gao xin			548	566	502	557	1097	1127
平阴县	Ping yin	517	681	853	764	880	938	993	839
商河县	Shang he	334	471	639	976	1015	1219	1451	1452

主要统计指标解释

人口统计资料主要有三个来源 人口普查、人口抽样调查和人口经常性登记。

人口普查 是在国家规定的统一时间内，用统一的方法，统一的调查项目，对全国或某一地区的人口进行的一种专门调查。

人口抽样调查 是从所要研究的总人口中，随机抽取部分人口，并根据对这些人口调查所得到的数据来推算该人口总体相应指标的方法。

人口经常性登记 是指对人口出生、死亡、婚姻、迁移等事件进行连续的、持久的、强制的全面登记制度。

人口数 指一定时点、一定地区范围内的有生命的个人的总和。

年度统计的年末人口数 指每年12月31日24时的人口数。

出生率（又称粗出生率） 指在一定时期内（通常为一年）平均每千人所出生的人数的比率，一般用千分率表示。计算公式为：

出生率＝年出生人数／年平均人数×1000‰

式中：出生人数指活产婴儿，即胎儿脱离母体时（不管怀孕月数），有过呼吸或其他生命现象。

出生人数 是指活产婴儿，即胎儿脱离母体时（不管怀孕月数），有过呼吸或其他生命现象。

年平均人数 是指年初、年底人口数的平均数，也可用年中人口数代替。

死亡率（又称粗死亡率） 指在一定时期内（通常为一年）一定地区的死亡人数与同期平均人数（或期中人数）之比，一般用千分率表示。计算公式为：

死亡率＝年死亡人数／年平均人数×1000‰

人口自然增长率 指在一定时期内（通常为一年）人口自然增加数（出生人数减死亡人数）与该时期内平均人数（或期中人数）之比，一般用千分率表示。计算公式为：

人口自然增长率＝（本年出生人数－本年死亡人数）／年平均人数×1000‰

人口自然增长率＝人口出生率－人口死亡率

机械增长率 是反映迁移变动的一个相对指标。它表明一个地区在一定时间内迁入人口数与迁出人口数相抵后的差额与总人口数的比率，一般用千分率表示。计算公式为：

机械增长率=一定时期的迁入迁出人口差额/该时期的平均人口×100%

人口密度 指一定时点，一定地区的人口数与该时点、该地区的面积之比，即一定时点的单位土地面积上的人口数，通常以每平方公里的居民人数来表示：

$$人口密度=\frac{该地区人口数}{该地区土地面积}\times100\%$$

性别比 反映两性人口间比例的指标，指在总人口中或各年龄组人口中，男性人数与女性人数之比。通常以每100个女性人口相对应的男性人口数。计算公式：

$$性别比=\frac{男性人口}{女生人口}\times100\%$$

Explanatory Notes on Main Statistical Indicators

Source of Demographic Data population census, sample survey of population and recurrent registration of population.

Population Census refers to an official survey of total population nationwide or in a given region by an official method within a given period of time in China.

Sample Survey of Population refers to the method of calculating corresponding indicators of total population pursuant to the data originated from the survey of partial population randomly extracted from the total population to be researched.

Recurrent registration of population refers to continuous, persistent and enforced registration system for population birth, death, marriage, and migration , etc.

Total Population refers to the total number of people alive at a certain point of time within a given area.

The Annual Statistics on Total Population is taken at midnight, the 31st of December.

Birth Rate (or Crude Birth Rate) refers to the ratio of births per one thousand people during a certain period of time (generally a year), expressed in permillage. The following formula is used:

Birth rate = number of births/annual average population *1,000‰

Wherein: Births refer to liveborn infants, namely those with breath or other vital signs when breaking away from the mother (regardless of number of months of pregnancy).

Births refer to liveborn infants, namely those with breath or other vital signs when breaking away from the mother (regardless of number of months of pregnancy).

Annual Average Population refers to the mean value of the number of people at the beginning and ending of the year, which can be replaced with the number of people in the middle of the year.

Death Rate (or Crude Death Rate) refers to the ratio of the number of deaths to the average population (or mid period population) during a certain period of time (usually a year), expressed in ‰. The following formula is used:

Death rate = number of deaths/annual average population *1,000‰

Natural Growth Rate of Population refers to the ratio of natural increase in population (number of births minus number of deaths) in a certain period of time (usually a year) to the average population (or mid period population) of the same period, expressed in ‰. The following formula is used:

Natural Growth Rate of Population=(number of births - number of deaths)/ annual average population * 1,000‰

Natural Growth Rate of Population=Birth Rate-Death Rate

Mechanical Growth Rate is a relative indicator that reflects changes in the population migration. It shows the ratio of the balance (between the people count moving in and out of a given area) to total population during a certain period of time, expressed in permillage. The following formula is used:

Mechanical growth rate = the balance between people count moving in and out of a given area during a certain period of time/average population * 100%

Population Density refers to the ratio of total population in a given area at a certain point of time to the area at this point of time, namely total population per area of land at a certain point of time, expressed in number of residents per square kilometers:

$$\text{Population density} = \frac{\text{Total population in the region}}{\text{Land area in the region}} \times 100\%$$

Sex ratio refers to the ratio of male to female population in total population or age groups, male population to per 100 female populations. The following formula is used:

$$\text{Sex ratio} = \frac{\text{Male n population}}{\text{Female population}} \times 100\%$$

综　合

GENERAL SURVEY

3-1 国民经济和社会

Principal Aggregate Indicators on National

指　标	Indicators	单位 Unit	1978
面　积	Area		
土地面积	Land Area	平方公里(sq.km)	
#市内八区建成区面积	Built-up Area of Eight Districts in the City	平方公里(sq.km)	85
人口	Population		
年末总户数（户籍人口）	Total year-end Households（Household Population）	万户(10 000 households)	102.93
年末总人口	Total year-end Population	万人(10 000 persons)	450.67
#市区	Population	万人(10 000 persons)	186.43
#男性	Male	万人(10 000 persons)	226.31
年末常住总人口	Total Resident Population at the Year-end	万人(10 000 persons)	
就业	Employment		
全社会从业人员	Employed Persons	万人(10 000 persons)	204.04
第一产业	Primary Industry	万人(10 000 persons)	136.30
第二产业	Secondary Industry	万人(10 000 persons)	46.06
第三产业	Tertiary Industry	万人(10 000 persons)	21.68
职工平均工资	Average Wage of Staff and Workers	元(yuan)	578
城镇登记失业人员数	Registered Urban Unemployed Persons	万人(10 000 persons)	
城镇登记失业率	Registered Urban Unemployment Rate	%	
国民经济核算	National Accounting		
地区生产总值	Gross Domestic Product	亿元(100 million yuan)	23.60
#非公有制经济	Non-ppublic Economy	亿元(100 million yuan)	
第一产业	Primary Industry	亿元(100 million yuan)	4.16
第二产业	Secondary Industry	亿元(100 million yuan)	13.32
第三产业	Tertiary Industry	亿元(100 million yuan)	6.12
人均地区生产总值	Per Capita GDP	元(yuan)	527
固定资产投资	Investment in Fixed Assets		
固定资产投资	Investment in Fixed Assets	亿元(100 million yuan)	3.19
第一产业	Primary Industry	亿元(100 million yuan)	0.55
第二产业	Secondary Industry	亿元(100 million yuan)	1.15
#工业	Industry	亿元(100 million yuan)	0.75
第三产业	Tertiary Industry	亿元(100 million yuan)	1.29
#房地产投资	Real Estate Investment	亿元(100 million yuan)	0.00
财政税收	Fiscal Tax Revenue		
一般公共预算收入	General Pubilic Budget Revenue	亿元(100 million yuan)	5.90
一般公共预算支出	General Pubilic Budget Expenditure	亿元(100 million yuan)	1.5
地域税收收入	Regional Tax Revenue	亿元(100 million yuan)	
国税税收收入	National Tax Revenue	亿元(100 million yuan)	
地税税收收入	Land Tax Revenue	亿元(100 million yuan)	

1990	1995	2000	2005	2010	2015	2017	2018
8227	8227	8154	8177	8177	7998	7998	7998
103	114	120	295	347	393	464	524
140.36	156.45	166.63	177.69	190.65	203.59	208.08	216.64
523.60	542.12	562.65	597.44	604.08	625.73	643.62	655.90
232.30	247.57	317.20	347.87	348.02	458.16	483.75	554.13
265.91	274.98	284.19	300.42	301.28	310.92	319.21	324.74
				681.80	713.20	732.12	746.04
270.54	324.22	347.37	360.00	373.70	388.70	405.38	419.27
125.73	116.13	109.98	99.10	76.66	71.80	69.50	68.80
87.75	106.68	110.81	114.20	120.20	124.70	129.35	132.17
57.06	101.41	126.58	146.70	176.84	192.20	206.53	218.30
2211	5851	10422	20866	31096	58578	70196	71142
	2.45	3.90	5.75	5.97	3.20	3.23	3.49
	2.30	3.70	3.86	3.84	2.04	2.08	2.06
138.24	473.52	944.13	1846.28	3910.53	6100.23	7201.96	7856.56
		238.32	768.50	1664.43	2599.60	3075.08	3237.50
23.93	67.64	96.02	134.34	215.17	305.39	317.40	272.42
67.36	220.37	414.74	847.47	1637.45	2307.00	2569.22	2829.31
46.95	185.51	433.38	864.47	2057.90	3487.84	4315.34	4754.83
2666	8773	16855	28900	57947	85919	98967	106302
30.60	112.76	305.95	857.00	1987.44	3498.42	4363.58	–
0.52	3.24	13.57	38.28	68.08	102.52	97.54	–
14.62	46.26	73.14	362.05	677.28	1217.39	1441.82	–
2.05	45.35	67.72	352.27	667.35	1147.87	1317.64	–
13.94	63.27	219.24	456.67	1242.08	2178.51	2824.22	–
2.18	16.46	50.53	121.09	484.50	1014.14	1232.57	1369.35
12.40	16.99	49.05	106.15	266.13	614.32	677.21	752.82
8.20	19.63	54.72	120.66	336.80	658.20	834.06	1018.32
	53.49	112.35	231.34	527.70	959.33	1134.93	1240.20
	39.55	72.54	144.20	309.87	494.43	745.63	755.63
	13.94	39.80	87.14	217.82	464.90	389.30	484.58

3-1 续 1

指　标	Indicators	单位 Unit	1978
金融保险	**Finance and Insurance**		
金融机构人民币存款余额	RMB Deposits Balance of Financial Institutions	亿元(100 million yuan)	15.43
#住户存款	Deposits of Households	亿元(100 million yuan)	1.14
金融机构人民币贷款余额	RMB Loans Balance of Financial Institutions	亿元(100 million yuan)	14.08
#短期贷款	Short-term Loans	亿元(100 million yuan)	-
保险承保额	Insurance Premium	亿元(100 million yuan)	
保险业务收入	Premium	万元(10 000 yuan)	
保险业务支出	Payment	万元(10 000 yuan)	
农业	**Agriculture**		
农林牧渔业总产值	Gross Output Value of Farming Forestry,Animal Husbandry and Fishery	亿元(100 million yuan)	6.57
农用机械总动力	total power of agricultural machinery	万千瓦(10 000kw)	69.70
年末实有耕地面积	Actural cultivated Area at Year-end	千公顷(1000 ha)	373.19
粮食总产量	Total Output of Grain	万吨(10 000 tons)	115.38
蔬菜总产量	Total Output of Vegetable	万吨(10 000 tons)	49.19
肉类总产量	Total Output of meat	万吨(10 000 tons)	2.50
奶类总产量	Total Output of Milk	万吨(10 000 tons)	0.40
棉花总产量	Total Output of Cotton	万吨(10 000 tons)	0.51
规模以上工业	**Industry Enterprises above Designated Size**		
单位数	Number of Enterprises	个(unit)	1319
工业总产值	Gross Industrial Output Value	亿元(100 million yuan)	37.67
主营业务收入	Revenue from Principal Business	亿元(100 million yuan)	31.39
利税总额	Total Profits and Taxes	亿元(100 million yuan)	6.80
利润总额	Total Profits	亿元(100 million yuan)	3.88
资产总计	Total Assets	亿元(100 million yuan)	25.68
所有者权益	Owner's Equities	亿元(100 million yuan)	7.47
建筑业	**Construction**		
资质以上企业个数	Number of Qualification Enterprises	个(unit)	10
建筑业总产值	Gross Output Value of Construction Enterprises	亿元(100 million yuan)	0.68
施工面积	Floor Space under Construction	万平方米(10 000 sq.m)	
竣工面积	Floor Space of Completed	万平方米(10 000 sq.m)	49
其中：住宅	Residential	万平方米(10 000 sq.m)	
交通运输	**Transport**		
货运量	Freight Traffic		
铁路	Railways	万吨(10 000 tons)	2191
公路	Highways	万吨(10 000 tons)	1670
航空	Airways	万吨(10 000 tons)	

1990	1995	2000	2005	2010	2015	2017	2018
117.95	438.01	1274.96	3483.34	7510.44	14174.72	15957.74	16571.87
51.08	222.06	463.04	1024.42	2187.68	3951.42	4465.73	5008.08
124.76	337.26	1069.31	3259.86	6319.09	11356.78	12883.66	14700.07
98.50	239.31	527.31	1240.49	1898.61	2692.81	2929.73	2865.97
		2169	5295	16802	97665	162712	256399
		124982	415338	1223791	2227474	3810660	4155535
		59618	141353	437708	656570	886699	1033980
36.92	114.07	154.30	230.46	361.24	493.04	505.08	514.90
183.40	241.20	349.47	426.76	509.68	584.98	442.90	454.62
347.56	339.30	333.72	366.99	362.30	358.57	355.66	353.65
181.47	252.48	240.27	260.11	289.43	264.55	255.57	251.42
126.09	253.54	405.95	529.37	572.05	626.23	591.63	527.22
11.38	28.68	31.82	37.93	31.79	34.18	32.50	29.82
1.87	3.48	7.09	19.61	31.20	23.27	26.36	32.84
5.00	2.91	2.73	3.55	2.94	0.74	0.20	0.29
2008	2648	1038	1670	2021	2021	2051	1889
174.89	526.48	680.04	2237.51	4485.61	5339.97	5770.91	4992.28
136.29	432.17	629.72	2142.84	4497.17	5417.16	5810.16	5192.15
15.57	53.59	64.62	244.61	584.53	685.71	686.80	535.39
3.23	16.30	21.69	131.30	339.76	396.13	415.23	307.98
125.25	578.55	958.10	1868.06	3904.42	4987.76	6319.64	5892.64
36.82	180.86	363.37	630.06	1481.75	2159.78	2268.27	2386.75
46	141	569	737	739	463	504	507
12.56	58.78	141.92	462.65	894.30	1663.83	2218.93	2823.47
269	1030	1611	3298	4655	10189	11363	12984
170	306	701	1400	1306	2039	2280	2366
77	141	396	884	773	1178	1258	1502
3416	3877	5168	7211	9913	15794	17865	18728
3970	6182	7024	8484	13029	20419	24058	25571
	0.4	1.3	2.0	3.4	4.2	5.0	5.6

3-1 续 2

指　标	Indicators	单位 Unit	1978
客运量	Passenger Traffic		
铁路	Railways	万人(10 000 persons)	1302
公路	Highways	万人(10 000 persons)	505
航空	Airways	万人(10 000 persons)	
民用汽车拥有量	Possession of Private Vehicles	辆(unit)	1684
# 载客	Passenger Vehicles	辆(unit)	1353
# 载货	Trucks	辆(unit)	224
邮电通信	**Post and Telecommunication Services**		
固定电话	Fixed Telephone	万户(10 000 households)	2.68
#城市	Urban	万户(10 000 households)	2.27
移动电话	Mobile Telephone	万户(10 000 households)	
互联网用户	Internet Broad Band	万户(10 000 households)	
国内贸易	**Domestic Trade**		
社会消费品零售总额	Total Retail Sales of Consumer Goods	亿元(100 million yuan)	8.13
#批发零售业	Wholesale and Retail Trade	亿元(100 million yuan)	7.07
#餐饮业	Catering Services	亿元(100 million yuan)	0.29
对外经济和国际旅游	**Foreign Economy and Trade,Tourism**		
全年货物进出口总额（海关）	Total Value of Imports and Exports（Customs）	万美元(10 000 USD)	
进口	Imports	万美元(10 000 USD)	
出口	Exports	万美元(10 000 USD)	
全年货物进出口总额	Total Value of Imports and Exports	亿元(100 million yuan)	
进口	Imports	亿元(100 million yuan)	
出口	Exports	亿元(100 million yuan)	
全年实际使用外资	Total Amount of Foreign Capital Actually Utilized	万美元(10 000 USD)	
全年实现合同外资	Total Amount of Contracted Foreign Capital	万美元(10 000 USD)	
入境游客人数	International Tourists	人(person)	
外国人	Foreigners	人(person)	
港澳台同胞	Compatriots from Hong Kong Macao and Taiwan	人(person)	
国际旅游（外汇）收入	Foreign Exchange Earnings	亿美元(100 million USD)	
教育	**Education**		
普通高等学校在校生	Total Enrollment of Regular Institutions of Higher Education	万人(10 000 persons)	1.09
普通高等学校专任教师	Full-time Teachers of Regular Institutions of Higher Education	人(person)	2947
中等专业学校在校生	Total Enrollment of Secondary Professional Schools	万人(10 000 persons)	0.68
中等专业学校专任教师	Full-time Teachers of Secondary Professional Schools	人(person)	1020
普通中学在校生	Total Enrollment of Regular Senior Secondary Schools	万人(10 000 persons)	30.61

1990	1995	2000	2005	2010	2015	2017	2018
1438	1519	1693	1924	3327	10681	13412	14548
1801	2611	4530	5364	12758	3663	3192	3149
2.6	37.0	62.0	140.0	379.2	533.1	785.6	894.1
39748	86766	129204	347687	807378	1541045	1949707	2160748
26032	33968	68625	196415	627849	1400588	1783848	1978951
12141	47790	56627	71588	117994	123801	151141	166277
9.87	39.18	106.34	258.90	213.30	165.30	153.10	135.27
9.12	36.48	83.08	206.30	177.40	141.00	132.55	118.70
	2.3	60.8	239.0	857.6	1090.4	971.1	1013.7
		11.57	74.34	117.30	231.66	298.75	344.70
52.82	188.02	354.71	807.88	1802.46	3410.31	4146.15	4404.46
38.20	134.53	228.75	657.55	1402.27	2875.48	3497.90	3716.58
2.56	13.35	37.76	108.44	308.11	513.80	622.96	661.14
	66587	143935	376213	743776	911424	1130449	1318209
	29812	86827	198370	338888	311763	379887	463119
	36775	57108	177843	404888	599661	750562	855090
						708.1	825.0
						257.1	519.3
						451.0	305.7
	25294	31981	54158	104011	157851	187623	272847
	47449	44074	112072	120903	303100	218692	556119
20583	54468	103990	120164	230985	332942	375469	398721
12705	30011	40990	69762	153327	205477	232260	247086
7878	24457	63000	50402	77658	127465	143209	151635
0.15	0.19	0.32	0.42	1.14	1.84	2.08	2.23
3.73	5.66	9.30	38.04	50.53	53.62	54.44	79.63
7245	7500	8267	18434	26870	30873	32559	37539
2.51	4.79	5.75	4.79	2.12	1.57	1.28	5.16
2890	2890	2916	1578	1334	763	716	3711
22.45	27.15	33.82	30.91	30.18	30.16	30.56	31.18

3-1 续 3

指　标	Indicators	单位 Unit	1978
普通中学专任教师	Full-time Teachers of Regular Senior Secondary Schools	人(person)	19275
小学在校生	Total Enrollment of Regular Primary Schools	万人(10 000 persons)	60.91
小学专任教师	Full-time Teachers of Regular Primary Schools	人(person)	24926
文化	**Culture**		
图书馆藏书量	Number of Books in Library	万册(10 000 copies)	341.0
图书出版种数	Number of Publication	种(kind)	389
图书量	Books	万册(10 000 copies)	20166
报纸量	Newspapers	万份(10 000 copies)	25055
杂志量	Magazines	万份(10 000 copies)	2209
卫生	**Public Health**		
卫生机构数	Number of Health Institutions	个(unit)	1017
#医院及卫生院	Hospitals and Township Hospitals	个(unit)	148
卫生机构床位数	Number of Beds	张(bed)	11496
#医院及卫生院	Hospitals and Township Hospitals	张(bed)	9856
卫生工作人员	Medical Personnel	人(person)	24949
# 卫生技术人员	Medical Technical Personnel	人(person)	19198
人民生活	**People's Livelihood**		
城镇居民人均可支配收入	Per Capita Disposable Income of Urban Residents	元(yuan)	337.8
城镇居民人均生活消费支出	Per Capita Life Consumption Expenditure of Urban Residents	元(yuan)	317.9
# 食品	Food	元(yuan)	181.6
农村居民人均可支配收入	Per Capita Disposable Income of Rural Residents	元(yuan)	110.5
农村居民人均生活消费支出	Per Capita Life Consumption Expenditure of Rural Residents	元(yuan)	83.2
#食品	Food	元(yuan)	58.2
农民人均住宅居住面积	Rural Residential Area Per Capita	平方米(sq.m)	9.6
社会治安	**Public security**		
交通事故起数	Number of Traffic Accidents	起(case)	
交通事故死伤人数	Deaths and Injuries from Traffic Accidents	人(person)	
交通事故损失折款	Property Losses from Traffic Accidents	万元(10 000 yuan)	
火灾事故起数	Number of Fire Accidents	起(case)	
火灾事故死伤人数	Deaths and Injuries from Fire Accidents	人(person)	
火灾事故损失折款	Property Losses from Fire Accidents	万元(10 000 yuan)	

注：1. “职工平均工资”2006 年以前为在岗职工口径，2006 年及以后为法人单位在岗职工口径

2. “市内八区建成区面积”，2017 年以前为市内七区口径，2015 年以前为市内六区口径

3. 工业统计指标 1997 年及以前统计口径为乡及乡以上工业企业，1998 年及以后为全部国有及年销售收入 500 万元以上工业企业，2011 年及以后为年主营业务收入 2000 万元及以上工业法人单位

4. 货运量、客运量中的“铁路”指标，2013 年 3 月铁路系统改革，铁路系统统计数据按新口径执行；“公路指标”自 2014 年起交通部门执行新的公路运输量统计方案，调查范围较老口径有所缩小，2014 年及 2013 年数据均为新口径下交通部反馈数据

5. 从 2015 年起，全市居民收支调查指标采用新口径。“农村居民人均可支配收入”2014 年以前为农民人均纯收入口径；“农村居民人均生活消费支出”2014 年以前为农民人均生活费支出口径

1990	1995	2000	2005	2010	2015	2017	2018
16065	17621	20585	21915	21943	23643	25676	26588
47.57	49.23	41.40	37.88	38.40	41.44	44.66	46.66
26922	27417	27417	25201	24801	25795	29109	30605
476.0	524.6	591.7	725.1	941.2	1195.0	1363.3	1442.3
2001	2603	3851	5389	6586	10234	12364	–
31685	39025	38471	27919	26603	43860	45501	–
46930	54460	109199	113751	184706	136480	99089	–
3321	4579	11177	7195	6995	8572	7809	–
1300	1185	1414	2138	5086	5947	5770	6030
178	216	231	246	277	269	289	293
18214	20747	21698	24695	31947	49311	54855	57460
17216	19534	20830	23524	29844	45195	50142	51207
41444	43648	45166	41499	54711	89117	97663	104347
31130	32848	35669	34129	39366	71778	76273	82834
1619.5	4720.6	8471.3	13578.5	25321.1	39888.7	46642.4	50146.5
1360.1	3830.4	6891.8	9226.6	15973.3	26318.7	30728.6	32977.1
781.6	1823.6	2387.1	3046.9	5051.2	6415.0	7229.3	7758.0
731.1	1812.7	3046.8	4812.3	8903.3	14231.8	16593.8	17924.4
569.8	1373.6	1976.8	2902.8	5406.6	8597.2	10327.3	11172.3
287.7	770.8	860.0	1134.8	1818.3	2775.5	3253.2	3409.0
22.5	24.7	28.6	33.8	40.2	52.6	55.2	54.3
509	1231	1306	911	774	2946	3075	3071
518	1345	1364	1186	1121	3885	3219	3618
64	369	357	316	189	840	1020	947
309	110	1281	1071	791	2609	1752	1539
67	87	26	3	9	12	11	12
166	925	471	76	462	1571	599	827

Note: 1. The average salary of employees is the caliber data of employees in the post before 2006, and the caliber data of employees in the legal entity in 2006 and later.

2. "The area of the built-up area in the eight districts of the city" , before 2017, it is the caliber of the seven districts in the city. Before 2015, it was the caliber of the six districts in the city.

3. Industrial statistical indicators In 1997 and before, the statistical caliber was industrial enterprises at or above the township level. In 1998 and after, they were all state-owned and with an annual sales income of more than 5 million yuan. In 2011 and beyond, the annual main business income was 20 million yuan and above industrial enterprises legal entities.

4. The "railway" indicator in freight volume and passenger volume, the railway system reform in March 2013, the railway system statistics are implemented according to the new caliber; the "road indicators" since 2014, the transportation department has implemented a new road traffic statistics program. The scope of the survey has been narrower than that of the old one. The data for 2014 and 2013 are the feedback data of the Ministry of Communications under the new caliber.

5. Starting from 2015, the city's residents' income and expenditure survey indicators adopt a new caliber. "per capita disposable income of Rural Residents" was the "per capita net income of Rural Residents" before 2014; "Per capita consumption expenditure of Rural Residents"was the "per capita living expenses of farmers" before 2014.

3-2 国民经济和社会

Indicators on Proportions and Efficiency in

指　标	Indicators	单　位 Unit	1978 年	1985 年
人　口	**Population**			
申报出生率	Birth Rate	‰	15.53	11.39
申报死亡率	Death Rate	‰	7.00	6.52
自然增长率	Natural Growth Rate	‰	8.53	4.87
就　业	**Employment**			
就业者负担人口	Dependency of Employed Population	人(person)	2.21	1.99
三次产业从业者比例	Composition of Employed Population			
第一产业	Primary Industry	%	66.8	47.5
第二产业	Secondary Industry	%	22.6	31.0
第三产业	Tertiary Industry	%	10.6	21.5
城镇登记失业率	Registered Unemployment Rate in Urban Areas	%		
国民经济核算	**National Accounting**			
三次产业增加值比例	Composition of Gross Domestic Product			
第一产业	Primary Industry	%		21.1
第二产业	Secondary Industry	%		51.8
第三产业	Tertiary Industry	%		27.1
人均生产总值	Per Capita GDP	元(yuan)		1263
资本形成率（投资率）	Capital Formation Rate	%		
最终消费率（消费率）	Final Consumption Rate	%		
固定资产投资	**Investment in Fixed Assets**			
固定资产投资占生产总值比重	Proportion of Fixed Assets Investment in GDP	%		23.7
财　政	**Finance**			
一般公共预算收入占生产总值比重	Proportion of General Public Budget Revenue in GDP	%	25.2	14.5
一般公共预算支出占生产总值比重	Proportion of General Public Budget Expenditure in GDP	%	6.3	5.6
农　业	**Agriculture**			
人均耕地面积	Per Cultivated Area	亩(mu)	1.24	1.10
每公顷耕地化肥施用量(折纯)	Consumption of Chemical Fertilizers per Hectare	千克(kg)		225

1990 年	1995 年	2000 年	2010 年	2015 年	2017 年	2018 年
12.88	10.03	11.08	11.13	11.82	17.83	14.57
6.54	6.32	7.05	8.35	6.73	9.86	6.98
6.34	3.71	4.03	2.78	5.09	7.96	7.59
1.94	1.67	1.62	1.62	1.61	1.34	1.4
46.5	35.8	31.7	20.5	18.5	17.1	16.4
32.4	32.9	31.9	32.2	32.1	31.9	31.5
21.1	31.3	36.4	47.3	49.4	51.0	52.1
	2.45	3.70	3.84	2.04	2.08	2.06
17.3	14.3	10.0	5.5	5.0	4.4	3.5
48.7	46.5	43.9	41.9	37.8	35.7	36.0
34.0	39.2	46.1	52.6	57.2	59.9	60.5
2666	8773	16999	57966	85919	98967	106302
39.1	39.5	40.2	52.6	63.0	66.8	–
37.8	41.9	56.9	46.9	52.3	52.5	–
22.1	23.8	32.1	50.8	57.3	60.6	–
9.0	3.6	5.2	15.2	10.1	9.4	9.6
5.9	4.1	5.8	16.9	10.8	11.6	13.0
1.00	0.94	0.88	0.90	0.87	0.83	0.82
330	569	641	646	626	589	564

3-2 续 1

指　标	Indicators	单 位 Unit	1978 年	1985 年
每公顷播种面积粮食产量	Grain Yield Per Hectare of Sown Area	千克(kg)	2475	3864
机耕率	Machine-cultivated Rate	%		
规模以上工业	**Industry Enterprises above Designated Size**			
产品销售率	Product Sales Rate	%		
总资产贡献率	Total Asset Contribution Rate	%		
流动资产周转次数	Turnover of Current Asset	次		
邮电通讯业	**Post and Telecommunication Services**			
每百人拥有电话机	Number of phones Per 100 Population	部(unit)	0.60	1.26
国内商业	**Domestic Commerce**			
人均消费品零售总额	Total Sales of Consumption Good Per Capita	元(yuan)	182	500
教　育	**Education**			
学龄儿童入学率	School-age Children Enrollment Rate	%		99.44
学校教师负担人数	Teacher-student Ratio	人(person)	21.28	16.75
高等教育	Higher Education	人(person)	2.47	6.55
中等教育	Secondary Education	人(person)	16.65	14.46
小学	Primary Schools	人(person)	34.99	20.33
卫　生	**Public Health**			
每万人拥有医院卫生院数	Number of Health Institutes per 10000 Population	个(unit)	0.33	0.34
每万人拥有医生数	Number of Doctors per 10000 Population	人(person)	23.3	26.3
每万人拥有医院床位数	Number of Hospitals Beds per 10000 Population	张(bed)	22.0	28.2
市政建设	**City Construction**			
城市人口用水普及率	Coverage Rate of Water Supply	%	99.0	100.0
城市用气普及率	Coverage Rate of Natural Gas Supply	%	17.8	26.3
建成区绿化覆盖率	Coverage Rate of Urban Green Areas	%	12.0	23.0
生　活	**Life**			
城镇居民恩格尔系数	Engel's Coefficient of Urban Residents	%	57.1	56.5
农村居民恩格尔系数	Engel's Coefficient of Rural Residents	%	69.9	51.8

注："一般公共预算收入占生产总值比重" 2012 年（含）以前为"地方财政收入"口径；"一般公共预算支出占生产总值比重" 2012 年（含）以前为"地方财政支出"口径

1990 年	1995 年	2000 年	2010 年	2015 年	2017 年	2018 年
4273	5512	5354	6192	6117	5660	5659
					87.3	96.7
	97.12	98.24	98.71	98.23	98.40	97.50
	12.25	8.45	15.98	13.37	17.63	9.93
	1.69	1.52	2.11	1.82	1.62	1.38
1.89	7.23	18.98	35.31	26.48	23.99	20.82
1009	3468	6332	28563	54687	64964	67786
99.03	99.40	99.93	100.00	100.00	100.00	100.00
14.20	15.60	15.24	17.40	17.37	17.09	16.68
5.15	7.55	11.25	21.76	22.53	23.79	21.21
12.99	15.30	16.78	14.72	13.33	12.04	12.87
17.67	18.20	15.10	15.48	16.07	15.35	15.25
0.34	0.40	0.41	0.46	0.43	0.45	0.45
29.2	27.9	29.5	29.1	46.0	39.7	43.1
32.9	36.0	38.6	52.9	69.1	74.9	77.0
100.0	100.0	100.0	100.0	99.00	99.64	99.78
45.7	72.2	90.7	95.5	97.73	99.85	99.87
30.0	30.5	36.1	36.9	39.94	40.57	40.52
57.5	47.6	34.6	31.6	24.4	23.5	23.5
50.5	56.1	43.5	33.6	32.3	31.5	30.5

Notes: "The proportion of general public budget revenue in total output value" was the caliber of "local financial revenue" before 2012 (inclusive); "The proportion of general public budget expenditure in total output value" was the caliber of "local financial expenditure"

3-3 平均每天主要

Selected Indicators on Average Daily Social

指　标	Indicators	单　位 Unit	1978 年	1985 年
每天创造的财富				
地区生产总值（当年价）	Gross Domestic Product	万元(10 000 yuan)	646	1682
第一产业	Primary Industry	万元(10 000 yuan)	114	354
第二产业	Secondary Industry	万元(10 000 yuan)	365	872
第三产业	Tertiary Industry	万元(10 000 yuan)	167	456
一般公共预算收入	General Pubilic Budget Revenue	万元(10 000 yuan)	163	244
一般公共预算支出	General Pubilic Budget Expenditure	万元(10 000 yuan)	41	94
固定资产投资	Investment in Fixed Assets	万元(10 000 yuan)		399
每天生产主要工、农业产品	**Production of Major Industrial Product and Agricultural Products on Average Daily**			
粮　食	Grain	吨(ton)	3161	4479
棉　花	Cotton	吨(ton)	14	136.2
蔬　菜	Vegetables	吨(ton)	1348	2304
猪　肉	Pork	吨(ton)	67	138
奶　类	Milk	吨(ton)	11	23
钢　材	Steel	吨(ton)	689	1197
发电量	Electric Energy Capacity	万千瓦时(10 000 kwh)	347	724
水　泥	Cement	吨(ton)	2399	3699
化　肥	Chemical Fertilizer	吨(ton)	494	313
金切机床	Metal-cutting Machine Tools	台(unit)	10	18
汽　车	Motor Vehicles	辆(unit)	12	31
服务器	server	台(unit)	—	—

1990 年	1995 年	2000 年	2010 年	2015 年	2017 年	2018 年
3787	12973	26087	107138	167130	197314	215248
656	1853	2603	5895	8367	8696	7464
1845	6257	11469	44862	63205	70390	77515
1286	5082	12015	56381	95557	118228	130269
339	465	1344	7291	16831	18554	20625
224	537	1499	9227	18032	22851	27899
838	3089	8382	54450	95847	119550	119550
4972	6917	6583	7930	7248	7002	6888
137	79.7	74.7	81	20.2	5.5	8
3455	6946	14733	16478	17157	16209	14444
215	390	478	597	508	460	425
51	95	194	855	638	722	900
1576	2856	6507	26857	19852	11226	6118
1225	1884	1898	3601	4818	4387	4189
5796	11644	13291	19994	21411	16561	16557
396	384	778	1345	644	575	569
14	11	8	6	10	16	16
17	16	8	581	263	553	636
—	—	—	271	1112	1547	2729

3-3 续 1

指　标	Indicators	单　位 Unit	1978 年	1985 年
布	Cloth	万米(10 000 m)	38	50
每天其他经济活动	**Other Economic Activity on Average Daily**			
最终消费量	Final Consumption	万元(10 000 yuan)		780
居民消费	Households Expense	万元(10 000 yuan)		638
农业居民	Rural Households	万元(10 000 yuan)		367
城镇居民	Urban Households	万元(10 000 yuan)		271
政府消费	Government Expense	万元(10 000 yuan)		142
社会消费品零售总额	Total Sales of Consumption Good Per Capita	万元(10 000 yuan)	261	640
公路货运量	Highways Freight Traffic	万吨(10 000 tons)	3.2	6.9
公路客运量	Highways Passenger Traffic	万人(10 000 persons)	1.4	3.1
自来水供水量	Water Supply	万吨(10 000 tons)	36.9	40
用电量	Electricity Consumption	万千瓦时(10 000 kwh)	754	747
市内公共车辆乘客人数	Number of City Bus Passengers	万人次(10 000 person-times)	34.0	62.2
实际使用外资额	Total Amount of Foreign Capital Actually Utilized	万美元(10 000 USD)		
港澳台及外国来济旅游人数	Compatriots from Hong Kong Macao and Taiwan	人(person)		27
每天人口变动和婚姻	**Daily Population Changes and Marriages**			
出　生	Birth	人(person)	191	152
死　亡	Death	人(person)	86	87
结　婚	Marriages	对(couple)		
离　婚	Divorces	对(couple)		

注：1、“一般公共预算收入” 指标 1978 年到 1995 年为“地方财政收入”口径，“一般公共预算支出”指标 1978 年到 1995 年为“地方财政支出”口径。

2、按照国家统计局经济普查年度数据使用规定，部分涉及国民经济核算的指标数据空缺。

1990 年	1995 年	2000 年	2010 年	2015 年	2017 年	2018 年
55	41	45	22	44	45	11
1580	5524	14833	50253	87412	103538	–
1274	4567	11098	39460	55221	76801	–
624	1938	3596	5142	7120	9878	–
650	2629	7502	34317	48101	66923	–
306	957	3735	10794	32192	26737	–
1447	5151	9718	49382	93433	113593	120670
10.9	16.9	19.2	35.7	55.9	65.9	70.1
4.9	7.2	12.4	35.0	10.0	8.7	8.6
45.3	57.5	76.7	64.5	87.2	98.3	107.5
1255	1779	2505	6713.3	7238.5	7569.5	7790.8
73.3	73.3	125.9	296.1	256.5	248.0	245.5
8.5	69.3	87.6	285.0	432.5	514.0	747.5
56	149	285	633	912.2	1029	1092.0
183	148	170	184	202	312	259
93	94	108	138	115	172	124
103	137	120	153	138	144	141
	17	20	50	70	89	87

Notes: 1. The indicator–"general public budget revenue" was the caliber of "local financial revenue" from 1978 to 1995 and the indicator–"general public budget expenditure" was the caliber of "local fiscal expenditure" from 1978 to 1995.

2. Part of index data regarding national economic accounting is missing according to economic census year data use provisions of National Bureau of Statistics.

指　标	Indicator	单　位 Unit	1978 年	1985 年
地区生产总值	**Gross Domestic Product**	元(yuan)	527	1263
主要农产品产量	**Output of Major Agricultural Products**			
粮　食	Grain	千克(kg)	258	336
棉　花	Cotton	千克(kg)	1.14	10.22
猪　肉	Pork	千克(kg)	5.44	10.33
水　果	Fruits	千克(kg)	12.65	14.70
禽　蛋	Eggs	千克(kg)		
蔬　菜	Vagatables	千克(kg)	109.84	173.02
牛　奶	Milk	千克(kg)	0.88	1.76
水产品	Aquatic Products	千克(kg)	0.29	0.41
主要工业产品产量	**Output of Major Industrial Products**			
钢　材	Steel	千克(kg)	48.1	69.6
发电量	Electric Energy Capacity	千瓦小时(kwh)	282.5	543.9
水　泥	Cement	千克(kg)	195.5	277.9
化　肥	Chemical Fertilizer	千克(kg)	29.5	18.7
服务器	server	台(unit)	–	–
布	Cloth	米(m)	30.8	37.2
其他经济活动	**Other Economic Activity**			
社会消费品零售总额	Total Sales of Consumption Good Per Capita	元(yuan)	182	500
一般公共预算收入	General Pubilic Budget Revenue	元(yuan)	133	183
一般公共预算支出	General Pubilic Budget Expenditure	元(yuan)	33	70
城乡居民人民币储蓄存款余额	RMB Deposits Balance of Urban and Rural Residents	元(yuan)	33	236
城镇居民人均可支配收入	Per Capita Disposable Income of Urban Residents	元(yuan)	338	732
城镇居民人均生活消费支出	Per Capita Life Consumption Expenditure of Urban Residents	元(yuan)	318	704
农村居民人均可支配收入	Per Capita Disposable Income of Rural Residents	元(yuan)	111	439
农村居民人均生活消费支出	Per Capita Life Consumption Expenditure of Rural Residents	元(yuan)	83	330

注：1、“一般公共预算收入” 指标 1978 年到 1995 年为“地方财政收入”口径。“一般公共预算支出”指标 1978 年到 1995 年为“地方财政支出”口径。
2、从 2015 年起，全市发布城乡住户调查一体化改革新口径数据，居民收支调查指标与 2014 年前分别实施的城镇和农村住户调查的调查范围、方法、指标口径、名称有所不同。

人 均 指 标

National Economic

1990 年	1995 年	2000 年	2010 年	2015 年	2017 年	2018 年
2666	8773	16999	57947	85919	98967	106302
350	468	429	479	424	400	340
9.64	5.38	4.87	4.87	2.36	1.49	0.39
15.13	26.33	31.15	36.10	36.46	32.13	20.97
12.88	35.81	66.56	78.58	85.00	80.70	124.02
18.27	41.29	74.29	59.68	56.86	51.83	44.96
243.10	469.77	960.06	996.29	1041.79	962.34	713.35
3.46	6.44	12.65	51.68	46.75	48.03	44.43
1.80	4.72	5.87	7.06	7.63	6.47	4.32
169.1	195.7	424.0	1623.8	1161.8	642.0	302.1
862.3	1237.0	1231.5	2177.5	2819.9	2508.9	2068.8
408.0	728.4	866.1	1208.9	1253.1	947.2	817.7
23.6	23.0	46.5	80.3	37.7	32.9	28.1
–	–	–	0.016	0.065	0.088	0.1
38.9	19.9	29.5	13.6	25.7	25.7	5.5
1009	3468	6332	28563	54687	64966	59594
239	315	876	4409	9850	10611	10186
158	363	977	5579	10553	13069	13778
985	4115	8266	36239	63358	70889	67761
1620	4721	8471	25321	39889	46642	50146
1369	3830	6892	15973	26319	30729	32977
731	1813	3047	8903	14232	16594	17924
570	1374	1977	5407	8597	10327	11172

Notes: 1. The indicator–"general public budget revenue" was the caliber of "local financial revenue" from 1978 to 1995 and the indicator–"general public budget expenditure" was the caliber of "local fiscal expenditure" from 1978 to 1995.

2. From 2015, new caliber data about urban and rural household survey integration reform was published by the city and the survey index of residents' income and expenditure was different from survey scope, method, indicator caliber and name of urban and rural residents implemented before 2014.

3-5 国民经济主要指标

Main Indicators of National Economy and Their

指　　标	Indicator	单 位 Unit	全 国 Country
区划面积	Area	万平方公里(10 000 sq.km)	960
年末总人口	Total year-end Population	万人(10 000 persons)	139538
生产总值(当年价)	Gross Domestic Product	亿元(100 million yuan)	900309.5
第一产业	Primary Industry	亿元(100 million yuan)	64734.0
第二产业	Secondary Industry	亿元(100 million yuan)	366000.9
第三产业	Tertiary Industry	亿元(100 million yuan)	469574.6
规模以上工业主营业务收入	Revenue from Principal Business of Industrial Enterprises above Designated Size	亿元(100 million yuan)	1022241.0
规模以上工业利润总额	Total Profits of Industrial Enterprises above Designated Size	亿元(100 million yuan)	66351.0
粮食总产量	Total Output of Grain	万吨(10 000 tons)	65789.2
棉花总产量	Total Output of Cotton	万吨(10 000 tons)	610.3
固定资产投资额	Investment in Fixed Assets	亿元(100 million yuan)	645675.0
公路货物周转量	Highways Freight Turnover	亿吨公里(100 million ton-km)	71249
社会消费品零售总额	Total Sales of Consumption Good Per Capita	亿元(100 million yuan)	380987.0
实际使用外资	Total Amount of Foreign Capital Actually Utilized	亿美元(100 million USD)	1349.7
一般公共预算收入	General Pubilic Budget Revenue	亿元(100 million yuan)	183351.8
一般公共预算支出	General Pubilic Budget Expenditure	亿元(100 million yuan)	220906.1
普通本专科在校学生	Enrollment of Regular Institutions of Higher Educatio	万人(10 000persons)	2831.0
中等职业教育在校学生	Enrollment of Secondary Professional Schools	万人(10 001persons)	1552
卫生机构数	Number of Health Institutions	个(unit)	997433
卫生技术人员	Medical Technical Personnel	万人(10 000persons)	951.9
#执业（助理）医师	Licensed Doctors	万人(10 000persons)	360.7
城镇居民人均可支配收入	Per Capita Disposable Income of Urban Residents	元(yuan)	39251
农村居民人均可支配收入	Per Capita Disposable Income of Rural Residents	元(yuan)	14617

及占全国、全省比重(2018)

Proportion in China and Shandong Province（2018）

全省 Province	济南 Ji'nan	济南占全国比重（%） Ji'nan Account for Proportion of Country(%)	济南占全省比重（%） Ji'nan Account for Proportion of Province(%)
15.8	0.7998	0.08	5.06
10047.2	655.9	0.47	6.53
76469.7	7856.56	0.87	10.27
4950.5	272.42	0.42	5.50
33641.7	2829.31	0.77	8.41
37877.4	4754.83	1.01	12.55
–	5192.2	0.51	
–	308.0	0.46	
5319.5	251.42	0.38	4.73
21.7	0.29	0.05	1.34
–	–		
6859.7	474.0	0.67	6.91
	4404.5	1.16	
123.9	27.3	2.02	22.03
6485.4	752.8	0.41	11.61
10099.0	1018.3	0.46	10.08
204.1	79.6	2.81	39.00
75	5.2	0.34	6.93
81517	6030	0.60	7.40
73.8	8.3	0.87	11.22
29.0	3.21	0.89	11.07
39549	50146		
16297	17924		

3-6 行政区划调整后济南市主要经济指标（2018）

Main Economic Indicators of Jinan after Administrative Division Adjustment（2018）

指　　标	Indicator	单 位 Unit	2018 年
面　积	Area		
土地面积	Land Area	平方公里(sq.km)	10244
人　口	Population		
年末户籍人口	Total Household Population at the Year-end	万人(10 000 persons)	785.3
年末常住人口	Total Resident Population at the Year-end	万人(10 000 persons)	883.9
国民经济核算	National Accounting		
地区生产总值	Gross Domestic Product	亿元(100 million yuan)	8862.2
第一产业	Primary Industry	亿元(100 million yuan)	332.7
第二产业	Secondary Industry	亿元(100 million yuan)	3395.4
第三产业	Tertiary Industry	亿元(100 million yuan)	5134.1
人均地区生产总值	Per Capita GDP	元(yuan)	101071
固定资产投资	Investment in Fixed Assets		
固定资产投资比上年增长	Growth rate Total Investment in Fixed Assets	%	9.3
第一产业	Primary Industry	%	-8.7
第二产业	Secondary Industry	%	-6.1
第三产业	Tertiary Industry	%	14.3
财　政	Fiscal		
一般公共预算收入	General Pubilic Budget Revenue	亿元(100 million yuan)	815.4
一般公共预算支出	General Pubilic Budget Expenditure	亿元(100 million yuan)	1118.6
金　融	Finance		
金融机构人民币存款余额	RMB Deposits Balance of Financial Institutions	亿元(100 million yuan)	17600.1
#住户存款	Deposits of Households	亿元(100 million yuan)	5638.3
金融机构人民币贷款余额	RMB Loans Balance of Financial Institutions	亿元(100 million yuan)	15515.3
农　业	Agriculture		
农林牧渔业总产值	Gross Output Value of Farming Forestry,Animal Husbandry and Fishery	亿元(100 million yuan)	623.8
农业机械总动力	total power of agricultural machinery	万千瓦(10 000kw)	543.1

3-6 续 1

指　　　标	Indicator	单 位 Unit	2018 年
农作物总播种面积	Total Sown Area of Farm Crops	千公顷(1000 ha)	612.1
粮食总产量	Total Output of Grain	万吨(10 000 tons)	276.9
蔬菜总产量	Total Output of Vegetable	万吨(10 000 tons)	659.0
肉类总产量	Total Output of meat	万吨(10 000 tons)	37.8
奶类总产量	Total Output of Milk	万吨(10 000 tons)	33.2
棉花总产量	Total Output of Cotton	万吨(10 000 tons)	0.4
规模以上工业	**Industry Enterprises above Designated Size**		
单位数	Number of Enterprises	个(unit)	2629
主营业务收入	Revenue from Principal Business	亿元(100 million yuan)	7264.9
利税总额	Total Profits and Taxes	亿元(100 million yuan)	647.5
利润总额	Total Profits	亿元(100 million yuan)	394.3
国内贸易	**Domestic Trade**		
社会消费品零售总额	Total Retail Sales of Consumer Goods	亿元(100 million yuan)	4777.6
#批发零售业	Wholesale and Retail Trade	亿元(100 million yuan)	4068.9
#住宿餐饮业	Hotels and Catering Services	亿元(100 million yuan)	708.7
对外经济和国际旅游	**Foreign Economy and Trade,Tourism**		
全年货物进出口总额	Total Value of Imports and Exports	亿元(100 million yuan)	936.4
出口	Exports	亿元(100 million yuan)	591.7
进口	Imports	亿元(100 million yuan)	344.7
全年实际使用外资	Total Amount of Foreign Capital Actually Utilized	亿元(100 million yuan)	178.9
入境游客人数	Number of Inbound Tourists	万人次(10 000 persons-time)	40.7
入境游客消费额	Inbound Tourists Consumption Amount	万美元(10 000 USD)	22955.1
人民生活	**People's Livelihood**		
城镇居民人均可支配收入	Per Capita Disposable Income of Urban Residents	元(yuan)	48364
城镇居民人均生活消费支出	Per Capita Life Consumption Expenditure of Urban Residents	元(yuan)	31344
农村居民人均可支配收入	Per Capita Disposable Income of Rural Residents	元(yuan)	17835
农村居民人均生活消费支出	Per Capita Life Consumption Expenditure of Rural Residents	元(yuan)	11385

主要统计指标解释

几点说明：

1.生产总值及一、二、三次产业增加值，历史数据有所调整，以本年鉴所列数据为准。

2.生产总值及一、二、三次产业增加值，全部工业增加值，农业总产值等指标的增长速度均以可比价格计算。

3.由于国家在1994 年开始财税体制改革，1994 年及以后各年的财政收支与以前年份不可比。另外，2000 年财政收入统计口径也有微调。

4.工业统计口径调整。1998年以前工业统计范围为乡及乡以上独立核算工业企业，1998年，统计范围调整为规模以上工业，即全部国有及年销售收入500万元以上的非国有工业单位，2011年，调整为年主营业务收入2000万元以上。

5.建筑业统计范围变化。建筑业统计范围1994–1995 年为县及县以上单位，1996–1997年为资质等级四级及以上独立核算建筑业企业，1998 年起为资质等级五级及以上独立核算建筑业企业。

企业（单位）登记注册类型 是以在工商行政管理机关登记注册的具有法人资格的各类企业为划分对象。行政机关、事业单位和社会团体及其他经济组织参照执行。

本项以工商行政管理部门对企业（单位）登记注册的类型为依据，将企业（单位）登记注册类型分为以下几种：

（1）国有企业是指企业全部资产归国家所有，并按《中华人民共和国企业法人登记管理条例》规定登记注册的非公司制的经济组织。不包括有限责任公司中的国有独资公司。

（2）集体企业是指企业资产归集体所有，并按《中华人民共和国企业法人登记管理条例》规定登记注册的经济组织。

（3）股份合作企业是指以合作制为基础，由企业职工共同出资入股，吸收一定比例的社会资产投资组建，实行自主经营，自负盈亏，共同劳动，民主管理，按劳分配与按股分红相结合的一种集体经济组织。

（4）联营企业是指两个及两个以上相同或不同所有制性质的企业法人或事业单位法人，按自愿、平等、互利的原则，共同投资组成的经济组织。

联营企业包括国有联营企业、集体联营企业、国有与集体联营企业和其他联营企业。

（5）有限责任公司是指根据《中华人民共和国登记管理条例》规定登记注册，由两个以上，五十个以下的股东共同出资，每个股东以其所认缴的出资额对公司承担有限责任，公司以其全部资产对其债务承担责任的经济组织。

有限责任公司包括国有独资公司以及其他有限责任公司。

①国有独资公司是指国家授权的投资机构或者国家授权的部门单独投资设立的有限责任公司。

②其他有限责任公司是指国有独资公司以外的其他有限责任公司。

（6）股份有限公司是指根据《中华人民共和国登记管理条例》规定登记注册，其全部注册资本由等额股份构成并通过发行股票筹集资本，股东以其认购的股份对公司承担有限责任，公司以其全部资产对其债务承担责任的经济组织。

（7）私营企业是指由自然人投资设立或由自然人控股，以雇佣劳动为基础的营利性经济组织。包括按照《公司法》、《合伙企业法》、《私营企业暂行条件》规定登记注册的私营有限责任公司、私营股份有限公司、私营合伙企业和私营独资企业。

①私营独资企业是指按《私营企业暂行条例》的规定，由一名自然人投资经营，以雇佣劳动为基础，投资者对企业债务承担无限责任的企业。

②私营合伙企业是指按《合伙企业法》或《私营企业暂行条例》的规定，由两个以上自然人按照协议共同投资、共同经营、共负盈亏，以雇佣劳动为基础，对债务承担无限责任的企业。

③私营有限责任公司是指按《公司法》、《私营企业暂行条例》的规定，由两个以上自然人投资或由单个自然人控股的有限责任公司。

④私营股份有限公司是指按《公司法》的规定，由五个以上自然人投资，或由单个自然人控股的有限公司。

（8）其他内资企业是指上述第（1）条至第（7）条之外的其他内资经济组织。

（9）与港澳台商合资经营企业是指港澳台地区投资者与内地的企业依照《中华人民共和国中外合资经营企业法》及有关法律的规定，按合同规定的比例投资设立、分享利润和分担风险的企业。

（10）与港澳台商合作经营企业是指港澳台地区投资者与内地企业依照《中华人民共和国中外合作经营企业法》及有关法律的规定，依照合作合同的约定进行投资或提供条件设立、分配利润和分担风险的企业。

（11）港澳台商独资经营企业是指依照《中华人民共和国外资企业法》及有关法律的规定，在内地由港澳台地区投资者全额投资设立的企业。

（12）港澳台商投资股份有限公司是指根据国家有关规定，经外经贸部依法批准设立，其中港、澳、台商的股本占公司注册资本的比例达25%以上的股份有限公司。凡其中港、澳、台商的股本占公司注册资本的比例小于25%的，属于内资企业中的股份有限公司。

（13）中外合资经营企业是指外国企业或外国人与中国内地企业依照《中华人民共和国中外合资经营企业法》及有关法律的规定，按合同规定的比例投资设立、分享利润和分担风险的企业。

（14）中外合作经营企业是指外国企业或外国人与中国内地企业依照《中华人民共和国中外合作经营企业法》及有关法律的规定，依照合作合同的约定进行投资或提供条件设立、分配利润和分担风险的企业。

（15）外资企业是指依照《中华人民共和国外资企业法》及有关法律的规定，在中国内地由外国投资者全额投资设立的企业。

（16）外商投资股份有限公司是指根据国家有关规定，经外经贸部依法批准设立，其中外资的股本占公司注册资本的比例达25%以上的股份有限公司。凡其中外资股本占公司注册资本的比例小于25%的，属于内资企业中的股份有限公司。

机关、事业单位和社会团体参照《企业登记注册类型与代码》，主要按其经费来源和管理方式划分。具体规定如下：

（1）机关包括国家机关和政党机关，原则上均列为“国有”。但有特殊规定的，如供销社等，则列为“集体”。

（2）事业单位包括经国家机构编制部门和有关业务主管部门批准成立的各类事业单位，不包括实行企业化管理的事业单位。事业单位的划分办法如下：

①由国家财政预算拨款或列入财政预算外资金管理以及经费主要来源于国有主管部门或国有上级单位的事业单位，列为“国有”。

②经费主要来源于集体单位的事业单位，列为“集体”。

③公民个人（或个人合伙）开办的事业单位，列为“私营”。

④上述以外的其他事业单位，如果其经费来源不明确，按管理方式进行归类。

（3）社会团体包括经民政部门批准成立以及未纳入社会团体管理条例范围的工会、妇联等各类社会团体。社会团体的划分办法如下：

①未纳入民政部社会团体管理条例范围的工会、妇联、共青团、青联、工商联、科协、侨联等社会团体，国家拨款设立的基金会或基金管理组织以及经费主要来源于国有业务主管部门或国有上级单位的社会团体，列为“国有”。

②经费主要来源于集体单位的社会团体，列为“集体”。

③公民个人（或个人合伙）开办的社会团体，划为“私营”。

④上述以外的其他社会团体，如果其经费来源不明确，改按管理方式进行归类。

平均增长速度 我国计算平均增长速度有两种方法：一种是习惯上经常使用的“水平法”，又称几何平均法，是以间隔期最后一年的水平同基期水平对比来计算平均每年增长（或下降）速度；另一种是“累计法”，又称代数平均法或方程法，是以间隔期内各年水平的总和同基期水平对比来计算平均每年增长（或下降）速度。在一般正常情况下，两种方法计算的平均每年增长速度比较接近；但在经济发展不平衡、出现大起大落时，两种方法计算的结果差别较大。

本《年鉴》内所列的平均增长速度，除固定资产投资用“累计法”计算外，其余均用“水平法”计算。从某年到某年平均增长速度的年份，均不包括基期年在内。如建国四十三年的平均增长速度是以1949年为基期计算的，则写为1950–1992年平均增长速度，其余类推。

Explanatory Notes on Main Statistical Indicators

Some explanations:

1. Historical data regarding total output value and value added of the primary industry, the secondary industry and the tertiary industry is adjusted and the data listed in the yearbooks shall prevail.

2. The growth rate of such indicators as total output value, value added of the primary industry, the secondary industry and the tertiary industry, total industrial added value and total value of agricultural output is calculated as per comparable price.

3. Because China started reform of fiscal and tax system from 1994, financial revenue and expenditure in 1994 and later are incomparable to those of previous years. Furthermore, fiscal revenue statistical caliber in 2000 was slightly adjusted.

4. Adjustment of industrial statistical caliber. Industrial statistical range before 1998 covered independent accounting industrial enterprises of township and above. The statistical range was adjusted to industrial enterprises above designated size in 1998, namely all state-owned industrial units and non-state-owned industrial units with annual sales revenue of above RMB 5 million and those with annual main business income of above RMB 20 million in 2011.

5. Change in statistical range in the construction industry. The statistical range in the construction industry covered county and above units from 1994 to 1995, construction enterprises with independent accounting whose qualification level was Level IV and above from 1996 to 1997 or construction enterprises with independent accounting whose qualification level was Level V and above from 1998.

Registration Status of Enterprises (Units) Enterprises are classified according to the registration status of an enterprise with the qualifications of legal person in industrial and commercial administration agencies. Government agencies, institutions, social organizations and other economic organizations shall follow the above classification.

Enterprises (units) are classified into the following categories according to the registration status of an enterprise in industrial and commercial administration agencies:

(1) **State-owned Enterprises** refer to non-corporation economic units that registered in accordance with the regulations of the people's republic of china for controlling the registration of enterprises as legal persons, where the entire assets are owned by the state. Excluded from this category are solely state-owned companies in the limited liability corporations.

(2) **Collective-owned Enterprises** refer to economic units where the enterprise assets are owned collectively and which have registered in accordance with the regulations of the people's republic of china for controlling the registration of enterprises as legal persons.

(3) **Cooperative Enterprises** refer to a form of collective economic units (enterprises) where capitals come mainly from employees as their shares, with certain proportion of capital from the outside, where production is organized on the basis of independent operation, independent accounting for profits and losses, joint work, democratic management, and a distribution system that integrates remuneration according to work with dividend according to capital share.

(4) **Joint Ownership Enterprises** refer to economic units established by two or more corporate enterprises or corporate institutions of the same or different ownership, through joint investment on the basis of equality, voluntary participation and mutual benefits. They include state joint ownership enterprises, collective joint ownership enterprises, joint state-collective enterprises, other joint ownership enterprises.

They include state joint ownership enterprise, collective joint ownership, joint state-collective enterprises and other joint operation enterprises.

(5) **Limited Liability Corporations** refer to economic units established with investment from 2-50 investors and registered in accordance with the Regulation of the People's Republic of China on the Management of Registration of Corporations, each investor bearing limited liability to the corporation depending on its share of investment, and the corporation bearing liability to its debt to the maximum of its total assets.

Limited Liability Corporations include exclusive state funded limited liability corporations and other limited liability corporations.

① **State-owned Exclusive Corporations** refer to limited liability corporations established with sole investment by the investment organizations or departments authorized by the State.

② **Other Limited Liability Corporations** refer to other limited liability corporations other than the state-owned exclusive corporations .

(6) Share-holding Corporations Ltd. refer to economic units registered in accordance with the Regulation of the People's Republic of China on the Management of Registration of Corporations, with total registered capitals divided into equal shares and raised through issuing stocks. Each investor bears limited liability to the corporation depending on the holding of shares, and the corporation bears liability to its debt to the maximum of its total assets.

(7) Private Enterprises refer to profit-making economic units invested and established by natural persons, or controlled by natural persons using employed labour. Included in this category are private limited liability corporations, private share-holding corporations Ltd., private partnership enterprises and private-funded enterprises registered in accordance with the Corporation Law, Partnership Enterprises Law and Interim Regulations on Private Enterprises.

① Private Exclusive Enterprises refer to enterprises invested and operated by one person using employed labour in accordance with Interim Regulations on Private Enterprises , where the investor bears unlimited liability for enterprise debts.

② Private Cooperative Enterprises refer to enterprises

jointly invested and managed by more than two natural persons in accordance with Partnership Enterprises Law or Interim Regulations on Private Enterprises using employed labour, where sharing of investment, operation, profits and debts is stipulated under contract. They bear unlimited liabilities for the enterprise debts.

③ **Private Limited Liability Corporations** refer to the limited liability corporations invested by more than two natural persons or controlled by one natural person according to the stipulations of the Corporations Law and Interim Regulations on Private Enterprises.

④ Private Stock Corporations Ltd. refer to the limited corporations invested by more than five natural persons, or controlled by one natural person in accordance with Corporations Law.

(8) **Other Domestic-funded Enterprises** refer to other domestic-funded economic organizations other than those specified from Article (1) to Article (7).

(9) Joint Venture Enterprises with Funds from Hong Kong, Macau and Taiwan established by investors from Hong Kong, Macau and Taiwan with enterprises in the mainland of China in accordance with the Law of the People's Republic of China on Sino-foreign Cooperative Enterprises and other relevant laws, where the establishment of investment and the sharing of profits and risks are stipulated under the joint venture contracts.

(10) Cooperative Enterprises with Funds from Hong Kong, Macau and Taiwan established by investors from Hong Kong, Macau and Taiwan with enterprises in the mainland of China in accordance with the Law of the People's Republic of China on Sino-foreign Cooperative Enterprises and other relevant laws, where the investment or provision of facilities, and the sharing of profits and risks are stipulated in the cooperative contracts.

(11) **Enterprises with Sole (exclusive) Investment from Hong Kong, Macau and Taiwan** refer to enterprises established in the mainland of China with exclusive investment from investors from Hong Kong, Macau and Taiwan in accordance with the Law of the People's Republic of China on Wholly Foreign-owned Enterprises and other relevant laws.

(12) Share-holding Corporations Ltd. with Investment from Hong Kong, Macau and Taiwan refer to share-holding corporations Ltd. established with the approved from the Ministry of Foreign Trade and Economic Cooperation in line with relevant State regulations, where the share of investment from Hong Kong, Macau and Taiwan exceeds 25% of the total registered capital of the corporation. In case the share of foreign investment is less than 25% of the total registered capital, the enterprise is to be classified as domestic-funded share-holding corporation Ltd..

(13) Joint Venture Enterprises with Foreign Investment refer to enterprises jointly established by foreign enterprises or foreigners with enterprises in the mainland of China in accordance with the Law of the People's Republic of China on Sino-Foreign Equity Joint Ventures and other relevant laws, where the sharing of investment, profits and risks is stipulated under contract.

(14) Cooperative Enterprises with Foreign Investment refer to enterprises jointly established by foreign enterprises or foreigners with enterprises in the mainland of China in accordance with the Law of the People's Republic of China on Sino-Foreign Contractual Joint Ventures and other relevant laws, where the investment or provision of facilities and the sharing of profits and risks are stipulated under cooperative contracts.

(15) Enterprises with Sole (exclusive) Foreign Investment refer to enterprises established in the mainland of China with exclusive investment from foreign investors in accordance with the Law of the People's Republic of China on Wholly Foreign-owned Enterprises and other relevant laws.

(16) Share-holding Corporations Ltd. with Foreign Investment refer to share-holding corporations Ltd. established with the approval from the Ministry of Foreign Trade and Economic Cooperation in line with relevant State regulations, where the share of investment from foreign investors exceeds 25% of the total registered capital of the corporation. In case the share of foreign investment is less than 25% of the total registered capital, the enterprise is to be classified as domestic-funded share-holding corporation Ltd.

Government Agencies, Institutions and Social Organizations are classified into the following categories by source of funds and manner of management taking reference of the registration status and code of enterprises:

(1) Government agencies: include State and party agencies, classified in principle as State-owned. There are exceptions, such as supply and marketing cooperatives which are classified as collective-owned.

(2) Institutions: include institutions of various types established with the approval by organization and staffing departments of the government, but exclude institutions where enterprise management system is introduced. Institutions are further classified as follows:

① Institutions for which their main budgets are from government budget appropriations or extra-budget funds, or allocated from the budget of their competent government agencies. Such institutions are classified as state-owned.

② Institutions for which their budget mainly come from collective units are classified as collective-owned.

③ Social institutions established by individual or a group of citizens, which are classified as private.

④ Institutions other than those mentioned above for which their sources of budget are not clear are classified by the manner of management.

(3) Social organizations: include social organizations established with the approved from the Ministry of Civil Affairs and organizations that are not covered by social organization management regulations such as trade unions, women's federations etc. Such organizations are further classified as follows:

① Social organizations that are not covered by social organization management regulations of the Ministry of Civil Affairs such as labor union, women federations, communist youth leagues, youth federation, industrial and commerce associations, scientist associations, overseas Chinese associations,etc., foundations and fund management organizations established with funds from the state, and social organizations whose funds mainly come from the budget of their competent government agencies. Such institutions are classified as State-owned.

② Social organizations for which their budget mainly

come from collective units are classified as collective-owned.

③ Social organizations established by individual or a group of citizens are classified as private.

④ Social organizations other than those mentioned above for which their sources of budget are not clear are classified by the manner of management.

Average speed of growth The average speed of growth in China is calculated based on two methods: Customarily, one method -- "level method" (also called as geometric method) is often used to calculate average annual growth (or decline) speed by comparing the level of the final year of the interval with the level during the base period; The other method is "cumulative method" (also called as method of algebraic or equation method) which is used to calculate average annual growth (decline) speed by comparing total level of all years within the interval with the level during the base period. In normal circumstances, average annual growth rates calculated based on these two method are relatively close; However, in case of unbalanced economic development and changing radically, big difference happens to results calculated based on these two methods.

Average speed of growth listed in the *Yearbooks* of fixed investments is calculated as per "cumulative method" and the rest is calculated pursuant to "level method". Years of average speed of growth from one year to one year are not included into the base period. For example, the average speed of growth in the 43 years after founding of China is calculated based on base period in 1949; average speed of growth from 1950 to 1992 is written down and the rest is analogized.

国民经济核算

NATIONAL ACCOUNTS

4-1 各时期生产总值(按当年价格计算)

Gross Domestic Product in Each Period

年份 Year	地区生产总值（万元）Gross Domestic Product (10 000 yuan)	第一产业 Primary Industry	第二产业 Secondary Industry	第三产业 Tertiary Industry	#工业 Industry	人均生产总值（元）Per Capita GDP (yuan)
1952	38282	14464	11300	12518	10907	121
1957	66616	19282	22378	24956	21840	194
1962	62056	10271	24346	27439	23610	177
1965	96827	18837	44395	33595	43388	262
1970	136085	21582	76949	37554	75571	337
1975	162427	28985	86500	46942	84614	373
"五五"时期						
1976	181751	33447	99797	48507	97215	413
1977	199814	35831	112347	51636	109811	450
1978	235993	41633	133172	61188	128910	527
1979	265619	50144	147679	67796	141048	586
1980	288001	59580	158591	69830	142369	630
"六五"时期						
1981	315623	65646	176516	73461	151131	681
1982	360552	88026	185548	86978	157894	765
1983	420075	116162	204758	99155	179572	881
1984	479948	103502	254684	121762	201017	997
1985	613741	129221	318193	166327	275447	1263
"七五"时期						
1986	712831	148165	344782	219884	286895	1451
1987	845431	175195	402857	267379	328783	1699
1988	1142249	222330	570722	349197	474895	2266
1989	1258319	237692	615209	405418	546591	2466
1990	1382350	239283	673593	469474	604274	2666
"八五"时期						
1991	1633920	253797	765582	614541	677340	3109
1992	2078386	277408	983638	817340	868539	3928
1993	2707637	326614	1331453	1049570	1153600	5088
1994	3718760	494413	1768214	1456133	1544940	6946
1995	4735176	676399	2203700	1855077	1941631	8773

年份 Year	地区生产总值（万元） Gross Domestic Product (10 000 yuan)	第一产业 Primary Industry	第二产业 Secondary Industry	第三产业 Tertiary Industry	#工业 Industry	人均生产总值（元） Per Capita GDP (yuan)
“九五”时期						
1996	5808366	742400	2749300	2316666	2383100	10701
1997	7099490	825200	3279700	2994590	2788668	12995
1998	8021619	902000	3664300	3455319	2984090	14549
1999	8813156	925171	3998006	3889979	3188000	15863
2000（调整前）	9521798	950125	4186077	4385596	3366075	16999
2000	9441315	960185	4147355	4333775	3319701	16855
“十五”时期						
2001	10579155	983242	4380564	5215349	3507175	18697
2002	11901167	1000514	5016352	5884300	4023830	20807
2003	13521540	1048068	5886754	6586718	4822007	23362
2004	16002700	1205800	7219300	7577600	6034000	27293
2005	18462792	1343400	8474679	8644713	7158669	28900
“十一五”时期						
2006	21615316	1451210	9971161	10192945	8441795	33480
2007	25001427	1502995	11287598	12210834	9548644	38301
2008	30067703	1750100	13130913	15186690	11152190	45563
2009	33409059	1870700	14335100	17203259	11913600	50219
2010	39105271	2151700	16374544	20579027	13524244	57947
“十二五”时期						
2011	44062889	2378573	18289700	23394616	15078800	64310
2012	48036696	2529161	19381399	26126136	16030799	69444
2013	52301948	2847088	20532400	28922460	16906300	74994
2013（新行业）	52301948	2769911	20950832	28581205	16906300	74994
2014	57705966	2902894	22616579	32186493	18221072	82052
2015	61002320	3053916	23070000	34878404	18443700	85919
“十三五”时期						
2016	65361165	3173113	23689000	38499052	18788300	90999
2017	72019553	3173969	25692200	43153384	20031000	98967
2018	78565600	2724200	28293100	47548300	21450700	106302

注：1、2013 年始使用新口径、新行业分类标准（GB–2011）。新行业中：第一产业不再包括 农林牧渔服务业；第二产业不再包括开采辅助活动，金属制品、机械和设备修理业；农林牧渔服务业，开采辅助活动，金属制品、机械和设备修理业归入第三产业。后同。

2、2013 年（新行业）、2014 年为普查口径数据，后同。

3、经济普查年度，2018 年相关指标为快报数据。

Note: 1.New caliber and industry classification standard started to be used from 2013 (GB–2011). In the new industries: The primary industry doesn't include agriculture, forestry, animal husbandry and fishery service industry any longer; The secondary industry doesn't include mining auxiliary activities, metalware and machinery and equipment repair industry; Agriculture, forestry, animal husbandry and fishery service industry, mining auxiliary activities, metalware and machinery and equipment repair industry fall into the tertiary industry. Similarly hereinafter.

2.Economic census survey caliber data in 2013 (new industry) and 2014 arises (the same below).

3.After 2005, the per capita gross domestic product (GDP) of the permanent population caliber(the same below).

4.In the economic census year, related indicator in 2018 is the express data.

4-2 各时期生产总值环比指数(以上年为 100)

Circle Indices of Gross Domestic Product (preceding year=100)

年份 Year	地区生产总值 Gross Domestic Product	第一产业 Primary Industry	第二产业 Secondary Industry	第三产业 Tertiary Industry	#工业 Industry	人均生产总值 Per Capita GDP
1952	123.9	119.1	153.2	132.7	126.2	118.0
1957	97.5	91.7	89.0	112.7	92.3	95.7
1962	105.6	116.7	82.7	121.9	81.3	105.9
1965	120.8	120.4	138.8	105.3	132.9	120.7
1970	113.7	95.9	131.9	100.5	130.8	108.7
1975	139.0	121.5	160.4	117.6	167.8	133.9
“五五”时期						
1976	104.9	93.2	114.6	104.5	113.1	104.6
1977	106.8	95.0	112.3	106.3	113.9	104.7
1978	113.0	99.3	114.2	119.0	111.9	109.1
1979	112.1	120.0	110.5	110.4	109.0	110.8
1980	113.6	124.5	112.5	107.9	105.7	112.6
“六五”时期						
1981	109.5	110.1	111.2	105.1	106.1	108.0
1982	116.0	136.2	106.7	120.2	106.1	114.1
1983	117.0	132.5	110.8	114.5	114.2	115.6
1984	118.4	92.3	128.9	127.3	116.0	117.3
1985	105.4	102.9	103.0	112.6	112.9	104.4
“七五”时期						
1986	110.8	109.4	103.4	126.1	99.4	109.6
1987	112.2	111.9	110.5	115.0	108.4	110.8
1988	119.0	111.8	124.8	115.0	127.2	117.5
1989	103.2	100.1	101.0	108.8	107.8	101.9
1990	108.3	99.2	107.9	114.2	109.0	106.6
“八五”时期						
1991	112.8	101.2	108.5	124.9	107.0	111.3
1992	122.8	105.5	124.0	128.4	123.8	122.0
1993	121.4	109.7	126.1	119.7	123.8	120.7
1994	118.9	131.0	115.0	120.1	115.9	118.2
1995	113.3	121.7	110.9	112.3	111.8	112.4

年份 Year	地区生产总值 Gross Domestic Product	第一产业 Primary Industry	第二产业 Secondary Industry	第三产业 Tertiary Industry	#工业 Industry	人均生产总值 Per Capita GDP
“九五”时期						
1996	114.9	102.8	116.9	117.0	115.0	114.3
1997	119.6	108.8	116.7	126.3	114.5	118.8
1998	113.8	110.1	112.6	116.3	107.8	112.8
1999	113.1	109.5	111.8	115.4	110.6	112.2
2000	112.1	106.1	110.8	114.9	112.2	111.2
“十五”时期						
2001	112.1	104.0	109.8	115.9	111.0	110.9
2002	113.2	102.6	114.8	113.9	115.2	112.0
2003	114.5	104.6	118.2	113.0	121.9	113.2
2004	115.6	107.8	119.8	113.0	121.9	114.1
2005	115.6	106.0	117.4	115.4	119.8	114.2
“十一五”时期						
2006	115.7	106.0	117.2	115.6	119.3	114.4
2007	115.8	100.0	115.3	118.5	116.0	114.5
2008	113.0	105.0	110.0	116.8	110.7	111.8
2009	112.2	105.1	112.1	113.1	110.5	111.3
2010	112.7	104.9	111.0	114.9	110.7	111.1
“十二五”时期						
2011	110.6	104.4	111.7	110.3	112.2	108.9
2012	109.5	104.7	109.2	110.1	109.7	108.4
2013	109.6	103.9	110.1	109.7	110.6	108.7
2013（新行业）	109.6	103.7	110.1	109.7	110.6	108.7
2014	108.8	103.9	108.8	109.1	108.9	107.9
2015	108.1	104.1	107.4	108.9	107.1	107.0
“十三五”时期						
2016	107.8	104.1	106.9	108.7	106.9	106.5
2017	108.0	103.3	108.4	108.2	108.9	106.6
2018	107.4	102.5	107.8	107.5	107.0	105.7

4-3 资本形成总额（按当年价格计算）

Gross Capital Formation(Calculated at Current Prices)

单位：万元 (10 000 yuan)

指标	Indicator	2012 年	2013 年	2014 年	2015 年	2016 年	2017 年
资本形成总额	Gross Capital Formation	24140144	30182535	34417750	38457600	40333673	48134888
一、固定资本形成总额	Gross fixed Capitai Formation	21390653	27194510	31268206	33457249	37051965	44000633
1、住宅	Residential	4209797	6274201	6617872	7438000	9945598	11719804
2、非住宅建筑物	Non-residential Buildings	9748694	13011712	15557997	14780097	15626960	17892869
3、机器和设备	Machinery and Equipment	3984376	4499778	5067899	6450000	5880359	6674207
4、土地改良支出	Land Improvement Expenditure	44788	62574	92567	136928	83868	51369
5、矿藏勘探费	Mineral Exploration Expenditure	4730	5198	6049	6979	6899	6821
6、计算机软件	Computer Software	2130000	2276970	2590812	2970366	3407010	3815852
7、其他	Others	1268268	1064077	1335012	1674879	2101270	2636211
二、存货增加	Changes in Inventories	2749492	2988025	3149544	5000351	3281707	4134254
1.农林牧渔业	Agriculture, Forestry, Animal Husbandry and Fishery	161773	163227	-1100	-16200	-31854	-13992
2.工业	Industry	248136	670461	685047	733000	8376	3468105
3.建筑业	Construction	188246	-532	-603	514751	399574	976845
4.交通运输、仓储和邮政业	Transport, Storage and Postal Services	1791	2508	2115	-17600	116139	-5000
5.批发和零售业	Wholesale and Retail Trade	175842	31828	110839	-79000	-104495	869398
6.住宿和餐饮业	Accommodations and Catering Services	157	-1866	-523	-26000	-21754	-23786
7.房地产业	Real Estate	1973546	2122399	2347812	4010000	2090306	-1226316
8.其他服务业	Other Services	0	0	5957	-118600	825415	89000

4-4 最终消费支出（按当年价格计算）

Final Consumption Expenditure(Calculated at Current Prices)

单位：亿元　　(100 million yuan)

指　　标	Indicator	2012 年	2013 年	2014 年	2015 年	2016 年	2017 年
最终消费支出	**Final Consumption Expenditures**	2448.32	2728.45	2936.20	3190.55	3466.81	3779.14
居民消费支出	Expense on Consumption of All Households	1574.06	1747.52	1856.00	2015.55	2227.92	2396.54
农村居民	Rural Households	206.67	226.28	243.72	259.87	282.02	299.67
食品类支出	Food,Tobacco and liquor	60.81	64.14	67.29	68.50	74.73	80.26
衣着类支出	Clothing	10.16	10.98	12.95	11.73	12.78	13.48
居住类支出	Residence	30.13	33.68	31.54	38.73	43.34	48.89
家庭设备、用品及服务类支出	Supplies and Services	10.88	13.45	15.99	13.94	15.32	16.17
医疗保健类支出	Health care	23.83	20.54	19.78	17.73	18.81	18.37
交通和通信类支出	Transport and Communications	24.73	30.40	36.10	36.83	39.26	40.44
文教娱乐用品及服务类支出	Recreation,Education and Cultural	10.75	14.17	16.18	21.61	23.93	24.50
金融中介服务虚拟支出	FIinancial Intermediary Services Virtual Expenditure	1.92	2.14	2.33	2.54	2.88	3.12
保险服务消费支出	Insurance Services Expenditure	7.74	8.03	9.42	11.05	11.56	12.68
自有住房服务虚拟支出	Private Housing Service Virtual Expenditure	24.03	26.68	28.02	29.42	30.89	32.43
其他商品和服务类支出	Other Goods and Services Expenditure	1.69	2.06	4.12	7.78	8.52	9.33
城镇居民	Urban Households	1367.39	1521.23	1612.27	1755.68	1945.90	2096.86
食品类支出	Food,Tobacco and liquor	336.42	367.27	377.92	415.71	447.72	468.76
衣着类支出	Clothing	138.84	152.42	152.72	155.01	136.57	138.61
居住类支出	Residence	123.43	138.63	172.32	181.63	232.57	266.76
家庭设备、用品及服务类支出	Supplies and Services	96.57	105.23	111.02	126.11	130.78	134.26
医疗保健类支出	Health care	100.39	110.48	110.26	125.36	144.54	155.09
交通和通信类支出	Transport and Communications	220.64	253.86	261.73	288.43	345.54	356.59
文教娱乐用品及服务类支出	Recreation,Education and Cultural	143.21	155.17	170.23	197.80	199.58	211.76
金融中介服务虚拟支出	FIinancial Intermediary Services Virtual Expenditure	38.25	47.12	51.26	55.78	68.43	79.89
保险服务消费支出	Insurance Services Expenditure	14.61	15.17	17.79	20.87	36.04	42.70
自有住房服务虚拟支出	Private Housing Service Virtual Expenditure	98.38	114.15	119.85	125.85	142.71	174.78
实物消费支出	Reality Consumption	5.71	6.18	6.56	9.67	14.28	22.75
其他商品和服务类支出	Other Goods and Services Expenditure	50.94	55.56	60.62	53.46	47.14	44.90
政府消费支出	Government Consumption Expenditure	874.26	980.93	1080.20	1175.00	1238.89	1382.60

4-5 实际最终消费（按当年价格计算）

Final Real Consumption(Calculated at Current Prices)

单位：亿元　　(100 million yuan)

指　　标	Indicator	2012 年	2013 年	2014 年	2015 年	2016 年	2017 年
最终消费	**Final Consumption**	2448.32	2728.45	2936.20	3190.55	3466.81	3779.14
居民消费	Expense on Consumption of All Households	1907.56	2066.16	2189.96	2378.21	2610.94	2803.24
农村居民	Rural Households	245.83	272.82	292.65	312.03	342.28	360.56
食品类消费	Food,Tobacco and liquor	61.32	65.67	68.89	70.13	76.51	82.17
衣着类消费	Clothing	10.24	11.24	13.26	12.01	13.08	13.80
居住类消费	Residence	30.24	34.32	32.14	39.46	44.16	49.81
家庭设备、用品及服务类消费	Supplies and Services	10.97	13.76	16.36	14.26	15.67	16.54
医疗保健类消费	Health care	42.55	40.63	39.13	35.07	37.21	36.34
交通和通信类消费	Transport and Communications	24.95	31.14	36.99	37.73	40.22	41.43
文教娱乐用品及服务类消费	Recreation,Education and Cultural	29.90	37.62	42.95	57.39	63.53	65.06
金融中介服务虚拟消费	FIinancial Intermediary Services Virtual Expenditure	1.94	2.14	2.33	2.53	2.88	3.11
保险服务消费支出	Insurance Services Expenditure	7.80	8.03	9.42	11.05	11.56	12.68
自有住房服务虚拟消费	Private Housing Service Virtual Expenditure	24.21	26.68	28.01	29.41	30.89	32.43
其他商品和服务类消费	Other Goods and Services Expenditure	1.71	1.59	3.18	6.01	6.58	7.21
城镇居民	Urban Households	1661.73	1793.34	1897.31	2066.06	2268.66	2442.68
食品类消费	Food,Tobacco and liquor	339.16	364.59	375.17	412.68	444.46	465.35
衣着类消费	Clothing	139.75	151.07	151.37	153.64	135.36	137.39
居住类消费	Residence	124.48	137.67	171.13	180.37	209.96	240.82
家庭设备、用品及服务类消费	Supplies and Services	97.28	104.39	110.13	125.10	129.73	133.19
医疗保健类消费	Health care	230.37	251.57	251.07	285.46	329.14	353.16
交通和通信类消费	Transport and Communications	222.24	251.79	259.60	286.08	322.30	332.62
文教娱乐用品及服务类消费	Recreation,Education and Cultural	298.85	318.87	349.80	406.47	410.13	435.15
金融中介服务虚拟消费	FIinancial Intermediary Services Virtual Expenditure	38.54	47.12	51.27	55.78	68.43	79.89
保险服务消费支出	Insurance Services Expenditure	14.73	15.17	17.79	20.87	36.05	42.71
自有住房服务虚拟消费	Private Housing Service Virtual Expenditure	99.33	114.15	119.86	125.85	142.71	174.79
实物消费消费	Reality Consumption	5.76	6.18	6.56	9.68	14.28	22.75
其他商品和服务类消费	Other Goods and Services Expenditure	51.24	30.77	33.57	29.60	26.11	24.87
政府消费	Government Consumption	540.76	662.28	746.25	811.74	855.87	975.90

4-6 生产总值分布

Distribution of Gross Domestic Product

单位：亿元 (100 million yuan)

年份 Year	政府最终消费 Government Final Consumption	居民最终消费 Household Final Consumption	国内总投资 Total Domestic Investment	国内储蓄总额 Gross Domestic Savings	资金差额 Funding Gap
ＧＤＰ分布					
1990	14.63	52.28	54.12	71.36	17.24
“八五”时期					
1991	16.43	60.70	56.35	86.26	29.91
1992	20.06	71.02	80.23	116.76	36.53
1993	22.75	90.63	122.66	157.38	34.71
1994	25.57	122.10	152.31	224.21	71.90
1995	34.93	197.61	190.05	240.98	50.93
“九五”时期					
1996	50.21	240.49	236.98	290.14	53.16
1997	98.69	291.30	246.44	319.96	73.52
1998	100.52	347.78	285.39	353.86	68.47
1999	126.27	362.71	347.37	392.34	44.97
2000	132.05	332.70	398.13	479.38	81.25
“十五”时期					
2001	146.90	357.84	418.38	553.18	134.79
2002	161.84	401.23	500.89	627.04	126.16
2003	184.97	430.62	562.41	736.57	174.15
2004	206.80	457.71	760.12	935.75	175.63
2005	223.46	522.10	1017.39	1100.72	83.33
“十一五”时期					
2006	285.51	621.65	1126.39	1254.37	127.98
2007	350.33	820.82	1286.16	1328.99	42.83
2008	431.26	940.61	1577.87	1634.90	57.03
2009	495.31	1022.07	1749.05	1823.53	74.48
2010	636.91	1197.34	2055.73	2076.28	20.55
“十二五”时期					
2011	747.23	1391.82	2360.99	2267.24	–93.75
2012	874.26	1574.06	2414.01	2355.35	–58.66
2013	980.93	1747.52	3018.25	3042.14	23.88
2014	1080.20	1856.00	3441.78	2834.40	–561.73
2015	1175.00	2015.55	3845.76	2909.68	–936.08
“十三五”时期					
2016	1238.89	2227.92	4033.37	3069.31	–964.06
2017	1382.60	2396.54	4813.49	3422.82	–1390.67

4-7 生产总值（2009 年—2013 年）(分行业、按当年价格计算)

Value of Gross Domestic Product（2009-2013）(Sub Industry、Calculated at Current Prices)

单位：亿元 (100 million yuan)

指　　标	Indicator	2009 年	2010 年	2011 年	2012 年	2013 年
地区生产总值	Gross Domestic Product	3340.91	3910.53	4406.29	4803.67	5230.19
第一产业	Primary Industry	187.07	215.17	237.86	252.92	284.71
农林牧渔业	Agriculture, Forestry, Animal Husbandry and Fishery	187.07	215.17	237.86	252.92	284.71
农业	Farming	120.34	149.43	152.55	160.77	186.98
林业	Forestry	8.34	4.73	5.69	6.68	7.89
畜牧业	Animal Husbandry	51.22	53.08	70.61	75.28	78.08
渔业	Fishery	2.88	3.02	3.35	3.54	4.04
农林牧渔服务业	Services of Agriculture,Forestry,Animal Husbandry and Fishing	4.29	4.91	5.66	6.65	7.72
第二产业	Secondary Industry	1433.51	1637.45	1828.97	1938.14	2053.24
工业	Industry	1191.36	1352.42	1507.88	1603.08	1690.63
采矿业	Mining	26.60	31.64	34.11	33.21	56.03
制造业	Manufacture	1073.42	1194.23	1299.80	1490.91	1539.44
电力、燃气及水的生产和供应业	Production and Supply of Electric, Gas and Water	91.34	126.56	173.98	78.96	95.16
建筑业	Construction	242.15	285.03	321.09	335.06	362.61
房屋和土木工程建筑业	Building Construction	193.94	233.87	265.87	279.09	280.86
建筑安装业	Construction Installment	36.02	38.26	38.41	40.22	59.54
建筑装饰业	Construction Decoration	7.51	7.78	11.77	13.03	19.00
其他建筑业	Others	4.69	5.12	5.04	2.72	3.21
第三产业	Tertiary Industry	1720.33	2057.90	2339.46	2612.61	2892.24
交通运输、仓储和邮政业	Transport, Storage and Postal Services	200.27	236.81	296.61	320.41	332.97
铁路运输业	Railway Transport	52.01	56.18	60.70	65.55	63.12
道路运输业	Road Transport	96.68	118.25	152.71	170.27	172.42
城市公共交通业	Public Transportation by City	13.62	14.71	17.08	18.99	18.28
水上运输业	Waterway Transport	0.60	0.73	0.94	1.05	1.18
航空运输业	Air Transport	17.01	24.76	33.73	27.71	31.87

指　　标	Indicator	2009 年	2010 年	2011 年	2012 年	2013 年
管道运输业	Pipeline Transport	1.20	1.36	1.37	1.40	1.65
装卸搬运和其他运输服务业	Loading and Unloading and Other Transport Services	11.84	13.55	21.59	21.64	26.47
仓储业	Storage	5.79	6.09	7.18	10.97	15.00
邮政业	Postal Services	1.52	1.19	1.30	2.83	2.98
信息传输、计算机服务和软件业	Information Transmission, Computer Services and Software	66.24	116.38	136.70	152.10	162.58
电信和其他信息传输服务业	Telecommunications, Radio and Television and Satellite Transmission Services	30.95	31.15	29.93	28.80	33.11
计算机服务业	Internet and related Services	17.95	25.14	31.67	37.99	44.56
软件业	Software and Information Technology Services	17.33	60.09	75.10	85.31	84.90
批发和零售业	Wholesale and Retail Trade	416.50	476.43	522.96	588.50	671.63
批发业	Wholesale	234.13	288.90	335.52	381.87	437.59
零售业	Retail Trade	182.37	187.53	187.44	206.64	234.04
住宿和餐饮业	Accommodations and Catering Services	125.55	142.81	143.73	149.52	168.18
住宿业	Accommodations	12.43	16.44	16.77	17.68	20.76
餐饮业	Catering Services	113.12	126.37	126.96	131.84	147.42
金融业	Financial Intermediation	240.21	288.33	330.14	411.34	461.00
银行业	Banking Sector	164.58	226.00	278.34	357.71	387.31
证券业	Securities Industry	60.51	47.28	32.05	26.87	33.74
保险业	Insurance	10.02	5.37	6.43	6.99	8.16
其他金融活动	Others	5.10	9.68	13.32	19.77	31.80
房地产业	Real Estate	172.63	220.79	254.98	273.94	320.56
房地产开发经营业	Real Estate Development and Management	62.40	83.08	99.19	100.31	124.98
物业管理业	Property Management	18.69	28.65	31.55	32.35	38.34
房地产中介服务业	Real Estate Intermediary Services	10.13	15.53	17.11	17.62	17.62
其他房地产活动	Other Real Estate Activity	7.21	11.05	12.20	13.03	22.87
居民自有住房服务业	Private Housing Service	74.20	82.48	94.94	110.62	116.74
租赁和商务服务业	Leasing and Business Services	88.71	107.32	131.18	145.29	153.19

4-7 续2

指　　标	Indicator	2009 年	2010 年	2011 年	2012 年	2013 年
租赁业	Leasing Services	4.92	7.01	8.39	12.30	15.05
商务服务业	Business Services	83.78	100.31	122.79	132.99	138.14
科学研究、技术服务和地质勘查业	Scientific Research,Technical Services and Geeological Prospecting Industry	57.79	63.63	69.22	69.36	75.62
研究与试验发展	Research and Experimental Development	19.95	18.95	22.14	22.85	27.12
专业技术服务业	Special Technical Services	27.36	32.94	33.95	33.78	32.72
科技交流和推广服务业	Science and Technology Promotion and Application Services	6.74	7.16	7.87	7.46	9.79
地质勘查业	Geeological Prospecting Industry	3.74	4.58	5.27	5.27	5.98
水利、环境和公共设施管理业	Management of Water Conservancy, Environment and Public Facilities	12.18	13.84	13.62	14.05	17.26
水利管理业	Management of Water Conservancy	5.06	6.06	5.91	6.21	9.06
环境管理业	Environmental Management	2.46	2.90	2.54	0.07	0.09
公共设施管理业	Management of Public Facilities	4.67	4.87	5.17	7.77	8.11
居民服务和其他服务业	Services to Households and Other Services	32.95	40.75	46.88	52.01	57.49
居民服务业	Services to Households	18.41	22.77	26.18	29.03	30.26
其他服务业	Other Services	14.53	17.98	20.70	22.98	27.24
教育	Education	109.66	116.49	123.09	128.09	140.75
卫生、社会保障和社会福利业	Health,Social Security and Social Welfare	64.87	87.30	105.00	127.60	134.11
卫生	Public Health	56.31	74.52	95.70	117.78	124.11
社会保障业	Social Security	6.37	9.46	7.11	7.48	7.60
社会福利业	Social Welfare	2.19	3.32	2.19	2.34	2.40
文化、体育和娱乐业	Culture, Sports and Recreation	23.60	28.01	28.40	32.21	36.29
新闻出版业	News and Publication	9.99	10.94	11.82	11.59	12.35
广播、电视、电影和音像业	Radio, Television, Film and Video	5.27	6.65	6.97	10.52	11.24
文化艺术业	Culture and Arts	4.26	5.84	4.46	4.19	5.04
体育	Sports	2.08	2.21	2.47	2.55	4.01
娱乐业	Recreation	2.01	2.37	2.68	3.37	3.65
公共管理和社会组织	Public Management and Social Organizations	109.18	119.01	136.93	148.19	160.61

注：旧行业分组（GB-2002）。

Note: Grouping of old industries (GB-2002)

4-8 生产总值（2013 年-2017 年）（分行业，按当年价格计算)

Value of Gross Domestic Product（2013-2017）(Sub Industry、Calculated at Current Prices)

单位：亿元 (100 million yuan)

指标	Indicator	2013 年	2014 年	2015 年	2016 年	2017 年
地区生产总值	**Gross Domestic Product**	5230.19	5770.60	6100.23	6536.12	7201.96
农、林、牧、渔业	Agriculture, Forestry, Animal Husbandry and Fishery	284.71	299.11	314.99	328.24	330.24
农业	Farming	186.98	199.53	210.14	215.11	215.11
林业	Forestry	7.89	8.85	9.96	11.19	11.19
畜牧业	Animal Husbandry	78.08	77.57	80.82	86.47	86.47
渔业	Fishery	4.04	4.33	4.47	4.55	4.63
农、林、牧、渔服务业	Services of Agriculture,Forestry,Animal Husbandry and Fishing	7.72	8.82	9.60	10.93	12.84
工业	Industry	1690.63	1822.11	1844.37	1878.83	2003.10
采矿业	Mining	27.95	30.13	36.89	45.80	49.88
#开采辅助活动	Mining Support Activities	0.03	0.03	0.03	0.03	0.03
制造业	Manufacture	1471.81	1586.27	1715.26	1749.57	1877.08
#金属制品、机械和设备修理业	Metal Products, Machinery and Equipment Repair Industry	3.08	3.32	3.40	3.46	3.60
电力、燃气及水的生产和供应业	Production and Supply of Electric, Gas and Water	190.87	205.71	92.22	83.46	76.14
建筑业	Construction	407.56	442.90	466.06	493.56	569.75
房屋建筑业	Building Construction	236.10	252.57	241.65	279.93	316.15
土木工程建筑业	Civil Engineering Construction	107.82	121.17	178.83	172.85	215.22
建筑安装业	Construction Installment	25.22	27.40	21.12	13.47	15.97
建筑装饰业和其他建筑业	Construction Decoration and Others	38.43	41.76	24.47	27.32	22.41
批发和零售业	Wholesale and Retail Trade	626.68	691.65	715.54	760.76	976.87
批发业	Wholesale	397.64	441.38	453.30	482.02	620.82
零售业	Retail Trade	229.04	250.27	262.24	278.74	356.05
交通运输、仓储和邮政业	Transport, Storage and Post	332.97	364.29	371.63	392.18	415.61
铁路运输业	Railway Transport	63.12	69.06	68.40	72.50	72.40
道路运输业	Road Transport	166.88	181.18	186.88	191.92	198.29

4-8 续1

指标	Indicator	2013 年	2014 年	2015 年	2016 年	2017 年
水上运输业	Waterway Transport	1.18	1.29	1.32	1.50	1.42
航空运输业	Air Transport	31.87	34.87	35.57	41.51	44.62
管道运输业	Pipeline Transport	21.47	23.49	23.96	24.35	29.71
装卸搬运和运输代理业	Loading, Unloading and Forwarding Agency	26.47	28.96	29.54	27.33	28.63
仓储业	Storage	15.00	16.41	16.74	21.68	27.20
邮政业	Postal Services	6.98	9.04	9.22	11.38	13.33
住宿和餐饮业	Accommodations and Catering Services	168.18	180.96	188.45	202.85	218.71
住宿业	Accommodations	20.76	22.45	22.68	23.99	25.21
餐饮业	Catering Services	147.42	158.51	165.77	178.86	193.50
信息传输、软件和信息技术服务和业	Information Transmission, Software and I nformation Technology	162.58	190.17	201.95	232.78	276.11
电信、广播电视和卫星传输服务	Telecommunications, Radio and Television and Satellite Transmission Services	101.79	119.07	126.45	125.49	164.15
互联网和相关服务	Internet and related Services	4.35	5.09	5.40	18.21	20.24
软件和信息技术服务业	Software and Information Technology Services	56.44	66.02	70.11	89.08	91.72
金融业	Financial Intermediation	461.00	541.88	641.86	719.98	776.01
货币金融服务	Monetary and Financial Services	387.31	437.25	517.93	589.41	657.35
资本市场服务	Capital Market Services	33.74	48.65	57.63	36.42	41.05
保险业	Insurance	8.16	9.59	11.36	23.06	26.76
其他金融业	Others	31.80	46.38	54.94	71.10	50.85
房地产业	Real Estate	320.56	369.23	415.00	463.21	500.05
房地产开发经营业	Real Estate Development and Management	136.61	169.38	190.37	218.55	220.66
物业管理业	Property Management	26.72	25.46	28.62	33.66	35.55
房地产中介服务业	Real Estate Intermediary Services	17.62	17.44	19.60	25.72	29.89
自有房地产经营活动	Own Real Estate Operating Activities	116.74	132.83	134.73	140.19	160.01
其他房地产业	Other Real Estate Industry	22.87	24.13	41.68	45.09	53.94
租赁和商务服务业	Leasing and Business Services	153.19	172.19	182.86	214.29	192.31
租赁业	Leasing Services	15.05	16.92	17.97	25.15	28.46
商务服务业	Business Services	138.14	155.27	164.90	189.14	163.85

指标	Indicator	2013 年	2014 年	2015 年	2016 年	2017 年
科学研究和技术服务业	Scientific Research and Technical Services	75.62	82.35	90.00	103.15	136.89
研究和试验发展	Research and Experimental Development	6.39	6.96	7.60	10.15	14.42
专业技术服务业	Special Technical Services	50.38	54.86	59.96	68.00	94.49
科技推广和应用服务业	Science and Technology Promotion and Application Services	18.85	20.53	22.43	25.00	27.98
水利、环境和公共设施管理业	Management of Water Conservancy, Environment and Public Facilities	17.26	18.80	20.54	24.95	28.81
水利管理业	Management of Water Conservancy	1.88	2.05	2.24	2.50	2.70
生态保护和环境治理业	Ecological Protection and Environmental Management	0.61	0.74	0.80	1.45	2.07
公共设施管理业	Management of Public Facilities	14.77	16.01	17.50	21.00	24.04
居民服务、修理和其他服务业	Services to Households, Repair and Other Services	57.49	64.63	68.63	80.79	78.46
居民服务业	Services to Households	30.26	32.21	34.21	39.47	36.39
机动车、电子产品和日用产品修理业	Repair of Motor Vehicle, Electronics and Household Products	9.12	10.25	10.89	13.07	13.44
其他服务业	Other Services	18.11	22.16	23.53	28.25	28.62
教育	Education	140.75	153.27	167.51	196.78	232.09
卫生和社会工作	Health,Social Security and Social Welfare	134.11	146.04	159.60	176.10	179.89
卫生	Public Health	124.11	135.15	147.70	161.56	164.89
社会工作	Social Work	10.00	10.89	11.90	14.53	15.00
文化、体育和娱乐业	Culture, Sports and Recreation	36.29	40.79	43.32	48.60	52.29
新闻和出版业	Journalism and Publishing Activities	12.35	13.88	14.74	17.30	20.63
广播、电视、电影和影视录音	Radio, Television, Motion Picture and Videotape Programme	11.24	14.43	15.33	15.50	15.47
文化艺术业	Culture and Arts	5.04	4.37	4.64	5.69	6.11
体育	Sports	4.01	4.51	4.79	5.55	5.74
娱乐业	Recreation	3.65	3.60	3.83	4.57	4.34
公共管理、社会保障和社会组织	Public Management, Social Security and Social Organization	160.61	190.24	207.91	219.08	234.78
第一产业	Primary Industry	276.99	290.29	305.39	317.31	317.40
第二产业	Secondary Industry	2095.08	2261.66	2307.00	2368.90	2569.22
第三产业	Tertiary Industry	2858.12	3218.65	3487.84	3849.91	4315.34

注：新行业分组（GB–2011）。
Note: Grouping of new industries (GB–2011)

4-9 生产总值贡献率（2009 年-2013 年）(分行业、按不变价格计算)

Distribution Rate of Gross Domestic Product(Calculated at Fixed Prices)（2009-2013）(Sub Industry、Calculated at Constant Prices)

单位：% (%)

指　　标	Indicator	2009 年	2010 年	2011 年	2012 年	2013 年
地区生产总值贡献率	Gross Domestic Product	100.0	100.0	100.0	100.0	100.0
第一产业	Primary Industry	2.3	1.9	2.3	2.6	2.0
农林牧渔业	Agriculture, Forestry, Animal Husbandry and Fishery	2.3	1.9	2.3	2.6	2.0
农业	Farming	1.3	2.3	-1.3	1.4	1.1
林业	Forestry	0.0	-0.6	0.2	0.2	0.2
畜牧业	Animal Husbandry	1.0	0.2	3.3	0.8	0.5
渔业	Fishery	0.0	0.0	0.0	0.0	0.0
农林牧渔服务业	Services of Agriculture,Forestry,Animal Husbandry and Fishing	0.0	0.1	0.1	0.2	0.2
第二产业	Secondary Industry	44.6	39.1	46.2	41.2	44.5
工业	Industry	33.8	32.6	39.9	36.0	38.8
采矿业	Mining	3.9	1.1	0.6	0.0	5.9
制造业	Manufacture	15.0	23.3	27.5	58.7	30.6
电力、燃气及水的生产和供应业	Production and Supply of Electric, Gas and Water	14.8	8.2	11.7	-22.7	2.4
建筑业	Construction	10.8	6.5	6.3	5.2	5.6
房屋和土木工程建筑业	Building Construction	11.5	6.3	5.8	4.7	-6.3
建筑安装业	Construction Installment	0.6	0.1	-0.2	0.6	10.5
建筑装饰业	Construction Decoration	-0.9	0.0	0.9	0.4	1.3
其他建筑业	Others	-0.4	0.0	-0.1	-0.5	0.1
第三产业	Tertiary Industry	53.1	59.0	51.5	56.2	53.5
交通运输、仓储和邮政业	Transport, Storage and Postal Services	12.4	6.4	13.0	5.4	2.9
铁路运输业	Railway Transport	1.2	1.1	0.8	1.1	-0.4
道路运输业	Road Transport	9.7	3.1	7.6	4.1	0.9
城市公共交通业	Public Transportation by City	0.1	0.2	0.5	0.4	-0.1
水上运输业	Waterway Transport	0.1	0.2	0.0	0.0	0.0
航空运输业	Air Transport	0.9	1.2	2.0	-1.5	0.8

指　　标	Indicator	2009 年	2010 年	2011 年	2012 年	2013 年
管道运输业	Pipeline Transport	0.1	0.0	0.0	0.0	0.1
装卸搬运和其他运输服务业	Loading and Unloading and Other Transport Services	0.5	0.4	1.8	0.0	0.8
仓储业	Storage	–0.1	0.1	0.2	0.9	0.7
邮政业	Postal Services	0.0	0.1	0.0	0.4	0.0
信息传输、计算机服务和软件业	Information Transmission, Computer Services and Software	2.9	7.7	4.7	3.5	2.3
电信和其他信息传输服务业	Telecommunications, Radio and Television and Satellite Transmission Services	–0.3	0.1	–0.3	–0.3	0.9
计算机服务业	Internet and related Services	2.9	2.6	1.5	1.5	1.4
软件业	Software and Information Technology Services	0.3	5.1	3.5	2.3	–0.1
批发和零售业	Wholesale and Retail Trade	10.5	12.4	7.6	13.5	15.7
批发业	Wholesale	10.6	11.8	9.5	9.4	11.2
零售业	Retail Trade	–0.1	0.6	–1.8	4.1	4.5
住宿和餐饮业	Accommodations and Catering Services	2.0	3.4	–0.6	1.0	2.5
住宿业	Accommodations	–0.1	1.1	0.1	0.2	0.3
餐饮业	Catering Services	2.1	2.4	–0.7	0.8	2.1
金融业	Financial Intermediation	8.7	8.8	7.0	17.5	13.9
银行业	Banking Sector	9.4	11.9	10.0	17.3	9.1
证券业	Securities Industry	0.1	–3.0	–4.0	–1.3	1.7
保险业	Insurance	–0.4	–1.0	0.2	0.1	0.3
其他金融活动	Others	–0.4	0.9	0.8	1.4	2.8
房地产业	Real Estate	5.3	8.3	4.9	3.5	8.3
房地产开发经营业	Real Estate Development and Management	0.7	3.6	3.1	0.0	4.4
物业管理业	Property Management	1.3	2.1	0.4	0.1	1.0
房地产中介服务业	Real Estate Intermediary Services	0.7	1.2	0.2	0.1	–0.1
其他房地产活动	Other Real Estate Activity	0.4	0.7	0.2	0.2	1.9
居民自有住房服务业	Private Housing Service	2.1	0.6	10.0	3.1	1.1
租赁和商务服务业	Leasing and Business Services	5.4	3.6	5.2	2.6	0.8

4-9 续2

指　　标	Indicator	2009 年	2010 年	2011 年	2012 年	2013 年
租赁业	Leasing Services	0.4	0.3	0.3	0.9	0.5
商务服务业	Business Services	5.1	3.2	4.9	1.7	0.3
科学研究、技术服务和地质勘查业	Scientific Research,Technical Services and Geeological Prospecting Industry	1.0	0.5	1.0	-0.4	0.9
研究与试验发展	Research and Experimental Development	0.4	-0.6	0.7	0.0	0.7
专业技术服务业	Special Technical Services	0.1	1.0	0.1	-0.3	-0.4
科技交流和推广服务业	Science and Technology Promotion and Application Services	0.4	0.1	0.1	-0.1	0.4
地质勘查业	Geeological Prospecting Industry	0.0	0.0	0.1	0.0	0.1
水利、环境和公共设施管理业	Management of Water Conservancy, Environment and Public Facilities	-0.3	-0.2	-0.1	0.0	0.6
水利管理业	Management of Water Conservancy	0.1	-0.1	-0.1	0.0	0.6
环境管理业	Environmental Management	0.1	0.0	-0.1	-0.6	0.0
公共设施管理业	Management of Public Facilities	-0.5	-0.1	0.0	0.6	0.0
居民服务和其他服务业	Services to Households and Other Services	0.7	1.8	1.3	0.9	0.9
居民服务业	Services to Households	0.4	1.0	0.7	0.5	0.1
其他服务业	Other Services	0.3	0.8	0.6	0.4	0.8
教育	Education	2.8	1.1	1.0	0.5	1.9
卫生、社会保障和社会福利业	Health,Social Security and Social Welfare	0.9	3.5	3.8	4.7	0.6
卫生	Public Health	0.6	2.6	4.7	4.7	0.6
社会保障业	Social Security	0.3	0.6	-0.6	0.0	0.0
社会福利业	Social Welfare	0.1	0.2	-0.3	0.0	0.0
文化、体育和娱乐业	Culture, Sports and Recreation	0.7	1.1	0.0	0.7	0.7
新闻出版业	News and Publication	0.3	0.2	0.2	-0.1	0.1
广播、电视、电影和音像业	Radio, Television, Film and Video	0.1	0.3	0.0	0.8	0.1
文化艺术业	Culture and Arts	0.1	0.4	-0.4	-0.1	0.2
体育	Sports	0.2	0.0	0.1	0.0	0.3
娱乐业	Recreation	0.0	0.1	0.1	0.1	0.0
公共管理和社会组织	Public Management and Social Organizations	0.1	0.7	2.6	2.8	1.7

注：旧行业分组（GB-2002）。
Note: Grouping of old industries (GB-2002)

4-10 生产总值贡献率（2013年-2017年）（分行业，按当年价格计算）

Value of Gross Domestic Product（2013-2017）(Sub Industry、Calculated at Current Prices)

单位：%　　(%)

指标	Indicator	2013年	2014年	2015年	2016年	2017年
地区生产总值贡献率	**Contribution Rate of Gross Domestic Product**	100.00	100.00	100.00	100.00	100.00
农、林、牧、渔业	Agriculture, Forestry, Animal Husbandry and Fishery	2.03	2.26	2.37	2.89	2.28
农业	Farming	1.13	3.36	3.51	1.85	0.94
林业	Forestry	0.20	0.09	0.09	0.29	0.31
畜牧业	Animal Husbandry	0.49	−1.36	−1.43	0.48	0.69
渔业	Fishery	0.03	0.05	0.05	0.03	0.03
农、林、牧、渔服务业	Services of Agriculture,Forestry,Animal Husbandry and Fishing	0.17	0.12	0.16	0.24	0.30
工业	Industry	38.69	36.05	31.40	26.92	33.80
采矿业	Mining	2.91	0.60	−0.36	2.41	1.00
#开采辅助活动	Mining Support Activities	0.00	0.00	0.00	0.00	0.00
制造业	Manufacture	31.06	26.58	26.89	25.49	33.95
#金属制品、机械和设备修理业	Metal Products, Machinery and Equipment Repair Industry	0.06	0.07	0.06	0.05	0.06
电力、燃气及水的生产和供应业	Production and Supply of Electric, Gas and Water	4.73	8.88	4.86	−0.98	−1.15
建筑业	Construction	6.70	7.52	8.58	6.75	5.77
房屋建筑业	Building Construction	4.31	−1.08	4.04	8.60	2.08
土木工程建筑业	Civil Engineering Construction	−3.32	7.07	9.30	−0.92	4.73
建筑安装业	Construction Installment	3.42	0.47	−1.20	−1.59	0.23
建筑装饰业和其他建筑业	Construction Decoration and Others	2.29	1.06	−3.56	0.66	−1.27
批发和零售业	Wholesale and Retail Trade	15.34	10.65	6.58	11.42	17.71
批发业	Wholesale	10.89	7.51	3.55	7.35	13.68
零售业	Retail Trade	4.44	3.13	3.03	4.07	4.02
交通运输、仓储和邮政业	Transport, Storage and Post	2.87	3.58	2.33	3.54	6.29
铁路运输业	Railway Transport	−0.35	−0.78	1.34	0.73	0.31
道路运输业	Road Transport	0.72	2.00	−0.55	0.67	2.11

4-10 续 1

指标	Indicator	2013 年	2014 年	2015 年	2016 年	2017 年
水上运输业	Waterway Transport	0.03	0.02	−0.01	0.04	−0.01
航空运输业	Air Transport	0.76	0.72	1.00	1.17	0.79
管道运输业	Pipeline Transport	0.57	0.16	0.11	0.03	1.13
装卸搬运和运输代理业	Loading, Unloading and Forwarding Agency	0.59	0.47	0.14	−0.52	0.38
仓储业	Storage	0.47	0.35	0.11	1.00	1.15
邮政业	Postal Services	0.10	0.65	0.21	0.43	0.42
住宿和餐饮业	Accommodations and Catering Services	2.45	2.28	1.16	2.04	2.05
住宿业	Accommodations	0.35	0.21	0.22	0.22	0.34
餐饮业	Catering Services	2.10	2.06	0.95	1.82	1.71
信息传输、软件和信息技术服务和业	Information Transmission, Software and I nformation Technology	2.27	3.82	1.92	5.69	13.79
电信、广播电视和卫星传输服务	Telecommunications, Radio and Television and Satellite Transmission Services	2.19	3.39	1.76	−0.65	10.70
互联网和相关服务	Internet and related Services	0.14	0.10	−0.01	2.64	0.79
软件和信息技术服务业	Software and Information Technology Services	−0.06	0.33	0.18	3.69	2.30
金融业	Financial Intermediation	13.84	16.01	22.21	15.56	6.25
货币金融服务	Monetary and Financial Services	9.10	7.35	13.63	14.35	9.08
资本市场服务	Capital Market Services	1.68	4.13	5.86	−4.52	0.64
保险业	Insurance	0.30	0.30	0.59	2.44	0.54
其他金融业	Others	2.74	4.23	2.13	3.29	−4.01
房地产业	Real Estate	8.28	6.70	10.89	7.55	−2.19
房地产开发经营业	Real Estate Development and Management	4.79	5.87	8.17	3.97	−3.86
物业管理业	Property Management	0.71	−0.37	0.67	0.76	−0.34
房地产中介服务业	Real Estate Intermediary Services	−0.11	−0.12	0.44	1.06	0.17
自有房地产经营活动	Own Real Estate Operating Activities	1.10	1.15	1.21	1.42	1.32
其他房地产业	Other Real Estate Industry	1.80	0.17	0.41	0.34	0.52
租赁和商务服务业	Leasing and Business Services	0.77	2.49	1.67	5.85	1.67
租赁业	Leasing Services	0.49	−0.10	0.37	1.43	1.45
商务服务业	Business Services	0.28	2.58	1.30	4.43	0.22

指标	Indicator	2013 年	2014 年	2015 年	2016 年	2017 年
科学研究和技术服务业	Scientific Research and Technical Services	0.89	0.81	1.40	1.75	3.77
研究和试验发展	Research and Experimental Development	0.18	0.24	0.24	0.44	0.54
专业技术服务业	Special Technical Services	-0.13	-0.36	0.74	1.02	3.22
科技推广和应用服务业	Science and Technology Promotion and Application Services	0.84	0.92	0.41	0.29	0.02
水利、环境和公共设施管理业	Management of Water Conservancy, Environment and Public Facilities	0.19	0.18	0.32	0.68	0.52
水利管理业	Management of Water Conservancy	0.11	0.02	0.01	0.03	0.02
生态保护和环境治理业	Ecological Protection and Environmental Management	0.03	0.04	0.01	0.12	0.10
公共设施管理业	Management of Public Facilities	0.05	0.12	0.29	0.53	0.40
居民服务、修理和其他服务业	Services to Households, Repair and Other Services	0.85	0.93	0.63	2.28	1.90
居民服务业	Services to Households	0.10	-0.22	0.51	0.97	0.51
机动车、电子产品和日用产品修理业	Repair of Motor Vehicle, Electronics and Household Products	0.33	0.10	-0.01	0.41	0.47
其他服务业	Other Services	0.42	1.05	0.12	0.90	0.92
教育	Education	1.85	1.51	2.60	4.23	3.51
卫生和社会工作	Health,Social Security and Social Welfare	0.62	1.42	2.48	1.49	-0.59
卫生	Public Health	0.64	1.05	2.38	1.08	-0.55
社会工作	Social Work	-0.02	0.37	0.10	0.41	-0.04
文化、体育和娱乐业	Culture, Sports and Recreation	0.67	0.59	0.40	0.94	2.23
新闻和出版业	Journalism and Publishing Activities	0.09	-0.10	-0.06	0.48	1.22
广播、电视、电影和影视录音	Radio, Television, Motion Picture and Videotape Programme	0.09	0.92	-0.01	-0.02	0.46
文化艺术业	Culture and Arts	0.15	-0.21	0.22	0.20	0.26
体育	Sports	0.29	0.03	0.13	0.14	0.21
娱乐业	Recreation	0.04	-0.05	0.12	0.14	0.09
公共管理、社会保障和社会组织	Public Management, Social Security and Social Organization	1.69	3.21	3.08	0.40	1.24
第一产业	Primary Industry	1.86	2.14	2.21	2.65	1.97
第二产业	Secondary Industry	45.33	43.50	39.92	33.63	39.52
第三产业	Tertiary Industry	52.81	54.36	57.88	63.72	58.51

注：新行业分组（GB-2011）。

Note: Grouping of new industries (GB-2011)

4-11 生产总值行业比重（2009 年-2013 年）(按当年价格计算)

Ratio of Gross Domestic Product by Sector(2009-2013)(Calculated at Current Prices)

单位：% (%)

指　　标	Indicator	2009 年	2010 年	2011 年	2012 年	2013 年
生产总值比重	Ratio of Gross Domestic Product	100.0	100.0	100.0	100.0	100.0
第一产业	Primary Industry	5.6	5.5	5.4	5.3	5.4
农林牧渔业	Agriculture, Forestry, Animal Husbandry and Fishery	5.6	5.5	5.4	5.3	5.4
农业	Farming	3.6	3.8	3.5	3.4	3.6
林业	Forestry	0.2	0.1	0.1	0.1	0.2
畜牧业	Animal Husbandry	1.5	1.4	1.6	1.6	1.5
渔业	Fishery	0.1	0.1	0.1	0.1	0.1
农林牧渔服务业	Services of Agriculture,Forestry,Animal Husbandry and Fishing	0.1	0.1	0.1	0.1	0.1
第二产业	Secondary Industry	42.9	41.9	41.5	40.3	39.3
工业	Industry	35.7	34.6	34.2	33.3	32.3
采矿业	Mining	0.8	0.8	0.8	0.7	1.1
制造业	Manufacture	32.1	30.5	29.5	31.0	29.4
电力、燃气及水的生产和供应业	Production and Supply of Electric, Gas and Water	2.7	3.2	3.9	1.6	1.8
建筑业	Construction	7.2	7.3	7.3	7.0	6.9
房屋和土木工程建筑业	Building Construction	5.8	6.0	6.0	5.8	5.4
建筑安装业	Construction Installment	1.1	1.0	0.9	0.8	1.1
建筑装饰业	Construction Decoration	0.2	0.2	0.3	0.3	0.4
其他建筑业	Others	0.1	0.1	0.1	0.1	0.1
第三产业	Tertiary Industry	51.5	52.6	53.1	54.4	55.3
交通运输、仓储和邮政业	Transport, Storage and Postal Services	6.0	6.1	6.7	6.7	6.4
铁路运输业	Railway Transport	1.6	1.4	1.4	1.4	1.2
道路运输业	Road Transport	2.9	3.0	3.5	3.5	3.3
城市公共交通业	Public Transportation by City	0.4	0.4	0.4	0.4	0.3
水上运输业	Waterway Transport	0.0	0.0	0.0	0.0	0.0
航空运输业	Air Transport	0.5	0.6	0.8	0.6	0.6

指　　标	Indicator	2009 年	2010 年	2011 年	2012 年	2013 年
管道运输业	Pipeline Transport	0.0	0.0	0.0	0.0	0.0
装卸搬运和其他运输服务业	Loading and Unloading and Other Transport Services	0.4	0.3	0.5	0.5	0.5
仓储业	Storage	0.2	0.2	0.2	0.2	0.3
邮政业	Postal Services	0.0	0.0	0.0	0.1	0.1
信息传输、计算机服务和软件业	Information Transmission, Computer Services and Software	2.0	3.0	3.1	3.2	3.1
电信和其他信息传输服务业	Telecommunications, Radio and Television and Satellite Transmission Services	0.9	0.8	0.7	0.6	0.6
计算机服务业	Internet and related Services	0.5	0.6	0.7	0.8	0.9
软件业	Software and Information Technology Services	0.5	1.5	1.7	1.8	1.6
批发和零售业	Wholesale and Retail Trade	12.5	12.2	11.9	12.2	12.8
批发业	Wholesale	7.0	7.4	7.6	7.9	8.4
零售业	Retail Trade	5.5	4.8	4.3	4.3	4.5
住宿和餐饮业	Accommodations and Catering Services	3.8	3.7	3.3	3.1	3.2
住宿业	Accommodations	0.4	0.4	0.4	0.4	0.4
餐饮业	Catering Services	3.4	3.2	2.9	2.7	2.8
金融业	Financial Intermediation	7.2	7.4	7.5	8.5	8.8
银行业	Banking Sector	4.9	5.8	6.3	7.4	7.4
证券业	Securities Industry	1.8	1.2	0.7	0.6	0.6
保险业	Insurance	0.3	0.1	0.1	0.1	0.2
其他金融活动	Others	0.2	0.2	0.3	0.4	0.6
房地产业	Real Estate	5.2	5.6	5.8	5.7	6.1
房地产开发经营业	Real Estate Development and Management	1.9	2.1	2.3	2.1	2.4
物业管理业	Property Management	0.6	0.7	0.7	0.7	0.7
房地产中介服务业	Real Estate Intermediary Services	0.3	0.4	0.4	0.4	0.3
其他房地产活动	Other Real Estate Activity	0.2	0.3	0.3	0.3	0.4
居民自有住房服务业	Private Housing Service	2.2	2.1	2.2	2.2	2.2
租赁和商务服务业	Leasing and Business Services	2.7	2.7	3.0	3.0	2.9

4-11 续2

指　　标	Indicator	2009年	2010年	2011年	2012年	2013年
租赁业	Leasing Services	0.1	0.2	0.2	0.3	0.3
商务服务业	Business Services	2.5	2.6	2.8	2.7	2.6
科学研究、技术服务和地质勘查业	Scientific Research,Technical Services and Geeological Prospecting Industry	1.7	1.6	1.6	1.4	1.4
研究与试验发展	Research and Experimental Development	0.6	0.5	0.5	0.5	0.5
专业技术服务业	Special Technical Services	0.8	0.8	0.8	0.6	0.6
科技交流和推广服务业	Science and Technology Promotion and Application Services	0.2	0.2	0.2	0.2	0.2
地质勘查业	Geeological Prospecting Industry	0.1	0.1	0.1	0.1	0.1
水利、环境和公共设施管理业	Management of Water Conservancy, Environment and Public Facilities	0.4	0.4	0.3	0.3	0.3
水利管理业	Management of Water Conservancy	0.2	0.2	0.1	0.1	0.2
环境管理业	Environmental Management	0.1	0.1	0.1	0.0	0.0
公共设施管理业	Management of Public Facilities	0.1	0.1	0.1	0.2	0.2
居民服务和其他服务业	Services to Households and Other Services	1.0	1.0	1.1	1.1	1.1
居民服务业	Services to Households	0.6	0.6	0.6	0.6	0.6
其他服务业	Other Services	0.4	0.5	0.5	0.5	0.5
教育	Education	3.3	3.0	2.8	2.7	2.7
卫生、社会保障和社会福利业	Health,Social Security and Social Welfare	1.9	2.2	2.4	2.7	2.6
卫生	Public Health	1.7	1.9	2.2	2.5	2.4
社会保障业	Social Security	0.2	0.2	0.2	0.2	0.1
社会福利业	Social Welfare	0.1	0.1	0.0	0.0	0.0
文化、体育和娱乐业	Culture, Sports and Recreation	0.7	0.7	0.6	0.7	0.7
新闻出版业	News and Publication	0.3	0.3	0.3	0.2	0.2
广播、电视、电影和音像业	Radio, Television, Film and Video	0.2	0.2	0.2	0.2	0.2
文化艺术业	Culture and Arts	0.1	0.1	0.1	0.1	0.1
体育	Sports	0.1	0.1	0.1	0.1	0.1
娱乐业	Recreation	0.1	0.1	0.1	0.1	0.1
公共管理和社会组织	Public Management and Social Organizations	3.3	3.0	3.1	3.1	3.1

注：旧行业分组（GB-2002）。
Note: Grouping of old industries (GB-2002)

4-12 生产总值行业比重（2013 年-2017 年）（按当年价格计算)

Ratio of Gross Domestic Product by Sector（2013-2017）(Calculated at Current Prices)

单位：%　　　　(%)

指标	Indicator	2013 年	2014 年	2015 年	2016 年	2017 年
地区生产总值贡献率	**Contribution Rate of Gross Domestic Product**	100.00	100.00	100.00	100.00	100.00
农、林、牧、渔业	Agriculture, Forestry, Animal Husbandry and Fishery	5.44	5.18	5.16	5.02	4.59
农业	Farming	3.57	3.46	3.44	3.29	2.99
林业	Forestry	0.15	0.15	0.16	0.17	0.16
畜牧业	Animal Husbandry	1.49	1.34	1.32	1.32	1.20
渔业	Fishery	0.08	0.08	0.07	0.07	0.06
农、林、牧、渔服务业	Services of Agriculture,Forestry,Animal Husbandry and Fishing	0.15	0.15	0.16	0.17	0.18
工业	Industry	32.32	31.58	30.23	28.75	27.81
采矿业	Mining	0.53	0.52	0.60	0.70	0.69
#开采辅助活动	Mining Support Activities	0.00	0.00	0.00	0.00	0.00
制造业	Manufacture	28.14	27.49	28.12	26.77	26.06
#金属制品、机械和设备修理业	Metal Products, Machinery and Equipment Repair Industry	0.06	0.06	0.06	0.05	0.05
电力、燃气及水的生产和供应业	Production and Supply of Electric, Gas and Water	3.65	3.56	1.51	1.28	1.06
建筑业	Construction	7.79	7.68	7.64	7.55	7.91
房屋建筑业	Building Construction	4.51	4.38	3.96	4.28	4.39
土木工程建筑业	Civil Engineering Construction	2.06	2.10	2.93	2.64	2.99
建筑安装业	Construction Installment	0.48	0.47	0.35	0.21	0.22
建筑装饰业和其他建筑业	Construction Decoration and Others	0.73	0.72	0.40	0.42	0.31
批发和零售业	Wholesale and Retail Trade	11.98	11.99	11.73	11.64	13.56
批发业	Wholesale	7.60	7.65	7.43	7.37	8.62
零售业	Retail Trade	4.38	4.34	4.30	4.26	4.94
交通运输、仓储和邮政业	Transport, Storage and Post	6.37	6.31	6.09	6.00	5.77
铁路运输业	Railway Transport	1.21	1.20	1.12	1.11	1.01
道路运输业	Road Transport	3.19	3.14	3.06	2.94	2.75

4-12 续1

指标	Indicator	2013 年	2014 年	2015 年	2016 年	2017 年
水上运输业	Waterway Transport	0.02	0.02	0.02	0.02	0.02
航空运输业	Air Transport	0.61	0.60	0.58	0.64	0.62
管道运输业	Pipeline Transport	0.41	0.41	0.39	0.37	0.41
装卸搬运和运输代理业	Loading, Unloading and Forwarding Agency	0.51	0.50	0.48	0.42	0.40
仓储业	Storage	0.29	0.28	0.27	0.33	0.38
邮政业	Postal Services	0.13	0.16	0.15	0.17	0.19
住宿和餐饮业	Accommodations and Catering Services	3.22	3.14	3.09	3.10	3.04
住宿业	Accommodations	0.40	0.39	0.37	0.37	0.35
餐饮业	Catering Services	2.82	2.75	2.72	2.74	2.69
信息传输、软件和信息技术服务和业	Information Transmission, Software and Information Technology	3.11	3.30	3.31	3.56	3.83
电信、广播电视和卫星传输服务	Telecommunications, Radio and Television and Satellite Transmission Services	1.95	2.06	2.07	1.92	2.28
互联网和相关服务	Internet and related Services	0.08	0.09	0.09	0.28	0.28
软件和信息技术服务业	Software and Information Technology Services	1.08	1.14	1.15	1.36	1.27
金融业	Financial Intermediation	8.81	9.39	10.52	11.02	10.77
货币金融服务	Monetary and Financial Services	7.41	7.58	8.49	9.02	9.13
资本市场服务	Capital Market Services	0.65	0.84	0.94	0.56	0.57
保险业	Insurance	0.16	0.17	0.19	0.35	0.37
其他金融业	Others	0.61	0.80	0.90	1.09	0.71
房地产业	Real Estate	6.13	6.40	6.80	7.09	6.94
房地产开发经营业	Real Estate Development and Management	2.61	2.94	3.12	3.34	3.06
物业管理业	Property Management	0.51	0.44	0.47	0.51	0.49
房地产中介服务业	Real Estate Intermediary Services	0.34	0.30	0.32	0.39	0.42
自有房地产经营活动	Own Real Estate Operating Activities	2.23	2.30	2.21	2.14	2.22
其他房地产业	Other Real Estate Industry	0.44	0.42	0.68	0.69	0.75
租赁和商务服务业	Leasing and Business Services	2.93	2.98	3.00	3.28	2.67
租赁业	Leasing Services	0.29	0.29	0.29	0.38	0.40
商务服务业	Business Services	2.64	2.69	2.70	2.89	2.28

4-12 续 2

指标	Indicator	2013 年	2014 年	2015 年	2016 年	2017 年
科学研究和技术服务业	Scientific Research and Technical Services	1.45	1.43	1.48	1.58	1.90
研究和试验发展	Research and Experimental Development	0.12	0.12	0.12	0.16	0.20
专业技术服务业	Special Technical Services	0.96	0.95	0.98	1.04	1.31
科技推广和应用服务业	Science and Technology Promotion and Application Services	0.36	0.36	0.37	0.38	0.39
水利、环境和公共设施管理业	Management of Water Conservancy, Environment and Public Facilities	0.33	0.33	0.34	0.38	0.40
水利管理业	Management of Water Conservancy	0.04	0.04	0.04	0.04	0.04
生态保护和环境治理业	Ecological Protection and Environmental Management	0.01	0.01	0.01	0.02	0.03
公共设施管理业	Management of Public Facilities	0.28	0.28	0.29	0.32	0.33
居民服务、修理和其他服务业	Services to Households, Repair and Other Services	1.10	1.12	1.13	1.24	1.09
居民服务业	Services to Households	0.58	0.56	0.56	0.60	0.51
机动车、电子产品和日用产品修理业	Repair of Motor Vehicle, Electronics and Household Products	0.17	0.18	0.18	0.20	0.19
其他服务业	Other Services	0.35	0.38	0.39	0.43	0.40
教育	Education	2.69	2.66	2.75	3.01	3.22
卫生和社会工作	Health,Social Security and Social Welfare	2.56	2.53	2.62	2.69	2.50
卫生	Public Health	2.37	2.34	2.42	2.47	2.29
社会工作	Social Work	0.19	0.19	0.20	0.22	0.21
文化、体育和娱乐业	Culture, Sports and Recreation	0.69	0.71	0.71	0.74	0.73
新闻和出版业	Journalism and Publishing Activities	0.24	0.24	0.24	0.26	0.29
广播、电视、电影和影视录音	Radio, Television, Motion Picture and Videotape Programme	0.21	0.25	0.25	0.24	0.21
文化艺术业	Culture and Arts	0.10	0.08	0.08	0.09	0.08
体育	Sports	0.08	0.08	0.08	0.08	0.08
娱乐业	Recreation	0.07	0.06	0.06	0.07	0.06
公共管理、社会保障和社会组织	Public Management, Social Security and Social Organization	3.07	3.30	3.41	3.35	3.26
第一产业	Primary Industry	5.30	5.03	5.01	4.85	4.41
第二产业	Secondary Industry	40.06	39.19	37.82	36.24	35.67
第三产业	Tertiary Industry	54.65	55.78	57.18	58.90	59.92

注：新行业分组（GB-2011）。
Note: Grouping of new industries (GB-2011)

4-13 分地区生产总值（2018年）

Value of Gross Domestic Product by Region（2018）

单位：亿元 (100 million yuan)

指　标	Indicator	济南市 Total City	历下区 Li xia	市中区 Shi zhong	槐荫区 Huai yin	天桥区 Tian qiao	历城区 Li cheng
地区生产总值	Gross Domestic Product	7856.6	1494.8	1042.8	531.7	529.5	864.5
第一产业	Primary Industry	272.4	0.0	2.3	2.6	3.7	18.2
第二产业	Secondary Industry	2829.3	233.1	213.2	151.8	143.2	297.6
第三产业	Tertiary Industry	4754.8	1261.7	827.3	377.2	382.6	548.7

4-13 续 1

指　标	Indicator	长清区 Chang qing	章丘区 Zhang qiu	济阳区 Ji yang	平阴县 Ping yin	商河县 Shang he	高新区 Gao xin	南部山区 Gao xin
地区生产总值	Gross Domestic Product	366.9	1072.7	295.7	284.9	180.8	1008.8	63.1
第一产业	Primary Industry	31.1	76.5	39.6	29.9	43.4	4.6	20.6
第二产业	Secondary Industry	153.4	615.7	145.4	162.4	69.8	619.1	16.7
第三产业	Tertiary Industry	182.4	380.6	110.8	92.6	67.6	385.1	25.9

注：经济普查年度，相关指标为快报数据

Note: In the economic census year, related indicator is the express data.

4-14 生产总值（2018年）（分行业，按当年价格计算）

Value of Gross Domestic Product（2018）(Sub Industry、Calculated at Current Prices)

单位：亿元 (100 million yuan)

指标	Indicator	2018 年
地区生产总值	Gross Domestic Product	7856.56
农、林、牧、渔业	Agriculture, Forestry, Animal Husbandry and Fishery	286.44
农、林、牧、渔服务业	Services of Agriculture,Forestry,Animal Husbandry and Fishing	14.02
工业	Industry	2145.07
#开采辅助活动	Mining Support Activities	0.03
#金属制品、机械和设备修理业	Metal Products, Machinery and Equipment Repair Industry	4.03
建筑业	Construction	688.30
批发和零售业	Wholesale and Retail Trade	1022.19
批发业	Wholesale	642.13
零售业	Retail Trade	380.06
交通运输、仓储和邮政业	Transport, Storage and Post	438.09
住宿和餐饮业	Accommodations and Catering Services	237.56
住宿业	Accommodations	26.91
餐饮业	Catering Services	210.65
金融业	Financial Intermediation	831.11
房地产业	Real Estate	549.60
房地产业(K门类)	Real estate industry (K category)	366.97
自有房地产经营活动	Own Real Estate Operating Activities	182.63
其他服务业	Other Services	1658.20
营利性服务业	Profit service industry	718.56
非营利性服务业	Non–profit service industry	939.64
第一产业	Primary Industry	272.42
第二产业	Secondary Industry	2829.31
第三产业	Tertiary Industry	4754.83

注：经济普查年度，2018年相关指标为快报数据

Note: In the economic census year, related indicator in 2018 is the express data.

4-15 规模以上服务业企业

Main Economic Indicators of Service Enterprise

指标	Indicator	单位 Unit	合计 Total	交通运输、仓储和邮政业 Transport, Storage and Postal Services
单位数	Number of Enterprises	个(unit)	1155	304
固定资产原价	Original Value of Fixed Assets	万元(10 000 yuan)	13310111	6247390
本年折旧	Depreciation in the Year	万元(10 000 yuan)	735617	293846
折旧率	Depreciation Rate	%	5.5	4.7
营业收入	Operating Income	万元(10 000 yuan)	13166010	4764405
税金及附加	Taxes and Other Surcharges	万元(10 000 yuan)	88900	22663
营业利润	Profits from Business	万元(10 000 yuan)	1936703	533062
利润总额	Total Profits	万元(10 000 yuan)	1885346	482600
应付职工薪酬（本年贷方累计发生额）	Total Wages Payable	万元(10 000 yuan)	2533485	847221
从业人员平均人数	Average Number of Employees	人(person)	235877	66431
人均工资	Per Capita Wages	元(yuan)	107407	127534
应交增值税	Value Added Tax Payable	万元(10 000 yuan)	347079	73706

分行业主要经济指标（2018年）

Above Designated Size by Sector（2018）

信息传输、软件和信息技术服务业 Information Transmission, Software and Information Technology	房地产业 Real Estate	租赁和商务服务业 Leasing and Business Services	科学研究和技术服务业 Scientific Research,Technical Services	水利、环境和公共设施管理业 Management of Water Conservancy, Environment and Public Facilities	居民服务、修理和其他服务业 services to Households, Repair and Other Services	教育 Education	卫生和社会工作 Health and Social Work	文化、体育和娱乐业 Culture, Sports and Recreation
161	134	182	203	25	30	22	39	55
3095342	462878	2341021	575846	241924	20023	43234	50304	232150
229311	24365	108219	45846	16391	1890	2256	4804	8689
7.4	5.3	4.6	8.0	6.8	9.4	5.2	9.6	3.7
2531581	551924	1685416	2563795	116781	77879	102034	189032	583162
12537	9789	17330	15976	802	404	670	72	8657
316465	76237	547632	298658	20189	–943	12666	20376	112362
330311	72948	528415	304206	20379	–593	12766	19481	114835
491270	192314	290320	512146	29378	16920	42278	32703	78934
41340	35858	33739	34853	4772	3970	4250	4997	5667
118836	53632	86049	146945	61564	42621	99477	65446	139286
90449	24455	50540	83087	3342	1670	3266	131	16433

主要统计指标解释

国内生产总值（GDP） 指一个国家（或地区）所有常住单位在一定时期内生产活动的最终成果。国内生产总值有三种表现形态，即价值形态、收入形态和产品形态。从价值形态看，它是所有常住单位在一定时期内生产的全部货物和服务价值超过同期中间投入的全部非固定资产货物和服务价值的差额，即所有常住单位的增加值之和；从收入形态看，它是所有常住单位在一定时期内创造并分配给常住单位和非常住单位的初次收入分配之和；从产品形态看，它是所有常住单位在一定时期内最终使用的货物和服务价值与货物和服务净出口价值之和。在实际核算中，国内生产总值有三种计算方法，即生产法、收入法和支出法。三种方法分别从不同的方面反映国内生产总值及其构成。国统字〔2004〕4号文规定：地区GDP的中文名称改为“地区生产总值”。

生产法 生产法是从生产过程中生产的货物和服务总产品价值入手，剔除生产过程中投入的中间产品的价值，得到增加价值的一种方法。计算公式为：

增加值=总产出-中间投入

将国民经济各行业的增加值相加，得到国内生产总值。

总产出、中间投入和增加值具有相同的生产范围，即常住生产单位货物和服务的生产。它不仅包括常住生产单位为其他单位提供的货物和服务的生产，而且包括为本单位使用的货物和服务的生产，但是，住户为自己最终消费生产的服务，只计算自有住房服务和付酬家庭雇员提供的服务，不包括住户成员为本住户最终消费而生产的自给性家庭服务。

收入法 收入法也称为分配法。按收入法计算生产总值是从生产过程创造收入的角度，对常住单位的生产活动成果进行核算。按照这种计算方法，增加值由劳动者报酬、生产税净额、固定资产折旧和营业盈余四个部分组成。计算公式为：

增加值=劳动者报酬+生产税净额+固定资产折旧+营业盈余

国民经济各部门的增加值之和等于生产总值。

在计算劳动者报酬时，需要注意作为劳动者报酬的实物性收入与中间消耗的界限。如果生产单位为其从事生产活动的劳动者提供的货物或服务，可以由劳动者在自己闲暇的时间里满足他们的需要，并且可以改善和提高他们的实际生活水平，同时，其他普通消费者也可以在市场上购买到这些货物和服务，那么就属于劳动者的实物收入。生产单位为了生产能正常进行，为劳动者购买的货物和提供的服务，如因特殊工作需要提供的服装或鞋，因公出差提供的运输和旅馆服务费用等，属于中间投入。

支出法 支出法是从最终使用的角度反映国内生产总值最终使用去向的一种方法。最终使用包括货物和服务的最终消费支出、资本形成总额、货物和服务净出口三部分，计算公式为：

国内生产总值=最终消费支出+资本形成总额+货物和服务净出口

按支出法计算的生产总值，在计算最终消费支出，包括居民消费支出和政府消费支出时，是从支出的最终承担者的角度计算的，而不是从最终实际消费者的角度计算的；在计算资本形成总额时，固定资本形成总额只包括通过生产活动生产出来的固定资产，不包括自然资产，存货增加不包括由于价格因素影响产生的持有收益。

按三种方法计算的国内生产总值反映的是同一经济总体在同一时期的生产活动成果，因此，从理论上讲，三种计算方法所得到的结果应该是一致的。但是，在实践中，由于受资料来源的口径限制和计算方法的影响，要保证这三种计算方法所得到的结果完全相等几乎是不可能的。在国内生产总值的三种计算方法中，生产法和收入法都是对各产业部门的增加值进行核算，为了就每一产业部门取得一致的增加值数据，根据资料来源状况，我国在核算实践中，有的产业部门，如农业、工业的增加值，确定以生产法的计算结果为准，有的产业部门，如部分服务业增加值，确定以收入法的计算结果为准，因此，我国的生产法国内生产总值等于收入法国内生产总值。但是，支出法国内生产总值与生产法和收入法国内生产总值之间存在统计误差，有的年份支出法国内生产总值大于生产法和收入法国内生产总值，有的年份结果相反。我国通常以生产法和收入法国内生产总值数据为准，将上述统计误差控制在一定范围。各种公开发表的国内生产总值总量和增长速度数据均是生产法和收入法的计算结果。按三种方法计算的国内生产总值数据之间具有如下关系：

国内生产总值=生产法国内生产总值

=收入法国内生产总值

=支出法国内生产总值+统计误差

可比价格 指计算各种总量指标所采用的扣除了价格变动因素的价格，可进行不同时期总量指标的对比。按可比价格计算总量指标有两种方法：一种是直接用产品产量乘某一年的不变价格计算；另一种是用价格指数进行缩减。

不变价格 指以同类产品某年的平均价格作为固定价格，用于计算各年的产品价值。按不变价格计算的产品价值消除了价格变动因素，不同时期对比可以反映生产的发展速度。新中国成立后，随着工农业产品价格水平的变化，国家统计局先后九次制定了全国统一的工业产品不变价格和农业产品不变价格。从1952年到1957年使用1952年工（农）业产品不变价格，从1957年到1970年使用1957年不变价格，从1971年到1980年使用1970年不变价格，从1981年到1990年使用1980年不变价格，从1991年到2000年使用1990年不变价格，从2001年到2005年使用2000年不变价格，从2006年到2010

年使用2005年不变价格，从2011年到2015年使用2010年不变价格，从2016年开始使用2015年不变价格。

三次产业 根据社会生产活动历史发展的顺序对产业结构的划分，产品直接取自自然界的部门称为第一产业，对初级产品进行再加工的部门称为第二产业。为生产和消费提供各种服务的部门称为第三产业。它是世界上通用的产业结构分类，但各国的划分不尽一致。我国的三次产业划分是：

第一产业是指农、林、牧、渔业（不含农、林、牧、渔服务业）。

第二产业是指采矿业（不含开采辅助活动），制造业（不含金属制品、机械和设备修理业），电力、热力、燃气及水生产和供应业，建筑业。

第三产业即服务业，是指除第一产业、第二产业以外的其他行业。第三产业包括：批发和零售业，交通运输、仓储和邮政业，住宿和餐饮业，信息传输、软件和信息技术服务业，金融业，房地产业，租赁和商务服务业，科学研究和技术服务业，水利、环境和公共设施管理业，居民服务、修理和其他服务业，教育，卫生和社会工作，文化、体育和娱乐业，公共管理、社会保障和社会组织，国际组织，以及农、林、牧、渔业中的农、林、牧、渔服务业，采矿业中的开采辅助活动，制造业中的金属制品、机械和设备修理业。

国内支出总额 指一个国家(或地区)所有常住单位在一定时期内用于最终消费和投资，以及净出口的货物和服务支出总额，它反映本期生产的国内生产总值的使用构成。这一总量就是支出法测算的国内生产总值，具体包括最终消费支出、资本形成总额、货物和服务净出口。

最终消费 指常住单位在一定时期内的货物和服务的全部最终消费。总消费分为居民消费和政府消费。

居民实际最终消费 指常住住户获得的所有消费品和消费服务的价值。包括以下二类(1)居民自身通过支出所得到的个人货物和服务，其价值即居民在个人消费品和消费服务上承担的支出，包括虚拟支出。(2)作为为居民服务的非营利机构和政府的实物转移得到的个人货物和服务。其价值即为居民非营利机构和政府在个人消费品和服务上的支出。包括虚拟支出。

资本形成总额 指常住单位在一定时期内获得减去处置的固定资产和存货的净额，包括固定资本形成总额和存货增加。

居民消费支出 居民消费支出包括居民实际最终消费中第(1)项内容。所以居民实际最终消费大于居民消费支出。

政府实际最终消费 指政府向社会或社会中某些部门提供的公共消费服务的价值。其价值即政府在公共服务上的支出。

政府消费支出 指(1)政府在个人消费品和消费服务。(2)在公共消费服务上承担的支出，包括虚拟支出。

总投资 指常住单位在一定时期内对固定资产和库存的投资支出合计，分为固定资产形成和库存增加两项。

（1）固定资本形成总额 指从常住单位在一定时期内购置、转入和自产自用的固定资产中，扣除已有固定资产的销售和转出后的价值。固定资产形成包括在一定时期内完成的建筑工程、安装工程和设备器具购置价值，以及新增役、种、奶、毛、娱乐用牲畜和新增经济林价值等。

(2)库存增加 指常住单位一定时期内库存实物量变动的市场价值。期初与期末差额为正值表示库存增加，负值表示库存减少。具体包括本期购买的原材料、燃料和储备物资等商品库存；本期生产的产成品、半成品和在制品等产品库存。

货物和服务净出口 指货物和服务出口减货物和服务进口的差额。出口包括常住单位向非常住单位出售或无偿转让的各种货物和服务的价值；进口包括常住单位从非常住单位购买或无偿得到的各种货物和服务的价值。由于服务活动的提供与使用同时发生，因此服务的进出口业务并不发生出入境现象，一般把常住单位从国外得到的服务作为进口，非常住单位从本国得到的服务作为出口。货物的出口和进口都按离岸价格计算。

来自国外的净要素收入 指一定国家（或地区）来自国外（地区外）的生产税及进口税（扣除生产及进口补贴）、劳动者报酬和财产收入，减去支付给国外（地区外）的生产税及进口税（扣除生产及进口补贴）、劳动者报酬和财产收入的差额。国内生产总值加上来自国外的净要素收入等于国民生产总值。

总产出 总产出是指一定时期内一个国家（或地区）常住单位生产的所有货物和服务的价值，即包括新增价值，也包括转移价值。它反映常住单位生产活动的总规模。总产出按生产者价格计算。

中间投入 中间投入是指常住单位在生产或提供货物与服务过程中，消耗和使用的所有非固定资产货物和服务的价值，中间投入也称为中间消耗。一般按购买者价格计算。

增加值 增加值是指常住单位生产过程创造的新增价值和固定资产的转移价值。它可以按生产法计算，也可以按收入法计算，按生产法计算，它等于总产出减去中间投入；按收入法计算，它等于劳动者报酬、生产税净额、固定资产折旧和营业盈余之和。

固定资产折旧 指一定时期内为弥补固定资产损耗而应提取的补偿价值，它反映了全部固定资产在本期生产中的资产转移价值。各类企业的固定资产折旧是指从成本费用中提取的折旧费。对不计提折旧的单位，如政府机关、事业单位、学校医院、部队和居民住房则应进行虚拟折旧。

劳动者报酬 指劳动者为常住单位提供劳务而获得的各种报酬，它反映劳动者参与增加值创造而获得的原始收入。具体包括从各种来源开支的货币工资和实物工资，即单位以工资、福利、社会保险等形式，从成本、费用和利润中为劳动者支付的各种开支，以及个体和其他劳动者通过参加社会生产活动所获得的各种劳动报酬。

生产税净额 指生产税与补贴之差，它反映政府从本期创造的增加值中所得到的原始收入份额。生产税是指政府对生产单位的生产经营活动所征收的各种税、附加和规费，具体包括销售（营业）税金及附加、增值税、管理费开支的税、应交纳的养路费、排污费和水电附加等，以及烟酒专卖上缴政府的专项收入。补贴与生产税相反，是政府对生产单位的单方面收入转移，因此视为负税处理，包括政策亏损补贴、粮食系统价格补贴、外贸企业出口退税收入等。

营业盈余 指常住单位创造的增加值扣除固定资产折旧价值、支付劳动者报酬和上缴政府生产税净额后的余额，它反映企业参与增加值创造而应得到的原始收入份额。该指标相当于企业的营业利润，但要扣除利税后项目中支付的工资、福利及公益金等。

非金融企业部门 非金融企业部门是指由以营利为目的、从事非金融经济活动的所有常住非金融企业组成的集合。包括农业企业、工业、建筑业企业、流通企业、服务企业、执行企业会计制度的事业单位;行政事业单位下属的独立核算单位(即企业化管理的事业单位）亦划入本部门。

金融机构部门 金融机构部门是指由从事金融活动的所有常住独立核算单位组成的集合。在我国的新国民经济核算体系中，将其分为三大类：银行机构、保险机构和非银行金融机构。

银行机构为中央银行（中国人民银行）、政策性银行（国家开发银行、农业开发银行、进出口银行）和商业银行（中国工商银行、中国农业银行、中国银行、中国建设银行、交通银行、中信实业银行、中国投资银行、光大银行、城市合作银行等），以及若干区域性银行或私营银行（如华夏银行、民生银行等）。

政府部门 政府部门是指由行使国家管理职能的行政单位和为社会提供非市场化服务的事业单位（即所谓非盈利性机构单位）组成的集合。包括国家机关、政党机关、社会团体及执行预算会计制度的事业单位等。军事单位及所属的非独立核算单位也包括在本部门中。由于目前在我国非盈利机构主要是由国家拨款资助的事业单位，因此我国将为政府和为居民服务的非盈利机构统一归进政府部门。

我国的政府部门由行政单位和非盈利的事业单位组成。其中“财政”作为一个特殊的部门归列于政府部门。

住户部门 住户部门是指由所有常住居民户组成的集体。包括城镇常住居民户、农村常住居民户和城乡个体经营单位。由于个体经营单位的资产负债及财务收支还不能完全独立于所属住户，因此把个体经营单位也划入住户部门。

住户内的成员共同享用其生活设施、共同消费一些货物和服务，其收入和财产的部门或全部被集中起来，因此他们也有权利参与或影响整个住户的经济活动。

国外部门 国外部门指与我国常住机构单位发生经济往来的所有非常住机构单位组成的集合，增列国外部门并不要求编制其整个资产负债表，而只限于记录常住机构单位与非常住机构单位之间所进行的交易及往来活动的累计存量，即仅仅是为了反映我国经济总体与国外进行经济往来活动及结果的总规模和结构关系。

非金融资产 根据我国新国民经济核算体系中有关资产负债项目的基本定义和联合国1993 年SNA 的定义，“非金融资产”是指机构单位单独或共同对其执行所有权或处置权，并通过在核算期内持有或使用它们可从中获得经济利益的，除金融资产以外的经济资产。

非金融资产按是否具有物质形态划分为有形资产和无形资产，按产生的方式或过程可划分为生产资产和非生产资产。在非金融资产中，“生产资产”由固定资产、存货和珍贵物品组成。“非生产资产”可大致分为两类，一类是资源资产，即有形非生产资产，由土地资产、水资源资产、地下资产和非培育生物资产组成；另一类是无形非生产资产，如专利权、租约和其他可转让合同、购买的商誉等。

由于我国目前在资产负债核算中所面临的资料来源和技术条件的限制，我们仅将非金融资产简单地划分为固定资产、存货和其他非金融资产三类。

贡献率 各产业的贡献率是分析经济效益的一个指标，它是指第一、二、三产业增量与生产总值增量之比。

规模以上服务业法人单位 包括：交通运输、仓储和邮政业，信息传输、软件和信息技术服务业，租赁和商务服务业，科学研究和技术服务业，水利、环境和公共设施管理业，居民服务业、修理和其他服务业，教育，卫生和社会工作，文化、体育和娱乐业；以及物业管理、房地产中介服务等行业。

Explanatory Notes on Main Statistical Indicators

GDP refers to the final products at market prices produced by all residents in a country (or a region) during a certain period of time. Gross domestic product is expressed in three different forms, i.e., value, income, and products respectively. GDP in its value form refers to the total value of all goods and services produced by all resident units during a certain period of time, minus the total value of input of goods of non-fixed assets and services; in other term, it is the sum of the value-added of all resident units. GDP in the form of income includes the income created by all resident units and distributed to resident and non-resident units. GDP in the form of products refers to the value of all goods and services for final consumption by all resident units minus the net exports of goods and services during a given period of time. In the practice of national accounting, gross domestic product is calculated with three approaches, i.e., production approach, income approach and expenditure approach, which reflect gross domestic product and its composition from different aspects. In the actual calculation, GDP is based on three calculation methods–production approach, income approach and expenditure approach. These three methods reflect GDP and its composition from different aspects. GTZi (2004) No. 4 document prescribes: Chinese name of regional GDP is "regional gross domestic product".

Production Approach focuses on the total value of goods and services produced in production activities. GDP by Production Approach equals the value of total output minus that of input consumed in production process. The calculation formula is:

GDP by Production Approach= gross output– intermediate input

The sum of value added made by different industries is GDP.

Gross output, intermediate input and value added have the same production scope, i.e., production of goods and services by resident units. It not only includes the production of goods and services by resident units for other units, but that used for the unit. However, services finally consumed and produced by households only include own housing services and services provided by paid family employees (excluding self-supporting family services produced by the household member for final consumption of the household).

Income Approach (also known as distribution approach): refers to the method measuring the final results of production activities from the perspective of income made by all residents. GDP of income approach includes laborers' remuneration, net taxes on production, depreciation of fixed assets and operating surplus. The calculation formula is:

GDP by income approach= laborers' remuneration + net taxes on production + depreciation of fixed assets+ operating surplus

The sum of value added made by different industries is GDP.

In the calculation of labourers' remunerations, it's necessary to define the limit between material incomes and intermediate consumption among labourers' remunerations. If goods or units provided by production units for its labourers engaging in production activity can be met by such labourers in their spare time, improve and raise their actual living level, and other ordinary consumers can purchase such goods and services in the market, these goods and services are classified into material incomes of labourers. Goods purchased by production units for labourers and relevant services for the purpose of successful production, such as clothes or shoes provided due to special work need and transportation and hotel service charges in the business trip, are classified into intermediate input.

Expenditure Approach refers to the method measuring the final results of production activities of a country during a given period from the perspective of final use. It includes final consumption expenditure, total capital formation and net export of goods and services.

GDP by expenditure approach = final consumption expenditure+ gross capital formation+ net export of goods and services

For GDP by expenditure approach, the final consumption expenditure, including household consumption expenditure and government consumption expenditure, is calculated from the perspective of final bearer of expenditure, not from the perspective of final consumers; in the calculation of gross capital formation, gross fixed capital formation only includes fixed assets produced by production activities, excluding natural assets, where increases in inventories do not include holding gains.

GDP by three approaches reflects the results of production activities of the same economic entity during the same period, so theoretically results from three calculation approaches shall be consistent. However, in practice, it's almost impossible to ensure results from these three approaches are completely equal due to the caliber limit of data source and the influence of calculation approaches. Among three calculation approaches of GDP, production approach and income approach are used for business accounting of the value added of each industry sector. For the purpose of consistent data regarding value added of each industrial sector, the value added of some industrial sectors (such as agriculture and industry) is subject to the calculation result of the production approach and the value added of some industry sectors (such as some service industries) is subject to the calculation result of the income approach in the accounting practice in China according to data source, thus China's GDP by production approach is equal to that by income approach. However, statistical error exists between GDP by expenditure approach and that by production approach and income approach. GDP by expenditure approach is more than that by production approach and income approach in some years and it turns out just the opposite in some other years. GDP by production approach and income approach prevail in China generally and the above statistical error shall be controlled to a certain range. Various data regarding total volume and growth rate of GDP published is the calculation result based on production approach and income approach. The following relationships between data regarding GDP calculated based on above-mentioned three methods are as follows:

GDP= GDP by production approach

= GDP by income approach

= GDP by expenditure approach+ statistical error

Constant Price refers to the price without the effect of price change. By using constant price, total amount of indices of different periods can be compared. There are two methods in which total amount indices are obtained, one using current price of some year to multiply the physical volume of certain products and the other using price index.

Fixed Price refers to the average price of similar products in a given period, with which the product value of different period can be calculated. The product value calculated at fixed price can show the growth rate of production in different periods. Since 1949, NBS has framed the united industrial and agricultural fixed price 8 times, including the fixed price of 1952 used from 1952 to 1957, the fixed price of 1957 used from 1957 to 1970, the fixed price of 1970 used from 1971 to 1980, the fixed price of 1980 used from 1981 to 1990, the fixed price of 1990 used from 1991 to 2000, the fixed price of 2000 used from 2001 to 2005, the fixed price of 2005 used from 2006 to 2010, the fixed price of 2010 used from 2011 to 2015, and the fixed price of 2015 used from 2016.

Three industries Classification of economic activities into three branches of industries is based on the development of production. Primary industry refers to the production activities that obtain products from nature. Secondary industry refers to the production activities that process primary goods. Tertiary industry refers to the production activities that provide primary and secondary industries with services. Classification of economic activities into three branches of industries is a common practice in the world, although the grouping varies to some extent from country to country.

Economic activities of China are categorized into following industries:

Primary industry refers to agriculture, forestry, animal husbandry and fishery (not contain agriculture, forestry, animal husbandry and fishery service industry).

Secondary industry refers to mining industry (not contain mining auxiliary activities), manufacturing industry (not contain metal products, machinery and equipment repair industry), electricity, heat, gas and water production and supply industry and construction industry.

The tertiary industry is the service industry, refers to all other economic activities not included in primary or secondary industry. According to the economic condition in China, tertiary industry includes Wholesale and Retail Trades, Transport, Storage and Post, Information Transmission, Computer Services and Software, Hotels and Catering Services, Financial Intermediation, Real Estate, Leasing and Business Services, Scientific Research, Technical Services and Geologic Prospecting, Management of Water Conservancy, Environment and Public Facilities, Services to Households and Other Services, Education, Health and Social Security and Social Welfare, Culture, Sports and Entertainment, Public Management and Social Organization, and International Organizations, as well as agriculture, forestry, animal husbandry and fishery services in the agriculture, forestry, animal husbandry and fishery, mining auxiliary activities in the mining industry, metalware, machinery and equipment repair industry in the manufacturing industry.

Gross Domestic Expenditure refers to total expenditures on goods and services of all resident units used for final consumption and investment and net export in a certain period of time in a country (or region) and reflects usage composition of GDP produced in the current period. The gross domestic expenditure is GDP by expenditure approach, including final consumption expenditure, gross capital formation and net export value of such goods and services.

Final Consumption refers to the final consumption of all goods and services of the resident unit within a certain period of time. Total consumption is classified into household consumption and government consumption.

Final Consumption of Households refers to the value of all consumer goods and consumption services obtained by permanent households, including two categories below (1) personal goods and services obtained by the resident based on expenditure whose value is the expenditure regarding individual consumer's goods and consumption services borne by the resident, including virtual expenditure and (2) personal goods and services obtained by physical transfer of non-profit organization and government serving the resident whose value is the expenditure regarding individual consumer's goods and consumption service borne by non-profit organization and government serving the resident, including virtual expenditure.

Total Capital Formation refers to the fixed assets acquired minus those disposed of and the net value of inventory, including the total fixed capital formation and the increase in inventory.

Household Consumption Expenditure includes Item (1) content in the residents' actual final consumption, so the residents' actual final consumption is more than household consumption expenditure.

Actual Final Consumption of Government refers to the value of public consumption services provided by the government to the society or some departments in the society whose value is the public service expenditure of the government.

Government Consumption Expenditure refers to the expenditure regarding (1) individual consumer's goods and consumption services and (2) public consumption services borne by the government, including virtual expenditure.

Total Investment refers to total investment expenditures of resident unit relating to fixed assets and inventories within a certain period of time, divided into formation of fixed assets and increase in inventories.

(1) Gross fixed capital formation refers to the value arising after deduction of sales and roll–out of existing fixed assets from fixed assets of the resident unit purchased, transferred in and produced independently within a certain period of time. Gross fixed capital formation includes the value of constructional engineering and installation project and equipment purchase completed within a certain period of time and the value of new livestock for service, breeding, milk, wool and recreation and economic forest.

(2) Increase in Inventory refers to the market value of the change in physical quantity of inventory of resident units within a certain period of time. In case that the difference between the beginning and the end is positive, it means an increase in inventories; in case that the difference between the beginning and the end is negative, it means decrease in inventories, including inventory of commodities such as raw material, fuel and restock purchased in the current period and inventory of such products as finished products, semi–finished products and products in process produced in the current period.

Net Export of Goods and Services refers to the difference of the exports of goods and services minus imports of goods and services. The exports include the value of various goods and services sold or gratuitously transferred by the resident units to the non– resident units; The imports include the value of various goods and services purchased or gratuitously obtained by the resident units from the non– resident units; Because the provision of services and the use of them happen simultaneously, the acquisition of services by the resident units from abroad is usually treated as import while the acquisition of services by non–resident units in this country is usually treated as export. The export and import of goods are calculated at FOB.

Net Factor Income from Abroad refers to the difference of net production tax and import tax (deducting production and import subsidies), labourers' remunerations and property income of a country (or region) from abroad minus production and import duties (deducting production and import subsidies), remuneration for labourers and property income paid to foreign country (region). The result after GDP plus foreign net factor income equals to GNP.

Gross Output Gross output refers to the value of all goods and services produced by resident units in a country (or region) within a certain period of time, including newly–increased value and transfer value which reflects the total scale of production activities of resident units. Gross output is calculated in line with producer's price.

Intermediate Input Intermediate input refers to the value of all non–permanent asset goods and services consumed and used in the process of resident units producing or providing goods and services, which is also called as intermediate consumption and is generally calculated pursuant to purchaser price.

Value Added refers to the newly–increased value created by the resident unit in the production process and transfer value of fixed assets which can be calculated based on production approach or income approach. The added value equals to the result after grass output is deducted by intermediate input in case of being calculated based on production approach or the sum of remuneration for labourers, net production tax, depreciation of fixed assets and operating surplus in case of being calculated based on income approach.

Depreciation of Fixed Assets refers to the compensated value extracted to make up for losses of fixed assets within a certain period of time which reflects the asset transfer value of all fixed assets in the production in the current period. Depreciation of fixed assets of various enterprises refers to the depreciation cost extracted from the cost. Units of no calculation of depreciation (such as government agency, public institution, school and hospital, troops and residents' housing) shall be subject to virtual depreciation.

Remuneration for Labourers refers to various remunerations because the worker provides the resident unit with labor service which reflects original income obtained by the worker due to participate in creation of value added, including monetary wages and wages in kind from various sources (namely various expenditures paid by the unit to the worker based on costs, expenses and profits in the form of salary, welfare and social insurance as well as various remunerations of labor obtained by individual and other labourers by participating in social production activity.

Net Production Tax refers to the balance between production tax and subsidy which reflects the original income share obtained by the government from the added value which is created in the current period. Net production tax refers to various taxes additional taxes and levies and charges levied against production and operation activities of production units by the government, including sales (business) taxes and surcharges, added–value tax, tax on overhead expenses, road toll, sewage charge and utility surcharge which shall be paid and special revenue of the government paid for a state monopoly of sales of tobacco and alcoholic drinks. The subsidy is contrary to the net production tax. The former is unilateral transfer of income of the government to the production unit, thus it's deemed negative tax, including policy loss subsidies, food system price subsidies, export tax rebate income of foreign trade enterprises.

Operating Surplus refers to the balance after the value added which is created by resident units is deducted by value of depreciation of fixed assets and used for payment of remuneration for labourers and net production tax of the government which reflects the original income share to be obtained after the enterprise participates in creating the value added. The indicator is equivalent to operating profit of the enterprise but deduction of salary, welfare and welfare fund paid in the after–tax project.

Non–financial Corporate Sectors Non–financial corporate

sectors refer to all resident non-financial businesses for a lucrative purpose which engage in non-financial economic activities, including agricultural enterprises, industrial enterprises, construction enterprises, circulation enterprises, service enterprises and public institutions implementing the enterprise accounting system; Independent accounting units (namely public institutions based on enterprise-style management) subordinate to the administrative institution are included into non-financial corporate sectors.

Financial Organization Departments Financial organization departments refer to all resident independent accounting units engaging in financial activities. In the new national economic accounting system in China, financial organization departments are divided into three categories: banking institution, insurance institute and non-bank financial institution.

Banking institutions include central bank (The People's Bank of China), policy banks (China Development Bank, Agricultural Development Bank of China and The Export-Import Bank of China), commercial banks (ICBC, ABC, Bank of China, CCB, Bank of Communications, China CITIC Bank, China Investment Bank, China Everbright Bank and Urban Partnership Bank) as well as several regional banks and private banks (such as Huaxia Bank and China Minsheng Bank).

Government Departments Government departments refer to administrative units exercising state administration functions and public institutions providing the society with non-market service (namely so-called non-profit organization), including state organs, Party organs, social organization and public institution implementing the budget accounting system. The military unit and non-independent accounting unit subordinate to the military unit are also included into government departments. Non-profit organizations in China are mainly public institution subsidized by state appropriation, so China uniformly classy non-profit organizations serving the government and residents into government departments.

Government departments in China are composed by administrative units and non-profit public institutions. "Financial department" (special department) is classified as government department.

Household Sector refers to the collective constituted by all resident households, including permanent urban households, permanent rural households and urban and rural self-employed units. Because assets and liabilities and financial revenues of individual business unit fail to be completely independent from corresponding household, the individual business unit is included into household sector.

Members in the household share domestic installation as well as consume some goods and services together whose income and property departments may be collected, so they also have the right to participate in or affect economic activities of the whole household.

Foreign Departments Foreign departments refer to all non-resident institutional units with economic exchanges with resident institutional units in China. In case of increasing foreign departments, preparation of the whole balance sheet isn't required, but it's necessary to record the cumulative stock of transactions and exchanges between resident institutional unit and non-resident institutional unit, namely only reflecting economic exchange between China's economic entity and foreign entity and total scale and structural relationship of corresponding results.

Non-financial Assets "Non-financial assets" refer to economic assets against which the institutional unit executes the ownership or disposal right independently or together with an economic interest obtained by holding or usage within the accounting period except for financial assets according to basic definition about assets and liabilities in the new national economic accounting system in China and definition regarding SNA of UN in 1993.

Non-financial assets can be classified into tangible assets and intangible assets based on whether physical form exists or productive assets and non-productive assets based on production way or process. In the non-financial assets, "productive assets" are constituted by fixed assets, inventories and valuables. "Non-productive assets" can be roughly divided into two categories, including resource assets (namely tangible non-productive assets, consisting of land assets, water resource assets, underground assets and non-breeding biological assets) and intangible non-productive assets (such as patent right, rental agreement and other transferrable contract and goodwill purchased).

Due to the restriction of data source and technical conditions in the assets and liabilities, accounting in China now, we only simply divide non-financial assets into three categories-fixed assets, inventories and other non-financial assets.

Rate of Contribution Rate of contribution of each industry is an indicator for analyzing economic benefit which refers to the ratio between the increment of primary, secondary and tertiary industries and increment of total output value.

Above State Designated Scale Service Industry Legal Entities include: transportation, warehousing and postal services, information transmission, software, and information technology service industry, leasing and business service, scientific research and technological services, water conservancy, environment and public facility management, resident service, repair and other service industries, education, health and social work, culture, sports and entertainment as well as property management, real estate agency service.

5

劳动就业

LABOR AND EMPLOYMENT

5-1 按三次产业分从业人员及构成

Number of Employed Persons and Structure by Type of Industry

年份 Year	从业人员（万人） Total Employed Persons(10 000 persons)				构成（合计＝100） Composition in Percentage(Total=100)		
	合计 Total	第一产业 Primary Industry	第二产业 Secondary Industry	第三产业 Tertiary Industry	第一产业 Primary Industry	第二产业 Secondary Industry	第三产业 Tertiary Industry
1952	134.26	109.87	5.86	18.53	81.8	4.4	13.8
1957	144.29	118.65	13.12	12.52	82.2	9.1	8.7
1962	137.58	106.50	16.45	14.63	77.4	12.0	10.6
1965	143.67	107.68	20.96	15.03	74.9	14.6	10.5
1970	161.18	118.15	30.32	12.71	73.3	18.8	7.9
1975	192.59	135.95	41.56	15.08	70.6	21.6	7.8
1978	204.04	136.30	46.06	21.68	66.8	22.6	10.6
1980	214.21	135.16	51.30	27.75	63.1	23.9	13.0
1985	245.32	116.59	76.08	52.65	47.5	31.0	21.5
1990	270.54	125.73	87.75	57.06	46.5	32.4	21.1
1991	276.18	130.36	87.99	57.83	47.2	31.9	20.9
1992	280.19	127.09	85.59	67.51	45.4	30.5	24.1
1993	285.69	124.25	89.91	71.53	43.5	31.5	25.0
1994	303.46	122.62	91.64	89.20	40.4	30.2	29.4
1995	324.22	116.13	106.68	101.41	35.8	32.9	31.3
1996	332.33	107.70	113.91	110.72	32.4	34.3	33.3
1997	337.43	108.17	113.93	115.33	32.0	33.8	34.2
1998	341.63	109.32	113.38	118.93	31.9	33.2	34.9
1999	344.48	109.56	112.98	121.94	31.8	32.8	35.4
2000	347.37	109.98	110.81	126.58	31.7	31.9	36.4
2001	350.10	109.99	109.24	130.87	31.4	31.2	37.4
2002	352.70	108.01	109.14	135.55	30.6	30.9	38.5
2003	355.30	104.90	110.60	139.80	29.5	31.1	39.4
2004	358.50	99.30	113.30	145.90	27.7	31.6	40.7
2005	360.00	99.10	114.20	146.70	27.5	31.7	40.8
2006	361.80	99.00	115.20	147.60	27.4	31.8	40.8
2007	364.30	98.80	116.30	149.20	27.1	31.9	41.0
2008	367.36	98.01	116.95	152.40	26.7	31.8	41.5
2009	372.25	97.80	119.15	155.30	26.3	32.0	41.7
2010	373.70	76.66	120.20	176.84	20.5	32.2	47.3
2011	375.50	74.95	120.70	179.85	20.0	32.1	47.9
2012	379.30	74.30	123.10	181.90	19.6	32.5	47.9
2013	382.30	73.40	122.19	186.71	19.20	32.00	48.80
2014	385.70	72.50	123.30	189.90	18.80	31.97	49.24
2015	388.70	71.80	124.70	192.20	18.47	32.08	49.45
2016	394.93	70.90	126.90	197.13	17.95	32.13	49.92
2017	405.38	69.50	129.35	206.53	17.14	31.91	50.95
2018	419.27	68.80	132.17	218.30	16.41	31.52	52.07

5-2 法人单位从业人员和平均工资

Number and Average Wage of Employed Persons in Various Units

指标	Indicator	2018 年		2017 年	
		从业人员（人）Employed Persons (person)	从业人员平均工资（元/人）Average Wage of Employed Persons (persons/yuan)	从业人员（人）Employed Persons (person)	从业人员平均工资（元/人）Average Wage of Employed Persons (persons/yuan)
全市法人单位	Total Corporate Unit	2134973	73535	2006930	69004
按国民经济行业分组	Grouped by Sector				
农、林、牧、渔业	Agriculture,Forestry,Animal Husbandry and Fishing	3935	34998	3625	35823
采矿业	Mining	2880	71582	2873	81333
制造业	Manufacturing	467784	63861	468188	56815
电力、热力、燃气及水生产和供应业	Production and Supply of Electricity, Heating Power, Gas and Water	15426	91932	15138	80713
建筑业	Construction	376736	69273	348252	63874
批发和零售业	Wholesale and Retail Trade	293919	51619	251409	45589
交通运输、仓储和邮政业	Traffic,Transport,Storage and Post	66513	60524	72174	82270
住宿和餐饮业	Hotels and Catering Services	46197	44503	42567	41608
信息传输、软件和信息技术服务业	Information Transmission, Software and Information Technology Services	136753	86531	119484	84069
金融业	Financial Intermediation	97469	120064	105504	110605
房地产业	Real Estate	78458	60437	71876	55910
租赁和商务服务业	Leasing and Business Services	102399	56210	89226	55933
科学研究和技术服务业	Scientific Research and Development,Technical Services	108987	80343	84856	73477
水利、环境和公共设施管理业	Management of Water Conservancy, Environment and Public Facilities	19946	59833	19434	56845
居民服务、修理和其他服务业	Resident Services, Repair and Other Services	17248	45677	11407	38105
教育	Education	106106	111372	110501	101528
卫生和社会工作	Health Care and Social Works	75041	114777	73916	106464
文化、体育和娱乐业	Culture,Sports and Entertainment	21661	94135	18562	95410
公共管理、社会保障和社会组织	Public Administration, Social Security and Social Organizations	97515	110801	97938	99294

注：本表统计口径为全部法人单位，包括非私营单位和私营单位。

Note: The statistical caliber of this table is all legal units, including non-private units and private units.

5-3 主要年份职工工资

Wage of Staff and Workers in Major Years

年份 Year	职工工资总额（万元） Total Wages of Staff and Workers(10 000yuan)				职工平均工资（元） Average Wage of Staff and Workers(yuan)			
	合计 Total	国有经济 State-owned Units	城镇集体经济 Urban ollective-owned Units	其他经济 Others	合计 Total	国有经济 State-owned Units	城镇集体经济 UrbanCollective-owned Units	其他经济 Others
1952	4881	4587	294	—	442	453	324	—
1957	14553	11654	2899	—	586	621	480	—
1962	19412	16409	3003	—	577	607	451	—
1965	20367	16821	3546	—	617	664	461	—
1970	21226	17314	3912	—	549	578	449	—
1975	29239	22662	6577	—	557	615	420	—
1978	37840	28733	9107	—	578	626	465	—
1980	55900	41809	14091	—	776	821	668	—
1985	92092	67756	24330	6	1104	1169	954	894
1986	111934	84269	27643	22	1298	1384	1092	882
1987	126263	96322	29673	268	1422	1515	1185	1603
1988	166206	130287	35515	404	1806	1946	1427	2304
1989	190106	150899	38654	553	2037	2199	1577	2614
1990	210618	166250	43003	1365	2211	2370	1751	2460
1991	229540	181185	46091	2264	2368	2535	1872	2658
1992	267295	214311	49565	3419	2710	2938	2020	2919
1993	327226	264252	54442	8532	3323	3547	2524	3553
1994	465966	371403	67351	27212	4736	5209	2975	4922
1995	581432	465311	79932	36189	5851	6561	3623	5663
1996	700636	562645	89126	48865	7031	7839	4290	6875
1997	792368	636694	67999	57675	7896	8761	4954	7303
1998	717927	578788	68455	70684	8326	9022	5459	7410
1999	756696	608052	67273	81371	9083	9929	5766	7818
2000	857337	639312	59468	158557	10422	11761	6211	8651

年份 Year	职工工资总额（万元） Total Wages of Staff and Workers(10 000yuan)				职工平均工资（元） Average Earning of Staff and Workers(yuan)			
	合计 Total	国有经济 State-owned Units	城镇集体经济 Urban ollective-owned Units	其他经济 Others	合计 Total	国有经济 State-owned Units	城镇集体经济 UrbanCollective-owned Units	其他经济 Others
2001	950851	713222	60818	176811	11980	13462	7061	9945
2002	1120837	846978	74672	199187	14395	16362	8188	11729
2003	1256160	930392	69554	256214	16027	18197	9331	12942
2004	1420491	1049033	73150	298308	18029	20759	10587	13974
2005	1966782	1126918	77722	762142	20866	24626	11890	18164
2006	2459044	1326412	140974	991658	21808	26550	12332	19305
2007	3086928	1680494	166960	1239474	26085	31910	15763	22500
2008	3735956	2049453	202995	1483509	30798	37191	19296	26645
2009	4241838	2227992	177020	1836825	34544	41239	21365	30368
2010	4695402	2462874	179365	2053164	36833	43339	22593	32740
2011	5569118	2647111	169476	2752531	41959	49342	26646	37851
2012	6458632	2811390	161513	3485729	45924	52845	32180	42294
2013	7927677	2766005	170176	4991497	53650	58842	37264	51891
2014	8464904	2912941	148424	5403539	59534	66810	40170	56945
2015	8885256	3282169	143078	5460009	67112	78733	47013	62283
2016	10068893	3715397	162695	6190800	74834	88887	51370	69107
2017	10694345	3776127	124702	6793516	82192	98770	54790	75814
2018	11496722	3869498	98327	7528898	89168	109052	62941	81935

注：本表中 1998 年及以后年份数据均为在岗职工口径，国有、集体、其他分组按 1998 年新标准。
2006 年及以后年份数据为非私营单位从业人员口径。

Note：In this table, the data for 1998 and subsequent years are the caliber of on–the–job workers, and the data of state–owned, collective and other groups base the new standard in 1998. Data for 2006 and subsequent years are the caliber of employees in non–private units.

5-4　城镇非私营单位从业人员人数（2018 年）

Number of Employed Persons in Urban Non Private Entities（2018）

单位：人　　(person)

指　　标	Indicator	从业人员 Employed Persons	在岗职工 Staff and Workers	劳务派遣人员 Labor Dispatch Personnel	其他从业人员 Others
合计	Total	1301723	1072823	123522	105378
按隶属关系分组	By Affiliation				
中央	Central	256709	167364	20981	68364
地方	Local	629640	534979	72919	21742
其他	Others	415374	370480	29622	15272
按国民经济行业分组	Grouped by Sector				
农、林、牧、渔业	Agriculture,Forestry,Animal Husbandry and Fishing	429	425	2	2
农业	Agriculture	100	98	2	0
林业	Forestry	231	229	0	2
畜牧业	Animal Husbandry	0	0	0	0
渔业	Fishing	19	19	0	0
农、林、牧、渔专业及辅助性活动	Service Activities for Agriculture, Forestry, Animal Production and Hunting, Fishing	79	79	0	0
采矿业	Mining	1200	1115	45	40
煤炭开采和洗选业	Mining and Washing of Coal	772	772	0	0
石油和天然气开采业	Extraction of Petroleum and Natural Gas	308	223	45	40
黑色金属矿采选业	Mining of Ferrous Metal Ores	0	0	0	0
有色金属矿采选业	Mining of Non-ferrous Metal Ores	0	0	0	0
非金属矿采选业	Mining and Processing of Nonmetal Ores	120	120	0	0
开采专业及辅助性活动	Mining Support Service Activities	0	0	0	0
其他采矿业	Mining of Other Ores	0	0	0	0
制造业	Manufacturing	251033	232412	14556	4065
农副食品加工业	Processing of Food from Agricultural Products	3004	2939	60	5
食品制造业	Manufacture of Foods	10054	9676	216	162
酒、饮料和精制茶制造业	Manufacture of Wine, Drinks and Refined Tea	5994	5853	65	76
烟草制品业	Manufacture of Tobacco	137	137	0	0
纺织业	Manufacture of Textile	4961	4876	85	0
纺织服装、服饰业	Manufacture of Textile Wearing Apparel and Finery	7271	7230	0	41
皮革、毛皮、羽毛及其制品业和制鞋业	Manufacture of Leather, Fur, Feather and Its Products,and Footwear	406	404	0	2
木材加工和木、竹、藤、棕、草制品业	Processing of Timbers, Manufacture of Wood, Bamboo,Rattan, Palm and Straw Products	435	435	0	0
家具制造业	Manufacture of Furniture	512	512	0	0

指　标	Indicator	从业人员 Employed Persons	在岗职工 Staff and Workers	劳务派遣人员 Labor Dispatch Personnel	其他从业人员 Others
造纸和纸制品业	Manufacture of Paper and Paper Products	1009	824	0	185
印刷和记录媒介复制业	Printing, Reproduction of Recording Media	4967	4800	141	26
文教、工美、体育和娱乐用品制造业	Manufacture of Articles for Culture, Education, Artwork,Sport and Entertainment Activities	695	645	30	20
石油、煤炭及其他燃料加工业	Processing of Petroleum, Coking, Processing of Nucleus Fuels	2039	1761	197	81
化学原料和化学制品制造业	Manufacture of Chemical Raw Material and Chemical Products	3806	3719	5	82
医药制造业	Manufacture of Medicines	18186	18099	22	65
化学纤维制造业	Manufacture of Chemical Fiber	479	479	0	0
橡胶和塑料制品业	Manufacture of Rubber and Plastic	2161	2137	15	9
非金属矿物制品业	Manufacture of Non-metallic Mineral Products	14522	13898	400	224
黑色金属冶炼和压延加工业	Manufacture and Processing of Ferrous Metals	15875	14849	6	1020
有色金属冶炼和压延加工业	Manufacture & Processing of Non-ferrous Metals	710	710	0	0
金属制品业	Manufacture of Metal Products	15961	15404	506	51
通用设备制造业	Manufacture of General Purpose Machinery	27427	24588	2073	766
专用设备制造业	Manufacture of Special Purpose Machinery	8522	8276	108	138
汽车制造业	Manufacture of Automotive	40480	31677	8464	339
铁路、船舶、航空航天和其他运输设备制造业	Manufacture of Railway Locomotives, Building of Ships and Boats, Manufacture of Air and Spacecrafts and Other Transportation Equipments	7688	7122	386	180
电气机械和器材制造业	Manufacture of Electrical Machinery & Equipment	15194	13451	1286	457
计算机、通信和其他电子设备制造业	Manufacture of Computers, Communication Equipment and Other Electronic Equipment	32737	32468	250	19
仪器仪表制造业	Manufacture of Measuring Instrument	5672	5315	241	116
其他制造业	Other Manufacture	95	95	0	0
废弃资源综合利用业	Comprehensive Utilization of Waste	19	18	0	1
金属制品、机械和设备修理业	Metal Products, Machinery and Equipment Repair Industry	15	15	0	0
电力、热力、燃气及水生产和供应业	Production and Distribution of Electricity, Heating Power, Gas and Water	11515	11144	236	135
电力、热力生产和供应业	Production and Supply of Electric Power and Heat Power	5762	5746	0	16
燃气生产和供应业	Production and Supply of Gas	2942	2708	183	51
水的生产和供应业	Production and Supply of Water	2811	2690	53	68
建筑业	Construction	286208	179923	62264	44021
房屋建筑业	Construction of Building	155933	86697	41551	27685
土木工程建筑业	Civil Engineering Construction	106752	74850	16778	15124
建筑安装业	Construction Installation	14719	12975	1025	719
建筑装饰、装修和其他建筑业	Building Completion, Finishing and Other Construction	8804	5401	2910	493

5-4 续2

指　　标	Indicator	从业人员 Employed Persons	在岗职工 Staff and Workers	劳务派遣人员 Labor Dispatch Personnel	其他从业人员 Others
批发和零售业	Wholesale and Retail Trade	92796	85779	5484	1533
批发业	Wholesale Trade	44624	40172	3710	742
零售业	Retail Trade	48172	45607	1774	791
交通运输、仓储和邮政业	Traffic,Transport,Storage and Post	36200	30558	2732	2910
铁路运输业	Railway Transport	1083	1067	16	0
道路运输业	Road Transport	25506	23232	1926	348
水上运输业	Waterway Transport	623	623	0	0
航空运输业	Air Transport	91	91	0	0
管道运输业	Pipeline Transport	1488	883	83	522
多式联运和运输代理业	Multimodal transport and transportation agency	126	101	6	19
装卸搬运和仓储业	Loading, Unloading, Portage and Storage	1128	1116	8	4
邮政业	Postal Services	6155	3445	693	2017
住宿和餐饮业	Hotels and Catering Services	25723	22126	593	3004
住宿业	Hotels	12460	11758	401	301
餐饮业	Catering Services	13263	10368	192	2703
信息传输、软件和信息技术服务业	Information Transfer, Software and Information Technology Services	85039	80440	4387	212
电信、广播电视和卫星传输服务	Telecommunications, Radio and Television and Satellite Transmission Services	58718	54865	3851	2
互联网和相关服务	Internet and related Services	751	655	91	5
软件和信息技术服务业	Software and Information Technology Services	25570	24920	445	205
金融业	Financial Intermediation	94818	58278	2047	34493
货币金融服务	Monetary and Financial Services	38682	37024	1288	370
资本市场服务	Capital Market Services	2498	2388	16	94
保险业	Insurance	52936	18186	726	34024
其他金融业	Others	702	680	17	5
房地产业	Real Estate	43871	41552	1261	1058
房地产开发经营	Real Estate Development and Management	17175	16247	502	426
物业管理	Property Management	20550	19502	748	300
房地产中介服务	Real Estate Intermediary Services	1856	1847	0	9
房地产租赁经营	Real Estate Leasing Business	4190	3856	11	323
其他房地产业	Others	0	0	0	0
租赁和商务服务业	Leasing and Business Services	26457	25280	1012	165
租赁业	Leasing Services	1515	1381	123	11
商务服务业	Business Services	24942	23899	889	154
科学研究和技术服务业	Scientific Research and Development,Technical Services	42985	37226	3320	2439

指　　标	Indicator	从业人员 Employed Persons	在岗职工 Staff and Workers	劳务派遣人员 Labor Dispatch Personnel	其他从业人员 Others
研究和试验发展	Research and Experimental Development	9464	8777	266	421
专业技术服务业	Special Technical Services	32097	27062	3036	1999
科技推广和应用服务业	Science and Technology Promotion and Application Services	1424	1387	18	19
水利、环境和公共设施管理业	Management of Water Conservancy, Environment and Public Facilities	14205	8037	3349	2819
水利管理业	Management of Water Conservancy	2040	2013	10	17
生态保护和环境治理业	Ecological Protection and Environmental Management	407	407	0	0
公共设施管理业	Management of Public Facilities	11758	5617	3339	2802
土地管理业	Land Management	0	0	0	0
居民服务、修理和其他服务业	Services to Households, Repair and Other Services	4379	3687	484	208
居民服务业	Services to Households	1132	1099	3	30
机动车、电子产品和日用产品修理业	Repair of Motor Vehicles, Electronics and Household Appliances	443	423	14	6
其他服务业	Other Services	2804	2165	467	172
教育	Education	101918	92907	5983	3028
卫生和社会工作	Health and Social Work	70791	65499	3848	1444
卫生	Health Care	70128	64864	3828	1436
社会工作	Social Work	663	635	20	8
文化、体育和娱乐业	Culture,Sports and Entertainment	14641	11569	2498	574
新闻和出版业	Journalism and Publishing	4069	3815	191	63
广播、电视、电影和录音制作业	Radio Broadcasting, Television, Movies and Sound Recording	5294	3291	1969	34
文化艺术业	Culture and Arts	3736	3140	338	258
体育	Sports	568	482	0	86
娱乐业	Recreation	974	841	0	133
公共管理、社会保障和社会组织	Public Administration, Social Security and Social Organizations	97515	84866	9421	3228
中国共产党机关	Organs of Communist Party of China	4396	4338	27	31
国家机构	Organs of State	89841	77442	9239	3160
人民政协、民主党派	Peole's Political Consultative Conference and Democratic Parties	806	657	116	33
社会保障	Social Security	400	381	19	0
群众团体、社会团体和其他成员组织	Mass Communities, Social Organizations and Other Membership Organizations	2072	2048	20	4
基层群众自治组织	Grass Roots Self-Government Organization	0	0	0	0

5-5 城镇非私营单位从业人员工资总额（2018 年）

Total Wage of Employed Persons in Urban Non Private Entities（2018）

单位：千元 (1000 yuan)

指　　标	Indicator	从业人员工资总额 Wage Bill of Employed Persons	在岗职工工资总额 Total Wage of Staff and Workers	劳务派遣人员工资总额 Total Wage of Labor Dispatch Personnel	其他从业人员工资总额 Total Wage of Other Staff
合计	Total	114967219	100607626	7916697	6442896
按隶属关系分组	By Affiliation				
中央	Central	25205144	18977434	1432957	4794753
地方	Local	60417234	54376209	5102483	938542
其他	Others	29344841	27253983	1381257	709601
按国民经济行业分组	Grouped by Sector				
农、林、牧、渔业	Agriculture,Forestry,Animal Husbandry and Fishing	32660	32649	11	0
农业	Agriculture	6316	6305	11	0
林业	Forestry	15721	15721	0	0
畜牧业	Animal Husbandry	0	0	0	0
渔业	Fishing	440	440	0	0
农、林、牧、渔专业及辅助性活动	Service Activities for Agriculture, Forestry, Animal Production and Hunting, Fishing	10183	10183	0	0
采矿业	Mining	108207	100691	6316	1200
煤炭开采和洗选业	Mining and Washing of Coal	72131	72131	0	0
石油和天然气开采业	Extraction of Petroleum and Natural Gas	30609	23093	6316	1200
黑色金属矿采选业	Mining of Ferrous Metal Ores	0	0	0	0
有色金属矿采选业	Mining of Non-ferrous Metal Ores	0	0	0	0
非金属矿采选业	Mining and Processing of Nonmetal Ores	5467	5467	0	0
开采专业及辅助性活动	Mining Support Service Activities	0	0	0	0
其他采矿业	Mining of Other Ores	0	0	0	0
制造业	Manufacturing	19372995	18268952	885480	218563
农副食品加工业	Processing of Food from Agricultural Products	141893	137467	4365	61
食品制造业	Manufacture of Foods	525663	511391	10380	3892
酒、饮料和精制茶制造业	Manufacture of Wine, Drinks and Refined Tea	392422	386109	2309	4004
烟草制品业	Manufacture of Tobacco	8709	8709	0	0
纺织业	Manufacture of Textile	232934	229349	3585	0
纺织服装、服饰业	Manufacture of Textile Wearing Apparel and Finery	399763	396451	0	3312
皮革、毛皮、羽毛及其制品业和制鞋业	Manufacture of Leather, Fur, Feather and Its Products,and Footwear	13101	13091	0	10
木材加工和木、竹、藤、棕、草制品业	Processing of Timbers, Manufacture of Wood, Bamboo,Rattan, Palm and Straw Products	17957	17909	0	48
家具制造业	Manufacture of Furniture	17687	17687	0	0
造纸和纸制品业	Manufacture of Paper and Paper Products	52764	49721	0	3043
印刷和记录媒介复制业	Printing, Reproduction of Recording Media	294167	285950	7394	823

指　标	Indicator	从业人员工资总额 Wage Bill of Employed Persons	在岗职工工资总额 Total Wage of Staff and Workers	劳务派遣人员工资总额 Total Wage of Labor Dispatch Personnel	其他从业人员工资总额 Total Wage of Other Staff
文教、工美、体育和娱乐用品制造业	Manufacture of Articles for Culture, Education, Artwork,Sport and Entertainment Activities	27647	25938	1080	629
石油、煤炭及其他燃料加工业	Processing of Petroleum, Coking, Processing of Nucleus Fuels	263466	244875	13000	5591
化学原料和化学制品制造业	Manufacture of Chemical Raw Material and Chemical Products	205285	202420	291	2574
医药制造业	Manufacture of Medicines	1437419	1432835	978	3606
化学纤维制造业	Manufacture of Chemical Fiber	25209	25209	0	0
橡胶和塑料制品业	Manufacture of Rubber and Plastic	102108	101129	741	238
非金属矿物制品业	Manufacture of Non-metallic Mineral Products	860562	829821	23012	7729
黑色金属冶炼和压延加工业	Manufacture and Processing of Ferrous Metals	1431986	1372262	1157	58567
有色金属冶炼和压延加工业	Manufacture & Processing of Non-ferrous Metals	57868	57868	0	0
金属制品业	Manufacture of Metal Products	857495	827731	26831	2933
通用设备制造业	Manufacture of General Purpose Machinery	1866579	1708626	121734	36219
专用设备制造业	Manufacture of Special Purpose Machinery	530274	516849	8302	5123
汽车制造业	Manufacture of Automotive	3275444	2722116	543569	9759
铁路、船舶、航空航天和其他运输设备制造业	Manufacture of Railway Locomotives, Building of Ships and Boats, Manufacture of Air and Spacecrafts and Other Transportation Equipments	646523	623443	14960	8120
电气机械和器材制造业	Manufacture of Electrical Machinery & Equipment	1307637	1182418	79045	46174
计算机、通信和其他电子设备制造业	Manufacture of Computers, Communication Equipment and Other Electronic Equipment	3927189	3914154	10017	3018
仪器仪表制造业	Manufacture of Measuring Instrument	444566	418771	12730	13065
其他制造业	Other Manufacture	5064	5064	0	0
废弃资源综合利用业	Comprehensive Utilization of Waste	505	480	0	25
金属制品、机械和设备修理业	Metal Products, Machinery and Equipment Repair Industry	3109	3109	0	0
电力、热力、燃气及水生产和供应业	Production and Distribution of Electricity, Heating Power, Gas and Water	1168264	1149447	12460	6357
电力、热力生产和供应业	Production and Supply of Electric Power and Heat Power	577846	577362	0	484
燃气生产和供应业	Production and Supply of Gas	324326	311998	10410	1918
水的生产和供应业	Production and Supply of Water	266092	260087	2050	3955
建筑业	Construction	21585631	13603232	4409684	3572715
房屋建筑业	Construction of Building	10898979	5333453	2951578	2613948
土木工程建筑业	Civil Engineering Construction	9470520	7246459	1310117	913944
建筑安装业	Construction Installation	773177	700480	48119	24578
建筑装饰、装修和其他建筑业	Building Completion, Finishing and Other Construction	442955	322840	99870	20245
批发和零售业	Wholesale and Retail Trade	5731334	5355996	320101	55237
批发业	Wholesale Trade	3229387	2983582	212795	33010
零售业	Retail Trade	2501947	2372414	107306	22227

5–5 续 2

指　标	Indicator	从业人员工资总额 Wage Bill of Employed Persons	在岗职工工资总额 Total Wage of Staff and Workers	劳务派遣人员工资总额 Total Wage of Labor Dispatch Personnel	其他从业人员工资总额 Total Wage of Other Staff
交通运输、仓储和邮政业	Traffic,Transport,Storage and Post	2672183	2425086	146253	100844
铁路运输业	Railway Transport	119786	118687	1099	0
道路运输业	Road Transport	1856264	1758939	82494	14831
水上运输业	Waterway Transport	45361	45361	0	0
航空运输业	Air Transport	14055	14055	0	0
管道运输业	Pipeline Transport	143562	125462	6762	11338
多式联运和运输代理业	Multimodal transport and transportation agency	14094	13059	303	732
装卸搬运和仓储业	Loading, Unloading, Portage and Storage	77118	76530	520	68
邮政业	Postal Services	401943	272993	55075	73875
住宿和餐饮业	Hotels and Catering Services	1153910	1090505	24966	38439
住宿业	Hotels	651866	625524	16794	9548
餐饮业	Catering Services	502044	464981	8172	28891
信息传输、软件和信息技术服务业	Information Transfer, Software and Information Technology Services	8841608	8523815	292930	24863
电信、广播电视和卫星传输服务	Telecommunications, Radio and Television and Satellite Transmission Services	6198630	5944265	254313	52
互联网和相关服务	Internet and related Services	87565	81737	5636	192
软件和信息技术服务业	Software and Information Technology Services	2555413	2497813	32981	24619
金融业	Financial Intermediation	11257918	9326539	148659	1782720
货币金融服务	Monetary and Financial Services	6505074	6377518	96222	31334
资本市场服务	Capital Market Services	529233	526193	909	2131
保险业	Insurance	4014540	2214916	50656	1748968
其他金融业	Others	209071	207912	872	287
房地产业	Real Estate	2927412	2811377	66555	49480
房地产开发经营	Real Estate Development and Management	1789544	1717071	37338	35135
物业管理	Property Management	837023	801745	28732	6546
房地产中介服务	Real Estate Intermediary Services	117860	114923	0	2937
房地产租赁经营	Real estate leasing business	176204	170857	485	4862
其他房地产业	Others	0	0	0	0
租赁和商务服务业	Leasing and Business Services	2009704	1951576	47160	10968
租赁业	Leasing Services	149092	142769	5953	370
商务服务业	Business Services	1860612	1808807	41207	10598
科学研究和技术服务业	Scientific Research and Development,Technical Services	4587443	4224176	207304	155963

指　标	Indicator	从业人员工资总额 Wage Bill of Employed Persons	在岗职工工资总额 Total Wage of Staff and Workers	劳务派遣人员工资总额 Total Wage of Labor Dispatch Personnel	其他从业人员工资总额 Total Wage of Other Staff
研究和试验发展	Research and Experimental Development	1022757	979941	13817	28999
专业技术服务业	Special Technical Services	3460591	3141805	192297	126489
科技推广和应用服务业	Science and Technology Promotion and Application Services	104095	102430	1190	475
水利、环境和公共设施管理业	Management of Water Conservancy, Environment and Public Facilities	962716	773675	110269	78772
水利管理业	Management of Water Conservancy	226490	225757	463	270
生态保护和环境治理业	Ecological Protection and Environmental Management	23102	23102	0	0
公共设施管理业	Management of Public Facilities	713124	524816	109806	78502
土地管理业	Land Management	0	0	0	0
居民服务、修理和其他服务业	Services to Households, Repair and Other Services	299003	283937	12537	2529
居民服务业	Services to Households	59745	58315	186	1244
机动车、电子产品和日用产品修理业	Repair of Motor Vehicles, Electronics and Household Appliances	24554	23527	846	181
其他服务业	Other Services	214704	202095	11505	1104
教育	Education	11496399	11050684	298357	147358
卫生和社会工作	Health and Social Work	8328111	7946860	284130	97121
卫生	Health Care	8264183	7884149	283095	96939
社会工作	Social Work	63928	62711	1035	182
文化、体育和娱乐业	Culture,Sports and Entertainment	1683402	1394612	267515	21275
新闻和出版业	Journalism and Publishing	490476	479431	8709	2336
广播、电视、电影和录音制作业	Radio Broadcasting, Television, Movies and Sound Recording	703898	457810	245175	913
文化艺术业	Culture and Arts	377856	358448	13631	5777
体育	Sports	53623	47579	0	6044
娱乐业	Recreation	57549	51344	0	6205
公共管理、社会保障和社会组织	Public Administration, Social Security and Social Organizations	10748319	10293817	376010	78492
中国共产党机关	Organs of Communist Party of China	736504	734651	1113	740
国家机构	Organs of State	9622649	9178581	367895	76173
人民政协、民主党派	Peole's Political Consultative Conference and Democratic Parties	109758	103585	4752	1421
社会保障	Social Security	55060	54219	841	0
群众团体、社会团体和其他成员组织	Mass Communities, Social Organizations and Other Membership Organizations	224348	222781	1409	158
基层群众自治组织	Grass Roots Self-Government Organization	0	0	0	0

5-6 城镇非私营单位从业人员平均工资（2018 年）

Average Wage of Employed Persons in Urban Non Private Entities（2018）

单位：元 (yuan)

指 标	Indicator	从业人员平均工资 Average Wage of Employed Persons	在岗职工平均工资 Average Wage of Total Wage of Staff	劳务派遣人员平均工资 Average Wage of Labor Dispatch Personnel	其他从业人员平均工资 Average Wage of Other Staff
合计	Total	89168	94988	63359	61227
按隶属关系分组	By Affiliation				
中央	Central	97701	112644	68816	69806
地方	Local	97077	103694	66329	44595
其他	Others	71749	74405	50782	45790
按国民经济行业分组	Grouped by Sector				
农、林、牧、渔业	Agriculture,Forestry,Animal Husbandry and Fishing	74737	75055	5500	0
农业	Agriculture	63798	65000	5500	0
林业	Forestry	65504	65504	0	0
畜牧业	Animal Husbandry	0	0	0	0
渔业	Fishing	23158	23158	0	0
农、林、牧、渔专业及辅助性活动	Service Activities for Agriculture, Forestry, AnimalProduction and Hunting, Fishing	128899	128899	0	0
采矿业	Mining	86566	86430	140356	30000
煤炭开采和洗选业	Mining and Washing of Coal	87857	87857	0	0
石油和天然气开采业	Extraction of Petroleum and Natural Gas	99380	103556	140356	30000
黑色金属矿采选业	Mining of Ferrous Metal Ores	0	0	0	0
有色金属矿采选业	Mining of Non–ferrous Metal Ores	0	0	0	0
非金属矿采选业	Mining and Processing of Nonmetal Ores	45182	45182	0	0
开采专业及辅助性活动	Mining Support Service Activities	0	0	0	0
其他采矿业	Mining of Other Ores	0	0	0	0
制造业	Manufacturing	77292	78887	60311	49889
农副食品加工业	Processing of Food from Agricultural Products	47408	47402	52590	6100
食品制造业	Manufacture of Foods	50789	51666	37338	22368
酒、饮料和精制茶制造业	Manufacture of Wine, Drinks and Refined Tea	63602	64042	35523	52684
烟草制品业	Manufacture of Tobacco	71385	71385	0	0
纺织业	Manufacture ofTextile	47335	47279	51214	0
纺织服装、服饰业	Manufacture of Textile Wearing Apparel and Finery	54316	54249	0	63692
皮革、毛皮、羽毛及其制品业和制鞋业	Manufacture of Leather, Fur, Feather and Its Products,and Footwear	31645	31774	0	5000
木材加工和木、竹、藤、棕、草制品业	Processing of Timbers, Manufacture of Wood, Bamboo,Rattan, Palm and Straw Products	39728	39798	0	24000
家具制造业	Manufacture of Furniture	40848	40848	0	0

指　　标	Indicator	从业人员平均工资 Average Wage of Employed Persons	在岗职工平均工资 Average Wage of Total Wage of Staff	劳务派遣人员平均工资 Average Wage of Labor Dispatch Personnel	其他从业人员平均工资 Average Wage of Other Staff
造纸和纸制品业	Manufacture of Paper and Paper Products	48496	59618	0	11980
印刷和记录媒介复制业	Printing, Reproduction of Recording Media	58751	59437	46797	21658
文教、工美、体育和娱乐用品制造业	Manufacture of Articles for Culture, Education, Artwork,Sport and Entertainment Activities	39952	40402	36000	31450
石油、煤炭及其他燃料加工业	Processing of Petroleum, Coking, Processing of Nucleus Fuels	127278	136649	65990	69025
化学原料和化学制品制造业	Manufacture of Chemical Raw Material and Chemical Products	52786	53170	58200	33429
医药制造业	Manufacture of Medicines	81463	81583	48900	58161
化学纤维制造业	Manufacture of Chemical Fiber	52085	52085	0	0
橡胶和塑料制品业	Manufacture of Rubber and Plastic	47228	47301	49400	26444
非金属矿物制品业	Manufacture of Non-metallic Mineral Products	59044	59520	55854	34973
黑色金属冶炼和压延加工业	Manufacture and Processing of Ferrous Metals	89387	91987	82643	53830
有色金属冶炼和压延加工业	Manufacture & Processing of Non-ferrous Metals	80039	80039	0	0
金属制品业	Manufacture of Metal Products	56296	56370	53026	69833
通用设备制造业	Manufacture of General Purpose Machinery	69135	70511	63238	43015
专用设备制造业	Manufacture of Special Purpose Machinery	63804	64030	74793	40023
汽车制造业	Manufacture of Automotive	80067	85453	62415	28287
铁路、船舶、航空航天和其他运输设备制造业	Manufacture of Railway Locomotives, Building of Ships and Boats, Manufacture of Air andSpacecrafts and Other Transportation Equipments	81601	84581	44260	37944
电气机械和器材制造业	Manufacture of ElectricalMachinery & Equipment	83072	84507	63034	93281
计算机、通信和其他电子设备制造业	Manufacture of Computers, Communication Equipment and Other Electronic Equipment	122190	122805	40068	177529
仪器仪表制造业	Manufacture of Measuring Instrument	78090	78716	52603	99733
其他制造业	Other Manufacture	52750	52750	0	0
废弃资源综合利用业	Comprehensive Utilization of Waste	26579	26667	0	25000
金属制品、机械和设备修理业	Metal Products, Machinery and quipment Repair Industry	207267	207267	0	0
电力、热力、燃气及水生产和供应业	Production and Distribution of Electricity, Heating Power, Gas and Water	101210	102712	53476	53420
电力、热力生产和供应业	Production and Supply of ElectricPower and Heat Power	99509	99700	0	30250
燃气生产和供应业	Production and Supply of Gas	112340	117072	57514	46780
水的生产和供应业	Production and Supply of Water	93398	95096	39423	63790
建筑业	Construction	78001	80450	68852	81943
房屋建筑业	Construction of Building	73722	69113	67756	96431
土木工程建筑业	Civil Engineering Construction	89146	97691	78356	59583
建筑安装业	Construction Installation	55077	56236	51964	37466
建筑装饰、装修和其他建筑业	Building Completion, Finishing and Other Construction	51375	61075	35190	40653

5-6 续 2

指标	Indicator	从业人员平均工资 Average Wage of Employed Persons	在岗职工平均工资 Average Wage of Total Wage of Staff	劳务派遣人员平均工资 Average Wage of Labor Dispatch Personnel	其他从业人员平均工资 Average Wage of Other Staff
批发和零售业	Wholesale and Retail Trade	61705	62520	56286	36150
批发业	WholesaleTrade	71572	73674	55560	41574
零售业	Retail Trade	52384	52521	57785	30282
交通运输、仓储和邮政业	Traffic,Transport,Storage and Post	73410	79135	51155	34810
铁路运输业	Railway Transport	112793	113467	68688	0
道路运输业	Road Transport	72703	76154	40026	39655
水上运输业	Waterway Transport	71322	71322	0	0
航空运输业	Air Transport	159716	159716	0	0
管道运输业	Pipeline Transport	93283	134472	81470	21679
多式联运和运输代理业	Multimodal transport and transportation agency	106773	123198	50500	36600
装卸搬运和仓储业	Loading, Unloading, Portage and Storage	67293	67487	65000	17000
邮政业	Postal Services	64147	75726	80401	37386
住宿和餐饮业	Hotels and Catering Services	45098	49460	43194	12982
住宿业	Hotels	52224	53091	45267	29021
餐饮业	Catering Services	38309	45293	39478	10977
信息传输、软件和信息技术服务业	Information Transfer, Software and I nformationTechnology Services	104099	106197	65753	115106
电信、广播电视和卫星传输服务	Telecommunications, Radio and Television and Satellite Transmission Services	104618	107538	64026	26000
互联网和相关服务	Internet and related Services	118171	125749	65535	38400
软件和信息技术服务业	Software and Information Technology Services	102446	102630	83076	117794
金融业	Financial Intermediation	118867	161203	70056	51328
货币金融服务	Monetary and Financial Services	169350	174068	68534	84686
资本市场服务	Capital Market Services	214351	222586	56813	23944
保险业	Insurance	75537	121732	74058	51038
其他金融业	Others	306556	315496	48444	57400
房地产业	Real Estate	66114	67271	49191	43672
房地产开发经营	Real Estate Development and Management	104811	106763	70716	75886
物业管理	Property Management	39737	40174	35297	22341
房地产中介服务	Real Estate Intermediary Services	63708	63882	0	57588
房地产租赁经营	Real estate leasing business	42053	44344	44091	14914
其他房地产业	Others	0	0	0	0
租赁和商务服务业	Leasing and Business Services	76229	77650	44323	65677
租赁业	Leasing Services	100942	106148	49198	33636
商务服务业	Business Services	74762	76039	43698	67936

指 标	Indicator	从业人员平均工资 Average Wage of Employed Persons	在岗职工平均工资 Average Wage of Total Wage of Staff	劳务派遣人员平均工资 Average Wage of Labor Dispatch Personnel	其他从业人员平均工资 Average Wage of Other Staff
科学研究和技术服务业	Scientific Research and Development,Technical Services	108489	114806	65210	67458
研究和试验发展	Research and Experimental Development	109316	112624	54398	72317
专业技术服务业	Special Technical Services	109888	117679	66264	66855
科技推广和应用服务业	Science and Technology Promotion andApplication Services	72439	73427	51739	25000
水利、环境和公共设施管理业	Management of Water Conservancy, Environment and Public Facilities	67535	95151	33234	28073
水利管理业	Management of Water Conservancy	110645	111761	46300	15882
生态保护和环境治理业	Ecological Protection and Environmental Management	57468	57468	0	0
公共设施管理业	Management of Public Facilities	60404	91928	33194	28147
土地管理业	Land management industry	0	0	0	0
居民服务、修理和其他服务业	Services to Households, Repair and Other Services	66445	72507	33343	12159
居民服务业	Services to Households	52639	52917	62000	41467
机动车、电子产品和日用产品修理业	Repair of Motor Vehicles, Electronics and Household Appliances	45219	44899	65077	30167
其他服务业	Other Services	76082	88251	31958	6419
教育	Education	114031	119746	53904	49136
卫生和社会工作	Health and Social Work	118939	122800	75206	63561
卫生	Health Care	119156	123040	75331	63776
社会工作	Social Work	96277	98602	51750	22750
文化、体育和娱乐业	Culture,Sports and Entertainment	114650	120246	105737	38333
新闻和出版业	Journalism and Publishing	120807	125967	45597	37079
广播、电视、电影和录音制作业	Radio Broadcasting, Television, Movies and Sound Recording	130618	137480	121074	26853
文化艺术业	Culture and Arts	101684	114010	43411	22391
体育	Sports	95755	100378	0	70279
娱乐业	Recreation	60072	60834	0	54430
公共管理、社会保障和社会组织	Public Administration, Social Security and Social Organizations	110801	121318	41283	25752
中国共产党机关	Organs of Communist Party of China	166856	168653	41222	23871
国家机构	Organs of State	107777	118617	41230	25561
人民政协、民主党派	Peole's Political Consultative Conference and Democratic Parties	133851	155067	39933	43061
社会保障	Social Security	137650	142307	44263	0
群众团体、社会团体和其他成员组织	Mass Communities, Social Organizations and Other Membership Organizations	107395	107884	70450	39500
基层群众自治组织	Grass Roots Self-Government Organization	0	0	0	0

5-7 国有单位从业人员和工资（2018 年）

Number and Wage of Employed Persons in State-owned Units（2018）

指　标	Indicator	从业人员（人）Number of Employed Persons(person)	从业人员工资总额（千元）Wage of Employed Persons(1000 yuan)	从业人员平均工资（元）Average Wage of Employed Persons(yuan)
总计	**Total**	359605	38694978	109052
按隶属关系分组	**By Affiliation**			
中央	Central Investment	47864	6003285	127078
地方	Local	305306	32284352	107221
其他	Others	6435	407341	62764
按国民经济行业分组	**Grouped by Sector**			
农、林、牧、渔业	Agriculture,Forestry,Animal Husbandry and Fishing	369	24705	65531
采矿业	Mining	0	0	0
制造业	Manufacturing	2980	266253	87641
电力、热力、燃气及水生产和供应业	Production and Distribution of Electricity, Heating Power, Gas and Water	992	52897	55044
建筑业	Construction	12994	868572	79011
批发和零售业	Wholesale and Retail Trade	2683	132417	50006
交通运输、仓储和邮政业	Transport, Storage and Post	16676	1377359	83330
住宿和餐饮业	Accommodation and Restaurants	5348	297960	55352
信息传输、软件和信息技术服务业	Information Transmission, Software and Information Technology Services	297	47881	157503
金融业	Financial Intermediation	17341	1923900	113793
房地产业	Real Estate	2307	123325	53226
租赁和商务服务业	Leasing and Business Services	4145	179908	43784
科学研究和技术服务业	Scientific Research and Development, Technical Services	16780	1933685	115831
水利、环境和公共设施管理业	Management of Water Conservancy, Environment and Public Facilities	10664	799387	74563
居民服务、修理和其他服务业	Resident Services, Repair and Other Services	2517	216583	85336
教育	Education	92308	10662761	116827
卫生和社会工作	Health Care and Social Works	63134	7833448	125480
文化、体育和娱乐业	Culture,Sports and Entertainment	10963	1247893	113177
公共管理、社会保障和社会组织	Public Administration, Social Security and Social Organizations	97107	10706044	110841

5-8 城镇集体单位从业人员和工资（2018 年）

Number and Wage of Employed Persons in Urban Collective-owned Units（2018）

指　标	Indicator	从业人员（人）Number of Employed Persons(person)	从业人员工资总额（千元）Wage of Employed Persons(1000 yuan)	从业人员平均工资（元）Average Wage of Employed Persons(yuan)
总计	**Total**	16294	983266	62941
按隶属关系分组	**By Affiliation**			
中央	Central Investment	0	0	0
地方	Local	8826	639858	73152
其他	Others	7468	343408	49950
按国民经济行业分组	**Grouped by Sector**			
农、林、牧、渔业	Agriculture,Forestry,Animal Husbandry and Fishing	57	7865	137982
采矿业	Mining	0	0	0
制造业	Manufacturing	684	25968	37472
电力、热力、燃气及水生产和供应业	Production and Distribution of Electricity, Heating Power, Gas and Water	81	2703	34654
建筑业	Construction	5154	242267	53481
批发和零售业	Wholesale and Retail Trade	1090	46609	44859
交通运输、仓储和邮政业	Transport, Storage and Post	86	2552	31122
住宿和餐饮业	Accommodation and Restaurants	675	31174	46184
信息传输、软件和信息技术服务业	Information Transmission, Software and Information Technology Services	0	0	0
金融业	Financial Intermediation	0	0	0
房地产业	Real Estate	819	39009	47341
租赁和商务服务业	Leasing and Business Services	963	39836	40941
科学研究和技术服务业	Scientific Research and Development, Technical Services	201	21140	104653
水利、环境和公共设施管理业	Management of Water Conservancy, Environment and Public Facilities	37	1958	51526
居民服务、修理和其他服务业	Resident Services, Repair and Other Services	33	1302	39455
教育	Education	2287	203011	88884
卫生和社会工作	Health Care and Social Works	3762	279433	74715
文化、体育和娱乐业	Culture,Sports and Entertainment	4	83	20750
公共管理、社会保障和社会组织	Public Administration, Social Security and Social Organizations	361	38356	103665

5-9 城镇其他单位从业人员和工资（2018 年）

Number and Wage of Employed Persons in Other Urban Collective-owned Units（2018）

指　标	Indicator	从业人员（人）Number of Employed Persons(person)	从业人员工资总额（千元）Wage of Employed Persons(1000 yuan)	从业人员平均工资（元）Average Wage of Employed Persons(yuan)
总计	Total	925824	75288975	81935
按隶属关系分组	By Affiliation			
中央	Central Investment	208845	19201859	91116
地方	Local	315508	27493024	87973
其他	Others	401471	28594092	72276
按国民经济行业分组	Grouped by Sector			
农、林、牧、渔业	Agriculture,Forestry,Animal Husbandry and Fishing	3	90	30000
采矿业	Mining	1200	108207	86566
制造业	Manufacturing	247369	19080774	77276
电力、热力、燃气及水生产和供应业	Production and Distribution of Electricity, Heating Power, Gas and Water	10442	1112664	105928
建筑业	Construction	268060	20474792	78384
批发和零售业	Wholesale and Retail Trade	89023	5552308	62248
交通运输、仓储和邮政业	Transport, Storage and Post	19438	1292272	65299
住宿和餐饮业	Accommodation and Restaurants	19700	824776	42233
信息传输、软件和信息技术服务业	Information Transmission, Software and Information Technology Services	84742	8793727	103907
金融业	Financial Intermediation	77477	9334018	119970
房地产业	Real Estate	40745	2765078	67216
租赁和商务服务业	Leasing and Business Services	21349	1789960	84107
科学研究和技术服务业	Scientific Research and Development, Technical Services	26004	2632618	103691
水利、环境和公共设施管理业	Management of Water Conservancy, Environment and Public Facilities	3504	161371	46159
居民服务、修理和其他服务业	Resident Services, Repair and Other Services	1829	81118	42052
教育	Education	7323	630627	86815
卫生和社会工作	Health Care and Social Works	3895	215230	55875
文化、体育和娱乐业	Culture,Sports and Entertainment	3674	435426	119197
公共管理、社会保障和社会组织	Public Administration, Social Security and Social Organizations	47	3919	83383

5-10 社会保障基本情况

Basic Conditions of Social Sewrity

单位：万人 (10 000 persons)

指标	Indicator	2013 年	2014 年	2015 年	2016 年	2017 年	2018 年
职工基本养老保险参保人数	Urban Basic Pension Insurance	232.54	250.63	266.14	284.28	304.63	331.66
# 企业	Enterpris	207.60	225.63	241.07	259.26	279.65	306.59
事业机关	Institution and Government Agency	24.94	25.01	25.08	25.02	24.98	25.06
职工基本医疗保险参保人数	Medcial Care Insurance	183.18	196.50	208.09	214.48	228.68	241.54
参加失业保险人数	Unemployment Insurance	119.96	125.04	130.08	135.78	147.19	158.29
工伤保险参保人数	Work Injury Insurance	135.69	139.42	144.46	161.22	187.51	220.47
生育保险参保人数	Maternity Insurance	107.80	129.43	136.43	142.17	152.73	163.97
城镇登记失业率(%)	Registered Urban Unemployment Rate(%)	2.40	2.24	2.04	2.17	2.08	2.06

注：“职工基本养老保险参保人数”、“企业”及“事业机关”2013 年以前不包含离退休人员，2013 年及以后包含离退休人员

Note: The caliber "number of employees with basic endowment insurance", enterprise" and "business organ" does not contain the emeritus and retired before 2013 and contains the emeritus and retired after 2013.

主要统计指标解释

Explanatory Notes on Main Statistical Indicators

从业人员 指在本单位工作，并取得工资或其他形式劳动报酬的人员。

城镇登记失业人员 是指具有本地城镇户口，有劳动能力，目前无业，有求职愿望并在街道(乡镇)劳动保障部门办理了求职登记的人员。

城镇登记失业率 指报告期末，登记失业人员期末实有人数占期末从业人员总数与登记失业人员期末实有人数之和的比重。

在岗职工 指在本单位工作且与本单位签订劳动合同，并由单位支付各项工资和社会保险、住房公积金的人员，以及上述人员中由于学习、病伤、产假等原因暂未工作仍由单位支付工资的人员。

在岗职工工资总额 指本单位在报告期内直接支付给本单位全部在岗职工的劳动报酬总额。

在岗职工平均工资 指本单位在岗职工在报告期内平均每人所得的工资额。

Explanatory Notes on Main Statistical Indicators

Employees refer to persons who work in the unit and receive remuneration payment or other forms of payment.

Registered Urban Unemployed Persons refer to persons with local urban registration and labor capacity who are unemployed currently, have the job-hunting desire and handle registering at an employment agency at the street (town) labor security department.

Registered Urban Unemployment Rate refers to the ratio of the actual number of unemployed people registered at the end of the reporting period to the sum of the total number of employees at the end of the reporting period and the sum of the actual number of unemployed people registered at the end of the reporting period.

Fully Employed staff and Workers refer to persons who work in the unit and sign a labor contract with working units for whom working units pays various wages, social insurances and housing provident fund, and persons who have their work posts, but are temporarily absent from work for reasons of study or on sick, injury or maternal leave and still receive wages from their working units.

Total Wages Bill refers to the total remuneration payment to staff and workers in working units during the reporting period.

Average Wage refers to average wage per person within the reporting period for staff and workers in working units.

固定资产投资

INVESTMENT IN FIXED ASSETS

6-1 固定资产投资

Total Investment in Fixed Assets

单位：万元 (10 000 yuan)

指　标	Indicator	2011年	2012年	2013年	2014年	2015年	2016年	2017年
固定资产投资额	**Investment in Fixed Assets**	19343389	21860756	26383337	30634425	34984158	39743278	43635821
按管理渠道分	**By Management Channels**							
城镇集体以上投资	Above Urban Collective Investment	13059328	14005706	18189147	20297503	23817574	27091510	30334660
房地产开发投资	Real Estate Development Investment	5271575	6633153	7211744	9173706	10141433	11639381	12325712
农村投资	Rural Investment	1012486	1221898	982446	1163216	1025151	1012387	975449
按经济类型分	**Registration Status**							
国有经济	State-owned	7334983	6595774	8770551	6421555	8236033	7175934	8700130
集体经济	Collective-owned	1802483	1920132	2165782	2309282	1809902	1298005	1458316
联营经济	Joint Ownership Units		195897	100213	17820	30882	1808	0
股份制经济	Share-holding	5682038	1234405	1448535	5814573	7403146	10826143	12722943
外商投资经济	Fund from Overseas	408736	466383	336618	384940	284944	771449	410019
港澳台投资经济	Fund from Hong Kong,Macao and Taiwan	586347	634574	546675	177167	270022	961601	1129955
个体经济	Self-employed	2956158	3318099	30342	4423319	4447149	6788160	39804
其他经济	Others	572644	1169661	2044857	1912063	2360647	1683680	1002734
按投资用途分	**By Investment Purpose**							
第一产业	Primary Industry	486482	624114	982446	1163216.064	1025151	1012387	975449
第二产业	Secondary Industry	6073178	7337047	9078831	10985385.51	12173905	13019930	14418169
#工业	Industry	5767374	7018465	8060463	10410562.18	11478708	12373806	13176351
第三产业	Tertiary Industry	12783729	13899596	16322060	18485823.43	21785102	25710961	28242203
投资资金来源	**Fund of Different Sources**							
国家资金	State Appropriations	1317777	1693582	1302138	1240862	691574	1360695	1353707
国内贷款	Domestic Loans	1579846	517431	2173131	341374	73212	3656032	3343213
债券	Bond							40902
利用外资	Overseas Funds	68300	226374	262823	32757	44835	327727	250555
自筹资金	Self-raised Fund	14843051	16405182	19166006	19058000	23594834	28216931	28042143
其他资金	Others	3469710	4139026	5741361	454265	342083	10839004	10267805

注：自2011年起固定资产投资统计口径由50万元调整为500万元。

Note: Statistical caliber of fixed-asset investment as of 2011 was adjusted to RMB 5 million from 0.5 million.

6-2 固定资产投资分类（2018年）

Classification of Fixed Assets Investment（2018）

指　　标	Indicator	比上年增长(%) Growth rate(%)	
		固定资产投资 Investment in Fixed Assets	#市辖区 Districts under City
本年完成投资	**Investment Completed This Year**	9.6	10.3
按构成分	**Investment by Structure**		
建筑安装工程	Construction and Installation	1.6	2.0
设备工器具购置	Purchase of Equipment and Instruments	28.8	33.1
#购置旧设备	Purchase of Second-hand Equipment	-34.7	274.3
其他费用	Others	42.3	43.2
按产业分	**Grouped by Three Strata of Industry**		
第一产业	Primary Industry	7.4	3.1
第二产业	Secondary Industry	-10.1	-9.6
第三产业	Tertiary Industry	14.3	14.7
按单位登记注册类型分	**Registration Status**		
内资	Domestically-invested	9.3	10.0
国有	State-owned	12.2	11.3
集体	Collective-owned	-64.1	14.5
股份合作	Joint-equity Cooperative	-11.3	-11.3
私营个体	Private Enterprises	54.7	57.5
港澳台投资	**Fund from Hong Kong,Macao and Taiwan**	3.2	3.9
#港澳台股份有限公司	Share-holding	-16.4	-16.4
外商投资	**Fund from Overseas**	66.2	67.6
#外商合资经营	Joint Venture	67.7	67.2
#外商独资	Foreign Funded	91.9	91.9
其他	Others	78.3	79.9
按建设性质分	**Investment by Type of Construction**		
新建	New Construction	23.5	25.0
扩建	Expansion	-26.6	-26.9
改建和技术改造	Reconstruction and Technical Transformation	-22.4	-18.5
其他	Others	51.8	55.4

6-2 续 1

指　　标	Indicator	比上年增长(%) Growth rate(%)	
		固定资产投资 Investment in Fixed Assets	#市辖区 Districts under City
按国民经济行业分	**Investments in Fixed Assets by Sector**		
农、林、牧、渔业	Farming, Forestry, Animal Husbandry and Fishery	8.4	5.8
采矿业	Mining	–6.5	11.3
制造业	Manufacture	–6.8	–6.8
电力、热力、燃气及水生产和供应业	Production and Supply of Electric, Heat, Gas and Water	1.3	5.0
建筑业	Construction	–54.1	–60.8
批发和零售业	Wholesale and Retail Trade	–23.7	–18.5
交通运输、仓储和邮政业	Transport, Storage and Postal Services	4.8	3.9
住宿和餐饮业	Accommodations and Catering Services	188.4	286.9
信息传输、软件和信息技术服务业	Information Transmission, Computer Services and Software	16.3	18.1
金融业	Finance	152.7	152.7
房地产业	Real Estate	14.6	14.1
租赁和商务服务业	Leasing and Business Services	–24.0	–25.5
科学研究和技术服务业	Scientific Research and Technical Services	–31.4	–27.3
水利、环境和公共设施管理业	Management of Water Conservancy,Environment and Public Facilities	44.7	80.7
居民服务、修理和其他服务业	Households services, Repair and Other Service	–72.8	–72.0
教育	Education	16.7	15.4
卫生和社会工作	Health and Social Work	–2.6	1.9
文化、体育和娱乐业	Culture, Sports and Recreation	404.7	408.2
公共管理、社会保障和社会组织	Public Management,Social Security and Social Organizations	57.2	45.5
新增固定资产	**Newly Increased Fixed Assets**	–24.0	–15.6
施工项目个数(个)	**Number of Project under Construction(unit)**	1166	866
#新开工	Started This Year	528	335
竣工项目个数(个)	**Number of Buildings Completed(unit)**	348	273
施工房屋面积（万平方米）	**Project under Construction(10 000 sq.m)**	631.1	553.6
#住　宅	Residential Buildings	119.5	111.2
竣工房屋面积（万平方米）	**Project Completed and Put into Use(10 000 sq.m)**	43.4	42.1
#住宅	Residential Buildings	3.0	3.0

6-3 房地产开发投资分类（2018年）

Classification of Estate Development Investment（2018）

指　　标	Indicator	房地产开发投资 Estate Development Investment
本年完成投资额(万元)	**Investment Completed This Year(10 000 yuan)**	13693456
按构成分	**Investment by Structure**	
建筑工程	Construction	7920264
安装工程	Installation	1409538
设备、工器具购置	Purchase of Equipment and Instruments	178895
其他费用	Others	4184759
按单位登记注册类型分	**Registration Status**	
内资	**Domestic Fund**	13108173
国有	State-owned	70692
集体	Collective-owned	
股份合作	Cooperative	
联营	Joint Ownership Units	
国有联营	State-owned Joint	
集体联营	Collective-owned Joint	
其他联营企业	Other Joint Ownership Units	
有限责任公司	Limited Liability	7519339
国有独资公司	Solely State-owned Company	589415
其他有限责任公司	other Limited Liability Company	6929924
股份有限公司	Share-holding Corporations Ltd.	16170
私营	Private	5492572
其它内资	Other Domestic Fund	9400
港澳台投资	**Fund from Hong Kong,Macao and Taiwan**	519285
港澳台商合资经营	Joint Venture	243352
港澳台商合作经营	Collaborative Operation	
港澳台商独资	Solely Foreign-owned	275933
港澳台股份有限公司	Share-holding	
外商投资	**Fund from Overseas**	65998
外商合资经营	Joint Venture	
外商合作经营	Collaborative Operation	
外商独资	Foreign Funded	65998
外商股份有限公司	Share-holding	
其他外商投资企业	Other Fund from Overseas	
个体经营	**Self-employed**	
新增固定资产（万元）	**Newly Increased Fixed Assets (10 000 yuan)**	4698943
施工项目个数(个)	**Number of Project under Construction(unit)**	657
#新开工	Started This Year	
竣工项目个数(个)	**Number of Buildings Completed(unit)**	
施工房屋面积（万平方米）	**Project under Construction(10 000 sq.m)**	9112.05
#住 宅	Residential Buildings	5932.70
竣工房屋面积（万平方米）	**Project Completed and Put into Use(10 000 sq.m)**	1203.81
#住宅	Residential Buildings	897.37

6-4 固定资产投资资金来源（2018年）

Investment by Source of Funds （2018）

指　　标	Indicator	固定资产投资比上年增长(%) Growth rate Investment in Fixed Assets(%)	房地产开发投资(万元) Estate Development Investment (10 000 yuan)
本年资金来源合计	Total Funds of All Sources	14.0	29343040
上年末结余资金	Fund Left from Last Year	28.6	7514467
本年资金来源小计	Fund of All Sources in Currrent Year	11.0	21828573
国家预算资金	State Budgetary Funds	-2.0	
国内贷款	Domestic Loans	57.7	4024357
债券	Bond	220.3	
利用外资	Foreign Investment	547.2	158514
其中：外商直接投资	Foreign Direct Investment		
自筹资金	Self-Raising Funds	0.6	6999639
其中：企、事业单位自有资金	Enterprise and Intitutions Own Funds		
其他资金来源	Others Capital Source	10.6	1028110

6-5 新增主要生产能力和效益（2018年）

Newly Increased Production Capacity and Administrative（2018）

项目 Item	单位 Unit	新增生产能力 Newly Increased This Year
年产1万吨W-203水剂型吕膏项目	吨/年(ton/year)	10000
年产500万吨包装制品项目	吨/年(ton/year)	500
年产1千吨石墨烯及3万吨功能纤维项目	吨/年(ton/year)	1000
济南至乐陵高速公路南延线工程	公里(km)	1.8
曹范街道黄旗山1号路道路工程建设	公里(km)	4
国道二二零东郑线陶庄至平阴东平界段改建工程	公里(km)	19.4
国电投商河一期100MW风电场项目	万千瓦(10 000kw)	1
国瑞新能源章丘九顶山风电场二期工程项目	万千瓦(10 001kw)	10

6-6 历年房地产开发建设情况

Basic Situations of Real Estate Development in Major Years

指　　标	Indicator	单 位 Unit	2013 年	2014 年	2015 年	2016 年	2017 年	2018 年
计划总投资	**Intended Investment**	万元(10 000 yuan)	40958297	47123834	55571721	65080572	75662272	90392774
本年完成投资	**Investment Completed in Current Year**	万元(10 000 yuan)	7211744	9173706	10141433	11639381	12325712	13693456
按构成分	**Grouped by Use of Funds**							
建筑工程	Construction	万元(10 000 yuan)	4774627	5444613	6083337	7329570	8643701	7920264
安装工程	Installation	万元(10 000 yuan)	728393	922515	1126053	1614742	1446801	1409538
设备、工器具购置	Purchase of Equipment and Instruments	万元(10 000 yuan)	75129	116907	78310	152443	172327	178895
其他费用	Others	万元(10 000 yuan)	1633595	2689671	2853733	2542621	2062883	4184759
#旧建筑物购置费	Purchase of Used Building	万元(10 000 yuan)	37192	18696	1892	35444	4742	196
土地购置	Purchase of Land	万元(10 000 yuan)	1134128	2356776	2545842	2241602	1683185	3780143
按工程用途分	**Grouped by Use of Buildings**							
住　宅	Residential Buildings	万元(10 000 yuan)	5135293	6136895	7254184	8055689	8227871	9285419
#安居工程	Comfortable Housing Project	万元(10 000 yuan)						
办公楼	Office Buildings	万元(10 000 yuan)	560175	1267961	1379919	1112954	1058113	1047097
商业营业用房	Buildings for Business	万元(10 000 yuan)	742425	1115138	833683	1665634	1907938	1879155
其　他	Others	万元(10 000 yuan)	773851	653712	673647	805104	1131790	1481785
本年新增固定资产	**Newly Increased Fixed Assets**	万元(10 000 yuan)	3055912	1865035	1815666	3770747	3061175	4698943
本年完成土地开发面积	Developed Floor Space Completed This year	万平方米 (10 000 sq.m)						
待开发土地面积	Space of Land to be Developed	万平方米 (10 000 sq.m)	250.54	179.81	291.87	225.80	138.80	302.35
本年购置土地面积	Space of Land Purchased in Current Year	万平方米 (10 000 sq.m)	217.71	273.89	274.45	170.34	144.77	265.91
房屋施工面积	Floor Space Under Construction	万平方米 (10 000 sq.m)	4806.99	5257.57	6625.90	7912.30	8006.85	9112.05
房屋竣工面积	Floor Space Completed	万平方米 (10 000 sq.m)	805.02	516.76	579.05	1134.10	631.29	1203.81
竣工房屋价值	Value of Buildings Completed	万元(10 000 yuan)	2058306	1204331	1389148	2639414	1615213	3172322
竣工住宅	Residential Buildings Completed	套(unit)	53075	29976	27877	68682	45775	70120

6-7 历年房地产开发公司经营情况

Real Estate Development and Managment in Major Years

指 标	Indicator	单 位 Unit	2013 年	2014 年	2015 年	2016 年	2017 年	2018 年
开发公司家数	Number of Real Estate Enterprises	家(unit)	494	524	570	622	646	706
企业资本金	Enterprises Funds	万元(10 000 yuan)	5490601	6756174	7612830	9270991	10505186	12994960
资产与负债	Property debt							
资产总计	Assets	万元(10 000 yuan)	40538425	47284278	57218796	72602423	85586496	113393735
负债总计	Liabilities	万元(10 000 yuan)	32646896	38185924	46478285	58406976	68738188	93511277
所有者权益	Owners' Equity	万元(10 000 yuan)	7891530	9098353	10740511	14195447	16848309	19882458
损益情况	Net Income or Loss							
经营收入	Revenues from Business	万元(10 000 yuan)	6583934	7146915	7076463	11913217	11218828	12495191
土地转让收入	Revenues from Land Transfer	万元(10 000 yuan)	8165	15595	14820	2409	1501	952885
商品房销售收入	Revenues from Commercial Housing Sale	万元(10 000 yuan)	63030345	6709472	6265506	11227539	10803498	11087179
房屋出租收入	Housing Rental Income	万元(10 000 yuan)	67931	86836	79458	106425	109982	90017
其他收入	Others	万元(10 000 yuan)	204804	335012	716679	576844	302963	126592
经营成本	Business Cost	万元(10 000 yuan)	4831143	5416141	5515583	968896	8352620	8570149
经营税金及附加	Business Tax and Extra Charges	万元(10 000 yuan)	555833	569221	573637	706161	658995	951196
利润总额	Total Profits	万元(10 000 yuan)	707966	525409	401995	606344	875949	2177983
房屋销售与出租								
本年实际销售房屋面积	Floor Space of Buildings to Lease	平方米(sq.m)	8201657	8648934	11911661	14242514	12152665	12346236
#住 宅	Residential Buildings	平方米(sq.m)	7028475	7234582	9234805	12316804	9737162	9636143
本年房屋实际销售额	Total Sales of Buildings	万元(10 000 yuan)	5875180	6374593	9159131	11750932	11725660	14737908
#住 宅	Residential Buildings	万元(10 000 yuan)	4937873	5179753	6954738	10357228	9462791	11728181
待售房屋面积	Floor Space of Waiting For Sale	平方米(sq.m)	1014400	1173463	1694588	1720232	1398451	980301
#住 宅	Residential Buildings	平方米(sq.m)	614943	607336	864938	931437	740636	542047
出租房屋面积	Floor Space of Buildings to Lease	平方米(sq.m)	137775	61250	229415	182137	66089	1794

6-8 房地产开发公司经营情况（2018年）

Real Estate Development and Management（2018）

单位：万元 (10 000 yuan)

指　标	Indicator	合计 Total	内资企业 Domestic Enterprise 小计 Total	#国有 State-owned	外资企业 Foreign-owned Enterprise 小　计 Total	#港澳台商 Hong kong,Macao and Taiwan Investment
开发公司家数	**Number of Real Estate Enterprises**	706	672	17	34	26
按资质分	**by Qualification Criteria**					
#一级资质	First Grade	20	20	0	0	0
二级资质	Second Grade	49	48	4	1	1
三级资质	Third Grade	116	109	7	7	5
四级资质	Forth Grade	13	12	1	1	0
企业资本金	**Enterprises Funds**	12994960	11021402	209485	1973559	1949068
资产与负债	**Property debt**					
资产总计	Assets	113393735	108546296	1182012	4847439	4572289
负债总计	Liabilities	93511277	90960973	985624	2550304	2287396
所有者权益	Owners' Equity	19882458	17585323	196388	2297135	2284893
损益情况	**Net Income or Loss**					
经营收入	Revenues from Business	12495191	11682127	64942	813064	806691
土地转让收入	Revenues from Land Transfer	952885	952885	4123	0	0
商品房销售收入	Revenues from Commercial Housing Sale	11087179	10324124	35537	763055	757729
房屋出租收入	Housing Rental Income	90017	74376	4669	15642	14595
其他收入	Others	126592	126159	0	434	433
经营成本	Business Cost	8570149	8066957	49213	503193	496517
经营税金及附加	Business Tax and Extra Charges	951196	857045	6425	94152	93913
利润总额	Total Profits	2177983	2021192	-5610	156791	158877

主要统计指标解释

固定资产投资额 指以货币形式表现的在一定时期内建造和购置固定资产的工作量以及与此有关的费用的总称。

房地产开发投资 指各种登记注册类型的房地产开发法人单位统一开发的住宅、厂房、仓库、饭店、宾馆、度假村、写字楼、办公楼等房屋建筑物，配套的服务设施，土地开发工程（如道路、给水、排水、供电、供热、通讯、平整场地等基础设施工程）和土地购置的投资；不包括单纯的土地开发和交易活动。

固定资产投资的资金来源 根据固定资产投资的资金来源不同，分为国家预算内资金、国内贷款、债券、利用外资、自筹资金和其他资金来源。

（1）国家预算内资金：指各级政府用于固定资产投资的财政资金，包括中央预算资金和地方预算资金。

（2）国内贷款：指报告期固定资产投资项目单位向银行及非银行金融机构借入用于固定资产投资的各种国内借款，包括银行利用自有资金及吸收存款发放的贷款、上级拨入的国内贷款、国家专项贷款，地方财政专项资金安排的贷款、国内储备贷款、周转贷款等。

（3）债券：指企业或金融机构为筹集用于固定资产投资的资金向投资者出具的承诺按一定发行条件还本付息的债务凭证，包括金融债券和企业债券。

（4）利用外资：指报告期收到的境外（包括外国及港澳台地区）资金(包括设备、材料、技术在内)。包括对外借款(外国政府贷款、国际金融组织贷款、出口信贷、外国银行商业贷款、对外发行债券和股票)、外商直接投资、外商其他投资(包括补偿贸易、加工装配由外商提供的设备价款、国际租赁，外商投资收益的再投资资金)。不包括我国自有外汇资金(国家外汇、地方外汇、留成外汇、调济外汇和中国境内银行自有资金发放的外汇贷款等)。各类外资按报告期的外汇牌价（中间价）折成人民币计算。

（5）自筹资金：指在报告期内筹集的用于项目建设和购置的资金。包括自有资金、股东投入资金和借入资金，但不包括各类财政性资金、从各类金融机构借入资金和国外资金。

（6）其他资金来源：指在报告期收到的除以上各种资金之外的用于固定资产投资的资金。包括社会集资、个人资金、无偿捐赠的资金及其他单位拨入的资金等。

固定资产投资按建设性质分 建设项目的性质一般分为新建、扩建、改建和技术改造、单纯建造生活设施、迁建、恢复、单纯购置。

（1）新建：指从无到有"平地起家"开始建设的项目。现有企业、事业、行政单位投资的项目一般不属于新建。但如有的单位原有基础很小，经过建设后新增的固定资产价值超过该企业、事业、行政单位原有固定资产价值（原值）三倍以上的，也应作为新建。

（2）扩建：指为扩大原有产品的生产能力（或效益）或增加新的产品生产能力，而增建的生产车间（或主要工程）、分厂、独立的生产线等项目。行政、事业单位在原单位增建业务性用房（如学校增建教学用房、医院增建门诊部、病房等）也作为扩建。

（3）改建和技术改造：指对原有设施进行技术改造或更新（包括相应配套的辅助性生产、生活福利设施）的建设项目。

（4）单纯建造生活设施：指在不扩建、改建生产性工程和业务用房的情况下，单纯建造职工住宅、托儿所、子弟学校、医务室、浴室、食堂等生活设施的项目。

（5）迁建：指为改变生产能力布局或由于城市环境保护和安全生产的需要等原因而搬迁到另地建设的项目。在搬迁另地的建设过程中，不论是维持原来规模还是扩大规模都按迁建来统计。

（6）恢复：指因自然灾害、战争等原因，使原有固定资产全部或部分报废，以后又投资恢复建设的项目。不论是按原规模恢复还是在恢复的同时进行扩建的都按恢复项目统计。尚未建成投产的建设项目因自然灾害而损坏重建的，仍按原有建设性质划分。

（7）单纯购置：指单纯购置不需要安装的设备、工具、器具而不进行工程建设的项目。有些调查单位当年虽然只从事一些购置活动，但其设计中规定有建筑安装活动，应根据设计文件的内容来确定建设性质，不得作为单纯购置统计。

固定资产投资按构成分 固定资产投资活动按其工作内容和实现方式分为建筑工程、安装工程、设备工器具购置、其他费用三个部分。

（1）建筑工程：指各种房屋、建筑物的建造工程，又称建筑工作量。这部分投资额必须兴工动料，通过施工活动才能实现，是固定资产投资额的重要组成部分。

（2）安装工程：指各种设备、装置的安装工程，又称安装工作量。

（3）设备工器具购置：指报告期内购置或自制的，达到固定资产标准的设备、工具、器具的价值。

（4）其他费用：指在固定资产建造和购置过程中发生的，除建筑安装工程和设备、工器具购置投资完成额以外的应当分摊计入固定资产投资项目的费用，不指经营中财务上的其他费用。

新增生产能力(或工程效益)名称 指建成投产项目或工程新增生产能力(或工程效益)的名称。

建设规模 指建设项目或工程设计文件中规定的全部设计能力(或工程效益)。包括已经建成投产和尚未建成投产的工程的生产能力(或工程效益)。它是以实物形态表示固定资产投资规模的指标，反映建设项目或工程全部建成投产（或交付使用）后，能够为社会提供多少设计能力（或工程效益）。

房屋施工面积 指报告期内施工的全部房屋建筑面积。

房屋竣工面积 指报告期内房屋建筑按照设计要求已全部完工，达到住人和使用条件，经验收鉴定合格或达到竣工验收标准，可正式移交使用的各栋房屋建筑面积的总和。

本年新增固定资产 指在报告期已经完成建造和购置过程，并已交付生产或使用单位的固定资产的价值，包括已经建成投入生产或交付使用的工程投资和达到固定资产标准的设备、工具、器具的投资及有关应摊入的费用。属于增加固定资产价值的其他建设费用，应随同交付使用的工程一并计入新增固定资产。

房地产开发本年完成投资 指各种登记注册类型的房地产开发法人单位本年内统一开发的住宅、厂房、仓库、饭店、宾馆、度假村、写字楼、办公楼等房屋建筑物，配套的服务设施，土地开发工程（如道路、给水、排水、供电、供热、通讯、平整场地等基础设施工程）和土地购置的投资；不包括单纯的土地开发和交易活动。

土地购置和开发情况

（1）待开发土地面积:指经有关部门批准，通过各种方式获得土地使用权，但尚未开工建设的土地面积。

（2）本年土地购置面积:指在本年内通过各种方式获得土地使用权的土地面积。

商品房屋销售与出租情况

（1）商品房销售面积:指报告期内出售商品房屋的合同总面积（即双方签署的正式买卖合同中所确定的建筑面积）。商品房销售面积由现房销售面积和期房销售面积两部分组成。

①现房销售面积：指在报告期内正式签订买卖合同、已经竣工达到入住条件的商品房屋建筑面积。包括以一次性付款方式和分期付款方式销售的现房建筑面积。

②期房销售面积：指在报告期内正式签订买卖合同、正在建设尚未竣工交付使用的商品房屋建筑面积。包括以一次性付款方式和分期付款方式销售的商品房屋建筑面积。期房销售建筑面积竣工后不再结转为现房销售建筑面积。

（2）待售面积:指报告期末已竣工的可供销售或出租的商品房屋建筑面积中，尚未销售或出租的商品房屋建筑面积，包括以前年度竣工和本期竣工的房屋面积，但不包括报告期已竣工的拆迁还建、统建代建、公共配套建筑、房地产公司自用及周转房等不可销售或出租的房屋面积。按照商品房待售时间的长短可以划分为待售一年以下、待售一到三年（含一年）和待售三年以上（含三年）。

（3）房屋出租面积:指在报告期末房屋开发单位出租的商品房屋的全部面积。

（4）商品房销售额：指报告期内出售商品房屋的合同总价款（即双方签署的正式买卖合同中所确定的合同总价）。该指标与商品房销售面积同口径，由现房销售额和期房销售额两部分组成。

①现房销售额：指报告期内销售的已竣工商品房屋的合同总价款。包括现房销售前期预收的定金、预收款、首付款及全部按揭贷款的本金等款项。该指标与现房销售面积同口径。

②期房销售额：指报告期内销售的正在建设尚未竣工的商品房屋的合同总价款。包括预售房屋前期预收的定金、预收款、首付款及全部按揭贷款的本金等项。该指标与期房销售面积同口径。

Explanatory Notes on Main Statistical Indicators

Total Investment in Fixed Assets refers to the volume of activities in construction and purchases of fixed assets and related fees during a certain period of time, expressed in monetary terms.

Investment in Real Estate Development refers to the investment by real estate development units of various types of ownership in buildings and structures (such as residence, factory, warehouse, restaurant, hotel, resort, office building and administration building), supporting service facilities and land development engineering (including infrastructure projects such as road, water supply, drainage, power supply, heat supply, communication and land grading) excluding activities in pure land transactions.

Source of Funds for Investment in Fixed Assets include national budgetary funds, domestic loans, foreign investment, self–raised funds, and others depending on the source of investment.

(1) National budgetary funds refers to financial funds used by governments at all levels for fixed–asset investment, including central budget funds and local budget funds.

(2) Domestic loans refer to loans of various forms borrowed by investing units from banks and non–bank financial institutions during the reference period for the purpose of investment in fixed assets, including the loan issued by the bank by self–owned funds and deposit taking, domestic loans appropriated by superior, national special loan, loan arranged by special funds for local finance, domestic reserve loan and revolving credit.

(3) Bonds: refer to the certificate of indebtedness issued by the enterprise or the financial institution to the investor for raising the capital of fixed–asset investment with capital and interest promised to be repaid as per certain issue terms, including financial bond and enterprise bond.

(4) Foreign investment: refer to overseas (including foreign countries, Hong Kong, Macau and Taiwan) funds (including equipment, materials and technology) received in the reporting period, including foreign borrowings (loans from foreign governments and international financial organizations, export credit, commercial loans from foreign banks and issue of bonds and stocks overseas), foreign direct investment and other foreign investments (including compensation trade, the price of processing and assembling the equipment provided by foreign business, international leasing, funds from foreign direct investment income that are reinvested in fixed assets domestically). Excluded from this category is capital in foreign exchanges owned by China (foreign exchanges owned by the central and local governments, foreign exchanges retained by enterprises, foreign exchanges by enterprises through the regulating mechanism, loans in foreign exchanges issued by the Bank of China with its own fund, etc.). In calculating the utilization of foreign capital, foreign currencies are converted into CNY applying the exchange rate (central parity rate) at the end of the reference period. .

(5) Self–raised funds: refer to the fund raised in the reporting period and used for construction and purchase of the project, including self–owned funds, capital invested by shareholders and borrowed funds other than various financial funds, capital borrowed from various financing institutions and offshore funds.

(6) Other refer to funds for investment in fixed assets received in the reporting period, except for the above–mentioned various capitals, including funds raised in society, personal money, voluntary donations and capital from other units.

Investment in Fixed Assets by Type of Construction The construction projects in general can be classified, by the type of construction, into new construction, expansion, reconstruction and technical transformation, simple construction of living facilities, relocation, recovery and simple purchase.

(1) New construction: refers to the project that started construction from scratch. Projects invested by the existing enterprises, institutions or agencies is not considered as new construction. In case the assets of the existing unit are quite small, and the value of newly added fixed assets exceeds the original value of assets by three times, the expansion will be considered as new construction.

(2) Expansion: refers to construction of new production workshops (or major projects), branch factories or independent production lines, for the purpose of increasing the production capacity (or improving efficiency) of the original products. Newly constructed houses for the operation of institutions and administrative organizations (such as the newly constructed buildings for teaching in schools, buildings for clinics or wards in hospitals, etc.) are also classified as expansion.

(3) Reconstruction and technical transformation: refer to the construction project for technical transformation or renewal for original facilities (including corresponding supporting auxiliary production and living welfare facilities).

(4) Simple construction of living facilities: refers to the project of simply constructing living facilities such as staff houses, nurseries, schools for children of employees, medical rooms, shower rooms and canteens, etc. without expanding or reconstructing productive engineering and business housing.

(5) Relocation: refer to the project moved to other place for construction for the purpose of changing production capacity layout or urban environment protection and safety production requirements. In the process of being moved to other places for construction, whether it is to maintain the original scale or augment the scale, it will be counted as relocation.

(6) Recovery: refers to the project with original fixed assets scrapped in whole or in part due to natural disaster or war which is invested to recover construction later. Regardless of recovery as per original size or expansion at the time of recovery, it will be counted as recovery. If the construction project which has not been completed and gone into operation is reconstructed due to being damaged by natural disaster, it is still classified according to the original type of construction.

(7) Simple purchase: refers to the project of simply purchasing equipment, tools and appliances which do not need to be installed without engineering construction. Although some investigating units only engaged in some purchase activities in that year, construction and installation activities were specified in their design, so it is necessary to confirm the type of construction in line with the content of the design document, and should not be counted as simple purchase.

Investment in fixed assets by Structure Fixed–asset investment activities are divided into construction engineering, installation engineering, purchase of equipment & tools and other expenses in terms of working content and implementation model.

(1) Construction engineering: refers to the construction of various houses and buildings, also called as construction workload. Such

investment volume must be implemented through construction activities based on utilization of materials, which is an important part of fixed investments.

(2) Installation engineering: refers to installation of various equipment and devices, also called as installation workload.

(3) Purchase of equipment and tools: refers to the value of purchased or home-made equipment, tools and appliances within the reporting period, which reach to fixed-asset standards.

(4) Other expenses: refer to expenses incurred in the construction and purchase process of fixed assets which shall be allocated and included into the fixed-asset investment project, except for the expenses of construction and installation engineering and purchase of equipment & tools, and not refer to other financial expenses in the operation.

Newly Increased Production Capacity (or Project Efficiency) refers to the name of new production capacity (or project benefit) of the project or the engineering completed and put into operation.

Scale of Construction refers to all design ability (or project benefit) specified in the design document for construction project or engineering, including production capacity (or project benefit) completed and put into production and not yet be completed and put into production. It is an indicator showing the scale of investment in fixed assets in the matter form and reflects the design capability (or project benefit) provided for the society after the construction project or engineering is completed and put into production (or delivered for use).

Construction area of the house refers to building area of all houses constructed in the reporting period.

Housing completion area refers to total building areas of all houses which have been completed in accordance with design requirements in the reporting period, reach to living and using conditions, pass acceptance and verification or reach to the completion acceptance standards and can be formally handed over for use.

New fixed assets in this year refer to the value of fixed assets having been delivered to the production or use unit with construction and purchase process completed in the reporting period, including investment in projects completed and put into production or delivered for use and investment in equipment, tools and appliances reaching to fixed-asset standards and related expenses which shall be included. Other construction costs falling into the added fixed-asset value shall be included into new fixed assets together with the project delivered for use.

Investment completed in current year in real estate development refers to buildings and structures (such as residence, factory, warehouse, restaurant, hotel, resort, office building and administration building), supporting service facilities and land development engineering (including infrastructure projects such as road, water supply, drainage, power supply, heat supply, communication and land grading) and investment in land purchase uniformly developed by real estate development legal entity in the current year based on all kinds of businesses; excluding simple land development and trading activities.

Land purchase and development

(1) Land area to be developed: refers to the area of the land approved by related department with land use right obtained by all means but not yet under construction.

(2) Land acquisition area in the current year: refers to the area of the land with land use right obtained by all means in the current year.

Sales and rental of the residential property

(1) Sales area of residential property: refers to the total area in the contract of residential properties sold within the reporting period (namely the building area set forth in the sales contract formally signed by both parties). Sales area of the residential property is composed by two parts -- sales area of completed houses and sales area of the property under construction.

① Sales area of completed houses: refers to the building area of the residential property which has been completed and reached to living conditions with the sales contract formally signed within the reporting period, including the building area of completed houses sold by one-off payment and installment payment.

② Sales area of property under construction: refer to the building area of residential properties under construction which has not yet been delivered for use with the sales contract formally signed within the reporting period, including the building area of residential properties sold by one-off payment and installment payment. The sales building area of the property under construction will not be transfered to the sales building area of the competed house after being completed.

(2) Area to be sold: refers to the building area of residential properties not sold or rented in the building area of residential properties available for sale or renting which has been completed at the end of the reporting period, including the area of houses completed before and in the current period, and other than the area of housings not available for sale or renting such as the housing built due to demolition, the housing uniformly built by the government, public matching buildings, the housing used by the real estate company and the relocation housing in the reporting period. As per the waiting time for sales of the residential property, the housings can be divided into the one waiting for sales for less than one year, the one waiting for sales for more than one year (one year included) but less than three years and the one waiting for sales for more than three years (three years included).

(3) Area of rental housing: refers to all areas of the residential property rented out by the house development unit at the end of the reporting period.

(4) Sales amount of residential property: refers to the total price in the contract of residential properties sold within the reporting period (namely the total contract price set forth in the sales contract formally signed by both parties). The indicator shares the same caliber with the sales area of the residential property, and it consists two parts -- sales amount of completed houses and sales amount of the property under construction.

① Sales amount of completed houses: refer to total contract price of residential properties completed and sold within the reporting period, including deposits, prepayments and down payment as well as all principal of all mortgage loans. The indicator shares the same caliber with the sales area of the completed houses.

② Sales amount of property under construction: refer to total contract price of residential properties under construction sold within the reporting period, including deposits, prepayments and down payment as well as all principal of all mortgage loans. The indicator shares the same caliber with the sales area of the property under construction.

7

城市公用事业和环境保护

URBAN PUBLIC UNILITIES
AND ENVIRONMENTAL
PROTECTION

7-1 城市道路与公共交通

Basic Statistics on Muncipal Engineering and Public Transportation

指　　标	Indicator	2013 年	2014 年	2015 年	2016 年	2017 年	2018 年
城市道路	City Roads						
道路长度(公里)	Length of Roads (km)	5222	5264	5350	5422	5663	5788
道路面积(万平方米)	Area of Roads(10 000 sq.m)	8572	9116	9523	9724	10224	10529
城市桥梁(座)	Number of Bridges(unit)	836	836	845	927	935	1021
#立交桥(座)	Interchange(unit)	81	76	77	82	82	85
路灯(盏)	Number of Streetlights(unit)	152361	162590	167462	170314	188598	195014
人均拥有道路面积(平方米)	Per Capita Road Arae(sq.m)	23.87	25.19	26.10	26.20	22.96	23.03
公共交通	Public Transportation						
年末营运车辆(辆)	Number of Operating Vehicles(unit)	13840	14650	15236	15539	16850	16644
公共汽车	Bus	4820	5099	5537	5846	7157	6951
#无轨电车	Trolley Bus	140	139	140	121	121	106
出租汽车	Number of Taxis	9020	9551	9699	9693	9693	9693
乘客人数(万人次)	Volume of Passenger Traffic (10 000 person-times)	104457	101698	93634	90776.1	90515.6	89619.7

7-2 水、电、气、热供应情况

Basic Statistics on Water、Electricity、Gas and Heating in Cities

指　　标	Indicator	单位 Unit	2013 年	2014 年	2015 年	2016 年	2017 年	2018 年
自来水	**Water**							
年末水厂生产能力	Production Capacity of Water Supply	万吨/日 (10 000 tons/day)	201.74	201.74	201.74	211.47	215.57	220.27
年末管线长度	Length of Water Supply Pioelines	公里(km)	4094	4222	4325.56	4241.04	4779.01	5277.13
全年供水量	Volume of Water Supply	万吨 (10 000 tons)	30357	31158	31826.63	33191.11	35865.07	39226.16
人均日生活用水	Per Capita Daily Water Consumption	升(litre)	137.3	143.9	138.95	142.78	139.58	140.37
城市人口用水普及率	Coverage Rate of Water Supply	%(%)	98.64	98.92	99	99.57	99.64	99.78
用电量	**Electricity Consumption**							
全社会用电量	Electricity Consumption	万千瓦时 (10 000 kwh)	2582682	2614124	2642035	2799221	2762869	2843630
工　业	Industrial Electricity Consumption	万千瓦时 (10 000 kwh)	1490436	1507683	1420304	1470794	1319975	1215034
城乡居民生活用电	Household　Electricity Consumption	万千瓦时 (10 000 kwh)	483401	488075	522513	554853	598578	667505
液化石油气和管道煤气	**Liquefied Petroleum Gas and Piped Gas**							
液化石油气全年供气量	Total Liquefied Petroleum Gas Supply	吨(tons)	52569	46693	46844.2	53086.2	49944.0	41110.0
生活用	Residential Use	吨(tons)	32310	21960	21866	19771	23462	20458
居民用气人口	Population Uses Gas	万人 (10 000 persons)	82.88	85	87.1	77.39	55.93	46.81
天然气供气量	Total Natural Gas Supply	万立方米 (10 000 cu.m)	54726	64904	75496.75	79325.47	90724.36	113945.56
生产用	Production Use	万立方米 (10 000 cu.m)	42454	45937	58196.06	60994.42	69361.61	88821.02
生活用	Residential Use	万立方米 (10 000 cu.m)	12272	17967	17300.69	18331.05	21362.75	25124.54
居民用气人口	Population Uses Gas	万人 (10 000 persons)	258	264	269.44	291.56	388.63	409.70
管道煤气供气量	Piped Gas Supply	万立方米 (10 000 cu.m)	3000	940	59	–	–	–
生产用	Production Use	万立方米 (10 000 cu.m)	900	796	59	–	–	–
生活用	Residential Use	万立方米 (10 000 cu.m)	2100	144	0	–	–	–
居民用气人口	Population Uses Gas	万人 (10 000 persons)	7	2	0	–	–	–
用气普及率	Coverage Rate of Gas Supply	%(%)	96.81	96.88	97.73	99.42	99.85	99.87
集中供热	**Central Heating**							
管道长度	Pipe Length	公里(km)	2334	2488	3277	2742	6104	7010
供热面积	Heating Area	万平方米 (10 000 sq.m)	10172	11786	14499	14917	18174	19834

注：本表指标为“–”的，是指济南市已不再使用“管道煤气”

Notes: The indicator"–",in this table refers Jinan no Longer Use Piped Gas.

7-3　环境状况及污染治理情况

Basic Statistics on Environment and Treatment of Pollution

指　　标	Indicator	单位 Unit	2013 年	2014 年	2015 年	2016 年	2017 年	2018 年
环境质量状况	**Environment Condition**							
环境空气细颗粒物（$PM_{2.5}$)浓度年均值	Annual Average Concentration of PM2.5	mg／m3	0.108	0.090	0.087	0.073	0.063	0.052
环境空气二氧化硫浓度年均值	Annual Average Concentration of SO2	mg／m3	0.093	0.072	0.050	0.038	0.025	0.017
环境空气二氧化氮浓度年均值	Annual Average Concentration of NO2	mg／m3	0.059	0.053	0.048	0.045	0.046	0.045
环境空气可吸入颗粒物(PM_{10})浓度年均值	Annual Average Concentration of PM10	mg／m3	0.191	0.172	0.157	0.141	0.130	0.112
集中式饮用水源地水质达标率	Standard rate of concentrate Water Source Area	%(%)	100.00	100.00	100.00	100.00	100.00	100.00
区域环境噪声昼间平均等效声级	Area Whole-day Average Noise Value	分贝(db)	52.5	54.2	53.7	53.1	53.7	53.3
道路交通噪声平均等效声级	Traffic Average Noise Value	分贝(db)	69.3	69.7	70.0	69.8	69.7	69.5
污染物排放情况	**Discharge of Major Pollutants**							
废水排放总量	Volume of Waste Water Discharged	万吨 (10 000 tons)	38402	38904	39454	34530	34693	34693
#工业废水排放量	Volume of Industrial Waste Water Discharged	万吨 (10 000 tons)	8596	7880	7415	5993	5949	5949
化学需氧量排放量	Volume of COD Emission	吨 (10 000 tons)	108889	104876	107743	30202	28701	28701
#工业化学需氧量排放量	Volume of Industrial COD Emission	吨(tons)	5413	5289	5515	2777	2594	2594
氨氮排放量	Volume of Ammonia Nitrogen	吨(tons)	8482	8224	9050	4306	4255	4255
#工业氨氮排放量	Volume of Industrial Ammonia Nitrogen	吨(tons)	380	346	360	186	197	197
二氧化硫排放量	Volume of Sulphur Dioxide Discharged	吨(tons)	107265	97171	99653	44403	32502	32502
#工业二氧化硫排放量	Volume of Industrial Sulphur Dioxide Discharged	吨(tons)	81118	67842	70327	28458	16545	16545
氮氧化物排放量	Volume of Nitrogen Oxides Discharged	吨(tons)	104265	95295	91614	61075	23316	23316
#工业氮氧化物排放量	Volume of Industrial Nitrogen Oxides Discharged	吨(tons)	72969	64861	63781	34502	21254	21254
机动车氮氧化物排放量	Volume of Vehicle Nitrogen Oxides	吨(tons)	27571	26703	24080	24472		
烟（粉）尘排放量	Volume of Soot and Dust Discharged	吨(tons)	58250	100899	108643	64253	32794	32794
#工业烟（粉）尘排放量	Volume of Industrial Soot and Dust Discharged	吨(tons)	47117	90082	92900	54677	25060	25060

注：1. 从 2014 年工业烟（粉）统计口径增加钢铁、水泥等行业无组织排放量。
2. “机动车氮氧化物排放量”指标，自 2017 年起，国家只核定到省级数据。
3. 污染物排放情况数据，根据生态环境部统一工作安排，暂时使用 2017 年已公布数据，2018 年数据待第二次全国污染源普查完成后统一发布。

Notes: 1. Industry unorganized emission (including steel and cement, etc.) was added to the statistical caliber of industrial smoke (powder) from 2014.
2. The indicator-"nitrogen oxide emission from motor vehicles" was only verified to provincial data by the state from 2017.
3. As for data on pollutant discharge, the data published in 2017 is temporarily used as per the unified arrangement of Ministry of Ecology and Environment and the data in 2018 will be uniformly published after completion of the 2nd national census of pollution sources.

7-4 城市园林绿化、环境卫生及其他

Basic Statistics on Parks、Gardens、Green Areas and Urban Sanitation in Cities

指标	Indicator	单位 Unit	2013年	2014年	2015年	2016年	2017年	2018年
园林绿化	**Parks Gardens and Green Areas**							
年末园林绿地面积	Garden Green Area at Year-end	公顷 (ha)	16226	17002	17561	18162.9	19528.6	20701.0
#公园面积	Area of Parks	万平方米 (10 000 sq.m)	2923	3116	3190	3190	3414	3930
人均公园绿地面积	Per Capita Public Green Areas	平方米/人 (sq.m/person)	11.3	11.5	11.6	11.8	11.8	12.6
建成区绿化覆盖率	Coverage of Green Area	%	39.03	39.62	39.94	40.12	40.57	40.52
城市卫生	**Urban Health**							
污水集中处理率	Centralized Sewage Treatment Rate	%	90.21	95.33	95.85	96.33	95.98	96.59
清运垃圾	Garbage Clearance	万吨 (10 000 tons)	122.79	114	158	179.68	192.22	202.64
清运粪便	Garbage Disposal	万吨 (10 000 tons)	63.79	58.5	48.2	10.5	-	-
公共厕所	Public Lavatory	座 (unit)	1006	1026	1060	1077	1075	1086
城市维护费收支	**Expenditure and Earning for City Maintenance**							
维护费收入	Earning for City Maintenance	万元 (10 000 yuan)	1574821	1546397	1693759	1843784	-	-
维护费支出	Expenditure for City Maintenance	万元 (10 000 yuan)	1597865	1559055	1681108	1571443	-	-

注：本表指标为"-"的，部门相关统计制度中已经不在进行统计

Notes: The indicator "-" in this table means statistics are no longer in the relevant statistical system of the department.

主要统计指标解释

年末自来水生产能力 指年底城建部门管理的自来水厂和自备水源的社会单位取水、净化、送水、出厂输水干管等环节的实际生产能力。

年末供水管道长度 指从送水泵到用户水表之间所有管道的长度。

全年供水总量 指公用自来水厂和自备水源的社会单位全年的供水总量，包括有效供水量及损失水量。

生活用水量 指居民日常生活与公共福利设施的用水量，包括居民、饮食店、旅馆、医院、理发店、浴池、洗衣店、游泳池、商店、学校、机关、部队等单位的用水量。

城市人口用水普及率 指城市用水的非农业人口数(不包括临时人口和流动人口)与城市非农业人口总数之比。计算公式为：

用水普及率 = 城市用水的非农业人口数 / 城市非农业人口数 × 100%

城市用气普及率 指使用煤气(包括人工煤气、液化石油气、天然气)的城市非农业人口数(不包括临时人口和流动口)与城市非农业人口总数之比。计算公式为：

城市用气普及率 = 城市用气的非农业人口数 / 城市非农业人口总数 × 100%

年底实有铺装道路长度 指除土路外，路面经过铺装宽度在3.5 米以上的道路，包括高级、次高级道路和普通道路。

城市桥梁 指城市范围内，修建在河道上的桥梁和道路与道路立交、道路跨越铁路的立交桥及人行天桥。包括永久性桥和半永久性桥，不包括临时性桥、铁路桥、涵洞。

城市污水日处理能力 指污水处理厂每昼夜处理污水量的设计能力。

年末实有公共汽（电）车 指年底可参加营运的全部车辆数，包括营运车辆数和库存查封未参加营运的车辆。不包括非营运车辆，如架线车、油罐车、工程车、货车及其他专用车辆和借入的客运车辆。

绿地面积 指报告期末用作园林和绿化的各种绿地面积。包括公园绿地、生产绿地、防护绿地、附属绿地和其他绿地的面积。

公园绿地 城市中向公众开放的、以游憩为主要功能，有一定的游憩设施和服务设施，同时兼有健全生态、美化景观、防灾减灾等综合作用的绿化用地。它是城市建设用地、城市绿地系统和城市市政公用设施的重要组成部分。

工业废水排放量 指报告期内经过企业厂区所有排放口排到企业外部的工业废水量。包括生产废水、外排的直接冷却水、废气治理设施废水、超标排放的矿井地下水和与工业废水混排的厂区生活污水，不包括独立外排的间接冷却水(清浊不分流的间接冷却水应计算在内)。

化学需氧量 (COD) 测量有机和无机物质化学分解所消耗氧的质量浓度的水污染指数。废气排放总量 指燃料燃烧和生产工艺过程中排放的各种废气总量，以标准状态下每年万标立方米表示。

二氧化硫排放量 指报告期内企业在燃料燃烧和生产工艺过程中排入大气的二氧化硫总质量。工业中二氧化硫主要来源于化石燃料(煤、石油等)的燃烧，还包括含硫矿石的冶炼或含硫酸、磷肥等生产的工业废气排放。

氮氧化物排放量 指报告期内企业在燃料燃烧和生产工艺过程中排入大气的氮氧化物总质量。

烟(粉)尘排放量 指报告期内企业在燃料燃烧和生产工艺过程中排入大气的烟尘及工业粉尘的总质量之和。烟尘或工业粉尘排放量可以通过除尘系统的排风量和除尘设备出口烟尘浓度相乘求得。

工业粉尘排放量 指企业在生产工艺过程中排放的颗粒物重量。如钢铁企业的耐火材料粉尘、焦化企业的筛焦系统粉尘、烧结机的粉尘、石灰窑的粉尘、建材企业的水泥粉尘等。不包括电厂排放大气的烟尘。

Explanatory Notes on Main Statistical Indicators

Year-end Tap Water Production Capacity refers to actual capacity of such links as water intaking, purification, water carriage and leaving factory water main pipe of the waterworks managed by urban construction department and social unit water source prepared at the end of the year.

Length of Water Supply Pipelines at the Year-end refers to the total length of all the pipelines between the water pumps and the user water meters.

Annual Volume of water supply refers to annual total water supply of public waterworks and social unit with water source prepared, including both the effective water supply and loss during the water supply.

Consumption of Water for Residential Use refers to water consumption in the daily life of residents and by public amenities and facilities, including water consumption by residents, eateries, hotels, hospitals, barber shops, common bathing pools, laundries, swimming pools, shops, schools, organs and troops, etc..

Urban Population Water Penetration Rate refers to the ratio between non-agricultural population of municipal water (excluding temporary and floating population) and total urban non-agricultural population. The calculation formula is:

Water penetration rate = non-agricultural population of municipal water / urban non-agricultural population * 100%

Urban Gas Popularizing Rate refers to the ratio between urban non-agricultural population (excluding temporary population and migrant population) using the coal gas (including manufactured gas, liquefied petroleum gas and natural gas) and total urban non-agricultural population. The calculation formula is:

Urban gas popularizing rate = non-agricultural population of municipal gas / total urban non-agricultural population * 100%

Year-end Actual Length of Paved Road refers to roads whose pavement width exceeds 3.5 m except for unsurfaced road (including senior, sub-senior and ordinary roads).

Urban Bridges refer to bridge and road built above the river, interchange between roads, highway interchange based on road spanning railway and pedestrian overpass, both permanent and semi-permanent bridges are included, other than temporary bridge, railway bridge and culvert in the scope of the city.

Daily Urban Sewage Treatment Capacity refers to the design capability of the sewage quantity treated by sewage treatment works every day and night.

Year-end Existing Buses (Public Trolleys) refer to all vehicles which can be put into operation at the end of the year, including number of vehicles put into operation and vehicles with inventory sealed up which are not put into operation other than non-operating vehicles, such as overhead line vehicle, oil tank truck, engineering vehicle, truck, other special vehicle and borrowed passenger service vehicle.

Green Area refers to a green area for gardening and greening. Including parks, green spaces, protective green, the accessory Greenbelt and other green areas at the end of referenced period.

Park Green Land refers to the green land which is open to the public for relaxation and has services facilities and is used for ecological protection, landscaping and disaster reduction. It is an important part of construction land, urban green space and municipal public facilities. public facilities.

Industrial Waste Water Discharged refers to the volume of industrial waste water discharged through all of the drainage system to the outside of factory complex by enterprises during the report period. It includes discharged waste water from production, direct cooling water, waste gas treatment facilities, mine groundwater beyond the standard and domestic sewage mixed with industrial waste water, does not include independently discharged indirect cooling water (voicing split-less indirect cooling water should be taken into account).

Chemical Oxygen Demand (COD) refers to index of water pollution measuring the mass concentration of oxygen consumed by the chemical breakdown of organic and inorganic matter. Total exhaust emission refers to total quantity of various exhaust gases discharged in the process of fuel burning and production which is expressed with 10,000 standard cubic meters each year under the standard state.

SO2 Emission refers to total volume of SO2 discharged into air during the process of fuel combustion and industrial production in enterprises in a given time, and is mainly caused by the combustion of fossil fuel, ore smelting and the discharge of industrial waste gas during the production of sulfuric acid and phosphate fertilizers.

Nitrogen Oxides Emission refers to total volume of nitrogen oxides discharged into air during the process of fuel combustion and industrial production.

Industrial Soot and Dust Emission refers to volume of soot and dust in smoke emitted in process of fuel burning and industrial production in premises of enterprises in the report period. It is calculated by multiplying exhaust volume of dust removal system by dust concentration.

Emission Load of Industrial Dust refers to the weight of particulate matters discharged in the process of production (such as fireproofing dust of the iron and steel enterprise, coke screening system dust of the coke making enterprise, dust of the sintering machine, dust of the lime kiln and cement dust of the building material industry), excluding smoke discharged by the power plant in to the atmosphere.

财政和金融保险

GOVERNMENT FINANCE
AND FINANCIAL INSURANCE

8-1 各时期地方财政收支及指数

Local Government Revenue、Expenditures and Indices of Major Years

年份 Year	一般公共预算收入 （万元） General Pubilic Budget Revenue (10 000yuan)	一般公共预算支出 （万元） General Pubilic Budget penditure (10 000yuan)	指数(%)（以上年为 100） (%)(Preceding Year=100)	
			一般公共预算收入 General Pubilic Budget Revenue	一般公共预算支出 General Pubilic Budget Expenditure
1999	460690	497667	119.9	110.8
2000	490485	547210	110.5	110.4
"十五" 时期				
2001	596061	703720	121.5	128.6
2002	662511	775046	115.4	110.2
2003	761064	884597	119.6	114.3
2004	890364	1016953	120.9	115.0
2005	1061547	1206643	120.7	118.7
"十一五" 时期				
2006	1284388	1469762	121.0	121.8
2007	1570192	1799787	122.3	122.5
2008	1860155	2213190	118.5	123.1
2009	2101923	2599178	113.0	117.4
2010	2661314	3368037	126.6	129.6
"十二五" 时期				
2011	3249315	3968831	122.1	117.8
2012	3808218	4656731	117.0	117.3
2013	4820722	5193190	113.9	111.5
2014	5431278	5714138	112.7	110.0
2015	6143172	6581813	113.1	115.2
"十三五" 时期				
2016	6412167	7412641	104.4	112.6
2017	6772100	8340600	105.6	112.5
2018	7528162	10183179	111.2	122.1

注：2013 年财政部门对一般公共预算收入口径进行调整，2013 年一般公共预算收入指数为可比口径。

Note: In 2013, the financial department adjusted the caliber of general public budget revenue. In 2013, the index of general public budget income index was comparable caliber.

8-2 地方财政收入 (2018年)

Local Financial Revenue（2018）

单位：万元 (10 000yuan)

指标	Indicator	全市合计 Total	市本级 Cities 小计 Total	市本级 Cities 市直 Departments Directiy Under the Municipal Government	市本级 Cities 高新区 Gaoxin	市本级 Cities 南部山区 Nanshan	县区级 Counties
一般公共预算收入	General Pubilic Budget Revenue	7528162	1725984	575403	1150507	74	5802178
增值税	Value-added Tax	2104828	380410	0	380410	0	1724418
营业税	Business Tax	4096	1	0	1	0	4095
企业所得税	Enterprise Income Tax	1080091	218516	0	218516	0	861575
个人所得税	Personal Income Tax	417546	81674	0	81674	0	335872
资源税	Resource Tax	28849	3552	0	3552	0	25297
城市维护建设税	Tax on City Maintenance and Construction	362205	94341	2725	91616	0	267864
房产税	Tax on Real Estates	206535	36955	0	36955	0	169580
印花税	Stamp Tax	112868	20724	0	20724	0	92144
城镇土地使用税	Holding tax on urban and county land	233482	28458	0	28458	0	205024
土地增值税	Land Value Added Tax	568478	68262	0	68262	0	500216
车船税	Tax on vehicles and Their Registration	91019	355	0	355	0	90664
耕地占用税	Farmland Occupation Tax	83483	22155	0	22155	0	61328
契税	Contract tax	897301	105952	0	105952	0	791349
环境保护税	Environmental Protection Tax	3801	52	0	52	0	3749
专项收入	Specific Revenue	363696	151235	89431	61804	0	212461
行政事业性收费收入	Income from Administrative Fees	361432	185225	177640	7585	0	176207
罚没收入	Penalty and Confiscatory Income	135141	80860	80355	505	0	54281
国有资本经营收入	Profits of State-owned Enterprises	-6631	-6735	-6735	0	0	104
国有资源（资产）有偿使用收入	Revenue of Compensable Use of State-owned Resources (Assets)	401972	192720	173664	18982	74	209252
捐赠收入	Donation Income	13237	409	409	0	0	12828
政府住房基金收入	Government Housing Fund Income	62450	61077	58128	2949	0	1373
其他收入	Others	2283	-214	-214	0	0	2497
政府性基金收入	Government Funds Income	13402089	10854192	10765913	88279	0	2547897
#城市基础设施配套收入	Urban Infrastructure Supporting Income	706720	500013	413309	86704	0	206707

8-3 各区财政收入（2018年）

Financial Revenue by District（2018）

单位：万元 (10 000yuan)

指标	Indicator	合计 Total	历下区 Li xia	市中区 Shi zhong	槐荫区 Huai yin	天桥区 Tian qiao	历城区 Li cheng	长清区 Chang qing	章丘区 Zhang qiu	济阳区 Zhang qiu
一般公共预算收入	**General Pubilic Budget Revenue**	5460652	1441898	933633	503447	451675	1041204	234995	603234	250566
增值税	Value-added Tax	1632074	442525	261050	179825	136117	287196	79521	174774	71066
营业税	Business Tax	3980	2611	196	468	261	327	52	7	58
企业所得税	Enterprise Income Tax	830325	249008	194738	54865	92438	125919	23172	66760	23425
个人所得税	Personal Income Tax	324997	119201	77635	25513	23750	39732	7205	25125	6836
资源税	Resource Tax	18963	743	7142	169	184	1343	1172	5700	2510
城市维护建设税	Tax on City Maintenance and Construction	256913	78096	39086	25514	19395	46193	11685	28575	8369
房产税	Tax on Real Estates	163095	59322	33375	16995	15521	13808	6157	13322	4595
印花税	Stamp Tax	88171	30139	16241	6196	6201	13376	2507	11102	2409
城镇土地使用税	Holding tax on urban and county land	179488	17718	16857	18907	15543	35423	19292	41608	14140
土地增值税	Land Value Added Tax	488846	127841	100444	33828	25692	136165	15495	35949	13432
车船税	Tax on vehicles and Their Registration	63192	26447	3880	196	807	1226	1604	5321	23711
耕地占用税	Farmland Occupation Tax	44443	144	877	4589	2163	11551	3099	15999	6021
契税	Contract tax	765693	193715	82833	101409	23657	225406	26191	78588	33894
环境保护税	Environmental Protection Tax	2462	99	204	38	107	550	122	1229	113
专项收入	Specific Revenue	192259	57754	26046	17074	12528	33329	9213	24980	11335
行政事业性收费收入	Income from Administrative Fees	146952	11478	6707	6899	44708	26703	5186	35575	9696
罚没收入	Penalty and Confiscatory Income	46138	1699	2239	1300	1537	7024	2829	21014	8496
国有资本经营收入	Profits of State-owned Enterprises	0	0	0	0	0	0	0	0	0
国有资源（资产）有偿使用收入	Revenue of Compensable Use of State-owned Resources (Assets)	205419	22580	63994	9407	31043	30773	20290	17007	10325
捐赠收入	Donation Income	5869	0	89	255	23	5160	203	4	135
政府住房基金收入	Government Housing Fund Income	1373	778	0	0	0	0	0	595	0
其他收入	Others	0	0	0	0	0	0	0	0	0
政府性基金收入	**Government Funds Income**	2098399	0	0	0	4861	137	24485	1443158	625758
#城市基础设施配套收入	Urban Infrastructure Supporting Income	157730	0	0	0	4861	0	23109	55086	74674

8-4 各县财政收入（2018年）

Financial Revenue by County（2018）

单位：万元 (10 000yuan)

指　　标	Indicator	合计 Totl	平阴县 Pingyin	商河县 Shanghe
一般公共预算收入	General Pubilic Budget Revenue	341526	218949	122577
增值税	Value-added Tax	92344	66164	26180
营业税	Business Tax	115	66	49
企业所得税	Enterprise Income Tax	31250	26450	4800
个人所得税	Personal Income Tax	10875	8129	2746
资源税	Resource Tax	6334	5890	444
城市维护建设税	Tax on City Maintenance and Construction	10951	7249	3702
房产税	Tax on Real Estates	6485	4101	2384
印花税	Stamp Tax	3973	2742	1231
城镇土地使用税	Holding tax on urban and county land	25536	10136	15400
土地增值税	Land Value Added Tax	11370	4377	6993
车船税	Tax on vehicles and Their Registration	27472	6100	21372
耕地占用税	Farmland Occupation Tax	16885	8623	8262
契税	Contract tax	25656	10580	15076
环境保护税		1287	1175	112
专项收入	Specific Revenue	20202	15156	5046
行政事业性收费收入	Income from Administrative Fees	29255	24792	4463
罚没收入	Penalty and Confiscatory Income	8143	6853	1290
国有资本经营收入	Profits of State-owned Enterprises	104	41	63
国有资源（资产）有偿使用收入	Revenue of Compensable Use of State-owned Resources (Assets)	3833	2509	1324
捐赠收入	Donation Income	6959	6816	143
政府住房基金收入	Government Housing Fund Income	0	0	0
其他收入	Others	2497	1000	1497
政府性基金收入	Government Funds Income	449498	145172	304326
#城市基础设施配套收入	Urban Infrastructure Supporting Income	48977	16688	32289

8-5 地方财政支出(2018年)

Local Financial Expenditures （2018）

单位：万元 (10 000yuan)

指标	Indicator	全市合计 total	市本级 Cities				县区级 Counties
			小计 Total	市直 Departments Directiy Under the Municipal Government	高新区 Gaoxin	南部山区 Nanshan	
一般公共预算支出	**General Pubilic Budget Expenditure**	10183179	4641976	3478263	959857	203856	5541203
一般公共服务支出	General Public Service	1053790	322091	223991	81154	16946	731699
国防支出	Defence Expenditure	12659	9417	9230	187	0	3242
公共安全支出	Public Security	623291	418320	405861	11603	856	204971
教育支出	Education	1530516	361705	274327	55899	31479	1168811
科学技术	Science andTechnology	210425	139863	31889	107864	110	70562
文化体育与传媒支出	Culture、Sports and Media	139534	69547	67327	1025	1195	69987
社会保障和就业支出	Social Security and Employment	1328725	558980	504086	28630	26264	769745
医疗卫生与计划生育支出	Health and Family Planning	691779	316582	282864	20035	13683	375197
节能环保支出	Energy-saving and Environment Protection	334104	193471	167515	9498	16458	140633
城乡社区支出	Urban and Rural Community Affairs	2463774	1561481	1153875	368206	39400	902293
农林水支出	Farming、Forestry and Irrigation Affairs	864211	156158	111101	10552	34505	708053
交通运输支出	Transport	197281	105087	79870	8043	17174	92194
资源勘探信息等支出	Exploration and Information Affairs	253655	195178	23327	171454	397	58477
商业服务业等支出	Commerce and Services Affairs	69227	46316	33190	12236	890	22911
金融支出	Financial Supervision Affairs	13199	8353	840	7513	0	4846
援助其他地区支出	Aid to Other Area	38280	27458	26107	1351	0	10822
国土海洋气象等支出	Land and Weather Affairs	144611	72997	22953	48390	1654	71614
住房保障支出	Housing Security Affairs	146265	47196	28134	16217	2845	99069
粮油物资储备支出	Grain and Oil Reserves	6678	2965	2965	0	0	3713
债务付息支出	Pay Principle and Interest for Public Debt	40703	15557	15557	0	0	25146
其他支出	Other Expenditure	20472	13254	13254	0	0	7218
政府性基金支出	**Government Funds Expenditure**	14522006	7544017	6481874	1038061	24082	6977989
#城乡社区支出	Urban and Rural Community Affairs	14246693	7336787	6277123	1037394	22270	6909906

8-6 各区地方财政支出(2018年)

Local Financial Expenditures by District（2018）

单位：万元 (10 000yuan)

指　标	Indicator	合 计 Total	历下区 Li xia	市中区 Shi zhong	槐荫区 Huai yin	天桥区 Tian qiao	历城区 Li cheng	长清区 Chang qing	章丘区 Zhang qiu	济阳区 Zhang qiu
一般公共预算支出	**General Pubilic Budget Expenditure**	4690250	807661	558305	423157	377710	685682	667967	706909	462859
一般公共服务支出	General Public Service	653128	151804	95176	69462	68714	99353	51101	73445	44073
国防支出	Defence Expenditure	2477	1142	367	5	5	442	253	260	3
公共安全支出	Public Security	171355	27090	19908	19806	14043	22569	9905	35783	22251
教育支出	Education	1024142	177389	152218	84868	94318	135798	100514	180365	98672
科学技术	Science andTechnology	68598	5314	4497	6207	5169	30541	2535	8554	5781
文化体育与传媒支出	Culture、Sports and Media	62795	28305	2782	2658	3050	3940	7179	11035	3846
社会保障和就业支出	Social Security and Employment	670298	101940	79701	79490	72475	81923	70250	124157	60362
医疗卫生与计划生育支出	Health and Family Planning	323769	49483	36733	37093	35475	36496	43417	54482	30590
节能环保支出	Energy-saving and Environment Protection	123218	15753	13753	20370	11865	13584	14777	22236	10880
城乡社区支出	Urban and Rural Community Affairs	743104	210233	108703	63612	44397	170824	20057	38789	86489
农林水支出	Farming、Forestry and Irrigation Affairs	556330	9416	19210	23218	11175	29058	295031	103473	65749
交通运输支出	Transport	63411	0	2919	273	633	11476	22752	12961	12397
资源勘探信息等支出	Exploration and Information Affairs	48122	8111	5084	5975	9198	5053	2569	10217	1915
商业服务业等支出	Commerce and Services Affairs	19604	2275	2364	3353	1739	3567	2093	2899	1314
金融支出	Financial Supervision Affairs	4590	2850	60	1324	80	0	56	0	220
援助其他地区支出	Aid to Other Area	10515	2733	2116	642	595	1930	0	2280	219
国土海洋气象等支出	Land and Weather Affairs	36485	6692	3777	2027	1117	2817	8675	8744	2636
住房保障支出	Housing Security Affairs	80811	259	7514	560	772	34761	14605	11194	11146
粮油物资储备支出	Grain and Oil Reserves	2807	0	0	0	0	353	1109	605	740
国债还本付息支出	Pay Principle and Interest for Public Debt	17473	79	1423	2214	2890	1082	779	5430	3576
其他支出	Other Expenditure	7218	6793	0	0	0	115	310	0	0
政府性基金支出	**Government Funds Expenditure**	6551118	856484	1032364	237418	45794	1636900	560795	1521080	660283
#城乡社区支出	Urban and Rural Community Affairs	6490788	853985	1026688	230587	42390	1628207	553598	1498185	657148

8-7 各县地方财政支出(2018年)

Local Financial Expenditures by County（2018）

单位：万元 (10 000yuan)

指　　标	Indicator	合计 Total	平阴县 Pingyin	商河县 Shanghe
一般公共预算支出	General Pubilic Budget Expenditure	850953	430987	419966
一般公共服务支出	General Public Service	78571	37829	40742
国防支出	Defence Expenditure	765	697	68
公共安全支出	Public Security	33616	16101	17515
教育支出	Education	144669	64699	79970
科学技术	Science andTechnology	1964	1148	816
文化体育与传媒支出	Culture、Sports and Media	7192	2962	4230
社会保障和就业支出	Social Security and Employment	99447	49321	50126
医疗卫生与计划生育支出	Health and Family Planning	51428	20646	30782
节能环保支出	Energy-saving and Environment Protection	17415	7287	10128
城乡社区支出	Urban and Rural Community Affairs	159189	80287	78902
农林水支出	Farming、Forestry and Irrigation Affairs	151723	85603	66120
交通运输支出	Transport	28783	15735	13048
资源勘探信息等支出	Exploration and Information Affairs	10355	8612	1743
商业服务业等支出	Commerce and Services Affairs	3307	594	2713
金融支出	Financial Supervision Affairs	256	25	231
援助其他地区支出	Aid to Other Area	307	201	106
国土海洋气象等支出	Land and Weather Affairs	35129	23770	11359
住房保障支出	Housing Security Affairs	18258	10562	7696
粮油物资储备支出	Grain and Oil Reserves	906	347	559
国债还本付息支出	Pay Principle and Interest for Public Debt	7673	4561	3112
其他支出	Other　Expenditure	0	0	0
政府性基金支出	Government Funds Expenditure	426871	159135	267736
#城乡社区支出	Urban and Rural Community Affairs	419118	155081	264037

8-8 金融机构本外币各项存、贷款期末余额

The Ending Balance of all Deposits and Loans in RMB and Foreign Currencies of Financial Institutions

单位：万元 (10 000yuan)

指　标	Indicator	2016年	2017年	2018年
金融机构本外币各项存款余额	**The Balance of RMB and Foreign Currencies Deposits in Financial Institutions**	155374463	165605979	170601377
#住户存款	Household Deposits	43448420	45241390	50672701
非金融企业存款	Non-financial Corporate Deposits	69796525	73973987	72213088
广义政府存款	General Government Deposits	30738367	35586733	36530329
非银行业金融机构存款	Non-bank Financial Intermediary Deposits	8457783	7083306	6729522
金融机构本外币各项贷款余额	**The Balance of RMB and Foreign Currencies Loans in Financial Institutions**	130961411	143502995	160599213
#住户贷款	Household Loans	24694440	31418600	37617608
非金融企业及机关团体贷款	Non-financial Corporate and Institution Loans	90455320	98004377	109865593
短期贷款	Short-term Loans	27912544	30184576	29398790
中长期贷款	Medium and Long-term Loans	51574175	61606175	72421049
票据融资	Bill Financing	9670794	3896507	4995957
融资租赁	Finance Lease	1129383	2181289	2870478
各项垫款	Bill Financing	168425	135831	179319
非银行业金融机构贷款	Non-bank Financial Intermediary Loans	73	50000	0

8-9 金融机构人民币各项存、贷款期末余额

The Ending Balance of all Deposits and Loans in RMB of Financial Institutions

单位：万元 (10 000yuan)

指　标	Indicator	2016 年	2017 年	2018 年
金融机构人民币各项存款余额	**The Balance of RMB Deposits in Financial Institutions**	150327948	159577448	165718671
#住户存款	Household Deposits	42799454	44657303	50080833
非金融企业存款	Non-financial Corporate Deposits	68394947	72288512	70776618
广义政府存款	General Government Deposits	30735405	35426387	36493478
非银行业金融机构存款	Non-bank Financial Intermediary Deposits	8232449	6942272	6630358
金融机构人民币各项贷款余额	**The Balance of RMB Loans in Financial Institutions**	113701787	128836570	147000678
#住户贷款	Household Loans	24693431	31417225	37616195
非金融企业及机关团体贷款	Non-financial Corporate and Institution Loans	88019574	96407415	108452714
短期贷款	Short-term Loans	27188058	29297325	28659735
中长期贷款	Medium and Long-term Loans	49896069	60896806	71747225
票据融资	Bill Financing	9670794	3896507	4995957
融资租赁	Finance Lease	1129383	2181289	2870478
各项垫款	Bill Financing	135271	135488	179319
非银行业金融机构贷款	Non-bank Financial Intermediary Loans	0	50000	-

8-10 保险业务情况

Insurance Business

指 标	Indicator	2013 年	2014 年	2015 年	2016 年	2017 年	2018 年
承保额(亿元)	**Insurance Value(100 million yuan)**	32896	63675	97665	112875	162712	256399
企业财产险	Enterprise Property insurance	6749	17723	36178	26150	32210	37260
家庭财产险	Family Property Insurance	118	321	1744	1568	3825	7799
运输工具及责任险	Motor Vehicle and Third Party Liability	4613	10470	13920	14443	17555	36904
货物运输险	Freight Transport Insurance	480	2021	1955	2769	2227	2589
养老金险	Pension Insurance	442	1017	1800	7187	6758	4262
人身意外伤害险	Accident Injury Insurance	17495	24686	34112	43834	66079	125181
简易人身险	Simple Life Insurance	1033	3620	4239	10871	29390	32025
农业险	Agriculture Insurance	18	28	30	36	52	138
其他险	Other Property Insurance	1948	3788	3687	6017	4617	10242
保险业务收入(万元)	**Insurance Revenue(10 000yuan)**	1414715	1628650	2227474	3474988	3810660	4155535
企业财产险	Enterprise Property Insurance	29628	30479	42535	53352	53503	52896
家庭财产险	Family Property Insurance	595	726	1757	2761	4997	5115
运输工具及责任险	Motor Vehicle and Third Party Liability	334114	386898	487124	547370	538780	554548
货物运输险	Freight Transport Insurance	2458	3042	4260	4035	3359	3118
养老金险	Pension Insurance	714798	809083	1322141	1818536	2470364	2579988
人身意外伤害险	Accident Injury Insurance	75971	56249	74259	71613	78836	146634
简易人身险	Simple Life Insurance	88527	120282	245598	827557	574080	638398
农业险	Agriculture Insurance	6569	5527	9389	9036	11121	23767
其他险	Other Property Insurance	162054	216365	40411	140728	75619	151071
保险业务支出(万元)	**Insurance Expenses(10 000yuan)**	472811	529707	656570	786752	886699	1033980
企业财产险	Enterprise Property Insurance	4833	860	7184	8843	7488	8186
家庭财产险	Family Property Insurance	129	15	80	705	1542	1539
运输工具及责任险	Motor Vehicle and Third Party Liability	127747	17016	151723	187490	170705	138639
货物运输险	Freight Transport Insurance	1111	204	1954	3455	1437	934
养老金险	Pension Insurance	249865	451243	392111	426820	545380	702446
人身意外伤害险	Accident Injury Insurance	13571	7389	16613	16603	15393	19719
简易人身险	Simple Life Insurance	29783	47425	69165	101695	110349	124070
农业险	Agriculture Insurance	5587	218	1795	6021	5199	11603
其他险	Other Property Insurance	40186	5337	15946	35120	29207	26846

8-11　证券机构及证券交易情况

Institution and Trading Summary for Stocks

单位：亿元　　(100 million yuan)

指　　标	Indicator	2013 年	2014 年	2015 年	2016 年	2017 年	2018 年
注册地在济南证券公司数（个）	Stocks Institutions in Ji'nan(Unit)	1	1	1	1	1	1
证券营业部（个）	Securities Business Department(Unit)	60	72	78	83	92	87
证券交易额	Trading Volume of Securities Business Department	8863	16077	54575	34687	30975	28482
股　票	Stock	5566	10165	38091	19183	15987	12126
基　金	Fund	353	1044	4568	1449	2361	2111
债　券	Bond	47	4857	11899	14045	12602	14119
其　他	Others	2897	11	17	10	25	126

注：数据由金融办提供。

Note: Data are provided by the Municipal financial office

主要统计指标解释

一般公共预算收入　指国家财政参与社会产品分配所取得的收入，是实现国家职能的财力保证。主要包括：（1）各项税收：包括国内增值税、国内消费税、进口货物增值税和消费税、出口货物退增值税和消费税、营业税、企业所得税、个人所得税、资源税、城市维护建设税、房产税、印花税、城镇土地使用税、土地增值税、车船税、船舶吨税、车辆购置税、关税、耕地占用税、契税、烟叶税等。（2）非税收入：包括专项收入、行政事业性收费、罚没收入和其他收入。财政收入按现行分税制财政体制划分为中央本级收入和地方本级收入。

一般公共预算支出　指国家财政将筹集起来的资金进行分配使用，以满足经济建设和各项事业的需要。主要包括：一般公共服务、外交、国防、公共安全、教育、科学技术、文化体育与传媒、社会保障和就业、医疗卫生与计划生育、节能环保、城乡社区、农林水、交通运输、资源勘探信息等、商业服务业等、金融、援助其他地区、国土海洋气象等、住房保障、粮油物资储备、政府债务付息等方面的支出。财政支出根据政府在经济和社会活动中的不同职权，划分为中央财政支出和地方财政支出。

存款　指企业、机关、团体或居民根据资金必须收回的原则，把货币资金存入银行或其他信贷机构保管并取得一定利息的一种信用活动形式。根据存款对象或性质的不同可划分为企业存款、财政存款、机关团体存款、基本建设存款、储蓄存款、农村存款、委托存款、其他存款等科目。它是银行信贷资金的主要来源。

贷款　指银行或其他信贷机构根据资金必须归还的原则，按一定利率，为企业、个人等提供资金的一种信用活动形式。我国银行贷款分为短期贷款、中期流动资金贷款、中长期贷款、信托贷款、融资租赁、委托贷款、票据融资、各项垫款等。

保险金额　指保险人承担赔偿或者给付保险金责任的最高限额。

保费　指投保人为取得保险人在约定范围内所承担赔偿责任而支付给保险人的费用。

赔款　指保险人根据保险合同的规定，向被保险人支付的赔偿保险责任损失的金额。

给付　包括死伤医疗给付和满期给付。死伤医疗给付是指保险人根据人寿保险及长期健康保险合同的规定，因被保险人在保险期内发生保险责任范围内的保险事故支付给被保险人(或受益人)的金额。满期给付是指被保险人生存期满，保险人按人寿保险合同规定支付给被保险人的满期保险金额。

Explanatory Notes on Main Statistical Indicators

General Public Budget Revenue refers to the revenue of the government finance by means of participating in the distribution of the social products, which is the financial resources for ensuring the government to function. The contents of government revenue have been changed several times. Now it includes the following main items : (1) Various tax revenues: Include domestic value-added tax, domestic excise duty, value-added tax and consumption tax on imported goods, VAT refund and consumption tax on exports, business tax, corporate income tax, individual income tax, resource tax, urban maintenance and construction tax, building taxes, stamp duty, city and town land use tax, land value increment tax, vehicle and vessel tax, tonnage tax, vehicle purchase tax, tariff, farmland conversion tax, deed tax and tobacco taxes. (2) Non-tax revenues: Included in this category are special revenue, revenue from administrative and institutional fees, confiscated income and other income. Fiscal revenues are divided into revenue at the central level and local income pursuant to the current tax-sharing financial system.

General Public Budget Expenditure refers to the distribution and use of the funds the government finances has raised, so as to meet the needs of economic construction and various causes. It includes the following main items: expenditures regarding general public service, diplomacy, national defense, public security, education, science and technology, culture, sports and media, social security and employment, health care and family planning, energy conservation and environment protection, urban and rural communities, agroforestry water, transportation, resource exploration information, commercial service industry, finance, assistance to other areas, territorial marine meteorology, housing security, reserves of grain, oil and materials and payment of government debt interest, etc. Fiscal expenditure is divided into central fiscal expenditure and local fiscal expenditure in accordance with different function and power of government in economic and social activities.

Deposit is a form of credit by which enterprises, institutions, organizations or households can put money into banks and other credit institutions for safekeeping and interest earning under the principle of free withdrawal. According to different depositors, deposits are divided into enterprise deposits, treasury deposits, deposits of government agencies and organizations, capital construction deposits, savings deposits, rural saving deposits, entrusted deposits and other deposits. Deposits are major sources of the credit funds of banks.

Loan is a form of credit by which banks and other credit institutions provide funds at certain interest rate to enterprises and individuals in the light of the principle of unconditional repayment. Loans from Chinese Banks include circulating capital loans, fixed assets loans, loans to urban and rural individuals engaged in industrial and commercial business and agricultural loans.

Amount Insured refers to the maximum that the insurant will get for the claim of the case insured.

Premium is the fee paid by the insurant to the insurer to obtain the obligation of compensation from the insurance within the agreed terms.

Settled Claim is the compensation paid by the insurer to the insurant in accordance with the insurance contract.

Payment includes payment for death, injury or medical treatment and mature payment. Payment for death, injury or medical treatment refers to the money paid to the insurant (or the beneficiary) in accordance with the life or health insurance contract when the insurant encounters accidents within the insured period covered in the contract. Mature payment refers to the mature payment to the insurant in accordance with the life insurance contract at the end of the insured period.

物 价

PRICE

9-1 主要年份物价指数（以上年价格为 100）

Price Indices of Major Years（Preceding Last Year=100）

年份 Year	居民消费价格指数 Consumer Price Index	#食品 Food	#服务项目 Services	零售物价指数 Retail Price Index
1951	108.5	105.3	98.7	109.8
1952	101.5	103.9	101.0	101.2
1955	101.6	101.3	103.4	101.4
1956	100.5	100.7	100.6	100.5
1965	107.3	111.5	97.5	108.0
1970	98.4	99.0	100.0	98.3
1971	100.0	100.5	100.0	100.0
1972	100.1	100.3	100.0	100.1
1973	99.5	99.6	97.9	99.7
1974	99.4	99.1	99.9	99.5
1975	100.2	100.0	100.0	100.2
1976	100.4	100.0	100.0	100.4
1977	99.2	99.9	91.2	100.0
1978	100.3	100.3	100.0	100.3
1979	101.1	101.7	100.5	101.1
1980	104.7	107.9	100.0	105.0
1981	101.9	102.2	100.1	102.0
1982	101.1	101.6	100.3	101.2
1983	100.1	100.3	100.9	100.1
1984	101.9	101.1	109.8	101.3
1985	108.7	112.2	103.3	109.1
1986	106.2	107.6	104.9	106.3
1987	109.5	111.9	104.9	109.8
1988	122.4	128.0	108.8	123.4
1989	116.2	111.2	113.5	116.4
1990	103.3	102.6	108.0	103.0

年份 Year	居民消费价格指数 Consumer Price Index	#食品 Food	#服务项目 Services	零售物价指数 Retail Price Index
1991	106.7	107.6	106.9	106.7
1992	110.4	108.7	122.2	109.3
1993	114.7	109.8	138.0	112.1
1994	124.8	133.9	114.5	122.7
1995	117.3	123.0	115.1	113.2
1996	109.1	109.7	116.2	106.3
1997	102.9	101.8	107.8	101.5
1998	100.9	99.4	119.0	98.9
1999	99.1	97.3	127.6	96.9
2000	100.6	97.9	129.0	98.0
2001	100.3	100.8	106.1	98.8
2002	98.8	100.2	101.3	97.8
2003	99.9	103.6	100.3	98.0
2004	102.5	107.4	101.2	100.6
2005	101.1	102.7	101.2	100.4
2006	100.9	102.4	100.9	100.3
2007	103.9	111.6	101.8	102.2
2008	105.7	115.5	101.8	104.5
2009	100.3	102.7	102.4	98.7
2010	102.1	107.3	100.6	101.3
2011	105.4	111.3	104.4	104.6
2012	102.4	103.6	102.2	101.8
2013	102.8	104.9	102.7	101.3
2014	102.2	103.2	102.9	101.2
2015	101.9	101.4	101.6	100.3
2016	102.7	103.9	103.5	100.8
2017	102.0	98.5	104.2	101.0
2018	102.6	102.8	102.1	102.6

9-2 主要年份物价指数（以1950年价格为100）

Price Indices of Major Years（Preceding 1950=100）

年份 Yaer	居民消费价格指数 Consumer Price Index	#食品 Food	#服务项目 Services	零售物价指数 Retail Price Index
1951	108.5	105.3	98.7	109.8
1952	110.1	109.4	103.7	111.1
1955	117.2	123.7	108.2	118.4
1956	117.8	124.6	108.8	119.0
1965	127.7	141.5	116.9	130.7
1970	123.0	141.6	110.1	126.0
1971	123.0	142.3	110.1	126.0
1972	123.1	142.7	110.1	126.1
1973	122.5	142.1	107.8	125.8
1974	121.8	140.9	107.7	125.1
1975	122.0	140.9	107.7	125.4
1976	122.5	140.9	107.7	125.9
1977	121.5	140.7	98.2	125.9
1978	121.9	141.1	98.2	126.3
1979	123.2	143.5	98.6	127.6
1980	129.0	154.9	98.6	134.0
1981	131.5	158.3	98.7	136.7
1982	132.9	160.8	99.0	138.3
1983	133.0	161.3	99.9	138.5
1984	135.6	163.1	109.7	140.3
1985	147.4	183.0	113.3	153.0
1986	156.5	195.8	118.9	162.7
1987	171.4	219.1	124.7	178.6
1988	209.8	280.4	135.7	220.4
1989	234.8	311.8	154.0	256.5
1990	251.8	319.9	166.3	264.2

年份 Yaer	居民消费价格指数 Consumer Price Index	#食品 Food	#服务项目 Services	零售物价指数 Retail Price Index
1991	268.7	344.2	177.8	281.9
1992	296.6	376.2	217.3	308.1
1993	340.2	413.1	299.8	345.4
1994	424.6	570.4	343.3	423.8
1995	498.1	709.7	395.1	479.7
1996	543.4	797.7	459.1	509.9
1997	559.2	782.5	494.9	551.6
1998	564.2	777.8	588.9	545.5
1999	559.1	756.8	751.4	528.6
2000	562.4	740.9	969.3	518.0
2001	564.1	746.8	1028.4	511.8
2002	557.3	748.3	1041.8	500.5
2003	556.7	775.2	1044.9	490.5
2004	570.6	832.6	1057.4	493.4
2005	576.9	855.1	1070.1	495.4
2006	582.1	875.6	1079.7	496.9
2007	604.8	977.2	1099.1	507.8
2008	639.3	1128.7	1118.9	530.7
2009	641.2	1159.2	1145.8	523.8
2010	654.7	1243.8	1152.7	530.6
2011	690.2	1384.7	1203.1	555.1
2012	706.8	1434.5	1229.5	565.1
2013	726.6	1504.8	1262.7	572.4
2014	742.6	1553.0	1299.3	579.3
2015	756.7	1574.7	1320.1	581.0
2016	777.1	1636.1	1366.3	585.6
2017	792.6	1611.6	1423.7	591.5
2018	813.3	1656.7	1453.6	606.8

9-3 分月居民消费价格指数

Consumer Price Indices by Month

指　　标	Indicator	全年 Total	一月 January	二月 February	三月 March	四月 April
居民消费价格总指数	Consumer Price Index	102.6	101.4	103.1	102.5	102.4
非食品烟酒价格指数	Non-food,tobacco and alcohol Price Index	102.3	102.5	102.6	102.3	102.1
服务价格指数	Services Price Index	102.1	103.3	104.2	102.7	102.0
工业品价格指数	Industrial Products Price Index	102.6	101.5	100.8	101.8	102.2
消费品价格指数	Consumer Goods Price Index	102.9	100.3	102.5	102.4	102.6
扣除食品和能源价格指数	Excluding Food and Energy Price Index	102.3	102.5	102.6	102.4	102.2
一、食品烟酒	Food,Tobacco and Liquor	103.2	98.9	104.3	103.1	103.1
1.食品	Food	102.8	97.0	105.1	102.8	102.8
(1)粮食	Grain	100.9	101.2	101.9	101.6	101.0
(2)薯类	Tuber	115.1	107.2	117.5	119.0	105.5
(3)豆类	Beans	111.1	107.1	106.9	114.9	111.0
(4)食用油	Edible Oil	101.0	100.9	100.9	99.9	100.8
食用植物油	Edible Vegetable Oil	101.4	101.4	101.4	100.3	101.4
(5)菜	Vegetables	116.1	82.9	124.4	118.3	125.6
鲜　菜	Fresh Vegetables	117.1	81.3	125.7	119.4	127.5
(6)畜肉类	Livestock Meat	95.4	92.2	94.1	90.8	89.5
猪　肉	Pork	91.9	86.9	90.3	85.7	83.6
(7)禽肉类	Poultry	107.7	105.8	104.7	108.3	105.1
(8)水产品	Aquatic Products	102.9	105.8	110.3	108.7	105.8
(9)蛋类	Eggs	114.3	115.7	125.5	117.7	118.0
鸡　蛋	Hen's Eggs	116.8	120.3	133.2	123.6	124.0
(10)奶类	Milk	102.6	103.7	102.6	101.8	103.8
(11)干鲜瓜果类	Dried and Fresh Melons and Fruits	100.0	97.6	102.9	101.8	101.9
鲜 瓜 果	Fresh Melons and Fruits	100.3	97.1	103.8	101.6	102.4
(12)糖果糕点类	Candy and Cakes	104.4	101.2	100.9	100.8	104.6
(13)调味品	Condiment	105.3	105.7	105.5	107.6	105.4
(14)其他食品类	Other Foods	98.7	97.8	99.4	100.9	99.4
2.茶及饮料	Tea and Beverages	100.6	100.2	99.9	99.6	99.8
3.烟酒	Tobacco and Liquor	103.8	102.9	102.6	102.8	103.2
(1)烟草	Tobacco	100.0	99.9	100.0	100.0	100.0
(2)酒类	Liquor	108.4	106.6	105.8	106.2	107.1
4.在外餐饮	Outside Catering	104.5	102.8	103.5	104.3	104.2
二、衣着	Clothing	103.8	103.0	102.8	103.6	104.1
1.服装	Garments	104.9	104.5	104.5	104.8	105.1
(1)男式服装	Men's Clothing	103.4	102.7	103.0	103.7	104.0
(2)女式服装	Women's Clothing	106.0	107.1	106.9	106.4	105.8
(3)儿童服装	Children's Clothing	104.5	99.1	99.5	101.5	105.3
2.服装材料	Clothing Material	107.9	105.0	106.4	106.4	106.4

（2018 年，以上年同期价格为 100）

（2018，Preceding Last Year=100）

五月 May	六月 June	七月 July	八月 August	九月 September	十月 October	十一月 November	十二月 December
102.6	102.6	102.4	102.9	103.2	103.2	102.4	102.2
102.4	102.6	102.4	102.4	102.3	102.5	102.2	101.5
102.1	101.9	101.6	101.7	101.5	101.7	101.4	101.0
102.8	103.5	103.4	103.3	103.3	103.5	103.1	102.1
102.9	103.1	103.0	103.7	104.3	104.2	103.0	102.9
102.4	102.5	102.3	102.4	102.3	102.3	102.0	101.8
103.1	102.6	102.5	104.1	105.5	105.0	102.8	103.9
102.6	101.8	101.3	103.7	105.9	105.1	102.3	103.9
101.4	101.7	100.1	98.3	99.8	100.9	101.8	101.6
129.0	130.0	117.3	117.1	112.7	103.0	108.8	114.0
112.9	112.8	114.3	113.4	113.0	114.1	109.3	104.4
101.0	98.8	101.1	101.1	100.2	102.3	102.0	102.6
101.6	99.2	101.6	101.5	100.8	102.9	102.4	102.9
132.5	117.4	108.8	115.7	129.3	121.1	109.8	120.7
135.6	118.7	109.1	116.6	131.4	122.5	110.6	122.6
91.0	93.8	95.3	100.8	101.2	100.7	99.0	97.1
85.7	88.9	91.9	99.8	100.3	100.2	97.3	94.9
109.6	108.9	107.2	105.4	105.6	108.3	111.4	112.2
104.6	101.4	98.8	99.4	100.7	99.4	100.1	100.8
123.1	115.5	113.8	113.2	108.3	110.9	109.9	105.5
130.4	119.8	117.3	114.0	107.4	110.1	109.2	103.5
104.0	103.3	103.6	101.7	102.1	102.5	101.9	100.5
92.1	95.8	99.8	101.0	104.2	105.4	96.2	103.8
89.7	95.4	100.7	102.7	106.6	107.9	94.6	105.2
105.4	104.5	104.1	106.0	105.6	106.6	107.4	105.9
103.9	103.3	103.8	102.9	105.4	107.5	105.6	107.1
99.5	98.6	97.3	98.6	97.4	97.2	98.7	99.4
100.3	100.5	100.3	100.7	100.9	101.5	102.0	101.4
103.9	104.1	104.0	104.7	104.6	104.5	104.2	104.0
100.0	100.0	100.0	100.0	100.0	100.0	100.0	100.0
108.6	109.1	108.9	110.2	110.0	109.8	109.1	108.7
104.4	104.4	105.3	105.6	105.7	105.6	103.8	104.2
105.2	105.3	104.3	103.9	104.1	103.2	103.0	102.7
106.1	106.6	106.0	105.3	105.2	103.6	103.7	103.2
105.0	105.2	104.1	103.4	102.9	101.5	103.6	101.4
107.0	107.6	107.3	106.6	106.5	104.4	103.4	103.9
105.7	106.4	106.2	105.5	106.8	106.7	105.7	105.5
108.2	109.8	109.8	106.8	109.6	109.6	109.3	107.8

指　　标	Indicator	全 年 Total	一月 January	二月 February	三月 March	四月 April
3.其他衣着及配件	Other Clothing and Accessories	101.5	101.7	101.5	101.3	101.3
4.衣着加工服务费	Clothing processing service fee	110.0	110.9	110.3	110.3	110.3
5.鞋类	Footwear	100.2	98.1	97.0	99.8	101.0
(1)鞋	Shoes	100.3	98.4	97.3	100.1	101.4
(2)鞋类加工服务	Footwear Processing Services	90.3	81.6	81.6	81.6	81.6
三、居住	Residence	103.5	105.3	104.7	104.5	104.0
1.租赁房房租	Rental Housing Rent	102.0	105.9	102.1	102.8	102.3
2.住房保养维修及管理	Housing Maintenance	101.5	100.9	100.9	101.4	101.5
(1)住房装潢材料	Housing Decoration Materials	103.9	102.4	102.5	103.6	103.8
(2)物业管理费	Property Management Fee	100.0	100.0	100.0	100.0	100.0
(3)住房装潢维修	Housing Decoration Maintenance	99.7	99.7	99.7	99.7	99.7
3.水电燃料	Water, Electricity and Fuels	100.6	100.0	100.3	100.5	100.5
(1)水	Water	100.0	100.0	100.0	100.0	100.0
(2)电	Electricity	100.0	100.0	100.0	100.0	100.0
(3)燃气	Gas	101.3	100.0	100.0	100.0	100.0
(4)取暖费	Heating Fee	100.0	100.0	100.0	100.0	100.0
(5)其他燃料	Other Fuel	106.7	100.0	105.9	108.8	108.8
4.自有住房	Self-owned House	105.4	108.8	108.0	107.2	106.3
四、生活用品及服务	Daily Necessities and Services	100.6	100.4	99.1	99.0	99.1
1.家具及室内装饰品	Furniture and Interior Decorations	102.4	104.0	102.3	101.0	101.7
(1)家具	Furniture and Interior Decorations	101.9	105.1	102.9	101.0	101.9
(2)室内装饰品	Interior Decorations	104.1	100.1	100.1	101.0	101.2
2.家用器具	Household Appliances	97.1	96.0	94.3	96.0	95.5
(1)大型家用器具	Large Household Appliances	97.2	95.8	94.0	95.9	95.3
(2)小家电	Small Household Appliances	96.6	97.1	95.9	96.7	96.2
3.家用纺织品	Home Textiles	105.3	101.6	101.7	101.6	100.5
(1)床上用品	Bedding Article	105.6	101.7	101.9	101.7	100.5
(2)窗帘门帘	Curtain	102.5	100.5	100.5	100.2	100.0
(3)其他家用纺织品	Other Household Textiles	105.8	101.6	101.7	101.6	101.2
4.家庭日用杂品	The Family Daily Sundry Goods	99.9	99.6	99.2	98.9	98.3
(1)洗涤卫生用品	Washing Sanitary Articles	100.4	99.0	98.8	98.5	98.7
(2)厨具餐具茶具	Kitchenware, Tableware, Tea Set	99.0	100.1	98.5	98.7	96.2
(3)家用手工工具	Home Hand Tools	98.3	100.0	100.0	100.0	100.0
(4)其他家庭日用杂品	Other Household Articles For Daily Use	99.6	101.0	101.2	100.0	98.5
5.个人护理用品	Personal Care Products	101.0	102.2	101.6	99.5	99.5
(1)化妆品	Cosmetics	100.3	100.5	100.3	96.9	97.7
(2)其他护理用品类	Other Nursing Products	101.7	104.0	103.0	102.1	101.4
6.家庭服务	Family Services	102.4	102.4	99.3	100.3	102.9
五、交通和通信	Transport and Communication	102.1	99.1	100.9	100.2	101.6
1.交通	Transport	103.3	99.4	102.3	101.1	102.8
(1)交通工具	Transport Tools	96.9	97.1	97.0	97.5	98.9

五月 May	六月 June	七月 July	八月 August	九月 September	十月 October	十一月 November	十二月 December
101.3	101.3	100.5	100.6	101.7	101.7	101.9	103.8
110.3	110.3	110.3	110.3	110.3	110.3	108.1	108.8
102.7	101.5	99.3	99.8	100.5	101.6	100.4	100.2
103.0	101.8	99.5	99.8	100.5	101.7	100.3	100.1
81.6	81.6	89.4	100.0	100.0	100.0	108.3	108.3
103.8	103.9	103.4	102.8	102.5	102.4	102.4	102.2
103.5	103.2	101.7	100.0	101.5	101.3	100.5	100.1
101.7	101.7	101.8	101.8	101.9	101.8	101.1	101.4
104.5	104.3	104.6	104.6	104.8	104.5	103.8	103.5
100.0	100.0	100.0	100.0	100.0	100.0	100.0	100.0
99.7	99.7	99.7	99.7	99.7	99.7	98.8	99.7
100.2	100.2	100.0	100.0	100.0	100.7	102.3	102.0
100.0	100.0	100.0	100.0	100.0	100.0	100.0	100.0
100.0	100.0	100.0	100.0	100.0	100.0	100.0	100.0
100.0	100.0	100.0	100.0	100.0	100.0	107.5	107.5
100.0	100.0	100.0	100.0	100.0	100.0	100.0	100.0
104.4	104.4	100.7	100.7	100.7	112.7	119.2	113.7
105.9	106.1	105.4	104.6	103.9	103.3	103.0	102.6
99.6	100.4	100.6	101.4	101.6	102.0	102.0	102.1
101.0	101.4	101.4	103.3	103.6	107.0	101.5	101.2
101.0	101.0	101.0	101.6	101.6	105.9	100.4	100.0
100.9	102.7	102.7	109.2	110.7	110.7	105.3	105.2
95.9	96.7	97.6	97.6	98.1	97.5	99.6	100.1
96.2	96.9	97.8	97.7	98.2	97.8	99.8	100.8
94.9	96.1	96.3	97.2	97.3	96.3	98.5	96.9
103.2	108.0	106.3	108.5	108.4	106.5	108.6	108.9
102.7	108.3	106.3	108.8	108.7	106.9	109.6	109.4
103.6	103.6	103.6	103.6	103.6	103.6	103.2	103.2
109.4	109.4	109.2	109.7	110.4	103.9	102.5	108.9
99.3	99.4	100.2	101.7	100.4	100.6	100.9	100.6
100.1	99.9	100.6	103.3	101.6	101.8	101.8	100.9
96.7	98.2	98.5	99.9	100.7	100.1	100.3	100.4
100.0	100.0	100.0	95.9	95.9	95.9	95.9	95.9
99.1	98.9	100.5	99.4	97.6	98.1	99.9	101.0
99.4	100.0	100.0	99.3	101.4	101.9	103.2	103.7
97.9	98.1	98.7	98.0	102.1	102.1	104.9	106.5
100.9	102.1	101.3	100.5	100.6	101.7	101.5	100.9
102.9	102.9	102.9	102.9	102.9	102.9	102.9	102.9
102.7	103.3	103.6	103.4	103.0	104.5	102.7	99.7
104.4	105.1	105.9	105.2	104.6	106.9	103.4	98.6
98.8	98.2	97.5	97.0	95.2	97.0	94.8	93.6

指 标	Indicator	全 年 Total	一月 January	二月 February	三月 March	四月 April
(2)交通工具用燃料	Transport Fuels	112.9	106.4	106.6	104.4	108.8
(3)交通工具使用和维修	Vehicle Use and Maintenance	111.3	103.0	112.0	112.0	112.7
(4)交通费	Travelling Expenses	101.0	91.2	106.2	99.1	97.2
2.通信	Signal Communication	99.9	98.6	98.6	98.8	99.6
(1)通信工具	Communication Tools	98.9	91.4	91.2	92.3	96.9
(2)通信服务	Communication Services	100.0	100.0	100.0	100.0	100.0
(3)邮递服务	Mailing Service	102.3	102.8	102.8	102.8	102.8
六、教育文化和娱乐	**Education Culture and Recreation**	99.6	101.7	103.6	99.8	98.5
1.教育	Education	103.3	102.7	102.6	103.1	102.7
(1)教育用品	Educational Supplies	101.1	105.4	101.0	101.1	101.1
(2)教育服务	Education Services	103.4	102.6	102.6	103.2	102.7
2.文化娱乐	Culture and Entertainment	96.3	100.7	104.5	96.9	94.8
(1)文娱耐用消费品	Recreational Consumer Durables	98.5	101.2	98.2	97.2	96.0
(2)其他文娱用品	Other Entertainment Products	101.7	101.0	100.8	101.4	101.6
(3)文化娱乐服务	Cultural and Recreational Services	100.9	101.2	101.6	103.6	103.1
(4)旅游	Tourism	92.7	100.2	108.4	93.3	90.0
七、医疗保健	**Health Care**	104.7	102.5	102.3	105.3	104.9
1.药品及医疗器具	Drugs and Medical Devices	109.4	105.3	104.8	111.2	110.2
(1)中药	Traditional Chinese Medicine	106.0	103.0	103.1	106.4	105.1
(2)西药	West Medicine	117.8	111.9	109.7	119.1	118.9
(3)滋补保健品	Western Medicine	100.8	98.8	100.2	103.9	102.1
(4)医疗卫生器具	Medical and Health Equipment	103.0	101.4	101.4	106.1	104.2
(5)保健器具	Healthcare Apparatus	105.3	99.2	99.2	106.8	106.9
2.医疗服务	Medical Services	100.3	100.0	100.0	100.0	100.0
(1)综合医疗类	Comprehensive Health Care	101.3	100.0	100.0	100.0	100.0
(2)诊断类	Diagnostic	100.0	100.0	100.0	100.0	100.0
(3)治疗类	Therapeutic	100.0	100.0	100.0	100.0	100.0
(4)康复类	Rehabilitation	100.0	100.0	100.0	100.0	100.0
(5)中医医疗服务类	Chinese Medicine Services	100.0	100.0	100.0	100.0	100.0
(6)其他医疗服务	Other Medical Services	100.0	100.0	100.0	100.0	100.0
八、其他用品和服务	**Other Supplies and Services**	99.6	101.2	98.3	99.2	98.7
1.其他用品类	Other Products	98.3	102.2	95.7	97.9	96.7
(1)首饰手表	Jewelry Watches	97.6	102.2	94.1	97.7	95.9
(2)其他杂项用品	Other Miscellaneous Supplies	100.4	101.9	100.5	98.4	99.4
2.其他服务类	Other Services	100.9	100.4	100.8	100.5	100.7
(1)旅馆住宿	Hotel Accommodation	101.4	96.8	96.8	96.8	98.4
(2)美容美发洗浴	Hairdressing Bath	101.2	102.3	104.0	103.1	103.1
(3)养老服务	Pension Services	103.6	100.0	100.0	100.0	100.0
(4)金融保险	Finance and Insurance	100.0	100.0	100.0	100.0	100.0
(5)其他服务类	Other Service	102.7	100.0	100.0	98.7	98.7

五月 May	六月 June	七月 July	八月 August	九月 September	十月 October	十一月 November	十二月 December
113.7	118.1	122.6	119.8	121.2	122.4	112.8	99.6
112.7	112.7	112.7	111.8	110.8	110.8	112.4	112.4
99.8	98.2	98.7	100.9	100.6	107.6	108.8	105.4
99.7	100.3	99.7	100.2	100.1	100.4	101.4	101.7
97.7	101.0	97.7	100.0	99.9	101.2	108.1	110.1
100.0	100.0	100.0	100.0	100.0	100.0	100.0	100.0
102.8	102.8	102.8	102.8	102.8	102.8	100.0	100.0
99.0	98.1	98.4	99.5	99.8	99.7	99.3	98.5
103.6	103.6	103.6	104.1	103.7	103.5	103.6	102.9
101.3	101.3	101.3	101.2	100.0	100.0	99.9	100.3
103.7	103.7	103.7	104.2	103.8	103.7	103.7	103.0
94.9	93.3	93.6	95.3	96.2	96.2	95.2	94.4
96.8	97.5	98.7	97.9	99.2	98.9	100.7	100.3
100.3	99.9	99.8	101.8	103.8	104.1	102.5	103.6
104.3	99.6	100.5	99.7	100.1	98.6	99.7	99.2
89.8	88.3	88.3	91.5	92.1	92.5	90.3	88.7
104.3	105.4	105.5	105.5	105.2	105.1	104.9	105.3
108.9	111.2	111.4	111.4	110.8	109.3	108.9	109.3
105.1	105.1	107.6	107.2	107.2	105.8	107.6	108.5
117.3	120.5	120.3	120.2	120.9	119.0	117.2	117.4
99.7	102.2	101.5	102.0	100.0	99.7	99.7	100.2
102.8	105.0	105.0	105.0	101.4	101.4	101.4	101.4
110.0	110.0	110.0	110.1	110.1	100.2	100.2	100.9
100.0	100.0	100.0	100.0	100.0	101.2	101.2	101.4
100.0	100.0	100.0	100.0	100.0	105.0	105.0	106.1
100.0	100.0	100.0	100.0	100.0	100.0	100.0	100.0
100.0	100.0	100.0	100.0	100.0	100.0	100.0	100.0
100.0	100.0	100.0	100.0	100.0	100.0	100.0	100.0
100.0	100.0	100.0	100.0	100.0	100.0	100.0	100.0
100.0	100.0	100.0	100.0	100.0	100.0	100.0	100.0
99.3	99.3	98.8	98.4	99.0	100.0	101.4	101.5
97.2	97.4	98.0	97.2	97.9	99.0	100.2	100.4
96.4	96.5	97.3	96.3	97.0	98.0	99.5	100.6
99.7	100.2	99.9	100.0	100.6	102.1	102.2	99.8
101.3	101.2	99.6	99.5	100.2	101.1	102.6	102.6
104.5	103.6	100.5	99.8	102.3	110.6	102.0	106.0
103.1	103.1	98.8	98.8	100.0	100.0	100.0	98.6
100.0	100.0	100.0	100.0	100.0	100.0	121.7	121.7
100.0	100.0	100.0	100.0	100.0	100.0	100.0	100.0
98.7	98.7	98.7	98.7	98.7	98.7	121.4	121.4

9-4 主要年份零售商品

Per Retail and Services

商品名称	Name	规格等级牌号 Grade	单位 Unit	1978年	1980年	1985年	1990年
面粉	Flour	特一	元/千克(yuan/kg)	0.50	0.50	0.50	0.50
粳米	Japonica	标一	元/千克(yuan/kg)	0.34	0.34	0.40	1.04
小米	Millet	一等	元/千克(yuan/kg)	0.27	0.27	0.44	1.32
土豆	Potato		元/千克(yuan/kg)	0.19	0.22	0.30	0.36
豆腐	Doufu	水豆腐	元/千克(yuan/kg)	0.16	0.18	0.26	0.70
猪肉	Pork	净肉	元/千克(yuan/kg)	1.72	1.95	2.65	5.52
牛肉	Beef	净肉	元/千克(yuan/kg)	1.26	1.76	2.91	5.43
羊肉	Mutton	净肉	元/千克(yuan/kg)	1.38	1.88	2.80	5.91
鸡蛋	Hen's Egg	新鲜完整	元/千克(yuan/kg)	1.58	2.20	2.60	4.96
海带	Kelp	盐干一级	元/千克(yuan/kg)	1.18	1.26	1.32	3.60
大白菜	Chinese Cabbage	一等	元/千克(yuan/kg)	0.11	0.07	0.09	0.13
菠菜	Spinage	一等	元/千克(yuan/kg)	0.08	0.09	0.28	0.50
油菜	Oilseed rape	一等	元/千克(yuan/kg)	0.05	0.07	0.26	0.63
芹菜	Celery	一等	元/千克(yuan/kg)	1.13	0.11	0.39	0.60
韭菜	Chinese Chives	一等	元/千克(yuan/kg)	0.15	0.16	0.54	1.01
黄瓜	Cucumber	一等	元/千克(yuan/kg)	0.19	0.18	0.47	0.99
西红柿	Tomato	一等	元/千克(yuan/kg)	0.15	0.18	0.53	1.02
茄子	Eggplant	一等	元/千克(yuan/kg)	0.14	0.11	0.27	0.89
青椒	Green Pepper	一等	元/千克(yuan/kg)	0.23	0.20	0.47	1.34
大葱	Allium Fistulosum	一等	元/千克(yuan/kg)	0.11	0.12	0.28	0.54
黑木耳	Black Fungus	甲级	元/千克(yuan/kg)	30.00	32.00	34.86	48.95

和服务项目年平均价格

Price of Major Years

1995 年	2000 年	2005 年	2010 年	2013 年	2014 年	2015 年	2016 年	2017 年	2018 年
2.24	1.78	2.86	4.14	5.07	5.41	5.43	5.46	5.64	8.54
3.33	2.03	3.08	4.76	5.91	5.91	6.04	6.05	6.00	6.06
2.66	2.07	3.26	6.99	8.58	14.10	14.63	10.51	11.49	10.87
1.48	1.48	1.92	4.53	3.61	3.72	3.80	3.84	3.53	3.84
1.43	1.55	2.14	4.31	5.21	5.99	6.24	5.97	5.88	6.11
12.91	12.87	14.90	25.18	33.04	30.57	32.37	35.78	35.49	32.88
12.06	10.99	16.34	36.47	64.52	65.00	66.58	69.02	69.46	69.25
15.49	15.04	22.07	44.80	75.33	79.23	76.29	76.85	69.67	79.86
5.99	3.99	5.72	7.48	8.52	10.87	9.25	8.41	8.18	9.75
5.35	5.36	8.76	19.29	30.35	33.43	32.50	28.87	27.15	25.51
0.72	0.91	1.64	3.23	2.77	2.29	2.84	2.80	2.41	2.93
0.90	1.57	2.21	6.69	7.61	6.53	7.91	8.53	7.41	8.81
1.11	1.26	1.83	5.05	5.84	5.17	6.43	7.14	6.08	7.46
1.22	1.25	2.28	4.99	5.46	4.07	5.62	5.06	5.13	5.68
1.80	1.98	2.99	6.55	7.05	6.47	7.42	5.33	4.97	5.59
2.45	2.53	3.16	5.67	6.26	5.36	5.96	6.03	5.67	7.53
2.66	2.07	2.90	6.01	6.60	6.37	7.02	6.97	7.24	7.69
2.67	2.51	3.07	6.05	6.34	5.60	6.14	6.66	6.14	7.48
4.13	3.15	4.10	6.45	7.48	6.38	8.07	7.61	7.00	9.03
1.46	1.31	2.51	6.16	6.95	5.94	6.56	9.59	6.44	6.19
59.16	68.57	65.13	86.80	121.45	128.14	122.59	118.11	122.67	128.34

9-4 续 1

商品名称	Name	规格等级牌号 Grade	单位 Unit	1978 年	1980 年	1985 年	1990 年
精 盐	Salt	再制盐	元/千克(yuan/500g)	0.16	0.16	0.14	0.31
酱 油	Soy Sauce	二 级	元/千克(yuan/kg)	0.22	0.22	0.34	0.68
味 精	Aginomoto	含麸酸钠 80%以上	元/千克(yuan/kg)	10.80	9.68	12.60	16.50
绵白糖	Soft Sugar	国产机制一级	元/千克(yuan/kg)	1.60	1.70	1.70	2.60
红 糖	Brown Sugar	一 级	元/千克(yuan/kg)	1.30	1.30	1.30	2.21
啤 酒	Beer	熟 12 度瓶装	元/瓶(yuan/unit)	0.58	0.58	0.73	1.41
苹 果	Apple	一 级	元/千克(yuan/kg)	0.82	0.90	1.19	2.48
桔 子	Orange	一 级	元/千克(yuan/kg)	1.30	1.52	2.35	2.27
西 瓜	watermelon	一 级	元/千克(yuan/kg)	0.24	0.28	0.32	0.58
香 蕉	Banana	一 级	元/千克(yuan/kg)	1.46	1.65	1.82	2.93
自来水	Tap Water	生活用水	元/吨(yuan/tons)	0.08	0.08	0.09	0.19
照明用电	Lighting Electricity	民用 220V	元/度(yuan/kwh)	0.18	0.18	0.18	0.18
平 信	Ordinary Mail	外 埠	元/封(yuan/unit)	0.08	0.08	0.08	0.13
注射费	Injection Fees	肌肉注射	元/次(yuan/unit)	0.10	0.10	0.10	0.20
住院费	Hospitalization Fees	普通床位	元/天(yuan/day)				2.50
学杂费	Tuition and Fees	高中学生	元/学期(yuan/semester)	2.50	2.50	2.50	12.00
公园门票	Park Tickets	大明湖	元/张(yuan/unit)	0.03	0.03	0.03	0.30
理 发	Haircut	男理一级全活	元/次(yuan/unit)	0.30	0.30	0.45	1.30
洗 澡	Bath		元/次(yuan/unit)	0.24	0.24	0.30	0.58
课 本	Textbook	高中语文一年级	元/本(yuan/unit)				2.00
银 花	Silver	一 等	元/千克(yuan/kg)	6.65	8.00	18.00	28.00

注：1、大明湖景区 2017 年开始免费入园
2、由于居民消费价格是指数比较，所以理发和洗澡所选的规格品与上年不一致，绝对价格无可比性

1995 年	2000 年	2005 年	2010 年	2013 年	2014 年	2015 年	2016 年	2017 年	2018 年
0.70	1.10	2.02	1.50	3.83	3.84	4.28	5.17	5.97	6.18
1.83	2.40	4.53	6.74	7.04	6.75	6.61	7.14	7.05	8.69
22.81	14.26	15.67	19.33	21.02	21.34	22.19	21.94	22.56	22.92
6.89	6.12	5.43	9.75	15.15	15.89	16.08	14.38	14.25	15.39
6.32	5.90	5.54	9.80	15.62	15.54	14.70	15.68	18.29	21.07
2.13	2.30	2.42	2.61	2.68	2.77	2.76	2.72	2.49	2.62
3.86	2.72	3.19	8.93	12.04	14.96	15.11	10.86	11.86	11.85
3.37	2.35	3.30	7.45	10.29	11.97	9.06	10.72	13.86	11.96
3.20	2.70	3.06	4.72	5.56	5.88	5.57	5.16	5.60	5.26
4.78	4.05	4.02	6.39	7.28	9.70	7.01	7.04	6.63	8.24
0.51	1.60	2.78	3.15	3.15	3.15	4.00	4.21	4.21	4.21
0.29	0.43	0.53	0.55	0.55	0.56	0.56	0.56	0.56	0.56
0.20	0.80	0.80	1.20	1.20	1.20	1.20	1.20	1.20	1.20
0.25	1.67	2.00	2.00	2.00	2.00	2.00	2.00	2.00	2.00
4.00	7.67	15.00	26.67	26.67	23.33	23.33	33.89	36.67	36.67
49.00	600.00	800.00	800.00	800.00	800.00	800.00	800.00	800.00	800.00
4.33	13.48	15.63	30.00	30.00	30.00	30.00	30.00		
5.63	10.00	17.50	20.50	25.00	25.21	25.21	32.38	25.10	27.70
5.00	8.00	12.00	30.00	38.00	53.00	58.00	58.00	68.00	68.00
2.55	6.41	4.60	6.47	6.47	6.47	6.47	6.47	6.44	6.39
70.00	93.00	87.22	325.00	314.10	361.17	352.71	325.00	324.39	403.83

Note: 1. Daming Lake Scenic spot has been free since 2017.
2. Because the consumer price of residents is an index comparison, the standard products selected for haircut and bath are inconsistent with the previous year, and the absolute price is incomparable.

9-5 工业生产者出厂价格总指数

Producer Price Index for Manufactured Goods

项目名称	Indicator	1月 January	2月 February	3月 March	4月 April
总指数	Total Price Indices	101.1	100.1	99.8	100.2
核心指数	Core Indices	101.2	100.0	100.0	100.1
高技术	High Technology	99.7	100.1	100.1	101.0
能源	Energy	101.4	101.2	97.9	101.5
㈠按轻重工业分	By Light and Heavy Industry				
(1)轻工业	Light Industry	100.9	99.4	100.3	100.5
1.以农产品为原料	Agricultural Products as Raw Materials	99.7	98.4	100.0	100.2
2.以非农产品为原料	Non-agricultural Products as Raw Materials	102.5	100.6	100.5	100.8
(2)重工业	Heavy Industry	101.1	100.2	99.7	100.2
1.采掘	Mining	100.0	100.0	100.0	100.0
2.原料	Raw Materials	102.2	100.2	98.1	100.9
3.加工	Processing	100.8	100.2	100.1	100.0
㈡按生产生活资料分	By Means of Production and Consumer Goods				
(1)生产资料	Means of Production	101.1	100.2	99.7	100.2
1.采掘	Mining	100.0	100.0	100.0	100.0
2.原料	Raw Materials	102.3	100.3	97.9	101.0
3.加工	Processing	100.9	100.2	100.2	100.0
(2)生活资料	Consumer Goods	100.8	99.3	100.2	100.5
1.食品	Food	99.4	97.8	99.8	100.2
2.衣着	Clothing	100.1	99.9	100.8	99.9
3.一般日用品	Articles for Daily Use	100.9	100.8	100.5	101.0
4.耐用消费品	Durable Consumer Goods	104.4	99.6	100.6	100.0
㈢按初级中间最终产品分	By Primary、Intermediate and Final Products				
(1)初级产品	Primary Products	100.0	100.0	100.0	100.0

（2018 年，以上月价格为 100）

(2018,Preceding last month=100)

5 月 May	6 月 June	7 月 July	8 月 August	9 月 September	10 月 October	11 月 November	12 月 December
100.2	100.9	99.8	100.0	100.5	100.6	100.1	98.9
100.0	101.0	99.7	100.1	100.4	100.3	100.2	99.7
100.4	101.8	99.3	99.8	100.7	98.3	99.8	99.8
102.4	100.5	100.9	100.3	102.0	102.8	96.5	93.5
100.3	100.2	100.0	99.3	99.9	100.2	102.2	98.9
100.2	99.9	100.4	99.2	100.2	100.4	103.7	98.2
100.5	100.7	99.5	99.4	99.6	100.0	100.3	99.9
100.2	101.0	99.7	100.2	100.6	100.7	99.6	98.9
100.0	100.0	100.0	100.0	100.0	100.0	100.0	100.0
101.4	99.9	99.6	100.6	101.5	102.1	98.1	95.3
99.8	101.3	99.8	100.0	100.4	100.3	100.1	99.9
100.2	101.0	99.8	100.1	100.6	100.7	99.7	98.8
100.0	100.0	100.0	100.0	100.0	100.0	100.0	100.0
101.5	99.9	99.6	100.6	101.5	102.3	97.9	95.0
99.8	101.3	99.8	100.0	100.4	100.3	100.1	99.7
100.3	100.0	99.8	99.3	99.9	100.2	102.0	99.4
99.7	99.3	100.3	98.6	100.5	100.5	104.2	97.6
100.3	100.0	100.3	100.5	99.7	100.0	104.7	100.0
101.6	100.8	99.2	99.6	99.3	99.7	99.9	100.9
99.2	100.0	100.0	100.0	99.9	100.8	100.8	100.3
100.0	100.0	100.0	100.0	100.0	100.0	100.0	100.0

9-5 续1

项目名称	Indicator	1月 January	2月 February	3月 March	4月 April
1.矿产品	Minerals	100.0	100.0	100.0	100.0
2.废料	Scrap				
(2)中间产品	Intermediate Products	100.9	100.2	99.7	100.3
(3)最终产品	Final Products	101.0	100.1	99.8	100.4
1.最终投资品	Investment Goods	101.3	100.3	99.7	100.3
2.最终消费品	Consumer Goods	99.9	99.8	100.2	100.4
(四)按工业门类分	Classification by Industrial Category				
(1)采矿业	Mining	100.0	100.0	100.0	100.0
(2)制造业	Manufacture	101.3	100.0	99.8	100.2
(3)电力、燃气及水生产和供应业	Production and Supply of Electric, Gas and Wate	96.8	101.6	100.0	100.3
(五)按工业部门分	By Industrial Department				
(1)冶金工业	Metallurgical Industry	99.7	99.7	100.3	100.5
(2) 电力工业	Power Industry	96.2	101.9	100.0	100.4
(3)煤炭及炼焦工业	Coal Industry				
(4)石油工业	Petroleum Industry	104.5	100.8	96.7	102.1
(5)化学工业	Chemical Industry	102.1	100.2	99.5	100.3
(6)机械工业	Machine Building Industry	101.0	100.2	100.0	100.1
(7)建筑材料工业	Building Materials Industry	100.6	100.3	100.9	99.1
(8)森林工业	Timber Industry	100.0	100.0	100.0	100.0
(9)食品工业	Food Industry	99.4	97.9	99.8	100.2
(10)纺织工业	Textile Industry	99.2	98.9	100.0	99.5
(11)缝纫工业	Tailoring Industry	100.1	99.9	100.8	99.9
(12)皮革工业	Leather Industry				
(13)造纸工业	Paper Industry	104.9	102.3	102.4	102.4
(14)文教艺术用品工业	Industry of Cultural, Educational & Handicrafts Articles	103.0	100.2	99.6	100.1
(15)其它工业	Others	103.9	99.7	100.9	99.4

5月 May	6月 June	7月 July	8月 August	9月 September	10月 October	11月 November	12月 December
100.0	100.0	100.0	100.0	100.0	100.0	100.0	100.0
100.4	101.3	99.7	100.0	100.7	100.7	99.7	98.7
100.2	100.9	100.0	99.9	100.3	100.4	100.0	99.0
100.1	101.3	100.0	100.1	100.4	100.5	99.5	98.8
100.3	99.8	99.8	99.4	99.9	100.3	101.7	99.4
100.0	100.0	100.0	100.0	100.0	100.0	100.0	100.0
100.2	100.9	99.8	100.0	100.5	100.6	100.1	98.9
100.2	99.5	99.5	100.2	100.3	100.4	100.4	99.5
99.8	100.4	100.2	100.6	100.4	100.7	99.9	99.2
100.2	99.3	99.4	100.0	100.3	99.5	100.5	99.4
103.6	101.2	101.6	100.5	102.8	104.5	94.5	90.5
100.6	100.4	98.4	100.0	100.5	100.8	100.2	98.7
99.8	101.6	99.6	99.9	100.1	99.8	99.9	99.9
99.1	101.1	101.8	100.6	101.9	103.5	102.2	102.4
96.8	100.0	100.0	100.0	100.0	100.0	100.0	100.0
99.7	99.4	100.6	98.6	100.3	100.7	104.5	97.7
102.6	100.8	99.9	99.9	100.3	99.9	102.4	99.9
100.3	100.0	100.3	100.5	99.7	100.0	104.7	100.0
99.0	102.3	99.6	101.7	99.2	98.2	98.1	97.8
100.2	100.1	100.0	100.0	99.9	100.2	99.8	100.1
99.5	99.0	99.5	100.3	100.8	100.7	100.6	98.9

9-6 工业生产者出厂价格总指数

Producer Price Index for Manufactured Goods

项目名称	Indicator	全年 Total	1月 January	2月 February	3月 March	4月 April
总指数	Total Price Indices	104.8	105.9	105.2	104.3	104.5
核心指数	Core Indices	105.0	106.5	105.8	105.0	104.9
高技术	High Technology	104.2	106.6	105.4	104.6	104.9
能源	Energy	106.5	102.4	103.3	101.6	103.9
(一)按轻重工业分	By Light and Heavy Industry					
(1)轻工业	Light Industry	102.1	102.2	101.4	101.6	102.0
1.以农产品为原料	Agricultural Products as Raw Materials	99.8	100.8	98.8	98.9	99.3
2.以非农产品为原料	Non-agricultural Products as Raw Materials	105.2	103.9	104.8	105.1	105.5
(2)重工业	Heavy Industry	105.3	106.7	106.0	104.9	105.1
1.采掘	Mining	93.5	83.0	79.4	78.3	88.2
2.原料	RawMaterials	108.6	112.1	109.6	107.4	107.9
3.加工	Processing	104.5	105.3	105.1	104.3	104.3
(二)按生产生活资料分	ByMeansofProductionandConsumerGoods					
(1)生产资料	MeansofProduction	105.3	106.4	105.8	104.8	105.0
1.采掘	Mining	93.5	83.0	79.4	78.3	88.2
2.原料	RawMaterials	109.0	112.8	110.2	107.8	108.3
3.加工	Processing	104.4	104.9	104.8	104.1	104.2
(2)生活资料	ConsumerGoods	102.2	103.2	101.9	102.1	102.2
1.食品	Food	98.7	103.3	99.5	99.3	99.3
2.衣着	Clothing	102.6	101.0	100.9	101.6	101.5
3.一般日用品	ArticlesforDailyUse	105.1	102.5	103.3	103.8	104.8
4.耐用消费品	DurableConsumerGoods	104.5	104.7	105.5	105.5	104.2
(三)按初级中间最终产品分	ByPrimary、IntermediateandFinalProducts					
(1)初级产品	PrimaryProducts	93.5	83.0	79.4	78.3	88.2

（2018 年，以上年同期价格为 100）

（2018,Preceding last year=100）

5 月 May	6 月 June	7 月 July	8 月 August	9 月 September	10 月 October	11 月 November	12 月 December
105.4	106.2	105.8	105.0	104.7	104.4	103.9	102.0
105.6	106.5	105.7	105.1	104.6	104.1	103.6	102.6
105.1	107.7	105.1	104.6	104.0	101.5	101.0	100.8
106.6	107.6	110.8	109.3	111.7	112.7	108.6	100.5
102.2	102.5	102.6	102.0	101.8	101.6	103.4	102.1
99.4	99.4	99.7	98.8	99.2	99.6	102.9	100.5
105.9	106.6	106.4	106.4	105.2	104.3	104.1	104.2
106.0	107.0	106.5	105.7	105.3	105.0	104.0	102.0
100.9	108.2	100.9	96.6	98.2	100.0	100.0	100.0
109.9	109.5	110.7	109.9	110.4	109.7	106.8	99.7
105.0	106.2	105.3	104.6	104.0	103.7	103.2	102.7
105.9	106.9	106.4	105.6	105.4	105.1	104.1	102.1
100.9	108.2	100.9	96.6	98.2	100.0	100.0	100.0
110.4	110.0	111.3	110.4	110.9	110.2	107.1	99.5
104.8	106.1	105.2	104.5	104.1	103.9	103.4	102.8
102.7	102.7	102.6	102.1	101.0	100.9	102.6	101.7
98.9	98.2	98.3	97.0	95.8	96.4	100.4	97.6
101.8	101.8	102.1	102.6	103.4	102.4	106.7	106.1
107.0	107.7	107.1	106.6	105.7	104.4	104.1	104.4
103.3	103.3	103.9	105.6	103.9	104.8	104.2	105.6
100.9	108.2	100.9	96.6	98.2	100.0	100.0	100.0

9-6 续 1

项目名称	Indicator	全年 Total	1月 January	2月 February	3月 March	4月 April
1.矿产品	Minerals	93.5	83.0	79.4	78.3	88.2
2.废料	Scrap					
(2)中间产品	IntermediateProducts	105.8	107.0	106.1	105.0	105.3
(3)最终产品	FinalProducts	103.8	104.4	104.0	103.4	103.7
1.最终投资品	InvestmentGoods	104.7	105.2	105.0	104.1	104.5
2.最终消费品	ConsumerGoods	101.2	101.9	101.0	101.3	101.3
(四)按工业门类分	ClassificationbyIndustrialCategory					
(1)采矿业	Mining	93.5	83.0	79.4	78.3	88.2
(2)制造业	Manufacture	105.1	106.3	105.6	104.7	104.9
(3)电力、燃气及水生产和供应业	ProductionandSupplyofElectric,GasandWate	97.9	97.0	97.4	98.2	97.8
(五)按工业部门分	ByIndustrialDepartment					
(1)冶金工业	MetallurgicalIndustry	103.5	102.2	101.2	99.2	101.2
(2)电力工业	PowerIndustry	97.1	96.6	97.1	98.0	97.5
(3)煤炭及炼焦工业	CoalIndustry					
(4)石油工业	PetroleumIndustry	112.2	105.9	107.0	103.6	107.7
(5)化学工业	ChemicalIndustry	109.1	116.1	112.1	111.2	110.7
(6)机械工业	MachineBuildingIndustry	103.1	103.5	103.8	103.0	103.0
(7)建筑材料工业	BuildingMaterialsIndustry	120.5	127.0	127.0	128.0	123.2
(8)森林工业	TimberIndustry	99.1	105.1	103.8	103.1	103.4
(9)食品工业	FoodIndustry	97.7	98.9	97.1	97.2	97.7
(10)纺织工业	TextileIndustry	100.6	103.1	98.5	97.7	97.1
(11)缝纫工业	TailoringIndustry	102.6	101.0	100.9	101.6	101.5
(12)皮革工业	LeatherIndustry					
(13)造纸工业	PaperIndustry	120.5	117.7	120.4	123.3	126.3
(14)文教艺术用品工业	IndustryofCultural,Educational&HandicraftsArticles	103.0	103.3	103.1	102.7	102.7
(15)其它工业	Others	104.2	108.7	107.3	107.4	105.7

5月 May	6月 June	7月 July	8月 August	9月 September	10月 October	11月 November	12月 December
100.9	108.2	100.9	96.6	98.2	100.0	100.0	100.0
106.6	107.9	107.4	106.4	106.0	105.6	104.6	102.3
103.9	105.0	104.8	104.1	103.7	103.6	103.3	102.0
104.7	106.1	106.0	105.0	104.8	104.6	103.8	102.3
101.7	101.5	101.3	101.1	100.5	100.3	101.8	101.0
100.9	108.2	100.9	96.6	98.2	100.0	100.0	100.0
105.7	106.6	106.2	105.4	105.0	104.7	104.1	102.2
97.9	97.4	96.5	97.5	98.7	98.4	99.0	98.6
107.1	107.5	106.7	104.8	103.9	103.9	103.9	101.4
97.7	97.0	96.0	96.9	97.7	96.3	97.6	97.1
111.9	114.0	120.1	116.7	120.1	122.5	115.1	102.5
111.4	110.5	109.4	109.5	107.8	105.7	104.4	101.6
103.1	104.9	103.8	103.3	103.1	102.5	102.0	101.9
120.3	120.7	122.3	119.5	114.1	118.6	115.3	114.2
97.2	96.8	96.8	96.8	96.8	96.8	96.8	96.8
97.7	97.0	97.5	96.2	96.3	97.2	101.5	98.7
98.3	100.0	100.4	100.1	102.6	102.6	103.5	103.3
101.8	101.8	102.1	102.6	103.4	102.4	106.7	106.1
125.1	128.0	124.6	123.6	120.4	118.1	113.2	108.0
102.8	103.0	103.0	103.1	103.1	103.3	103.0	103.2
104.5	102.7	102.0	101.8	102.2	102.1	103.3	103.0

9-7 工业生产者购进价格指数

Purchasing Price Index for Industrial Producers

项目名称	Category	1月 January	2月 February	3月 March	4月 April
总指数	Total Price Indices	100.3	100.6	99.5	99.7
(一)按初级中间最终产品分	By Primary and Intermediate Products				
(1)初级产品	Primary Products	101.3	102.9	96.8	98.4
1.农产品	Farm Produce	102.0	99.9	100.4	101.1
2.矿产品	Minerals	101.1	103.6	96.0	97.7
3.废料	Scrap				
(2)中间产品	Intermediate Products	99.9	99.8	100.5	100.1
(二)九大类原材料购进价格指数	By Nine Categories of Raw Material				
(1)燃料、动力类	Fuel and Power	100.6	102.4	98.6	98.7
(2)黑色金属材料类	Ferrous Metals	98.8	99.4	100.2	99.2
1.钢材	Steel	99.7	99.9	100.5	99.7
2.其它	Others	97.9	98.9	99.8	98.7
(3)有色金属材料及电线类	Nonferrous Metals	99.5	100.3	98.8	97.8
(4)化工原料类	Raw Chemical Materials	97.9	97.5	100.2	99.1
(5)木材及纸浆类	Timber and Paper Pulp	101.4	101.2	101.6	101.4
(6)建筑材料及非金属类	Building Materials and Nonmetal Ores	101.4	100.0	101.9	97.6
(7)其它工业原材料及半成品类	Other Industrial Raw Materials and	100.9	99.7	99.8	102.4
(8)农副产品类	Semi-finished Products Agricultural Products	102.0	99.9	100.4	101.1
(9)纺织原料类	Textile Materials	99.7	99.8	99.6	99.7

（2018 年，以上月价格为 100）

（2018，Preceding Last Month=100）

5 月 May	6 月 June	7 月 July	8 月 August	9 月 September	10 月 October	11 月 November	12 月 December
100.5	101.6	100.3	101.0	100.6	101.8	101.4	97.0
103.0	105.6	101.2	102.0	99.9	103.4	103.8	93.3
98.6	100.6	99.6	100.4	100.2	99.5	99.9	100.8
104.2	106.8	101.6	102.3	99.8	104.2	104.6	91.8
99.7	100.3	99.9	100.6	100.9	101.2	100.5	98.4
101.4	102.9	101.1	101.4	99.8	103.0	103.1	95.4
100.6	100.5	100.0	101.3	101.3	99.6	99.1	97.6
100.7	100.5	100.6	100.5	100.5	99.7	99.2	97.5
100.5	100.5	99.4	102.0	102.1	99.5	98.9	97.6
100.4	101.5	100.0	97.1	98.8	102.4	99.0	99.5
98.3	103.7	94.6	102.2	103.2	103.9	102.7	90.3
106.6	100.0	102.4	100.0	99.4	99.3	99.2	98.2
97.5	99.8	103.4	99.6	102.3	102.8	101.5	100.8
100.2	100.2	100.4	100.8	100.7	100.5	100.2	99.6
98.6	100.6	99.6	100.4	100.2	99.5	99.9	100.8
100.6	100.5	98.8	100.4	100.4	100.9	99.5	99.8

9 -8 工业生产者购进价格指数

Purchasing Price Index for Industrial Producers

项目名称	Category	全年 Total	1 月 January	2 月 February	3 月 March	4 月 April
总指数	Total Price Indices	108.3	107.3	107.6	106.2	105.4
(一)按初级中间最终产品分	By Primary and Intermediate Products					
(1)初级产品	Primary Products	117.0	110.9	114.3	107.1	107.2
1.农产品	Farm Produce	101.9	99.9	100.6	101.7	102.9
2.矿产品	Minerals	120.5	113.3	117.4	108.1	107.9
3.废料	Scrap					
(2)中间产品	Intermediate Products	105.5	106.0	105.4	105.8	104.8
(二)九大类原材料购进价格指数	By Nine Categories of Raw Material					
(1)燃料、动力类	Fuel and Power	112.4	107.3	110.5	107.2	105.8
(2)黑色金属材料类	Ferrous Metals	107.5	112.4	111.1	110.9	109.8
1.钢材	Steel	105.8	107.1	106.2	106.3	106.6
2.其它	Others	108.5	116.7	115.0	114.5	112.0
(3)有色金属材料及电线类	Nonferrous Metals	104.0	118.4	113.9	109.1	101.5
(4)化工原料类	Raw Chemical Materials	105.2	111.2	105.0	102.5	100.6
(5)木材及纸浆类	Timber and Paper Pulp	118.6	117.2	117.8	116.2	117.0
(6)建筑材料及非金属类	Building Materials and Nonmetal Ores	116.2	125.5	125.5	127.3	121.3
(7)其它工业原材料及半成品类	Other Industrial Raw Materials and	102.2	97.9	97.6	97.9	100.2
(8)农副产品类	Semi-finished Products Agricultural Products	101.9	99.9	100.6	101.7	102.9
(9)纺织原料类	Textile Materials	98.9	99.6	97.4	98.6	98.3

(2018 年，以上年同期价格为 100)

（2018,Preceding Last Year=100）

5 月 May	6 月 June	7 月 July	8 月 August	9 月 September	10 月 October	11 月 November	12 月 December
107.5	110.2	111.8	111.7	109.5	109.4	109.5	104.2
111.2	119.5	125.1	127.1	122.8	124.0	124.6	111.4
102.2	102.8	102.3	102.7	101.6	101.3	102.1	102.8
113.1	123.4	130.6	133.0	127.9	129.4	130.1	113.5
106.2	107.2	107.6	106.8	105.2	104.8	104.6	101.7
109.0	114.5	118.5	120.3	115.7	115.5	116.7	108.6
111.2	110.9	111.1	107.0	104.9	103.7	102.3	97.3
108.3	108.9	108.9	106.8	105.1	104.5	103.2	98.9
113.1	112.0	112.3	106.8	104.5	102.8	101.3	95.8
103.7	108.2	109.7	104.9	96.1	96.7	95.4	95.2
102.0	108.3	104.4	106.8	108.8	111.2	110.7	92.7
123.9	123.4	124.8	122.0	119.2	117.4	114.4	111.1
116.6	114.5	118.1	110.6	110.4	112.4	108.9	108.8
102.6	103.0	103.4	104.1	104.9	104.7	104.8	105.4
102.2	102.8	102.3	102.7	101.6	101.3	102.1	102.8
99.2	98.8	97.9	99.1	98.9	99.6	99.3	99.8

9-9 住宅销售价格指数（2018 年，以上月价格为 100）

Sales Price of Residential Buildings（2018,Preceding last month=100）

指 标	Indicator	1月 January	2月 February	3月 March	4月 April	5月 May	6月 June
新建住宅	New Residential Buildings	100.5	99.9	100.2	100.1	100.4	103.6
新建商品住宅	New Commercial Residential Buildings	100.5	99.9	100.2	100.1	100.4	103.6
90 平方米及以下	Buildings below 90sq.m	100.3	100.1	100.1	100.2	100.3	101.3
90–144 平方米	Buildings 90–144 sq.m	100.2	99.9	100.2	100.1	100.4	101.6
144 平方米以上	Buildings above 144sq.m	101.4	100.1	100.2	100.1	100.2	101.5
二手住宅	Second-hand House	99.6	100.0	100.3	100.2	100.5	101.0
90 平方米及以下	Buildings below 90sq.m	99.6	99.8	100.2	100.4	100.2	101.1
90–144 平方米	Buildings 90–144 sq.m	99.6	100.3	100.4	100.0	100.7	101.0
144 平方米以上	Buildings above 144sq.m	100.0	100.0	100.3	100.1	100.5	100.6

9-9 续 1

指 标	Indicator	7月 July	8月 August	9月 September	10月 October	11月 November	12月 December
新建住宅	New Residential Buildings	103.0	102.8	101.3	100.7	101.7	100.7
新建商品住宅	New Commercial Residential Buildings	103.0	102.8	101.3	100.7	101.7	100.7
90 平方米及以下	Buildings below 90sq.m	103.4	103.1	100.8	100.9	101.7	101.0
90–144 平方米	Buildings 90–144 sq.m	102.9	102.9	101.6	100.6	101.6	100.8
144 平方米以上	Buildings above 144sq.m	103.0	102.4	100.9	101.0	101.8	100.6
二手住宅	Second-hand House	102.5	102.8	101.2	100.6	100.5	100.5
90 平方米及以下	Buildings below 90sq.m	102.3	102.3	100.8	100.7	100.9	100.6
90–144 平方米	Buildings 90–144 sq.m	102.8	103.2	101.5	100.6	100.1	100.4
144 平方米以上	Buildings above 144sq.m	102.2	103.3	101.4	100.4	100.5	100.8

9-10 住宅销售价格指数(2018年，以上年同期价格为100)

Sales Price of Residential Buildings （2018,Preceding last year=100）

指　标	Indicator	1月 January	2月 February	3月 March	4月 April	5月 May	6月 June
新建住宅	New Residential Buildings	100.9	101.4	100.9	100.6	100.5	103.9
新建商品住宅	New Commercial Residential Buildings	100.9	101.4	100.9	100.6	100.5	103.9
90平方米及以下	Buildings below 90sq.m	99.4	100.4	99.7	99.7	99.2	106.0
90–144平方米	Buildings 90–144 sq.m	101.0	100.9	100.6	100.2	100.1	105.8
144平方米以上	Buildings above 144sq.m	101.3	103.7	102.9	102.3	102.6	103.3
二手住宅	Second–hand House	102.3	101.8	100.8	99.9	99.8	100.0
90平方米及以下	Buildings below 90sq.m	102.8	101.8	100.7	99.7	99.3	99.6
90–144平方米	Buildings 90–144 sq.m	101.7	101.6	100.5	99.8	100.1	100.2
144平方米以上	Buildings above 144sq.m	102.6	102.5	102.0	101.0	100.3	100.4

9–9 续1

指　标	Indicator	7月 July	8月 August	9月 September	10月 October	11月 November	12月 December
新建住宅	New Residential Buildings	106.9	110.2	112.3	113.3	115.4	115.9
新建商品住宅	New Commercial Residential Buildings	106.9	110.2	112.3	113.3	115.4	115.9
90平方米及以下	Buildings below 90sq.m	106.5	110.1	111.3	113.4	115.7	116.8
90–144平方米	Buildings 90–144 sq.m	105.9	109.2	111.8	112.6	114.6	115.4
144平方米以上	Buildings above 144sq.m	110.4	113.6	114.7	116.0	117.7	116.9
二手住宅	Second–hand House	102.7	106.3	107.8	108.6	109.4	110.1
90平方米及以下	Buildings below 90sq.m	102.1	105.0	106.2	107.0	108.4	109.3
90–144平方米	Buildings 90–144 sq.m	103.3	107.6	109.3	110.0	110.3	110.8
144平方米以上	Buildings above 144sq.m	102.9	106.6	108.4	109.1	109.8	110.7

9-11 主要年份工业生产者出厂、购进价格指数（以上年价格为100）

Purchasing Price Index for Industrial Producers and Producer Price Index for Manufactured Goods in Main Years（Preceding last year=100）

年份 Year	工业生产者出厂价格指数 Producer Price Indices for Industrial Products	工业生产者购进价格指数 Industrial Producer Purchasing Price Indices
1998	94.5	95.2
1999	98.9	97.6
2000	104.8	114.5
2001	99.8	101.4
2002	97.9	100.4
2003	103.2	111.2
2004	106.7	116.4
2005	102.3	111.3
2006	100.2	105.6
2007	103.9	105.0
2008	109.2	116.9
2009	96.2	94.3
2010	104.7	109.9
2011	105.3	108.2
2012	98.4	99.4
2013	98.8	97.8
2014	99.0	98.0
2015	95.0	92.7
2016	99.8	99.0
2017	105.7	113.9
2018	104.8	108.3

主要统计指标解释

Explanatory Notes on Main Statistical Indicators

居民消费价格 是指城乡居民购买并用于日常生活消费的商品和服务项目的价格。

居民消费价格指数 是反映一定时期内城乡居民所购买的生活消费品价格和服务项目价格变动趋势和程度的相对数，是对城市居民消费价格指数和农村居民消费价格指数进行综合汇总计算的结果。利用居民消费价格指数，可以观察和分析消费品的零售价格和服务价格变动对城乡居民实际生活费支出的影响程度。

调查内容是城乡居民购买并用于日常生活消费的商品和服务项目的价格。调查内容根据全国城乡居民家庭消费支出调查资料以及居民消费结构和消费习惯确定，按用途划分为8个大类，262个基本分类，包括食品烟酒、衣着、居住、生活用品及服务、交通和通信、教育文化和娱乐、医疗保健、其他用品和服务。

商品零售价格 是商品在流通过程中最后一个环节的价格，是工业、商业、餐饮业和其他零售企业向城乡居民、机关团体出售生活消费品和办公用品的价格。

商品零售价格指数 是反映城乡商品零售价格变动趋势的一种经济指数。零售物价的调整变动直接影响到城乡居民的生活支出和国家的财政收入，影响居民购买力和市场供需平衡，影响消费与积累的比例。因此，计算零售价格指数，可以从一个侧面对上述经济活动进行观察和分析。

调查内容是工业、商业、餐饮业和其他行业的零售商品以及农民对非农业居民出售商品的价格。包括食品、饮料烟酒、服装鞋帽、纺织品、家用电器及音像器材、文化办公用品、日用品、体育娱乐用品、交通通信用品、家具、化妆品、金银饰品、中西药品及医疗保健用品、书报杂志及电子出版物、燃料、建筑材料及五金电料等16个大类，197个基本分类的商品零售价格。

工业生产者价格 工业生产者价格包括工业企业产品第一次出售时的出厂价格和企业作为中间投入的原材料、燃料、动力购进价格（简称工业生产者购进价格）。工业生产者价格调查的目的在于及时、准确、科学地反映各工业行业产品价格水平及其变动趋势和幅度，为国民经济核算、计算工业发展速度、宏观经济分析和调控、理顺价格体系等提供科学、准确的依据。

工业生产者价格指数 是由工业生产者出厂价格指数和工业生产者购进价格指数两部分组成。

工业生产者出厂价格指数 是反映一定时期内工业企业产品第一次出售时的出厂价格总水平的变动趋势和程度的相对数，包括工业企业售给本企业以外所有单位的各种产品和直接售给居民用于生活消费的产品。该指数可以观察出厂价格变动对工业总产值及增加值的影响。

工业生产者购进价格指数 是反映工业企业作为生产投入，而从物资交易市场和能源、原材料生产企业购买原材料、燃料和动力产品时，所支付的价格水平变动趋势和程度的统计指标，是扣除工业企业物质消耗成本中的价格变动影响的重要依据。

住宅销售价格 指房产所有权转移时买卖双方实际成交的价格（合同价格）。房产买卖时，买房人购买的是房产的所有权，卖房人将房产所有权出让，同时要获得房产所有权出让的价格补偿。它主要包括新建住宅销售和二手住宅销售两部分。

住宅销售价格指数 是综合反映住宅商品价格总体变化趋势和变化幅度的相对数。各市住宅销售价格指数是由新建住宅销售价格指数和二手住宅销售价格指数组成。

Explanatory Notes on Main Statistical Indicators

Consumer Price refers to the price of goods and services purchased and used for daily life consumption by urban and rural residents.

Consumer Price index reflects the trend and degree of changes in prices of consumer goods and services purchased by urban households during a given period. It is the result after comprehensive summary and calculation of urban consumer price index and rural consumer price index. It can be used to observe and analyze the impact of price changes in consumer goods and services on the actual expenditure of urban and rural residents.

The investigation content is the price of goods and services purchased and used for daily life consumption by urban and rural residents. The investigation content is confirmed pursuant to survey data regarding national urban and rural residents' household consumption expenditure and resident consumption structure as well as consumption habit which is divided into 8 categories (262 basic types) as per purpose, including food, alcohol and tobacco, clothing, housing, daily necessities and services, transportation and communication, education, culture and entertainment, health care and other goods and services.

Retail Price refers to the prices in the last link of the production circulation process. It is the prices that industrial, commercial, catering and other retail enterprises sell daily consumer goods and products for office use to urban and rural residents and institutions and social organizations.

The research content involves the prices of retail goods in industry, business, catering and other industries as well as the prices of goods sold by the farmer to the non–agricultural residents, including the commodities of 16 categories (including 197 basic types) –– food, beverage alcohol & tobacco, clothing & shoes, textile, household appliances and audio & video equipment, cultural & office goods, daily necessities, sports & entertainment goods, transportation & communication supplies, furniture, cosmetics, gold & silver accessories, traditional Chinese and western medicines & healthcare supplies, newspapers & magazines and electronic publications, fuel, building materials & hardware.

Industrial Producer Price covers the ex–factory price when products of industrial enterprises are sold for the first time and the purchase price (called as industrial producer purchase price for short) of raw materials, fuels and power which are intermediate inputs of the enterprise. The investigation of industrial producer price is aimed at timely, accurately and scientifically reflecting the price level of products and the corresponding trend and range of changing in various industries, and providing scientific and accurate basis for national economic accounting, computing industry development speed, macroeconomic analysis and regulation and straightening out the price system, etc.

Industrial Producer Price Index is constituted by Producer Price Indices for Industrial Products and Industrial Producer Purchasing Price Index.

Producer Price Indices for Industrial Products reflect the trend and degree of changes in price of all industrial products for the first time to sell during a given period, including sales of industrial products by an industrial enterprise to all units outside the enterprise, as well as sales of consumer goods to residents. It can be used to analyze the impact of ex–factory prices on gross output value and value added of the industrial sector.

Industrial Producer Purchasing Price Index reflects changes in the level and degree of prices paid by industrial enterprises when they purchase production input such as raw materials, fuels and power from the material market. These indices provide important basis for measuring the material consumption cost of industrial enterprises after removing influence of price changes.

The Sales Price of Residential refers to the actual price (contract price) of the transaction between the buyer and the seller when the house ownership is transferred. When the house property is sold, the house buyer purchases the ownership of the house property and the house seller transfers the ownership of the house property with price compensation for house property ownership transfer obtained at the same time. Housing sales mainly include sales of newly built house and sales of second–hand house.

Price Index for Residential reflects the trend and degree of changes in prices of real estate. The price index for real estate is constituted by the price index for the new houses and the price index for the second–hand house.

10

人民生活

PEOPLE´S LIVELIHOOD

10-1 人民物质文化

Improvement in People`s Material

指标	Indicator	单位 (unit)	1978 年
就业	**Employment**		
每一农村劳动力负担人数	Average Dependents Per Labor Force	人(person)	1.70
每一城镇就业者负担人数	Dependents Per Urban Employee	人(person)	1.89
城镇登记失业率	Registered Urban Unemployment Rate	%(%)	
收入与支出	**Income and Expenditure**		
农村居民人均可支配收入	Per Capita Disposable Income of Rural Inhabitant	元(yuan)	111
农村居民人均生活消费支出	Per Capita Consumer Expenditure of Rural Inhabitant	元(yuan)	83
农村居民恩格尔系数	Engel's Coefficient of Rural Inhabitant	%(%)	69.9
城镇居民人均可支配收入	Per Capita Disposable Income of Urban Inhabitant	元(yuan)	338
城镇居民人均生活消费支出	Per Capita Consumer Expenditure of Urban Inhabitant	元(yuan)	318
城镇居民恩格尔系数	Engel's Coefficient of Urban Inhabitant	%(%)	57.1
居民储蓄	**Household Savings**		
城乡居民年末储蓄存款余额	Deposits of Urban and Rural Residents	亿元(100 million yuan)	1.3
人均储蓄存款余额	Per Capita Savings Balance	元(yuan)	28.5
住房面积	Area of Building		
农村人均住房建筑面积	Rural Per Capita Living Space	平方米(sq.m)	9.6
城镇人均住房建筑面积	Urban Per Capita Living Space	平方米(sq.m)	4.1
交通通讯	**Traffic and Communication**		
农村每百户拥有摩托车	Number of Motorcycles Owned by Per 100 Rural Households	辆(unit)	
城市每百户拥有摩托车	Number of Motorcycles Owned by Per 100 Urban Households	辆(unit)	
城市公用事业	Urban Utilities		
城市人口用水普及率	Urban water Penetration Rate	%(%)	99
每万人拥有公园绿地面积	Green Area of Park Per 10000 Population	公顷(ha)	1.6
文化生活	**Culture Life**		
城市每百户拥有彩色电视机	Number of Color TV Sets Owned by Per 100 Rural Households	台(set)	-
农村每百户拥有彩色电视机	Number of Color TV Sets Owned by Per 100 Urban Households	台(set)	-
教育卫生	Education and Public Health		
每万人口中在校大学生数	Number of College Students Per 10 000 Population	人(person)	22
每万人拥有卫生技术人员	Number of Health Technical Personnel Per 1oooo Population	人(person)	10.98
每万人拥有医院病床	Number of Beds of Hospitals and Health Centers Per 1oooo Population	张(unit)	22.01

注：1.“城镇居民人均生活消费支出”1990 年以前为“生活费支出”

2.“人均住宅建筑面积”，2009 年以前（不含）为“使用面积”口径，2002 年以前（不含）为“居住面积”口径。

3. 从 2015 年起，全市发布城乡住户调查一体化改革新口径数据，居民收支调查指标与 2014 年前分别实施的城镇和农村住户调查的调查范围、方法、指标口径、名称有所不同。（以下相关表同）

4.“农村居民人均可支配收入”2014 年以前为“农民人均纯收入”口径。

生活提高情况

and Cultural Life

1990年	2000年	2010年	2015年	2016年	2017年	2018年
1.61	1.40	1.35	1.38	1.42	1.31	1.4
1.72	1.71	1.67	1.80	1.87	1.35	1.4
	3.70	3.84	2.04	2.17	2.08	2.06
731	3047	8903	14232	15346	16594	17924
570	1977	5407	8597	9396	10327	11172
50.5	43.5	33.6	32.3	32.2	31.5	30.5
1620	8471	25321	39889	43052	46642	50146
1360	6892	15973	26319	28537	30729	32977
57.5	34.6	31.6	24.4	24.2	23.5	23.5
51.1	463.0	2187.7	3951.4	4279.9	4465.7	5008.1
975.5	8229.6	36239.0	63358.0	68012.6	69971.2	77076.2
22.5	28.6	40.2	52.6	53.8	55.2	54.3
7.5	10.5	29.7	44.9	45.5	47.8	46.5
4.0	61.0	84.9	79.1	75.8	76.3	51.7
7.7	34.3	13.3	15.1	13.5	16.1	11.6
100	100	100	99.00	99.57	99.64	99.78
4	7.2	11.3	11.55	11.81	11.79	12.59
61.3	132.3	115.5	110.5	110.6	111.1	106.0
70.0	125.0	122.2	114.0	118.3	118.4	114.1
71	165	1064	1141	1154	1241	1226
59.45	63.40	65.2	100.6	105.6	104.2	111.0
32.88	38.57	52.9	69.1	72.2	74.9	77.0

Note: 1. "Per capita living expenditure of urban residents" was "cost of living expenses" before 1990;

2. "Per capita housing area" was the caliber of "usable area" before 2009 (excluding) and was the caliber of "living area" before 2002

3. Since 2015, the city has released new caliber data for the integrated reform of urban and rural household surveys. The survey indicator of residents' income and expenditure was different from the survey scope, method, index caliber and name of urban and rural households carried out before 2014. (The same below)

4. "Per capita disposable income of rural residents" was the caliber of "rural per capita net income" before 2014.

10-2 各时期城镇居民生活情况

Basic Conditions of Urban Households in Each Period

年 份 Year	人均可支配收入（元） Per Capita Annual isposable Income(yuan)	人均生活消费支出(元) Per Capita Consumer Expenditure(yuan)		就业者负担人数（人） Average Dependents Per Employee(person)	人均住宅建筑面积（平方米） Per Capita Floor Space (sq.m)
		小计 Total	#人均食品支出 Per Capita Food Expenditure		
1949	64.53	61.30	37.39		4.09
1978	337.80	317.88	181.56	1.89	4.06
1981	487.19	452.77	256.67	1.73	4.40
1982	502.97	468.03	275.30	1.70	4.57
1983	552.37	484.87	293.32	1.66	4.93
1984	671.89	537.27	326.97	1.69	5.10
1985	783.00	703.82	397.33	1.68	5.21
"七五"时期					
1986	946.46	836.50	474.62	1.70	7.40
1987	1057.48	943.58	534.12	1.73	7.30
1988	1272.83	1150.44	635.11	1.70	7.50
1989	1487.91	1355.64	745.32	1.71	7.50
1990	1619.50	1360.08	781.58	1.72	7.50
"八五"时期					
1991	1854.33	1569.26	896.62	1.71	7.60
1992	2148.49	1781.21	979.03	1.73	7.65
1993	2873.94	2394.03	1146.02	1.74	7.80
1994	3951.94	3224.73	1566.59	1.72	7.90
1995	4720.55	3830.38	1823.64	1.80	8.00
"九五"时期					
1996	5681.49	4422.91	2161.00	1.71	8.00
1997	6261.21	5210.40	2185.11	1.62	8.10
1998	6757.12	5440.10	2179.99	1.61	9.89

年 份 Year	人均可支配收入 （元） Per Capita Annual isposable Income(yuan)	人均生活消费支出(元) Per Capita Consumer Expenditure(yuan)		就业者负担人数（人） Average Dependents Per Employee(person)	人均住宅建筑面积（平方米） Per Capita Floor Space (sq.m)
		小计 Total	#人均食品支出 Per Capita Food Expenditure		
1999	7162.48	6415.39	2204.76	1.66	10.00
2000	8471.32	6891.75	2387.06	1.71	10.50
“十五”时期					
2001	9564.99	7465.04	2386.84	1.74	10.70
2002	10094.13	7818.33	2575.21	1.72	17.83
2003	11012.86	8395.36	2610.75	1.68	18.85
2004	12005.06	8580.54	2784.87	1.65	19.50
2005	13578.46	9226.61	3046.93	1.73	19.55
“十一五”时期					
2006	15340.17	10713.13	3335.31	1.74	20.1
2007	18005.10	12389.69	3900.91	1.72	21.0
2008	20802.17	13904.59	4466.18	1.87	21.5
2009	22721.65	14764.28	4836.78	1.86	29.4
2010	25321.06	15973.32	5051.18	1.67	29.7
“十二五”时期					
2011	28891.97	18045.58	5722.65	1.71	30.3
2012	32569.75	20031.67	6162.16	1.72	–
2013	35647.59	21666.94	6624.32	–	–
2014	38762.77	22980.67	6814.14	2.04	–
2015	39888.71	26318.72	6415.00	1.80	44.9
“十三五”时期					
2016	43052.16	28536.93	6908.01	1.87	45.5
2017	46642.40	30728.60	7229.30	1.35	47.8
2018	50146	32977	7758	1.4	46.5

注：1. 可支配收入 1983 年以前为生活费收入,消费性支出 1992 年以前为生活费支出。

2. “人均住宅建筑面积”，2009 年以前（不含）为“使用面积”口径，2002 年以前（不含）为“居住面积”口径。

Note: 1. The disposable income was living expenditure income before 1983, and the consumption expenditure was previously the cost–of–living expenditure before 1992.

2. "Per capita housing area", was the caliber of "usable area" before 2009 (excluding) and was the caliber of "living area" before 2002

10-3 主要年份农村居民生活情况

Basic Conditions of Rural Households in Major Years

年份 Year	人均可支配收入（元） Per Capita Annual Disposable Income(yuan)	人均生活消费支出（元） Per Capita Consumer Expenditure(yuan)		每一劳动力负担人数（人） Average Dependents Per Labor Force(person)	人均住宅建筑面积（平方米） Per Capita Floor Space (sq.m)
		小计 Total	#人均食品支出 Per Capita Food Expenditure		
1952	49.4	39.2	29.2	1.8	7.5
1957	63.6	57.9	34.8	1.8	7.8
1962	67.7	59.9	36.3	1.8	8.0
1965	92.6	69.7	46.1	1.8	8.2
1970	82.7	67.2	42.2	1.7	8.5
1975	79.1	59.5	40.8	1.7	9.0
1978	110.5	83.2	58.2	1.7	9.6
1980	168.9	127.1	85.8	1.6	10.5
1985	439.2	330.5	171.1	1.6	16.9
1990	731.1	569.8	287.7	1.6	22.5
1991	810.1	610.6	303.7	1.6	23.7
1992	865.3	660.5	335.1	1.6	21.1
1993	1031.4	724.8	371.4	1.6	22.9
1994	1401.0	942.5	511.0	1.6	24.1
1995	1812.7	1373.6	770.8	1.4	24.7
1996	2328.1	1728.1	926.2	1.4	26.9
1997	2600.0	1799.7	922.0	1.4	27.1
1998	2826.4	1872.5	935.9	1.4	27.4

年份 Year	人均可支配收入（元） Per Capita Annual Disposable Income(yuan)	人均生活消费支出（元） Per Capita Consumer Expenditure(yuan)		每一劳动力负担人数（人） Average Dependents Per Labor Force(person)	人均住宅建筑面积（平方米） Per Capita Floor Space (sq.m)
		小计 Total	#人均食品支出 Per Capita Food Expenditure		
1999	2943.7	1841.2	876.7	1.4	28.3
2000	3046.8	1976.8	860.0	1.4	28.6
2001	3215.7	2057.8	852.5	1.5	29.9
2002	3355.8	2133.9	849.5	1.4	30.6
2003	3619.3	2316.2	900.7	1.4	32.5
2004	4198.7	2543.1	1040.4	1.4	32.9
2005	4812.3	2902.8	1134.8	1.4	33.8
2006	5480.0	3415.3	1199.8	1.4	35.3
2007	6300.1	3789.8	1423.0	1.4	37.3
2008	7180.2	4385.4	1628.2	1.4	38.7
2009	7804.8	4733.1	1686.3	1.4	39.4
2010	8903.3	5406.6	1818.3	1.4	40.2
2011	10411.8	5905.1	2147.3	1.4	41.2
2012	11786.2	6932.2	2465.4	1.4	42.9
2013	13247.6	7798.7	2640.8	1.4	43.9
2014	14726.0	8581.4	2831.4	1.4	–
2015	14231.8	8597.2	2775.5	1.4	52.6
2016	15345.6	9396.3	3028.0	1.4	53.8
2017	16593.8	10327.3	3253.2	1.3	55.2
2018	17924	11172	3409	1.4	54.3

注：1、“人均可支配收入”2014 年以前为“农民人均纯收入”口径。
2、“人均住宅建筑面积”，2009 年以前（不含）为“使用面积”口径，2002 年以前（不含）为“居住面积”口径。

Note: 1. "Per capita disposable income" was the caliber of "rural per capita net income" before 2014.
2. "Per capita housing area" was the caliber of "usable area" before 2009 (excluding) and was the caliber of "living area"before 2002 (excluding).

10-4 每百户城镇居民家庭主要耐用消费品拥有量

Number of Durable Consumer Goods Owned Per 100 Urban Households in Major Years

商品名称	Indicator	单位 Unit	1995 年	2000 年	2005 年	2010 年	2015 年	2016 年	2017 年	2018 年
摩托车	Motorcycles	辆(Unit)	13.0	34.3	30.1	13.3	15.1	13.5	16.1	11.6
助力车	Moped	辆(Unit)			18.1	40.2	72.0	73.1	75.7	80.8
家用汽车	Automobiles	辆(Unit)			5.4	22.7	47.6	49.8	53.7	53.7
洗衣机	Washing Machines	台(set)	91.5	100.0	97.0	93.2	98.5	97.9	99.5	99.3
电冰箱	Refrigerators	台(set)	92.0	99.3	97.0	96.7	101.8	101.4	101.9	103.2
彩色电视机	Color TV Sets	台(set)	95.0	132.3	126.8	115.5	110.5	110.6	111.1	106.0
家用电脑	Computers	台(set)		20.0	54.2	81.0	90.8	90.0	91.3	80.6
组合音响	Music Center	台(set)	10.5	29.0	26.8	16.2	–	9.1	0.0	0.0
摄像机	Pickup Cameras	台(set)		2.3	4.0	10.8	16.9	16.1	0.0	0.0
照相机	Cameras	台(set)	40.5	76.0	59.2	54.0	56.1	52.8	52.3	36.4
其它中高档乐器	High-grade Instruments	件(Unit)	6.5	12.3	6.4	3.5	5.7	7.2	7.9	13.1
微波炉	Microwave Oven	台(set)		32.3	53.2	55.8	58.7	62.7	63.6	61.0
空调器	Air Conditioner	台(set)	16.0	65.0	104.4	121.5	146.3	152.3	156.4	172.8
淋浴热水器	Water Heaters	台(set)	36.5	81.3	79.3	82.0	100.3	100.8	101.4	101.1
消毒碗柜	Sterilized Cupboard	台(set)			5.4	6.5	6.2	7.6	0.0	0.0
洗碗机	Dish-washing Machine	台(set)			1.0	0.3	2.1	4.4	4.9	2.6
健身器材	Fitness Equipment	台(set)		4.7	6.4	4.3	10.2	10.6	11.7	7.8
住宅电话	Fixed-line Phones	台(set)	38.0	86.7	88.6	46.3	54.7	57.0	54.8	26.5
移动电话	Mobile Phones	台(set)		28.7	145.2	179.7	213.5	209.4	212.5	219.5

10-5 农村每百户居民家庭主要耐用消费品拥有量

Number of Major Durable Consumer Goods Owend Per 100 Rural Households

商品名称	Indicator	单位 Unit	2010年	2011年	2012年	2013年	2015年	2016年	2017年	2018年
洗衣机	Washing Machines	台(set)	79	82	86	88	86	90	90	95
电冰箱	Refrigerators	台(set)	83	88	91	92	91	97	97	97
摩托车	Motorcycles	辆(unit)	85	71	62	65	79	76	76	52
家用汽车	Automobiles	辆(unit)								42
彩色电视机	Color TV Sets	台(set)	120	116	118	119	114	118	118	114
照相机	Cameras	台(set)	14	15	14	16	8	9	9	6
抽油烟机	Range Hoods	台(set)	22	27	28	34	28	36	38	45
空调器	Air Conditioner	台(set)	36	36	39	46	56	67	74	87
热水器	Water Heaters	台(set)	55	64	69	69	74	79	82	87
电话机	Phones	部(set)	80	60	58	55	47	48	46	26
移动电话	Mobile Phones	部(set)	153	175	186	195	214	224	231	245
家用计算机	Computers	台(set)	28	36	39	43	40	43	43	41

10-6 居民人均可支配收入和消费性支出（2018年）

Per Capital Annual Income and Per Capital Annual Expenditure(2018)

单位：元 (yuan)

指标名称	Item	全体居民 All Households	城镇居民 Urban households	农村居民 Rural households
可支配收入	**Disposable Income**	39944	50146	17924
工资性收入	Income of Wages and Salaries	22438	28108	10200
经营净收入	Net Business Income	3878	2758	6295
财产净收入	Income from Properties	6719	9616	465
转移净收入	Income from Transfer	6910	9664	965
消费支出	**Consumption Expenditure**	26073	32977	11172
食品烟酒	Food,Tobacco and liquor	6381	7758	3409
衣着	Clothing	1480	1911	551
居住	Residence	7893	10368	2551
生活用品及服务	Household Appliances and Services	1900	2446	721
交通通信	Transport and Communications	3513	4340	1728
教育文化娱乐	Recreation,Education and Cultural Services	2682	3411	1109
医疗保健	Health care and Medical Services	1693	2047	927
其他用品和服务	Miscellaneous Goods and Services	532	696	176

主要统计指标解释

可支配收入 指调查户在调查期内获得的、可用于最终消费支出和储蓄的总和，即调查户可以用来自由支配的收入。可支配收入既包括现金，也包括实物收入。按照收入的来源，可支配收入包含四项，分别为：工资性收入、经营净收入、财产净收入、转移净收入。计算公式为：

可支配收入 = 工资性收入 + 经营净收入 + 财产净其中：经营净收入 = 经营收入 - 经营费用 - 生产性固定资产折旧-生产税净额(生产税-生产补贴)

财产净收入 = 财产性收入 - 财产性支出

转移净收入 = 转移性收入 - 转移性支出

工资性收入 指就业人员通过各种途径得到的全部劳动报酬和各种福利，包括受雇于单位或个人、从事各种自由职业、兼职和零星劳动得到的全部劳动报酬和福利。

经营净收入 指住户或住户成员从事生产经营活动所获得的净收入，是全部经营收入中扣除经营费用、生产性固定资产折旧和生产税之后得到的净收入。

财产净收入 指住户或住户成员将其所拥有的金融资产、住房等非金融资产和自然资源交由其他机构单位、住户或个人支配而获得的回报并扣除相关的费用之后得到的净收入。财产净收入包括利息净收入、红利收入、储蓄性保险净收益、转让承包土地经营权租金净收入、出租房屋净收入、出租其他资产净收入和自有住房折算净租金等。

转移性收入 指国家、单位、社会团体对住户的各种经常性转移支付和住户之间的经常性收入转移。包括政府、非行政事业单位、社会团体对居民转移的养老金或退休金、社会救济和补助、惠农补贴、政策性生活补贴、救灾款、经常性捐赠和赔偿以及报销医疗费等；住户之间的赡养收入、经常性捐赠和赔偿以及农村地区(村委会)在外(含国外)工作的本住户非常住成员寄回带回的收入等。转移性收入不包括住户之间的实物馈赠。

转移性支出 指调查户对国家、单位、住户或个人的经常性或义务性转移支付。包括缴纳的税款、各项社会保障支出、赡养支出、经常性捐赠和赔偿支出以及其他经常转移支出等。

消费支出 指住户用于满足家庭日常生活消费需要的全部支出，包括用于消费品的支出和用于服务性消费的支出。根据用途不同，消费支出可划分为食品烟酒、衣着、居住、生活用品及服务、交通通信、教育文化娱乐、医疗保健、其他用品及服务八大类。根据来源不同，消费支出可划分为现金消费支出、实物消费支出(含自产自用、来自单位、来自政府和其他社会组织)。

食品烟酒 指用于各种食品和烟草、酒类的支出，包括食品和烟酒两个中类。

衣着 指与居民穿着有关的支出，包括服装、服装材料、鞋类、其他衣类及配件、衣着相关加工服务的支出。

居住 指与居住有关的支出，包括房租、水、电、燃料、物业管理等方面的支出，也包括自有住房折算租金。

生活用品及服务 指家庭及个人的各类生活品及家庭服务。包括家具及室内装饰品、家用器具、家用纺织品、家庭日用杂品、个人用品和家庭服务。

交通通信 指用于交通和通信工具及相关的各种服务费、维修费和车辆保险等支出。

教育文化和娱乐 指用于教育和文化娱乐方面的支出。

医疗保健 指用于医疗和保健的药品、用品和服务的总费用。包括医疗器具及药品，以及医疗服务。

其他用品及服务 指无法直接归入上述各类支出的其他用品与服务支出。

就业者负担人数 指家庭人口与就业人口之比。

城镇家庭可支配收入(老口径) 指家庭成员得到可用于最终消费支出和其它非义务性支出以及储蓄的总和，即居民家庭可以用来自由支配的收入。它是家庭总收入扣除交纳的所得税、个人交纳的社会保障支出以及记账补贴后的收入。计算公式为：

可支配收入=家庭总收入-交纳所得税-个人交纳的社会保障支出-记帐补贴

农村居民纯收入(老口径) 指农村住户当年从各个来源得到的总收入相应地扣除所发生的费用后的收入总和。计算方法：

纯收入=总收入-家庭经营费用支出-税费支出-生产性固定资产折旧

纯收入主要用于再生产投入和当年生活消费支出，也可用于储蓄和各种非义务性支出。“农民人均纯收入”按人口平均的纯收入水平，反映的是一个地区或一个农户农村居民的平均收入水平。

农村居民人均可支配收入与改革前的农民纯收入指标的主要区别是：可支配收入扣除了赠送农村以外亲友支出、农村居民用于购买住房、汽车等生活性贷款的利息支出，以及个人交纳的养老、医疗等社会保障支出，纯收入则不扣。同时，计算农村居民人均收入的分母调整为农村常住人口，调整了外出农民工寄带回收入的归类。

Explanatory Notes on Main Statistical Indicators

Disposable Income refers to the sum of households income that can be used for final consumption expenditure and savings during the period of investigation. Disposable income includes cash and real income. According to sources of income, disposable income includes the wage income, net operating income, net property income, and net transfer income. The formula for computing:

Disposable income = the wage income + net operating income + net property income + net transfer income

Net operating income = Income – operating costs – depreciation of productive fixed assets – net taxes on production (production tax – production subsidies)

Net property income = income from property – property expenditure

The transfer of net income = income from transfer – transfer expenditure

Wage Income refers to income and all kinds of welfare obtained by labors employed by different establishments, working independently or part–time.

Net Operating Income refers to the net income from operation run by the members of households, and it equals to total income minus operating costs and depreciation of productive fixed assets and taxes on production.

Net Property Income refers to the net income obtained from the financial assets, non–financial assets such as housing and natural resources provided by its owners to other establishments, households or individuals. It includes net interest income, bonus, net income from saving insurance, net income from the transfer of the right to land contractual management, income from house renting, income from renting of other assets and net rental income of home ownership.

Income from Transfer refers to the current transaction between government, establishments, social organization and households, and to the income transaction between households. It includes annuity, pension, social relief, agricultural subsidy, disaster relief fund, and medical expense, which are provided by governments, institutions, social organizations. It also includes supporting expense, regular donations, and income provided by non–permanent population. It does not include donations between households.

Transfer Expenditure refers to the regular or obligatory expenditure provided by the households to governments, institutions, other households or residents. It includes taxes, social security expenditure, supporting expenditure, regular donation and compensation expenditure, etc.

Expenditure refers to the consumption of all expenditures needs to meet the family daily life, including the expenditures on consumer goods and services. According to different purposes, consumption can be divided into tobacco & food, clothing, housing, daily necessities & services, transportation & communication, education & culture & entertainment, health care, and other goods & services. According to different sources, consumption expenditures can be divided into cash consumption and physical consumption expenditures (including self–occupied, from the unit, from the government and other social organizations).

Tobacco & Food refers to all kinds of expenditure on foods, tobaccos and beverages, including food and tobacco.

Clothing refers to the expenditure on clothes, clothing materials, shoes, accessories and charges for clothing production process.

Housing refers to the expenditure related to residing, including the expenditure on rent, water, fuel, power and real estate management and net rental income of home ownership.

Daily Necessities & Services refer to the expenditure on daily necessities and home service, including the expenditure on furniture, decoration, appliance, textile, personal items and home service.

Transportation & Communication refer to the expenditure on transportation, communication, related service, maintenance, and vehicle insurance.

Education & Culture & Entertainment refer to the expenditure on education, culture and entertainment.

Health Care refers to the sum of the expenditure on health care, medicine, related products and service, including the medical devices, drug as well as medical services.

Other Services refer to the expenditure on the goods and services that cannot be included in the categories mentioned above.

Number of Dependents per Employee refers to the ratio between number of persons in households and the number of employers in the household.

Urban Households Disposable Income (in previous cope) refers to the sum of households' income used for final consumption expenditure and savings during the period of investigation, meaning the income that is disposable for households. Disposable income is the general income of households minus income tax, social security expenditure and subsidy for account–keeping. The formula for computing:

Disposable Income of Households = General income – income tax – personal social security expenditure – subsidy for account keeping

Rural Households Net Income (in previous cope) refers to the total income of rural households from all sources minus all corresponding expenses. The formula for calculation is as follows:

Net income = total income – household operation expenses – taxes and fees – depreciation of fixed assets for production

Net income is mainly used as input for reproduction and as consumption expenditure of the year, and also used for savings and non–compulsory expenses of various forms. "Per capita net income of farmers" is the level of net income averaged by population which reflects the average income level of rural households in a given area.

The main difference between rural household disposable income and rural household net income is that the disposable income does not include the expenditure of donations to urban relatives, the expenditure on houses and vehicles purchasing, interest expenditure on consumer loans, and expenditure on pension and health care, but the net income includes all the expenditure mentioned above. When calculating the average income of rural household, the denominator is changed to permanent rural residents, and the classification of income brought back by migrant workers is also changed.

11

农 业

AGRICULTURE

11-1 各时期农业主要经济指标

Major Economic Indicators of Agriculture in Each Period

年份 Year	农村劳动力 (万人) Rural Labor (10 000 persons)	农林牧渔业总产值 (亿元) Gross Output Value of Farming,Forestry,Animal Husbandry and Fishery (100 million yuan)	农业机械总动力 (万千瓦) Total power of agricultural machinery (10 000 kw)	年末实有耕地面积 (千公顷) Actual Cultivated Area (1000 ha)	粮食总产量 (万吨) Output of Grain (10 000 tons)	蔬菜总产量 (万吨) Output of Vegetables (10 000 tons)	肉类总产量 (万吨) Output of Meat (10 000 tons)	粮食单产 (千克/公顷) Output Per Hectare of Grain (kg/ha)
1949	106.51	1.50	–	469.85	51.63	10.72	0.24	825
1952	112.35	1.91	–	481.17	62.75	8.61	0.40	960
1957	121.09	2.79	0.32	479.58	67.92	15.86	0.66	1065
1962	108.44	1.33	2.98	412.34	39.74	27.67	0.72	765
1965	111.74	2.61	4.84	410.02	73.80	29.12	1.12	1350
1970	123.91	2.75	14.32	396.49	75.47	31.81	1.21	1470
1975	141.00	4.07	48.04	382.05	100.46	42.00	2.07	2025
1978	140.05	6.57	69.70	373.19	115.38	49.19	2.50	2475
1979	141.60	7.48	80.63	372.45	122.56	49.42	2.92	2610
1980	143.19	7.79	88.45	370.87	116.54	58.13	3.69	2565
“六五”时期								
1981	146.52	11.73	94.47	369.80	121.27	49.85	3.99	2865
1982	149.07	14.47	106.60	369.22	121.13	63.45	4.31	3060
1983	152.39	18.07	112.19	368.45	147.41	65.66	4.66	3570
1984	158.23	19.00	123.92	367.35	160.60	86.91	5.03	3915
1985	162.51	18.36	130.41	357.41	163.50	84.11	5.43	3915
“七五”时期								
1986	165.86	20.91	147.36	353.96	168.16	118.86	6.44	3855
1987	168.56	24.65	156.23	352.18	167.25	101.52	7.13	3945
1988	171.44	34.24	172.89	350.56	167.95	122.83	8.68	4080
1989	173.38	35.14	182.40	349.59	162.45	117.99	9.70	3945
1990	176.83	36.92	183.40	347.56	181.47	126.09	11.38	4273
“八五”时期								
1991	180.09	40.13	191.00	344.76	207.55	146.87	13.50	4779
1992	182.51	45.14	191.50	343.29	198.29	170.61	15.36	4655
1993	183.78	57.81	194.40	341.54	232.21	205.62	19.12	4963
1994	183.42	85.37	207.40	339.97	237.66	226.39	26.14	5237
1995	183.55	114.07	241.20	339.30	252.48	253.54	28.68	5512

年份 Year	农村劳动力 (万人) Rural Labor (10 000 persons)	农林牧渔业总产值 (亿元) Gross Output Value of Farming,Forestry,Animal Husbandry and Fishery (100 million yuan)	农业机械总动力 (万千瓦) Total power of agricultural machinery (10 000 kw)	年末实有耕地面积 (千公顷) Actual Cultivated Area (1000 ha)	粮食总产量 (万吨) Output of Grain (10 000 tons)	蔬菜总产量 (万吨) Output of Vegetables (10 000 tons)	肉类总产量 (万吨) Output of Meat (10 000 tons)	粮食单产 (千克/公顷) Output Per Hectare of Grain (kg/ha)
"九五"时期								
1996	184.68	117.65	247.07	337.25	267.08	350.36	30.43	5602
1997	186.68	131.69	258.50	335.90	240.34	328.64	24.75	5064
1998	186.54	141.45	273.30	334.83	273.10	344.67	27.38	5634
1999	188.27	148.61	297.55	333.72	279.01	366.78	29.89	5752
2000	189.15	154.30	349.47	333.72	240.27	405.95	31.82	5354
"十五"时期								
2001	189.87	162.27	409.07	331.75	239.08	435.20	33.23	5480
2002	190.98	167.99	410.17	329.35	189.86	478.34	31.87	4440
2003	192.71	180.30	417.43	325.18	220.56	504.81	33.29	5448
2004	191.31	204.39	418.54	324.89	242.74	515.26	35.35	5807
2005	190.21	230.46	426.76	366.99	260.11	529.37	37.93	5932
"十一五"时期								
2006	190.80	247.70	429.62	361.74	267.91	536.28	38.74	6042
2007	191.16	262.51	446.60	358.80	268.01	522.24	31.85	6064
2008	190.45	302.00	466.00	361.33	281.50	520.25	30.22	6230
2009	195.56	318.06	486.00		289.47	560.83	31.39	6246
2010	196.85	361.24	509.68	362.30	289.43	572.05	31.79	6192
"十二五"时期								
2011	197.38	399.90	527.39	361.25	295.84	590.02	32.43	6315
2012	198.74	422.75	538.66	360.28	286.03	606.11	33.22	6285
2013	199.80	470.55	552.06	361.01	266.60	629.54	33.59	5997
2014	199.73	479.50	567.02	360.24	271.19	638.22	34.10	6109
2015	200.45	493.04	584.98	358.57	264.55	626.23	34.18	6117
"十三五"时期								
2016	200.46	501.72	447.83	357.60	275.43	611.25	31.72	5778
2017	198.91	505.08	442.90	355.66	255.57	591.63	32.50	5660
2018	189.10	514.90	454.62	353.65	251.42	527.22	29.82	5659

注：1. 自 2005 年始年末实有耕地面积有国土资源局提供，暂无 2009 年数据。
2. 依据 2006 年农业普查数据，对 1997 年至 2007 年蔬菜面积、产量做了相应调整。
3. 粮食作物产量、播种面积自 2012 年开始由山东调查总队反馈。
4. 按照国务院农普办要求，由国家统计局山东调查总队根据第三次农业普查数据，对 2016-2017 年市、县（区）粮食播种面积、单产和总产量等数据进行了修订。
5. 依据 2016 年农业普查数据，对 2007 年至 2017 年农林牧渔业总产值做了相应调整。
6. 依据 2016 年农业普查数据，对 2008 年至 2017 年蔬菜总产量、肉类总产量做了相应调整。

Note: 1. Since 2005, the actual cultivated area has been provided by Land Resources Bureau. No data for 2009.
2. According to the data of the agricultural census in 2006, the area and yield of the vegetables from 1997 to 2007 were adjusted accordingly.
3. Grain crop yield and sown area have been reported by Shandong Survey Team since 2012.
4. According to the requirements of Agricultural Census Office of the State Council, Shandong Survey Team of National Bureau of Statistics revised the grain sown area, yield per unit and total yield of each city and country (district) from 2016-2017 based on the data from the third agricultural census.
5. According to the data of the agricultural census in 2016, the total output value of agriculture, forestry, animal husbandry and fishery in the period from 2007 to 2017 was adjusted accordingly.
6. According to the data of the agricultural census in 2016, the total output value of agriculture, vegetable and meat in the period from 2008 to 2017 was adjusted accordingly.

11-2 农村基层组织和农业基本情况

Basic Conditions of Rural Grassroots Units and Agriculture

指 标	Indicator	单 位 Unit	2013 年	2014 年	2015 年	2016 年	2017 年	2018 年
乡镇数量	Number of Towns	个(Unit)	53	53	48	39	29	29
#镇	Towns	个(Unit)	51	51	46	39	29	29
村民委员会	Village Committee	个(Unit)	4532	4547	4546	4547	4548	4546
乡村户数	Rural Households	万户 (10 000 households)	101.11	101.31	101.96	103.14	102.31	101.96
乡村人口	Rural Numbers	万人 (10 000 persons)	357.43	357.42	360.29	362.55	359.18	355.74
家庭从业人员	FamilyPractitioner	万人 (10 001 persons)	199.81	199.73	200.45	200.46	198.91	189.10
男	Male	万人 (10 002 persons)	106.34	105.89	106.07	106.06	105.38	99.96
女	Female	万人 (10 003 persons)	93.47	93.84	94.38	94.40	93.52	89.15
地类面积	Land Category Area	公顷(ha)	799841	799841	799841	799841	799841	799841
耕地	Cultivated Land	公顷(ha)	361012	360241	358568	357601	355659	353652
其中水浇地	Irrigated Land	公顷(ha)	265725	265119	264016	263310	261894	263885
园地	Garden Land	公顷(ha)	26233	26180	26054	25957	25801	25675
林地	Forest Land	公顷(ha)	85100	84963	84676	84484	84175	83947
草地	Grazing and Pasture Land	公顷(ha)	57520	57430	57250	57151	57018	56879
城镇村及工矿用地	Land for Urban Village, Mining and Manufacturing	公顷(ha)	140218	140772	142969	144219	146819	149020
交通运输用地	Land for Transport Facilities	公顷(ha)	28740	29068	29135	29319	29617	30216
水域及水利设施用地	Land for Water Conservancy Facilities	公顷(ha)	51155	51039	50962	50875	50696	50531
其它土地	Other Land	公顷(ha)	49863	50150	50227	50236	50055	49921
年末耕地总资源	Total Cultivated Area	公顷(ha)	398999	398132	396365	395292	393224	391040
农业机械总动力	total power of agricultural machinery	万千瓦 (10 000 kw)	552.06	567.02	584.98	447.83	442.90	454.62
农用大中型拖拉机	Large and Medium-sized Tractors	台(set)	22717	23906	24328	25574	24329	20208
农用小型拖拉机	Small Tractors	台(set)	39099	37503	36964	35492	27179	30152
谷物联合收割机	Combine Harvester	台(set)	10902	12734	12933	14365	13948	14380
柴油机	Diesel Engine	台(set)	84915	85395	85775	84583	82173	
割晒机	Cutter-Rower	台(set)	3783	3768	3357	3103	2935	
脱粒机	Thresher	台(set)	19464	20901	20178	20450	19917	19660
农村用电量	Electricity Consumption in Rural Area	亿千瓦小时 (100 million kwh)	26.35	26.42	26.51	25.66	24.40	23.58
农作物总播种面积	Total Sown Area of Farm Crops	千公顷 (1000 ha)	583.4	578.1	562.4	598.9	566.1	549.0

注：按照国务院农普办要求，由国家统计局山东调查总队根据第三次农业普查数据，对 2016-2017 年市、县（区）粮食播种面积数据进行了修订。

Note: According to the requirements of Agricultural Census Office of the State Council, Shandong Survey Team of National Bureau of Statistics revised the grain sown area, of each city and country (district) from 2016-2017 based on the data from the third agricultural census.

11-3 分地区农村基层组织

Basic Conditions of Rural Grassrootsunits

指　标	Indicator	单　位 Unit	济南市 Ji'nan	历下区 Li xia
乡镇数量	Number of Towns	个(Unit)	29	
#镇	Towns	个(Unit)	29	
村民委员会	Village Committee	个(Unit)	4546	20
乡村户数	Rural Households	万户(10 000 households)	101.96	
乡村总人口	Rural Numbers	万人(10 000 persons)	355.74	
乡村劳动力	FamilyPractitioner	万人(10 001 persons)	189.10	
男	Male	万人(10 002 persons)	99.96	
女	Female	万人(10 003 persons)	89.15	
地类面积	Land Category Area	公顷(ha)	799841	10118
耕地	Cultivated Land	公顷(ha)	353652	276
其中水浇地	Irrigated Land	公顷(ha)	263885	78
园地	Garden Land	公顷(ha)	25675	25
林地	Forest Land	公顷(ha)	83947	1901
草地	Grazing and Pasture Land	公顷(ha)	56879	436
城镇村及工矿用地	Land for Urban Village, Mining and Manufacturing	公顷(ha)	149020	7262
交通运输用地	Land for Transport Facilities	公顷(ha)	30216	59
水域及水利设施用地	Land for Water Conservancy Facilities	公顷(ha)	50531	38
其它土地	Other Land	公顷(ha)	49921	120
年末耕地总资源	Total Cultivated Area	公顷(ha)	391040	276
农业机械总动力	total power of agricultural machinery	万千瓦(10 000 kw)	455	3.67
农用大中型拖拉机	Large and Medium-sized Tractors	台(set)	20208	60
农用小型拖拉机	Small Tractors	台(set)	30152	615
谷物联合收割机	Combine Harvester	台(set)	14380	41
柴油机	Diesel Engine	台(set)		
割晒机	Cutter-Rower	台(set)		
脱粒机	Thresher	台(set)	19660	26
农村用电量	Electricity Consumption in Rural Area	亿千瓦小时(100 million kwh)	23.58	
农作物总播种面积	Total Sown Area of Farm Crops	千公顷(1000 ha)	548.97	

和农业基本情况（2018年）

and Agriculture by Region（2018）

市中区 Shi zhong	槐荫区 Huai yin	天桥区 Tian qiao	历城区 Li cheng	长清区 Chang qing	章丘区 Zhang qiu	济阳区 Ji yang	平阴县 Ping yin	商河县 Shang he
			2	3	3	4	6	11
77	92	120	520	580	890	811	336	948
4.39	1.50	2.53	20.96	12.80	24.70	12.43	8.80	13.85
15.07	5.86	9.13	69.29	43.58	82.08	47.64	29.89	53.20
7.05	3.19	4.56	36.31	22.30	47.48	27.90	12.09	28.22
3.78	1.82	2.40	17.06	11.13	25.17	14.96	8.41	15.23
3.27	1.37	2.16	15.28	11.16	22.31	12.93	7.68	12.99
28149	15161	25897	130121	120859	171909	109881	71506	116240
5401	3263	9477	31801	46147	78263	70253	33201	75570
1436	1416	8940	17390	20489	52301	67022	19745	75067
1104	40	88	13632	4392	3782	377	1949	286
3698	431	1767	23091	20691	14624	4391	10398	2954
4149	118	130	15628	15154	16428	494	3997	345
10163	7783	9066	29872	14746	28793	15852	9747	15736
867	723	1337	5033	3772	6205	4130	2806	5284
358	2625	3773	4600	4911	8011	11563	3207	11446
2411	179	258	6465	11046	15802	2820	6200	4619
6659	3549	10716	39401	52628	90141	73396	37036	77238
12.68	5	16.18	53.00	48.19	91.24	96.42	41.28	86.86
359	279	530	1606	2841	3229	4493	1590	5221
385	350	2261	5644	3489	2243	3298	5013	6854
114	157	340	1298	1307	3631	2471	692	4329
121	2772	1158	1285	886	2193	6040	780	4399
1.61	0.50	0.61	3.90	2.86	8.67	1.22	2.30	1.91
5.04	2.70	14.53	27.33	58.11	138.22	119.27	47.20	136.56

11 - 4 各时期农林牧渔业增加值(按当年价格计算)

Added Value of Agriculture, Forestry, Animal Husbandry and Fishery in Each Period(Calculated at Current Prices)

单位：亿元 (100 million yuan)

年 份 Year	合计 Total	农业 Farming	林业 Forestry	牧业 Animal Husbandry	渔业 Fishery	农林牧渔服务业 Services of Agriculture,Forestry,Animal Husbandry and Fishing
1957	1.89	1.42	-	0.47	-	-
1962	1.01	0.76	–	0.25	–	–
1965	1.85	1.39	–	0.46	–	–
1970	2.11	1.58	–	0.53	–	–
1975	2.84	2.13	–	0.71	–	–
1978	4.08	2.94	0.19	0.89	0.06	–
1980	5.84	4.21	0.27	1.28	0.08	–
1985	12.16	8.75	0.57	2.66	0.18	–
"七五" 时期						
1986	13.94	10.03	0.65	3.05	0.21	–
1987	16.21	11.66	0.76	3.55	0.24	–
1988	22.05	15.87	1.03	4.83	0.32	–
1989	22.74	16.37	1.06	4.98	0.33	–
1990	22.70	16.34	1.06	4.97	0.33	–
"八五" 时期						
1991	24.68	18.00	0.95	5.31	0.42	–
1992	27.74	19.52	1.31	6.38	0.53	–
1993	35.66	23.83	1.45	9.72	0.66	–
1994	49.44	33.39	2.02	13.48	0.55	–
1995	67.24	49.59	1.97	14.95	0.75	–
"九五" 时期						
1996	72.74	55.35	2.68	13.49	1.22	–
1997	81.07	62.25	2.95	14.66	1.21	–
1998	88.06	67.07	2.67	16.92	1.40	–
1999	92.52	67.30	2.21	21.33	1.68	–
2000	95.01	67.57	2.51	23.56	1.37	–

年 份 Year	合计 Total	农业 Farming	林业 Forestry	牧业 Animal Husbandry	渔业 Fishery	农林牧渔服务业 Services of Agriculture,Forestry,Animal Husbandry and Fishing
"十五" 时期						
2001	97.17	68.96	2.25	24.49	1.47	-
2002	98.74	68.88	2.44	25.99	1.43	-
2003	104.90	70.71	2.87	28.51	1.22	1.60
2004	120.47	80.17	3.15	33.86	1.50	1.77
2005	134.34	88.66	4.05	38.14	1.59	1.90
"十一五" 时期						
2006	145.12	95.80	4.54	40.32	1.77	2.69
2007	148.53	95.54	5.26	42.19	1.98	3.56
2008	171.05	105.38	7.58	51.14	3.11	3.83
2009	180.67	114.54	8.12	50.27	3.24	4.50
2010	205.01	139.90	4.57	51.77	3.53	5.24
"十二五" 时期						
2011	224.58	140.49	5.45	68.43	4.08	6.14
2012	236.29	145.64	6.34	72.50	4.48	7.33
2013	262.72	166.61	7.42	74.73	5.30	8.65
2014	272.90	174.90	8.25	73.78	5.93	10.05
2015	284.25	181.19	9.20	76.39	6.36	11.11
"十三五" 时期						
2016	284.92	189.87	9.28	68.36	6.16	11.26
2017	279.91	185.71	10.72	66.27	4.86	12.36
2018	286.44	195.16	12.86	59.27	5.13	14.02
2018 年分地区 Region						
历下区 Li xia						
市中区 Shi zhong	2.36	0.74	0.45	0.98	0.10	0.08
槐荫区 Huai yin	2.68	1.86	0.37	0.16	0.25	0.05
天桥区 Tian qiao	3.72	2.44	0.17	0.90	0.17	0.03
历城区 Li cheng	45.36	35.52	3.97	3.16	0.66	2.05
长清区 Chang qing	32.01	21.31	1.54	8.06	0.21	0.89
章丘区 Zhang qiu	80.85	54.00	2.77	18.56	1.15	4.37
济阳区 Ji yang	40.56	30.17	1.04	7.29	1.07	0.98
平阴县 Ping yin	32.27	22.16	1.03	6.45	0.28	2.34
商河县 Shang he	46.63	26.96	1.53	13.70	1.22	3.22

注：依据 2016 年农业普查数据，对 2007 年至 2017 年农林牧渔业增加值做了相应调整。

Note: According to the data of the agricultural census in 2016, the value added of agriculture, forestry, animal husbandry and fishery in the period from 2007 to 2017 was adjusted accordingly.

11-5 各时期农林牧渔业总产值(按当年价格计算)

Gross Output Value of Agriculture, Forestry, Animal Husbandry and Fishery in Each Period(Calculated at Current Prices)

单位：亿元 (100 million yuan)

年份 Year	合计 Total	农业 Farming	林业 Forestry	牧业 Animal Husbandry	渔业 Fishery	农林牧渔服务业 Services of Agriculture,Forestry,Animal Husbandry and Fishing
1952	1.91	1.67	0.04	0.18	0.02	–
1957	2.79	2.41	0.09	0.28	0.01	–
1962	1.33	1.18	0.03	0.12	…	–
1965	2.61	2.25	0.07	0.28	0.01	–
1970	2.75	2.32	0.10	0.32	0.01	–
1975	4.07	3.48	0.13	0.44	0.02	–
1978	6.57	5.63	0.20	0.72	0.02	–
1980	7.78	6.66	0.18	0.93	0.01	–
1985	18.36	14.63	0.75	2.93	0.05	–
“七五”时期						
1986	20.91	16.81	0.79	3.23	0.08	–
1987	24.65	19.50	0.99	4.05	0.11	–
1988	34.24	24.83	1.42	7.67	0.32	–
1989	35.14	25.04	1.24	8.47	0.39	–
1990	36.92	24.70	1.41	10.36	0.45	–
“八五”时期						
1991	40.13	26.44	1.47	11.64	0.58	–
1992	45.14	29.01	1.70	13.71	0.72	–
1993	57.81	36.00	1.98	18.86	0.97	–
1994	85.37	52.36	2.80	29.38	0.83	–
1995	114.07	71.48	2.71	38.69	1.19	–
“九五”时期						
1996	117.65	77.16	3.35	35.25	1.89	–
1997	131.69	87.91	3.86	38.04	1.88	–
1998	141.45	93.56	3.55	42.17	2.17	–
1999	148.61	96.81	3.12	46.27	2.41	–
2000	154.30	100.18	3.64	48.34	2.14	–

年 份 Year	合计 Total	农业 Farming	林业 Forestry	牧业 Animal Husbandry	渔业 Fishery	农林牧渔服务业 Services of Agriculture,Forestry,Animal Husbandry and Fishing
"十五"时期						
2001	162.27	105.54	3.27	51.16	2.30	–
2002	167.99	106.27	3.51	55.84	2.37	–
2003	180.30	109.41	4.11	60.90	2.05	3.83
2004	204.39	121.28	4.49	71.87	2.50	4.25
2005	230.46	137.01	5.56	80.56	2.69	4.64
"十一五"时期						
2006	247.72	147.98	6.44	84.86	2.89	5.55
2007	262.51	154.32	7.28	91.33	3.18	6.41
2008	302.00	173.32	10.63	104.53	4.54	8.97
2009	318.06	192.96	11.16	98.96	4.79	10.18
2010	361.24	231.08	6.87	106.40	5.31	11.58
"十二五"时期						
2011	399.90	240.80	7.98	131.55	6.05	13.51
2012	422.75	251.57	9.00	139.90	6.88	15.39
2013	470.55	284.66	10.34	149.46	8.01	18.07
2014	479.50	291.94	11.19	147.57	8.76	20.03
2015	493.04	296.93	12.15	153.12	9.32	21.52
"十三五"时期						
2016	501.72	298.63	13.20	156.28	9.88	23.74
2017	505.08	296.75	15.25	159.23	7.80	26.06
2018	514.90	318.55	17.72	141.48	7.28	29.88
2018 年分地区 Region						
历下区 Li xia						
市中区 Shi zhong	4.20	1.06	0.62	2.22	0.15	0.16
槐荫区 Huai yin	4.59	3.26	0.49	0.39	0.35	0.09
天桥区 Tian qiao	6.35	3.61	0.26	2.19	0.23	0.06
历城区 Li cheng	80.76	62.09	5.49	7.72	0.91	4.55
长清区 Chang qing	59.05	35.34	2.08	19.49	0.28	1.86
章丘区 Zhang qiu	145.11	86.41	3.87	44.21	1.69	8.93
济阳区 Ji yang	72.49	49.86	1.39	17.68	1.38	2.18
平阴县 Ping yin	57.26	35.52	1.39	14.89	0.41	5.04
商河县 Shang he	85.10	41.38	2.14	32.70	1.86	7.02

注：依据 2016 年农业普查数据，对 2007 年至 2017 年农林牧渔业总产值做了相应调整。

Note: According to the data of the agricultural census in 2016, the total output value of agriculture, forestry, animal husbandry and fishery in the period from 2007 to 2017 was adjusted accordingly.

11-6 各时期农林牧渔业总产值定基指数（以1952年为100）

Gross Output Value and Indices of Farming、Forestry、Animal Husbandry in Each Period(1952=100)

年 份 Year	合计 Total	农业 Farming	林业 Forestry	牧业 Animal Husbandry	渔业 Fishery
1952	100.00	100.00	100.00	100.00	100.00
1957	116.18	114.55	170.35	119.90	109.96
1962	73.32	74.42	69.10	69.25	20.68
1965	123.31	121.76	147.34	141.38	28.95
1970	151.35	146.28	254.82	184.02	58.65
1975	201.09	196.80	317.61	226.74	78.38
“五五”时期					
1976	198.67	185.64	340.19	269.52	118.70
1977	197.95	190.19	373.20	218.87	56.26
1978	208.10	203.90	304.32	239.93	57.89
1979	233.93	224.05	316.47	293.89	53.70
1980	264.53	259.07	286.30	330.80	43.98
“六五”时期					
1981	279.36	279.29	281.28	377.56	55.36
1982	312.68	308.75	346.83	460.13	51.95
1983	402.03	369.18	434.91	460.59	57.98
1984	493.28	436.59	572.67	651.29	69.52
1985	505.48	460.68	992.56	841.94	161.47
“七五”时期					
1986	531.29	488.47	964.62	857.25	229.32
1987	560.14	506.85	1075.00	960.76	291.92
1988	585.14	510.86	992.11	1191.92	383.08
1989	571.95	483.32	886.96	1320.55	495.30
1990	607.77	449.63	1126.99	1931.15	695.49
“八五”时期					
1991	670.19	488.17	1189.04	2204.93	830.45
1992	712.62	491.78	1298.34	2574.55	1007.33

年 份 Year	合计 Total	农业 Farming	林业 Forestry	牧业 Animal Husbandry	渔业 Fishery
1993	844.31	566.55	1420.51	3221.58	1209.21
1994	945.74	603.90	1671.10	2864.71	1064.29
1995	1093.57	657.49	1508.72	4905.57	1945.11
"九五"时期					
1996	1197.20	727.03	1818.36	5258.95	2224.25
1997	1273.56	820.27	2002.99	5116.96	2202.07
1998	1426.28	914.05	1858.14	5907.41	2516.54
1999	1486.09	934.64	2110.21	6277.65	2639.47
2000	1569.90	991.58	2255.81	6620.62	2441.73
"十五"时期					
2001	1599.32	1005.16	1700.16	6905.18	2646.43
2002	1638.09	997.16	1826.57	7349.57	2712.97
2003	1711.88	1072.24	1977.78	7726.93	2324.25
2004	1804.32	1132.29	1979.76	8121.00	2803.05
2005	1930.62	1188.90	2237.13	8770.68	2802.30
"十一五"时期					
2006	2046.15	1249.31	2454.25	9245.35	3003.10
2007	2046.15	1334.26	2610.83	9006.43	3540.65
2008	2148.45	1422.32	2783.14	9231.59	3204.85
2009	2260.17	1524.73	2964.04	9342.35	3323.43
2010	2367.76	1584.02	1815.08	10311.68	3416.48
"十二五"时期					
2011	2471.94	1658.47	2016.56	10600.40	3508.72
2012	2588.12	1724.80	2216.20	11151.62	3768.36
2013	2689.05	1762.74	2491.01	11809.56	3877.64
2014	2801.99	1845.58	2724.66	12116.60	3916.41
2015	2919.67	1924.93	2986.23	12540.68	4033.90
"十三五"时期					
2016	3045.21	2007.70	3317.70	12967.06	4187.19
2017	3157.88	2126.15	3689.28	13278.26	4203.93
2018	3095.96	2215.44	4105.56	12733.85	4330.04

11-7 主要农作物播种面积及产量

Sown Areas and Output of Main Farm Crops

指标	Indicator	2013 年	2014 年	2015 年	2016 年	2017 年	2018 年
农作物总播种面积(万公顷)	**Total Sown Area of Crops(10 000 ha)**	58.34	57.81	56.24	59.89	56.61	54.90
粮食作物	Grain	44.47	44.39	43.25	47.67	45.15	44.43
谷物	Cereals	42.94	42.80	41.65	46.05	43.79	43.25
小麦	Wheat	21.04	21.05	20.99	22.00	21.58	21.38
稻谷	Rice	0.45	0.34	0.21	0.20	0.18	0.14
玉米	Corn	20.85	20.81	19.82	22.93	21.07	20.84
谷子	Millet	0.50	0.49	0.54	0.86	0.91	0.86
高粱	Chinese Sorghum	0.09	0.09	0.09	0.05	0.05	0.02
其他	Others	0.01	0.01	0.01	0.01	0.00	0.01
豆类	Beans	0.69	0.69	0.71	0.85	0.70	0.62
薯类	Tubers	0.84	0.91	0.88	0.77	0.66	0.56
油料作物	Oil-bearing Crops	1.52	1.36	1.30	1.00	1.00	1.02
#花生	Peanuts	1.33	1.21	1.13	0.88	0.87	0.90
棉花	Cotton	1.17	0.89	0.71	0.62	0.20	0.28
蔬菜	Vegetable	9.61	9.61	9.42	9.13	8.86	7.89
果用瓜	Melon	1.31	1.29	1.28	1.20	1.16	1.07
其他作物	Other Farm Crops	0.26	0.27	0.28	0.26	0.25	0.21
果园种植面积(万公顷)	**Orchard Area(10 000 ha)**	3.42	3.41	3.35	3.20	3.16	3.09
#苹果	Apple	1.33	1.33	1.29	1.18	1.18	1.13
梨	Pear	0.17	0.16	0.16	0.14	0.14	0.16
葡萄	Grape	0.10	0.10	0.10	0.10	0.10	0.11
桃	Peach	0.47	0.49	0.47	0.49	0.49	0.72
农作物总产量(万吨)	**Total Output of Farm Crops(10 000 tons)**						
粮食作物产量	Output of Grain Crops	266.61	271.19	264.55	275.43	255.57	251.42
谷物	Cereals	259.98	264.64	257.65	268.30	249.47	246.12
小麦	Wheat	123.86	126.37	129.75	127.31	123.79	121.78
稻谷	Rice	2.89	2.33	1.52	1.55	1.36	1.18
玉米	Corn	131.40	134.26	124.39	136.65	121.25	119.82
谷子	Millet	1.59	1.45	1.74	2.64	2.97	3.27
高粱	Chinese Sorghum	0.20	0.19	0.22	0.11	0.11	0.04
其他	Other Cereals	0.04	0.04	0.03	0.04	0.00	0.03

指　　标	Indicator	2013 年	2014 年	2015 年	2016 年	2017 年	2018 年
豆类	Beans	1.87	1.71	1.92	2.25	1.82	1.67
薯类	Tubers	4.76	4.85	4.99	4.87	4.28	3.63
油料作物	Oil-bearing Crops	5.69	4.95	4.59	3.53	3.59	4.15
#花生	Peanuts	5.33	4.63	4.23	3.25	3.31	3.87
棉花	Cotton	1.16	0.97	0.74	0.69	0.20	0.29
蔬菜	Vegetable	629.54	638.22	626.23	611.25	591.63	527.22
果用瓜	Melon	78.75	77.79	77.00	70.74	67.51	59.65
水果总产量(万吨)	**Output of Fruits(10 000 tons)**	43.29	44.11	43.94	41.08	43.15	42.19
#苹果	Apple	20.65	20.98	20.62	18.33	18.59	16.00
梨	Pear	4.76	4.70	4.83	4.26	3.98	3.40
葡萄	Grape	3.08	3.10	3.16	2.86	3.00	3.00
桃	Peach	11.02	10.82	10.71	11.08	13.10	11.86
杏	Apricot	0.73	0.85	0.83	0.78	0.75	3.02
枣(鲜)	Jujube	0.98	1.02	1.00	1.02	1.02	0.89
柿子(鲜)	Persimmon	0.26	0.26	0.24	0.23	0.23	1.24
山楂	Hawthorn	0.54	0.54	0.54	0.55	0.55	0.63
樱桃	Cherry	0.95	1.05	1.59	1.49	1.45	1.51
其他	Others	0.50	0.50	0.50	0.48	0.47	0.64
农作物单位面积产量(公斤/公顷)	**Output per Hectare of Farm Crops(kg/ha)**						
粮食作物单位面积产量	Output per Hectare of Grain Crops	5995	6109	6117	5778	5660	5659
谷物	Cereals	6054	6184	6186	5826	5697	5690
小麦	Wheat	5887	6002	6182	5787	5736	5696
稻谷	Rice	6422	6799	7259	7698	7645	8288
玉米	Corn	6302	6452	6276	5960	5754	5748
谷子	Millet	3180	2965	3220	3071	3252	3809
高粱	Chinese Sorghum	2222	2149	2497	2097	2228	2074
其他	Others	4000	2974	3000	2716	0	3062
豆类	Beans	2710	2474	2683	2659	2614	2716
薯类	Tubers	5667	5341	5673	6371	6462	6462
油料作物	Oil-bearing Crops	3753	3627	3545	3531	3609	4083
#花生	Peanuts	4004	3830	3747	3713	3795	4327
棉花	Cotton	995	1080	1040	1106	1037	1029
蔬菜	Vegetable	65495	66434	66460	66918	66798	66852
果用瓜	Melon	60056	60506	60263	46939	58724	55628

注：1. 依据 2006 年农业普查数据，对 1997 年至 2007 年蔬菜面积、产量做了相应调整。

2. 按照国务院农普办要求，由国家统计局山东调查总队根据第三次农业普查数据，对 2016-2017 年市、县（区）粮食播种面积、单产和总产量等数据进行修订。

3、依据 2016 年农业普查数据，对 2008 年至 2017 年种植业相关品种面积、产量做了相应调整。

Note: 1. According to the data of the agricultural census in 2006, the area and yield of the vegetables from 1997 to 2007 were adjusted accordingly.

2. According to the requirements of Agricultural Census Office of the State Council, Shandong Survey Team of National Bureau of Statistics revised the grain sown area, yield per unit and total yield of each city and country (district) from 2016-2017 based on the data from the third agricultural census.

3. According to the agricultural census data in 2016, the area and yield of planting related varieties from 2008 to 2017 were adjusted accordingly.

11-8 林、牧、渔业生产情况

Basic Statistics on Forestry、Animal Husbandry and Fishery

指　　标	Indicator	单位 Unit	2013 年	2014 年	2015 年	2016 年	2017 年	2018 年
林业生产	**Production of Forestry**							
造林面积	Forested Area	公顷(ha)	13637	14881	12013	3504	3809	4902
四旁植树	Surrounding Tree Planting	万株(10000 trees)	1377	1366	1311	1312	1301	1306
育苗面积	Area of Nursery Garden	公顷(ha)	8900	12073	14439	11773	10645	10174
果品产量	Output of Fruits	吨(tons)	535625	574248	573064	539475	596994	555042
木材采伐量	Timber Cut	立方米(stere)	167433	143896	132014	157238	214946	283354
牧业生产	**Production of Animal Husbandry**							
大牲畜存栏	Stocked Large Livestock	万头(10 000 heads)	26.05	26.30	28.11	28.97	31.63	26.30
#役畜	Draught Animal	万头(10 000 heads)	1.49	1.37	0.26	0.19	0.02	0.02
#牛	Cattle	万头(10 000 heads)	25.46	25.71	27.86	28.69	31.36	26.17
猪存栏	Stocked Pigs	万头(10 000 heads)	136.26	136.56	128.51	116.73	120.13	102.95
羊存栏	Stocked Sheep	万只(10 000 heads)	88.04	88.78	89.71	93.27	96.60	87.61
家禽存栏	Stocked Poultry	万只(10 000 heads)	2701.65	2723.53	2784.87	2743.90	2467.54	2300.42
猪出栏数	Slaughtered Pigs	万头(10 000 heads)	214.59	223.04	214.97	194.15	198.43	185.59
羊出栏数	Slaughtered Sheep and Goats	万只(10 000 heads)	121.14	129.91	132.07	149.03	153.23	143.84

指　标	Indicator	单 位 Unit	2013 年	2014 年	2015 年	2016 年	2017 年	2018 年
肉类总产量	Output of Meat	吨(tons)	335868	340975	341829	317201	325036	298180
#猪牛羊肉	Meat	吨(tons)	248845	259678	259954	235990	246561	223735
猪肉	Pork	吨(tons)	180114	188921	185546	162114	168054	155005
牛肉	Beef	吨(tons)	51272	51902	55852	53203	57206	46438
羊肉	Mutton	吨(tons)	17459	18854	18557	20673	21301	22292
禽肉	Poultry Meat	吨(tons)	83473	76781	81113	80447	77809	74164
奶类	Milk	吨(tons)	243649	258085	232705	214620	263642	328412
#牛奶	Cow Milk	吨(tons)	243649	258082	232702	214617	263638	328410
禽蛋	Poultry Eggs	吨(tons)	342797	347254	378577	386440	394001	332303
#鸡蛋	Hen's Eggs	吨(tons)	327293	332092	362017	368636	375517	313234
渔业生产	**Aquatic Products**							
水产品产量	Total Aquatic Products	吨(tons)	46048	47018	47565	46709	41279	31911
捕捞	Fishing	吨(tons)	905	759	650	465	186	289
养殖	Cultured	吨(tons)	45143	46259	46915	46244	41093	31622
养殖面积	Breeding Area of Aquatic Products	公顷(ha)	7428	7360	7285	7079	6673	5228
养殖单产	Aquaculture Yield	公斤/公顷(kg/ha)	6077	6285	6440	6533	6158	6049

注：依据 2016 年农业普查数据，对 2008 年至 2017 年牧业生产有关指标做了相应调整。
Note: According to the data of agricultural census in 2016, the relevant indicators of animal husbandry production from 2008 to 2017 were adjusted accordingly.

11-9 分地区主要农作物

Sown Areas and Output of

指标	Indicator	济南市 Total City	历下区 Li xia	市中区 Shi zhong
农作物播种总面积(公顷)	Total Sown Area of Crops(ha)	548971		5043
粮食	Grain	444308		4835
谷物	Cereals	432529		4792
小麦	Wheat	213798		2287
稻谷	Rice	1427		0
玉米	Corn	208447		2293
谷子	Millet	8573		212
高粱	Chinese Sorghum	184		0
其他	Others	100		0
豆类	Beans	6165		29
薯类	Tubers	5614		14
油料作物	Oil-bearing Crops	10171		19
#花生	Peanuts	8950		15
棉花	Cotton	2845		30
蔬菜	Vegetable	78863		152
果用瓜	Melon	10723		7
其他作物	Other Farm Crops	2061		0
果园种植面积(公顷)	Orchard Area(ha)	30939		198
#苹果	Apple	11285		49
梨	Pear	1590		1
葡萄	Grape	1074		14
桃	Peach	7226		91
农作物产量(吨)(tons)	Total Output of Farm Crops			
粮食作物产量	Output of Grain Crops	2514197		19493
谷物	Cereals	2461175		19364
小麦	Wheat	1217824		8539
稻谷	Rice	11829		0
玉米	Corn	1198184		10416
谷子	Millet	32650		408
高粱	Chinese Sorghum	382		0
其他	Other Cereals	305		0

播种面积及产量（2018年）

Main Farm Crops by Region（2018）

槐荫区 Huai yin	天桥区 Tian qiao	历城区 Li cheng	长清区 Chang qing	章丘区 Zhang qiu	济阳区 Ji yang	平阴县 Ping yin	商河县 Shang he
2702	14532	27335	58110	138222	119270	47199	136559
2305	13878	20612	44680	105714	99813	33615	118857
2259	13821	20079	42435	101671	98984	29746	118741
1176	7655	8181	17842	50831	52829	15307	57690
296	34	0	55	113	930	0	0
786	6132	10597	21073	48277	45226	13011	61051
0	0	1298	3363	2284	0	1416	0
0	0	2	4	167	0	12	0
0	0	1	99	0	0	0	0
46	57	244	899	2245	797	1762	87
0	0	289	1346	1798	32	2107	29
103	181	438	4375	1939	721	2325	69
36	181	435	4167	1754	721	1572	69
0	85	51	226	849	102	632	870
292	351	5145	8507	24750	15590	8576	15499
2	37	1085	322	4962	2977	1000	333
0	0	4	0	8	67	1051	931
0	83	11735	3372	6473	707	7833	537
0	11	2842	95	2705	338	5119	127
0	63	882	70	280	68	58	168
0	3	88	19	388	157	304	101
0	6	4692	1151	923	89	210	64
12239	68867	101968	247617	575878	574336	171980	741819
12138	68736	99552	234300	557562	571910	156317	741297
6161	41344	43142	88934	280571	315236	73861	360036
2275	234	0	482	959	7878	0	0
3701	27157	52055	127524	269744	248796	77529	381260
0	0	4347	17047	5946	0	4902	0
0	0	3	12	342	0	25	0
0	0	4	300	0	0	0	0

11-9 续1

指　　标	Indicator	济南市 Total City	历下区 Li xia	市中区 Shi zhong
豆类	Beans	16745		43
薯类	Tubers	36278		86
油料作物	Oil-bearing Crops	41534		35
#花生	Peanuts	38729		28
棉花	Cotton	2928		31
蔬菜	Vegetable	5272163		7733
果用瓜	Melon	596519		284
水果总产量(吨)	**Output of Fruits(tons)**	421865		3484
#苹果	Apple	159960		1430
梨	Pear	34002		0
葡萄	Grape	30040		449
桃	Peach	118553		1298
杏	Apricot	30153		238
枣(鲜)	Jujube	8880		33
柿子(鲜)	Persimmon	12424		3
山楂	Hawthorn	6316		29
樱桃	Cherry	15140		6
其他	Others	6399		0
农作物单位面积产量(公斤/公顷)	**Output per Hectare of Farm Crops(kg/ha)**			
粮食作物单位面积产量	Output per Hectare of Grain Crops	5659		4032
谷物	Cereals	5690		4041
小麦	Wheat	5696		3733
稻谷	Rice	8288		0
玉米	Corn	5748		4543
谷子	Millet	3809		1929
高粱	Chinese Sorghum	2074		0
其他	Others	3062		0
豆类	Beans	2716		1483
薯类	Tubers	6462		6336
油料作物	Oil-bearing Crops	4083		1814
#花生	Peanuts	4327		1935
棉花	Cotton	1029		1042
蔬菜	Vegetable	66852		50917
果用瓜	Melon	55628		41801

槐荫区 Huai yin	天桥区 Tian qiao	历城区 Li cheng	长清区 Chang qing	章丘区 Zhang qiu	济阳区 Ji yang	平阴县 Ping yin	商河县 Shang he
101	131	682	2453	6529	2218	4286	301
0	0	1734	10864	11787	208	11378	221
311	484	1889	19125	6434	3730	9181	346
109	484	1886	18517	6133	3730	7496	346
0	58	71	208	911	94	633	921
14201	18697	339974	525495	1782791	998871	656415	927985
88	1922	54287	11951	247759	193426	64691	22111
0	1165	153302	52313	72538	19307	99768	19987
0	262	22223	2203	38594	12057	80050	3142
0	543	18332	2096	2699	934	1766	7632
0	23	1923	774	10636	3553	7753	4930
0	285	86287	13286	10999	1117	3524	1757
0	6	14419	13721	500	646	246	378
0	44	304	107	5750	158	402	2082
0	3	2245	8815	140	756	404	59
0	0	4927	90	586	0	676	8
0	0	860	11173	2579	3	519	0
0	0	1783	48	56	84	4428	0
5310	4962	4947	5542	5448	5754	5116	6241
5374	4973	4958	5521	5484	5778	5255	6243
5238	5401	5273	4985	5520	5967	4825	6241
7688	6879	0	8806	8506	8474	0	0
4706	4429	4912	6051	5588	5501	5959	6245
0	0	3348	5069	2604	0	3462	0
0	0	2194	3099	2046	0	2126	0
0	0	4442	3048	0	0	0	0
2191	2307	2801	2728	2909	2784	2433	3484
0	0	6007	8069	6557	6485	5400	7628
3020	2670	10525	4371	3317	5174	3948	5030
3002	2670	10561	4444	3496	5174	4769	5030
0	690	4413	921	1074	916	1002	1059
48601	53218	190736	61770	72032	64071	76537	59874
48778	52500	141963	37168	49932	64965	64708	66400

11-10 分地区林、牧、渔

Basic Statistics on Forestry、Animal Husbandry

指　　标	Indicator	单　位 Unit	济南市 Total City	历下区 Li xia
林业生产	**Production of Forestry**			
造林面积	Forested Area	公顷(ha)	4902	69
四旁植树	Surrounding Tree Planting	万株(10000 trees)	1306	95
育苗面积	Area of Nursery Garden	公顷(ha)	10174	
果品产量	Output of Fruits	吨(tons)	555042	
木材采伐量	Timber Cut	立方米(stere)	283354	
牧业生产	**Production of Animal Husbandry**			
大牲畜存栏	Stocked Large Livestock	万头(10 000 heads)	26.30	
#役畜	Draught Animal	万头(10 000 heads)	0.02	
#牛	Cattle	万头(10 000 heads)	26.17	
猪存栏	Stocked Pigs	万头(10 000 heads)	102.95	
羊存栏	Stocked Sheep	万只(10 000 heads)	87.61	
家禽存栏	Stocked Poultry	万只(10 000 heads)	2300.42	
猪出栏数	Slaughtered Pigs	万头(10 000 heads)	185.59	
羊出栏数	Slaughtered Sheep and Goats	万只(10 000 heads)	143.84	
肉类总产量	Output of Meat	吨(tons)	298180	
#猪牛羊肉	Meat	吨(tons)	223735	
猪肉	Pork	吨(tons)	155005	
牛肉	Beef	吨(tons)	46438	
羊肉	Mutton	吨(tons)	22292	
禽肉	Poultry Meat	吨(tons)	74164	
奶类	Milk	吨(tons)	328412	
#牛奶	Cow Milk	吨(tons)	328410	
禽蛋	Poultry Eggs	吨(tons)	332303	
#鸡蛋	Hen's Eggs	吨(tons)	313234	
渔业生产	**Aquatic Products**			
水产品产量	Total Aquatic Products	吨(tons)	31911	
捕捞	Fishing	吨(tons)	289	
养殖	Cultured	吨(tons)	31622	
养殖面积	Breeding Area of Aquatic Products	公顷(ha)	5228	
养殖单产	Aquaculture Yield	公斤/公顷(kg/ha)	6049	

业生产情况（2018年）

and Fishery by Region（2018）

市中区 Shi zhong	槐荫区 Huai yin	天桥区 Tian qiao	历城区 Li cheng	长清区 Chang qing	章丘区 Zhang qiu	济阳区 Ji yang	平阴县 Ping yin	商河县 Shang he
583	0	0	1200	504	768	542	209	1027
90	80	21	170	160	320	100	120	150
89	33	137	2965	3125	747	913	132	2033
12089	0	2620	367986	29710	25026	35900	62725	18986
0	380	6110	9678	80105	44694	35348	24039	83000
0.07		0.05	0.34	4.30	11.08	4.96	2.33	3.17
				0.02				
0.07		0.05	0.34	4.20	11.06	4.96	2.32	3.17
0.24	0.02	0.69	1.63	18.18	35.13	13.31	10.11	23.64
0.47	0.17	0.66	2.65	18.13	23.32	10.09	15.82	16.30
12.62	3.00	35.89	125.08	255.60	886.68	232.34	306.71	442.50
1.09	0.06	2.83	2.80	27.91	59.70	13.56	20.58	57.06
0.47	0.41	2.57	3.20	23.80	33.15	10.16	44.50	25.58
1474	171	4354	6896	36587	100244	30943	42179	75332
1245	125	3202	2806	29544	72818	24147	31270	58578
892	53	2264	2015	20153	50156	12405	17761	49306
269		578	362	6472	18040	10317	6195	4205
84	72	360	429	2919	4622	1425	7314	5067
230	45	1151	4090	6891	27379	6795	10835	16748
837	21	305	7319	38735	83158	26940	40426	130671
837	21	305	7319	38733	83158	26940	40426	130671
1122	858	4919	9780	27117	180663	18962	43326	45556
1122	858	4911	9771	25581	176814	17953	43064	33160
	1600	2142	488	1248	4542	10302	1200	10389
	0	0	0	120	40	115	0	14
	1600	2142	488	1128	4502	10187	1200	10375
	153	260	43	344	1240	1502	446	1240
	10457	8238	11349	3279	3631	6782	2691	8367

11-11 农业“四化”情况（2018年）

Basic Statistics on Four Modernization of Agriculture（2018）

指　标 Indicator	机耕面积（千公顷）Machine-cultivated Area (1000 hectares)	有效灌溉面积（千公顷）Effective Irrigated Area (1000 hectares)	农用化肥施用量（吨折纯）Consumption of Chemical Fertilizer (tons convert to pure volume)	每公顷耕地化肥施用量（公斤折纯）Consumption of Chemical Fertilizers per Hectare (kg convert to pure volume)	农药施用量（吨）Pesticides mption (tons)	每公顷耕地农药施用量（公斤）Consumption of Pesticides per Hectare (kg)
全　市 Total City	273.2	256.6	199591	564.4	2692.9	7.6
历下区 Li xia						
市中区 Shi zhong	2.0	2.7	1121	207.6	45.8	8.5
槐荫区 Huai yin	1.5	2.1	1030	315.7	16.2	5.0
天桥区 Tian qiao	13.2	8.5	4951	522.4	47.1	5.0
历城区 Li cheng	15.2	25.0	15169	477.0	437.9	13.8
长清区 Chang qing	33.1	25.1	13059	283.0	344.1	7.5
章丘区 Zhang qiu	62.5	57.5	48274	616.8	411.1	5.3
济阳区 Ji yang	55.2	53.0	41810	595.1	841.1	12.0
平阴县 Ping yin	36.7	18.7	14526	437.5	140.5	4.2
商河县 Shang he	53.9	63.9	59651	789.3	409.1	5.4

11-12 主要农副产品产量与上年和历史最高年份比较

Output of Major Agricultral Products in Comparision with Last Year and Maximum Year

指　标	Indicator	2018年	2017年	历史最高年 Maximum Year		2018年为历史最高年的% 2018 Account for Historic High	2018年为2017年的% 2018 Account for 2017
				年份 Year	产量 Output		
农产品产量(万吨)	Total Output of Farm Crops(10 000 tons)						
粮食总产量	Output of Grain Crops	251.42	255.57	2011	295.84	85.0	98.4
#小麦	Wheat	121.78	123.79	2015	129.75	93.9	98.4
稻谷	Rice	1.18	1.36	2000	9.89	12.0	87.0
玉米	Corn	119.82	121.25	2011	143.96	83.2	98.8
薯类	Tubers	3.63	4.28	1995	23.10	15.7	84.8
经济作物(万吨)	Commercial Crop(10 000 tons)						
#棉花	Cotton	0.29	0.20	1999	5.00	5.8	145
油料花生	Peanuts	3.87	3.31	2009	5.75	67.3	116.9
蔬菜总产量	Output of Vegetables	527.22	591.63	2014	638.22	82.6	89.1
水果总产量	Output of Fruits	42.19	43.15	2014	44.11	95.6	97.8
水产品总产量(万吨)	Total Aquatic Products(10 000 tons)	3.2	4.1	2015	4.80	66.67	78.1

注：按照国务院农普办要求，由国家统计局山东调查总队根据第三次农业普查数据，对2016–2017年市、县（区）粮食播种面积、单产和总产量等数据进行修订

Note: According to the requirements of Agricultural Census Office of the State Council, Shandong Survey Team of National Bureau of Statistics revised the grain sown area, yield per unit and total yield of each city and country (district) from 2016–2017 based on the data from the third agricultural census.

主要统计指标解释

Explanatory Notes on Main Statistical Indicators

农林牧渔业总产值 是以货币表现的农、林、牧、渔业全部产品的总量，它反映一定时期内农林牧渔业生产的总规模和总成果。

农、林、牧、渔四业的统计范围是辖区内各种经济组织类型、各个系统的全部农林牧渔业生产单位和非农行业单位附属的农林牧渔业生产活动单位。不包括农业科学试验机构进行的农业生产。

农林牧渔业总产值的核算范围是本辖区内在一定时期内生产的农业、林业、牧业、渔业产品的价值和对农林牧渔业生产活动进行的各种支持性服务活动的价值总和，执行日历年度。

（1）农业产值，包括谷物和其他作物产值：蔬菜，园艺作物产值：水果，坚果，饮料和香料产值；中药材产值。其中谷物和其他作物产值包括谷物、薯类、豆类、棉花、油料，糖料，麻类、烟叶和其他农作物的产值。其他农作物包括青饲料，绿肥、牧草、桑叶及采集的野生植物。

（2）林业，包括林木的培育和种植（不包括茶园、桑园和果园的栽培，管理和收获等活动）。林产品的采集和竹木采伐。

（3）牧业，包括除渔业养殖以外的一切动物饲养和放牧以及捕猎野兽野禽产值。

（4）渔业，包括水生动物和海藻类植物的养殖和捕捞。

（5）农林牧渔服务业，包括灌溉，农产品初加工。农机服务，病虫害防治、森林防火、兽医服务、鱼苗及鱼种场等对农林牧渔业生产活动进行的各种支持性服务活动。但不包括各种科学技术和专业技术服务活动。农林牧渔业总产值核算采用“产品法”进行计算，即用产品产量乘以价格以求出各种产品产值，然后加总求得各业产值，最后各业相加求得农林牧渔业总产值。

1957 年以前的农业总产值中包括了厩肥和农民自给性手工业（如农民自制衣服、鞋、袜，自己从事粮食初步加工等）。1958 年及以后的农业总产值，林业中增加了村及村以下竹木采伐产值；牧业中取消了厩肥产值；副业中取消了农民自给性手工业产值，增加了村及村以下办的工业产值；渔业中增加了海洋捕捞水产品产值。1980 年及以后的农业总产值，在副业中增加了农民家庭兼营工业商品性部分的产值。从1984 年起村及村以下办工业产值划归工业。从1993 年起取消副业，将采集野生植物产值和农民家庭兼营商品性工业产值划归农业产值，捕猎野兽、野禽产值划入牧业产值。2003 年根据新的国民经济行业分类，农林牧渔服务业划归第一产业。原农业产值中的农民家庭兼营商品性工业产值划归工业产值；林业中竹木采伐产值统计范围由村及村以下改为全社会。

农林牧渔业增加值 是指农、林、牧、渔及农林牧渔服务业生产货物或提供服务活动而增加的价值，为农林牧渔业现价总产值扣除农林渔业现价中间投入后的余额。

农林牧渔业增加值的核算范围同农林牧渔业总产值的核算范围相同。

农林牧渔业增加值的计算方法：采用生产法和分配法（收入法)两种。

1. 生产法计算公式：

农林牧渔业增加值=农林牧渔业总产值-农林牧渔业中间消耗

2. 分配法计算公式：

农林牧渔业增加值=固定资产折旧+劳动者报酬+生产税净额+营业盈余

其中：生产税净额=生产税收-生产补贴

粮食产量 指全社会的粮食作物产量。包括国营农场等全民所有制经营的、集体统一经营和农民家庭经营的粮食产量，还包括工矿企业家属办的农场和其他生产单位的产量粮食除包括稻谷、小麦、玉米、高粱、谷子及其他杂粮外，还包括薯类和大豆。其产量计算方法，豆类按去豆荚后的干豆计算；薯类包括甘薯和马铃薯，不包括芋头和木薯。1963年以前按每4公斤鲜薯1公斤粮食计算，从1964年以后按5公斤鲜薯折1公斤粮食计算。其他粮食一律按脱粒后的原粮计算。

油料产量 指全部油料作物的生产量。包括花生、油菜籽、芝麻、向日葵籽、胡麻籽（亚麻籽）和其他油料。不包括大豆、木本油料和野生油料。花生以带壳干花生计算。

水产品产量 指人工养殖的水产品和天然生长的水产的捕捞量。包括海水的鱼类、虾蟹类、贝类和藻类以及淡水的鱼类、虾蟹类和贝类，不包括淡水水生植物。

猪、牛、羊肉产量 指当年出栏并已屠宰的猪、牛、羊的肉产量。即屠宰后除去头蹄下水后带骨肉(即胴体重)的重量。

耕地面积 指年初可以用来种植农作物、经常进行耕锄的田地，包括熟地、当年新开荒地、连续撂荒未满三年的耕地和当年的休闲地（轮歇地)，还包括以种植农作物为主并附带种植桑树、茶树、果树和其他林木的土地，以及沿海、沿湖地区已围垦利用的“海涂”、“湖田”等面积。

不包括属于专业性的桑园、茶园、果园、果木苗圃、林地、芦苇地、天然或人工草地面积。

农作物播种面积 指实际播种或移植有农作物的面积。凡是实际种植有农作物的面积，不论种植在耕地上还是种植在非耕地上，均包括在农作物播种面积中。在播种季节基本结束后，因遭灾而重新改种和补种的农作物面积，也包括在内。

灌溉面积 有效灌溉面积，指具有一定的水源，地块比较平整，灌溉工程或设备已经配套，在一般年景下半年能够进行正常灌溉的耕地面积。

农用化肥施用量 指本年内实际用于农业生产的化肥数量，包括氮肥、磷肥、钾肥和复合肥。化肥施用量要求按折纯量计算数量。折纯量是指把氮肥、磷肥、钾肥分别按含氮、含五氧化二磷、含氧化钾的百分之一百成份进行折算后的数量。复合肥按其所含主要成分折算。

农业机械总动力 指主要用于农、林、牧、渔业的各种动力机械的动力总和。包括耕作机械、排灌机械、收获机械、农产品加工机械、运输机械、植物保护机械、牧业机械、林业机械、渔业机械和其他农业机械（内燃机按引擎马力折成瓦(特)计算），电动机按功率折成瓦特计算。不包括专门用于乡办工业、基本建设、非农业运输、科学试验和教学等非农业生产方面用的动力机械与作业机械。

Explanatory Notes on Main Statistical Indicators

Gross Output Value of Farming, Forestry, Animal Husbandry and Fishery refers to the total volume of products of farming, forestry, animal husbandry and fishery in monetary expression, which reflects the total scale and the total result of farming, forestry, animal husbandry and fishery production during a given period.

The scope of statistics of farming, forestry, animal husbandry and fishing covers various economic organizations in the area under administration as well as agriculture, forestry, animal husbandry and fishery production activity units which all agriculture, forestry, animal husbandry and fishing production units and units in non–agricultural industries of all systems are subordinate to, excluding agricultural production by agricultural science experiment organization.

The scope of accounting of the gross output value of farming, forestry, animal husbandry and fishery is the sum of the value of agriculture, forestry, animal husbandry and fishery products produced in the area under administration within a certain period and the value of various supportive service activities in agriculture, forestry, animal husbandry and fishery production activities based on a calendar year.

(1) The value of agricultural production includes the output value of cereal and other crop: output value of vegetables and horticultural plants: output value of fruits, nuts, beverages and spices; output value of traditional Chinese medicinal materials. Output value of cereal and other crops includes that of cereal, potato, bean, cotton, oil plants, sugar, bast fiber plants, tobacco and other crops. Other crops include green feed, green manure, pasture, folium mori and collected wild plants.

(2) Forestry includes cultivation and plantation of the forest (excluding cultivation, management and harvesting of tea plantation, mulberry plantation and orchard). Acquisition of forest products and bamboo and wood cutting.

(3) Animal husbandry includes output value of animal feeding and grazing and hunting wild animals and wildfowls except for fishery breeding.

(4) Fishery includes breeding and fishing of aquatic animals and seaweed plants.

(5) Farming, forestry, animal husbandry and fishery service industry include irrigation and primary processing of agricultural products. Various supportive service activities (such as agricultural machinery service, pest control, forest fire prevention, veterinary service and fry and seed farm) for agriculture, forestry, animal husbandry and fishery production activities, excluding various service activities of scientific technology and professional technology. The gross output value of farming, forestry, animal husbandry and fishery is calculated by "product approach", which means the gross output value of agriculture, forestry, animal husbandry and fishery is obtained after adding the output value of all industries obtained by adding the output value of various products originating from the production output multiplying by the price.

Gross output value of farming before 1957 includes animal manure and peasant self–catering handicraft industry (including homemade clothes, shoes and socks of farmers as well as preliminary processing of grain by farmers). As for the gross output value of agriculture in 1958 and later, the output value of bamboo and wood cutting of the village and below is added in the forestry; output value of animal manure is cancelled in the animal husbandry; output value of peasant self–catering handicraft industry is cancelled and output value of the industry of the village and below is added in the sideline; output value of aquatic products based on marine fishing is added in the fishery. As for gross output value of agriculture in 1980 and later, output value of industrial commodities concurrently operated by the peasant family is added in the sideline. Output value of the industry of the village and below from 1984 was incorporated into value of industrial output. The sideline was cancelled from 1993. The output value of wild plants acquired and output of commercial industry concurrently operated by peasant family are classified into value of agricultural production and output of wild animals and wild birds hunted is included into output of animal husbandry. Agriculture, forestry, animal husbandry and fishery service industry was classified into the primary industry in 2003 pursuant to the new classification of national economy industries. Output value of the commercial industry concurrently operated by the peasant family in the original value of agricultural production is included into value of industrial output; the scope of statistics of the output value of bamboo and wood cutting in the forestry is changed to the whole society.

Value added of agriculture, forestry, animal husbandry and fishery refers to the value added due to production of goods or provision of service in agriculture, forestry, animal husbandry and fishing and agriculture, it is the balance of the total output value at the current price of agriculture, forestry, animal husbandry and fishery minus by intermediate input at the current price of agriculture, fishing and forestry.

The scope of accounting of the value added of agriculture, forestry, animal husbandry and fishery is the same to the gross output value of farming, forestry, animal husbandry and fishery.

The method for computing the value added of farming, forestry, animal husbandry and fishery: Production approach and distribution approach (income approach) are adopted:

1. Calculation formula of production approach:

Value added of agriculture, forestry, animal husbandry and fishery = gross output value of agriculture, forestry, animal husbandry and fishery – intermediate consumption of agriculture, forestry, animal husbandry and fishery

2. Calculation formula of distribution approach:

Value added of agriculture, forestry, animal husbandry and fishery = depreciation of fixed assets + remuneration for workers + net production tax + operating surplus

Wherein: Net production tax = production tax – production subsidy

Grain output refers to food crop yield of the whole society, including output of grain operated by ownership by the whole people (such as state farm), based on collective unified management and operated by peasant family and output of the farm operated by family members of industrial and mining enterprises and other production units. Grains include rice, wheat, corn, sorghum, millet and other coarse cereals as well as potato and soybean. As for output calculation method, bean shall be calculated as per dried bean after removal of the pod; potatoes include sweet potato and potato other than taro and cassava. Calculation was conducted based on 4kg fresh potatoes regarding as 1kg grain before 1963 and calculation was conducted based on 5kg fresh potatoes regarding as 1kg grain from 1964. Other grain shall be calculated after threshing.

Output of Oil–bearing Crops refers to the total production of oil bearing crops of various kinds, including peanuts, sesame, sunflower seeds, flax seeds, and other oil bearing crops. Soybeans, oil bearing woody plants, and wild oil–bearing crops are not included. Only shelled dry peanuts are included.

Output of Aquatic Products refers to catches of both artificially cultured and naturally grown aquatic products, including fish, shrimps, crabs, shellfish and algae in sea and fish, shrimps, crabs and shellfish in fresh water. Freshwater plants are not included.

Output of Pork, Beef, and Mutton refers to the output of meat of slaughtered hogs, cattle, sheep and goats with head, feet, and offal taken away.

Cultivated Area refers to area of the farmland used to plant crops at the beginning of the year which is often plowed, including cultivated land, new cultivated land that very year, arable land abandoned for less than three years consecutively, fallow land (rotation land) that very year, the land mainly planting crops complemented by plantation of white mulberry, tea tree, fruit tree and other forest as well as "shoal" and "shoaly land" having been subject to reclamation and utilization in coastal and lake–side areas.

Excluded from this category are professional mulberry field, tea garden, orchard, nurseries of young plants, woods, reeds, natural or artificial grass area.

Sown Area of Crops refers to area of land sown or transplanted with crops regardless of being in cultivated area or non–cultivated area. Area of land re–sown due to natural disasters is also included.

Irrigation effective irrigation area refers to cultivated area with some water sources, which is smooth, provided with irrigation engineering or equipment and capable of normal irrigation in the latter half of general year.

Consumption of Chemical Fertilizers in Agriculture refers to the quantity of chemical fertilizers applied in agriculture in the year, including nitrogenous fertilizer, phosphate fertilizer, potash fertilizer, and compound fertilizer. The consumption of chemical fertilizers is required in calculation to convert the gross weight into weight containing 100% effective component (e.g. 100% nitrogen content in nitrogenous fertilizer, 100% phosphorous pent oxide contents in phosphate fertilizer, 100% potassium oxide contents in potash fertilizer). Compound fertilizer is converted with its major component.

Total Power of Farm Machinery refers to total mechanical power of machinery used in farming, forestry, animal husbandry, and fishery, including ploughing, irrigation and drainage, harvesting, transport, plant protection, stock breeding, forestry and fishery. The power of internal combustion engines is required to convert horsepower into watts and the power of electric motors is required to be converted into watts. Machinery employed for non– agricultural purposes, such as the machines used in township run and village run industry, construction, non–agricultural transport, scientific experiments and teaching, is excluded.

工　业

INDUSTRY

12 - 1 各时期全部工业基本情况

Basic Statistics on Total Industry in Each Period

年份 Year	全部工业单位数(个) Number of Industial Enterprises(Unit)		工业总产值(亿元) Gross Industrial Output Value(100 million yuan)		工业增加值(亿元) Value Added of Industry Enterprises(100 million yuan)		国有独立核算工业(万元) State-owned Independent Accounting Industrial(10 000 yuan)	
	合 计 Total	#国有单位 State-owned	合 计 Total	#国有单位 State-owned	合计 Total	#国有单位 State-owned	利润总额 Total Profits	利税总额 Total Profits and Taxes
1949	52	—	1.20	0.52	0.40	0.15	190	541
1952	92	—	2.97	1.65	1.09	0.52	1616	2761
1957	399	—	6.90	6.13	2.18	1.84	5742	10065
1962	847	286	6.67	5.61	2.36	1.80	3293	8242
1965	724	247	11.99	10.09	4.34	3.39	16246	22906
1970	828	285	23.12	17.93	7.56	5.64	19347	31834
1975	1041	326	26.41	18.87	8.46	5.50	11555	27846
1978	1319	398	39.06	25.87	12.89	7.11	28852	53031
1979	1353	359	42.95	28.90	14.10	8.01	31875	57532
1980	1535	356	45.31	30.37	14.24	8.85	32909	59572
"六五"时期								
1981	1538	350	47.61	31.72	15.11	9.47	35077	62657
1982	1619	357	51.98	33.91	15.79	10.01	32062	64673
1983	1674	369	59.06	36.99	17.96	11.49	35870	60308
1984	1981	325	66.96	39.78	20.10	13.17	45869	83520
1985	2584	477	74.41	44.66	27.54	16.97	61274	112154
"七五"时期								
1986	3005	369	86.93	48.71	28.69	17.53	54804	115006
1987	3957	361	107.63	56.16	32.88	19.40	58715	125775
1988	5252	372	138.05	68.58	47.49	25.09	80173	156056
1989	7655	380	158.53	76.19	54.66	30.51	76571	170703
1990	11020	394	222.63	116.92	60.43	37.11	25084	125522
"八五"时期								
1991	12211	376	245.73	131.35	67.73	43.35	36715	151718
1992	15374	373	303.33	162.35	86.85	48.97	55463	193000
1993	19392	376	448.25	230.93	115.36	69.65	57984	223445
1994	22009	366	614.08	236.40	154.49	69.64	60393	240473
1995	24621	495	752.23	279.16	194.16	83.12	65335	316289

12-1 续 1

年份 Year	全部工业单位数(个) Number of Industial Enterprises(Unit)		工业总产值(亿元) Gross Industrial Output Value(100 million yuan)		工业增加值(亿元) Value Added of Industry Enterprises(100 million yuan)		国有独立核算工业(万元) State-owned Independent Accounting Industrial(10 000 yuan)	
	合 计 Total	#国有单位 State-owned	合 计 Total	#国有单位 State-owned	合计 Total	#国有单位 State-owned	利润总额 Total Profits	利税总额 Total Profits and Taxes
"九五"时期								
1996	32902	425	834.45	260.16	238.31	91.30	79615	337807
1997	33000	325	897.59	263.34	278.87	92.99	95267	343426
1998	32793	227	966.62	234.03	298.41	94.28	42152	292991
1999	29319	211	981.78	212.95	318.80	79.51	-2340	254619
2000	30899	195	994.00	237.14	336.61	81.00	34824	292198
"十五"时期								
2001	34135	169	1090.70	140.44	356.72	64.69	49222	226242
2002	30064	155	1302.00	144.78	410.98	49.16	28011	234986
2003	30258	126	1544.50	167.30	494.55	68.80	53363	302975
2004	31163	115	1981.80	150.70	620.14	37.21	-3943	72684
2005	31370	102	2447.51	177.00	786.11	66.49	268573	354111
"十一五"时期								
2006	35370	86	2806.94	193.10	861.48	73.95	315323	458191
2007	36112	76	3389.09	283.32	985.78	103.65	364790	751182
2008	36416	80	4829.16	338.24	1140.14	136.55	418265	853091
2009	37656	77	5096.98	345.44	1191.36	166.36	422898	885006
2010	37521	66	5800.39	404.38	1352.42	284.75	643216	1162785
"十二五"时期								
2011	36750	54	5544.60	478.10	1507.88		561683	1217350
2012	35917	52	5535.25	491.20	1603.08		646193	1401892
2013	38443	30	5711.48	280.63	1690.63		551967	665206
2014	38753	25	5861.98	246.26	1822.11		507491	611865
2015	38793	24	5877.28	204.79	1844.37		517575	571354
"十三五"时期								
2016	34310	16	6059.16	157.83	1878.83		540739	622714
2017	33725	12	6395.21	147.27	2003.10		583734	589999
2018	31270	13	5641.61	15.50	2145.10		-4140	5014

注：1、工业增加值、工业总产值按当年价格计算。
2、1985、1995 年因工业普查对教育局校办工厂统计方法的规定，故国有单位较多。
3、2001 年后炼油、浪潮、将军等原国有企业陆续改制，故国有数字较以前年份有所减小。
4、2004 年第一次经济普查后，统计年鉴包含济南供电公司年报数据。

Note: 1. Industrial value added and total industrial output value are calculated according to the current year's prices.
2. There were many state-owned units in 1985 and 1995 due to the provisions regarding statistical approach for school-run factories of Education Bureau from industrial census.
3. Original state-owned enterprises such as Oil Refining, Inspur and General were subject to restructuring in succession after 2001, so the quantity of state-owned enterprises decreased in comparison to that of previous years.
4. After the economic census for the first time in 2004, statistical yearbook includes annual report data of Ji'nan Power Supply Company.

12-2 各时期规模以上工业基本情况

Basic Statistics of Industrial Enterprises Above Designated Size in Each Period

单位：亿元 (100 million yuan)

年份 Year	单位数(个) Number of Industial Enterprises(unit)	工业总产值 Gross Industrial Output Value	工业增加值 Value Added of Industry Enterprises	主营业务收入 Revenue from Principal Business	利税总额 Total Profits and Taxes	利润总额 Total Profits	资产总计 Total Assets	所有者权益 Owner's Equities
1949	52	1.06	0.40	0.91	0.07	0.03	0.58	0.17
1952	92	2.83	1.02	2.40	0.32	0.18	1.89	0.55
1957	399	6.04	2.08	5.85	1.04	0.60	2.85	0.83
1962	847	6.65	2.15	6.87	0.92	0.39	5.66	1.65
1965	724	11.89	4.07	9.49	2.47	1.73	5.93	1.73
1970	828	22.94	7.29	19.30	3.66	2.22	10.67	3.10
1975	1041	26.16	7.94	19.70	3.47	1.55	17.21	5.01
1978	1319	37.67	9.94	31.39	6.80	3.88	25.68	7.47
1979	1353	38.79	11.18	35.51	7.21	4.13	27.19	7.91
1980	1535	43.60	12.15	36.90	7.51	4.26	29.22	8.50
"六五"时期								
1981	1538	42.26	12.77	39.84	7.98	4.37	31.49	9.20
1982	1619	45.58	13.63	42.94	8.13	4.18	34.52	10.08
1983	1674	49.64	14.86	46.38	8.84	4.74	38.09	11.12
1984	1981	55.95	17.91	52.16	10.46	5.82	41.66	12.16
1985	1915	66.98	23.10	64.76	13.98	7.62	47.09	13.75
"七五"时期								
1986	2036	75.67	24.54	73.98	14.38	7.07	56.79	16.70
1987	2004	88.17	27.24	86.19	15.88	7.52	64.21	18.88
1988	1984	107.76	35.39	113.84	19.65	10.37	81.67	24.01
1989	1993	118.88	43.20	131.86	20.88	9.73	104.34	30.68
1990	2008	174.89	41.63	136.29	15.57	3.23	125.25	36.82
"八五"时期								
1991	1985	194.29	44.84	160.58	18.46	4.97	138.34	40.81
1992	1941	236.37	60.16	200.54	23.48	7.84	167.44	49.39
1993	2156	319.49	104.43	309.91	31.88	10.26	338.15	99.61
1994	2202	414.81	113.71	346.13	41.69	13.61	462.34	136.14
1995	2648	526.48	130.88	432.17	53.59	16.30	578.55	180.86

12-2 续 1

年份 Year	单位数(个) Number of Industial Enterprises(unit)	工业总产值 Gross Industrial Output Value	工业增加值 Value Added of Industry Enterprises	主营业务收入 Revenue from Principal Business	利税总额 Total Profits and Taxes	利润总额 Total Profits	资产总计 Total Assets	所有者权益 Owner's Equities
"九五"时期								
1996	2301	549.40	175.21	494.99	66.82	27.83	705.50	225.53
1997	1843	603.30	194.42	605.81	70.12	26.99	882.36	286.59
1998	1060	593.83	189.88	539.29	58.56	18.62	882.38	297.81
1999	1064	628.59	201.38	579.64	59.17	15.97	931.22	302.21
2000	1038	680.04	219.19	629.72	64.62	21.69	958.10	363.37
"十五"时期								
2001	1015	786.70	252.61	746.92	77.79	28.45	984.71	369.40
2002	1125	1009.04	325.98	917.31	92.71	32.13	1120.60	407.36
2003	1319	1318.54	426.30	1223.76	132.84	54.71	1312.97	440.85
2004	1512	1781.78	560.15	1677.93	175.98	83.68	1473.90	507.63
2005	1670	2237.51	722.11	2142.84	244.61	131.30	1868.06	630.06
"十一五"时期								
2006	1752	2591.65	797.70	2490.94	289.78	153.74	2000.62	702.78
2007	1820	3189.09	926.58	3086.85	358.87	199.73	2337.09	903.87
2008	2016	3862.64	1052.48	3766.93	425.72	220.79	2899.47	1123.03
2009	2156	3950.77	1154.01	3868.70	500.63	275.85	3478.94	1572.11
2010	2021	4485.61	1313.00	4497.17	584.53	339.76	3904.42	1481.75
"十二五"时期								
2011	1417	4028.49	–	4165.19	453.47	242.63	3932.90	1407.89
2012	1647	4248.29	–	4454.97	498.24	253.06	4109.29	1582.77
2013	1901	4777.47	–	4926.11	539.49	312.95	4249.79	1671.91
2014	1984	5253.05	–	5406.67	606.60	357.82	4564.86	1846.32
2015	2021	5339.97	–	5417.16	685.71	396.13	4987.76	2159.78
"十三五"时期								
2016	1962	5486.56	–	5714.29	729.75	421.11	5501.88	2301.94
2017	2051	5770.91		5810.16	686.80	415.23	6319.64	2268.27
2018	1889	4992.28		5192.15	535.39	307.98	5892.64	2386.75

注：1. 工业增加值、工业总产值按当年价格计算。

2. 1997 年及以前统计口径为乡及乡以上工业企业，1998 年及以后为全部国有及年销售收入 500 万元以上工业企业，2011 年及以后为年主营业务收入 2000 万元以上工业企业。

3. 1991 年及以前"工业增加值"指标为"工业净产值"指标。

4. 2004 年第一次经济普查后，统计年鉴包含济南供电公司年报数据。

Note: 1. Industrial value added and total industrial output value are calculated according to the current year's prices.

2. Industrial statistical indicators In 1997 and before, the statistical caliber was industrial enterprises at or above the townshi level. In 1998 and after, they were all state–owned and with an annual sales income of more than 5 million yuan. In 2011 and beyond, the annual main business income was 20 million yuan and above industrial enterprises legal entities.

3. The index of "industrial added value" in 1991 and before is "net industrial output value".

4. After the economic census for the first time in 2004, statistical yearbook includes annual report data of Ji'nan Power Supply Company.

12-3 各时期主要工业产品产量

Output of Major Industrial Products in Each Period

年份 Year	钢 (万吨) Steel (10 000 tons)	发电量 (亿千瓦小时) Electric Energy Production (100 million kwh)	水泥 (万吨) Cement (10 000 tons)	化肥 (万吨) Chemical Fertilizer (10 000 tons)	金切机床 (台) Metal-cutting Machine Tools(unit)	汽车 (辆) Motor ehicles (unit)	服务器 (万台) Servers (10 000 unit)	布 (万米) Cloth (10 000 m)
1949	—	0.29	0.15	—	40	—	—	2682
1952	—	0.55	1.08	1.62	565	—	—	5104
1957	0.03	1.07	1.29	0.48	2312	—	—	5573
1962	0.57	4.20	4.85	0.81	1140	12	—	2160
1965	0.54	5.65	19.24	3.79	2061	335	—	4853
1970	7.01	11.28	38.06	4.87	4718	1775	—	11665
1975	22.81	11.07	58.48	9.06	3994	3507	—	12547
1978	34.54	12.65	87.55	18.02	3610	4025	—	13806
1979	33.19	11.92	93.77	11.07	3771	4515	—	14300
1980	36.34	11.95	98.86	12.78	4414	5641	—	15236
"六五"时期							—	
1981	34.23	11.12	96.50	11.62	3336	5099		16290
1982	34.96	11.15	104.64	13.23	4262	5993	—	17657
1983	41.24	13.01	112.38	15.37	4816	7249	—	17963
	43.80	23.49	117.17	14.53	5533	7947	—	16522
1985	52.64	26.44	135.10	11.44	6686	9400	—	18082
"七五"时期							—	
1986	57.24	27.01	154.51	12.31	7472	7600		12346
1987	64.09	28.83	158.92	13.00	7007	5225	—	20137
1988	75.23	42.97	182.80	13.69	7280	6741	—	19374
1989	81.58	43.98	198.95	14.48	6806	7701	—	21744
1990	87.68	44.71	211.56	14.44	5121	6239	—	20155
"八五"时期								
1991	105.42	56.43	248.33	14.90	5330	7096		20119
1992	113.34	61.46	335.61	14.64	7443	8544	—	14896
1993	139.35	69.00	340.35	14.47	6724	10132	—	13205
1994	166.19	66.87	384.00	15.62	3297	9380	—	16062
1995	172.72	68.75	425.02	14.03	4109	5657	—	15046

12-3 续 1

年份 Year	钢 (万吨) Steel (10 000 tons)	发电量 (亿千瓦小时) Electric Energy Production (100 million kwh)	水泥 (万吨) Cement (10 000 tons)	化肥 (万吨) Chemical Fertilizer (10 000 tons)	金切机床 (台) Metal-cutting Machine Tools(unit)	汽车 (辆) Motor ehicles (unit)	服务器 (万台) Servers (10 000 unit)	布 (万米) Cloth (10 000 m)
"九五"时期								
1996	205.49	63.50	379.32	13.73	3855	7125	—	13710
1997	237.70	59.14	392.23	13.89	2526	5656	—	14213
1998	267.33	60.06	379.40	17.29	1508	3615	—	11286
1999	265.29	64.24	474.47	22.91	1955	3738	—	14782
2000	277.04	69.29	485.12	28.41	2908	3078	—	16493
"十五"时期								
2001	293.83	69.81	572.28	28.71	3528	7395	—	14107
2002	394.41	69.12	867.71	28.29	4522	12152		16027
2003	507.70	77.60	925.20	28.50	6751	19989	—	17040
2004	688.30	74.70	1343.90	40.30	8904	29648	—	16336
2005	1046.60	90.80	1595.70	28.90	7166	42214	—	14018
"十一五"时期							—	
2006	1131.26	100.14	1960.64	31.44	10057	59242	—	22852
2007	1214.90	130.37	733.98	40.31	9473	100133	—	27469
2008	1123.20	124.25	734.58	48.52	5110	109107	8.3	11786
2009	1051.67	128.76	761.72	57.77	2400	129900	9.7	7500
2010	959.33	131.45	729.79	49.09	2165	212047	9.9	8191
"十二五"时期								
2011	835.80	154.48	824.70	44.20	2024	170717	13.0	11461
2012	694.50	156.60	776.00	55.20	4237	141269	14.7	14908
2013	711.14	162.55	782.20	33.29	4297	165963	17.1	14574
2014	746.20	178.47	832.40	28.60	4902	139751	28.1	14070
2015	699.80	175.87	781.50	23.50	3807	96184	40.6	15539
"十三五"时期								
2016	805.70	177.20	719.80	32.50	4679	124200	46.8	15585
2017	452.03	160.12	604.48	21.00	6013	201883	56.5	16407
2018	160.92		604.32	20.77	5964	232082	99.6	4032

注：按经济普查规定汽车产量不含底盘。

Note: The automotive output excludes chassis in line with the provisions of economic census.

12-4 规模以上工业主要经济指标(2018年)

Main Economic Indicators of Industrial Enterprises Above Designated Size（2018）

指标	Indicator	企业单位数（个）Number of Industial Enterprises (unit)	亏损企业数（个）Loss Enterprises (unit)	工业总产值（现价）（亿元）Gross Industrial Output Value (Calculated at Current Prices) (100 million yuan)	工业销售产值（现价）（亿元）Industrial Output Value of Products Sold(Calculated at Current Prices) (100 million yuan)	平均用工人数（万人）Average of Employed Persons (10 000 persons)
总计	**Total**	1889	281	4992.28	4818.62	36.88
按登记注册类型分组	**by Status of Registration**					
内资企业	Domestic Funded Enterprises	1765	258	4607.90	4434.71	32.51
国有企业	State-owned Enterprises	13	5	15.47	15.55	0.25
中央企业	Central Enterprises	2	0	1.89	1.89	0.05
地方企业	Local Enterprises	11	5	13.58	13.67	0.20
集体企业	Collective-owned Enterprises	9	1	7.40	7.29	0.17
股份合作企业	Cooperative Enterprises	5	0	2.20	2.10	0.06
有限责任公司	Private Limited Liability Corporations	545	96	2811.63	2695.22	18.36
国有独资公司	State Sole funded Corporations	31	8	1192.67	1144.57	6.32
其他有限责任公司	Other Limited Liability Corporations	514	88	1618.96	1550.65	12.04
股份有限公司	Share-holding Corporations Limited	80	16	467.30	455.04	2.45
私营企业	Private Enterprises	1113	140	1303.90	1259.50	11.22
私营独资企业	Private-funded Enterprises	53	3	38.43	38.17	0.28
私营合伙企业	Private Partnership Enterprises	1	0	4.05	4.05	0.01
私营有限责任公司	Private Limited Liability Corporations	1005	130	918.32	891.52	9.05
私营股份有限公司	Private Share-holding Corporations Ltd.	54	7	343.10	325.77	1.88
港、澳、台商投资企业	Enterprises with Funds from Hong Kong, Macao and Taiwan	40	6	144.14	145.83	1.95
合资经营企业(港或澳、台资)	Joint-ventures Enterprises	18	2	80.12	80.58	0.91
合作经营企业(港或澳、台资)	Cooperative Enterprises	1	0	8.13	12.76	0.12
港澳台商独资经营企业	Enterprises with Sole Investment	19	3	38.49	35.78	0.69
港澳台商投资股份有限公司	Share-holding Corporations Ltd. With Funds From Hong Kong, Macao and Taiwan	1	0	16.99	16.35	0.22
其他港澳台商投资企业	Other Enterprises with Funds from Hong Kong,Macao and Taiwan	1	1	0.41	0.36	0.01
外商投资企业	Foreign Funded Enterprises	84	17	240.23	238.09	2.41

12-4 续 1

指标	Indicator	企业单位数（个）Number of Industial Enterprises (unit)	亏损企业数（个）Loss Enterprises (unit)	工业总产值（现价）（亿元）Gross Industrial Output Value (Calculated at Current Prices) (100 million yuan)	工业销售产值（现价）（亿元）Industrial Output Value of Products Sold(Calculated at Current Prices) (100 million yuan)	平均用工人数（万人）Average of Employed Persons (10 000 persons)
中外合资经营企业	Joint-venture Enterprises	39	9	91.34	90.83	1.18
中外合作经营企业	Cooperation Enterprises	3	1	2.55	2.98	0.04
外资企业	Enterprises with Sole Foreign Funds	40	6	126.50	124.43	1.09
外商投资股份有限公司	Share-holding Corporations Ltd. With Foreign Investment	2	1	19.85	19.85	0.11
按轻重工业分	**by Light & Heavy Industry**					
轻工业	Light Industry	548	92	900.94	859.62	10.07
重工业	Heavy Industry	1341	189	4091.33	3959.00	26.80
按企业规模分	**by Enterprise Size**					
大型企业	Large-sized Enterprises	39	5	2753.70	2634.73	14.98
中型企业	Medium-sized Enterprises	148	24	847.78	805.83	7.91
小型企业	Small-sized Enterprises	1473	204	1328.04	1315.46	13.23
微型企业	Micro-sized Enterprises	229	48	62.75	62.61	0.75
按工业行业分	**by Sector**					
煤炭开采和洗选业	Mining and Washing of Coal	1	0	3.27	3.16	0.09
石油和天然气开采业	Extraction of Petroleum and Natural Gas	3	1	9.80	9.80	0.08
非金属矿采选业	Mining and Processing of Nonmetal Ores	8	0	7.01	7.01	0.05
农副食品加工业	Processing of Food from Agricultural Products	57	10	49.05	48.54	0.52
食品制造业	Manufacture of Foods	66	16	115.10	111.37	1.60
酒、饮料和精制茶制造业	Manufacture of Wine, Drinks and Refined Tea	21	4	51.09	53.64	0.63
烟草制品业	Manufacture of Tobacco	1	0	1.10	1.10	0.01
纺织业	Manufacture of Textile	40	12	40.11	39.76	0.63
纺织服装、服饰业	Manufacture of Textile Wearing Apparel and Finery	30	7	16.85	16.81	0.84
皮革、毛皮、羽毛及其制品和制鞋业	Manufacture of Leather, Fur, Feather & Its Products and Footwear	7	1	8.14	8.00	0.08
木材加工和木、竹、藤、棕、草制品业	Processing of Timbers, Manufacture of Wood, Bamboo, Rattan, Palm, and Straw Products	11	0	10.91	11.05	0.06
家具制造业	Manufacture of Furniture	12	0	9.42	9.34	0.13

指标	Indicator	企业单位数（个）Number of Industial Enterprises (unit)	亏损企业数（个）Loss Enterprises (unit)	工业总产值（现价）（亿元）Gross Industrial Output Value (Calculated at Current Prices) (100 million yuan)	工业销售产值（现价）（亿元）Industrial Output Value of Products Sold(Calculated at Current Prices) (100 million yuan)	平均用工人数（万人）Average of Employed Persons (10 000 persons)
造纸和纸制品业	Manufacture of Paper and Paper Products	27	5	23.53	23.01	0.27
印刷和记录媒介复制业	Printing, Reproduction of Recording Media	50	6	54.79	55.23	0.64
文教、工美、体育和娱乐用品制造业	Manufacture of Culture, Education,Arts and crafts , Sport and Entertainment Goods	28	6	18.80	18.96	0.25
石油、煤炭及其他燃料加工业	Processing of Petroleum, Coal and Other fuels	10	1	254.74	253.49	0.23
化学原料和化学制品制造业	Manufacture of Chemical Raw Material and Chemical Products	103	15	349.39	352.59	2.04
医药制造业	Manufacture of Medicines	60	6	285.70	256.97	2.21
化学纤维制造业	Manufacture of Chemical Fiber	5	1	8.03	7.39	0.06
橡胶和塑料制品业	Manufacture of Rubber and Plastic	63	3	33.34	33.08	0.41
非金属矿物制品业	Manufacture of Non–metallic Mineral Products	186	22	370.83	359.74	2.67
黑色金属冶炼和压延加工业	Manufacture and Processing of Ferrous Metals	12	0	80.91	86.19	0.29
有色金属冶炼和压延加工业	Manufacture & Processing of Non–ferrous Metals	17	3	14.28	14.00	0.12
金属制品业	Manufacture of Metal Products	235	20	263.34	259.78	2.77
通用设备制造业	Manufacture of General Purpose Machinery	269	45	313.38	307.54	3.94
专用设备制造业	Manufacture of Special Purpose Machinery	169	21	181.90	167.29	1.77
汽车制造业	Manufacture of Automotive	109	10	1168.37	1120.48	5.87
铁路、船舶、航空航天和其他运输设备制造业	Manufacture of Railroad,Marine, Aerospace and Other Transportation Equipment	32	8	115.79	115.14	1.02
电气机械和器材制造业	Manufacture of Electrical Machinery & Equipment	95	28	272.78	262.72	1.81
计算机、通信和其他电子设备制造业	Manufacture of Computer, Communications and Other Electronic Equipment	48	13	662.78	610.31	3.44
仪器仪表制造业	Manufacture of Measuring Instrument	64	8	51.70	52.95	0.90
其他制造业	Other Manufacture	1	0	0.22	0.22	0.00
废弃资源综合利用业	Comprehensive Utilization of Waste	2	0	0.76	0.76	0.01
金属制品、机械和设备修理业	Metal Products, Machinery and Equipment Repair Industry	3	0	6.81	6.71	0.18
电力、热力生产和供应业	Production and Supply of Electric Power and Heat Power	21	5	84.56	84.34	0.67
燃气生产和供应业	Production and Distribution of Gas	14	2	30.41	30.40	0.29
水的生产和供应业	Production and Supply of Water	9	2	20.29	19.80	0.27

12 - 5 规模以上国有及国有控股工业主要经济指标(2018 年)

Main Economic Indicators of State-Owned and State-Controlled Industrial Enterprises Above Designated Size（2018）

指标	Indicator	企业单位数（个）Number of Industial Enterprises (unit)	#亏损企业数（个）Loss Enterprises (unit)	工业总产值(现价)(万元) Gross Industrial Output Value (Calculated at Current Prices) (10 000 yuan)	工业销售产值(现价)(万元) Industrial Output Value of Products Sold(Calculated at Current Prices) (10 000 yuan)	平均用工人数（万人）Average of Employed Persons (10 000 persons)
总计	**Total**	147	34	24454849	23441051	12.83
按登记注册类型分	**by Status of Registration**					
内资企业	Domestic Funded Enterprises	134	30	23822903	22764976	12.21
国有企业	State-owned Enterprises	13	5	154746	155530	0.25
中央企业	Central Enterprises	2	0	18896	18878	0.05
地方企业	Local Enterprises	11	5	135850	136653	0.20
有限责任公司	Private Limited Liability Corporations	107	23	20907817	19882900	11.20
国有独资公司	State Sole funded Corporations	31	8	11926738	11445668	6.32
其他有限责任公司	Other Limited Liability Corporations	76	15	8981078	8437231	4.88
股份有限公司	Share-holding Corporations Limited	14	2	2760341	2726546	0.76
港、澳、台商投资企业	Enterprises with Funds from Hong Kong, Macao and Taiwan	4	1	319035	361491	0.35
合资经营企业(港或澳、台资)	Joint-ventures Enterprises	3	1	237735	233873	0.23
合作经营企业(港或澳、台资)	Cooperative Enterprises	1	0	81300	127618	0.12
外商投资企业	Foreign Funded Enterprises	9	3	312911	314585	0.27
中外合资经营企业	Joint-venture Enterprises	7	2	291611	288945	0.24
中外合作经营企业	Cooperation Enterprises	2	1	21300	25640	0.02
按轻重工业分	**by Light & Heavy Industry**					
轻工业	Light Industry	34	9	507609	544750	1.02
重工业	Heavy Industry	113	25	23947240	22896301	11.81
按企业规模分	**by Enterprise Size**					
大型企业	Large-sized Enterprises	17	4	20883651	19924400	9.50
中型企业	Medium-sized Enterprises	42	9	2278944	2216133	2.16
小型企业	Small-sized Enterprises	86	20	1280448	1285384	1.14
微型企业	Micro-sized Enterprises	2	1	11806	15134	0.03
按工业行业分	**by Sector**					
煤炭开采和洗选业	Mining and Washing of Coal	1	0	32716	31633	0.09
石油和天然气开采业	Extraction of Petroleum and Natural Gas	2	1	81388	81388	0.05

指标	Indicator	企业单位数（个）Number of Industial Enterprises (unit)	亏损企业数（个）Loss Enterprises (unit)	工业总产值(现价)(万元) Gross Industrial Output Value (Calculated at Current Prices) (10 000 yuan)	工业销售产值(现价)(万元) Industrial Output Value of Products Sold(Calculated at Current Prices) (10 000 yuan)	平均用工人数（万人）Average of Employed Persons (10 000 persons)
非金属矿采选业	Mining and Processing of Nonmetal Ores	1	0	1657	1627	0.01
农副食品加工业	Processing of Food from Agricultural Products	2	1	12459	8518	0.02
食品制造业	Manufacture of Foods	5	1	25296	25469	0.10
酒、饮料和精制茶制造业	Manufacture of Wine, Drinks and Refined Tea	3	0	174132	219670	0.22
烟草制品业	Manufacture of Tobacco	1	0	10999	10999	0.01
纺织业	Manufacture of Textile	2	1	10943	10266	0.04
纺织服装、服饰业	Manufacture of Textile Wearing Apparel and Finery	4	3	30958	30747	0.22
造纸和纸制品业	Manufacture of Paper and Paper Products	1	0	18970	18970	0.01
印刷和记录媒介复制业	Printing, Reproduction of Recording Media	7	3	85521	88070	0.20
石油、煤炭及其他燃料加工业	Processing of Petroleum, Coal and Other fuels	1	0	2446070	2433556	0.16
化学原料和化学制品制造业	Manufacture of Chemical Raw Material and Chemical Products	6	1	443500	424635	0.29
医药制造业	Manufacture of Medicines	3	0	56502	55627	0.09
非金属矿物制品业	Manufacture of Non-metallic Mineral Products	1	0	21629	17178	0.02
黑色金属冶炼和压延加工业	Manufacture and Processing of Ferrous Metals	11	1	320729	321092	0.17
金属制品业	Manufacture of Metal Products	1	0	75809	78249	0.04
通用设备制造业	Manufacture of General Purpose Machinery	8	2	191679	193616	0.16
专用设备制造业	Manufacture of Special Purpose Machinery	14	3	764851	733746	1.22
汽车制造业	Manufacture of Automotive	8	0	249827	241195	0.21
铁路、船舶、航空航天和其他运输设备制造业	Manufacture of Railroad,Marine, Aerospace and Other Transportation Equipment	4	1	10137617	9727425	4.19
电气机械和器材制造业	Manufacture of Electrical Machinery & Equipment	9	2	785118	781243	0.67
计算机、通信和其他电子设备制造业	Manufacture of Computer, Communications and Other Electronic Equipment	18	5	1121899	1087883	0.67
仪器仪表制造业	Manufacture of Measuring Instrument	7	3	6142899	5622267	2.74
废弃资源综合利用业	Comprehensive Utilization of Waste	5	1	141272	125576	0.18
金属制品、机械和设备修理业	Metal Products, Machinery and Equipment Repair Industry	1	0	11640	11640	0.02
电力、热力生产和供应业	Production and Supply of Electric Power and Heat Power	10	2	712164	712164	0.55
燃气生产和供应业	Production and Supply of Gas	6	1	194231	194231	0.24
水的生产和供应业	Production and Supply of Water	5	2	152374	152374	0.23

12-6 规模以上私营工业企业主要经济指标（2018年）

Main Economic Indicators of Private Industrial Enterprises Above Designated Size（2018）

指标	Indicator	企业单位数（个）Number of Industial Enterprises (unit)	#亏损企业数（个）Loss Enterprises (unit)	工业总产值（现价）（万元）Gross Industrial Output Value (Calculated at Current Prices) (10 000 yuan)	工业销售产值（现价）（万元）Industrial Output Value of Products Sold(Calculated at Current Prices) (10 000yuan)	平均用工人数（万人）Average of Employed Persons (10 000 persons)
总计	**Total**	1113	140	13038959	12595038	11.22
按登记注册类型分组	**by Status of Registration**					
内资企业	Domestic Funded Enterprises	1113	140	13038959	12595038	11.22
私营企业	Private Enterprises	1113	140	13038959	12595038	11.22
私营独资企业	Private-funded Enterprises	53	3	384264	381691	0.28
私营合伙企业	Private Partnership Enterprises	1	0	40485	40485	0.01
私营有限责任公司	Private Limited Liability Corporations	1005	130	9183222	8915155	9.05
私营股份有限公司	Private Share-holding Corporations Ltd.	54	7	3430989	3257707	1.88
按轻重工业分	**by Light & Heavy Industry**					
轻工业	Light Industry	313	43	4183285	3932093	4.00
重工业	Heavy Industry	800	97	8855674	8662944	7.22
按企业规模分	**by Enterprise Size**					
大型企业	Large-sized Enterprises	5	1	3555606	3364733	1.99
中型企业	Medium-sized Enterprises	34	8	1437514	1292870	1.54
小型企业	Small-sized Enterprises	909	100	7576139	7469493	7.19
微型企业	Micro-sized Enterprises	165	31	469699	467941	0.49
按工业行业分	**by Sector**					
非金属矿采选业	Mining and Processing of Nonmetal Ores	5	0	43867	43900	0.03
农副食品加工业	Processing of Food from Agricultural Products	41	3	315799	314103	0.37
食品制造业	Manufacture of Foods	30	10	304693	296674	0.57
酒、饮料和精制茶制造业	Manufacture of Wine, Drinks and Refined Tea	6	2	9718	9272	0.03
纺织业	Manufacture of Textile	23	5	98821	96443	0.14
纺织服装、服饰业	Manufacture of Textile Wearing Apparel and Finery	12	1	40343	40119	0.13
皮革、毛皮、羽毛及其制品和制鞋业	Manufacture of Leather, Fur, Feather & Its Products and Footwear	4	0	66250	65233	0.04
木材加工和木、竹、藤、棕、草制品业	Processing of Timbers, Manufacture of Wood, Bamboo, Rattan, Palm, and Straw Products	8	0	77637	78990	0.05
家具制造业	Manufacture of Furniture	12	0	94169	93382	0.13

指标	Indicator	企业单位数（个）Number of Industial Enterprises (unit)	亏损企业数（个）Loss Enterprises (unit)	工业总产值（现价）（万元）Gross Industrial Output Value (Calculated at Current Prices) (10 000 yuan)	工业销售产值（现价）（万元）Industrial Output Value of Products Sold(Calculated at Current Prices) (10 000yuan)	平均用工人数（万人）Average of Employed Persons (10 000 persons)
造纸和纸制品业	Manufacture of Paper and Paper Products	21	3	160312	156046	0.19
印刷和记录媒介复制业	Printing, Reproduction of Recording Media	28	1	240256	238490	0.18
文教、工美、体育和娱乐用品制造业	Manufacture of Culture, Education,Arts and crafts，Sport and Entertainment Goods	20	4	170026	171232	0.20
石油、煤炭及其他燃料加工业	Processing of Petroleum, Coal and Other fuels	5	1	81293	81439	0.04
化学原料和化学制品制造业	Manufacture of Chemical Raw Material and Chemical Products	64	6	1762271	1799622	0.79
医药制造业	Manufacture of Medicines	29	5	2080169	1857067	1.32
化学纤维制造业	Manufacture of Chemical Fiber	1	0	7130	5141	0.01
橡胶和塑料制品业	Manufacture of Rubber and Plastic	43	3	211636	209452	0.24
非金属矿物制品业	Manufacture of Non-metallic Mineral Products	114	13	1888279	1837191	1.23
黑色金属冶炼和压延加工业	Manufacture and Processing of Ferrous Metals	6	0	59449	62957	0.03
有色金属冶炼和压延加工业	Manufacture & Processing of Non-ferrous Metals	12	1	84358	82724	0.04
金属制品业	Manufacture of Metal Products	154	16	1023282	1012624	1.17
通用设备制造业	Manufacture of General Purpose Machinery	173	29	1160704	1140249	1.40
专用设备制造业	Manufacture of Special Purpose Machinery	108	12	1202719	1073487	1.04
汽车制造业	Manufacture of Automotive	66	4	651299	641334	0.57
铁路、船舶、航空航天和其他运输设备制造业	Manufacture of Railroad,Marine, Aerospace and Other Transportation Equipment	14	2	307880	305704	0.15
电气机械和器材制造业	Manufacture of Electrical Machinery & Equipment	42	10	264251	259918	0.28
计算机、通信和其他电子设备制造业	Manufacture of Computer, Communications and Other Electronic Equipment	20	4	284671	285223	0.34
仪器仪表制造业	Manufacture of Measuring Instrument	44	4	265582	261499	0.44
其他制造业	Other Manufacture	1	0	2201	2201	0.00
废弃资源综合利用业	Comprehensive Utilization of Waste	1	0	4243	4243	0.01
金属制品、机械和设备修理业	Metal Products, Machinery and Equipment Repair Industry	1	0	2791	2791	0.00
电力、热力生产和供应业	Production and Supply of Electric Power and Heat Power	1	0	16212	14578	0.01
燃气生产和供应业	Production and Supply of Gas	2	1	37507	37507	0.01
水的生产和供应业	Production and Supply of Water	2	0	19143	14203	0.02

12-7 规模以上工业

Capital Power of Industrial Enterprises

单位：亿元

指　　标	Indicator	流动资产合计 Total Current Assets	应收账款 Receivable	存货 Inventory	固定资产合计 Total Fixed Assets
总计	**Total**	3824.08	781.96	830.42	956.77
按登记注册类型分	**by Status of Registration**				
内资企业	Domestic Funded Enterprises	3552.84	724.53	779.22	842.06
国有企业	State-owned Enterprises	21.86	8.33	4.11	9.35
中央企业	Central Enterprises	4.01	1.10	0.98	1.40
地方企业	Local Enterprises	17.85	7.23	3.14	7.95
集体企业	Collective-owned Enterprises	1.82	0.60	0.42	2.40
股份合作企业	Cooperative Enterprises	2.58	0.74	0.45	0.37
有限责任公司	Private Limited Liability Corporations	2627.59	438.58	570.57	554.59
国有独资公司	State Sole funded Corporations	1479.87	116.02	306.69	191.24
其他有限责任公司	Other Limited Liability Corporations	1147.72	322.57	263.88	363.35
股份有限公司	Share-holding Corporations Limited	213.46	63.13	46.86	85.10
私营企业	Private Enterprises	685.53	213.16	156.80	190.25
私营独资企业	Private-funded Enterprises	4.74	1.82	1.04	3.59
私营合伙企业	Private Partnership Enterprises	0.28	0.01	0.03	0.73
私营有限责任公司	Private Limited Liability Corporations	451.08	156.64	112.89	122.15
私营股份有限公司	Private Share-holding Corporations Ltd.	229.44	54.69	42.84	63.79
港、澳、台商投资企业	Enterprises with Funds from Hong Kong, Macao and Taiwan	127.14	19.63	16.71	55.27
合资经营企业(港或澳、台资)	Joint-ventures Enterprises	86.94	12.50	8.33	29.87
合作经营企业(港或澳、台资)	Cooperative Enterprises	3.17	0.20	0.87	3.35
港澳台商独资经营企业	Enterprises with Sole Investment	18.33	4.71	5.85	16.73
港澳台商投资股份有限公司	Share-holding Corporations Ltd. With Funds From Hong Kong, Macao and Taiwan	18.08	2.22	1.27	5.30
其他港澳台商投资企业	Other Enterprises with Funds from Hong Kong,Macao and Taiwan	0.63	0.00	0.39	0.01
外商投资企业	Foreign Funded Enterprises	144.10	37.79	34.48	59.43
中外合资经营企业	Joint-venture Enterprises	60.09	16.30	13.99	21.07
中外合作经营企业	Cooperation Enterprises	2.64	0.45	0.61	0.81
外资企业	Enterprises with Sole Foreign Funds	73.95	18.08	17.63	29.10
外商投资股份有限公司	Share-holding Corporations Ltd. With Foreign Investment	7.41	2.97	2.25	8.46
按轻重工业分	**by Light & Heavy Industry**				
轻工业	Light Industry	550.58	123.79	123.29	183.96
重工业	Heavy Industry	3273.50	658.16	707.12	772.81
按企业规模分	**by Enterprise Size**				
大型企业	Large-sized Enterprises	2359.06	293.36	518.97	480.09
中型企业	Medium-sized Enterprises	598.46	203.47	129.13	207.77
小型企业	Small-sized Enterprises	825.35	272.00	174.26	252.92
微型企业	Micro-sized Enterprises	41.21	13.12	8.06	15.99

资产实力（2018年）

Above Designated Size（2018）

(100 million yuan)

固定资产原价 Original Value of Fixed Assets	流动负债合计 Current Liabilities Total	非流动负债合计 Non-Current Liabilities Total	所有者权益合计 Total Owner'sEquities	实收资本 Paid- up Capital	国家资本 Official Capital
1813.95	2989.70	503.78	2386.75	1046.21	312.69
1576.64	2807.92	454.63	2136.85	930.77	303.02
18.54	21.32	2.49	11.35	3.82	2.79
2.31	2.98	0.00	2.43	0.57	0.12
16.23	18.34	2.48	8.92	3.25	2.67
4.42	1.26	0.91	3.82	0.36	0.04
0.64	1.45	0.02	1.53	0.16	0.00
1031.03	2111.02	395.64	1359.65	652.94	265.62
400.54	1241.53	180.93	636.74	393.31	152.71
630.49	869.49	214.71	722.91	259.63	112.91
171.69	155.81	14.69	212.60	80.60	34.21
350.31	517.05	40.89	547.90	192.90	0.37
6.20	3.60	0.36	7.23	2.36	0.00
1.45	0.45	0.00	0.56	0.08	0.00
227.07	367.02	31.63	292.82	140.33	0.29
115.60	145.98	8.90	247.29	50.13	0.09
105.16	77.32	19.46	127.78	45.37	8.51
58.00	47.25	11.69	79.95	25.33	8.20
5.21	3.81	0.07	3.16	0.40	0.30
28.85	16.57	5.60	27.33	17.35	0.00
13.04	9.64	2.09	16.74	2.23	0.00
0.06	0.04	0.00	0.61	0.05	0.00
132.16	104.46	29.69	122.12	70.07	1.16
53.02	46.36	11.37	38.76	24.82	0.53
2.02	1.09	0.00	4.36	1.78	0.64
64.67	49.39	13.32	73.24	40.42	0.00
12.45	7.61	5.00	5.76	3.05	0.00
355.91	369.06	24.10	578.88	163.16	13.64
1458.04	2620.64	479.67	1807.87	883.05	299.05
902.76	1843.21	351.94	1309.95	527.45	196.69
424.71	417.74	52.69	513.81	198.96	66.88
464.07	697.11	89.35	536.16	303.37	47.45
22.41	31.64	9.79	26.83	16.43	1.67

12-7 续 1

指　　标	Indicator	流动资产合计 Total Current Assets	应收账款 Receivable	存货 Inventory	固定资产合计 Total Fixed Assets
按工业行业分	by Sector				
煤炭开采和洗选业	Mining and Washing of Coal	0.69	0.26	0.08	6.17
石油和天然气开采业	Extraction of Petroleum and Natural Gas	38.15	34.44	0.12	7.28
非金属矿采选业	Mining and Processing of Nonmetal Ores	2.50	0.75	0.24	1.81
农副食品加工业	Processing of Food from Agricultural Products	16.03	3.13	6.04	5.33
食品制造业	Manufacture of Foods	59.79	10.35	13.04	27.53
酒、饮料和精制茶制造业	Manufacture of Wine, Drinks and Refined Tea	20.37	3.95	6.75	17.79
烟草制品业	Manufacture of Tobacco	1.76	0.22	0.05	1.00
纺织业	Manufacture ofTextile	17.81	4.51	5.89	12.94
纺织服装、服饰业	Manufacture of Textile Wearing Apparel and Finery	13.48	1.65	4.43	8.17
皮革、毛皮、羽毛及其制品和制鞋业	Manufacture of Leather, Fur, Feather & Its Products and Footwear	2.32	0.54	0.75	0.38
木材加工和木、竹、藤、棕、草制品业	Processing of Timbers, Manufacture of Wood, Bamboo, Rattan, Palm, and Straw Products	3.12	0.89	1.49	2.00
家具制造业	Manufacture of Furniture	2.33	0.29	0.76	1.58
造纸和纸制品业	Manufacture of Paper and Paper Products	10.62	2.41	4.49	3.52
印刷和记录媒介复制业	Printing, Reproduction of Recording Media	30.65	9.31	5.07	14.14
文教、工美、体育和娱乐用品制造业	Manufacture of Culture, Education,Arts and crafts，Sport and Entertainment Goods	6.37	1.41	2.63	1.67
石油、煤炭及其他燃料加工业	Processing of Petroleum, Coal and Other fuels	21.69	4.14	9.03	39.66
化学原料和化学制品制造业	Manufacture of Chemical Raw Material and Chemical Products	173.59	29.15	32.51	107.54
医药制造业	Manufacture of Medicines	225.80	56.87	45.37	62.53
化学纤维制造业	Manufacture of Chemical Fiber	6.75	1.10	2.11	2.28
橡胶和塑料制品业	Manufacture of Rubber and Plastic	13.04	4.11	3.27	4.68
非金属矿物制品业	Manufacture of Non-metallic Mineral Products	214.20	83.89	30.60	54.70
黑色金属冶炼和压延加工业	Manufacture and Processing of Ferrous Metals	26.73	2.53	14.72	7.11
有色金属冶炼和压延加工业	Manufacture & Processing of Non-ferrous Metals	6.01	1.57	2.93	0.91
金属制品业	Manufacture of Metal Products	142.12	47.33	32.93	52.97
通用设备制造业	Manufacture of General Purpose Machinery	259.51	63.13	69.26	60.33
专用设备制造业	Manufacture of Special Purpose Machinery	144.16	42.50	38.27	23.87
汽车制造业	Manufacture of Automotive	1320.30	92.31	282.06	123.07
铁路、船舶、航空航天和其他运输设备制造业	Manufacture of Railroad,Marine,Aerospace and Other Transportation Equipment	68.58	24.94	12.93	26.34
电气机械和器材制造业	Manufacture of ElectricalMachinery & Equipment	255.35	94.79	53.61	55.30
计算机、通信和其他电子设备制造业	Manufacture of Computer, Communications and Other Electronic Equipment	491.98	116.49	125.86	44.05
仪器仪表制造业	Manufacture of Measuring Instrument	55.15	21.81	12.07	10.10
其他制造业	Other Manufacture	0.09	0.04	0.01	0.00
废弃资源综合利用业	Comprehensive Utilization of Waste	0.54	0.11	0.01	0.26
金属制品、机械和设备修理业	Metal Products, Machinery and Equipment Repair Industry	4.81	2.26	1.32	2.88
电力、热力生产和供应业	Production and Supply of ElectricPower and Heat Power	78.77	12.44	6.67	115.51
燃气生产和供应业	Production and Supply of Gas	45.64	1.76	1.04	22.81
水的生产和供应业	Production and Supply of Water	43.31	4.58	2.00	28.55

固定资产原价 Original Value of Fixed Assets	流动负债合计 Current Liabilities Total	非流动负债合计 Non-Current Liabilities Total	所有者权益合计 Total Owner's Equities		
				实收资本 Paid- up Capital	国家资本 Official Capital
9.82	8.82	0.00	–0.99	2.50	2.50
30.48	1.28	2.24	45.04	5.18	0.70
2.45	1.36	0.34	3.52	1.20	0.50
8.32	15.97	1.75	9.12	4.34	0.33
57.44	49.05	5.88	57.10	22.42	0.22
35.88	18.77	1.26	23.04	13.89	5.97
1.22	0.58	0.00	2.41	0.95	0.95
25.23	22.50	0.79	14.51	7.36	0.43
13.66	8.98	1.67	13.95	5.13	0.51
0.74	2.77	0.00	0.16	0.28	0.00
3.49	4.86	0.04	1.47	1.30	0.00
2.03	2.10	0.02	3.07	1.76	0.00
6.87	10.34	0.94	5.21	3.60	0.80
34.45	22.34	2.03	33.64	15.92	1.74
2.58	4.90	0.20	4.56	2.53	0.00
87.58	41.57	0.04	23.32	28.39	27.01
185.26	151.35	72.11	105.79	40.22	4.15
114.23	137.74	5.67	261.46	53.31	0.00
3.36	6.21	0.00	5.80	1.95	1.00
12.97	5.88	1.44	16.23	7.50	0.06
115.34	160.12	13.09	133.22	43.02	7.86
14.42	15.47	1.16	18.69	15.33	0.40
1.48	3.99	0.06	4.71	1.09	0.00
85.96	93.77	12.23	133.63	40.00	2.84
137.09	188.07	14.52	189.05	125.06	66.33
46.89	97.16	13.93	95.05	37.49	5.34
255.97	1105.96	127.80	521.91	306.00	49.15
49.75	86.81	9.32	45.39	31.01	21.29
97.54	215.52	20.68	153.64	78.74	39.90
72.95	271.36	87.30	265.08	40.45	6.93
16.23	34.99	1.11	38.65	17.00	4.28
0.03	0.03	0.00	0.06	0.09	0.00
0.30	2.60	0.00	0.42	0.30	0.00
5.84	2.11	0.00	6.06	2.26	1.22
195.41	110.78	55.02	84.19	53.24	45.56
32.19	38.86	10.10	41.37	15.37	5.57
48.49	44.72	41.03	27.23	20.03	9.16

12-8 规模以上国有及国有控

Capital Power of State-Owned and State-Controlled

单位：万元

指　　标	Indicator	流动资产合计 Total Current Assets	应收账款 Receivable	存货 Inventory	固定资产合计 Total Fixed Assets
总计	**Total**	22798094	3456327	4878039	4694249
按登记注册类型分	**by Status of Registration**				
内资企业	Domestic Funded Enterprises	22154023	3359022	4791014	4412027
国有企业	State-owned Enterprises	218640	83255	41134	93494
中央企业	Central Enterprises	40114	10981	9776	14008
地方企业	Local Enterprises	178526	72274	31358	79486
有限责任公司	Private Limited Liability Corporations	21360788	3095327	4574312	3825741
国有独资公司	State Sole funded Corporations	14798744	1160154	3066891	1912431
其他有限责任公司	Other Limited Liability Corporations	6562044	1935174	1507421	1913310
股份有限公司	Share-holding Corporations Limited	574594	180440	175568	492793
港、澳、台商投资企业	Enterprises with Funds from Hong Kong, Macao and Taiwan	402277	29411	31096	198748
合资经营企业(港或澳、台资)	Joint-ventures Enterprises	370625	27430	22402	165226
合作经营企业(港或澳、台资)	Cooperative Enterprises	31652	1982	8694	33521
外商投资企业	Foreign Funded Enterprises	241794	67893	55929	83474
中外合资经营企业	Joint-venture Enterprises	218104	64206	51156	75718
中外合作经营企业	Cooperation Enterprises	23689	3688	4773	7757
按轻重工业分	**by Light & Heavy Industry**				
轻工业	Light Industry	452090	75475	121078	191176
重工业	Heavy Industry	22346003	3380852	4756961	4503072
按企业规模分	**by Enterprise Size**				
大型企业	Large-sized Enterprises	19245264	1983961	4190478	3147838
中型企业	Medium-sized Enterprises	2051018	955237	403360	963769
小型企业	Small-sized Enterprises	1488240	510895	281980	570124
微型企业	Micro-sized Enterprises	13572	6234	2222	12518
按工业行业分	**by Sector**				
煤炭开采和洗选业	Mining and Washing of Coal	6889	2562	770	61690

股工业资产实力(2018 年)

Industrial Enterprises Above Designated Size (2018)

(10 000 yuan)

固定资产原价 Original Value of Fixed Assets	流动负债合计 Current Liabilities Total	非流动负债合计 Non-Current Liabilities Total	所有者权益合计 Total Owner's Equities		
				实收资本 Paid- up Capital	国家资本 Official Capital
9024023	18606638	3656440	11201501	5900851	2956318
8552837	18093449	3525056	10639316	5651721	2888576
185400	213234	24861	113475	38215	27864
23084	29842	31	24299	5727	1205
162316	183391	24831	89177	32488	26659
7301649	17252136	3467410	10007887	5222762	2529835
4005400	12415272	1809300	6367436	3933107	1527149
3296248	4836864	1658109	3640451	1289655	1002685
1065788	628079	32785	517953	390744	330877
281003	296541	98799	396029	157704	60996
228881	258392	98114	364460	153667	57970
52122	38149	685	31570	4037	3026
190183	216647	32585	166156	91426	6747
170777	206114	32585	125301	74257	364
19406	10534	0	40855	17170	6383
393031	378420	34849	364731	194623	129876
8630992	18228218	3621591	10836770	5706228	2826442
6175145	15568272	3182553	8741463	4440212	1947031
1869001	1508089	199064	1685500	885934	651123
953252	1465675	272730	800871	542347	357863
26624	64602	2092	-26333	32359	300
98234	88227	0	-9915	25000	25000

12-8 续 1

指 标	Indicator	流动资产合计 Total Current Assets	应收账款 Receivable	存货 Inventory	固定资产合计 Total Fixed Assets
石油和天然气开采业	Extraction of Petroleum and Natural Gas	348394	340182	1115	65432
非金属矿采选业	Mining and Processing of Nonmetal Ores	8715	1063	363	5010
农副食品加工业	Processing of Food from Agricultural Products	30712	1708	16096	4118
食品制造业	Manufacture of Foods	13244	3626	1372	5942
酒、饮料和精制茶制造业	Manufacture of Wine, Drinks and Refined Tea	87376	4858	20014	65746
烟草制品业	Manufacture of Tobacco	17636	2213	489	9952
纺织业	Manufacture of Textile	9438	1384	6015	1920
纺织服装、服饰业	Manufacture of Textile Wearing Apparel and Finery	68033	3797	15898	15751
造纸和纸制品业	Manufacture of Paper and Paper Products	11937	1541	1600	0
印刷和记录媒介复制业	Printing, Reproduction of Recording Media	73833	25702	14380	33917
石油、煤炭及其他燃料加工业	Processing of Petroleum, Coal and Other fuels	163426	27356	76674	388020
化学原料和化学制品制造业	Manufacture of Chemical Raw Material and Chemical Products	262070	31804	52998	269853
医药制造业	Manufacture of Medicines	56067	7495	9406	34704
化学纤维制造业	Manufacture of Chemical Fiber	29330	607	15266	16884
非金属矿物制品业	Manufacture of Non-metallic Mineral Products	212176	74741	25040	60615
黑色金属冶炼和压延加工业	Manufacture and Processing of Ferrous Metals	11764	450	4976	396
金属制品业	Manufacture of Metal Products	202249	67888	56218	32971
通用设备制造业	Manufacture of General Purpose Machinery	1084495	214563	224022	219165
专用设备制造业	Manufacture of Special Purpose Machinery	348830	119460	74022	70074
汽车制造业	Manufacture of Automotive	12405038	576402	2630827	961697
铁路、船舶、航空航天和其他运输设备制造业	Manufacture of Railroad,Marine,Aerospace and Other Transportation Equipment	553166	176642	101959	216833
电气机械和器材制造业	Manufacture of Electrical Machinery & Equipment	1112293	560616	307571	397284
计算机、通信和其他电子设备制造业	Manufacture of Computer, Communications and Other Electronic Equipment	4430640	1011958	1131771	280948
仪器仪表制造业	Manufacture of Measuring Instrument	128481	66420	27263	40439
金属制品、机械和设备修理业	Metal Products, Machinery and Equipment Repair Industry	11280	3639	5061	3884
电力、热力生产和供应业	Production and Supply of Electric Power and Heat Power	462487	88834	43932	1025220
燃气生产和供应业	Production and Supply of Gas	312646	4674	9862	179426
水的生产和供应业	Production and Supply of Water	335449	34142	3059	226361

固定资产原价 Original Value of Fixed Assets	流动负债合计 Current Liabilities Total	非流动负债合计 Non-Current Liabilities Total	所有者权益合计 Total Owner's Equities	实收资本 Paid- up Capital	国家资本 Official Capital
285104	10195	15897	403004	44800	0
8863	2932	3016	8326	5000	5000
7612	32281	4154	-257	3281	3281
9953	12043	951	7561	2900	1720
118015	56891	5866	101855	61317	59676
12153	5809	0	24068	9500	9500
6707	9040	0	3164	2360	1860
41804	38131	1289	57265	7505	5070
6059	14643	5382	2454	8000	8000
121294	53290	5462	77443	59167	17396
863561	373932	103	207895	270054	270054
406294	430526	377771	-165429	53581	41526
46515	66915	11679	57882	16169	0
17793	50157	0	10767	10000	10000
145485	169503	8897	172051	86927	63358
5827	5979	0	8412	4000	0
66557	175601	16341	69365	43600	27420
657755	683197	87355	826178	692815	642188
105530	243860	31167	170624	79690	46679
2051310	10301934	1230181	4769853	2864110	490333
390206	694440	88928	354815	255096	212561
613632	1111641	97547	651599	451665	393698
476582	2414414	814375	2202057	195618	68392
61787	91258	527	89435	52977	42691
6697	6634	0	8784	2000	1600
1739942	854513	407612	577460	374160	368265
255177	251062	98933	350481	113146	49438
397575	357593	343007	164306	106413	91613

12-9 规模以上工业

Profit、Loss and Distribution of Industrial

单位：亿元

指标	Indicator	主营业务收入 Revenue from Principal Business	主营业务成本 Cost of Principal Business	主营业务税金及附加 Taxes and Other Charges on Principal Business	销售费用 Selling Expenses
总计	**Total**	5192.15	4001.40	94.04	259.64
按登记注册类型分	**by Status of Registration**				
内资企业	Domestic Funded Enterprises	4819.14	3709.37	90.74	238.53
国有企业	State-owned Enterprises	274.27	15.83	0.36	0.15
中央企业	Central Enterprises	260.46	3.05	0.02	0.02
地方企业	Local Enterprises	13.81	12.79	0.34	0.13
集体企业	Collective-owned Enterprises	7.51	6.62	0.07	0.04
股份合作企业	Cooperative Enterprises	2.09	1.22	0.02	0.43
有限责任公司	Private Limited Liability Corporations	2838.45	2400.70	18.79	116.51
国有独资公司	State Sole funded Corporations	1288.97	1131.02	6.79	42.26
其他有限责任公司	Other Limited Liability Corporations	1549.48	1269.68	12.00	74.25
股份有限公司	Share-holding Corporations Limited	444.46	320.10	60.81	22.54
私营企业	Private Enterprises	1252.35	964.90	10.69	98.86
私营独资企业	Private-funded Enterprises	37.87	33.27	0.33	0.51
私营合伙企业	Private Partnership Enterprises	4.05	3.00	0.00	0.42
私营有限责任公司	Private Limited Liability Corporations	881.52	741.31	7.56	31.95
私营股份有限公司	Private Share-holding Corporations Ltd.	328.91	187.32	2.80	65.99
港、澳、台商投资企业	Enterprises with Funds from Hong Kong, Macao and Taiwan	145.58	109.10	1.46	13.27
合资经营企业(港或澳、台资)	Joint-ventures Enterprises	79.88	60.08	0.64	7.45
合作经营企业(港或澳、台资)	Cooperative Enterprises	12.76	8.99	0.10	2.65
港澳台商独资经营企业	Enterprises with Sole Investment	37.07	28.59	0.42	2.68
港澳台商投资股份有限公司	Share-holding Corporations Ltd. With Funds From Hong Kong, Macao and Taiwan	15.53	11.21	0.29	0.45
其他港澳台商投资企业	Other Enterprises with Funds from Hong Kong,Macao and Taiwan	0.34	0.23	0.01	0.05
外商投资企业	Foreign Funded Enterprises	227.43	182.93	1.84	7.83
中外合资经营企业	Joint-venture Enterprises	88.12	74.16	0.91	3.09
中外合作经营企业	Cooperation Enterprises	3.00	2.30	0.04	0.03
外资企业	Enterprises with Sole Foreign Funds	121.73	97.06	0.84	4.01
外商投资股份有限公司	Share-holding Corporations Ltd. With Foreign Investment	14.59	9.42	0.05	0.70
按轻重工业分	**by Light & Heavy Industry**				
轻工业	Light Industry	986.21	591.30	9.38	120.15
重工业	Heavy Industry	4205.94	3410.11	84.67	139.48
按企业规模分	**by Enterprise Size**				
大型企业	Large-sized Enterprises	3032.70	2233.73	72.36	155.67
中型企业	Medium-sized Enterprises	787.86	614.05	8.56	56.36
小型企业	Small-sized Enterprises	1310.73	1099.74	12.34	46.42
微型企业	Micro-sized Enterprises	60.86	53.87	0.79	1.18
按工业行业分	**by Sector**				
煤炭开采和洗选业	Mining and Washing of Coal	3.97	2.48	0.19	0.02
石油和天然气开采业	Extraction of Petroleum and Natural Gas	9.80	6.08	0.95	0.00
非金属矿采选业	Mining and Processing of Nonmetal Ores	8.01	6.32	0.30	0.30
农副食品加工业	Processing of Food from Agricultural Products	47.79	42.86	0.12	1.65

损益及分配(2018 年)

Enterprises Above Designated Size（2018）

(100 million yuan)

管理费用 Cost of Management	利息支出 Interest Expense	利润总额 Total Profits	所得税费用 Income Tax Payable	亏损企业亏损总额 Total Loss of Loss Enterprises	利税总额 Total Profits and Taxes	应交增值税 Value-added Tax Payable
294.87	54.84	307.98	46.38	23.79	535.39	138.42
268.27	52.30	274.74	39.36	22.15	488.98	128.72
2.32	0.25	6.13	0.13	0.96	0.50	0.55
0.20	0.00	6.96	0.10	0.00	0.57	0.13
2.11	0.25	–0.83	0.03	0.96	–0.07	0.42
0.65	0.00	0.30	0.01	0.00	0.61	0.25
0.31	0.03	0.19	0.02	0.00	0.35	0.14
160.51	42.62	140.68	22.83	14.80	234.44	73.78
51.43	17.67	68.59	13.40	6.61	98.76	22.99
109.07	24.95	72.09	9.43	8.20	135.69	50.79
23.50	2.44	29.85	3.65	1.48	107.04	16.33
80.99	6.95	97.59	12.71	4.90	146.03	37.67
0.72	0.10	2.82	0.14	0.00	4.51	1.36
0.49	0.00	0.15	0.00	0.00	0.15	0.00
47.90	4.18	49.29	5.73	4.59	79.58	22.67
31.88	2.67	45.33	6.83	0.31	61.79	13.64
10.61	0.67	14.94	3.49	0.47	21.29	4.81
6.74	0.16	8.88	1.97	0.09	11.94	2.34
0.04	0.00	1.04	0.26	0.00	1.51	0.37
1.99	0.36	3.16	0.76	0.24	4.91	1.33
1.75	0.15	1.99	0.51	0.00	3.04	0.76
0.09	0.00	–0.13	0.00	0.13	–0.12	0.00
15.99	1.88	18.31	3.54	1.17	25.12	4.90
5.33	0.81	4.37	0.92	0.61	7.60	2.25
0.40	0.00	0.27	0.05	0.01	0.41	0.10
9.44	0.87	12.10	2.33	0.46	15.45	2.50
0.82	0.19	1.56	0.24	0.09	1.66	0.04
63.06	4.37	109.77	14.76	3.23	146.00	31.68
231.82	50.48	198.22	31.62	20.56	389.39	106.74
159.14	36.33	170.61	28.09	8.51	314.49	77.25
53.86	6.36	67.66	9.70	3.89	98.82	22.21
79.20	11.10	68.18	8.53	9.86	118.28	37.48
2.67	1.05	1.53	0.06	1.52	3.81	1.48
0.99	0.01	0.13	0.00	0.00	0.74	0.43
0.65	0.05	2.06	0.55	0.03	3.95	0.93
0.36	0.08	0.65	0.13	0.00	1.24	0.28
1.54	0.22	1.46	0.23	0.34	2.15	0.56

12-9 续 1

指标	Indicator	主营业务收入 Revenue from Principal Business	主营业务成本 Cost of Principal Business	主营业务税金及附加 Taxes and Other Charges on Principal Business	销售费用 Selling Expenses
食品制造业	Manufacture of Foods	116.93	93.09	0.72	7.38
酒、饮料和精制茶制造业	Manufacture of Wine, Drinks and Refined Tea	53.08	39.43	1.83	6.09
烟草制品业	Manufacture of Tobacco	117.26	0.67	0.00	0.01
纺织业	Manufacture of Textile	43.45	39.62	0.25	0.90
纺织服装、服饰业	Manufacture of Textile Wearing Apparel and Finery	20.19	15.47	0.28	2.23
皮革、毛皮、羽毛及其制品和制鞋业	Manufacture of Leather, Fur, Feather & Its Products and Footwear	7.88	7.31	0.12	0.03
木材加工和木、竹、藤、棕、草制品业	Processing of Timbers, Manufacture of Wood, Bamboo, Rattan, Palm, and Straw Products	11.10	9.85	0.11	0.10
家具制造业	Manufacture of Furniture	10.69	9.35	0.09	0.52
造纸和纸制品业	Manufacture of Paper and Paper Products	23.00	20.53	0.10	0.59
印刷和记录媒介复制业	Printing, Reproduction of Recording Media	56.62	47.04	0.50	1.78
文教、工美、体育和娱乐用品制造业	Manufacture of Culture, Education,Arts and crafts, Sport and Entertainment Goods	21.16	18.22	0.18	0.90
石油、煤炭及其他燃料加工业	Processing of Petroleum, Coal and Other fuels	253.38	179.96	59.09	0.69
化学原料和化学制品制造业	Manufacture of Chemical Raw Material and Chemical Products	356.75	306.58	2.14	9.32
医药制造业	Manufacture of Medicines	259.39	96.18	3.32	81.46
化学纤维制造业	Manufacture of Chemical Fiber	7.16	6.05	0.08	0.15
橡胶和塑料制品业	Manufacture of Rubber and Plastic	33.27	28.59	0.35	1.00
非金属矿物制品业	Manufacture of Non-metallic Mineral Products	358.12	301.17	3.04	11.96
黑色金属冶炼和压延加工业	Manufacture and Processing of Ferrous Metals	85.82	82.53	0.29	1.60
有色金属冶炼和压延加工业	Manufacture & Processing of Non-ferrous Metals	13.90	12.39	0.16	0.18
金属制品业	Manufacture of Metal Products	254.16	207.88	2.34	7.76
通用设备制造业	Manufacture of General Purpose Machinery	306.08	243.33	2.58	14.37
专用设备制造业	Manufacture of Special Purpose Machinery	156.17	117.45	1.57	8.46
汽车制造业	Manufacture of Automotive	1226.91	1074.74	6.34	38.98
铁路、船舶、航空航天和其他运输设备制造业	Manufacture of Railroad,Marine,Aerospace and Other Transportation Equipment	112.76	97.91	0.99	2.40
电气机械和器材制造业	Manufacture of Electrical Machinery & Equipment	258.15	218.32	1.54	16.11
计算机、通信和其他电子设备制造业	Manufacture of Computer, Communications and Other Electronic Equipment	620.25	505.67	1.87	33.04
仪器仪表制造业	Manufacture of Measuring Instrument	53.96	35.70	0.58	5.50
其他制造业	Other Manufacture	0.22	0.18	0.00	0.02
废弃资源综合利用业	Comprehensive Utilization of Waste	0.76	0.60	0.00	0.02
金属制品、机械和设备修理业	Metal Products, Machinery and Equipment Repair Industry	6.70	4.34	0.12	0.06
电力、热力生产和供应业	Production and Supply of Electric Power and Heat Power	226.45	78.34	0.95	0.59
燃气生产和供应业	Production and Supply of Gas	32.02	28.53	0.11	2.42
水的生产和供应业	Production and Supply of Water	18.85	16.68	0.83	1.04

管理费用 Cost of Management	利息支出 Interest Expense	利润总额 Total Profits	所得税费用 Income Tax Payable	亏损企业亏损总额 Total Loss of Loss Enterprises	利税总额 Total Profits and Taxes	应交增值税 Value-added Tax Payable
5.96	0.26	10.76	2.62	0.95	14.17	2.69
1.96	0.21	3.73	0.93	0.00	7.95	2.39
0.19	0.00	5.17	0.08	0.00	0.31	0.00
1.99	0.54	0.21	0.02	0.35	1.01	0.54
1.56	0.09	0.76	0.23	0.24	1.90	0.85
0.20	0.00	0.21	0.03	0.05	0.49	0.16
0.14	0.14	0.78	0.01	0.00	1.16	0.28
0.32	0.00	0.56	0.06	0.00	0.99	0.34
1.12	0.13	0.65	0.14	0.08	1.10	0.35
3.56	0.16	5.33	0.57	0.27	7.80	1.96
0.99	0.05	0.74	0.10	0.09	1.41	0.50
5.67	0.41	7.46	1.88	0.02	77.36	10.81
13.71	8.23	16.78	2.52	2.47	25.67	6.27
30.67	1.97	54.57	6.96	0.07	73.58	15.69
0.56	0.00	0.42	0.07	0.05	0.47	–0.04
1.55	0.20	1.77	0.30	0.12	3.09	0.97
16.24	2.55	22.36	3.31	0.58	35.69	10.28
1.22	0.02	1.20	0.38	0.00	2.59	1.10
0.31	0.02	0.75	0.02	0.01	1.15	0.24
12.77	1.83	20.28	2.44	0.41	31.09	8.46
27.80	1.16	20.62	2.57	2.93	32.39	8.92
14.00	1.85	15.51	2.23	0.84	21.85	4.76
42.39	17.80	71.14	12.98	1.77	99.50	21.99
8.05	1.31	2.86	0.40	0.66	6.75	2.77
18.38	3.16	11.37	1.24	3.89	18.77	5.52
60.98	7.80	15.49	0.52	2.39	40.57	23.13
8.87	0.51	4.70	0.45	0.61	7.79	2.50
0.02	0.00	0.00	0.00	0.00	0.02	0.01
0.05	0.00	0.10	0.01	0.00	0.12	0.02
1.66	0.02	0.73	0.11	0.00	1.22	0.37
4.41	3.40	3.05	1.20	4.13	4.36	1.99
2.07	0.05	3.05	0.87	0.16	3.10	–0.06
1.96	0.62	0.56	0.22	0.31	1.90	0.47

12-10 规模以上国有及国有

Profit、Loss and Distribution of State-Owned and State-

单位：万元

指标	Indicator	主营业务收入 Revenue from Principal Business	主营业务成本 Cost of Principal Business	主营业务税金及附加 Taxes and Other Charges on Principal Business	销售费用 Selling Expenses
总计	Total	27486187	20894118	729653	902571
按登记注册类型分	by Status of Registration				
内资企业	Domestic Funded Enterprises	26810336	20347579	726306	835333
国有企业	State-owned Enterprises	2742720	158316	3645	1491
中央企业	Central Enterprises	2604573	30455	232	185
地方企业	Local Enterprises	138147	127861	3413	1306
有限责任公司	Private Limited Liability Corporations	21317133	18243254	128195	800879
国有独资公司	State Sole funded Corporations	12889722	11310224	67940	422635
其他有限责任公司	Other Limited Liability Corporations	8427411	6933030	60255	378244
股份有限公司	Share-holding Corporations Limited	2750483	1946009	594466	32964
港、澳、台商投资企业	Enterprises with Funds from Hong Kong, Macao and Taiwan	384702	305741	1506	55793
合资经营企业(港或澳、台资)	Joint-ventures Enterprises	257084	215830	549	29343
合作经营企业(港或澳、台资)	Cooperative Enterprises	127618	89911	957	26451
外商投资企业	Foreign Funded Enterprises	291148	240798	1841	11445
中外合资经营企业	Joint-venture Enterprises	265318	220447	1503	11191
中外合作经营企业	Cooperation Enterprises	25830	20351	338	254
按轻重工业分	by Light & Heavy Industry				
轻工业	Light Industry	1716030	394381	15615	73009
重工业	Heavy Industry	25770157	20499737	714038	829562
按企业规模分	by Enterprise Size				
大型企业	Large-sized Enterprises	23802449	17848808	676687	738751
中型企业	Medium-sized Enterprises	2321011	1893975	36624	113901
小型企业	Small-sized Enterprises	1349892	1137900	15763	49116
微型企业	Micro-sized Enterprises	12836	13436	578	803
按工业行业分	by Sector				
煤炭开采和洗选业	Mining and Washing of Coal	39723	24758	1880	167

控股工业损益及分配(2018年)

Controlled Industrial Enterprises Above Designated Size（2018）

(10 000 yuan)

管理费用 Cost of Management	利息支出 Interest Expense	利润总额 Total Profits	所得税费用 Income Tax Payable	亏损企业亏损总额 Total Loss of Loss Enterprises	利税总额 Total Profits and Taxes	应交增值税 Value-added Tax Payable
1391712	364600	1121750	193518	122240	2475991	680330
1336253	362222	1082898	183265	119530	2426630	674611
23155	2533	61260	1344	9631	5014	5509
2020	0	69556	1043	0	5734	1346
21135	2533	–8296	300	9631	–720	4163
1225073	350725	933017	161752	107668	1620093	550833
514338	176702	685922	134031	66063	987585	229924
710735	174023	247095	27721	41605	632508	320909
88024	8964	88621	20169	2231	801524	118270
28157	0	31986	8903	807	35214	973
27744	0	21536	6345	807	20076	–2759
414	0	10449	2558	0	15138	3732
27302	2379	6867	1350	1902	14146	4746
23791	2367	5143	1068	1766	11229	3890
3511	12	1724	282	136	2918	856
48059	2745	82583	8340	5228	72093	22458
1343653	361855	1039168	185178	117012	2403898	657873
1102735	300617	914270	161996	78070	2160333	564728
179269	21681	109954	20768	10192	222953	72464
105248	39567	37348	10794	28692	96757	42549
4461	2735	–5221	–40	5285	–4053	590
9862	79	1258	0	0	7395	4256

12-10 续 1

指标	Indicator	主营业务收入 Revenue from Principal Business	主营业务成本 Cost of Principal Business	主营业务税金及附加 Taxes and Other Charges on Principal Business	销售费用 Selling Expenses
石油和天然气开采业	Extraction of Petroleum and Natural Gas	81388	50355	7566	0
非金属矿采选业	Mining and Processing of Nonmetal Ores	12097	8037	673	1084
农副食品加工业	Processing of Food from Agricultural Products	12907	11828	125	1064
食品制造业	Manufacture of Foods	25534	19354	114	1895
酒、饮料和精制茶制造业	Manufacture of Wine, Drinks and Refined Tea	221123	155356	11290	29826
烟草制品业	Manufacture of Tobacco	1172623	6706	34	75
纺织业	Manufacture of Textile	10146	9476	28	242
纺织服装、服饰业	Manufacture of Textile Wearing Apparel and Finery	31774	24368	765	1171
造纸和纸制品业	Manufacture of Paper and Paper Products	18970	17549	55	561
印刷和记录媒介复制业	Printing, Reproduction of Recording Media	89018	71671	1206	3102
石油、煤炭及其他燃料加工业	Processing of Petroleum, Coal and Other fuels	2430659	1710247	590107	1559
化学原料和化学制品制造业	Manufacture of Chemical Raw Material and Chemical Products	404515	346721	2594	14096
医药制造业	Manufacture of Medicines	55724	20456	1268	26599
化学纤维制造业	Manufacture of Chemical Fiber	18684	17877	222	87
非金属矿物制品业	Manufacture of Non-metallic Mineral Products	343300	300685	2643	4726
黑色金属冶炼和压延加工业	Manufacture and Processing of Ferrous Metals	68657	66497	291	140
金属制品业	Manufacture of Metal Products	273766	254498	1785	3661
通用设备制造业	Manufacture of General Purpose Machinery	793603	589130	5253	45100
专用设备制造业	Manufacture of Special Purpose Machinery	224286	163183	2811	8890
汽车制造业	Manufacture of Automotive	10899057	9585953	52287	347158
铁路、船舶、航空航天和其他运输设备制造业	Manufacture of Railroad,Marine,Aerospace and Other Transportation Equipment	742140	626898	5876	21141
电气机械和器材制造业	Manufacture of Electrical Machinery & Equipment	1154246	1015265	6452	46707
计算机、通信和其他电子设备制造业	Manufacture of Computer, Communications and Other Electronic Equipment	5740880	4692598	15809	301096
仪器仪表制造业	Manufacture of Measuring Instrument	132587	96260	2034	11254
金属制品、机械和设备修理业	Metal Products, Machinery and Equipment Repair Industry	11640	8152	125	77
电力、热力生产和供应业	Production and Supply of Electric Power and Heat Power	2132489	682723	8260	163
燃气生产和供应业	Production and Supply of Gas	209346	187681	806	20971
水的生产和供应业	Production and Supply of Water	135310	129839	7295	9960

管理费用 Cost of Management	利息支出 Interest Expense	利润总额 Total Profits	所得税费用 Income Tax Payable	亏损企业亏损总额 Total Loss of Loss Enterprises	利税总额 Total Profits and Taxes	应交增值税 Value-added Tax Payable
5159	393	17964	5376	260	32983	7375
1186	130	1101	494	0	2842	1069
1242	232	–916	11	980	–710	82
3232	90	1249	272	200	1967	603
5325	542	20110	5281	0	40461	9061
1944	0	51737	769	0	3101	0
769	0	–357	0	377	–148	170
7963	300	–991	0	2151	2544	2770
751	0	45	17	0	100	0
11690	468	3927	842	1519	10656	5435
50868	3871	72890	18317	0	768732	105735
15318	38334	–13127	435	17401	1568	10707
7914	0	4377	520	0	8252	2607
467	0	161	0	0	–431	–814
11777	920	23551	939	1391	33832	7638
776	–5	1077	269	0	2179	811
8620	5500	2119	680	232	8059	4155
107718	3260	68598	11038	11303	105402	28931
20887	10260	20983	4225	0	34829	11035
333059	169024	649766	120425	2666	890715	188663
66880	12618	16589	3213	3554	42147	18445
83027	18586	–8389	1785	30051	25894	24828
548347	71786	148934	2784	4163	383978	218478
22117	724	4437	358	4467	14528	8058
1873	71	1734	201	0	2595	736
32202	25110	9579	7560	37578	19671	18533
16824	0	24880	7162	850	23540	–2146
13917	2307	–1533	544	3097	9311	3111

12-11 分地区规模以上工

Main Economic Indicators of Industrial Enterprises

指 标	Indicator	全 市 Total	历下区 Li xia	市中区 Shi zhong	槐荫区 Huai yin
企业单位数（个）	Number of Industial Enterprises(unit)	1889	32	30	49
工业总产值（万元）	Gross Industrial Output Value(10 000 yuan)	49922768	2961994	6333298	2019608
资产与负债（万元）	Assets and Liabilities(10 000 yuan)				
资产总计	Total Assets	58926421	1635607	10439366	2965081
流动资产合计	Total Fixed Assets	38240845	792202	7738632	1956271
存货	Inventory	8304161	195918	1603893	350233
应收账款	Receivable	7819586	260386	670472	367398
固定资产合计	Total Fixed Assets	9567692	574189	786681	349596
流动负债合计	Current Liabilities Total	29896959	939067	6392475	1488446
非流动负债合计	Non-Current Liabilities Total	5037759	107472	979445	164704
所有者权益合计	Total Owner's Equities	23867474	589069	3061172	1299742
实收资本	Paid- up Capital	10462103	390978	1836198	381763
国家资本	Official Capital	3126942	291286	448108	260537
损益及分配（万元）	Profit,Loss and Distribution				
主营业务收入	Revenue from Principal Business	51921489	2995321	6797222	1982295
主营业务成本	Cost of Principal Business	40014017	2200499	5959819	1613676
主营业务税金及附加	Taxes and Other Charges on Principal Business	940449	594380	35702	11451
管理费用	Cost of Management	2948740	99688	243053	152071
利润总额	Total Profits	3079824	70221	377303	185061
应交所得税	Income Tax Payable	463832	23954	71223	17290
亏损企业亏损总额	Losses of Loss Enterprises	237890	24726	2284	7275
利税总额	Total Profits and Taxes	5353920	782264	531458	245572
本年应交增值税	Value-added Tax Payable	1384207	117173	117860	48550

业主要经济指标(2018年)

Above Designated Size By Region（2018）

天桥区 Tian qiao	历城区 Li cheng	长清区 Chang qing	章丘区 Zhang qiu	济阳区 Ji yang	平阴县 Ping yin	商河县 Shang he	高新区 Gao xin	南部山区 Nan shan
77	103	203	646	94	197	156	290	12
1006241	2750470	2022429	13927660	1448188	3008361	992919	13338380	113221
2117600	4253354	3084332	12183003	1951329	3407580	1170845	15581908	136418
995628	2623801	1836123	7432899	1160852	2047639	648221	10926823	81754
192113	398051	453775	1776879	162646	453810	159126	2515868	41850
241067	739942	533232	1066176	483040	492925	161363	2794910	8675
677394	774330	595740	2526921	431001	745356	315469	1769084	21932
1205462	2083862	1569166	5958997	769215	1271902	608448	7526272	83648
537601	256634	240021	1025652	109769	163387	77914	1370254	4905
374535	1908074	1266327	5157006	1072843	1967813	465211	6657817	47865
336193	780647	1145208	2256062	437048	431579	205973	2242779	17676
136165	272198	669514	367128	35514	41478	26836	578179	0
1012367	2793555	1994577	14244439	1350217	2788879	962288	12325885	106644
903543	1901113	1632488	12258782	1053590	2080914	837235	9491887	80471
6185	23173	14452	126560	18237	23841	10621	71179	4666
88127	236735	154985	479672	92663	182361	50654	1160403	8328
−35323	284222	91965	835847	130869	311437	28584	729090	5147
4901	47605	18572	109973	32544	50030	2352	84364	1024
61815	10496	27549	25734	9363	6912	5957	55526	253
−2175	409989	159019	1322856	193641	429432	51473	1216623	13768
25433	101323	49822	356646	44241	94100	11947	413159	3955

12-12 规模以上大中型工

Main Indicators of Large and

指标	Indicator	企业单位数（个）Number of Industial Enterprises (unit)	亏损企业（个）Loss nterprises (unit)	工业总产值（当年价格）（万元）Gross Industrial Output Value (10 000 yuan)	工业销售产值（当年价格）（万元）Industrial Output Value of Products Sold (10 000 yuan)
总计	**Total**	187	29	36014842	34405553
按登记注册类型分	**by Status of Registration**				
内资企业	Domestic Funded Enterprises	150	26	33307816	31717708
国有企业	State-owned Enterprises	1	1	18800	18308
地方企业	Local Enterprises	1	1	18800	18308
集体企业	Collective-owned Enterprises	2	0	36202	35708
股份合作企业	Cooperative Enterprises	1	0	11877	11283
有限责任公司	Private Limited Liability Corporations	82	13	25907874	24566185
国有独资公司	State Sole funded Corporations	15	6	11569146	11089337
其他有限责任公司	Other Limited Liability Corporations	67	7	14338728	13476848
股份有限公司	Share-holding Corporations Limited	26	3	4222901	4096873
私营企业	Private Enterprises	38	9	3110163	2989351
私营有限责任公司	Private Limited Liability Corporations	35	9	1866654	1695771
私营股份有限公司	Private Share-holding Corporations Ltd.	3	0	1243509	1293580
港、澳、台商投资企业	Enterprises with Funds from Hong Kong, Macao and Taiwan	16	1	1193727	1211073
合资经营企业(港或澳、台资)	Joint-ventures Enterprises	10	1	747438	751702
合作经营企业(港或澳、台资)	Cooperative Enterprises	1	0	81300	127618
港澳台商独资经营企业	Enterprises with Sole Investment	4	0	195105	168263
港澳台商投资股份有限公司	Share-holding Corporations Ltd. With Funds From Hong Kong, Macao and Taiwan	1	0	169884	163490
外商投资企业	Foreign Funded Enterprises	21	2	1513300	1476771
中外合资经营企业	Joint-venture Enterprises	11	1	563689	556364
外资企业	Enterprises with Sole Foreign Funds	9	1	752089	722886
外商投资股份有限公司	Share-holding Corporations Ltd. with Foreign Investment	1	0	197522	197522
按轻重工业分	**by Light & Heavy Industry**				
轻工业	Light Industry	57	7	5762978	5384673
重工业	Heavy Industry	130	22	30251864	29020879
按企业规模分	**by Enterprise Size**				
大型企业	Large-sized Enterprises	39	5	27537040	26347274

业企业经营情况(2018 年)

Medium-Sized Enterprises（2018）

资产总计（万元）Total Assets (10 000 yuan)	负债合计（万元）Total Liabilities (10 000 yuan)	主营业务收入（万元）Revenue fromPrincipal Business (10 000 yuan)	利润总额（万元）Total Profits (10 000 yuan)	利税总额（万元）Total Profits and Taxes(10 000 yuan)	平均用工人数（万人）Average of Employed Persons (10 000 persons)
44893500	26655871	38205613	2382775	4133048	22.90
41475933	25043006	35590573	2136709	3796763	19.66
57067	17778	2586108	64662	879	0.05
57067	17778	18308	-738	879	0.05
27456	3783	36039	642	2208	0.12
22680	13770	11877	1448	2814	0.04
35915843	22365367	26040691	1599912	2492177	15.13
20072251	13842198	12462595	677566	969710	6.11
15843592	8523170	13578096	922346	1522467	9.02
3023623	1316194	3989003	271990	1026576	1.85
2429263	1326114	2926855	198055	272109	2.48
1574915	977243	1633868	130311	175238	2.05
854348	348872	1292987	67745	96871	0.43
1850548	793255	1230949	129855	185787	1.67
1300500	537425	743636	87542	116880	0.85
70405	38835	127618	10449	15138	0.12
194913	99617	204353	11998	23361	0.48
284731	117378	155341	19866	30407	0.22
1567018	819611	1384092	116212	150498	1.56
644368	393947	546227	27859	47252	0.79
743626	303986	693047	71803	85865	0.68
179025	121678	144818	16550	17381	0.09
7012574	2562097	6630590	935645	1191186	5.92
37880926	24093774	31575023	1447130	2941861	16.97
35051018	21951483	30326970	1706137	3144851	14.98

指　标	Indicator	企业单位数（个）Number of Industial Enterprises (unit)	亏损企业（个）Loss nterprises (unit)	工业总产值（当年价格）（万元）Gross Industrial Output Value (10 000 yuan)	工业销售产值（当年价格）（万元）Industrial Output Value of Products Sold (10 000 yuan)
中型企业	Medium-sized Enterprises	148	24	8477802	8058279
按工业行业分	**by Sector**				
煤炭开采和洗选业	Mining and Washing of Coal	1	0	32716	31633
石油和天然气开采业	Extraction of Petroleum and Natural Gas	1	0	73875	73875
农副食品加工业	Processing of Food from Agricultural Products	3	0	94465	94352
食品制造业	Manufacture of Foods	11	2	900851	871416
酒、饮料和精制茶制造业	Manufacture of Wine, Drinks and Refined Tea	9	0	492937	517878
纺织业	Manufacture of　Textile	2	0	157122	157205
纺织服装、服饰业	Manufacture of Textile Wearing Apparel and Finery	6	2	106425	106930
家具制造业	Manufacture of Furniture	1	0	38049	38049
造纸和纸制品业	Manufacture of Paper and Paper Products	1	0	31122	29551
印刷和记录媒介复制业	Printing, Reproduction of Recording Media	4	1	146337	148691
石油、煤炭及其他燃料加工业	Processing of Petroleum, Coal and Other fuels	1	0	2446070	2433556
化学原料和化学制品制造业	Manufacture of Chemical Raw Material and Chemical Products	11	1	2562509	2606797
医药制造业	Manufacture of Medicines	10	0	2480557	2201530
非金属矿物制品业	Manufacture of Non-metallic Mineral Products	18	3	1574144	1489021
黑色金属冶炼和压延加工业	Manufacture and Processing of Ferrous Metals	2	0	701871	751642
有色金属冶炼和压延加工业	Manufacture & Processing of Non-ferrous Metals	1	0	40425	39424
金属制品业	Manufacture of Metal Products	12	2	996991	979012
通用设备制造业	Manufacture of General Purpose Machinery	22	4	1500871	1457252
专用设备制造业	Manufacture of Special Purpose Machinery	10	0	733480	604755
汽车制造业	Manufacture of Automotive	11	3	10645577	10173241
铁路、船舶、航空航天和其他运输设备制造业	Manufacture of Railroad,Marine,Aerospace and Other Transportation Equipment	7	3	744340	740810
电气机械和器材制造业	Manufacture of Electrical　Machinery & Equipment	16	4	1998169	1884970
计算机、通信和其他电子设备制造业	Manufacture of Computer, Communications and Other Electronic Equipment	10	3	6317019	5793555
仪器仪表制造业	Manufacture of Measuring Instrument	8	0	211943	194379
金属制品、机械和设备修理业	Metal Products, Machinery and Equipment Repair Industry	1	0	53650	52703
电力、热力生产和供应业	Production and Supply of Electric　Power and Heat Power	4	1	655876	655876
燃气生产和供应业	Production and Supply of Gas	2	0	158552	158552
水的生产和供应业	Production and Supply of Water	2	0	118896	118896

资产总计（万元）Total Assets (10 000 yuan)	负债合计（万元）Total Liabilities (10 000 yuan)	主营业务收入（万元）Revenue fromPrincipal Business (10 000 yuan)	利润总额（万元）Total Profits (10 000 yuan)	利税总额（万元）Total Profits and Taxes (10 000 yuan)	平均用工人数（万人）Average of Employed Persons (10 000 persons)
9842482	4704388	7878643	676638	988197	7.91
78312	88227	39723	1258	7395	0.09
407791	23206	73875	18224	32410	0.05
34340	22570	99226	1877	2373	0.15
764811	342714	923220	102518	129826	1.14
401257	186270	513117	36268	77751	0.57
171488	111813	193908	511	4690	0.28
180377	75926	142992	6922	15663	0.63
16679	10602	38047	1581	3004	0.04
26937	19537	29344	1569	2797	0.04
306513	115296	156705	30017	38194	0.21
581929	374035	2430659	72890	768732	0.16
2465296	1718377	2659829	117006	177700	1.27
3617906	1248520	2226666	497414	666812	1.72
1555484	707363	1506350	138729	197966	1.27
270409	109748	742049	7771	18091	0.23
60033	30979	39448	2105	2467	0.05
1241562	442569	900312	127882	169366	1.14
2372578	1112182	1460096	112949	167632	2.02
819507	451638	586416	78191	93335	0.56
16885851	11915796	11261633	666233	905040	4.95
1068951	745094	696012	11389	33133	0.70
2603239	1361232	1830537	101634	154243	1.14
5652697	3319109	5887650	144093	380470	3.04
264279	126123	201514	16361	29828	0.40
64107	12913	52565	5429	9311	0.16
1657520	1106915	2075811	10815	19396	0.51
609622	311022	175199	22343	20133	0.20
714024	566097	101832	130	5292	0.17

12 - 13 规模以上大中型工业企业一览表（2018 年）

Summary of Large and Medium-Sized Enterprises（2018）

企业名称 Number of Industial Enterprises	登记注册类型 Status of Registration	企业规模 Enterprise Size	所属行业 Sector
中国重型汽车集团有限公司	国有独资公司	大型	汽车制造
浪潮集团有限公司	其他有限责任公司	大型	计算机整机制造
中国石油化工股份有限公司济南分公司	股份有限公司	大型	生产汽油产品
齐鲁制药有限公司	其他有限责任公司	大型	抗生素原料药及制剂
济南圣泉集团股份有限公司	私营有限股份公司	大型	呋喃树脂等铸造辅助材料
山东闽源钢铁有限公司	其他有限责任公司	大型	钢铁加工
山东晋煤明水化工集团有限公司	其他有限责任公司	大型	生产尿素
中车山东机车车辆有限公司	其他有限责任公司	大型	铁路货车
玫德集团有限公司	其他有限责任公司	大型	各类管件制造
济南二机床集团有限公司	国有独资公司	大型	金属成形机床
华能济南黄台发电有限公司	其他有限责任公司	大型	火力发电
山东佳宝集团有限公司	其他有限责任公司	大型	乳制品制造
费斯托气动有限公司	外资企业	大型	液压和气动动力机械及元件制造业
济南万瑞炭素有限责任公司	私营有限责任公司	大型	石墨及碳素制品制造
山东晋煤日月化工有限公司	其他有限责任公司	大型	生产尿素
济南热电有限公司	国有独资公司	大型	蒸汽、热水等热力的生产与供热
济南裕兴化工有限责任公司	其他有限责任公司	大型	钛白粉制造业
济南达利食品有限公司	私营有限责任公司	大型	焙烤食品制造
中国石油集团济柴动力有限公司	国有独资公司	大型	内燃机生产、销售
山东山水水泥集团有限公司	港澳台商投资股份有限公司	大型	生产水泥
齐鲁宏业纺织集团有限公司	其他有限责任公司	大型	制造、批发/零售棉纱
积成电子股份有限公司	股份有限公司	大型	电力调度自动化系统
中粮可口可乐饮料(济南)有限公司	与港澳台商合作经营	大型	碳酸饮料
卧龙电气章丘海尔电机有限公司	与港澳台商合资经营	大型	洗衣机电机
山东济华燃气有限公司	与港澳台商合资经营	大型	燃气供应业
济南轻骑铃木摩托车有限公司	中外合资经营	大型	摩托车制造
福士汽车零部件（济南）有限公司	外资企业	大型	汽车零部件制造
山东齐鲁电机制造有限公司	国有独资公司	大型	汽轮发电机
山东省章丘鼓风机股份有限公司	股份有限公司	大型	风机制造
安莉芳(山东)服装有限公司	港澳台商独资	大型	制造服装
济南邦德激光股份有限公司	股份有限公司	大型	激光应用设备的生产
山东小鸭集团有限责任公司	国有独资公司	大型	制冷空调设备制造
济南金麒麟刹车系统有限公司	其他有限责任公司	大型	制造业刹车片
济南水务集团有限公司	国有独资公司	大型	自来水生产业及供应业
山东福牌制药有限公司	其他有限责任公司	大型	煎膏剂、口服液、颗粒剂、酒剂、片剂、硬胶

企业名称 Number of Industial Enterprises	登记注册类型 Status of Registration	企业规模 Enterprise Size	所属行业 Sector
济南沃德汽车零部件有限公司	中外合资经营	大型	生产、销售、批发气门
济南重工股份有限公司	股份有限公司	大型	环保脱硫设备
山东太古飞机工程有限公司	与港澳台商合资经营	大型	飞机维修
济南锅炉集团有限公司	私营有限责任公司	大型	电站锅炉
山东电力设备有限公司	国有独资公司	中型	生产、检修变压器
九阳股份有限公司	股份有限公司	中型	豆浆机批发
山东圣泉新材料股份有限公司	其他有限责任公司	中型	酚醛树脂及复合材料
济南澳海炭素有限公司	其他有限责任公司	中型	炭素制品制造
临工集团济南重机有限公司	私营有限责任公司	中型	生产矿用自卸车
济南伊利乳业有限责任公司	其他有限责任公司	中型	乳制品生产
华电章丘发电有限公司	其他有限责任公司	中型	火力发电
山东旺旺食品有限公司	外资企业	中型	液体乳及乳制品制造
山东输变电设备有限公司	其他有限责任公司	中型	变压器制造
山东新升实业发展有限责任公司	国有独资公司	中型	电力、供热、供汽
山东伊莱特重工有限公司	外商投资股份有限公司	中型	风电法兰
山东国舜绿色钢结构有限公司	私营有限责任公司	中型	环境保护专用设备制造
济南港华燃气有限公司	与港澳台商合资经营	中型	天然气生产供应
山东鲁能智能技术有限公司	其他有限责任公司	中型	其他输配电及控制设备制造
东港股份有限公司	股份有限公司	中型	防伪票据印刷品制造
华润双鹤利民药业（济南）有限公司	其他有限责任公司	中型	西药生产制造
济南圣泉铸造材料有限公司	与港澳台商合资经营	中型	铸造用磺酸固化剂生产
济南迈克管道科技股份有限公司	其他有限责任公司	中型	管道及管道接头制造
华熙福瑞达生物医药有限公司	其他有限责任公司	中型	透明质酸钠
济南吉利汽车有限公司	其他有限责任公司	中型	汽车零配件、发动机零配件的生产
济南龙山炭素有限公司	私营有限责任公司	中型	预焙阳极制造
平阴山水水泥有限公司	与港澳台商合资经营	中型	熟料、水泥制造
济南中海炭素有限公司	其他有限责任公司	中型	石墨及炭素制品制造
山东绿霸化工股份有限公司	股份有限公司	中型	化学农药原药制造
山东大汉建设机械有限公司	其他有限责任公司	中型	固定式塔机、自升式塔机、施工升降机
山东银鹭食品有限公司	外资企业	中型	八宝粥生产
浪潮商用机器有限公司	与港澳台商合资经营	中型	计算机制造
山东华森建材集团有限公司	其他有限责任公司	中型	混凝土搅拌、批发销售
济阳县济北石化有限责任公司	其他有限责任公司	中型	石油开采
济南黄河特钢有限责任公司	其他有限责任公司	中型	钢压延加工
山东爱普电气设备有限公司	其他有限责任公司	中型	电气机械和器材制造业
济南轻骑摩托车有限公司	国有独资公司	中型	摩托车制造
山东电工电气日立高压开关有限公司	中外合资经营	中型	GIS 制造
济南西门子变压器有限公司	中外合资经营	中型	设计和制造变压器

12–13 续 2

企业名称 Number of Industial Enterprises	登记注册类型 Status of Registration	企业规模 Enterprise Size	所属行业 Sector
济南百事可乐饮料有限公司	与港澳台商合资经营	中型	碳酸饮料制造
济南海川投资集团有限公司	私营有限责任公司	中型	碳素产品制造
济南统一企业有限公司	港澳台商独资	中型	饮料、方便面生产
济南汇丰炭素有限公司	私营有限责任公司	中型	制造业碳素制品
济南圣泉倍进陶瓷过滤器有限公司	中外合资经营	中型	陶瓷过滤网
山东科兴生物制品有限公司	其他有限责任公司	中型	生物药品依普定
济南新峨嵋实业有限公司	其他有限责任公司	中型	滑动水口砖
青岛啤酒(济南)有限公司	其他有限责任公司	中型	生产加工
山东力诺特种玻璃股份有限公司	股份有限公司	中型	药用安瓶
中电装备山东电子有限公司	其他有限责任公司	中型	电工仪器仪表
济南镁碳砖厂有限公司	股份有限公司	中型	优质镁碳砖
山东宏济堂制药集团股份有限公司	股份有限公司	中型	中成药的生产
山东宏业纺织股份有限公司	股份有限公司	中型	棉纱生产
西电济南变压器股份有限公司	股份有限公司	中型	变压器制造
山东力诺瑞特新能源有限公司	中外合资经营	中型	太阳能热水器
山东博士伦福瑞达制药有限公司	与港澳台商合资经营	中型	润舒滴眼液
山东奥太电气有限公司	其他有限责任公司	中型	逆变焊机
山东福贞金属包装有限公司	外资企业	中型	空罐生产
平阴鲁西装备科技有限公司	其他有限责任公司	中型	制造业金属压力容器制造
山推建友机械股份有限公司	股份有限公司	中型	砼搅拌站、楼
济南帅潮实业有限公司	私营有限责任公司	中型	汽车配件制造批发
山东同欣电子有限公司	私营有限责任公司	中型	电阻电容电感元件制造
山东和美华集团有限公司	私营有限责任公司	中型	饲料生产
山东宝雅新能源汽车股份有限公司	股份有限公司	中型	新能源汽车、电动汽车生产批发零售
山东华凌电缆有限公司	私营有限责任公司	中型	电力电缆
济南中维世纪科技有限公司	私营有限责任公司	中型	中维监控软件
山东新阳能源有限公司	国有独资公司	中型	煤炭开采
济南市冶金科学研究所有限责任公司	其他有限责任公司	中型	硬质合金
山东胜邦绿野化学有限公司	其他有限责任公司	中型	农药制造
济南宇飞食品有限公司	私营有限责任公司	中型	农林牧渔业
山东欧克家具有限公司	私营有限责任公司	中型	家具制造(陈设)
济南迈克阀门科技有限公司	其他有限责任公司	中型	阀门配件制造
济南市琦泉热电有限责任公司	其他有限责任公司	中型	电力、汽供应
章丘重型锻造有限公司	私营有限责任公司	中型	其他通用设备制造
济南泓泉制水有限公司	其他有限责任公司	中型	生活饮用水集中式供水
济南趵突泉酿酒有限责任公司	其他有限责任公司	中型	白酒制造
山东桑乐太阳能有限公司	其他有限责任公司	中型	生产太阳能热水器
济南娃哈哈恒枫饮料有限公司	中外合资经营	中型	营养快线、纯净水、爽歪歪

企业名称 Number of Industial Enterprises	登记注册类型 Status of Registration	企业规模 Enterprise Size	所属行业 Sector
章丘华明水泥有限公司	其他有限责任公司	中型	水泥生产
济南宜和食品有限公司	中外合资经营	中型	调味品制造
山东金钟科技集团股份有限公司	股份有限公司	中型	称重设备及零配件
济南弘正科技有限公司	港澳台商独资	中型	摩托车无级变速器制造
山东百脉泉酒业有限公司	其他有限责任公司	中型	白酒制造
山东大旺食品有限公司	外资企业	中型	饼干、果冻、饮料
山东北辰机电设备股份有限公司	私营有限股份公司	中型	压力容器制造
济南天辰机器集团有限公司	私营有限责任公司	中型	数控塑铝窗设备
济南台有玻璃制品有限公司	私营有限责任公司	中型	日用玻璃制品(工艺品)
济南轻骑标致摩托车有限公司	中外合资经营	中型	生产摩托车
济南泉华包装制品有限公司	与港澳台商合资经营	中型	制造包装制品
济南市平阴县玛钢厂	集体	中型	玛钢管件制造
济南华阳炭素有限公司	私营有限责任公司	中型	炭素、炭素制品生产
山东山大电力技术股份有限公司	其他有限责任公司	中型	微机电力故障录波装置
山东鲁信天一印务有限公司	其他有限责任公司	中型	盒类产品
山东明仁福瑞达制药股份有限公司	股份有限公司	中型	颈痛颗粒
山东博科生物产业有限公司	其他有限责任公司	中型	生化试剂
山东上好佳食品工业有限公司	港澳台商独资	中型	膨化食品生产
中集车辆（山东）有限公司	中外合资经营	中型	制造冷藏车
神思电子技术股份有限公司	股份有限公司	中型	身份认证解决方案
山东科芯电子有限公司	私营有限责任公司	中型	晶粒 STD1-6A、FR1-6A、SF(电视接收)
山东天鹅棉业机械股份有限公司	股份有限公司	中型	棉花加工设备
山东科源制药股份有限公司	股份有限公司	中型	格列齐特
济南桃李面包有限公司	其他有限责任公司	中型	面包、烘烤类糕点制造
济南中燃科技发展有限公司	其他有限责任公司	中型	振动筛的研发生产
济南实达紧固件有限公司	私营有限责任公司	中型	标准紧固件生产
济南冶金化工设备有限公司	其他有限责任公司	中型	冶金专用设备制造
济南二机床铸造有限公司	国有独资公司	中型	机床铸造
山东福瑞达生物工程有限公司	其他有限责任公司	中型	生产化妆品、生产消毒卫生用品
山东汉方制药有限公司	私营有限责任公司	中型	复方黄柏液涂剂
山东华氟化工有限责任公司	其他有限责任公司	中型	生产氟化物
山东镭鸣数控激光装备有限公司	私营有限责任公司	中型	金属切削机床制造
山东山大华天科技集团股份有限公司	股份有限公司	中型	EPS 电源
济南瑞通铁路电务有限责任公司	其他有限责任公司	中型	生产铁路电缆
山东冠世针织有限公司	外资企业	中型	针织衫裤
山东小鸭零售设备有限公司	其他有限责任公司	中型	生产超市冷冻柜
济南晶恒电子有限责任公司	国有独资公司	中型	半导体分立器件
山东法因智能设备有限公司	其他有限责任公司	中型	数控机床生产

企业名称 Number of Industial Enterprises	登记注册类型 Status of Registration	企业规模 Enterprise Size	所属行业 Sector
山东重骑摩托车(集团)厂	国有	中型	摩托车整车制造
济南森峰科技有限公司	私营有限责任公司	中型	激光雕刻机、打标机、激光切割机的研发生产
济南界龙科技有限公司	外资企业	中型	精密电子零配件
山东银鹰炊事机械有限公司	其他有限责任公司	中型	炊具机械制造
山东华光光电子股份有限公司	股份有限公司	中型	半导体激光二极管芯片
济南汇智电力科技有限公司	其他有限责任公司	中型	一体化直流电源系统生产
山东神戎电子股份有限公司	股份有限公司	中型	激光夜视仪
济南奥图自动化股份有限公司	私营有限责任公司	中型	自动化设备
山东普利思饮用水股份有限公司	股份有限公司	中型	生产瓶装桶装饮用水
济南元首针织股份有限公司	股份有限公司	中型	针织内衣
济南圣都食品有限公司	私营有限责任公司	中型	烤肠酱卤产品
山东耀华玻璃有限公司	私营有限责任公司	中型	其他玻璃制造
迈大食品（山东）有限公司	外资企业	中型	饼干及其他焙烤食品制造
山东小鸭精工机械有限公司	其他有限责任公司	中型	汽车零部件制造
济南瑞泉电子有限公司	私营有限责任公司	中型	电子远传水表
山东通发实业有限公司	私营有限责任公司	中型	建筑工程用机械制造
济南科盛电子有限公司	其他有限责任公司	中型	半导管电子器件制造
山东宏达科技集团有限公司	其他有限责任公司	中型	压力容器制造
山东越宫钢构件有限公司	其他有限责任公司	中型	钢结构件建筑配套制造
国机铸锻机械有限公司	其他有限责任公司	中型	铸造机械制造
济南市长清计算机应用公司	股份合作	中型	可燃气体报警控制器
济南沃德机械制造有限公司	股份有限公司	中型	汽车零部件及配件
济南银鹰食品机械有限公司	其他有限责任公司	中型	活面机制造
山东新华印务有限责任公司	国有独资公司	中型	多色印刷品
中闻集团山东印务有限公司	其他有限责任公司	中型	报纸印刷
山东金德利集团快餐连锁配送有限责任公司	其他有限责任公司	中型	米面制品制造
济南第一机床有限公司	其他有限责任公司	中型	金属切削机床制造
章丘市鲁洪化工有限公司	私营有限股份公司	中型	制造氯化钙
山东平安建筑工业化科技有限公司	私营有限责任公司	中型	建筑产业化 PC 构件生产
济南思迈迩制衣有限公司	私营有限责任公司	中型	服装制造
济南巨鑫机车车辆配件有限公司	私营有限责任公司	中型	机车车辆配件
章丘市铜铝铸造厂	集体	中型	铜铝件锻压
济阳元首针织有限责任公司	其他有限责任公司	中型	针纺织品制造
济南恒升工程机械有限公司	私营有限责任公司	中型	塔机的生产制造
山东省兴业发展有限公司	国有独资公司	中型	服装加工
山东明威起重设备有限公司	私营有限责任公司	中型	起重机设备塔机
济南轻骑大韩摩托车有限责任公司	中外合资经营	中型	摩托车整车制造
济南野风酥食品有限公司	私营有限责任公司	中型	糕点制造

12-14 主要工业产品生产量（2018年）

Output of Major Industrial Products（2018）

主要工业产品名称	Major Industrial Products above Designated Size	单 位 Unit	生产量 Proction
石灰石	Lime Powder	万吨（10 000 tons)	75.1
高岭土（瓷土）	kaolin	万吨（10 000 tons)	5.5
小麦粉	Wheat Flour	万吨（10 000 tons)	8.5
饲料	Feed	万吨（10 000 tons)	60.9
配合饲料	Formula Feed	万吨（10 000 tons)	15.7
混合饲料	Mixed Feed	万吨（10 000 tons)	17.2
精制食用植物油	Refined Edible Vegetable Oil	万吨（10 000 tons)	0.3
鲜、冷藏肉	Frozen,Fresh Meat	万吨（10 000 tons)	8.4
冻肉	Frozen meat	万吨（10 000 tons)	1.6
冷冻蔬菜	Frozen Vegetable	吨(ton)	19466.0
糖果	Candies	万吨（10 000 tons)	1.1
速冻食品	Quick-frozen Food	万吨（10 000 tons)	0.3
速冻米面食品	Quick-frozen rice and Noodles	万吨（10 000 tons)	0.3
乳制品	Milk Products	万吨（10 000 tons)	46.9
液体乳	Liquid Milk	万吨（10 000 tons)	46.9
固体及半固体乳制品	Solid and Semi-soild Dairy Products	吨(ton)	94
乳粉	Milk Powder	吨(ton)	94
罐头	Canned Food	吨(ton)	5.7
营养、保健食品	Nutrition and Health Food	吨(ton)	442.3
酱油	Soy Sauce	万吨（10 000 tons)	9.5
饲料添加剂	Feed Additive	万吨（10 000 tons)	2.9
食品添加剂	Food Additives	万吨（10 000 tons)	0.9
饮料酒	Liquor	万千升（10 000 kiloliter)	26.4
白酒（折66度，商品量）	White Spirit	万千升（10 000 kiloliter)	1.1
啤酒	Beer	万千升（10 000 kiloliter)	25.3
饮料	Drinks	万吨（10 000 tons)	154.9
碳酸型饮料（汽水）	Carbonated Drinks	万吨（10 000 tons)	45.9
包装饮用水	Bottled Drinking Water	万吨（10 000 tons)	45.0
果汁和蔬菜汁类饮料	Juice and Vegetable Juice Beverage	万吨（10 000 tons)	19.3
精制茶	Refined Tea	吨(ton)	18.9
纱	Yarn	万吨（10 000 tons)	11.3
棉纱	Cotton Yarn	万吨（10 000 tons)	6.0
棉混纺纱	Cotton Blended Yarn	万吨（10 000 tons)	4.5
化学纤维纱	Chemical Fiber Yarn	万吨（10 000 tons)	0.8
布	Cloth	亿米(100 million m)	0.4

12-14 续 1

主要工业产品名称	Major Industrial Products above Designated Size	单 位 Unit	生产量 Proction
棉布	Cotton Cloth	亿米(100 million m)	0.1
非织造布（无纺布）	Nonwovens	万吨 (10 000 tons)	4.0
棉混纺布	Cotton Blended Cloth	万米(10 000 m)	469.2
化学纤维短纤布	Chemical Fiber Cloth	亿米(100 million m)	0.3
服装	Garments	万件(10 000 pieces)	6419.4
梭织服装	Woven Garments	万件(10 000 pieces)	2447.6
其中羽绒服装	Down Wear	万件(10 000 pieces)	37.4
衬衫	Shirts	万件(10 000 pieces)	39.0
针织服装	Knitted Clothing	万件(10 000 pieces)	3971.8
人造板	Manmade Plates	万立方米(10 000 cu.m)	21.9
纤维板	Fiberboard	万立方米(10 000 cu.m)	21.9
家具	Furniture	万件(10 000 pieces)	32.1
木质家具	Wood Furniture	万件(10 000 pieces)	23.9
金属家具	Metal Furniture	万件(10 000 pieces)	6.1
纸制品	Paper Products	万吨 (10 000 tons)	16.2
瓦楞纸箱	Corrugated Box	万吨 (10 000 tons)	4.3
单色印刷品	Monochrome Print	万令(10 000 ream)	268.2
多色印刷品	Ploychrome Print	万对开色令(10 000 color folio ream)	810.1
精甲醇	Extracted Methanol	万吨 (10 000 tons)	98.0
合成氨（无水氨）	Synthetic Ammonia	万吨 (10 000 tons)	60.5
农用氮、磷、钾化学肥料（折纯）	Chemical Fertilizer	万吨 (10 000 tons)	20.8
氮肥（折含氮 100%）	Nitrogen Fertilizer	万吨 (10 000 tons)	20.8
尿素（折含氮 100%）	Urea	万吨 (10 000 tons)	20.8
化学农药原药（折有效成分 100%）	Chemical Pesticide	万吨 (10 000 tons)	0.9
杀虫剂（杀螨剂）原药	Insecticides Pesticide	吨(ton)	372.7
杀菌剂原药	Fungicides	吨(ton)	47.8
除草剂原药	Herbicide	万吨 (10 000 tons)	0.9
兽用药品	Veterinary Drugs	吨(ton)	382.5
涂料	Paint	万吨 (10 000 tons)	0.9
初级形态塑料	Primary Plastic	万吨 (10 000 tons)	57.7
聚丙烯树脂	Polypropylene Colophony	万吨 (10 000 tons)	9.5
合成橡胶	Synthetic Rubber	万吨 (10 000 tons)	0.7
化学试剂	Chemical Reagent	吨 (ton)	46
单晶硅	Monocrystalline Silicon	万千克(10 000 kg)	8.1
多晶硅	Ploycrystalline Silicon	万千克(10 000 kg)	228.0
合成洗涤剂	Synthetic Detergents	万吨 (10 000 tons)	1.0
化学药品原药	Chemical Medicine	万吨 (10 000 tons)	1.0

主要工业产品名称	Major Industrial Products above Designated Size	单 位 Unit	生产量 Proction
中成药	Traditional Chemical Medicine	万吨 (10 000 tons)	0.2
化学纤维	Chemical Fiber	万吨 (10 000 tons)	3.1
合成纤维	Synthetic Fiber Polymers	万吨 (10 000 tons)	3.1
涤纶纤维	Polyester Fiber	万吨 (10 000 tons)	2.8
锦纶纤维	Polyamide Fiber	万吨 (10 000 tons)	0.4
塑料制品	Plastic Articles	万吨 (10 000 tons)	8.0
塑料薄膜	Plastic Film	万吨 (10 000 tons)	1.3
农用薄膜	Agricultural Film	万吨 (10 000 tons)	0.6
泡沫塑料	Foam	万吨 (10 000 tons)	0.5
硅酸盐水泥熟料	Portland Cement Clinker	万吨 (10 000 tons)	403.1
窑外分解窑水泥熟料	Precalciner Kiln Clinker	万吨 (10 000 tons)	403.1
水泥	Cement	万吨 (10 000 tons)	604.3
强度等级 42.5 水泥（含 R 型）	Strength Grade42.5Cement	万吨 (10 000 tons)	49.8
商品混凝土	Concrete	万立方米(10 000 cu.m)	1499.9
水泥混凝土压力管	Cement and Concrete Pressure Pipes	千米(km)	74.8
水泥混凝土排水管	Cement and Concrete Drainage Pipes	千米(km)	64.0
砖	Brick	亿块(100 million unit)	2.5
纤维增强塑料制品	Fiber Reinforced Plastic Products	吨(ton)	372.4
天然花岗石建筑板材	Natural Marble Building Block	万平方米(10 000 cu.m)	1.3
隔热、隔音人造矿物材料及其制品	Insulation and sound Insulation Materials and Products	万吨 (10 000 tons)	0.6
钢化玻璃	Stalinite	万平方米(10 000 sq.m)	47.9
夹层玻璃	Sandwich Glass	万平方米(10 000 sq.m)	40.0
中空玻璃	Hollow Glass	万平方米(10 000 sq.m)	38.8
日用玻璃制品	Household Glass	万吨 (10 000 tons)	10.8
玻璃包装容器	Glass Container	万吨 (10 000 tons)	1.6
耐火材料制品	Refractory Product	万吨 (10 000 tons)	52.3
石墨及炭素制品	Graphite and Carbon Products	万吨 (10 000 tons)	191.3
粗钢	Crude Steel	万吨 (10 000 tons)	160.9
铸铁件	Iron Casting	万吨 (10 000 tons)	49.4
铸钢件	Steel Casting	万吨 (10 000 tons)	21.3
钢材	Steel	万吨 (10 000 tons)	223.3
中小型型钢	Small and Medium Steel	万吨 (10 000 tons)	21.0
棒材	Bar	万吨 (10 000 tons)	184.3
焊接钢管	Welded Steel Tube	万吨 (10 000 tons)	18.0
用外购国产钢材再加工生产钢材	Steel in Process of Foreign-purchased Domestic Steel	万吨 (10 000 tons)	26.9
用外购钢材再加工生产钢材	Steel in Process of Foreign-purchased Steel	万吨 (10 000 tons)	26.9

12-14 续3

主要工业产品名称	Major Industrial Products above Designated Size	单 位 Unit	生产量 Proction
铁合金	Iron Alloy	万吨 (10 000 tons)	1.2
铝合金	Aluminium Alloy	万吨 (10 000 tons)	0.2
铜材	Copper Product	万吨 (10 000 tons)	0.4
铝材	Aluminium Product	万吨 (10 000 tons)	0.8
钢结构	Steel Structure	万吨 (10 000 tons)	6.5
金属切削工具	Metal Cutting Tool	万件 (10 000 unit)	51.3
锻件	Forge Piece	万吨 (10 000 tons)	71.4
粉末冶金零件	Sintered Metal Products	万吨 (10 000 tons)	0.1
电站锅炉	Utility Boilers	万蒸发量吨 (10 000 evaporation ton)	0.9
工业锅炉	Industrial Boilers	蒸发量吨 (evaporation ton)	807.6
发动机	Engine	万千瓦(10 000kw)	3172.6
汽车用发动机	Automotive Engine	万千瓦(10 000kw)	3079.6
电站用汽轮机	Turbine Power Plant	万千瓦(10 000kw)	22.0
金属切削机床	Metal-cutting Machine Tools	台(unit)	5964
数控金属切削机床	CNC Metal cuttingMachine	台(unit)	1100
金属成形机床	Metal Forming Machine	台(unit)	271
数控金属成形机床（数控锻压设备）	CNC Metal Forming Machine	台(unit)	241
铸造机械	Casting Machinery	台(unit)	140
机床数控装置	Machine Tool Control Device	万套(10 000 unit)	1.0
金属轧制设备	Metal Rolling Equipment	万吨 (10 000 tons)	0.3
起重机	Lifting Equipment	万吨 (10 000 tons)	13.9
电焊机	Electric Welding Machine	万台(10 000 unit)	7.1
泵	Pumps	万台(10 000 unit)	1.3
真空泵	Vacuum Pumps	万台(10 000 unit)	0.6
气体压缩机	Gas Compressor	台(unit)	192
非制冷设备用压缩机	Compressor for Non-refrigeration Equipment	台(unit)	192
阀门	Valves	万吨 (10 000 tons)	0.4
液压元件	Hydraulic Components	万件(10 000 unit)	33.8
气动元件	Pneumatic Components	万件(10 000 unit)	292.1
滚动轴承	Rolling Bearings	万套(10 000 unit)	2426.9
齿轮	Wheel Gear	万吨 (10 000 tons)	1.7
工业电炉	Industrial Furnace	台(unit)	33
风机	Fans	万台(10 000 unit)	6.5
鼓风机	Air Blower	万台(10 000 unit)	5.7
真空应用设备	Vacuum Application Equipment	台(unit)	266
工商用制冷、空调设备	Commercial Refrigeration Equipment	万台(套)	2.1
衡器（秤）	Scales	万台(10 000 unit)	0.4

主要工业产品名称	Major Industrial Products above Designated Size	单 位 Unit	生产量 Proction
金属密封件	Metal Seal	万件 (10 000 unit)	0.4
金属紧固件	Metal Fastener	万吨 (10 000 tons)	2.4
弹簧	Spring	万吨 (10 000 tons)	6.2
矿山专用设备	Mining Equipment	万吨 (10 000 tons)	4.3
建筑工程用机械	Construction Engineering Machinery	台(unit)	251
水泥专用设备	Cement Special Equipment	吨(ton)	10593.0
混凝土机械	Concrete Machinery	台(unit)	5052
金属冶炼设备	Metal Smelting Equipment	吨(ton)	26159.0
炼油、化工生产专用设备	Special Equipment for Oil Refining and Chemical Protection	万吨 (10 000 tons)	0.7
模具	Matrix	万套(10 000 unit)	0.1
食品制造机械	Food Manufacturing Machinery	台(unit)	712
农产品初加工机械	Agricultural Primary Processing Machinery	万台(10 000 unit)	4.8
农产品加工专用设备	Special Equipment for Agricultural Products Processing	万台(10 000 unit)	1.2
印刷专用设备	Printing Special Equipment	吨(ton)	2065.0
电子工业专用设备	Special Equipment for Electrionic Industry	台(unit)	106944
棉花加工机械	Cotton Processing Machinery	台(unit)	790
医疗仪器设备及器械	Medical Instruments	台(unit)	1266
环境污染防治专用设备	Special Equipment for Environmental Protection	台（套）(unit)	2031
大气污染防治设备	Air Pollution Control Equipment	台（套）(unit)	1279
高压开关设备（11 万伏以上）	High Voltage Switchgear (over 110,000 volts)	万台(10 000 unit)	1.8
水质污染防治设备	Water Pollution Control Equipment	台（套）(unit)	22
固体废弃物处理设备	Soild Waste Dis posal Equipment	台（套）(unit)	730
工业机器人	Industrial Robot	套(unit)	1003
光缆	Optical Cable	芯千米(core km)	666.0
锂离子电池	Lithium Ion Battery	万只（万自然只）(10 000 unit)	32.7
电光源	Electric Light Source	万只(10 000 unit)	193.2
汽车	Motor Vehicles	万辆(10 000 unit)	23.2
基本型乘用车（轿车）	Basic Passenger Car (Car)	辆(unit)	11452
轿车（1 升 < 排量≤1.6 升）	Car (1 liter < Displacement < 1.6 liter)	辆(unit)	11452
载货汽车	Trucks	万辆(10 000 unit)	17.6
新能源汽车	New Energy Automobile	辆(unit)	44663
改装汽车	Modified Cars	万辆(10 000 unit)	0.7
铁路货车	Railway Freight Wagons	辆(unit)	4998
摩托车整车	Motorcycles	万辆(10 000 unit)	32.4
发电机组（发电设备）	Power Generating Equipment	万千瓦(10 000kw)	505.6
汽轮发电机组	Steam Turbogenerator	万千瓦(10 000kw)	505.6
电动机	Electromotor	万千瓦(10 000kw)	217.9

12-14 续 5

主要工业产品名称	Major Industrial Products above Designated Size	单 位 Unit	生产量 Proction
交流电动机	AC Motors	万千瓦(10 000kw)	217.9
变压器	Transformers	万千伏安(10 000 KVA pm)	15845.0
电力变压器，额定容量≥8000kVA，电压≥500kV	power Transformer	万千伏安(10 000 KVA pm)	7563.5
互感器	Mutual Inductor	台(unit)	68
高压开关板	High Voltage Switch Plate	面(unit)	175
低压开关板	Low Voltage Switch Plate	面(unit)	1478
通信及电子网络用电缆	Cable for Communications and Electronic Network	万对千米(10 000 couples.km)	22.1
电力电缆	Power Cable	万千米(10 000 km)	13.4
家用洗衣机	Household Washing Machines	万台(10 000 unit)	65.0
太阳能热水器	Solar Water Heater	万平方米(10 000 sq.m)	139.7
灯具及照明装置	Lamps and Lighting Fixtures	万套(台个)(10 000 unit)	9.3
电子计算机整机	Computers	万台(10 000 unit)	101.4
微型计算机设备	Microcomputer Equipment	万台(10 000 unit)	0.7
服务器	Servers	万台(10 000 unit)	99.6
显示器	Display	万台(10 000 unit)	0.8
半导体分立器件	Discrete Semiconductor Devices	亿只(100 million unit)	29.3
集成电路	Integrated Circuit	万块(10 000 unit)	1427.6
电子元件	Eletronic Components	亿只(100 million unit)	31.7
印制电路板	Print-circuit Board	万平方米(10 000 sq.m)	84.1
工业自动调节仪表与控制系统	Industrial Automatic Instrument and Control System	万台(套)(10 000 unit)	2.8
电工仪器仪表	Electrical Instrument	万台(10 000 unit)	378.1
分析仪器及装置	Analytical Instruments and Devices	万台(套)(10 000 unit)	0.4
试验机	Testing Machine	万台(10 000 unit)	0.4
汽车仪器仪表	Automobile Instrument	万台(10 000 unit)	89.7
钟	Clock	万只(10 000 unit)	100.4
自来水生产量	Tap Water Production	亿立方米(100 million cu.m)	6.1
原油加工量	Crude Processing Volume	万吨 (10 000 tons)	442.1
汽油	Gasoline	万吨 (10 000 tons)	142.2
柴油	Diesel Oil	万吨 (10 000 tons)	136.7
燃料油	Fuel Oil	万吨 (10 000 tons)	2.8
石脑油	Naphtha	万吨 (10 000 tons)	7.4
液化石油气	Liquefied Petroleum	万吨 (10 000 tons)	22.4
石油焦	Petroleum Coke	万吨 (10 000 tons)	19.9
石油沥青	Asphalt	万吨 (10 000 tons)	15.4
发电量	Power Generating Capacity	亿千瓦时(100 million kwh)	152.9
其中：火力发电量	Thermal Power Generation	亿千瓦时(100 million kwh)	146.1
风力发电量	Wind Power Generation	亿千瓦时(100 million kwh)	6.3
垃圾发电量	Garbage Power Generation	亿千瓦时(100 million kwh)	3.7
煤气生产量	Gas Power Generation	亿立方米(100 million cu.m)	21.2

12-15 工业企业能源购进、消费及库存（2018年）

Purchases、Consumption and Invetory of Main Energy Source in Industrial Enterprises(2018)

能源名称	Energy	计量单位 Unit	年初库存量 Beginning Stock	本年购进量 Purchases This Year	本年消费 Consumption of This Year			年末库存量 Year-end Stock
					合计 Total	工业生产消费 Industrial Consumption	非工业生产消费 Non-Industrial Consumption	
能源合计	Total Energy	吨标准煤 (tons of SCE)	0	0	20165016	20111394	53622	0
原煤	Raw Coal	吨(ton)	471021	8446013	9260077	9256293	3784	303719
洗精煤	Cleaned Coal	吨(ton)	0	0	0	0	0	0
其他洗煤	Other Cleaned Coal	吨(ton)	90003	2835978	2774868	2774708	160	151113
煤制品	Coal Product	吨(ton)	32738	349504	339099	339099	0	43142
焦炭	Coke	吨(ton)	3913	554369	523629	523629	0	3443
天然气	Natural Gas	万立方米 (10 000 cu.m)	50	63351	63397	63006	391	0
液化天然气	Liquefied Nutural Gas	吨(ton)	7	2678	3165	3159	7	10
原油	Crude Oil	吨(ton)	83445	4417540	4420603	4420603	0	80382
汽油	Gasoline	吨(ton)	743	7142	7254	4444	2809	753
煤油	Kerosene	吨(ton)	6	101	108	108	0	4
柴油	Diesel Oil	吨(ton)	2502	29002	29284	19493	9791	2280
燃料油	Fuel Oil	吨(ton)	0	178	885	885	0	0
液化石油气	Liquefied Petroleum	吨(ton)	0	40	40	34	5	2
炼厂干气	Refinery Dry Gas	吨(ton)	0	135	192018	192018	0	0
其他石油制品	Other Petroleum Product	吨(ton)	26	47497	386512	386512	0	0
热力	Heating	百万千焦 (mkj)	0	7354826	10560184	10334842	225342	0
电力	Electricity	万千瓦时 (10 000 kwh)	0	875035	1052815	1036998	15817	0
其他燃料	Other Fuel	吨标准煤 (tons of SCE)	1200	8345	8419	8419	0	0

注：按照经济普查要求，免填能源合计中，年初库存、购进量、年末库存。

Note: According to requirements of economic census, it's unnecessary to fill in inventory and volume of purchase at the beginning of the year and the inventory at the end of the year in the total energy.

12-16 工业分行业主要能源消费量（2018年）

Consumption of Main Energy Source in Industrial Enterprises by Sector（2018）

指　标	Indicator	原煤(吨) Coal (ton)	汽油(吨) Gasoline (ton)	煤油(吨) Kerosene (ton)	柴油(吨) Diesel Oil (ton)	燃料油(吨) Fuel Oil (ton)	热力(百万千焦) Heating (mkj)	电力(万千瓦时) Electricity (10 000 kwh)
总计	**Total**	9260077	7254	108	29284	885	10560184	1052815
采矿业	**Mining**							
煤炭开采和洗选业	Mining and Washing of Coal	670199	0	0	112	0	5198	2574
石油和天然气开采业	Extraction of Petroleum and Natural Gas	0	21	0	14	0	0	3952
黑色金属矿采选业	Mining of Ferrous Metal Ores	0	0	0	0	0	0	0
非金属矿采选业	Mining and Processing of Nonmetal Ores	0	0	0	1754	0	0	3320
制造业	**Manufacture**							
农副食品加工业	Processing of Food from Agricultural Products	41	113	0	174	0	13550	6487
食品制造业	Manufacture of Foods	0	128	0	758	0	317108	20856
酒、饮料和精制茶制造业	Manufacture of Wine, Drinks and Refined Tea	0	63	0	204	0	227415	10535
纺织业	Manufacture of Textile	0	55	0	57	0	126979	32480
纺织服装、服饰业	Manufacture of Textile Wearing Apparel and Finery	80	63	0	6	0	54940	3627
皮革、毛皮、羽毛(绒)及其制品业	Manufacture of Leather, Fur, Feather & Its Products and Footwear	0	20	0	0	0	0	560
木材加工及木、竹、藤、棕、草制品业	Processing of Timbers, Manufacture of Wood, Bamboo, Rattan, Palm, and Straw Products	0	16	0	1	0	139	5097
家具制造业	Manufacture of Furniture	0	19	0	28	0	0	1387
造纸及纸制品业	Manufacture of Paper and Paper Products	0	19	0	13	0	213201	7131
印刷业和记录媒介的复制	Printing, Reproduction of Recording Media	0	231	0	110	0	35512	11216
文教体育用品制造业	Manufacture of Culture, Education,Arts and crafts，Sport and Entertainment Goods	0	20	0	24	0	0	1907
石油加工、炼焦及核燃料加工业	Processing of Petroleum, Coking and Nucleus Fuel	0	119	5	180	707	611770	45071

指　标	Indicator	原煤 (吨) Coal (ton)	汽油 (吨) Gasoline (ton)	煤油 (吨) Kerosene (ton)	柴油 (吨) Diesel Oil (ton)	燃料油 (吨) Fuel Oil (ton)	热力 (百万千焦) Heating (mkj)	电力 (万千瓦时) Electricity (10 000 kwh)
化学原料及化学制品制造业	Manufacture of Chemical Raw Material and Chemical Products	2821792	91	0	1086	0	2426985	174837
医药制造业	Manufacture of Medicines	52976	313	0	247	0	5602719	65739
化学纤维制造业	Manufacture of Chemical Fiber	10164	20	0	20	0	0	2921
橡胶和塑料制品业	Manufacture of Rubber and Plastic	0	66	0	89	0	47788	9092
非金属矿物制品业	Manufacture of Non-metallic Mineral Products	609205	473	0	15113	178	1312	115120
黑色金属冶炼及压延加工业	Manufacture and Processing of Ferrous Metals	0	13	0	7	0	244991	64992
有色金属冶炼及压延加工业	Manufacture & Processing of Non-ferrous Metals	62	17	0	70	0	0	2789
金属制品业	Manufacture of Metal Products	5786	352	0	1051	0	0	86029
通用设备制造业	Manufacture of General Purpose Machinery	1	945	53	1910	0	142	53063
专用设备制造业	Manufacture of Special Purpose Machinery	4	608	0	223	0	0	13873
汽车制造业	Manufacture of Automotive	239	341	36	3597	0	422669	82089
铁路、船舶、航空航天和其他运输设备制造业	Manufacture of Railroad,Marine,Aerospace and Other Transportation Equipment	0	316	1	268	0	40035	14489
电气机械及器材制造业	Manufacture of Electrical Machinery & Equipment	2	1210	12	65	0	22529	16118
计算机、通信和其他电子设备制造业	Manufacture of Computer, Communications and Other Electronic Equipment	0	430	0	37	0	858	15869
仪器仪表制造业	Manufacture of Measuring Instrument	0	682	0	58	0	3610	2802
其他制造业	Other Manufacture	0	24	0	0	0	29	591
金属制品、机械和设备修理业	Metal Products, Machinery and Equipment Repair Industry	0	0	0	0	0	0	454
电力、热力、燃气及水生产和供应业	**Production and Supply of Electric Power and Heat Power**							
电力、热力生产和供应业	Production and Supply of Electric Power and Heat Power	5089526	63	0	1865	0	140706	152699
燃气生产和供应业	Production and Supply of Gas	0	181	0	70	0	0	1102
水的生产和供应业	Production and Supply of Water	0	222	0	73	0	0	21948

主要统计指标解释

按照国家统计方法制度规定，1998 年独立核算工业统计范围由原乡及乡以上调整为全部国有及年销售收入500 万元以上非国有工业企业，2011 年规模以上工业企业统计范围调整为年主营业务收入2000 万元以上。同时，统计分类中的原经济组织类型分组相应地调整为按企业登记注册类型分组。

工业 指从事自然资源的开采，对采掘品和农产品进行加工和再加工的物质生产部门。具体包括：(1)对自然资源的开采，如采矿、晒盐等(但不包括禽兽捕猎和水产捕捞)；(2)对农副产品的加工、再加工，如粮油加工、食品加工、缫丝、纺织、制革等；(3)对采掘品的加工、再加工，如炼铁、炼钢、化工生产、石油加工、机器制造、木材加工等，以及电力、自来水、煤气的生产和供应等；(4)对工业品的修理、翻新，如机器设备的修理、交通运输工具(如汽车)的修理等。

工业统计调查单位为独立核算法人工业企业。

独立核算法人工业企业指从事工业生产经营活动的单位。独立核算法人工业企业应同时具备以下条件：①依法成立，有自己的名称、组织机构和场所，能够承担民事责任；②独立拥有和使用资产，承担负债，有权与其他单位签订合同；③独立核算盈亏，并能够编制资产负债表。

本年鉴中涉及的企业登记注册类型：

国有及国有控股企业 指国有企业加上国有控股企业。国有企业(即原全民所有制工业或国营工业)指企业全部资产归国家所有，并按《中华人民共和国企业法人登记管理条例》规定登记注册的非公司制的经济组织。包括国有企业、国有独资公司和国有联营企业。1957年以前的公私合营和私营工业，后均改造为国营工业，1992年改为国有工业，这部分工业的资料不单独分列时，均包括在国有企业内。国有控股企业是对混合所有制经济的企业进行的“国有控股”分类。它是指这些企业的全部资产中国有资产(股份)相对其他所有者中的任何一个所有者占资(股)最多的企业。该分组反映了国有经济控股情况。

集体企业 指企业资产归集体所有，并按《中华人民共和国企业法人登记管理条例》规定登记注册的经济组织。

股份合作企业 指以合作制为基础，由企业职工共同出资入股，吸收一定比例的社会资产投资组建，实行自主经营，自负盈亏，共同劳动，民主管理，按劳分配与按股分红相结合的一种集体经济组织。

联营企业 指两个及两个以上相同或不同所有制性质的企业法人或事业单位法人，按自愿、平等、互利的原则，共同投资组成的经济组织。联营企业包括：

国有联营企业指国有企业与国有企业间的联营；

集体联营企业指集体企业与集体企业间的联营；

国有与集体联营企业指国有企业与集体企业间的联营。

有限责任公司 指根据《中华人民共和国公司登记管理条例》规定登记注册，由两个以上，五十个以下的股东共同出资，每个股东以其所认缴的出资额对公司承担有限责任，公司以其全部资产对其债务承担责任的经济组织。

有限责任公司包括国有独资公司以及其他有限责任公司。

股份有限公司 指根据《中华人民共和国企业法人登记管理条例》规定登记注册，其全部注册资本由等额股份构成并通过发行股票筹集资本，股东以其认购的股份对公司承担有限责任，公司以其全部资产对其债务承担责任的经济组织。

私营企业 指由自然人投资设立或由自然人控股，以雇佣劳动为基础的营利性经济组织。包括按照《公司法》、《合伙企业法》、《私营企业暂行条例》规定登记注册的私营有限责任公司、私营股份有限公司、私营合伙企业、私营独资企业和个人独资企业。

港、澳、台商投资企业 指企业注册登记类型中的港、澳、台资合资、合作、独资经营企业和股份有限公司之和。

外商投资企业 指企业注册登记类型中的中外合资、合作经营企业、外资企业和外商投资股份有限公司之和。

“三资”企业系指港、澳、台商投资企业和外资企业的简称。

轻工业 指主要提供生活消费品和制作手工工具的工业。按其所使用的原料不同，可分为两大类：(1)以农产品为原料的轻工业，是指直接或间接以农产品为基本原料的轻工业。主要包括食品制造、饮料制造、烟草加工、纺织、缝纫、皮革和毛皮制作、造纸以及印刷等工业；(2)以非农产品为原料的轻工业，是指以工业品为原料的轻工业。主要包括文教体育用品、化学药品制造、合成纤维制造、日用化学制品、日用玻璃制品、日用金属制品、手工工具制造、医疗器械制造、文化和办公用机械制造等工业。

重工业 指为国民经济各部门提供物质技术基础的主要生产资料的工业。按其生产性质和产品用途，可以分为下列三类：(1)采掘(伐)工业，是指对自然资源的开采，包括石油开采、煤炭开采、金属矿开采、非金属矿开采等工业；(2)原材料工业，指向国民经济各部门提供基本材料、动力和燃料的工业。包括金属冶炼及加工、炼焦及焦炭、化学、化工原料、水泥、人造板以及电力、石油和煤炭加工等工业；(3)加工工业，是指对工业原材料进行再加工制造的工业。包括装备国民经济各部门的机械设备制造工业、金属结构、水泥制品等工业，以及为农业提供的生产资料如化肥、农药等工业。

根据上述划分原则，修理业中以重工业产品为修理作业对象的划为重工业，反之划为轻工业。

工业总产值 是以货币表现的工业企业在一定时期内生产的已出售或可供出售工业产品总量，它反映一定时间内工业生产的总规模和总水平。它包括：在本企业内不再进行加工，经检验、包装入库（规定不需包装的产品除外）的成品价值，对外加工费收入，自制半成品、在产品期末初差额价值。工业总产值采用“工厂法”计算，即以工业企业作为一个整体，按企业工业生产活动的最终成果来计算，企业内部不允许重复计算，不能把企业内部各个车间（分厂）生产的成果相加。但在企业之间、行业之间、地区之间存在着重复计算。

轻重工业总产值的划分也是按“工厂法”计算的，即一个工业企业在正常情况下生产的主要产品的性质属于轻工业，则该企业的全部总产值作为轻工业总产值。如生产的主要产品的性质属于重工业，则该企业的全部总产值作为重工业总产值。

工业增加值 是指工业行业在报告期内以货币表现的工业生产活动的最终成果。

实收资本 指企业实际收到的投资人投入的资本。按投资主体可分为国家资本、集体资本、法人资本、个人资本、港澳台资本和外商资本等。

资产总计 指企业拥有或控制的能以货币计量的经济资源。包括各种财产、债权和其他权利。资产按其流动性划分为流动资产、长期投资、固定资产、无形及递延资产和其他资产。

（1）流动资产指企业可以在一年内或者超过一年的一个生产周期内变现或耗用的资产合计。包括现金及各种存款、短期投资、应收及预付款项、存货等。

（2）固定资产指企业固定资产净值、固定资产清理、在建工程、待处理固定资产损失所占用的资金合计。

（3）无形资产指企业长期使用而没有实物形态的资产。包括专利权、非专利技术、商标权、著作权、土地使用权、商誉等。

负债合计 指企业承担的能以货币计量，将以资产或劳务偿付的债务。负债一般按偿还期长短分为流动负债和长期负债、递延税项等。

（1）流动负债指企业在一年内或者超过一年的一个营业周期内需要偿还的债务合计，其中包括短期借款、应付及预收款项、应付工资、应交税金和应交利润等。

（2）长期负债指企业在一年以上或者超过一年的一个营业周期以上需要偿还的债务合计，其中包括长期借款、应付债务、长期应付款项等。

所有者权益 指企业投资人对企业净资产的所有权。企业净资产等于企业全部资产减去全部负债后的余额，其中包括投资者对企业的最初投入，以及资本公积金、盈余公积金和未分配利润，对股份制企业即为股东权益。

固定资产原价 指企业在建造、购置、安装、改建、扩建、技术改造某项固定资产时所支出的全部货币总额。它一般包括买价、包装费、运杂费和安装费等。

主营业务收入 指企业确认的销售商品、提供劳务等主营业务的收入。根据会计“主营业务收入”科目的本年各月贷方余额（结转前）之和填报。如未设置该科目，以“营业收入”代替填报。

主营业务成本 指企业经营主要业务所发生的成本总额。根据会计“主营业务成本”科目的本年各月借方余额（结转前）之和填报。如未设置该科目，以“营业成本”代替填报。

主营业务税金及附加 指企业经营主要业务应负担的消费税、城市维护建设税、资源税、教育费附加及房产税、土地使用税、车船使用税、印花税等相关税费。根据会计“主营业务税金及附加”科目的本年各月借方余额（结转前）之和填报。如未设置该科目，以“税金及附加”代替填报。

利润总额 指企业在一定会计期间的经营成果，是生产经营过程中各种收入扣除各种耗费后的盈余，反映企业在报告期内实现的盈亏总额。利润总额为营业利润加上营业外收入，减去营业外支出后的金额，根据会计“利润表”中“利润总额”项目的本年累计数填报。

平均用工人数 是指报告期平均实际拥有的，参与本企业生产经营活动的人员数。

利税总额 指企业产品销售税金及附加、利润总额和应交增值税之和。

本年应交增值税 指按照税法规定，以销售货物、服务、无形资产、不动产或提供加工、修理修配劳务的增值额和货物进口金额为计税依据而课征的一种流转税。

Explanatory Notes on Main Statistical Indicators

As per provisions of national system of statistical method, the scope of statistics of the independent accounting industry in 1998 was adjusted to all state-owned enterprises and non-state industrial enterprises with above RMB 5 million annual sales revenue from those of village and above and the scope of statistics of above state designated scale industrial enterprises in 2011 was adjusted to above RMB 20 million annual income of main business. Meanwhile, grouping of original economic organizations in the statistical classification is adjusted to grouping based on enterprise registration type accordingly.

Industry refers to the material production sector which is engaged in extraction of natural resources and processing and reprocessing of minerals and agricultural products, including (1) extraction of natural resources, such as mining, salt production (but not including hunting and fishing); (2) processing and reprocessing of farm and sideline produces, such as rice husking, flour milling, wine making, oil pressing, silk reeling, spinning and weaving, and leather making; (3) manufacture of industrial products, such as steel making, iron smelting, chemicals manufacturing, petroleum processing, machine building, timber processing; water and gas production and electricity generation and supply; (4)repairing of industrial products such as the repairing of machinery and means of transport (including cars).

Units of industrial statistics survey corporate are industrial enterprises with independent accounting system.

Corporate industrial enterprises with independent accounting system refer to enterprises engaging in industrial production activities, which meet the following requirements: (1)They are established legally, having their own names, organizations, location, able to take civil liability; (2)They possess and use their assets independently, assume liabilities, and are entitled to sign contracts with other units; (3)They are financially independent and compile their own balance sheets.

Enterprises covered in the industrial statistics in this Yearbook include following categories by their registration:

State-owned and State-holding Enterprises refer to state owned enterprises plus state holding enterprises. State owned enterprises (originally known as state run enterprises with ownership by the whole society) are non-corporate economic entities registered in accordance with the Regulation of the People's Republic of China on the Management of Registration of Legal Enterprises, where all assets are owned by the state. Included in this category are state owned enterprises, state funded corporations and state owned joint operation enterprises. Public-private partnerships industries and private industries, which existed before 1957, were transformed into state run industries since 1957, and into state owned industries after 1992. Statistics on those enterprises are included in the state owned industries instead of grouping them separately. State-holding enterprise is a sub-classification of enterprises with mixed ownership, referring to enterprises where the percentage of state assets (or shares by the state) is larger than any other single shareholder of the same enterprise. This sub-classification illustrates the control of the state over a particular industry.

Collective-owned Enterprises refer to economic entities registered in accordance with the Regulation of the People's Republic of China on the Management of Registration of Legal Enterprises, where assets are owned by collectively.

Share-holding Cooperative Enterprises refer to economic units set up on cooperative basis, with funding partly from members of the enterprise and partly from outside investment, which are collective economic organizations with characteristics of self-employed, self-financing, working together, democratic management, distributing by work and shares.

Joint Operation Enterprises refer to economic units that are established by joint investment by two or more corporate enterprises or institutions of the same or different types of ownership on voluntary, equal and mutual beneficial basis. They include:

State owned joint operation enterprises (joint operation between state owned enterprises);

Collective joint operation enterprises (joint operation between collective enterprises, and

State collective joint operation enterprises (joint operation between state and collective enterprises)

Limited Liability Corporations refer to economic units registered in accordance with the Regulation of the People's Republic of China on the Management of Registration of Corporations, with capitals from 2 to 49 investors, each investor bears limited liability to the corporation depending on his/her holding of shares, and the corporation bears liability to its debt to the maximum of its total assets.

Limited liability corporations cover state-owned exclusive company and other limited liability corporations.

Share-holding Corporations Ltd. refer to economic units registered in accordance with the Regulation of the People's Republic of China on the Management of Registration of Corporate Enterprises, with total registered capitals divided into equal shares and raised through issuing stocks. Each investor bears limited liability to the corporation depending on the holding of shares, and the corporation bears liability to its debt to the maximum of its total assets.

Private Enterprises refer to economic units invested on controlled (by holding the majority of the shares) by natural persons who hire labors for profit making activities. Included in this category are private limited liability corporations, private share-holding corporations Ltd., private partnership enterprises and private sole investment enterprises registered in accordance with the Corporation Law, Partnership Enterprise Law and Tentative Regulation on Private Enterprises.

Enterprises with Funds from Hong Kong, Macao and Taiwan refers to all industrial enterprises registered as the joint venture, cooperative, sole investment industrial enterprises and limited liability corporations with funds from Hong Kong, Macao and Taiwan.

Foreign Funded Enterprises refers to all industrial enterprises registered as the joint venture, cooperative, foreign companies and foreign investment Co. Ltd..

Enterprise with Hong Kong, Macao, Taiwan and foreign fund refer to all the enterprises with funds from Hong Kong Macao and Taiwan and foreign funded enterprises.

Light industry refers to the industry that produces consumer goods and hand tools. It consists of two categories, depending on the materials used: (1) Industries using farm products as raw materials. These are branches of light industry which directly or indirectly use farm products as basic raw materials, including the manufacture of food and beverages, tobacco processing, textile, clothing, fur and leather manufacturing, paper making, printing, etc.(2) Industries using non-farm products as raw materials. These are branches of light industry which use manufactured goods as raw materials, including the manufacture of cultural, educational articles and sports goods, chemicals, synthetic fiber, chemical products for daily use, glass products for daily use, metal products for daily use, hand tools, medical apparatus and instruments, and the manufacture of cultural and clerical machinery.

Heavy Industry refers to the industry which produces capital goods, and provides various sectors of the national economy with necessary material and technical basis. It consists of the following three branches according to the purpose of production or the use of products:

(1) Mining, quarrying and logging industry refers to the industry that extracts natural resources, including extraction of petroleum, coal, metal and non–metal ores. (2) Raw materials industry refers to the industry that provides various sectors of the national economy with raw materials, fuels and power. It includes smelting and processing of metals, coking and coke chemistry, chemical materials, cement, plywood, power, petroleum refining and coal dressing. (3) Manufacturing industry refers to the industry that processes raw materials. It includes machine building industry which equips sectors of the national economy, industries of metal structure and cement products, industries producing means of agricultural production, such as chemical fertilizers and pesticides.

According to the above principle of classification, the repairing trades, which are engaged primarily in repairing products of heavy industry are classified into heavy industry while these engaged in repairing products of light industry are classified into light industry.

Gross Industrial Output Value refers to total industrial products which were sold or are available for sale produced by industrial enterprise within a certain period of time and expressed with currency and reflects total scale and total level of industrial production within a certain period of time. It includes: value of finished product not processed in the enterprise which are put in storage after inspection and packaging (except products specified not to be packaged), external processing fee income and the value of the difference between the end of the period and the beginning of the period of self–made semi–manufactured goods. Gross industrial output value is calculated as per "factory approach", that is to say that gross industrial output value is calculated according to final result of industrial production activities of enterprises based on industrial enterprise as a whole. Repeated calculation in the enterprise and adding production results of all workshops (branch factories) in the enterprise are forbidden. However, the repeated calculation between enterprises, industries and regions exists.

Gross output value of light and heavy industries is also calculated according to "factory approach", that is to say that total output value of the enterprise is used as gross output of the light industry if major products produced by an industrial enterprise under normal circumstances fall into light industry. Gross output value of the enterprise is use as gross output value of heavy industry if major products produced fall into heavy industry.

Value–added of Industry refers to the final results of industrial production of industrial enterprises in currency during the reference period

Paid–up capital refers to the capital actually received by the enterprise and invested by the investor. Paid–up capital can be divided into national capital, collectively owned capital, corporate capital, personal capital, Hong Kong, Macao and Taiwan capital and foreign capital as per investors.

Total Assets refer to all economic resources, in monetary terms, that is owned or controlled by enterprises, including properties, creditors equity and other economic rights of all forms. Classified by the degree of equitability, total assets include circulating assets, long–term investment, fixed assets, intangible assets and deferred assets, and other assets.

(1)Current assets refer to assets that an enterprise can convert into cash or use during one year or one production cycle that may exceeds one year, including cash and savings deposits of various forms, short–term investment, receivable and prepaid money, inventories, etc..

(2) Fixed assets refer to the total amount of net fixed assets of the enterprise, disposal of fixed assets, project under construction and losses on pending fixed assets.

(3) Intangible assets refer to the assets without physical form used by the enterprise for a long time. It consists of patent right, non–patent technology, trademark right, copyright, chartered right, land use right, etc..

Total Liabilities refer to the liabilities borne by the enterprise which can be measured with currency and repaid by assets or labor services. Liabilities are generally divided into current liabilities, long–term liabilities and deferred tax on the basis of repayment period.

(1) Current liabilities (also called quick liabilities or immediate liabilities) refer to enterprises' total debt payable within an operating cycle of one year or over one year, including short term loans, payables and advance payments, wages payable, taxes payable and profit payable, etc..

(2) Long–term liabilities refers enterprises' total debt payable within an operating cycle of one year or over one year, including long–term loans, payable liabilities, long–term payables, etc..

Owner's Equity refers to the ownership of net assets of enterprise by its investors. The net assets equal the total assets minus total liabilities of the enterprise, including the actual assets invested into the enterprise by investors, accumulation of capitals and operating surplus and non–distributed profits (namely stockholders' equity for corporate enterprise).

Original Value of Fixed Assets refers to the total value, in monetary terms, that an enterprise spent on fixed assets, through construction, purchase, installation, transformation, expansion or technical upgrading. Generally, it covers cost of purchase, packing, transportation and installation, etc..

Revenue from Principal Business refers to the income of main business such as sales of commodities and provision of labor service confirmed by the enterprise which shall be filled in and reported according to the sum of credit balances (before carry–over) of all the months of the current year in the item "main business income". In case of no such item, "operating income" shall be used to replace it for filling in.

Cost of Principal Business refers to total cost incurred by main businesses operated by the enterprise. It shall be filled in and reported according to the sum of debit balances (before carry–over) of all the months of the current year in the item "main business cost". In case of no such item, "operating cost" shall be used to replace it for filling in.

Taxes and Surcharges of Principal Business refer to related expenses of taxation, such as consumption tax, city maintenance and construction tax, resource tax, education surcharge and property tax, land use tax, vehicle and vessel use tax and stamp tax borne due to main businesses operated by the enterprise. They shall be filled in and reported according to the sum of debit balances (before carry–over) of all the months of the current year in the item "taxes and surcharges of principal business". In case of no such item, "taxes and surcharges" shall be used to replace it for filling in.

Total Profits refer to the operating result of the enterprise during a certain accounting period, they are the balance of the production and operation process after all incomes are deducted by various costs, reflect the total amount of profit and loss achieved within the reporting period. Total profit is the amount after operating profit plus non–business income and then minus non–business expenditure, which shall be filled in and reported pursuant to the cumulative data in the current year in the item "total profit" in the "profit statement".

Average Number of Workers refers to the average number of personnel actually owned and participating in production and operation activities of the enterprise within the reporting period.

Total Profits and Taxes refer to the sum of sales taxes, charges, revenues and VAT of the products in the enterprise.

VAT payable this year refers to a turnover tax that pursuant to the VAT of goods and services sales, invisible assets, real estate, machining provided, repair services and to the amount of goods import in accordance with the taxes laws.

13

建 筑 业

CONSTRUCTION

13-1 建筑业主要指标

Main Indicators of Construction Enterprises

指 标	Indicator	单位 Unit	2013年	2014年	2015	2016年	2017	2018年
汇总单位数	Number of Enterprises	个(unit)	486	454	463	460	504	507
建筑业增加值	Construction Inscreased	万元(10 000 yuan)	2986331	3014387	2826306	2805982	3308084	5136408
建筑业总产值	Gross Output Value	万元(10 000 yuan)	13867631	15422095	16638332	18647972	22189343	28234734
按隶属关系分	by Ownership							
中央属	Central	万元(10 000 yuan)	6026998	6781707	7693792	9079591	11379540	14747883
省 属	Provincial	万元(10 000 yuan)	1497316	1549456	1664077	1853736	2391026	3039149
市 属	Region	万元(10 000 yuan)	2723246	2978560	3222554	3676145	5195869	6391344
县及县以下	County	万元(10 000 yuan)	1525039	1654785	1608569	1711315	570463	641220
其 他	Others	万元(10 000 yuan)	2095032	2457587	2449340	2327185	2652445	3415138
按工程性质分	by Sector							
建筑工程	Building and Civil Engineering Construction	万元(10 000 yuan)	12174551	13708876	14422832	16291789	19476820	25182882
安装工程	Construction Installation	万元(10 000 yuan)	1190377	1392597	1744180	1998465	2051423	2329541
其他产值	Others	万元(10 000 yuan)	502703	320622	471320	357718	661100	722311
竣工产值	Value of Construction Completed	万元(10 000 yuan)	6457841	6398538	7613104	7415119	7987351	8691856
房屋施工面积	Floor Space Completed	万平方米(10 000 sq.cm)	7696	9183	10189	10293	11363	12984
#本年新开工	Startde This year	万平方米(10 000 sq.cm)	3008	3420	2991	3222	3694	4842
房屋竣工面积	Floor Space Completed	万平方米(10 000 sq.cm)	2012	1772	2039	2298	2280	2366
#住 宅	Residential	万平方米(10 000 sq.cm)	1281	1157	1178	1379	1258	1502
所有者权益	Creditors'Equity	万元(10 000 yuan)	3214727	3516583	4015082	4433678	5900444	6269077
利润总额	Total Profits	万元(10 000 yuan)	499818	516686	568473	573258	836297	810897
工资总额	Total wages	万元(10 000 yuan)	1711089	1917170	1638141	1812042	2185631	3480056

注：建筑业增加值2006年起采用以企业营业利润为主的收入法计算。

Note: The value added of construction output was calculated as per income method mainly involving enterprise operating profit as of 2006.

13-2 建筑业增加值构成(2018年)

Value Added of Construction by Structure（2018）

单位：万元 (10 000yuan)

指标 （总承包与专业承包）	Indicator	建筑业增加值 Construction Inscreased	本年提取固定资产折旧 Fixed Assets Depreciation in the Year	税金及附加 Taxes and Other Charges	营业利润 Profits from Business	应付职工薪酬（本年贷方累计发生额） Total Wages Payable
总计	Total	5136408	175391	685311	795650	3480056
其中：国有及国有控股企业	State-owned and State-controlled Enterprises	3650444	114259	426470	599927	2509788
一、按登记注册类型分组	Grouped by Registration Status					
内资企业	Domestic Funded	5131393	175067	685016	794565	3476745
国有企业	State-owned	117787	3503	30148	23790	60346
集体企业	Collective-owned	37385	731	6966	3726	25963
股份合作企业	Stock-holding Cooperation	6629	128	2366	1098	3037
联营企业	Joint-owned	383	6	142	24	211
其他联营企业	Others	383	6	142	24	211
有限责任公司	Company with Limited Liabilition	3933257	130575	537739	630999	2633945
国有独资公司	State-owned	1057162	39714	132738	166140	718571
其他有限责任公司	Others	2876095	90861	405001	464859	1915374
股份有限公司	Stock-holding Company limited	635309	27272	33180	82880	491977
私营企业	Private Enterprises	400644	12854	74475	52048	261267
私营独资企业	Solely Owned	0	0	0	0	0
私营有限责任公司	Private Limited Liability Corporations	377381	12162	71150	51197	242872
私营股份有限公司	Private Share-holding Corporations Ltd.	23263	692	3325	851	18395
其他企业	Others	0	0	0	0	0
港、澳、台商投资企业	Enterprises with Funds from Hong Kong, Macao and Taiwan	0	0	0	0	0
与港澳台商合资经营	Joint-venture Enterprises	0	0	0	0	0
港、澳、台商独资	Enterprises with Sole Fund	0	0	0	0	0
外商投资企业	Foreign Funded Enterprises	5015	324	295	1085	3311
中外合资经营企业	Joint-venture Enterprises	417	4	54	22	337
外资企业	Enterprises with Sole Fund	4598	320	241	1064	2973
二、按国民经济行业分组	by Sector					
房屋建筑业	Building Construction	2365067	36841	344935	339068	1644222
土木工程建筑业	Civil Engineering Construction	2425070	116290	271734	374781	1662266
建筑安装业	Construction Installation	176676	12237	30124	50555	83760
建筑装饰和其他建筑业	Construction Decoration and Others	169595	10023	38518	31247	89807
三、按隶属关系分组	by Ownership					
中央	Central	2464318	80485	307268	339841	1736724
地方	Local	1497349	50245	179295	302777	965032
其他	Others	1174741	44661	198748	153032	778300
四、按企业资质等级分组	by Qualification Criteria					
施工总承包	Construction Contract	4842523	151503	624405	750458	3316157
特级	Special Grade	2975824	78219	302823	516688	2078094
一级	First Grade	1456707	48402	251267	179725	977313
二级	Second Grade	258752	20919	38589	39460	159784
三级以下	Third Grade and below	151241	3964	31726	14585	100966
专业承包	Professional Contract	293885	23888	60906	45192	163898
一级	First Grade	125287	7018	27551	22147	68572
二级	Second Grade	92270	5556	23053	15781	47881
三级以下	Third Grade and below	76327	11314	10302	7265	47446

13-3 建筑企业

Assets of Construction

单位：万元

指 标 （总承包与专业承包）	Indicator	流动资产合计 LiquidAssets	# 存货 Inventory	固定资产合计 Fixed Assets
总计	**Total**	25141635	5074093	1065484
其中：国有及国有控股企业	State-owned and State-controlled Enterprises	19579403	3936989	724837
一、按登记注册类型分组	**Grouped by Registration Status**			
内资企业	Domestic Funded	25135829	5073699	1063114
国有企业	State-owned	568943	181716	42303
集体企业	Collective-owned	133164	39861	13283
股份合作企业	Stock-holding Cooperation	153506	108688	1004
联营企业	Joint-owned	7481	959	77
其他联营企业	Others	7481	959	77
有限责任公司	Company with Limited Liabilition	19299670	4362785	810047
国有独资公司	State-owned	5248876	882408	262563
其他有限责任公司	Others	14050793	3480376	547484
股份有限公司	Stock-holding Company limited	3189924	97764	72693
私营企业	Private Enterprises	1783141	281927	123707
私营独资企业	Solely Owned	0	0	0
私营有限责任公司	Private Limited Liability Corporations	1643947	263548	110375
私营股份有限公司	Private Share-holding Corporations Ltd.	139194	18379	13332
其他企业	Others	0	0	0
港、澳、台商投资企业	Enterprises with Funds from Hong Kong,Macao and Taiwan	0	0	0
与港澳台商合资经营	Joint-venture Enterprises	0	0	0
港、澳、台商独资	Enterprises with Sole Fund	0	0	0
外商投资企业	Foreign Funded Enterprises	5806	394	2371
中外合资经营企业	Joint-venture Enterprises	4043	368	33
外资企业	Enterprises with Sole Fund	1763	27	2338
二、按国民经济行业分组	**by Sector**			
房屋建筑业	Building Construction	7750770	1500885	256831
土木工程建筑业	Civil Engineering Construction	15564276	3276450	678689
建筑安装业	Construction Installation	859396	191466	85174
建筑装饰和其他建筑业	Construction Decoration and Others	967193	105293	44790
三、按隶属关系分组	**by Ownership**			
中央	Central	11628649	1814987	460266
地方	Local	8468392	2359331	295800
其他	Others	5044594	899774	309418
四、按企业资质等级分组	**by Qualification Criteria**			
施工总承包	Construction Contract	23409563	4805898	957337
特级	Special Grade	15003404	3009671	436920
一级	First Grade	6325754	1228234	365925
二级	Second Grade	1506412	477262	107634
三级以下	Third Grade and below	573993	90730	46858
专业承包	Professional Contract	1732072	268195	108147
一级	First Grade	828797	143284	38361
二级	Second Grade	417492	51850	27976
三级以下	Third Grade and below	485783	73061	41810

资 产 实 力（2018 年）

Enterprises （2018）

(10 000 yuan)

固定资产原价 Original Value of Fixed Assets	流动负债合计 Current Liabilities Total	非流动负债合计 Non-Current Liabilities Total	负债合计 Total Liabilitie	所有者权益合计 Total Creditors' Equity	#国家资本 Official Capital
2204854	22455914	1215603	23850914	6269077	1904439
1565405	18434666	1082635	19517718	4090687	1888801
2201595	22448977	1215603	23843977	6261353	1904439
75750	448208	22201	470834	165593	107461
18877	111488	279	112902	51023	0
3967	162338	0	170638	-10290	65
153	7210	0	7210	348	0
153	7210	0	7210	348	0
1667681	17479892	917868	18545616	4287513	1388589
508163	5135171	271639	5406810	929993	606521
1159518	12344721	646229	13138806	3357521	782067
207784	3157583	222101	3379684	881491	407950
227382	1082260	53154	1157094	885674	375
0	0	0	0	0	0
206488	1006499	14854	1042504	842202	375
20894	75761	38300	114591	43473	0
0	0	0	0	0	0
0	0	0	0	0	0
0	0	0	0	0	0
0	0	0	0	0	0
3260	6937	0	6937	7725	0
208	2423	0	2423	1653	0
3052	4515	0	4515	6071	0
485395	6350243	188452	6685936	1905482	385573
1483853	14776783	951692	15736114	3611632	1422930
153013	644935	17606	663372	407900	55289
82593	683954	57853	765492	344063	40648
1042751	11283916	649923	11933839	2259302	1462151
609250	7404963	429267	7959537	2024058	363540
552854	3767036	136413	3957539	1985718	78749
2001458	21129915	1131417	22414175	5633299	1866101
991598	14161019	839788	15000808	3226076	1362622
734735	5438120	254443	5806689	1570690	415150
206226	1152009	16806	1187958	559207	22045
68899	378767	20380	418720	277326	66285
203396	1325999	84186	1436739	635779	38338
65519	647184	13960	676435	233132	27516
59095	295592	6824	311040	191865	6773
78783	383223	63401	449265	210781	4050

13-4 建筑业施工产值构成（2018 年）

Output Value of Construction by Structure（2018）

单位：万元 (10 000 yuan)

指 标（总承包与专业承包）	Indicator	合计 Total	建筑工程 Constructional Engineering	安装工程 Installation Project	其他产值 Other Value	竣工产值 Value of Construction Completed
总计	Total	28234734	25182882	2329541	722311	8691856
其中：国有及国有控股企业	State-owned and State-controlled Enterprises	22116040	20256023	1320648	539369	5477995
一、按登记注册类型分组	Grouped by Registration Status					
内资企业	Domestic Funded	28223528	25182882	2318335	722312	8691576
国有企业	State-owned	1786951	1156469	570963	59519	614474
集体企业	Collective-owned	109032	105367	2107	1558	58883
股份合作企业	Stock-holding Cooperation	2913	2303	610	0	610
联营企业	Joint-owned	312020	312020	0	0	128826
其他联营企业	Others	0	0	0	0	0
有限责任公司	Company with Limited Liabilition	20336893	18840831	931287	564775	5056937
国有独资公司	State-owned	6137339	5659891	466975	10473	2068747
其他有限责任公司	Others	14199554	13180940	464312	554302	2988190
股份有限公司	Stock-holding Company limited	354416	301846	51466	1105	125828
私营企业	Private Enterprises	5319623	4462367	761901	95355	2706018
私营有限责任公司	Private Limited Liability Corporations	4938937	4081681	761901	95355	2562414
私营股份有限公司	Private Share-holding Corporations Ltd.	380686	380686	0	0	143604
港、澳、台商投资企业	Funded from Hong Kong,Macao and Taiwan	0	0	0	0	0
与港澳台商合资经营	Joint Ventures	0	0	0	0	0
外商投资企业	Foreign Funded	11206	0	11206	0	281
中外合资经营企业	Chinese-foreign Joint Venture	3391	0	3391	0	281
二、按国民经济行业分组	by Sector					
房屋建筑业	Building Construction	12130518	11380243	487367	262907	5487061
土木工程建筑业	Civil Engineering Construction	14286063	12741723	1177673	366668	2328334
建筑安装业	Construction Installation	772414	148432	585846	38136	360683
建筑装饰和其他建筑业	Construction Decoration and Others	1045739	912484	78655	54601	515777
三、按隶属关系分组	by Ownership					
中央	Central	14747883	13327373	1157576	262934	3789880
省(自治区、直辖市)	Provincial	3039149	2575947	111369	351833	317962
地区(州、盟、省辖市)及以下、其他	Region	10447702	9279562	1060595	107545	4584014
四、按企业资质等级分组	by Qualification Criteria					
施工总承包	Construction Contract	26482305	24064036	1950272	467997	7778015
特级	Special Grade	17360977	16430499	875207	55270	4741027
一级	First Grade	7689772	6365547	929877	394349	2346617
二级	Second Grade	980755	881264	93799	5693	462901
三级及以下	Third Grade and below	450801	386726	51389	12686	227470
专业承包	Professional Contract	1752430	1118846	379269	254315	913841
一级	First Grade	935725	549599	164699	221426	436301
二级	Second Grade	513781	327331	158641	27810	311647
三级及以下	Third Grade and below	302924	241916	55929	5079	165893

13-5 建筑企业损益及分配（2018年）

Output Value of Construction by Structure（2018）

单位：万元 (10 000 yuan)

指标（总承包与专业承包）	Indicator	营业收入 Business Revenue	利税总额 Total Profits and Taxes	营业利润 Profits from Business	利润总额 Total Profits	应付职工薪酬（本年贷方累计发生额） Total Wages Payable
总计	**Total**	27671340	1496208	795650	810897	3480056
其中：国有及国有控股企业	State-owned and State-controlled Enterprises	21368313	1024487	599927	598017	2509788
一、按登记注册类型分组	**Grouped by Registration Status**					
内资企业	Domestic Funded	27660879	1494824	794565	809808	3476745
国有企业	State-owned	630539	54544	23790	24396	60346
集体企业	Collective-owned	144353	10513	3726	3548	25963
股份合作企业	Stock-holding Cooperation	37550	3364	1098	998	3037
联营企业	Joint-owned	8173	166	24	24	211
其他联营企业	Others	8173	166	24	24	211
有限责任公司	Company with Limited Liabilition	20955816	1177317	630999	639578	2633945
国有独资公司	State-owned	6960479	300748	166140	168011	718571
其他有限责任公司	Others	13995337	876568	464859	471568	1915374
股份有限公司	Stock-holding Company limited	3884402	110589	82880	77408	491977
私营企业	Private Enterprises	2000046	138330	52048	63856	261267
私营独资企业	Solely Owned	0	0	0	0	0
私营有限责任公司	Private Limited Liability Corporations	1879041	134086	51197	62936	242872
私营股份有限公司	Private Share-holding Corporations Ltd.	121005	4244	851	919	18395
其他企业	Others	0	0	0	0	0
港、澳、台商投资企业	Enterprises with Funds from Hong Kong, Macao and Taiwan	0	0	0	0	0
与港澳台商合资经营	Joint-venture Enterprises	0	0	0	0	0
港、澳、台商独资	Enterprises with Sole Fund	0	0	0	0	0
外商投资企业	Foreign Funded Enterprises	10461	1384	1085	1090	3311
中外合资经营企业	Joint-venture Enterprises	2647	75	22	22	337
外资企业	Enterprises with Sole Fund	7815	1309	1064	1068	2973
二、按国民经济行业分组	**by Sector**					
房屋建筑业	Building Construction	11131841	684972	339068	340037	1644222
土木工程建筑业	Civil Engineering Construction	14493869	646113	374781	374379	1662266
建筑安装业	Construction Installation	921992	83284	50555	53161	83760
建筑装饰和其他建筑业	Construction Decoration and Others	1123638	81839	31247	43320	89807
三、按隶属关系分组	**by Ownership**					
中央	Central	14999018	639659	339841	332391	1736724
地方	Local	7295526	488296	302777	309001	965032
其他	Others	5376796	368254	153032	169506	778300
四、按企业资质等级分组	**by Qualification Criteria**					
施工总承包	Construction Contract	25737319	1374964	750458	750559	3316157
特级	Special Grade	16769971	818199	516688	515376	2078094
一级	First Grade	7436715	431778	179725	180511	977313
二级	Second Grade	1034777	78722	39460	40134	159784
三级以下	Third Grade and below	495855	46265	14585	14538	100966
专业承包	Professional Contract	1934021	121245	45192	60339	163898
一级	First Grade	1025952	63483	22147	35932	68572
二级	Second Grade	550487	39630	15781	16577	47881
三级以下	Third Grade and below	357583	18132	7265	7830	47446

13 - 6　施工工程个数及施工面积（2018 年）

Number of Projects and Floor Space Under Construction（2018）

单位：万平方米　　10 000 sq.m

指标（总承包与专业承包）	Indicator	房屋建筑施工面积 Floor Space under Construction	# 本年新开工面积 Started This Year	房屋建筑竣工面积 Floor Space Completed	# 住宅房屋 Residential	竣工房屋价值（万元）Value of Construction Completed (10 000 yuan)
总计	Total	12984	4842	2366	1502	4171041
其中：国有及国有控股企业	State-owned and State-controlled Enterprises	8331	2632	1359	800	2289391
一、按登记注册类型分组	Grouped by Registration Status					
内资企业	Domestic Funded	12984	4842	2366	1502	4171041
国有企业	State-owned	134	67	63	10	146314
集体企业	Collective-owned	85	48	24	16	49171
股份合作企业	Stock-holding Cooperation	0	0	0	0	0
有限责任公司	Company with Limited Liabilition	8793	2907	1489	934	2396330
国有独资公司	State-owned	3350	968	521	274	254483
其他有限责任公司	Others	5444	1940	969	660	2141847
股份有限公司	Stock-holding Company limited	298	152	46	46	91787
私营企业	Private Enterprises	3392	1629	710	470	1382725
私营有限责任公司	Private Limited Liability Corporations	2951	1443	647	428	1244323
私营股份有限公司	Private Share-holding Corporations Ltd.	442	186	63	41	138402
二、按国民经济行业分组	by Sector					
房屋建筑业	Building Construction	12680	4675	2271	1477	3992948
土木工程建筑业	Civil Engineering Construction	219	96	76	10	170527
建筑安装业	Construction Installation	49	42	2	0	2546
建筑装饰和其他建筑业	Construction Decoration and Others	37	30	16	15	5021
三、按隶属关系分组	by Ownership					
中央	Central	6027	1571	922	508	1491146
省(自治区、直辖市)	Provincial	278	144	75	74	163913
地区(州、盟、省辖市)及以下、其他	Region	6680	3126	1369	920	2515982
四、按企业资质等级分组	by Qualification Criteria					
施工总承包	Construction Contract	12956	4818	2361	1502	4160691
特级	Special Grade	8194	2620	1320	760	2352361
一级	First Grade	3950	1695	801	599	1441048
二级	Second Grade	513	283	122	73	239124
三级以下	Third Grade and below	300	221	118	69	128157
专业承包	Professional Contract	28	23	5	0	10351
一级	First Grade	3	3	0	0	0
二级	Second Grade	12	11	3	0	8020
三级以下	Third Grade and below	13	10	1	0	2331

13-7 济南市建筑业特级、一级资质企业一览表（2018年）

Summary of Construction Enterprises with Grade Ⅰ Qualification（2018）

企业名称 Name	隶属关系 Ownership	经济类型 Economic Type	所属行业 Sector
山东省建设建工（集团）有限责任公司	地（区、市、州、盟）	私营有限责任公司	住宅房屋建筑
中建八局第一建设有限公司	中央	国有独资公司	住宅房屋建筑
中建八局第二建设有限公司	中央	其他有限责任公司	住宅房屋建筑
济南四建(集团)有限责任公司	地（区、市、州、盟）	其他有限责任公司	住宅房屋建筑
山东平安建设集团有限公司	地（区、市、州、盟）	私营有限责任公司	住宅房屋建筑
山东三箭建设工程股份有限公司	地（区、市、州、盟）	私营股份责任公司	住宅房屋建筑
山东省路桥集团有限公司	省（自治区、直辖市）	其他有限责任公司	其他道路、隧道和桥梁工程建筑
山东省公路建设(集团)有限公司	其他	其他有限责任公司	公路工程建筑
中铁十四局集团有限公司	中央	其他有限责任公司	铁路工程建筑
中铁十四局集团第三工程有限公司	中央	私营有限责任公司	铁路工程建筑
中铁十局集团有限公司	中央	其他有限责任公司	铁路工程建筑
中国电建集团山东电力建设第一工程有限公司	中央	国有	架线及设备工程建筑
中国电建集团核电工程有限公司	中央	国有	架线及设备工程建筑
济南城建集团有限公司	地（区、市、州、盟）	国有独资公司	铁路工程建筑
山东高速齐鲁建设集团公司	省（自治区、直辖市）	其他有限责任公司	其他房屋建筑
山东天宝建设集团有限公司	其他	其他有限责任公司	住宅房屋建筑
山东省城建工程集团公司	省（自治区、直辖市）	国有	住宅房屋建筑
山东鲁建工程集团有限公司	省（自治区、直辖市）	其他有限责任公司	住宅房屋建筑
山东三箭建设工程管理有限公司	地（区、市、州、盟）	其他有限责任公司	住宅房屋建筑
山东泉景建设有限公司	地（区、市、州、盟）	其他有限责任公司	住宅房屋建筑
济南华海建设集团有限公司	其他	股份有限公司	住宅房屋建筑
济南二建集团工程有限公司	地（区、市、州、盟）	其他有限责任公司	住宅房屋建筑
普利置业集团股份有限公司	省（自治区、直辖市）	股份有限公司	住宅房屋建筑
中铁十局集团建筑工程有限公司	中央	国有与集体联营	住宅房屋建筑
山东中恒建设集团有限公司	其他	私营有限责任公司	住宅房屋建筑
济南建工总承包集团有限公司	地（区、市、州、盟）	其他有限责任公司	住宅房屋建筑
济南一建集团有限公司	地（区、市、州、盟）	国有独资公司	住宅房屋建筑
山东港基建设集团有限公司	地（区、市、州、盟）	其他有限责任公司	住宅房屋建筑
山东长箭建设集团有限公司	县级及以下	私营有限责任公司	住宅房屋建筑
山东汇富建设集团有限公司	地（区、市、州、盟）	其他有限责任公司	住宅房屋建筑
山东长泰建设集团工程有限公司	其他	私营有限责任公司	住宅房屋建筑
济南长兴建设集团有限公司	地（区、市、州、盟）	私营有限责任公司	住宅房屋建筑
章丘市第二建筑安装(集团)有限责任公司	地（区、市、州、盟）	其他有限责任公司	住宅房屋建筑

13-7 续 1

企业名称 Name	隶属关系 Ownership	经济类型 Economic Type	所属行业 Sector
济南铸诚建筑工程集团有限公司	县级及以下	私营有限责任公司	住宅房屋建筑
山东科信达建筑安装有限公司	县级及以下	私营有限责任公司	住宅房屋建筑
山东信达建设工程有限公司	其他	私营有限责任公司	其他房屋建筑
山东省建设集团有限公司	其他	私营有限责任公司	其他房屋建筑
中铁十四局集团第四工程有限公司	中央	国有独资公司	铁路工程建筑
山东省公路桥梁建设有限公司	省（自治区、直辖市）	其他有限责任公司	公路工程建筑
山东省高速路桥养护有限公司	省（自治区、直辖市）	其他有限责任公司	其他道路、隧道和桥梁工程建筑
山东省大通公路工程有限责任公司	地（区、市、州、盟）	私营有限责任公司	公路工程建筑
济南金曰公路工程有限公司	地（区、市、州、盟）	其他有限责任公司	公路工程建筑
济南通达公路工程有限公司	县级及以下	国有独资公司	公路工程建筑
山东鲁桥建设有限公司	其他	其他有限责任公司	公路工程建筑
山东琴通路桥集团有限公司	地（区、市、州、盟）	其他有限责任公司	公路工程建筑
山东省齐鲁装饰设计院	省（自治区、直辖市）	集体联营	公共建筑装饰和装修
山东万得福装饰工程有限公司	其他	其他有限责任公司	公共建筑装饰和装修
济南舜联建设集团有限公司	其他	私营有限责任公司	其他房屋建筑
山东黄河工程集团有限公司	中央	国有	港口及航运设施工程建筑
山东水总有限公司	省（自治区、直辖市）	国有独资公司	河湖治理及防洪设施工程建筑
山东省水利工程局有限公司	省（自治区、直辖市）	私营有限责任公司	河湖治理及防洪设施工程建筑
山东黄河顺成水利水电工程有限公司	中央	其他有限责任公司	管道工程建筑
山东送变电工程有限公司	中央	其他有限责任公司	架线及设备工程建筑
山东电建建设集团有限公司	其他	其他有限责任公司	架线及设备工程建筑
济钢集团山东建设工程有限公司	省（自治区、直辖市）	股份有限公司	电气安装
济南普利供水工程有限公司	地（区、市、州、盟）	私营有限责任公司	管道工程建筑
中铁十四局集团隧道工程有限公司	中央	其他有限责任公司	铁路工程建筑
山东汇通建设集团有限公司	地（区、市、州、盟）	其他有限责任公司	市政道路工程建筑
中铁十局集团第一工程有限公司	中央	其他有限责任公司	公路工程建筑
济南黄河路桥建设集团有限公司	地（区、市、州、盟）	国有独资公司	市政道路工程建筑
山东省邮电工程有限公司	其他	私营有限责任公司	架线及设备工程建筑
山东宏业发展集团有限公司	其他	私营有限责任公司	架线及设备工程建筑
山东省工业设备安装有限公司	省（自治区、直辖市）	其他有限责任公司	其他建筑安装
中铁十四局集团电气化工程有限公司	中央	国有独资公司	架线及设备工程建筑
中铁十局集团电务工程有限公司	中央	私营有限责任公司	铁路工程建筑
山东亚特尔集团股份有限公司	省（自治区、直辖市）	股份有限公司	管道和设备安装
山东国舜建设集团有限公司	地（区、市、州、盟）	私营有限责任公司	其他建筑安装
山东福源设备安装有限公司	地（区、市、州、盟）	私营有限责任公司	管道和设备安装
山东正元建设工程有限责任公司	中央	其他有限责任公司	其他房屋建筑

企业名称 Name	隶属关系 Ownership	经济类型 Economic Type	所属行业 Sector
中铁济南工程技术有限公司	中央	私营有限责任公司	铁路工程建筑
山东省机械施工有限公司	地（区、市、州、盟）	私营有限责任公司	场地准备活动
山东建勘集团有限公司	省（自治区、直辖市）	国有独资公司	场地准备活动
山东省装饰集团总公司	省（自治区、直辖市）	国有	公共建筑装饰和装修
山东省鸿鑫工程有限公司	其他	私营有限责任公司	公共建筑装饰和装修
中炬装饰工程集团有限公司	省（自治区、直辖市）	私营有限责任公司	公共建筑装饰和装修
绿城永隆装饰工程有限公司	其他	其他有限责任公司	公共建筑装饰和装修
山东华森装饰工程有限公司	其他	其他有限责任公司	公共建筑装饰和装修
济南万泰建筑装饰工程有限公司	其他	私营有限责任公司	住宅装饰和装修
山东通海装饰工程有限公司	其他	私营有限责任公司	公共建筑装饰和装修
济南宏铁建筑装饰工程有限公司	中央	其他有限责任公司	住宅装饰和装修
山东福缘来装饰有限公司	其他	私营有限责任公司	住宅装饰和装修
山东福思特建筑装饰有限公司	其他	私营有限责任公司	建筑幕墙装饰和装修
山东盛顺装饰有限公司	其他	私营有限责任公司	住宅装饰和装修
沃尔德项目管理有限公司	其他	其他有限责任公司	住宅装饰和装修
山东鑫龙装饰工程有限公司	其他	私营有限责任公司	公共建筑装饰和装修
济南金鼎电力安装有限公司	县级及以下	其他有限责任公司	电气安装
山东国宸装饰工程有限公司	地（区、市、州、盟）	私营有限责任公司	公共建筑装饰和装修
德泰建设有限公司	其他	私营有限责任公司	公共建筑装饰和装修
山东省鲁美建材装饰有限公司	其他	私营有限责任公司	建筑幕墙装饰和装修
山东津单幕墙有限公司	其他	私营有限责任公司	建筑幕墙装饰和装修
济南长兴安装工程公司	其他	集体	其他建筑安装
济南凯诚消防自控设备有限公司	其他	私营有限责任公司	电气安装
山东费尔消防技术工程有限公司	其他	私营有限责任公司	电气安装
山东宏雁电子系统工程有限公司	其他	私营有限责任公司	电气安装
山东华森建筑消防项目管理有限公司	其他	私营有限责任公司	电气安装
济南消防工程有限公司	地（区、市、州、盟）	私营有限责任公司	电气安装
山东润诚机电工程有限公司	其他	私营有限责任公司	电气安装
山东华尔泰建筑工程有限公司	其他	私营有限责任公司	电气安装
山东正晨科技股份有限公司	省（自治区、直辖市）	股份有限公司	电气安装
嘉林建设集团有限公司	其他	私营有限责任公司	建筑幕墙装饰和装修
济南长城空调公司	地（区、市、州、盟）	股份合作	管道和设备安装
济南建设设备安装有限责任公司	地（区、市、州、盟）	其他有限责任公司	管道和设备安装
优士科技发展有限公司	其他	私营有限责任公司	电气安装
中广核宏达环境科技有限责任公司	中央	其他有限责任公司	环保工程施工
山东海威装饰工程有限公司	其他	私营有限责任公司	公共建筑装饰和装修

主要统计指标解释

建筑业统计单位 指从事房屋、构筑物建造和设备安装活动的法人企业。建筑业法人企业应同时具备的条件是：①依法成立，有自己的名称、组织机构和场所，能够承担民事责任；②独立拥有和使用资产，承担负债，有权与其他单位签订合同；③独立核算盈亏，能够编制资产负债表。

建筑业总产值（即自行完成施工产值） 是以货币表现的建筑安装企业在一定时期内生产的建筑业产品的总和。建筑业总产值包括：

（1）建筑工程产值：指列入建筑工程预算内的各种工程价值。

（2）设备安装工程产值：指设备安装工程价值，不包括被安装设备本身价值。

（3）房屋、构筑物修理产值：指房屋、构筑物修理所完成的价值，但不包括被修理房屋、构筑物本身的价值和生产设备的修理价值。

（4）非标准设备制造产值：指加工制造没有定型的、非标准的生产设备的加工费和原材料价值，以及附属加工厂为本企业承建工程制作的非标准设备的价值。

建筑业增加值 指建筑业企业在报告期内以货币表现的建筑业生产经营活动的最终成果。目前建筑业增加值采用分配法（收入法）计算，即从收入的角度出发，根据生产要素在生产过程中应得的收入份额计算。具体计算公式为：

建筑业增加值＝本年提取的固定资产折旧+应付工资+应付福利费+管理费用中的劳动待业保险金、税金+工程结算税金及附加+工程结算利润

房屋建筑施工面积 指在报告期内施工的全部房屋建筑面积，包括本期新开工的房屋面积、上期施工跨入本期继续施工的房屋面积、上期停缓建在本期恢复施工的房屋面积、本期竣工的房屋面积及本期施工后又停缓建的房屋面积。

房屋建筑竣工面积 指在报告期内房屋建筑按照设计要求全部完工，达到了住人和使用条件，经验收鉴定合格，正式移交使用单位的房屋建筑面积。

营业收入 指企业经营主要业务和其他业务所确认的收入总额。营业收入合计包括“主营业务收入”和“其他业务收入”。根据会计“利润表”中“营业收入”项目的本期总额数填报。

营业利润 指企业从事生产经营活动所取得的利润。执行2006年《企业会计准则》的企业，营业利润为营业收入减去营业成本、营业税金及附加、销售费用、管理费用、财务费用、资产减值损失，再加上公允价值变动收益和损益收益。未执行2006年《企业会计准则》的企业，营业利润为主营业务收入减去主营业务成本、主营业务税金及附加，加上其他业务利润后，再减支销售费用、管理费用、财务费用后的金额。

Explanatory Notes on Main Statistical Indicators

Statistical Unit in Construction refers to corporate enterprise engaged in the construction of buildings, structures and the installation of equipment. A corporate construction enterprise should meet the following requirements: ① being set up in line with relevant legal basis, having its full name, organization and location, and capable of taking civil liabilities; ② independently possessing and using its assets and assuming its liabilities, and entitled to sign contracts with other institutions; ③ making independent accounts of its profits and losses, and capable of compiling its own balance sheet.

Gross Output Value of Construction (i.e. complete construction output value independently) is the sum of construction products produced by construction and installation enterprises embodied with currency within a certain period. It includes:

(1) Output value of construction projects: the value of projects covered by the project budgets;

(2) Value of equipment installation projects: the value of the installation of equipment, (excluding the own value of the equipment to be installed);

(3) Output value of repair of buildings and structures: the value created through the repairs of buildings or structures. It does not include the value of buildings or structures being repaired and the value of the repair of production equipment;

(4) Output value of manufactured non-standard equipment: the value of non-standard production equipment including raw materials and manufacturing cost, made for the construction project. It also includes the output value of equipment manufactured by subsidiary workshops.

Value added of Construction refers to the final result of the activities of production and operation of enterprises of construction industry in monetary terms during the reporting period. Now, the construction value added is calculated in terms of distribution approach (income approach), namely calculation based on earned income of production factors in the production process from the perspective of the income. Specific calculation formula is:

Construction value added= depreciation of fixed assets extracted this year+ wages payable+ welfare payable+ unemployment insurance and taxes in the administration expense + project settlement tax and surcharge + project settlement profits

Floor Space of Buildings under Construction refers to floor space of buildings under construction during the reporting period, including newly started buildings, buildings started earlier and continued during the reporting period, and buildings suspended earlier but restarted during the reporting period, buildings completed during the reporting period, and buildings under construction and then suspended during the reporting period.

Floor Space of Buildings Completed refers to the floor space of buildings that are completed in the reporting period in accordance with the requirements of the design, up to the standard for living in and putting into use, and have been checked and accepted by concerned departments as qualified ones.

Operating Income refers to the total income of main business or other businesses of the enterprise confirmed. Total operating incomes include "main business income" and "other business income" which is filled in pursuant to total amount of "operating income" in the "profit statement" in the current period.

Operating Profit refers to the profit obtained by the enterprise after engaging in production and operation activities. As for enterprises subject to 2006 *Accounting Standards for Business Enterprises*, the operating profit is the result after the operating income minus operating cost, business tax and surcharge, selling expense, administration expense, financial expense and assets impairment loss and then plus income from fair value changes and income from profit and loss. As for enterprises do not subject to 2006 *Accounting Standards for Business Enterprises*, the operating profit is the amount after main business income minus main business cost and tax and extra charges of main business and then plus profit from other business and finally minus selling expense, administration expense and financial expense.

14

运输与邮电

TRANSPORTATION POST AND TELECOMMUNICATIONS

14-1 邮 电 业 务 量

Postal and Telecommunications Services

指　　标	Indicator	单 位 Unit	2013 年	2014 年	2015 年	2016 年	2017 年	2018 年
国内分类业务量	**Domestic Classified Business Volume**							
固定电话数	Number of Fixed Telephone	万户 (10 000 subscribers)	180.05	176.90	165.30	155.90	153.10	135.27
年末市内电话	Urban Fixed Telephone Subscribers at Year-end	万户 (10 000 subscribers)	150.32	150.17	141.00	135.89	132.55	118.70
年末农村电话	Rural Telephone Subscribers at Year-end	万户 (10 000 subscribers)	29.73	26.73	24.30	19.07	19.23	16.47
年末住宅电话	Number of Fixed Telephone Subscribers at Year-end	万户 (10 000 subscribers)	103.57	102.61	86.40	71.79	79.54	67.64
年末移动电话用户	Number of Mobile Telephone Subscribers at Year-end	万户 (10 000 subscribers)	1243.57	1177.87	1090.40	1087.71	971.10	1013.65
4G 电话用户数	4G Mobile Phone Subscribers	万户 (10 000 subscribers)		74.30	306.60	442.10	623.50	725.01
宽带互联网接入用户数	Subscribers of Broad Band Internet	户 (subscriber)	1758710	2027279	2316600	2618800	2987500	3447000
每百人互联网用户数	Number of Internet User per 100 Population	户/百人 (subscriber/100 person)	28.68	32.61	37.02	41.38	46.81	53.05
邮电局所	Post & Telecommunication offices	处(place)	215	216	204	204	207	207
国际及港澳分类业务量	**International,Hong kong and Macao Classified Business Volume**							
函　件	Letters	万件(10 000 pieces)	42.70	115.40	19.49	16.10	27.67	51.95
包　件	Package	万件(10 000 pieces)	1.26	0.92	0.84	1.24	1.35	0.76

14-2 交通运输业基本情况

Basic Conditions of Transportation

指　　标	Indicator	2013 年	2014 年	2015 年	2016 年	2017 年	2018 年
铁路客运量(万人)	Railways Passenger Traffic(10 000 persons)	8483.5	9507.8	10681.1	11923.7	13411.8	14547.7
铁路客运周转量(亿人公里)	Railways Passenger Turnover(100 million passengers-km)	549.9	617.3	662.5	703.8	754.6	784.6
铁路货运量(万吨)	Railways Freight Traffic(10 000 tons)	19045.9	16792.3	15793.8	16749.1	17865.2	18728.0
铁路货运周转量(亿吨公里)	Railways Freight Turnover(100 million ton-km)	1393.5	1238.1	1088.0	1153.0	1254.9	1288.4
公路客运量(万人)	Highways Passenger Traffic(10 000 persons)	3670.0	3729.0	3663.0	3212.0	3192.0	3149.0
公路旅客周转量(亿人公里)	Highways Passenger Turnover(100 million passengers-km)	50.7	51.6	54.2	52.2	52.7	52.9
公路货运量(万吨)	Highways Freight Traffic(10 000 tons)	19050.0	19359.0	20419.0	21212.0	24058.0	25571.0
公路货物周转量(亿吨公里)	Highways Freight Turnover(100 million ton-km)	371.3	392.0	393.8	419.0	459.5	474.0
民航客运量(万人)	Civil Aviation Passenger Traffic (10 000 persons)	452.8	488.1	533.1	645.1	785.6	894.1
民航客运周转量(亿人公里)	Civil Aviation Passenger Turnover(100 million passengers-km)	176.2	195.3	227.7	272.9	334.3	368.5
民航货运量(万吨)	Civil Aviation Freight Turnover(10 000 tons)	3.8	3.9	4.2	5.1	5.0	5.6
公路通车里程(公里)	Length of Highways in Operation						
公路通车里程	Length of Highways in Operation	12697	12846	13104	12730.2	12856.8	12637.7
#高速公路	Expressway	355	419	419	462.2	488.5	488.5
有铺装、简易铺装路面	Poved Road	12422	12602	12906	12603.9	12735.7	12579.4
未铺装路面	UnPoved Road	274	245	198	126.3	121.1	58.3
民用航空	Civil Aviation						
执行航线（条）	Perform Routes	150	103	152	125	150	182
通航城市（个）	Navigable City	59	53	55	64	82	96
起飞架次（架次）	Plane Flights	80746	83551	86158	100152	115529	126828
民用车辆(辆)	Civil Vehicles						
民用汽车	Civil Vehicles	1213611	1382459	1541045	1742313	1949707	2160748
私人汽车	Private Vehicles	1051529	1217636	1505308	1573761	1764574	1948815
载客汽车	Passenger Vehicles	1052540	1224763	1400588	1592737	1783848	1978951
#大型	Large	11205	11966	11194	12206	13539	14002
载货汽车	Trucks	136874	134929	123801	134741	151141	166277
#重型	Heavy	24860	26303	24653	27303	31632	36720
其它汽车	Others	24197	22767	16656	14835	14718	15520
摩托车	Motorcycle	197767	174618	126540	73568	106168	133743
挂车	Wheeler	7299	7398	7497	8191	9102	9851

注：1.公路通车里程自 2006 年起调整统计口径，增加了村道公路统计。

2.因省交通厅公路局统计口径变化，自 2012 年起，公路通车里程按路面类型分为有铺装路面、简易铺装路面和未铺装路面。

3.铁路系统统计数据来自中国铁路济南局集团有限公司。

4.自 2014 年起，交通部门执行新的公路运输量统计方案，调查范围较老口径有所缩小，2013 年及 2014 年数据均为新口径下交通部反馈数据。

Note: 1. The mileage in highway open to traffic was adjusted to be statistical caliber as of 2006, increasing statistics of village road highway.

2. Due to the change in statistical caliber of provincial communications department and highway administration bureau, the mileage in highway open to traffic was divided into dry pavement, easy pavement and unpaved road in light of pavement type as of 2012.

3. Statistical data of railway system comes from China Railway Jinan Group Co., Ltd.

4. Traffic departments started to execute new statistical project of highway transport volume with survey scope decreasing compared to old caliber as of 2014 and the data in 2014 and 2013 is the date reported by traffic departments based on new caliber.

14-3 规模以上交通运输仓储邮政业企业财务指标（2018年）

Main Financial Indicators of Transport,Storage and Postal Services above Designated Size（2018）

单位：万元 (10 000 yuan)

指标	Indicator	交通运输、仓储和邮政业 Transport,Storage and Postal Services
单位数	Number	304
年初存货	Inventory at Beginning of year	136828
流动资产合计	Total Liquid Assets	3048488
其中：应收账款	Receivable	288512
其中：存货	Inventory	135896
固定资产原价	Original Value of Fixed Assets	6247390
本年折旧	Depreciation in the Year	293846
资产总计	Total Assets	13029388
负债合计	Total Liabilities	7537114
所有者权益合计	Total Creditors'Equity	5492274
营业收入	Revenue	4764405
其中：主营业务收入	Revenue from Principal Business	4619685
营业成本	Cost	4003727
其中：主营业务成本	Cost of Principal Business	3982149
税金及附加	Taxes and Other Surcharges	22663
销售费用	Sales Expenses	137367
管理费用	Management Expenses	258842
财务费用	Financial Expenses	103423
投资收益	Investment Interests	172995
营业利润	Profits from Business	533062
营业外收入	Profits from Non-Business	19537
营业外支出	Expense from Non-Business	69846
利润总额	Total Profits	482600
所得税费用	Income Tax Expense	123877
应付职工薪酬（本年贷方累计发生额）	Total Wages Payable	847221
应交增值税	Value-added Tax Payable	73706
从事服务业活动的从业人员平均人数（人）	Average of Empolyed Persons	66431

14-4 分地区公路交通(2018年)

Road Transportation by Region(2018)

指　　标	Indicator	济南市 Ji'nan	市　区 Urban	平阴县 Ping yin	商河县 Shang he
公路通车里程(公里)	Length of Highways in Operation	12637.7	9254.2	904.6	2478.9
#高速公路	Expressway	488.5	420.3	35.5	32.7
有铺装、简易铺装路面	Poved Road	12579.4	9195.9	904.6	2478.9
未铺装路面	UnPoved Road	58.3	58.3	0.0	0.0

主要统计指标解释

公路里程 指在一定时期内实际达到《公路工程技术标准JTJ01-88》规定的等级公路，并经公路主管部门正式验收交付使用的公路里程数。包括大中城市的郊区公路以及通过小城镇街道部分的公路里程和桥梁、渡口的长度，不包括大中城市的街道、厂矿、林区生产用道和农业生产用道的里程。两条或多条公路共同经由同一路段，只计算一次，不得重复计算里程长度。它是反映公路建设发展规模的重要指标，也是计算运输网密度等指标的基础资料。

民用航空航线里程 指民航运输定期班机飞行的航线长度的总和。航线长度按机场之间的距离计算，通常有两种计算方法：一是将每条航线长度相加称为重复计算航线里程；一是将两线或两条以上航线经过同一区段里程，只计算一次航线长度称为不重复计算航线里程。一般常用的是后者，它能确切反映民航运输网的规模，是表明民航事业为国民经济服务和方便人民生活程度的主要指标。

货(客)运量 指在一定时期内，各种运输工具实际运送的货物(旅客)数量。它是反映运输业为国民经济和人民生活服务的数量指标，也是制定和检查运输生产计划、研究运输发展规模和速度的重要指标。货运按吨计算，客运按人计算。货物不论运输距离长短、货物类别，均按实际重量统计。旅客不论行程远近或票价多少，均按一人一次客运量统计；半价票、小孩票也按一人统计。

货物(旅客)周转量 指在一定时期内，由各种运输工具运送的货物(旅客)数量与其相应运输距离的乘积之总和。它是反映运输业生产总成果的重要指标，也是编制和检查运输生产计划，计算运输效率、劳动生产率以及核算运输单位成本的主要基础资料。计算货物周转量通常按发出站与到达站之间的最短距离，也就是计费距离计算。计算公式为：

货物(旅客)周转量=Σ(货物(旅客)运输量×运输距离)

移动电话用户 指在移动电话营业部门登记，通过移动电话交换机进入移动电话网、占有移动电话号码的电话用户。用户数量以实际办理登记手续进入邮电部门移动电话网的户数进行计算，一部或一台移动电话统计为一户。

电话用户 指接入国家公众固定电话网，并按固定电话业务进行经营管理的电话用户。1997年以前，电话用户分为市内电话用户和农村电话用户。市内电话用户是指接入县城及县以上城市电话网上的电话用户；农村电话用户是指接入县邮电局农话台及县以下农村电话交换点，以县城为中心(除市话用户外)联通县、乡(镇)、行政村、村民小组的用户。从1997年起，电话用户数分组调整为以用户所在区域划分为“城市电话用户”和“乡村电话用户”，与过去的按市内电话和农村电话划分方法不同。而电话用户数、电话机部数统计方法不变。

Explanatory Notes on Main Statistical Indicators

Length of Highways refers to the length of highways which are built in conformity with the grades specified in the *Technical Standard JTJ01–88 for Highway Engineering* within a certain period of time, and have been formally checked and accepted by the departments of highways and put into use. The length of highways includes that of the suburb highways at large and medium sized cities, highways passing through streets at small cities and towns, and also the length of bridges and ferries. It does not include the length of streets in big and medium sized cities and highways built for the production purpose at factories, mines, forest areas and agricultural areas. If two or more highways go to the same section of the way, the length of the section is only calculated for once and no duplication is allowed. The length of highways is an important indicator to show the development of the highway construction and to provide essential information to calculate the transport network density.

Mileage of Civil Aviation Routes refers to the sum of the length of the route of scheduled civil aviation flight. The length of the route is calculated as the distance between airports. There are usually two calculation methods: First, repeated calculation of route mileage is deemed in case of adding the length of each route; Second, no repeated calculation of route mileage is deemed if the length of the route is only calculated once when no less than two routes pass the same zone. The second one is usually used, as it can precisely show the size of the civil aviation network and also is the major indicator of indicating the extent of civil aviation serving the national economy and the people.

Freight (Passenger) Traffic refers to the volume or freight (passenger) transported with various means in a certain period. It provides a quantitative measure to show how the transportation industry serves the national economy and people, and is also an important indicator for planning the transport industry and for studying the development scale and speed of the transport industry. Freight transport is calculated in tons and passenger traffic is calculated in the number of persons. Despite the type of freight and traveling distance, the freight transport is calculated in the actual weight of the goods. And despite the traveling distance and ticket price, the passenger traffic is calculated by the principle that one person can be counted only once in one travel. The passengers who travel with a half–price ticket or a child ticket is also calculated as one person.

Tonnage Mileage (Passenger turnover) refers to the sum of the products of the volume of transported cargos (passengers) multiplying by the transport distance. It is an important indicator to reflect the achievement of transportation industry, to prepare and examine the transport plan and to measure the efficiency, the labor productivity and the unit cost of transport. Normally, the shortest distance between the departure station and the destination station (i.e., the payable distance) is the basis to calculate the Tonnage mileage. The formula is as follows:

Tonnage mileage (passenger turnover) = Σ(freight (passenger) traffic* distance of transportation)

Wireless Subscribers refer to persons who have registered at the mobile phone business department and hence connected with the mobile telephone communication network through the mobile telephone switchboards and occupy mobile telephone numbers. The number of subscribers is calculated in line with the number of users actually handling the registration procedures and entering the mobile telephone network of the post and telecommunications departments. One mobile telephone is deemed as one household.

Telephone Subscribers refer to telephone subscribers entering the national public fixed telephone network and undergoing operating management based on fixed telephone services. Before 1997, telephone subscribers were divided into local telephone subscribers and rural telephone subscribers. Local telephone subscribers refer to telephone subscribers accessing to the urban telephone network of county and above; Rural telephone subscribers refer to telephone subscribers accessing to the agricultural telephone station of the county post and telecommunications office and the rural telephone exchange of those below country, and connecting with county, township (town), administrative village and group of villagers based on the county as the center (except for city telephone users). From 1997, grouping of telephone users is adjusted to "city telephone subscribers" and "rural telephone subscribers" in light of regions where subscribers are, which is different from partition method -- local call and rural call in the past. The statistical approaches for counting telephone subscribers and telephones numbers remain unchanged.

15

国 内 贸 易

DOMESTIC TRADE

15 - 1 各时期分行业社会消费品零售

Total Retail Sales of Consumer Goods by Section in Each Period

单位：万元 (10 000 yuan)

年份 Year	社会消费品零售总额 Retail Sale of Consumer Goods						
	总计 Total	批发零售业 Wholesale and Retail Trades	住宿业 Hotels Services	餐饮业 Catering Services	制造业 Manufacture	其 他 Others	农民对非农业居民 Farmers to Non-agricultural Residents
1949	11426	7312		556	3514	–	44
1952	22248	16985		1223	3592	–	448
1957	34568	29279		1935	2381	3	970
1962	41436	35784		1655	2946	266	785
1965	40795	36470		1829	1856	287	353
1970	42993	39397		1537	1468	321	270
1975	60105	53239		2565	2914	1217	170
1978	81335	70661		2907	5120	2222	425
1979	96036	80703		4000	9060	823	1450
1980	119775	95121		4392	16489	1299	2474
“六五时期”							
1981	135236	103303		5388	21353	2157	3035
1982	152094	116241		8165	21398	2778	3512
1983	167948	127884		9225	23569	2953	4317
1984	200301	150233		11342	29563	4506	4657
1985	243080	181867		14823	32342	5535	8513
“七五时期”							
1986	294102	219730		17880	35565	5456	15471
1987	331504	240192		20305	45386	8963	16658
1988	425984	300090		30808	60463	12300	22323
1989	484392	343978		28634	71653	9729	30398
1990	528221	382047		25599	71505	10886	38184
“八五时期”							
1991	597989	424836		27443	78452	14186	53072
1992	732882	535080		37096	77951	21108	61647
1993	1013726	723914		56059	80101	28475	125177

年份 Year	社会消费品零售总额 Retail Sale of Consumer Goods						
	总计 Total	批发零售业 Wholesale and Retail Trades	住宿业 Hotels Services	餐饮业 Catering Services	制造业 Manufacture	其 他 Others	农民对非农业居民 Farmers to Non-agricultural Residents
1994	1454386	1037687		86141	99621	27914	203023
1995	1880151	1345321		133501	115105	42533	243691
"九五时期"							
1996	2256851	1570947		176100	141201	22261	346342
1997	2618976	1744014		216727	177219	50392	430624
1998	2911018	1893486		255616	207595	76994	477327
1999	3175983	2043078		305333	225132	83892	518548
2000	3547062	2287545		377550	233128	102535	546304
"十五时期"							
2001	3975320	2574216		485494	237545	118179	559886
2002	4464927	2935804		613178	231947	143702	540296
2003	5371750	4373831		741565	–	256354	–
2004	6984935	5691288	57973	940191	–	295483	–
2005	8078776	6575543	66490	1084425	–	352318	–
"十一五时期"							
2006	9393436	7571831	78098	1324135	–	419372	–
2007	11031462	8791908	86322	1648409	–	504823	–
2008	13566824	10684195	96391	2142271	–	643968	–
2009	15956509	12710608	105378	2438279	–	702244	–
2010	18024610	14022650	150810	3081114	–	770036	–
"十二五时期"							
2011	21142868	16338362	175067	3717616	–	911823	–
2012	24202475	18740304	187466	4308195	–	966510	–
2013	27433506	22006709	177160	4154845	–	1094792	–
2014	30876494	26004226	196307	4675960	–	–	–
2015	34103088	28754816	210316	5137956	–	–	–
"十三五时期"							
2016	37647762	31752379	230502	5664881	–	–	–
2017	41461481	34978973	252921	6229587	–	–	–
2018	44044641	37165791	267447	6611403	–	–	–

15-2 限额以上批发零售业法人企业商品销售情况（2018年）

Total Purchase Sales and Inventory by Sector Above Designated Size（2018）

单位：万元 (10 000 yuan)

指标	Indicator	商品销售总额 Total Sale Value		
		合计 Total	批发 Wholesalel	零售 Retail
总计	Total	39106320.0	26406905.8	12699414.2
一、批发业	Wholesalel Trade	28069712.5	25842322.2	2227390.3
农、林、牧产品批发	Wholesale of Farm Produce and Livestock Products	189258.1	188928.6	329.5
谷物、豆及薯类批发	Wholesale of Grain,Beans and Tubers	41877.0	41797.0	80.0
种子批发	Wholesale of Seed	42381.0	42168.3	212.7
饲料批发	Wholesale of Fodder	50636.7	50636.7	0.0
棉、麻批发	Wholesale of Cotton and Linen	39002.5	39002.5	0.0
林业产品批发	Wholesale of Forestery Products	0.0	0.0	0.0
牲畜批发	Wholesale of Livestocks	5795.0	5795.0	0.0
其他农牧产品批发	Wholesale of Other Agricultural Products	9565.9	9529.1	36.8
食品、饮料及烟草制品批发	Wholesale of Food, Beverages and Tobaccos	2942969.9	2885200.1	57769.8
米、面制品及食用油批发	Wholesale of Rice,Noodles and Oil	1513216.4	1492009.5	21206.9
糕点、糖果及糖批发	Wholesale of Cake,Candyand Sugar	30832.1	30832.1	0.0
果品、蔬菜批发	Wholesale of Fruits and Vegetables	38168.5	38145.3	23.2
肉、禽、蛋、奶及水产品批发	Wholesale of Meat,Poultry,Egg,Mik and Aquatic Products	114167.5	111165.3	3002.2
盐及调味品批发	Wholesale of Salt and Spices	52518.1	51904.8	613.3
营养和保健品批发	Wholesale of nutrition and health products	93219.9	88573.9	4646.0
酒、饮料及茶叶批发	Wholesale of Wine,Drink and Tea	148276.5	130168.2	18108.3
烟草制品批发	Wholesale of Tobacco Products	841263.2	841263.2	0.0
其他食品批发	Wholesale of Other Food	111307.7	101137.8	10169.9
纺织、服装及家庭用品批发	Wholesale of Textiles, Garments and Daily Consumer Articles	2173122.0	2066854.8	106267.2
纺织品、针织品及原料批发	Wholesale of Textiles, Garments and Row Material	51954.8	51854.8	100.0
服装批发	Wholesale of Garments	155874.4	145779.3	10095.1
鞋帽批发	Wholesale of Shoes and Hats	31047.0	30032.0	1015.0
化妆品及卫生用品批发	Wholesale of Cosmetic and Hygiene Products	66386.0	58832.2	7553.8
厨房、卫生间用具及日用杂货批发	Wholesale of Kitchen,Bathroom Equipment and Groceries	17166.9	12016.8	5150.1
灯具、装饰物品批发	Wholesale of Lamps and Decorative Items	11392.3	11168.5	223.8
家用视听设备批发	Wholesale of household aquipments	17827.4	17827.4	0.0
日用家电批发	Wholesale of household appliances	1817297.4	1735168.0	82129.4
其他家庭用品批发	Wholesale of Other Household Articles	4175.8	4175.8	0.0
文化、体育用品及器材批发	Wholesale of Culture, Sports Appliances and Equipments	1942333.2	1271126.3	671206.9
文具用品批发	Wholesale of Culture Products	125131.1	124648.1	483.0
体育用品及器材批发	Wholesale of Sports Appliances and Equipments	2749.4	2749.4	0.0
图书批发	Wholesale of Books	1228207.3	558174.0	670033.3
音像制品及电子出版物批发	Wholesale of Audiovisual Products and Electronic Publications	4515.2	4515.2	0.0

指　　标	Indicator	商品销售总额 Total Sale Value		
		合　计 Total	批 发 Wholesalel	零售 Retail
首饰、工艺品及收藏品批发	Wholesale of Jewelry,Crafts and Collectibles	578953.3	578437.1	516.2
其他文化用品批发	Wholesale of Other Culture Products	2776.9	2602.5	174.4
医药及医疗器材批发	Wholesale of Medicines and Medical Appliances	4822223.4	4799257.0	22966.4
西药批发	Wholesale of Western Medicine	1609341.8	1607954.9	1386.9
中药批发	Wholesale of Traditional Chinese Medicine	2253955.5	2249743.4	4212.1
动物用药品批发	Wholesale of veterinary drugs	39488.7	39488.7	0.0
医疗用品及器材批发	Wholesale of Medicines Products and Medical Appliances	919437.4	902070.0	17367.4
矿产品、建材及化工产品批发	Wholesale of Mineral Products, Building Materials and Chemical Products	10959717.1	9843221.0	1116496.1
煤炭及制品批发	Wholesale of Coal and Its Products	1873381.5	1866587.0	6794.5
石油及制品批发	Wholesale of Petroleum and Its Products	3931293.4	2858922.2	1072371.2
非金属矿及制品批发	Wholesale of Non-metal Mine and Its Products	70057.9	70057.9	0.0
金属及金属矿批发	Wholesale of Metal and Metal Mine	3511643.2	3492871.1	18772.1
建材批发	Wholesale of Construction Materials	491855.0	479720.4	12134.6
化肥批发	Wholesale of Chemical Fertilizer	15553.7	13819.6	1734.1
农药批发	Wholesale of Pesticide	304620.7	304620.7	0.0
其他化工产品批发	Wholesale of Other　Chemical Products	761311.7	756622.1	4689.6
机械设备、五金产品及电子产品批发	Wholesale of Machinery, Hardware and Electronic Equipment	4412718.2	4167145.6	245572.6
农业机械批发	Wholesale of Agricultural Machinery	19359.7	7984.2	11375.5
汽车及零配件批发	Wholesale of Automobile and Spare Parts	1727834.4	1702403.5	25430.9
摩托车及零配件批发	Wholesale of Motorbike and Spare Parts	26034.8	25745.8	289.0
五金产品批发	Wholesale of Hardware	148200.4	131759.9	16440.5
电气设备批发	Wholesale of Electronic Equipment	709334.4	704713.4	4621.0
计算机、软件及辅助设备批发	Wholesale of Computer,Software and Auxiliary Equipment	348124.9	289986.2	58138.7
通讯设备批发	Wholesale of Communication Equipment	193749.9	188091.2	5658.7
广播影视设备批发	Wholesale of Broadcast Television Equipment	34164.0	34164.0	0.0
其他机械设备及电子产品批发	Wholesale of Other Machinery and Electronic Equipment	1205915.7	1082297.4	123618.3
贸易经纪与代理	Trade Broker and Agency	45247.7	45247.7	0.0
贸易代理	Trade Agency	45247.7	45247.7	0.0
其他批发业	Other Wholesale not Classified Elsewhere	582122.9	575341.1	6781.8
再生物资回收与批发	Renewable Resources Recycle and Wholesale	16716.6	14941.5	1775.1
互联网批发	Internet wholesale	0.0	0.0	0.0
其他未列明批发业	Other Wholesale	565406.3	560399.6	5006.7
内资企业	Domestic Funded Enterprises	25767681.6	23540532.5	2227149.1
国有企业	State-owned	93799.8	90303.9	3495.9
集体企业	Collective-owned	8914.2	8282.6	631.6

指　　标	Indicator	商品销售总额 Total Sale Value		
		合　计 Total	批 发 Wholesalel	零售 Retail
有限责任公司	Limited Liability Corporations	13830791.0	12339522.3	1491268.7
国有独资公司	State Sole funded Corporations	3123542.5	3121347.4	2195.1
其他有限责任公司	Other Limited Liability Corporations	10707248.5	9218174.9	1489073.6
股份有限公司	Share-holding Corporations Limited	1070212.6	763937.1	306275.5
私营企业	Private Enterprises	10763964.0	10338486.6	425477.4
私营独资企业	Private-funded Enterprises	24440.5	24440.5	0.0
私营有限责任公司	Private Limited Liability Corporations	10588138.1	10172005.6	416132.5
私营股份有限公司	Private Share-holding Corporations Ltd	151385.4	142040.5	9344.9
其他企业	Others	0.0	0.0	0.0
港、澳、台商投资企业	Hong Kong,Macao and Taiwan investment enterprises	2086384.5	2086143.3	241.2
与港澳台商合资经营企业	Enterprises with Funds from Hong Kong,Macao and Taiwan	0.0	0.0	0.0
港澳台商独资企业	Sole Investment	2086384.5	2086143.3	241.2
外商投资企业	Foreign Funded Enterprises	215646.4	215646.4	0.0
中外合资经营企业	Joint-venture	152530.2	152530.2	0.0
中外合作经营企业	Cooperative	22911.5	22911.5	0.0
外资企业	Sole Foreign Investment	40204.7	40204.7	0.0
二、零售业	**Retail Trade**	11036607.5	564583.6	10472023.9
综合零售	Integrated Retail	2627008.4	54997.1	2572011.3
百货零售	Commodity Retail	2147850.2	1432.2	2146418.0
超级市场零售	Supermarket Retail	424581.8	36943.6	387638.2
便利店零售	Convenience Store Retail	4089.3	0.0	4089.3
其他综合零售	Other Retail	50487.1	16621.3	33865.8
食品、饮料及烟草制品专门零售	Retail of Food, Beverages and Tobaccos	439006.5	46206.3	392800.2
粮油零售	Retail of Grain and Oil	29610.2	823.3	28786.9
糕点、面包零售	Retail of Cake and Bread	10785.4	0.0	10785.4
果品、蔬菜零售	Retail of Fruits and Vegetables	39326.4	2420.0	36906.4
肉、禽、蛋、奶及水产品零售	Retail of Meat,Poultry,Egg,Mik and Aquatic Products	172395.8	21484.1	150911.7
营养和保健品零售	Retail of Nutrition and Health Care Products	35308.3	1240.6	34067.7
酒、饮料及茶叶零售	Retail of Wine,Drink and Tea	68004.4	4775.1	63229.3
烟草制品零售	Retail of Tobacco Products	14749.8	0.0	14749.8
其他食品零售	Retail of Other Food	68826.2	15463.2	53363.0
纺织、服装及日用品专门零售	Special Retail of Textiles, Garments and Daily Consumer Articles	399105.1	43298.6	355806.5
纺织品及针织品零售	Retail of Textiles, Garments and Row Material	6665.6	22.6	6643.0
服装零售	Retail of Garments	276028.3	29342.4	246685.9
鞋帽零售	Retail of Shoes and Hats	6289.7	555.5	5734.2
化妆品及卫生用品零售	Retail of Cosmetic and Hygiene Products	50233.3	9015.2	41218.1
厨具卫具及日用杂品零售	Retail of Kitchen,Bathroom Equipment and Groceries	5920.6	1547.7	4372.9

15-2 续 3

指　　标	Indicator	商品销售总额 Total Sale Value		
		合　计 Total	批 发 Wholesalel	零售 Retail
钟表、眼镜零售	Retail of Clock and Glasses	23171.4	0.0	23171.4
箱包零售	Retail of bags and suitcases	0.0	0.0	0.0
自行车等代步设备零售	Retail of bicycle and other equipments	891.3	891.3	0.0
其他日用品零售	Retail of Household Appliances	29904.9	1923.9	27981.0
文化、体育用品及器材专门零售	Retail of Culture, Sports Appliances and Equipments	325607.0	41975.2	283631.8
文具用品零售	Retail of Culture Products	16107.1	9732.9	6374.2
体育用品及器材零售	Retail of Sports Appliances and Equipments	1409.9	0.0	1409.9
图书、报刊零售	Retail of Books,Magazines and Newspapers	69179.5	3759.7	65419.8
音像制品、电子和数字出版物零售	Retail of audiovisual products,electronic and digital publications	19343.5	2321.3	17022.2
珠宝首饰零售	Retail of Jewelry	137707.8	8823.3	128884.5
工艺美术品及收藏品零售	Retail of Crafts and Collectibles	5493.8	2322.5	3171.3
乐器零售	Retail of Music Instruments	2764.8	0.0	2764.8
照相器材零售	Retail of Photographic Apparatus	15381.1	0.0	15381.1
其他文化用品零售	Retail of Other Culture Products	58219.5	15015.5	43204.0
医药及医疗器材专门零售	Retail of Medicines and Medical Appliances	495559.1	12174.3	483384.8
西药零售	Retail of Western Medicine	435466.2	6218.1	429248.1
中药零售	Retail of Traditional Chinese Medicine	6088.5	0.0	6088.5
动物用药品零售	Retail of veterinary drugs	5936.2	4511.5	1424.7
医疗用品及器材零售	Retail of Medical Appliances	48068.2	1444.7	46623.5
汽车、摩托车、零配件和燃料及其他动力销售	Cars,motorcycles,spare part and fuel and other power sales	4919865.8	187246.8	4732619.0
汽车新车零售	Retail of new cars	3964608.4	102112.5	3862495.9
汽车旧车零售	Retail of used cars	3081.9	0.0	3081.9
汽车零配件零售	Retail of Automobile Spare Parts	62074.6	2658.1	59416.5
摩托车及零配件零售	Retail of Motorbike and Its Spare Parts	23125.6	0.0	23125.6
机动车燃油零售	Retail of motor fuel oil	842064.8	78870.4	763194.4
机动车燃气零售	Retail of motor gas	24910.5	3605.8	21304.7
家用电器及电子产品专门零售	Special Retail of Household Electric Appliances and Electronic Products	1123249.6	29004.4	1094245.2
家用视听设备零售	Retail of Household Electric Appliances	782908.2	301.1	782607.1
日用家电设备零售	Retail of Daily Household Equipment	73301.0	12175.5	61125.5
计算机、软件及辅助设备零售	Retail of Computer,Software and Auxiliary Equipment	117347.5	8254.3	109093.2
通信设备零售	Retail of Communication　Equipment	108681.8	6495.7	102186.1
其他电子产品零售	Retail of Other Electronic Equipment	41011.1	1777.8	39233.3
五金、家具及室内装饰材料专门零售	Special Retail of Hardware, Furniture and Decoration Materials	128091.0	10905.4	117185.6
五金零售	Retail of Hardware	33911.7	10905.4	23006.3
灯具零售	Retail of lamps	695.6	0.0	695.6

指　　标	Indicator	商品销售总额 Total Sale Value		
		合　计 Total	批 发 Wholesalel	零售 Retail
家具零售	Retail of Furniture	78137.3	0.0	78137.3
涂料零售	Retail of Coating	0.0	0.0	0.0
木质装饰材料零售	Retail of Wood Decorative Material	2014.4	0.0	2014.4
陶瓷、石材装饰材料零售	Retail of Ceramics and Stone Decorative Material	13332.0	0.0	13332.0
其他室内装饰材料零售	Retail of Other Decoration Materials	0.0	0.0	0.0
货摊、无店铺及其他零售业	Non-shop and Other Retails	579115.0	138775.5	440339.5
流动货摊零售	Retail of mobile stalls	0.0	0.0	0.0
互联网零售	Internet Retail	478959.3	115421.3	363538.0
邮购及电视、电话零售	Mail,Television and Telephone Retail	56465.4	16640.4	39825.0
自动售货机零售	Retail of vending machine	0.0	0.0	0.0
生活用燃料零售	Retail of Domestic Fuel	11277.9	0.0	11277.9
其他未列明零售业	Other Retails	32412.4	6713.8	25698.6
内资企业	**Domestic Funded Enterprises**	10130692.5	526664.5	9604028.0
国有企业	State-owned	9152.2	0.0	9152.2
集体企业	Collective-owned	15074.2	0.0	15074.2
股份合作企业	Cooperative	4676.1	0.0	4676.1
联营企业	Joint venture	0.0	0.0	0.0
国有与集体联营企业	State-owned enterprises and collective enterprises	0.0	0.0	0.0
有限责任公司	Limited Liability Corporations	3200955.3	211271.2	2989684.1
国有独资公司	State Sole funded Corporations	39072.0	0.0	39072.0
其他有限责任公司	Other Limited Liability Corporations	3161883.3	211271.2	2950612.1
股份有限公司	Share-holding Corporations Limited	2835567.4	79277.7	2756289.7
私营企业	Private Enterprises	4037920.6	233695.6	3804225.0
私营独资企业	Private-funded Enterprises	11038.7	775.9	10262.8
私营有限责任公司	Private Limited Liability Corporations	3937591.3	230222.4	3707368.9
私营股份有限公司	Private Share-holding Corporations Ltd.	89290.6	2697.3	86593.3
其他企业	Other Enterprises	27346.7	2420.0	24926.7
港、澳、台商投资企业	**Enterprises with Funds from Hong Kong, Macao and Taiwan**	405024.8	36943.6	368081.2
与港澳台商合资经营企业	Joint-ventures Enterprises	80517.1	0.0	80517.1
港澳台商独资企业	Enterprises with Sole Investment	324507.7	36943.6	287564.1
外商投资企业	**Foreign Funded Enterprises**	500890.2	975.5	499914.7
中外合资经营企业	Joint-venture Enterprises	103669.8	0.0	103669.8
中外合作经营企业	Cooperation Enterprises	78321.4	0.0	78321.4
外资企业	Enterprises with Sole Foreign Funds	106343.4	0.0	106343.4
外商投资股份有限公司	Share-holding Corporations Ltd. With Foreign Investment	212555.6	975.5	211580.1

15-3 限额以上批发零售

Capital Power of Wholesales and Retail

单位：万元

指标名称	Indicator	法人企业数（个）Number of Corporation Enterprises (unit)	流动资产合计 Total Working Capitals	存货 Inventory	固定资产原价 Original Value of Fixed Assets	累计折旧 Depreciation
总计	Total	1553	21457532.9	2998611.4	2089676.9	826159.0
一、批发业	Wholesalel Trade	851	15665141.6	2133652.6	1121665.9	421836.6
农、林、牧产品批发	Wholesale of Farm Produce and Livestock Products	23	92385.8	52723.1	36691.7	10491.9
谷物、豆及薯类批发	Wholesale of Grain,Beans and Tubers	4	38071.6	27498.7	17418.3	4089.7
种子批发	Wholesale of Seed	7	26233.0	14503.2	12107.4	3870.3
饲料批发	Wholesale of Fodder	4	7094.8	2198.3	143.8	90.9
棉、麻批发	Wholesale of Cotton and Linen	3	11288.3	5018.4	143.0	134.8
林业产品批发	Wholesale of Forestery Products	0	0.0	0.0	0.0	0.0
牲畜批发	Wholesale of Livestocks	1	1910.5	14.7	164.3	99.6
其他农牧产品批发	Wholesale of Other Agricultural Products	4	7787.6	3489.8	6714.9	2206.6
食品、饮料及烟草制品批发	Wholesale of Food, Beverages and Tobaccos	68	1250361.4	379050.9	236436.0	80390.5
米、面制品及食用油批发	Wholesale of Rice,Noodles and Oil	11	731193.6	289891.4	62662.3	22962.2
糕点、糖果及糖批发	Wholesale of Cake,Candyand Sugar	1	3000.7	1054.5	77.6	53.2
果品、蔬菜批发	Wholesale of Fruits and Vegetables	10	8769.7	513.2	882.0	566.1
肉、禽、蛋、奶及水产品批发	Wholesale of Meat,Poultry,Egg,Mik and Aquatic Products	10	46672.7	17826.9	64686.9	17551.8
盐及调味品批发	Wholesale of Salt and Spices	6	23858.8	2443.7	5906.1	2996.0
营养和保健品批发	Wholesale of nutrition and health products	7	68887.6	12780.4	19804.3	4720.0
酒、饮料及茶叶批发	Wholesale of Wine,Drink and Tea	11	63948.8	18565.4	1802.5	1491.0
烟草制品批发	Wholesale of Tobacco Products	3	248988.0	31415.5	54079.3	22451.3
其他食品批发	Wholesale of Other Food	9	55041.5	4559.9	26535.0	7598.9
纺织、服装及家庭用品批发	Wholesale of Textiles, Garments and Daily Consumer Articles	58	1098992.7	387361.1	71702.7	18631.4
纺织品、针织品及原料批发	Wholesale of Textiles, Garments and Row Material	4	2887.0	1376.7	535.9	315.6
服装批发	Wholesale of Garments	13	53599.3	29861.8	2053.6	1677.9
鞋帽批发	Wholesale of Shoes and Hats	6	15677.4	7121.6	382.4	315.5
化妆品及卫生用品批发	Wholesale of Cosmetic and Hygiene Products	10	40839.9	15380.9	739.3	438.3
厨房、卫生间用具及日用杂货批发	Wholesale of Kitchen,Bathroom Equipment and Groceries	1	10596.0	2236.3	339.6	175.3
灯具、装饰物品批发	Wholesale of Lamps and Decorative Items	4	3377.3	953.1	133.3	113.0
家用视听设备批发	Wholesale of household aquipments	3	4744.0	2293.5	42.4	36.4
日用家电批发	Wholesale of household appliances	16	963609.4	327047.8	66228.8	14436.4
其他家庭用品批发	Wholesale of Other Household Articles	1	3662.4	1089.4	1247.4	1123.0
文化、体育用品及器材批发	Wholesale of Culture, Sports Appliances and Equipments	24	922901.3	233938.2	240861.8	90610.6
文具用品批发	Wholesale of Culture Products	11	30365.7	4729.5	2914.4	1374.5

贸易企业资产实力（2018年）

Sales Trade Above Designated Size（2018）

(10 000 yuan)

本年折旧 Depreciation in the Year	资产总计 Total Assets	负债合计 Total Liabilities	所有者权益合计 totalCreditors' Equity	实收资本 Paid-up Capital				
					国家资本 Official Capital	集体资本 Collective Capital	法人资本 Corporate Capital	个人资本 Personal Capital
147024.4	25499073.7	18638493.1	7067197.7	4493525.1	1285499.6	50268.2	2194161.7	760954.5
75207.5	18179358.8	12882648.3	5502948.6	2507412.8	1223875.2	37909.3	648097.5	491425.5
1720.7	131116.9	76510.5	54606.4	27928.0	7453.2	226.4	2499.9	17748.5
439.0	54947.9	37949.5	16998.4	1869.5	1768.0	0.0	1.5	100.0
974.9	43135.2	18591.3	24543.9	19456.1	5098.7	226.4	296.0	13835.0
27.9	7151.7	3586.8	3564.9	2402.4	0.0	0.0	1322.4	1080.0
15.4	11296.5	9743.9	1552.6	1200.0	0.0	0.0	200.0	1000.0
0.0	0.0	0.0	0.0	0.0	0.0	0.0	0.0	0.0
18.6	1975.2	1330.4	644.8	500.0	0.0	0.0	0.0	500.0
244.9	12610.4	5308.6	7301.8	2500.0	586.5	0.0	680.0	1233.5
22526.1	1576266.6	1068378.6	507888.0	156951.3	8174.8	1524.1	136189.5	10757.0
3207.5	796063.2	727039.1	69024.1	11863.4	1961.5	1180.0	4816.0	3600.0
4.3	3026.0	3973.3	−947.3	2000.0	0.0	0.0	1700.0	300.0
91.6	9751.3	8227.5	1523.8	1684.1	0.0	44.1	540.0	1100.0
5066.4	181604.9	41939.6	139665.3	89073.2	2163.2	0.0	86275.0	635.0
2758.0	30438.0	19232.9	11205.1	3161.2	2631.2	0.0	227.0	303.0
1046.7	119904.9	119044.4	860.5	2599.0	0.0	0.0	1298.0	1301.0
585.0	64549.6	51617.1	12932.5	11603.0	0.0	300.0	8000.0	3303.0
2416.5	296505.5	58352.3	238153.2	14218.9	1418.9	0.0	12800.0	0.0
7350.1	74423.2	38952.4	35470.8	20748.5	0.0	0.0	20533.5	215.0
5472.0	1270760.4	1159859.7	110900.7	32181.3	500.0	10700.0	11204.9	9776.4
62.5	3424.6	1167.3	2257.3	1160.0	0.0	0.0	160.0	1000.0
224.2	55975.5	60935.5	−4960.0	2593.0	0.0	0.0	1419.0	1174.0
23.2	15979.2	15428.0	551.2	567.0	0.0	0.0	90.6	476.4
82.0	42296.6	31243.2	11053.4	5461.2	0.0	0.0	4471.2	990.0
23.4	10760.3	10603.1	157.2	300.0	0.0	0.0	300.0	0.0
3.4	3405.6	1268.8	2136.8	1708.0	0.0	0.0	300.0	1408.0
4.6	5148.7	4612.4	536.3	555.0	0.0	0.0	245.0	310.0
3925.7	1129908.8	1032254.4	97654.4	19706.1	500.0	10700.0	4219.1	4287.0
1123.0	3861.1	2347.0	1514.1	131.0	0.0	0.0	0.0	131.0
10103.7	1379047.1	927000.9	452046.2	88071.6	56000.0	0.0	11636.3	20435.3
374.1	32998.0	28196.2	4801.8	5279.0	0.0	0.0	825.5	4453.5

指标名称	Indicator	法人企业数（个）Number of Corporation Enterprises (unit)	流动资产合计 Total Working Capitals	存货 Inventory	固定资产原价 Original Value of Fixed Assets	累计折旧 Depreciation
体育用品及器材批发	Wholesale of Sports Appliances and Equipments	1	768.9	30.6	42.4	26.1
图书批发	Wholesale of Books	6	867188.5	228369.9	237211.3	88785.3
音像制品及电子出版物批发	Wholesale of Audiovisual Products and Electronic Publications	1	3878.4	199.0	187.6	74.2
首饰、工艺品及收藏品批发	Wholesale of Jewelry,Crafts and Collectibles	3	20425.0	543.7	397.8	317.5
其他文化用品批发	Wholesale of Other Culture Products	2	274.8	65.5	108.3	33.0
医药及医疗器材批发	Wholesale of Medicines and Medical Appliances	138	2722697.0	391359.8	189483.9	62899.3
西药批发	Wholesale of Western Medicine	47	925468.0	170593.5	61369.4	26837.0
中药批发	Wholesale of Traditional Chinese Medicine	20	1227271.6	155301.1	97952.9	20022.7
动物用药品批发	Wholesale of veterinary drugs	5	14152.0	3344.4	566.9	358.1
医疗用品及器材批发	Wholesale of Medicines Products and Medical Appliances	66	555805.4	62120.8	29594.7	15681.5
矿产品、建材及化工产品批发	Wholesale of Mineral Products, Building Materials and Chemical Products	330	7230578.4	304640.3	255875.4	124295.7
煤炭及制品批发	Wholesale of Coal and Its Products	45	613376.4	49131.4	17458.6	7027.9
石油及制品批发	Wholesale of Petroleum and Its Products	33	4648502.0	58372.6	159204.5	80033.9
非金属矿及制品批发	Wholesale of Non-metal Mine and Its Products	3	25791.5	2378.0	80.7	38.3
金属及金属矿批发	Wholesale of Metal and Metal Mine	149	1177148.8	145244.9	37012.6	17796.2
建材批发	Wholesale of Construction Materials	32	273946.2	19698.3	13235.7	4195.4
化肥批发	Wholesale of Chemical Fertilizer	6	143955.3	7233.6	12745.6	7012.8
农药批发	Wholesale of Pesticide	12	146966.8	7410.7	6806.3	3154.8
其他化工产品批发	Wholesale of Other Chemical Products	50	200891.4	15170.8	9331.4	5036.4
机械设备、五金产品及电子产品批发	Wholesale of Machinery, Hardware and Electronic Equipment	191	2119591.8	331242.6	70762.8	29525.8
农业机械批发	Wholesale of Agricultural Machinery	7	10199.5	4014.2	837.4	657.2
汽车及零配件批发	Wholesale of Automobile and Spare Parts	52	884872.2	178568.8	6897.9	3477.8
摩托车及零配件批发	Wholesale of Motorbike and Its Spare Parts	4	5912.7	3749.0	296.2	197.1
五金产品批发	Wholesale of Hardware	16	74916.6	7447.3	5609.6	2626.1
电气设备批发	Wholesale of Electronic Equipment	18	489775.0	7825.1	7051.2	3613.5
计算机、软件及辅助设备批发	Wholesale of Computer,Software and Auxiliary Equipment	26	96504.2	20911.2	6110.9	1781.1
通讯设备批发	Wholesale of Communication Equipment	13	34914.2	8723.1	1136.9	736.0
广播影视设备批发	Wholesale of Broadcast Television Equipment	1	64019.8	12.0	6053.3	1855.9
其他机械设备及电子产品批发	Wholesale of Other Machinery and Electronic Equipment	54	458477.6	99991.9	36769.4	14581.1
贸易经纪与代理	Trade Broker and Agency	1	6953.0	1867.1	93.2	88.5
贸易代理	Trade Agency	1	6953.0	1867.1	93.2	88.5
其他批发业	Other Wholesale not Classified Elsewhere	18	220680.2	51469.5	19758.4	4902.9
再生物资回收与批发	Renewable Resources Recycle and Wholesale	5	12437.9	756.7	5074.4	74.4
互联网批发	Internet wholesale	0	0.0	0.0	0.0	0.0
其他未列明批发业	Other Wholesale	13	208242.3	50712.8	14684.0	4828.5

本年折旧 Depreciation in the Year	资产总计 Total Assets	负债合计 Total Liabilities	所有者权益合计 totalCreditors' Equity	实收资本 Paid-up Capital	国家资本 Official Capital	集体资本 Collective Capital	法人资本 Corporate Capital	个人资本 Personal Capital
4.1	785.2	242.5	542.7	508.0	0.0	0.0	0.0	508.0
9667.7	1319289.3	887362.6	431926.7	73256.0	56000.0	0.0	2610.7	14645.3
11.0	5078.6	4048.7	1029.9	775.6	0.0	0.0	564.1	211.5
35.4	20545.9	7059.0	13486.9	8000.0	0.0	0.0	7500.0	500.0
11.4	350.1	91.9	258.2	253.0	0.0	0.0	136.0	117.0
20383.4	3114889.2	2539392.5	575496.7	364733.1	33438.6	4664.3	202287.0	124043.2
10155.3	1076489.9	832857.5	243632.4	196063.4	15830.7	380.0	85100.3	94752.4
6306.8	1409773.2	1190400.1	219373.1	103466.5	4962.9	4134.3	80221.1	14148.2
51.4	14398.9	13800.8	598.1	701.4	0.0	0.0	150.0	551.4
3869.9	614227.2	502334.1	111893.1	64501.8	12645.0	150.0	36815.6	14591.2
9518.1	8157085.3	5042112.7	3321210.7	1458392.8	1047686.5	20776.0	160749.0	203041.7
981.9	684668.3	632509.1	52159.2	76835.5	30000.0	0.0	21453.0	25382.5
3693.1	5096509.0	2522091.3	2781482.5	984657.2	914366.5	0.0	34040.2	23306.0
1.5	25833.9	20554.9	5279.0	2010.0	0.0	0.0	910.0	1100.0
2296.8	1430507.6	1132984.1	297523.5	302674.3	100920.0	300.0	86059.7	102199.5
871.8	310648.6	269052.5	41596.1	33530.2	0.0	14858.0	5913.2	12759.0
159.4	212823.4	201161.1	11662.3	7800.3	2400.0	0.0	1422.0	3978.3
674.6	187056.0	100824.4	86231.6	16938.8	0.0	5618.0	4247.0	7073.8
839.0	209038.5	162935.3	45276.5	33946.5	0.0	0.0	6703.9	27242.6
4863.8	2276788.1	1936926.2	339861.9	296887.7	30622.1	18.5	97959.9	88927.4
7.3	12550.9	10326.8	2224.1	2183.2	3.0	18.5	50.0	2111.7
541.1	902728.9	795676.9	107052.0	115579.1	4009.1	0.0	19359.0	16111.0
48.3	6011.8	5455.9	555.9	857.0	0.0	0.0	151.0	706.0
554.9	80375.9	69762.2	10613.7	12326.0	0.0	0.0	7719.0	4607.0
1070.2	494512.1	459914.1	34598.0	26454.5	5000.0	0.0	4743.2	13451.5
197.6	125270.1	86047.6	39222.5	22547.2	2000.0	0.0	7412.9	13134.3
118.8	35824.4	21945.8	13878.6	13646.4	0.0	0.0	2015.0	11631.4
291.2	70727.2	58686.8	12040.4	10000.0	0.0	0.0	10000.0	0.0
2034.4	548786.8	429110.1	119676.7	93294.3	19610.0	0.0	46509.8	27174.5
8.5	6964.1	5439.1	1525.0	1000.0	0.0	0.0	1000.0	0.0
8.5	6964.1	5439.1	1525.0	1000.0	0.0	0.0	1000.0	0.0
611.2	266441.1	127028.1	139413.0	81267.0	40000.0	0.0	24571.0	16696.0
30.2	17857.2	4518.4	13338.8	2917.0	0.0	0.0	571.0	2346.0
0.0	0.0	0.0	0.0	0.0	0.0	0.0	0.0	0.0
581.0	248583.9	122509.7	126074.2	78350.0	40000.0	0.0	24000.0	14350.0

15-3 续 2

指标名称	Indicator	法人企业数（个）Number of Corporation Enterprises (unit)	流动资产合计 Total Working Capitals	存货 Inventory	固定资产原价 Original Value of Fixed Assets	累计折旧 Depreciation
内资企业	Domestic Funded Enterprises	840	14292493.5	1747512.3	1034163.4	398399.5
国有企业	State-owned	9	63203.2	40104.0	29200.7	9441.5
集体企业	Collective-owned	3	1657.2	34.3	185.0	57.2
有限责任公司	Limited Liability Corporations	185	5844810.9	759443.5	652159.7	248986.9
国有独资公司	State Sole funded Corporations	18	790800.9	154359.7	114507.6	49239.4
其他有限责任公司	Other Limited Liability Corporations	167	5054010.0	605083.8	537652.1	199747.5
股份有限公司	Share-holding Corporations Limited	15	3995909.6	13668.1	54579.9	30025.0
私营企业	Private Enterprises	628	4386912.6	934262.4	298038.1	109888.9
私营独资企业	Private-funded Enterprises	3	1425.8	734.5	413.3	174.9
私营有限责任公司	Private Limited Liability Corporations	611	4226682.3	913775.1	273283.0	100767.2
私营股份有限公司	Private Share-holding Corporations Ltd	14	158804.5	19752.8	24341.8	8946.8
其他企业	Others	0	0.0	0.0	0.0	0.0
港、澳、台商投资企业	Hong Kong,Macao and Taiwan investment enterprises	7	1273725.5	368154.7	83054.2	20426.0
与港澳台商合资经营企业	Enterprises with Funds from Hong Kong,Macao and Taiwan	0	0.0	0.0	0.0	0.0
港澳台商独资企业	Sole Investment	7	1273725.5	368154.7	83054.2	20426.0
外商投资企业	Foreign Funded Enterprises	4	98922.6	17985.6	4448.3	3011.1
中外合资经营企业	Joint-venture	1	74315.0	14407.2	4286.2	2887.2
中外合作经营企业	Cooperative	1	9879.0	3489.2	91.4	86.3
外资企业	Sole Foreign Investment	2	14728.6	89.2	70.7	37.6
二、零售业	Retail Trade	702	5792391.3	864958.8	968011.0	404322.4
综合零售	Integrated Retail	55	2885982.6	101196.6	423701.6	212955.5
百货零售	Commodity Retail	33	2751940.9	86526.9	326807.1	165920.1
超级市场零售	Supermarket Retail	15	122004.7	8793.2	94955.0	46197.3
便利店零售	Convenience Store Retail	2	3177.8	373.9	1063.1	73.6
其他综合零售	Other Retail	5	8859.2	5502.6	876.4	764.5
食品、饮料及烟草制品专门零售	Retail of Food, Beverages and Tobaccos	109	174361.1	46442.9	108049.7	32898.9
粮油零售	Retail of Grain and Oil	15	8252.4	866.1	8732.4	2928.2
糕点、面包零售	Retail of Cake and Bread	2	1326.1	36.8	699.6	602.6
果品、蔬菜零售	Retail of Fruits and Vegetables	21	5451.1	941.6	7485.9	1729.2
肉、禽、蛋、奶及水产品零售	Retail of Meat,Poultry,Egg,Mik and Aquatic Products	23	45502.1	21717.9	56980.8	18451.2
营养和保健品零售	Retail of Nutrition and Health Care Products	12	34234.2	8479.5	10096.6	1120.2
酒、饮料及茶叶零售	Retail of Wine,Drink and Tea	15	54300.1	7960.5	18024.5	5884.6
烟草制品零售	Retail of Tobacco Products	5	5282.5	1341.5	2331.8	873.5
其他食品零售	Retail of Other Food	16	20012.6	5099.0	3698.1	1309.4
纺织、服装及日用品专门零售	Special Retail of Textiles, Garments and Daily Consumer Articles	64	153265.3	60192.4	39917.7	6888.8
纺织品及针织品零售	Retail of Textiles, Garments and Row Material	2	1484.4	912.7	7.7	3.7

本年折旧 Depreciation in the Year	资产总计 Total Assets	负债合计 Total Liabilities	所有者权益合计 totalCreditors' Equity	实收资本 Paid-up Capital	国家资本 Official Capital	集体资本 Collective Capital	法人资本 Corporate Capital	个人资本 Personal Capital
69452.7	16635153.2	11619056.3	5222335.0	2301603.3	1223875.2	37909.3	548393.3	491425.5
3350.4	94015.6	60477.1	33538.5	6855.0	6853.5	0.0	1.5	0.0
30.8	1846.3	1566.3	280.0	322.0	51.5	270.5	0.0	0.0
36598.3	7323132.1	5788974.7	1534157.4	706652.4	330525.4	20580.7	223533.8	132012.5
5826.8	1009044.1	645861.3	363182.8	103696.9	47971.1	1180.0	54545.8	0.0
30771.5	6314088.0	5143113.4	1170974.6	602955.5	282554.3	19400.7	168988.0	132012.5
2478.7	4171162.3	1671130.8	2707096.3	923274.5	886171.9	4358.0	4207.0	28537.6
26994.5	5044996.9	4096907.4	947262.8	664499.4	272.9	12700.1	320651.0	330875.4
19.0	1664.2	432.2	1232.0	210.0	0.0	0.0	0.0	210.0
26088.9	4849073.6	3955269.6	892977.3	627114.0	0.0	10875.8	302541.0	313697.2
886.6	194259.1	141205.6	53053.5	37175.4	272.9	1824.3	18110.0	16968.2
0.0	0.0	0.0	0.0	0.0	0.0	0.0	0.0	0.0
5610.0	1432616.1	1208420.1	224196.0	162905.9	0.0	0.0	85600.0	0.0
0.0	0.0	0.0	0.0	0.0	0.0	0.0	0.0	0.0
5610.0	1432616.1	1208420.1	224196.0	162905.9	0.0	0.0	85600.0	0.0
144.8	111589.5	55171.9	56417.6	42903.6	0.0	0.0	14104.2	0.0
120.2	79535.1	42556.0	36979.1	25192.8	0.0	0.0	12848.3	0.0
12.9	9889.8	5338.6	4551.2	1883.9	0.0	0.0	1255.9	0.0
11.7	22164.6	7277.3	14887.3	15826.9	0.0	0.0	0.0	0.0
71816.9	7319714.9	5755844.8	1564249.1	1986112.3	61624.4	12358.9	1546064.2	269529.0
29150.7	3607652.4	3086320.3	521332.1	280332.3	3058.0	3184.3	216536.4	37191.3
15002.5	3366821.2	2949308.2	417513.0	133150.8	1058.0	3184.3	98807.2	30101.3
13500.0	226703.4	115891.0	110812.4	144680.5	2000.0	0.0	115818.2	6500.0
69.9	5120.1	8217.5	−3097.4	1000.0	0.0	0.0	500.0	500.0
578.3	9007.7	12903.6	−3895.9	1501.0	0.0	0.0	1411.0	90.0
5285.1	287796.1	175904.0	111892.1	77930.3	7733.3	15.5	51858.2	16382.7
396.7	18238.6	5202.6	13036.0	8219.7	4553.3	0.0	1277.8	2388.6
30.7	1445.1	385.6	1059.5	100.0	0.0	0.0	0.0	100.0
231.0	15537.9	5441.8	10096.1	6056.7	0.0	15.5	1793.3	4247.9
1619.3	108435.8	76176.7	32259.1	30600.9	0.0	0.0	26587.2	4013.7
668.2	44903.0	33615.8	11287.2	5093.9	0.0	0.0	3700.0	1393.9
1359.8	66714.6	35831.5	30883.1	16402.6	0.0	0.0	11301.0	3161.0
150.5	6748.5	2697.4	4051.1	3343.4	3180.0	0.0	87.3	76.1
828.9	25772.6	16552.6	9220.0	8113.1	0.0	0.0	7111.6	1001.5
2349.6	194493.6	161065.2	33428.4	38209.4	1.0	0.0	26713.6	11494.8
3.2	1514.4	800.8	713.6	61.0	0.0	0.0	51.0	10.0

15-3 续 3

指标名称	Indicator	法人企业数（个）Number of Corporation Enterprises (unit)	流动资产合计 Total Working Capitals	存货 Inventory	固定资产原价 Original Value of Fixed Assets	累计折旧 Depreciation
服装零售	Retail of Garments	34	97891.5	37761.1	33429.5	3613.7
鞋帽零售	Retail of Shoes and Hats	4	7660.9	6188.3	354.0	227.1
化妆品及卫生用品零售	Retail of Cosmetic and Hygiene Products	13	15125.9	6513.2	1140.1	681.1
厨具卫具及日用杂品零售	Retail of Kitchen,Bathroom Equipment and Groceries	2	1527.9	602.2	27.6	15.2
钟表、眼镜零售	Retail of Clock and Glasses	5	17989.4	4561.0	2153.9	976.8
箱包零售	Retail of bags and suitcases	0	0.0	0.0	0.0	0.0
自行车等代步设备零售	Retail of bicycle and other equipments	1	484.0	232.9	1325.3	517.6
其他日用品零售	Retail of Household Appliances	3	11101.3	3421.0	1479.6	853.6
文化、体育用品及器材专门零售	Retail of Culture, Sports Appliances and Equipments	41	170118.7	74975.5	20235.7	6618.7
文具用品零售	Retail of Culture Products	7	7628.9	1443.0	1047.5	667.2
体育用品及器材零售	Retail of Sports Appliances and Equipments	1	896.6	198.3	48.7	34.1
图书、报刊零售	Retail of Books,Magazines and Newspapers	10	25498.8	8358.7	2113.3	965.7
音像制品、电子和数字出版物零售	Retail of audiovisual products,electronic and digital publications	1	11309.7	6960.0	168.6	83.8
珠宝首饰零售	Retail of Jewelry	10	92226.5	50126.7	6541.0	2523.2
工艺美术品及收藏品零售	Retail of Crafts and Collectibles	4	6306.3	924.9	131.7	83.8
乐器零售	Retail of Music Instruments	2	1242.0	1124.9	33.4	27.9
照相器材零售	Retail of Photographic Apparatus	3	2968.2	2475.5	295.6	274.3
其他文化用品零售	Retail of Other Culture Products	3	22041.7	3363.5	9855.9	1958.7
医药及医疗器材专门零售	Retail of Medicines and Medical Appliances	41	264423.6	68282.6	28544.4	10135.0
西药零售	Retail of Western Medicine	24	231844.0	63695.9	25328.9	8763.4
中药零售	Retail of Traditional Chinese Medicine	3	3590.3	1737.0	253.6	174.4
动物用药品零售	Retail of veterinary drugs	1	2110.4	138.3	1511.9	295.7
医疗用品及器材零售	Retail of Medical Appliances	13	26878.9	2711.4	1450.0	901.5
汽车、摩托车、零配件和燃料及其他动力销售	Cars,motorcycles,spare part and fuel and other power sales	255	1621698.4	441433.9	260598.4	112789.9
汽车新车零售	Retail of new cars	177	1455307.3	407930.2	179773.2	75077.3
汽车旧车零售	Retail of used cars	1	708.8	224.2	0.6	0.2
汽车零配件零售	Retail of Automobile Spare Parts	16	24326.8	4562.5	2077.6	897.8
摩托车及零配件零售	Retail of Motorbike and Its Spare Parts	4	5575.5	2632.6	383.2	79.5
机动车燃油零售	Retail of motor fuel oil	54	122786.8	25674.2	62897.3	24371.3
机动车燃气零售	Retail of motor gas	3	12993.2	410.2	15466.5	12363.8
家用电器及电子产品专门零售	Special Retail of Household Electric Appliances and Electronic Products	88	330267.4	25013.3	11712.4	6144.4
家用视听设备零售	Retail of Household Electric Appliances	13	219346.2	3567.0	4861.4	2764.8
日用家电设备零售	Retail of Daily Household Equipment	29	31222.9	9909.5	1892.7	1049.0
计算机、软件及辅助设备零售	Retail of Computer,Software and Auxiliary Equipment	21	37138.2	4301.2	3413.3	1421.5
通信设备零售	Retail of Communication Equipment	15	28948.4	5810.5	1097.0	655.4
其他电子产品零售	Retail of Other Electronic Equipment	10	13611.7	1425.1	448.0	253.7

本年折旧 Depreciation in the Year	资产总计 Total Assets	负债合计 Total Liabilities	所有者权益合计 totalCreditors' Equity	实收资本 Paid-up Capital	国家资本 Official Capital	集体资本 Collective Capital	法人资本 Corporate Capital	个人资本 Personal Capital
1303.6	131591.3	105886.6	25704.7	25124.6	0.0	0.0	19572.0	5552.6
54.9	7960.0	10231.1	–2271.1	530.0	0.0	0.0	110.0	420.0
82.0	18572.4	14723.2	3849.2	3996.3	1.0	0.0	2060.3	1935.0
3.9	1606.7	1233.1	373.6	225.0	0.0	0.0	0.0	225.0
550.5	19245.8	18148.5	1097.3	3652.3	0.0	0.0	620.3	3032.0
0.0	0.0	0.0	0.0	0.0	0.0	0.0	0.0	0.0
64.6	1737.3	2182.4	–445.1	300.0	0.0	0.0	300.0	0.0
286.9	12265.7	7859.5	4406.2	4320.2	0.0	0.0	4000.0	320.2
1669.4	197661.0	87567.3	110093.7	42285.3	3100.0	4600.0	15499.2	19086.1
139.0	8634.0	6187.3	2446.7	2191.2	0.0	0.0	1078.3	1112.9
10.0	911.2	659.0	252.2	370.1	0.0	0.0	0.0	370.1
203.0	28195.2	14452.8	13742.4	8984.7	3100.0	0.0	2996.3	2888.4
28.2	16010.3	6219.7	9790.6	5053.0	0.0	0.0	1350.0	3703.0
255.3	100540.5	33251.4	67289.1	21997.4	0.0	4600.0	9246.4	8151.0
19.4	6424.6	4835.8	1588.8	1482.7	0.0	0.0	0.0	1482.7
3.5	1303.8	876.4	427.4	250.0	0.0	0.0	200.0	50.0
6.6	2989.5	2304.8	684.7	751.0	0.0	0.0	251.0	500.0
1004.4	32651.9	18780.1	13871.8	1205.2	0.0	0.0	377.2	828.0
2374.1	328040.1	188515.5	139524.6	53975.3	2338.7	520.0	10686.5	40430.1
2143.1	292799.1	160423.8	132375.3	49351.9	2011.7	0.0	9589.2	37751.0
31.2	3944.1	3201.8	742.3	1320.0	306.0	520.0	396.0	98.0
54.5	3779.3	640.2	3139.1	673.9	0.0	0.0	216.0	457.9
145.3	27517.6	24249.7	3267.9	2629.5	21.0	0.0	485.3	2123.2
24472.6	2040541.7	1604345.2	436575.5	1333170.0	40421.8	4039.1	1149232.3	106514.3
18632.0	1732036.1	1448261.1	284154.0	1254898.5	28778.0	3271.2	1119961.8	89925.0
0.1	709.2	471.0	238.2	390.9	0.0	0.0	0.0	390.9
159.4	29488.7	19293.3	10195.4	3649.9	0.0	200.0	1778.5	1671.4
35.1	6182.0	3329.9	2852.1	2399.3	0.0	0.0	1049.3	1350.0
5262.5	254042.5	118939.0	135103.5	66311.4	9123.8	567.9	23442.7	13177.0
383.5	18083.2	14050.9	4032.3	5520.0	2520.0	0.0	3000.0	0.0
1595.1	348030.5	272022.7	76007.8	47360.1	2008.0	0.0	32540.7	12811.4
856.9	224121.3	182041.9	42079.4	9952.6	0.0	0.0	8345.0	1607.6
382.4	33059.4	24488.6	8570.8	8692.8	0.0	0.0	3618.5	5074.3
178.0	43750.4	16458.3	27292.1	20378.4	2008.0	0.0	15204.9	3165.5
135.1	32311.8	37839.3	–5527.5	5377.9	0.0	0.0	4014.9	1363.0
42.7	14787.6	11194.6	3593.0	2958.4	0.0	0.0	1357.4	1601.0

15-3 续4

指标名称	Indicator	法人企业数（个）Number of Corporation Enterprises (unit)	流动资产合计 Total Working Capitals	存货 Inventory	固定资产原价 Original Value of Fixed Assets	累计折旧 Depreciation
五金、家具及室内装饰材料专门零售	Special Retail of Hardware, Furniture and Decoration Materials	21	26763.4	8582.0	37751.6	3460.7
五金零售	Retail of Hardware	13	12714.6	3408.6	1795.5	587.5
灯具零售	Retail of lamps	1	186.9	67.5	12.3	8.7
家具零售	Retail of Furniture	3	8815.7	4631.8	35701.9	2723.3
涂料零售	Retail of Coating	0	0.0	0.0	0.0	0.0
木质装饰材料零售	Retail of Wood Decorative Material	1	134.8	29.7	102.7	47.1
陶瓷、石材装饰材料零售	Retail of Ceramics and Stone Decorative Material	3	4911.4	444.4	139.2	94.1
其他室内装饰材料零售	Retail of Other Decoration Materials	0	0.0	0.0	0.0	0.0
货摊、无店铺及其他零售业	Non-shop and Other Retails	28	165510.8	38839.6	37499.5	12430.5
流动货摊零售	Retail of mobile stalls	0	0.0	0.0	0.0	0.0
互联网零售	Internet Retail	16	125359.6	27906.9	25718.1	6527.3
邮购及电视、电话零售	Mail,Television and Telephone Retail	3	27909.2	6654.8	3682.7	2766.4
自动售货机零售	Retail of vending machine	0	0.0	0.0	0.0	0.0
生活用燃料零售	Retail of Domestic Fuel	2	2018.1	93.9	5557.4	2328.5
其他未列明零售业	Other Retails	7	10223.9	4184.0	2541.3	808.3
内资企业	**Domestic Funded Enterprises**	688	5612646.6	831066.7	796500.2	343596.7
国有企业	State-owned	5	8130.8	1078.9	2579.7	2035.1
集体企业	Collective-owned	11	5729.2	336.7	5051.0	917.7
股份合作企业	Cooperative	3	565.5	102.0	494.9	261.8
联营企业	Joint venture	0	0.0	0.0	0.0	0.0
国有与集体联营企业	State-owned enterprises and collective enterprises	0	0.0	0.0	0.0	0.0
有限责任公司	Limited Liability Corporations	191	1303026.8	292937.0	283232.4	107659.8
国有独资公司	State Sole funded Corporations	8	28214.4	1311.0	18020.9	13965.1
其他有限责任公司	Other Limited Liability Corporations	183	1274812.4	291626.0	265211.5	93694.7
股份有限公司	Share-holding Corporations Limited	21	3086433.2	180072.1	331394.6	162641.5
私营企业	Private Enterprises	440	1204298.5	356423.4	169533.4	69402.9
私营独资企业	Private-funded Enterprises	13	3572.4	793.0	1333.9	248.1
私营有限责任公司	Private Limited Liability Corporations	418	1179697.8	345441.5	165282.9	68340.0
私营股份有限公司	Private Share-holding Corporations Ltd.	9	21028.3	10188.9	2916.6	814.8
其他企业	Other Enterprises	17	4462.6	116.6	4214.2	677.9
港、澳、台商投资企业	**Enterprises with Funds from Hong Kong, Macao and Taiwan**	6	73396.2	25106.4	66058.2	20287.0
与港澳台商合资经营企业	Joint-ventures Enterprises	1	16725.0	6694.3	8193.5	5167.2
港澳台商独资企业	Enterprises with Sole Investment	5	56671.2	18412.1	57864.7	15119.8
外商投资企业	**Foreign Funded Enterprises**	8	106348.5	8785.7	105452.6	40438.7
中外合资经营企业	Joint-venture Enterprises	2	26801.9	57.1	9965.5	5122.3
中外合作经营企业	Cooperation Enterprises	1	52758.1	0.0	20968.2	15276.3
外资企业	Enterprises with Sole Foreign Funds	4	12655.1	4764.3	44718.6	9050.8
外商投资股份有限公司	Share-holding Corporations Ltd. With Foreign Investment	1	14133.4	3964.3	29800.3	10989.3

本年折旧 Depreciation in the Year	资产总计 Total Assets	负债合计 Total Liabilities	所有者权益合计 totalCreditors' Equity	实收资本 Paid-up Capital				
					国家资本 Official Capital	集体资本 Collective Capital	法人资本 Corporate Capital	个人资本 Personal Capital
2266.6	94526.6	66678.0	27848.6	35147.6	0.0	0.0	2344.1	2803.5
317.2	13955.1	11971.5	1983.6	3284.1	0.0	0.0	619.0	2665.1
3.0	190.5	2.1	188.4	188.4	0.0	0.0	50.0	138.4
1949.8	75206.5	51098.3	24108.2	30303.0	0.0	0.0	303.0	0.0
0.0	0.0	0.0	0.0	0.0	0.0	0.0	0.0	0.0
0.5	208.3	25.7	182.6	62.1	0.0	0.0	62.1	0.0
-3.9	4966.2	3580.4	1385.8	1310.0	0.0	0.0	1310.0	0.0
0.0	0.0	0.0	0.0	0.0	0.0	0.0	0.0	0.0
2653.7	220972.9	113426.6	107546.3	77702.0	2963.6	0.0	40653.2	22814.8
0.0	0.0	0.0	0.0	0.0	0.0	0.0	0.0	0.0
1510.4	166366.2	81189.4	85176.8	58270.0	0.0	0.0	27532.8	21914.8
453.3	34020.3	20843.9	13176.4	11431.0	2963.6	0.0	8467.4	0.0
0.0	0.0	0.0	0.0	0.0	0.0	0.0	0.0	0.0
486.4	8606.1	3351.8	5254.3	5300.0	0.0	0.0	2352.0	500.0
203.6	11980.3	8041.5	3938.8	2701.0	0.0	0.0	2301.0	400.0
55067.5	6915180.8	5496252.9	1419306.9	1879233.4	61624.4	12358.9	1523950.7	269529.0
71.5	9077.6	5366.3	3711.3	2048.0	1778.0	0.0	270.0	0.0
71.8	10639.2	1213.6	9425.6	3822.1	0.0	3465.7	350.3	6.1
39.3	1190.7	822.8	367.9	422.7	0.0	372.0	0.0	50.7
0.0	0.0	0.0	0.0	0.0	0.0	0.0	0.0	0.0
0.0	0.0	0.0	0.0	0.0	0.0	0.0	0.0	0.0
17125.9	1690279.4	1239601.9	450677.5	1287852.9	58520.7	7920.0	1171746.3	46717.9
692.4	34212.9	21170.2	13042.7	12354.0	7629.0	0.0	4725.0	0.0
16433.5	1656066.5	1218431.7	437634.8	1275498.9	50891.7	7920.0	1167021.3	46717.9
16020.5	3766189.3	3134376.0	631813.3	232314.4	1325.7	520.0	117523.5	104122.8
21605.0	1428471.8	1113174.3	315676.5	348664.4	0.0	81.2	233070.8	115512.4
60.5	4681.8	3168.7	1513.1	877.1	0.0	0.0	119.3	757.8
21126.4	1394613.3	1093762.6	301229.7	340824.3	0.0	81.2	230561.5	110181.6
418.1	29176.7	16243.0	12933.7	6963.0	0.0	0.0	2390.0	4573.0
133.5	9332.8	1698.0	7634.8	4108.9	0.0	0.0	989.8	3119.1
5136.6	128011.8	81035.3	46976.5	19348.1	0.0	0.0	3152.5	0.0
621.6	22117.8	14305.3	7812.5	3831.1	0.0	0.0	2868.6	0.0
4515.0	105894.0	66730.0	39164.0	15517.0	0.0	0.0	283.9	0.0
11612.8	276522.3	178556.6	97965.7	87530.8	0.0	0.0	18961.0	0.0
4574.6	37542.8	18694.7	18848.1	14142.9	0.0	0.0	10842.9	0.0
813.1	58489.8	34983.8	23506.0	16387.9	0.0	0.0	1618.1	0.0
3598.0	84470.9	58684.4	25786.5	37000.0	0.0	0.0	6500.0	0.0
2627.1	96018.8	66193.7	29825.1	20000.0	0.0	0.0	0.0	0.0

15-4 限额以上批发零售贸易

Profit Loss and Distribution of Wholesales and

单位：万元

指标名称	Indicator	法人企业数（个）Number of Corporation Enterprises (unit)	主营业务收入 Revenue from Principal Business	主营业务成本 Cost from Principal Business	主营业务税金及附加 Taxes and Other Charges on Principal Business
总计	**Total**	1553	34106025.4	31264242.5	157394.9
一、批发业	**Wholesalel Trade**	851	24745223.6	23026231.0	123644.1
农、林、牧产品批发	Wholesale of Farm Produce and Livestock Products	23	178135.2	166645.6	62.1
谷物、豆及薯类批发	Wholesale of Grain,Beans and Tubers	4	36116.5	35116.8	8.0
种子批发	Wholesale of Seed	7	42345.7	37658.6	22.2
饲料批发	Wholesale of Fodder	4	46451.7	44414.3	21.5
棉、麻批发	Wholesale of Cotton and Linen	3	38402.9	37779.6	2.2
林业产品批发	Wholesale of Forestery Products	0	0.0	0.0	0.0
牲畜批发	Wholesale of Livestocks	1	5252.5	4771.8	8.2
其他农牧产品批发	Wholesale of Other Agricultural Products	4	9565.9	6904.5	0.0
食品、饮料及烟草制品批发	Wholesale of Food, Beverages and Tobaccos	68	2590006.1	2251536.5	92600.1
米、面制品及食用油批发	Wholesale of Rice,Noodles and Oil	11	1336213.1	1280302.3	434.6
糕点、糖果及糖批发	Wholesale of Cake,Candyand Sugar	1	26579.4	25545.3	34.7
果品、蔬菜批发	Wholesale of Fruits and Vegetables	10	36760.9	33381.4	46.7
肉、禽、蛋、奶及水产品批发	Wholesale of Meat,Poultry,Egg,Mik and Aquatic Products	10	109580.3	83509.3	55.9
盐及调味品批发	Wholesale of Salt and Spices	6	43911.2	35669.1	97.6
营养和保健品批发	Wholesale of nutrition and health products	7	80356.3	64866.5	468.6
酒、饮料及茶叶批发	Wholesale of Wine,Drink and Tea	11	136323.1	115228.1	272.2
烟草制品批发	Wholesale of Tobacco Products	3	723120.2	531484.6	90806.6
其他食品批发	Wholesale of Other Food	9	97161.6	81549.9	383.2
纺织、服装及家庭用品批发	Wholesale of Textiles, Garments and Daily Consumer Articles	58	1884280.9	1783417.0	1722.0
纺织品、针织品及原料批发	Wholesale of Textiles, Garments and Row Material	4	51016.7	49146.8	9.9
服装批发	Wholesale of Garments	13	138007.9	121214.6	265.0
鞋帽批发	Wholesale of Shoes and Hats	6	26725.5	23808.6	36.6
化妆品及卫生用品批发	Wholesale of Cosmetic and Hygiene Products	10	59771.0	52175.2	99.8
厨房、卫生间用具及日用杂货批发	Wholesale of Kitchen,Bathroom Equipment and Groceries	1	14767.1	13269.4	23.7
灯具、装饰物品批发	Wholesale of Lamps and Decorative Items	4	9951.3	9350.8	10.0
家用视听设备批发	Wholesale of household aquipments	3	12487.4	12165.2	18.1
日用家电批发	Wholesale of household appliances	16	1567587.0	1500019.8	1237.4
其他家庭用品批发	Wholesale of Other Household Articles	1	3967.0	2266.6	21.5
文化、体育用品及器材批发	Wholesale of Culture, Sports Appliances and Equipments	24	1851957.3	1581901.6	4542.0
文具用品批发	Wholesale of Culture Products	11	113503.7	109057.5	84.1

企业损益及分配（2018年）

Retail Sales Trade Above Designated Size（2018）

(10 000 yuan)

销售费用 Cost of Sales	管理费用 Cost of Management	财务费用 Cost of Finance	营业利润 Profits from Business	利润总额 Total Profits	应交所得税 Income Tax Payable	应付职工薪酬(本年贷方累计发生额) Total Wages Payable	应交增值税 Value-added Tax Payable
1536846.7	778076.1	151015.0	500750.9	491692.7	96181.9	832740.9	338004.5
807947.6	509946.9	82999.1	378936.9	370816.7	61431.8	437578.8	204441.2
5296.1	6445.8	1268.8	-898.4	-293.8	389.0	3853.5	-294.9
477.8	1874.6	1092.9	-2458.5	-2460.3	102.8	1057.3	13.1
2309.2	2918.5	80.6	-139.6	381.3	14.6	1184.5	17.4
1118.3	349.2	-13.2	559.4	560.0	187.3	298.0	123.5
207.0	293.6	31.1	284.8	309.0	77.9	213.0	-498.9
0.0	0.0	0.0	0.0	0.0	0.0	0.0	0.0
340.0	98.2	3.0	31.3	25.4	6.4	198.7	50.0
843.8	911.7	74.4	824.2	890.8	0.0	902.0	0.0
80372.8	103065.0	-2868.8	93830.8	93989.3	16651.0	79263.1	43987.4
19446.3	56835.6	-1078.0	12435.6	13050.0	2712.2	15803.6	4375.4
659.6	211.0	140.2	-74.4	-75.0	0.0	255.1	231.6
2578.9	666.0	38.2	102.3	83.2	17.5	1971.9	193.3
5788.0	2607.4	476.6	7892.4	7815.8	67.7	4622.0	241.3
4286.5	3770.6	34.5	473.5	506.1	387.8	3547.1	732.6
17629.3	1700.7	657.8	-7021.5	-7013.2	-1891.3	6536.8	813.3
12691.7	4757.5	603.2	3018.4	3090.6	1249.8	3025.8	4399.9
14186.0	30335.9	-3772.6	67165.7	66743.3	11687.0	35337.7	30812.9
3106.5	2180.3	31.3	9838.8	9788.5	2420.3	8163.1	2187.1
50248.3	20969.3	7675.9	31860.4	31568.2	4034.5	27306.5	9337.9
817.7	272.3	31.3	253.1	267.0	15.0	422.8	76.8
10050.3	3965.7	1482.5	692.5	678.2	209.6	5795.0	2860.8
1856.2	750.4	183.1	41.8	43.5	15.3	1386.2	274.8
3088.1	2809.7	592.9	920.3	968.1	39.7	2855.0	656.7
1423.1	116.4	-79.6	14.2	14.2	0.0	335.7	191.8
464.5	70.4	0.9	61.0	61.0	6.1	243.1	64.2
307.0	133.4	26.2	-156.1	-156.1	10.9	371.0	20.0
31639.8	11249.1	5438.2	30558.6	30417.7	3737.9	15191.0	4984.0
601.6	1601.9	0.4	-525.0	-725.4	0.0	706.7	208.8
86605.1	93688.6	-1860.3	108886.3	108279.5	2415.7	103064.4	5457.7
2866.2	1079.8	582.6	-226.7	-106.3	148.6	1649.6	530.6

指标名称	Indicator	法人企业数（个）Number of Corporation Enterprises (unit)	主营业务收入 Revenue from Principal Business	主营业务成本 Cost from Principal Business	主营业务税金及附加 Taxes and Other Charges on Principal Business
体育用品及器材批发	Wholesale of Sports Appliances and Equipments	1	2401.1	2237.2	-3.4
图书批发	Wholesale of Books	6	1215529.8	956454.7	4138.2
音像制品及电子出版物批发	Wholesale of Audiovisual Products and Electronic Publications	1	4469.7	4068.4	5.8
首饰、工艺品及收藏品批发	Wholesale of Jewelry,Crafts and Collectibles	3	511361.6	505533.8	296.9
其他文化用品批发	Wholesale of Other Culture Products	2	4691.4	4550.0	13.6
医药及医疗器材批发	Wholesale of Medicines and Medical Appliances	138	4227618.6	3780066.9	10127.5
西药批发	Wholesale of Western Medicine	47	1432871.5	1303593.7	2904.2
中药批发	Wholesale of Traditional Chinese Medicine	20	1937058.8	1804448.0	3799.2
动物用药品批发	Wholesale of veterinary drugs	5	34511.5	29541.0	75.5
医疗用品及器材批发	Wholesale of Medicines Products and Medical Appliances	66	823176.8	642484.2	3348.6
矿产品、建材及化工产品批发	Wholesale of Mineral Products, Building Materials and Chemical Products	330	9460519.9	9150621.6	9875.7
煤炭及制品批发	Wholesale of Coal and Its Products	45	1590702.8	1529696.0	1769.8
石油及制品批发	Wholesale of Petroleum and Its Products	33	3343195.7	3241684.9	3082.1
非金属矿及制品批发	Wholesale of Non-metal Mine and Its Products	3	67610.5	63439.4	56.8
金属及金属矿批发	Wholesale of Metal and Metal Mine	149	3047658.4	2972406.4	3630.5
建材批发	Wholesale of Construction Materials	32	437814.1	417162.4	579.2
化肥批发	Wholesale of Chemical Fertilizer	6	13983.2	12481.0	134.8
农药批发	Wholesale of Pesticide	12	297106.2	272982.8	192.1
其他化工产品批发	Wholesale of Other Chemical Products	50	662449.0	640768.7	430.4
机械设备、五金产品及电子产品批发	Wholesale of Machinery, Hardware and Electronic Equipment	191	4006617.3	3789987.2	4173.1
农业机械批发	Wholesale of Agricultural Machinery	7	18278.0	17616.6	3.5
汽车及零配件批发	Wholesale of Automobile and Spare Parts	52	1646143.3	1563349.7	1036.6
摩托车及零配件批发	Wholesale of Motorbike and Its Spare Parts	4	23464.9	21941.9	27.7
五金产品批发	Wholesale of Hardware	16	132540.3	124167.0	167.9
电气设备批发	Wholesale of Electronic Equipment	18	617634.7	596792.7	596.3
计算机、软件及辅助设备批发	Wholesale of Computer,Software and Auxiliary Equipment	26	307604.2	289302.0	255.5
通讯设备批发	Wholesale of Communication Equipment	13	173489.7	168448.5	110.4
广播影视设备批发	Wholesale of Broadcast Television Equipment	1	31818.4	26538.5	11.7
其他机械设备及电子产品批发	Wholesale of Other Machinery and Electronic Equipment	54	1055643.8	981830.3	1963.5
贸易经纪与代理	Trade Broker and Agency	1	39006.7	37308.6	51.0
贸易代理	Trade Agency	1	39006.7	37308.6	51.0
其他批发业	Other Wholesale not Classified Elsewhere	18	507081.6	484746.0	490.6
再生物资回收与批发	Renewable Resources Recycle and Wholesale	5	14850.2	13962.1	184.2
互联网批发	Internet wholesale	0	0.0	0.0	0.0
其他未列明批发业	Other Wholesale	13	492231.4	470783.9	306.4

销售费用 Cost of Sales	管理费用 Cost of Management	财务费用 Cost of Finance	营业利润 Profits from Business	利润总额 Total Profits	应交所得税 Income Tax Payable	应付职工薪酬 (本年贷方累计发生额) Total Wages Payable	应交增值税 Value-added Tax Payable
128.7	0.0	2.6	28.9	28.9	1.6	59.6	21.7
82360.3	91972.9	-2603.6	104562.8	103490.0	1020.5	100327.7	3565.7
333.8	78.4	3.0	-19.7	8.2	0.4	113.5	46.1
870.8	475.8	153.9	4541.3	4859.0	1244.2	848.6	1280.4
45.3	81.7	1.2	-0.3	-0.3	0.4	65.4	13.2
236585.9	118234.7	39918.1	59004.5	59052.0	12900.1	99535.0	78419.7
66113.5	43272.8	10285.7	19980.4	20034.2	3930.8	31406.4	31858.1
53599.1	29720.6	23464.0	27024.1	27164.2	6416.0	36039.6	19891.5
1651.5	2651.1	78.2	514.2	536.0	98.4	759.4	604.3
115221.8	42590.2	6090.2	11485.8	11317.6	2454.9	31329.6	26065.8
207212.2	110704.0	40577.6	57068.3	46974.1	16572.9	60169.6	45438.5
36076.2	9071.3	6186.0	-1950.4	-1219.1	882.5	4806.6	11532.4
103005.0	44233.8	12942.6	28868.5	27197.8	11982.0	24839.7	16161.5
3086.9	138.1	-201.4	1090.6	1128.6	199.0	177.8	550.0
30986.5	31257.0	13118.3	18647.9	8539.1	1614.0	11722.4	8448.0
9446.7	5202.0	3017.7	2380.3	2505.5	896.1	3096.2	2432.2
810.5	1580.7	2031.8	-2990.6	-2964.2	24.1	1230.2	101.4
11992.7	12763.5	976.0	8545.3	9241.3	522.6	10484.8	418.3
11807.7	6457.6	2506.6	2476.7	2545.1	452.6	3811.9	5794.7
133210.3	50126.1	-4031.4	21994.8	23888.6	7625.5	59938.8	19476.4
609.3	380.9	40.3	-419.5	-25.6	14.5	363.1	34.1
66956.5	11591.9	-8615.8	878.1	1330.4	3227.0	18453.8	1777.6
549.9	820.9	92.5	32.1	36.5	8.7	622.6	194.4
3262.4	4287.3	1059.3	-284.6	-185.1	85.0	2767.0	1004.8
9203.5	6893.9	32.4	3320.3	3383.7	813.8	6813.4	2432.9
6310.2	7275.0	874.7	3928.8	4601.6	1044.8	6664.6	1738.4
1572.4	2684.6	302.2	389.0	440.1	124.4	1799.8	836.4
1294.3	987.9	125.2	2970.8	2924.2	75.0	302.4	67.6
43451.8	15203.7	2057.8	11179.8	11382.8	2232.3	22152.1	11390.2
1113.5	0.0	299.8	231.5	232.9	3.1	60.0	374.3
1113.5	0.0	299.8	231.5	232.9	3.1	60.0	374.3
7303.4	6713.4	2019.4	6958.7	7125.9	840.0	4387.9	2244.2
165.3	301.2	42.9	194.3	194.3	19.7	254.4	359.1
0.0	0.0	0.0	0.0	0.0	0.0	0.0	0.0
7138.1	6412.2	1976.5	6764.4	6931.6	820.3	4133.5	1885.1

15-4 续 2

指标名称	Indicator	法人企业数（个）Number of Corporation Enterprises (unit)	主营业务收入 Revenue from Principal Business	主营业务成本 Cost from Principal Business	主营业务税金及附加 Taxes and Other Charges on Principal Business
内资企业	Domestic Funded Enterprises	840	22594070.1	21016203.2	122267.5
国有企业	State-owned	9	84167.8	79404.8	162.7
集体企业	Collective-owned	3	8954.1	8441.0	37.2
有限责任公司	Limited Liability Corporations	185	12138264.2	11207865.5	109235.3
国有独资公司	State Sole funded Corporations	18	2704391.8	2483021.5	92014.8
其他有限责任公司	Other Limited Liability Corporations	167	9433872.4	8724844.0	17220.5
股份有限公司	Share-holding Corporations Limited	15	943564.4	889111.1	818.5
私营企业	Private Enterprises	628	9419119.6	8831380.8	12013.8
私营独资企业	Private-funded Enterprises	3	22467.0	21864.3	57.1
私营有限责任公司	Private Limited Liability Corporations	611	9258865.4	8697105.3	11624.5
私营股份有限公司	Private Share-holding Corporations Ltd	14	137787.2	112411.2	332.2
其他企业	Others	0	0.0	0.0	0.0
港、澳、台商投资企业	Hong Kong,Macao and Taiwan investment enterprises	7	1965087.5	1836977.2	1001.7
与港澳台商合资经营企业	Enterprises with Funds from Hong Kong,Macao and Taiwan	0	0.0	0.0	0.0
港澳台商独资企业	Sole Investment	7	1965087.5	1836977.2	1001.7
外商投资企业	Foreign Funded Enterprises	4	186066.0	173050.6	374.9
中外合资经营企业	Joint-venture	1	131065.4	126875.6	241.9
中外合作经营企业	Cooperative	1	19989.8	16771.7	15.6
外资企业	Sole Foreign Investment	2	35010.8	29403.3	117.4
二、零售业	Retail Trade	702	9360801.8	8238011.5	33750.8
综合零售	Integrated Retail	55	2174505.6	1925746.6	9646.5
百货零售	Commodity Retail	33	1715236.3	1543645.0	8541.9
超级市场零售	Supermarket Retail	15	407485.1	333042.9	977.1
便利店零售	Convenience Store Retail	2	3838.0	3310.2	9.4
其他综合零售	Other Retail	5	47946.2	45748.5	118.1
食品、饮料及烟草制品专门零售	Retail of Food, Beverages and Tobaccos	109	341809.7	261455.9	1595.4
粮油零售	Retail of Grain and Oil	15	28790.4	20421.6	240.7
糕点、面包零售	Retail of Cake and Bread	2	9282.1	8110.5	18.9
果品、蔬菜零售	Retail of Fruits and Vegetables	21	34324.9	27061.0	198.8
肉、禽、蛋、奶及水产品零售	Retail of Meat,Poultry,Egg,Mik and Aquatic Products	23	115198.5	86336.5	758.8
营养和保健品零售	Retail of Nutrition and Health Care Products	12	29028.0	19677.9	102.0
酒、饮料及茶叶零售	Retail of Wine,Drink and Tea	15	55355.0	37993.3	202.4
烟草制品零售	Retail of Tobacco Products	5	13096.6	11783.2	29.7
其他食品零售	Retail of Other Food	16	56734.2	50071.9	44.1
纺织、服装及日用品专门零售	Special Retail of Textiles, Garments and Daily Consumer Articles	64	354211.9	283402.3	1254.4
纺织品及针织品零售	Retail of Textiles, Garments and Row Material	2	6417.6	5182.2	19.6

销售费用 Cost of Sales	管理费用 Cost of Management	财务费用 Cost of Finance	营业利润 Profits from Business	利润总额 Total Profits	应交所得税 Income Tax Payable	应付职工薪酬 (本年贷方累计发生额) Total Wages Payable	应交增值税 Value-added Tax Payable
740986.7	448628.3	95828.3	360069.0	351745.5	56520.0	412858.9	199981.8
3132.5	6159.3	1075.1	−2230.5	−2187.9	511.4	5326.8	392.7
154.2	182.3	38.6	88.7	83.1	0.0	86.0	66.3
371180.7	224237.4	50411.2	242100.2	240520.0	28488.7	256210.7	117054.3
37675.1	42088.5	965.3	62117.1	62485.5	10636.9	49833.8	35513.4
333505.6	182148.9	49445.9	179983.1	178034.5	17851.8	206376.9	81540.9
71529.5	44279.0	6863.7	16564.1	17187.3	7324.7	15380.2	14429.6
294989.8	173770.3	37439.7	103546.5	96143.0	20195.2	135855.2	68038.9
320.6	145.0	25.2	54.6	54.6	2.0	93.5	172.4
284037.9	165653.9	36007.6	98464.5	90909.1	19735.0	128050.7	66801.2
10631.3	7971.4	1406.9	5027.4	5179.3	458.2	7711.0	1065.3
0.0	0.0	0.0	0.0	0.0	0.0	0.0	0.0
61862.6	57516.2	−12924.1	15491.9	15539.1	4298.2	22482.3	2595.1
0.0	0.0	0.0	0.0	0.0	0.0	0.0	0.0
61862.6	57516.2	−12924.1	15491.9	15539.1	4298.2	22482.3	2595.1
5098.3	3802.4	94.9	3376.0	3532.1	613.6	2237.6	1864.3
1114.8	1329.2	202.3	1587.7	1743.1	76.2	1034.7	967.2
52.4	994.3	−6.9	1645.5	1646.2	413.2	426.6	55.1
3931.1	1478.9	−100.5	142.8	142.8	124.2	776.3	842.0
728899.1	268129.2	68015.9	121814.0	120876.0	34750.1	395162.1	133563.3
206463.3	54139.5	31631.5	19261.3	15500.6	6357.6	96944.1	27754.2
125389.5	40359.0	30110.0	21041.3	17215.5	4674.7	67894.4	21460.9
75337.9	11972.6	1078.6	900.3	956.9	1679.0	25529.2	5922.8
2708.7	1377.5	27.3	−3584.2	−3583.9	0.0	2044.9	11.6
3027.2	430.4	415.6	903.9	912.1	3.9	1475.6	358.9
44177.3	18763.0	2257.2	20136.1	20734.9	4216.9	24436.0	6884.4
4731.5	1539.2	113.6	1938.6	1946.1	65.2	2767.7	92.7
458.2	585.3	−0.6	108.4	108.3	26.6	472.2	148.5
2048.2	920.6	168.7	2330.5	2332.1	21.7	1916.5	148.3
16847.8	7428.5	713.8	11397.6	11697.5	3085.8	8519.8	3251.3
8849.3	1610.0	116.1	1092.9	1213.2	6.9	1965.9	1168.2
7639.0	3295.6	1037.9	2408.1	2393.4	934.7	4526.9	1510.3
520.3	644.0	1.6	193.8	194.6	57.4	309.3	181.9
3083.0	2739.8	106.1	666.2	849.7	18.6	3957.7	383.2
54582.6	16281.4	851.7	−125.8	−192.7	415.3	24298.9	6298.3
909.5	29.7	10.1	266.7	266.7	65.3	276.4	109.1

15-4 续 3

指标名称	Indicator	法人企业数（个）Number of Corporation Enterprises (unit)	主营业务收入 Revenue from Principal Business	主营业务成本 Cost from Principal Business	主营业务税金及附加 Taxes and Other Charges on Principal Business
服装零售	Retail of Garments	34	238189.8	193605.8	886.7
鞋帽零售	Retail of Shoes and Hats	4	5876.9	4531.7	2.7
化妆品及卫生用品零售	Retail of Cosmetic and Hygiene Products	13	45506.8	35627.9	200.5
厨具卫具及日用杂品零售	Retail of Kitchen,Bathroom Equipment and Groceries	2	4900.3	4274.0	3.6
钟表、眼镜零售	Retail of Clock and Glasses	5	20656.2	16238.8	64.1
箱包零售	Retail of bags and suitcases	0	0.0	0.0	0.0
自行车等代步设备零售	Retail of bicycle and other equipments	1	781.0	731.0	2.8
其他日用品零售	Retail of Household Appliances	3	31883.3	23210.9	74.4
文化、体育用品及器材专门零售	Retail of Culture, Sports Appliances and Equipments	41	341988.3	255352.1	5111.8
文具用品零售	Retail of Culture Products	7	14172.9	12586.2	19.7
体育用品及器材零售	Retail of Sports Appliances and Equipments	1	1220.0	919.3	1.4
图书、报刊零售	Retail of Books,Magazines and Newspapers	10	67297.2	58137.1	91.6
音像制品、电子和数字出版物零售	Retail of audiovisual products,electronic and digital publications	1	19343.5	4005.3	18.9
珠宝首饰零售	Retail of Jewelry	10	167888.5	124774.7	4875.8
工艺美术品及收藏品零售	Retail of Crafts and Collectibles	4	5181.2	4916.5	3.1
乐器零售	Retail of Music Instruments	2	2380.7	1989.1	5.3
照相器材零售	Retail of Photographic Apparatus	3	13900.7	13577.6	7.5
其他文化用品零售	Retail of Other Culture Products	3	50603.6	34446.3	88.5
医药及医疗器材专门零售	Retail of Medicines and Medical Appliances	41	435549.6	340421.3	1914.7
西药零售	Retail of Western Medicine	24	381120.0	295760.1	1749.7
中药零售	Retail of Traditional Chinese Medicine	3	5650.3	3563.7	17.6
动物用药品零售	Retail of veterinary drugs	1	5773.2	3779.0	27.1
医疗用品及器材零售	Retail of Medical Appliances	13	43006.1	37318.5	120.3
汽车、摩托车、零配件和燃料及其他动力销售	Cars,motorcycles,spare part and fuel and other power sales	255	4324887.9	3990725.4	10813.8
汽车新车零售	Retail of new cars	177	3504185.1	3273735.8	8416.4
汽车旧车零售	Retail of used cars	1	3081.9	2768.9	0.0
汽车零配件零售	Retail of Automobile Spare Parts	16	54355.3	51576.3	95.7
摩托车及零配件零售	Retail of Motorbike and Its Spare Parts	4	19914.8	17662.5	72.4
机动车燃油零售	Retail of motor fuel oil	54	721249.4	626859.3	2166.4
机动车燃气零售	Retail of motor gas	3	22101.4	18122.6	62.9
家用电器及电子产品专门零售	Special Retail of Household Electric Appliances and Electronic Products	88	807018.3	729778.3	1024.8
家用视听设备零售	Retail of Household Electric Appliances	13	524218.0	470208.7	501.4
日用家电设备零售	Retail of Daily Household Equipment	29	63143.1	58017.7	149.8
计算机、软件及辅助设备零售	Retail of Computer,Software and Auxiliary Equipment	21	87080.4	78936.7	184.7
通信设备零售	Retail of Communication Equipment	15	96639.4	90611.4	128.5
其他电子产品零售	Retail of Other Electronic Equipment	10	35937.4	32003.8	60.4

销售费用 Cost of Sales	管理费用 Cost of Management	财务费用 Cost of Finance	营业利润 Profits from Business	利润总额 Total Profits	应交所得税 Income Tax Payable	应付职工薪酬 (本年贷方累计发生额) Total Wages Payable	应交增值税 Value-added Tax Payable
34615.7	11645.9	403.9	−1173.1	−1102.8	30.1	16044.5	3589.6
1159.5	472.5	43.9	−206.2	−333.6	−1.0	1038.6	6.7
8016.5	1995.6	154.5	−490.0	−487.4	48.7	2609.2	1503.8
381.3	214.8	−5.4	32.6	32.3	4.2	208.8	28.8
2933.1	699.5	240.3	480.2	480.3	262.2	2241.5	479.7
0.0	0.0	0.0	0.0	0.0	0.0	0.0	0.0
18.1	106.1	0.8	−58.5	−58.5	0.0	74.5	14.1
6548.9	1117.3	3.6	1022.5	1010.3	5.8	1805.4	566.5
46794.3	13155.6	864.8	22251.6	22390.8	4396.7	26697.1	7921.1
716.7	843.1	−9.1	783.4	815.5	12.8	600.0	144.7
0.0	226.3	−0.6	74.1	74.1	0.0	68.8	8.7
3532.9	2291.4	−78.4	3234.6	3296.1	322.2	3031.2	61.6
10406.6	1787.7	75.8	3019.7	3007.4	364.4	1874.1	0.0
20709.2	3105.0	666.2	13700.9	13696.4	3475.8	10754.7	6942.8
175.3	44.7	1.4	39.8	39.8	1.5	79.3	32.6
129.1	215.0	7.1	38.7	38.7	3.4	128.6	44.2
118.0	195.1	5.0	−0.5	3.6	3.7	170.3	45.0
11006.5	4447.3	197.4	1360.9	1419.2	212.9	9990.1	641.5
60469.7	17366.9	685.4	16021.4	16875.7	4661.4	41467.2	5516.9
57001.9	12915.7	521.7	14573.8	15329.2	4407.2	38891.3	4428.9
810.5	1115.3	18.8	118.6	116.9	2.5	677.1	36.4
1131.5	607.8	26.7	204.1	264.2	138.4	910.6	177.8
1525.8	2728.1	118.2	1124.9	1165.4	113.3	988.2	873.8
174832.8	95896.6	27760.5	35927.2	36917.3	12035.8	115131.2	51532.2
119879.6	68119.3	24142.2	20748.2	20900.0	8849.1	86589.6	36553.1
183.5	144.2	26.5	−41.2	−41.2	0.0	106.5	0.0
1406.4	1441.3	−154.7	38.3	79.3	31.0	1344.9	165.0
1013.0	830.4	93.1	267.3	277.1	97.5	316.0	612.5
50204.8	24407.1	3536.1	14318.7	15135.3	2875.7	24785.7	13903.4
2145.5	954.3	117.3	595.9	566.8	182.5	1988.5	298.2
47606.9	21754.4	2001.0	608.0	697.8	449.1	25216.1	9663.7
33530.8	9173.0	957.5	2348.3	2267.5	9.3	14698.9	5999.7
3063.5	4203.3	368.8	−710.9	−611.5	48.5	2364.1	624.7
4138.9	3811.4	122.2	441.0	497.3	348.4	4237.9	1655.2
4904.4	3061.4	502.4	−1923.9	−1911.1	24.5	3065.8	1027.6
1969.3	1505.3	50.1	453.5	455.6	18.4	849.4	356.5

指标名称	Indicator	法人企业数（个）Number of Corporation Enterprises (unit)	主营业务收入 Revenue from Principal Business	主营业务成本 Cost from Principal Business	主营业务税金及附加 Taxes and Other Charges on Principal Business
五金、家具及室内装饰材料专门零售	Special Retail of Hardware, Furniture and Decoration Materials	21	111094.4	82958.9	142.2
五金零售	Retail of Hardware	13	29873.4	29086.8	40.0
灯具零售	Retail of lamps	1	688.9	521.8	1.1
家具零售	Retail of Furniture	3	67351.4	42076.1	57.2
涂料零售	Retail of Coating	0	0.0	0.0	0.0
木质装饰材料零售	Retail of Wood Decorative Material	1	1736.6	1524.3	6.4
陶瓷、石材装饰材料零售	Retail of Ceramics and Stone Decorative Material	3	11444.1	9749.9	37.5
其他室内装饰材料零售	Retail of Other Decoration Materials	0	0.0	0.0	0.0
货摊、无店铺及其他零售业	Non-shop and Other Retails	28	469736.1	368170.7	2247.2
流动货摊零售	Retail of mobile stalls	0	0.0	0.0	0.0
互联网零售	Internet Retail	16	384310.8	301317.0	1963.0
邮购及电视、电话零售	Mail,Television and Telephone Retail	3	47236.2	34473.6	196.6
自动售货机零售	Retail of vending machine	0	0.0	0.0	0.0
生活用燃料零售	Retail of Domestic Fuel	2	10214.8	8729.2	15.4
其他未列明零售业	Other Retails	7	27974.3	23650.9	72.2
内资企业	**Domestic Funded Enterprises**	688	8539133.5	7550086.2	30215.4
国有企业	State-owned	5	9397.0	7420.3	67.8
集体企业	Collective-owned	11	13114.8	11176.9	100.8
股份合作企业	Cooperative	3	4021.9	3287.2	17.9
联营企业	Joint venture	0	0.0	0.0	0.0
国有与集体联营企业	State-owned enterprises and collective enterprises	0	0.0	0.0	0.0
有限责任公司	Limited Liability Corporations	191	2772843.8	2420272.0	11147.1
国有独资公司	State Sole funded Corporations	8	35365.0	27400.8	125.6
其他有限责任公司	Other Limited Liability Corporations	183	2737478.8	2392871.2	11021.5
股份有限公司	Share-holding Corporations Limited	21	2340162.4	2048045.5	10799.1
私营企业	Private Enterprises	440	3375600.5	3040189.2	7792.5
私营独资企业	Private-funded Enterprises	13	9603.5	8238.6	21.6
私营有限责任公司	Private Limited Liability Corporations	418	3288427.8	2984730.0	7674.2
私营股份有限公司	Private Share-holding Corporations Ltd.	9	77569.2	47220.6	96.7
其他企业	Other Enterprises	17	23993.1	19695.1	290.2
港、澳、台商投资企业	**Enterprises with Funds from Hong Kong, Macao and Taiwan**	6	362347.8	315065.2	2379.5
与港澳台商合资经营企业	Joint-ventures Enterprises	1	67716.2	60828.6	406.1
港澳台商独资企业	Enterprises with Sole Investment	5	294631.6	254236.6	1973.4
外商投资企业	**Foreign Funded Enterprises**	8	459320.5	372860.1	1155.9
中外合资经营企业	Joint-venture Enterprises	2	102569.4	81215.9	338.9
中外合作经营企业	Cooperation Enterprises	1	76556.1	64211.8	143.4
外资企业	Enterprises with Sole Foreign Funds	4	95480.2	68229.0	91.4
外商投资股份有限公司	Share-holding Corporations Ltd. With Foreign Investment	1	184714.8	159203.4	582.2

销售费用 Cost of Sales	管理费用 Cost of Management	财务费用 Cost of Finance	营业利润 Profits from Business	利润总额 Total Profits	应交所得税 Income Tax Payable	应付职工薪酬 (本年贷方累计发生额) Total Wages Payable	应交增值税 Value-added Tax Payable
13615.1	12557.8	1902.0	−471.6	−416.3	264.5	6565.7	1716.6
730.6	1028.5	19.2	−1029.0	−1042.1	18.6	878.7	160.5
11.6	11.1	0.0	43.0	43.0	0.0	36.0	8.8
11447.4	11140.5	1757.2	471.2	531.3	242.3	4962.5	1271.8
0.0	0.0	0.0	0.0	0.0	0.0	0.0	0.0
40.1	9.7	6.0	150.1	150.1	0.0	41.6	40.3
1385.4	368.0	119.6	−106.9	−98.6	3.6	646.9	235.2
0.0	0.0	0.0	0.0	0.0	0.0	0.0	0.0
80357.1	18214.0	61.8	8205.8	8367.9	1952.8	34405.8	16275.9
0.0	0.0	0.0	0.0	0.0	0.0	0.0	0.0
62759.3	13579.5	114.1	11368.1	11353.7	1778.5	26117.2	13298.6
14070.0	3248.3	−161.6	−3368.4	−3306.3	0.0	5566.4	1610.2
0.0	0.0	0.0	0.0	0.0	0.0	0.0	0.0
1122.9	412.5	31.7	−83.2	18.0	5.8	685.2	971.4
2404.9	973.7	77.6	289.3	302.5	168.5	2037.0	395.7
632701.6	238496.9	64008.5	106426.9	104824.0	30590.0	370158.3	121233.0
645.9	2629.9	4.2	277.5	277.0	59.1	1075.3	191.5
856.9	771.2	27.9	170.6	177.3	9.8	988.2	229.0
516.6	101.8	4.2	94.1	98.1	8.2	230.6	100.6
0.0	0.0	0.0	0.0	0.0	0.0	0.0	0.0
0.0	0.0	0.0	0.0	0.0	0.0	0.0	0.0
214085.1	78900.7	16983.4	45749.8	46553.0	15184.7	120506.0	46969.4
3969.7	2182.3	−14.2	1779.8	1753.6	444.0	3391.2	963.7
210115.4	76718.4	16997.6	43970.0	44799.4	14740.7	117114.8	46005.7
199565.6	58252.0	30779.7	44867.6	41290.4	9810.4	107105.8	34766.8
215530.4	97628.8	16150.2	13038.1	14197.4	5508.5	138816.4	38867.9
518.7	455.1	43.1	283.5	282.2	19.6	467.7	137.2
195447.0	89980.2	15949.1	8380.8	9570.2	5064.4	129579.5	38304.9
19564.7	7193.5	158.0	4373.8	4345.0	424.5	8769.2	425.8
1501.1	212.5	58.9	2229.2	2230.8	9.3	1436.0	107.8
30216.0	4347.6	322.7	16261.4	16339.6	4222.1	8748.5	4018.0
2398.7	1315.2	402.2	3872.8	3893.5	1034.2	1760.2	126.5
27817.3	3032.4	−79.5	12388.6	12446.1	3187.9	6988.3	3891.5
65981.5	25284.7	3684.7	−874.3	−287.6	−62.0	16255.3	8312.3
19746.5	8273.4	139.3	1580.3	1583.0	219.5	7877.9	3224.3
9829.8	169.8	151.3	2050.0	2147.1	536.8	2507.0	190.4
14724.7	10283.9	1954.5	551.0	650.0	382.6	4970.4	574.3
21680.5	6557.6	1439.6	−5055.6	−4667.7	−1200.9	900.0	4323.3

15-5 限额以上餐饮业

Main Economic Indicators of Enterprises in

单位：万元

指标名称	Indicator	法人企业数（个）Number of Corporation Enterprises (unit)	资产总计 Total Assests	负债合计 Total Liabilities	所有者权益合计 Total Owners' Equities	实收资本 Paid-in Capital
总计	**Total**	211	406301.0	362379.5	43921.5	96743.9
正餐服务	Dinner service	185	344074.5	307342.1	36732.4	66016.8
快餐服务	Fast Food Service	20	51562.8	51189.6	373.2	28254.7
餐饮配送及外卖送餐服务	Catering Distribution and Takeaway service	5	10583.7	3817.8	6765.9	2462.4
餐饮配送服务	Catering and Distribution Service	4	10561.0	3808.1	6752.9	2449.4
外卖送餐服务	Takeaway service	1	22.7	9.7	13.0	13.0
其他餐饮业	Other Catering Services	1	80.0	30.0	50.0	10.0
小吃服务	Snack Service	1	80.0	30.0	50.0	10.0
内资企业	**Domestic Funded Enterprises**	209	389786.6	331306.4	58480.2	94055.5
国有企业	State-owned	9	19954.8	17808.3	2146.5	2198.4
集体企业	Collective-owned	3	4733.3	5100.8	-367.5	2332.5
股份合作企业	Cooperative	1	1153.6	255.5	898.1	876.8
有限责任公司	Limited Liability Corporations	61	146437.3	106486.3	39951.0	53359.5
国有独资公司	State Sole funded Corporations	1	14030.7	4438.4	9592.3	9592.3
其他有限责任公司	Other Limited Liability Corporations	60	132406.6	102047.9	30358.7	43767.2
股份有限公司	Share-holding Corporations Limited	3	1023.5	1455.4	-431.9	225.9
私营企业	Private Enterprises	132	216484.1	200200.1	16284.0	35062.4
私营独资企业	Private-funded Enterprises	11	2161.6	1945.3	216.3	147.5
私营有限责任公司	Private Limited Liability Corporations	119	211820.3	197720.3	14100.0	30889.1
私营股份有限公司	Private Share-holding Corporations Ltd.	2	2502.2	534.5	1967.7	4025.8
其他企业	Other Enterprises	0	0.0	0.0	0.0	0.0
港、澳、台商投资企业	**Enterprises with Funds from Hong Kong, Macao and Taiwan**	2	16514.4	31073.1	-14558.7	2688.4
港澳台商独资企业	Enterprises with Sole Investment	2	16514.4	31073.1	-14558.7	2688.4

主要经济指标（2018年）

Cataring Trades Above Designated Size（2018）

(10 000 yuan)

主营业务收入 Revenue from Principal Business	主营业务成本 Cost of Principal Business	销售费用 Cost of Sales	管理费用 Cost of Management	财务费用 Cost of Finance	营业利润 Profits from Business	利润总额 Total Profits	应付职工薪酬 (本年贷方累计发生额) Total Wages Payable
343719.8	154947.5	119388.3	55398.7	7592.8	5074.9	5415.6	84834.2
249125.0	103587.9	93565.4	48303.1	6354.8	−773.7	−274.9	66803.3
69230.2	33586.9	24406.6	4589.4	1198.2	2421.9	2079.8	15837.6
25036.5	17517.6	1415.8	2478.0	39.8	3383.1	3567.1	2007.3
24553.4	17267.4	1415.8	2249.7	39.8	3380.4	3564.4	1829.9
483.1	250.2	0.0	228.3	0.0	2.7	2.7	177.4
328.1	255.1	0.5	28.2	0.0	43.6	43.6	186.0
328.1	255.1	0.5	28.2	0.0	43.6	43.6	186.0
312289.8	145294.5	101227.9	54170.2	6420.3	3880.7	4552.9	78785.2
16442.5	4550.8	5732.1	6605.9	48.1	−60.7	−97.2	5797.1
3065.1	1050.2	426.9	1955.2	113.5	−110.1	−35.7	1887.7
1319.9	445.7	422.6	422.2	−0.7	25.6	28.0	346.9
135574.3	72249.4	37859.5	18287.7	863.3	4368.6	4880.3	30491.2
8036.4	6765.8	2141.6	497.3	234.6	−188.9	138.4	364.1
127537.9	65483.6	35717.9	17790.4	628.7	4557.5	4741.9	30127.1
2712.4	1389.5	1222.4	101.6	35.4	−55.0	−50.0	1043.4
153175.6	65608.9	55564.4	26797.6	5360.7	−287.7	−172.5	39218.9
5129.4	2373.2	1810.9	838.5	2.5	57.1	66.1	1670.0
146519.3	62439.8	53450.4	25290.0	5356.2	−93.4	15.8	37129.9
1526.9	795.9	303.1	669.1	2.0	−251.4	−254.4	419.0
0.0	0.0	0.0	0.0	0.0	0.0	0.0	0.0
31430.0	9653.0	18160.4	1228.5	1172.5	1194.2	862.7	6049.0
31430.0	9653.0	18160.4	1228.5	1172.5	1194.2	862.7	6049.0

15-6 限额以上住宿业

Main Economic Indicators of Enterprises in

单位：万元

指标名称	Indicator	法人企业数（个）Number of Corporation Enterprises (unit)	资产总计 Total Assests	负债合计 Total Liabilities	所有者权益合计 Total Owners' Equities	实收资本 Paid-in Capital
总计	**Total**	103	564577.6	451455.9	113121.8	109803.2
旅游饭店	Tourist Hotels	52	444847.2	292984.8	151862.4	85755.5
一般旅馆	General Hotels	45	118377.0	157885.9	-39508.8	23675.7
经济型连锁酒店	Economical chain hotels	13	59236.9	85570.5	-26333.5	6642.0
其他一般旅馆	Other general hotels	32	59140.1	72315.4	-13175.3	17033.7
其他住宿业	Other Accommodation Services	6	1353.4	585.2	768.2	372.0
内资企业	**Domestic Funded Enterprises**	99	545985.4	427438.4	118547.1	103014.8
国有企业	State-owned	14	211479.0	105226.3	106252.7	32759.6
集体企业	Collective-owned	2	3015.2	3038.5	-23.3	1583.4
股份合作企业	Cooperative	2	14170.1	12170.8	1999.3	1394.0
有限责任公司	Limited Liability Corporations	33	180247.0	184374.2	-4127.2	44061.9
国有独资公司	State Sole funded Corporations	6	38450.6	16264.1	22186.5	2653.0
其他有限责任公司	Others	27	141796.4	168110.1	-26313.7	41408.9
股份有限公司	Share-holding Corporations Ltd.	5	2129.1	1277.6	851.5	761.0
私营企业	Private Enterprises	43	134945.0	121351.0	13594.1	22454.9
私营有限责任公司	Private Limited Liability Corporations	42	134910.2	121323.5	13586.8	22418.3
私营股份有限公司	Private Share-holding Corporations Ltd.	1	34.8	27.5	7.3	36.6
港、澳、台商投资企业	**Enterprises with Funds from Hong Kong, Macao and Taiwan**	4	18592.2	24017.5	-5425.3	6788.4
与港澳台商合资经营企业	Joint-ventures Enterprises	3	17942.7	22034.5	-4091.8	6522.8
港澳台商独资企业	Enterprises with Sole Investment	1	649.5	1983.0	-1333.5	265.6

主要经济指标（2018年）

Quartering Trades Above Designated Size（2018）

(10 000 yuan)

主营业务收入 Revenue from Principal Business	主营业务成本 Cost of Principal Business	销售费用 Cost of Sales	管理费用 Cost of Management	财务费用 Cost of Finance	营业利润 Profits from Business	利润总额 Total Profits	应付职工薪酬 (本年贷方累计发生额) Total Wages Payable
277576.5	69854.1	137464.7	70120.6	6782.2	−2717.9	−3945.8	84489.5
202548.6	56721.8	86835.7	53721.0	6232.3	724.2	506.6	65534.4
72658.5	12337.2	49575.4	15930.3	548.9	−3512.1	−4533.2	18627.3
47780.5	3391.0	41509.9	5925.1	466.0	−3346.7	−4352.1	12984.5
24878.0	8946.2	8065.5	10005.2	82.9	−165.4	−181.1	5642.8
2369.4	795.1	1053.6	469.3	1.0	70.0	80.8	327.8
269894.9	68861.4	134522.3	66710.0	6805.0	−2726.6	−3971.9	81352.2
75591.9	17952.5	37608.9	26380.8	−1554.5	782.0	445.4	27808.4
3332.1	971.1	1566.9	826.7	18.5	−33.0	−32.8	1346.0
5372.2	2533.5	1429.8	1255.9	114.3	16.3	22.5	910.7
135874.8	30137.9	76656.7	27931.7	2431.7	−1695.1	−2719.5	42009.1
18533.2	9797.7	2884.9	5215.2	317.7	116.7	112.9	7964.3
117341.6	20340.2	73771.8	22716.5	2114.0	−1811.8	−2832.4	34044.8
2607.2	494.5	2055.2	136.7	32.0	−125.6	−130.8	710.1
47116.7	16771.9	15204.8	10178.2	5763.0	−1671.2	−1556.7	8567.9
46863.2	16539.8	15184.9	10177.8	5763.0	−1671.3	−1560.7	8446.4
253.5	232.1	19.9	0.4	0.0	0.1	4.0	121.5
7681.6	992.7	2942.4	3410.6	−22.8	8.7	26.1	3137.3
6955.1	687.2	2822.4	3054.0	−22.8	64.3	81.7	2887.7
726.5	305.5	120.0	356.6	0.0	−55.6	−55.6	249.6

15 - 7 限额以上住宿业和餐饮业

Main Economic Indicators of Enterprises in Quartering

指标名称	Indicator	法人企业数（个）Number of Corporation Enterprises (unit)	从业人员期末人数（人）Engaged Persons at Year-end (person)	营业额（万元）Business Revenue (10 000yuan)	客房收入 From Hotel Rooms
总计	Total	314	31491	642813.6	208300.4
一、住宿业	Hotels	103	14037	286596.4	148770.2
旅游饭店	Tourist Hotels	52	10010	207865.7	90960.1
一般旅馆	General Hotels	45	3955	76352.9	56514.2
经济型连锁酒店	Economical chain hotels	13	2828	50201.4	39000.7
其他一般旅馆	Other general hotels	32	1127	26151.5	17513.5
其他住宿业	Other Accommodation Services	6	72	2377.8	1295.9
内资企业	Domestic Funded Enterprises	99	13603	278330.9	144694.9
国有企业	State-owned	14	3799	75527.1	30996.6
集体企业	Collective-owned	2	253	3492.8	1699.7
股份合作企业	Cooperative	2	241	5631.3	1867.4
有限责任公司	Limited Liability Corporations	33	7379	142017.8	78566.9
国有独资公司	State Sole funded Corporations	6	1157	20391.9	6641.1
其他有限责任公司	Others	27	6222	121625.9	71925.8
股份有限公司	Share-holding Corporations Ltd.	5	156	2598.4	2230.1
私营企业	Private Enterprises	43	1775	49063.5	29334.2
私营有限责任公司	Private Limited Liability Corporations	42	1747	48802.4	29073.1
私营股份有限公司	Private Share-holding Corporations Ltd.	1	28	261.1	261.1
港、澳、台商投资企业	Enterprises with Funds from Hong Kong, Macao and Taiwan	4	434	8265.5	4075.3
与港澳台商合资经营企业	Joint-ventures Enterprises	3	354	7260.0	3439.9
港澳台商独资企业	Enterprises with Sole Investment	1	80	1005.5	635.4
二、餐饮业	Catering Services	211	17454	356217.2	59530.2
正餐服务	Dinner service	185	13686	254689.1	59530.2
快餐服务	Fast Food Service	20	3361	73263.3	0.0
餐饮配送及外卖送餐服务	Catering Distribution and Takeaway service	5	361	27926.8	0.0
餐饮配送服务	Catering and Distribution Service	4	349	27414.7	0.0
外卖送餐服务	Takeaway service	1	12	512.1	0.0
其他餐饮业	Other Catering Services	1	46	338.0	0.0
小吃服务	Snack Service	1	46	338.0	0.0
内资企业	Domestic Funded Enterprises	209	15898	322891.9	59530.2
国有企业	State-owned	9	1240	16080.7	8708.1
集体企业	Collective-owned	3	312	3172.3	1237.8
股份合作企业	Cooperative	1	86	1379.3	727.8
有限责任公司	Limited Liability Corporations	61	6013	137816.9	15610.7
国有独资公司	State Sole funded Corporations	1	44	1379.7	361.5
其他有限责任公司	Other Limited Liability Corporations	60	5969	136437.2	15249.2
股份有限公司	Share-holding Corporations Limited	3	252	2794.0	272.8
私营企业	Private Enterprises	132	7995	161648.7	32973.0
私营独资企业	Private-funded Enterprises	11	415	5558.8	641.9
私营有限责任公司	Private Limited Liability Corporations	119	7481	154541.0	31533.8
私营股份有限公司	Private Share-holding Corporations Ltd.	2	99	1548.9	797.3
其他企业	Other Enterprises	0	0	0.0	0.0
港、澳、台商投资企业	Enterprises with Funds from Hong Kong, Macao and Taiwan	2	1556	33325.3	0.0
港澳台商独资企业	Enterprises with Sole Investment	2	1556	33325.3	0.0

法人企业经营情况（2018 年）

Trades and Cataring Trades Above Designated Size（2018）

			客房数（间）Number of Room(room)	床位数（个）Number of Beds(bed)	餐位数（位）Number of dining-seats(seat)	年末餐饮营业面积(平方米) Business Area of Catering Services at Year-end(sq.m)
餐费收入 From Meals	商品销售收入 Revenue from Commodities	其他收入 Other Revenue				
379746.0	10233.3	44533.9	40312	64670	128501	651840
101660.1	3811.6	32354.5	26105	38798	32302	179490
94355.4	2545.5	20004.7	9838	15956	25195	103246
6959.8	1264.7	11614.2	15927	22359	6989	70086
788.6	1076.2	9335.9	10328	15036	4514	20059
6171.2	188.5	2278.3	5599	7323	2475	50027
344.9	1.4	735.6	340	483	118	6158
99524.3	3811.6	30300.1	25413	37741	29732	173390
34654.0	485.5	9391.0	2466	4266	7527	33754
1767.7	0.0	25.4	297	534	1300	4707
3411.7	87.3	264.9	280	530	800	4200
43887.2	2710.3	16853.4	14435	21800	15939	74673
11102.3	1225.5	1423.0	789	1314	2527	8414
32784.9	1484.8	15430.4	13646	20486	13412	66259
184.8	23.5	160.0	664	1088	210	9240
15618.9	505.0	3605.4	7271	9523	3956	46816
15618.9	505.0	3605.4	7220	9451	3956	46816
	0.0	0.0	51	72	0	0
2135.8	0.0	2054.4	692	1057	2570	6100
1765.7	0.0	2054.4	544	800	1370	4100
370.1	0.0	0.0	148	257	1200	2000
278085.9	6421.7	12179.4	14207	25872	96199	472350
181090.7	2856.7	11211.5	14207	25872	73635	396538
71474.5	1300.7	488.1	0	0	22544	64194
25182.7	2264.3	479.8	0	0	0	11438
24670.6	2264.3	479.8	0	0	0	11438
512.1	0.0	0.0	0	0	0	0
338.0	0.0	0.0	0	0	20	180
338.0	0.0	0.0	0	0	20	180
244760.6	6421.7	12179.4	14207	25872	91339	453152
7061.8	1.7	309.1	1394	2608	5478	23568
1781.3	153.2	0.0	347	623	1242	4990
631.9	19.6	0.0	76	140	380	1000
110081.1	3385.2	8739.9	7026	13153	38341	145923
817.4	34.4	166.4	102	198	1350	9591
109263.7	3350.8	8573.5	6924	12955	36991	136332
2521.2	0.0	0.0	245	320	1235	4700
122683.3	2862.0	3130.4	5119	9028	44663	272971
4842.9	69.0	5.0	117	212	1911	10186
117088.8	2793.0	3125.4	4788	8430	41552	251855
751.6	0.0	0.0	214	386	1200	10930
0.0	0.0	0.0	0	0	0	0
33325.3	0.0	0.0	0	0	4860	19198
33325.3	0.0	0.0	0	0	4860	19198

15-8 商品交易市场分类情况（2018年）

Free Markets in Urban and Rural Areas（2018）

单位：个 (unit)

指 标	Indicator	合 计 Total	城 市 Urban	农 村 Rural
商品交易市场个数总计(个)	Total Number of Commodity Transaction Market	419	249	170
消费品市场	consumer products Markets	350	201	149
消费品综合市场	consumer products Comprehensive Markets	33	11	22
农副产品市场	Farmer Produces Markets	202	81	121
农副产品综合市场	Farmer Produces Comprehensive Markets	161	65	96
农副产品专业市场	Farmer Produces Special Markets	51	26	25
工业消费品市场	Industrial consumer products Markets	111	106	5
工业消费品综合市场	Industrial consumer products Comprehensive Markets	84	81	3
工业消费品专业市场	Industrial consumer products Special Markets	27	25	2
其 他	Others	4	3	1
生产资料市场	Means of Production Markets	69	48	21
生产资料综合市场	Means of Production Comprehensive Markets	10	3	7
工业生产资料市场	Industrial Production Markets	40	32	8
农业生产资料市场	Agricultural Production Markets	10	4	6
农业生产资料综合市场	Agricultural Production Comprehensive Markets	6	2	4
农业生产资料专业市场	Agricultural Production Special Markets	4	2	2
其 他	Others	9	9	0

15-9 销售过亿元的商品交易市场一览表（2018年）

Summary of Consumer Goods Markets with Annual Transaction Value Above 100 Million Rmb Yuan（2018）

市场名称 Name	市场类别 Category	年末营业面积（平方米） Operating Area at Year-End(sq.m)	市场总摊位（个） Number of ooths (unit)	年成交额(万元) Annual Turnover (10 000 yuan)
济南海鲜大市场	水产品市场	30000	1200	425000
济南博茗茶叶市场	茶叶市场	82000	680	187100
山东匡山汽车大世界	汽车市场	130000	71	413519
山东匡山钢材市场	金属材料市场	10000	60	21000
山东老屯汽车配件城	机动车零配件市场	35000	489	25320
山东老屯茶城	茶叶市场	8000	120	11521
济南西市场小商品批发市场	工业消费品综合市场	26000	620	12628
山东匡山农产品综合交易市场	蔬菜市场	21000	793	210246
槐荫区红旗钢材市场	金属材料市场	35000	112	78350
济南中恒商场	工业消费品综合市场	71565	2269	45885
山东齐鲁鞋城	鞋帽市场	19176	600	124200
济南泺口服装批发市场	服装市场	200000	2775	205652
济南众鑫鞋城	鞋帽市场	38765	640	130540
山东东亚金星家居	家具市场	69000	457	43856
山东建材市场	建材市场	32000	390	96000
山东济南重汽配件城	机动车零配件市场	61938	435	380000
济南市堤口路果品批发市场	干鲜果品市场	110000	215	101347
济南黄台家居广场	家具市场	15000	200	22000
济南红星美凯龙世博家居生活广场	家具市场	97741	441	152303
七里堡蔬菜综合批发市场	农产品综合市场	150000	1800	313500
济南永君钢材市场	金属材料市场	37000	92	11000
山东济南维尔康肉类水产综合批发市场	水产品市场	20000	820	1200070
济南曲堤蔬菜销售市场	蔬菜市场	23310	75	15014
商河县小商品批发城	工业消费品综合市场	19000	300	22196
商河县富东农贸综合市场	农产品综合市场	27000	502	21392
章丘市刁镇蔬菜批发市场	蔬菜市场	40600	600	150360
济南金田义乌小商品交易市场	小商品市场	45000	1500	103146

主要统计指标解释

社会消费品零售总额 指企业（单位、个体户）通过交易直接售给个人、社会集团非生产、非经营用的实物商品金额，以及提供餐饮服务所取得的收入金额。个人包括城乡居民和入境人员，社会集团包括机关、社会团体、部队、学校、企事业单位、居委会或村委会等。

商品销售额 指对本单位以外的单位和个人出售的商品金额（包括售给本单位消费用的商品，含增值税），在批发和零售业中，本指标反映在国内市场上销售商品以及出口商品的总价。

商品销售包括：（1）售给个人和社会集团消费用的商品；（2）售给农业、工业、建筑业、服务业等国民经济各行业用于生产、经营用的商品，包括售予批发和零售业作为转卖或加工后转卖的商品；（3）对国（境）外直接出口的商品。

商品销售不包括：（1）未通过买卖行为付出的商品，如因机构变动移交给其他企业单位的商品、借出的商品、归还受其他单位委托代保管的商品、付出的加工原料和赠送给其他单位的样品等；（2）促销返券所销售的、不计入营业收入的商品；（3）经本单位介绍，由买卖双方直接结算，本单位只收取手续费的业务；（4）未发生所有权转移的商品预付卡销售，如加油卡；（5）汽车维修、电话卡销售等服务性经济活动；（6）购货退回的商品；（7）商品损耗和损失；（8）出售本单位自用的废旧物资；（9）期货交易商品；（10）自来水供应企业、电力企业、天然气供应企业提供的水、电、气。

批发额 指售给国民经济各行业用于生产、经营用的商品金额。

商品批发包括：（1）售给农业、工业、建筑业等行业用于生产的各种机器设备、工具、原料、材料、燃料、建筑材料，售给农民的农业生产资料，售给交通运输、仓储和邮政业用于业务活动的设备、车辆和燃料等；（2）售给信息传输、软件和信息技术服务，科学研究和技术服务业，水利、环境和公共设施管理业等行业用于生产经营、勘察设计、科研试验等业务经营使用的商品，售给批发和零售业、住宿和餐饮业使用的各种设备、工具、原材料、燃料、仓储运输用的商品；（3）售给居民服务、修理和其他服务业各种营业用品，如售给理发业的理发工具、毛巾等，日用品修理业的设备、工具、材料、零配件等，售给民政部门救灾用的商品等；（4）售给批发和零售业作为转卖用的商品；售给餐饮业用于烹饪、调制加工后出售的商品和转卖的商品；售给服务业转卖的商品；（5）出口的商品。

零售额 指售给个人用于生活消费和社会集团用于公共消费的商品金额。

商品零售包括：（1）售给城乡居民和入境外国人、华侨、港澳台同胞的各类生活消费品；（2）售给行政事业单位、社会团体、军队和武警等机构的商品，以及以零售方式售给各类企业的商品。具体包括：用于非生产和社会交往的办公用品，如通讯设备、计算器具和设备、电讯网络设备、文印设备、音像视听器材和设备、纸张、本册、文具及装订文印材料、家具、日用电器、针纺织品、清洁卫生用品、文体用品、奖品、纪念品、礼品等；供内部人员乘坐的交通工具和燃料；用于办公设施修缮的各类配件、材料、工具等；用于取暖和防暑降温的设备、燃料、材料及食品等；专用于教学的用品和设备；非专用的劳动保护用品；不对外营业的内部食堂用的餐具、炊具、设备、清洁卫生工具和食品、燃料等；军队、武警用于其人员生活的衣着品和个人用品；其他各类非生产性设备和用品。

商品零售不包括：（1）售给城乡居民已确知是用于生产、经营的商品；（2）售给各类农业生产者的生产资料类商品，如农机、农药化肥、农膜、种子饲料等商品；（3）售给企业单位生产用具及生产上专用的劳动保护用品；（4）专用于科研的用品和设备；（5）售给医疗机构的中、西药品、中药材和医疗设备器材；（6）以投资为目的的商品，如黄金、收藏品等。

住宿餐饮业营业额 指住宿和餐饮业单位在经营活动中，因提供服务或销售商品等取得的全部收入（含增值税），收入主要来源于提供客房、餐费服务、商品销售和其他服务，如商务服务。不包括多产业法人企业附营的其他行业产业活动单位的餐费收入、商品销售收入等各项收入。

Explanatory Notes on Main Statistical Indicators

Total Retail Sales of Consumer Goods refer to the amount obtained by enterprises (units, self–employed individuals) through the direct sales of non–production & non–business physical commodity to individuals, social institutions, and the revenue from providing catering services. Individuals include rural and urban households, population from abroad, social institutions include government agencies, social organizations, military units, schools, institutions. neighborhood or village committees.

Total Sales of Commodities refers to value of commodities sold by the establishments to other establishments and individuals (including commodities sold to their own establishments for consumption, including VAT). This indicator is used to show the total value of sales of commodities at domestic markets and export.

The commodities includes: (1) commodities sold to urban and rural residents and social groups for their consumption; (2) commodities sold to establishments in agriculture, industry, construction, service and various sectors of national economy for their production and operation, including commodities sold to wholesale and retail establishments for re–selling with or without further processing; (3) commodities for directing export to other countries.

Commodities exclude: (1) Commodities given not based on purchase and sale activities, such as commodities handed over to other enterprises due to the change in the institution, commodities lent, commodities which are kept by other unit based on entrustment returned, raw materials for processing given and samples given away to other units; (2) Commodities sold based on promotion coupons and not included into operating income; (3) Businesses introduced by the unit based on direct settlement by the buyer and the seller for which the unit only charges for the service charges; (4) Sales of the prepaid card of commodities without transfer of ownership (such as oil filling card); (5) Service economic activities such as vehicle maintenance and repair and sales of phone card; (6) Commodities returned; (7) Commodity loss and damage; (8) Sale of self–used waste and old materials of the unit; (9) Futures trading commodity; (10) Water, electricity and gas provided by the tap water supply enterprise, the power enterprise and the natural gas supply enterprise.

Wholesale Amount refers to the amount of commodities sold to all industries of national economy for production and operation.

The wholesale includes: (1) Various machines and equipment, tools, raw materials, materials, fuel and building materials sold to agriculture, industry and construction industry, etc. for production as well as equipment, vehicles and fuel sold to transportation, warehousing and mail business for business activities; (2) Commodities sold to information transmission, software and information technology services, scientific research and technological services, water conservancy, environment and public facilities management for production, operation, survey and design, scientific research and test, various equipment, tools, raw materials and fuel sold to the wholesale and retail and accommodation and catering industries for use as well as commodities for warehousing and transportation; (3) Various operating supplies sold to neighborhood services, repair and other service industries, such as barber tools and towels sold to the hairdressing industry; equipment, tools, materials and spare and accessory parts for the commodity repair industry and commodities sold to the civil administration department for relieving the victims of a disaster; (4) Commodities sold to wholesale and retail industries for reselling; commodities sold to the catering industry for cooking, selling after processing and reselling; commodities sold to the service industry for reselling; (5) Exported commodities.

Retail Sales refer to the amount of commodities sold to individuals for living consumption and social groups for public consumption.

Commodity retail includes: (1) Various consumer goods sold to urban and rural residents, inbound foreigners, overseas Chinese and compatriots from Hong Kong, Macao and Taiwan; (2) Commodities sold to such institutions as administrative institution, social organization, army and armed police as well as commodities sold to various enterprises in the form of retails. Specifically include: Office supplies not for production and social interaction, such as communication equipment, calculation appliances and equipment, telecommunication network equipment, printing equipment, audio–visual devices and equipment, paper, books, stationery, binding and printing materials, furniture, household electrical appliance, knitwear and textile, sanitary articles, stationery and sporting goods, prizes, souvenirs and presents; communication media for internal personnel and fuel; various accessories, materials and tools for repair of office facilities; equipment, fuel, materials and food for heating and heatstroke prevention; supplies and equipment for teaching; non–special labor protection appliances; tableware, cooking utensils, equipment, cleaning and sanitation tools, food and fuel for internal canteen only; clothing and personal belongings for personnel from the army and armed police living; all other kinds of nonproductive equipment and supplies.

Commodity retail excludes: (1) Commodities sold to urban and rural residents, having been confirmed to be used for production and operation; (2) Means of production (such as agricultural machinery, pesticide and fertilizer, agricultural film and seed feed) sold to various agricultural producers; (3) Production equipment sold to enterprises and special labor protection articles for production; (4) Supplies and equipment for scientific research; (5) Traditional Chinese and Western medicines, traditional Chinese medicinal materials, and medical equipment and supply sold to medical establishments; (6) Commodities for investment, such as gold and collection.

Sales Revenue of Accommodation and Catering industry refers to the total revenue (included VAT) received by accommodation and catering industries from services provided and goods sold, where the main sources are: guest rooms provided, catering services, goods sold and other services such as business services, other than catering income, goods sold income or income from other activities of other industry activity units additive by multi–industry corporate enterprises.

16

对外贸易与国际旅游

FOREIGN TRADE AND INTERNATIONAL TOURISM

16-1 海关进出口商品总额

Total Value of Imports and Exports by Category of Commodities

单位：万美元 (10 000 USD)

指　标	Indicator	2018年 进出口总额 Total Value of Imports and Exports in 2018	出　口 Export	进　口 Import	2017年 进出口总额 Total Value of Imports and Exports in 2017	出　口 Export	进　口 Import
总　额	Total	1318209	855090	463119	1130449	750562	379887
按贸易方式分	By Trade						
一般贸易	General Trade	1163296	740340	422956	1007848	662548	345300
援助物资	Aid Material	–	–	–	643	643	–
捐赠物资	Donation Material	–	–	–	–	–	–
补偿贸易	Compensation Trate	–	–	–	–	–	–
来料加工装配贸易	Processing and Assembling Trade with Sent Materials	2750	1770	980	3660	2162	1498
进料加工贸易	Processing Trade with Imported Materials	63425	48804	14622	61741	47202	14539
对外承包工程出口货物	Export of Contracted projects	50279	50279		28844	28844	–
投资设备	Investment Goods	603	–	603	265	–	265
出料加工贸易	Export Processing Trate	–	–	–	–	–	–
海关特殊监管区域进口设备	Import of Equipment in Special Customs Supervision Area	95	–	95	9	–	9
海关特殊监管区域物流货物	Logistics Freight of Equipment in Special Customs Supervision Area	8852	2473	6379	7119	1288	5831
易货贸易	Barter Trate	–	–	–	–	–	–
保税监管场所进出境货物	Bonded Supervision Entry and Exit Goods	26940	10030	16910	18925	7257	11668
来料加工装配进口设备	Imported Equipment for Processing Incoming Materials	–	–	–	153	–	153
租赁贸易	Leasing Trate	–	–	–	–	–	–
其他贸易	Other Trate	838	265	573	1242	618	624
按运输方式分	By Ways of Transport						
水路运输	Waterway Transport	932819	698290	234529	839251	646055	193196
铁路运输	Railway Transport	15897	10611	5285	10681	7051	3630
公路运输	Road Transport	187772	44792	142980	150211	38118	112093
航空运输	Air Transport	181597	101326	80271	129999	59312	70687
邮件运输	Mail Transport	47	10	37	42	8	34
其他运输	Others	77	61	16	265	18	247
按企业性质分	By Natural of Enterprises						
国有企业	State-owned Enterprises	269741	61894	207847	233898	58602	175296
集体企业	Collective-owned Enterprises	22820	21906	913	15239	14324	915
外商投资企业	Foreign Funded Enterprises	306258	218474	87785	281424	202975	78449
中外合资	Joint-venture Enterprises	106127	75603	30524	94979	66115	28864
中外合作	Cooperation Enterprises	597	551	46	2606	2552	54
外商独资	Wholly Foreign-owned Enterprises	199535	142320	57214	183838	134308	49530
其　他	Others	719389	552815	166574	599888	474661	125227

16-2 主要国别（地区）海关进出口商品总额

Total Value of Imports and Exports by Category of Commodities

单位：万美元 (10 000 USD)

国别(地区)	Country (region)	2018年 进出口总值 Total Value of Imports and Exports in 2018	出口 Export	进口 Import	2017年 进出口总值 Total Value of Imports and Exports in 2017	出口 Export	进口 Import
总额	Total	1318209	855090	463119	1130449	750562	379887
亚洲	Asia	587966	379039	208927	522097	348177	173920
香港	Hong kong	12382	11306	1076	10240	10161	79
印度	India	39895	35204	4692	37857	35786	2071
印度尼西亚	Indonesia	66731	59207	7525	24186	19169	5017
日本	Japan	61049	44098	16950	58816	40002	18814
马来西亚	Malaysia	66735	20138	46597	87444	20090	67354
巴基斯坦	Pakistan	8517	8396	121	12859	12850	9
菲律宾	Philippines	37277	32594	4683	40118	37513	2605
卡塔尔	Katar	1905	1143	762	1431	1240	191
沙特阿拉伯	Saudi Arabia	11458	5309	6150	13588	7967	5621
新加坡	Singapore	31746	22805	8942	12065	8203	3862
韩国	Repulic of Korea	38631	27410	11221	40577	30751	9826
泰国	Thailand	74476	13062	61414	44252	11885	32367
土耳其	Kurtey	7832	7680	151	8412	8279	133
阿拉伯联合酋长国	The United Arab Emirates	10489	8095	2394	13588	7967	5621
越南	Vietnam	19388	17754	1634	30499	29154	1345
台湾省	Taiwan	18681	10804	7877	18263	11464	6799
非洲	Africa	117829	112174	5655	114499	104408	10091
埃及	Egypt	4581	4572	9	5344	5331	13
南非	South Africa	12492	8856	3636	8126	6908	1218
尼日利亚	Nigeria	17761	17760	1	14680	14460	220

16–2 续 1

国别(地区)	Country (region)	2018 年 进出口总值 Total Value of Imports and Exports in 2018	出 口 Export	进 口 Import	2017 年 进出口总值 Total Value of Imports and Exports in 2017	出 口 Export	进 口 Import
欧 洲	**Europe**	253350	140935	112415	217478	117593	99885
比利时	Belgium	5859	4663	1196	5731	4506	1225
英 国	United Kingdom	19406	11647	7759	20118	11709	8409
德 国	Germany	80690	24293	56398	69061	17985	51076
法 国	France	14796	10039	4757	10760	7212	3548
意大利	Italy	17212	13190	4022	16857	12858	3999
荷 兰	Netherlands	8592	6479	2113	6643	4979	1664
西班牙	Spain	9941	8434	1508	8298	6872	1426
芬 兰	Finland	1622	1323	299	1599	1207	392
瑞 典	Sweden	8246	2917	5329	13104	2271	10833
瑞 士	Switzerland	5701	724	4976	5807	1009	4798
俄罗斯	Russia	26015	22227	3788	21075	19851	1224
拉丁美洲	**Latin America**	104765	63436	41329	84060	62130	21930
阿根廷	Argentina	6846	4226	2620	3994	3863	131
巴 西	Brazil	32383	13720	18662	30347	18702	11645
智 利	Chile	19018	6376	12641	11654	4517	7137
墨西哥	Mexico	13212	12872	340	10044	9739	305
北美洲	**North America**	189906	140622	49284	143253	100798	42455
加拿大	United States	32309	22802	9508	27659	18433	9226
美 国	Canada	156999	117816	39183	115580	82351	33229
大洋洲	**Oceanic**	64361	18883	45478	49016	17455	31561
澳大利亚	Australia	52399	13780	38619	38309	12924	25385
新西兰	New Zealand	9231	2375	6856	7960	1790	6170

16-3 海关进出口商品分类金额

Value of Imports and Exports by Category of Commodities

单位：万美元 (10 000 USD)

商品类别	Indicator	2018年 出口 Export	2018年 进口 Import	2017年 出口 Export	2017年 进口 Import
总　额	**Total**	855090	463119	750562	379947
活动物；动物产品	**Live Animals & Animal Products**	489	22849	261	5451
活动物	Live Animals	0	0	0	0
肉及食用杂碎	Meat and Edible Met Offal	0	9582	0	496
鱼、甲壳动物、软体动物及其他水生无脊椎动物	Fish,Crustacean,Mollusc and Other Aquatic Invertebrates	80	9241	48	564
乳品；蛋品；天然蜂蜜；其他食用动物产品	Milk,eggs,Natural Honey and Other Edible Animal Products	55	4023	49	4391
其他动物产品	Other Animal Products	354	4	164	0
植物产品	**Plant Products**	4401	4075	5804	4844
活树及其他活植物；鳞茎、根及类似品；插花及装饰用簇叶	Plant,root,Flower Arrangement	3	55	0	3
食用蔬菜、根及块茎	Vegetable,root and Tuber	1725	58	2548	82
食用水果及坚果；柑桔属水果或甜瓜的果皮	Fruit and Nut	1732	439	2255	845
咖啡、茶、马黛茶及调味香料	Coffee,tea and Aromatic flavouring	766	98	545	132
谷物	Cereal	2	0	1	1
制粉工业产品；麦芽；淀粉、菊粉；面筋	Powder Industrial Products,Starch ,Malt	15	174	6	346
含油子仁及果实；杂项子仁及果实；工业用或药用植物；	Industrial or Medical Plants	90	3230	326	3421
稻草、秸秆及饲料	Straw and Fodder	0	0		
虫胶；树胶、树脂及其他植物液、汁	Gum,Resin and Other Juice from Plants	69	13	121	0
编结用植物材料；其他植物产品	Plant Material for Weaving	0	9	2	14
动、植物油、脂及其分解产品；精制的食用油脂；动、植物蜡	**Animal and Vegetable Oils; Fats and Wax;Edible Oils and Fats**	34	2749	155	711
动、植物油、脂及其分解产品；精制的食用油脂；动、植物蜡	Animal and Vegetable Oils; Fats and Wax;Edible Oils and Fats	34	2749	155	711
食品；饮料、酒及醋；烟草、烟草及烟草用品的制品	**Food; Beverages; Liquor and Vinegar;Tobacco and Tobacco Substitutes**	1953	4193	2314	3054
肉、鱼、甲壳动物、软体动物及其他水生无脊椎动物的制品	Meat,Fish Crustaceans,Mollusks and Other Aquatic Invertebrates	1	1	0	0
糖及糖食	Sugar and Sugar Products	105	37	28	26
可可及可可制品	Cocoa and cocoa Products	0	6	3	5
谷物、粮食粉、淀粉或乳的制品；糕饼点心	Grain,Flour,Starch and Milk Products,Cakes	99	19	61	110
蔬菜、水果、坚果或植物其他部分的制品	Vegetables,Fruits,Nuts Products	935	75	975	80
杂项食品	Miscellaneous Food	448	1354	930	348
饮料、酒及醋	Drink,Wine and Vinegar	13	2273	16	2106
食品工业的残渣及废料；配制的动物饲料	Food Industrial Waste,Animal Feed	352	428	301	380
烟草、烟草及烟草代用品的制品	Tobaccoa and Tobaccoa Products	0	0	0	0

16-3 续 1

商品类别	Indicator	2018年 出口 Export	2018年 进口 Import	2017年 出口 Export	2017年 进口 Import
矿产品	**Minerals**	221	72805	135	51098
盐；硫磺；泥土及石料；石膏料、石灰及水泥	Salt,asaulfer,Stone,cement	96	624	88	543
矿砂、矿渣及矿灰	Ore,Slag,Ash	1	59419	0	43803
矿物燃料、矿物油及其蒸馏产品；沥青物质；矿物蜡	Fossil Fuels,Mineral oil,Asphalt,Mineral Wax	124	12762	47	6752
化学工业及其相关工业的产品	**Chemicals and Related Products**	109403	7364	89386	7126
无机化学品；贵金属、稀土金属、放射性元素及其同位素的	Inorganic chemical,precious metals, radioactive elements	3508	398	3969	639
有机及无机化合物	Organic and Inorganic Compounds				
有机化学品	Organic chemicals	40449	2109	32753	550
药　品	Drugs	24257	951	17124	1111
肥　料	Fertilizer	3102	0	1442	0
鞣料浸膏及染料浸膏；鞣酸及其衍生物；染料、颜料	Dye,Ink,Graphite	17410	653	14346	520
精油及香膏；芳香料制品及化妆盥洗品	Essential ois and ointments,cosmetic	260	462	142	697
肥皂、有机表面活性剂、洗涤剂、润滑剂、人造蜡、调制蜡、光洁剂、蜡烛及类似品、塑料用膏、"牙科用蜡"及牙科用熟石膏制剂	Soap,surfactant,detergents,lubrifiants,cire artificielle Candles,Plaster	986	279	1502	286
蛋白类物质；改性淀粉；胶；酶	Protein,starch,glue,enzymes	1064	42	1090	60
炸药；烟火制品；火柴；引火合金；易燃材料制品	Explosives,matches,flammable materials	0	0	0	0
照相及电影用品	Photographic and Film supplies	18	1	21	1
杂项化学产品	Miscellaneous chemical Products	18347	2470	16997	3262
塑料及其制品；橡胶及其制品	**Plastics and Related Products;Rubber and Related Products**	27305	21175	31325	24808
塑料及其制品	Plastics and Related Products	24310	19635	21575	22842
橡胶及其制品	Rubber and Related Products	2995	1540	3522	1436
生皮、皮革、毛皮及其制品；鞍具及挽具；旅行用品、手提包及类似容器、动物肠线（蚕胶丝除外）制品	**Leather,fur Products,saddle and harness,Travel acessories**	3969	32	3114	265
生皮（毛皮除外）及皮革	Leather,fur	4	4	33	226
皮革制品；鞍具及挽具；旅行用品、手提包及类似容器；动物肠线（蚕胶丝除外）制品	fur Products,saddle and harness,Travel acessories Animal intestine products	2803	27	2300	37
毛皮、人造毛皮及其制品	Leather,artificial fur and its products	1163	1	781	2
木及木制品；木炭；软木及软木制品；稻草、秸秆、针茅或其他编结材料制品；蓝筐及柳条编结品	**Wood and Wooden Products; Cork and Cork Products Straw and other woven product**	11084	3446	18197	2032
木及木制品；木炭	Wood and Wooden Products;	9346	3446	16154	2032
软木及软木制品	Cork and Cork Products	14	0	19	0
稻草、秸秆、针茅或其他编结材料制品；蓝筐及柳条编结品	Straw and other woven product	1724	0	2024	0
木浆及其他纤维状纤维素浆；回收（废碎）纸或纸板；纸、纸板及其制品	**Paper Pulp and Cellulose Pulp; Paper and Waste Paper; Paperboard and Related Products**	3101	33005	3122	31166
木浆及其他纤维状纤维素浆；回收（废碎）纸或纸板	Paper Pulp and Cellulose Pulp,	17	29174	29	29957

商品类别	Indicator	2018年		2017年	
		出口 Export	进口 Import	出口 Export	进口 Import
纸及纸板；纸浆、纸或纸板制品	Paper and paper products	2929	3804	2962	1166
书籍、报纸、印刷图画及其他印刷品；手稿、打字稿及设计图纸	Books,Newspapers,print paintings,manuscripts	154	27	131	43
纺织原料及纺织制品	**Textile Materials and Products**	43444	3701	55071	3232
蚕丝	Silk	13	0	2	3
羊毛、动物细毛或粗毛；马毛纱线及其机织物	Wool and other Textile Materials	195	26	266	19
棉花	Cotton	1016	1994	1150	1673
其他植物纺织纤维；纸纱线及其机织物	Other Vegetable Textile Fibers and its Products	174	3	16	9
化学纤维长丝	Chemical Fiber Filament	2170	249	1942	244
化学纤维短纤	Chemical Fiber Staple	4292	462	6981	354
絮胎、毡呢及无纺织物；特种纱线；线、绳、索、缆及其制品	Wadding,Nonwoven Fabrics,Wire and Other Related Products	5642	284	5243	384
地毯及纺织材料的其他铺地制品	Carpet and Other Floor Covering Products	2040	16	2080	23
特种机织物；簇绒织物；花边；装饰毯；装饰带；刺绣品	Textile,Lace,Tapestry,Embroidery	640	161	401	123
浸渍、涂布、包覆或层压的纺织物；工业用纺织制品	Textile and other Industrial Textile	1244	21	1129	23
针织物或钩编织物	Knitted fabric	258	202	334	156
针织或钩编的服装及衣着附件	Accessory of Knitted fabric	10853	23	14268	36
非针织或非钩编的服装及衣着附件	Accessory of UnKnitted fabric	8149	42	11009	40
其他纺织制成品；成套物品；旧衣着及旧纺织品；碎织物	Other Knitted fabric,Pieces of Fabric	6761	218	10250	145
鞋、帽、伞、杖、鞭及其零件；已加工的羽毛及其制品；人造花；人发制品	**Footwear; Headgear; Umbrellas; Canes;Whips; Feather and Wigs and Related Products**	3986	45	3566	22
鞋靴、护腿和类似品及其零件	Shoes and Other Related Products	1293	42	1100	19
帽类及其零件	Hats and Other Related Products	423	3	631	0
雨伞、阳伞、手杖、鞭子、马鞭及其零件	Umbrellas,Cane,Whip and Other Related Products	22	0	9	0
已加工羽毛、羽绒及其制品；人造花；人发制品	Feather and Wigs and Related Products	2248	0	1826	3
石料、石膏、水泥、石棉、云母及类似材料的制品；陶瓷产品；玻璃及其制品	**Gypsum; Cement; Asbestos; Mica; Ceramic Glass and Its Products**	24528	1760	23606	1037
石料、石膏、水泥、石棉、云母及类似材料的制品	Gypsum, Cement, Asbestos, Mica	7740	194	5850	124
陶瓷产品	Ceramic Products	4016	655	4894	334
玻璃及其制品	Glass and Its Products	12772	911	12862	579
天然或养殖珍珠、宝石或半宝石、贵金属、包贵金属及其制品；仿手饰；硬币	**Pearls and Precious Stones;Precious Metal and Related Products; Artificial Jewelry**	752	255	384	330
天然或养殖珍珠、宝石或半宝石、贵金属、包贵金属及其制品；仿手饰；硬币	Pearls and Precious Stones;Precious Metal and Related Products;Artificial Jewelry	752	255	384	330
贱金属及其制品	**Base Metals and Related Products**	116488	10044	106303	8948
钢铁	Steel	13223	533	12810	483
钢铁制品	Steel Products	84709	2815	76791	3358

16-3 续3

商品类别	Indicator	2018年		2017年	
		出口 Export	进口 Import	出口 Export	进口 Import
铜及其制品	Coper and Related Products	3980	3981	2589	3128
镍及其制品	Nickel and Related Products	18	23	18	66
铝及其制品	Aluminum and Related Products	11770	1714	11531	1111
铅及其制品	Plumbum and Related Products	2	3	1	1
锌及其制品	Zinc and Related Products	34	30	26	32
锡及其制品	Stannum and Related Products	0	0	0	0
其他贱金属、金属陶瓷及其制品	Other Base Metals,Metal Ceramic and Related Products	42	239	78	219
贱金属工具、器具、利口器、餐匙、餐叉及其零件	Base Metals Equipment,Tableware and its Part	1612	387	1290	262
贱金属杂项制品	Base Metals Miscellaneous Products	1099	320	1169	288
机器、机械器具、电气设备及其零件；录音机及放声机、电视图像、 声音的录制和重放设备及其零件、附件	**Machinery; Electric Equipment;TV Sets and Audio**	309148	227510	211990	198464
核反应堆、锅炉、机器、机械器具及其零件	Nuclear Reator,Boiler ,Machinery and Other Parts	236524	155376	150104	93230
电机、电气设备及其零件；录音机及放声机、电视图像、声音的录制和重放设备及其零件、附件	Electric Equipment and Its Part TV Sets and Audio and Its Part	72624	72134	61886	105234
车辆、航空器、船舶及有关运输设备	**Locomotives; Vehicles; Aircraft; Ship and Related Transportation Equipment**	168611	12110	174520	12490
铁道及电车道机车、车辆及其零件；铁道及电车道轨道固定装置及其零件、附件；各种机械（包括电动机械）交通信号设备	Railway and Vehicles and Its Part Machinery and Transportation Equipment	4468	515	3444	597
车辆及其零件、附件，但铁道及电车道车辆除外	Vehicles and Its Part	161708	8427	168837	8923
航空器、航空器及其零件	Aircraftand Its Part	1940	3123	1668	2914
船舶及浮动结构体	Ship and Floating Structures	495	44	571	56
光学、照相、电影、计量、检验、医疗或外科用仪器及设备、精密仪器及设备；钟表；乐器；上述物品的零件、附件	**Photographic,Measuring and Medical Instruments and Equipment Presion Instrument and Machinery**	11762	35451	11471	24292
光学、照相、计量、检验、医疗或外科用仪器 及设备、精密仪器及设备；上述物品的零件、 附件	Photographic,Measuring and Medical Instruments and Equipment Presion Instrument and Machinery	10927	35253	10764	24083
钟表及其零件	Clock Equipment	35	49	56	45
乐器及其零件、附件	Musical Instruments Equipment	800	149	651	164
武器、弹药及其零件、附件	**Weapons and Ammunition; Related Parts and Accessories**	84	0	0	0
武器、弹药及其零件、附件	Weapons and Ammunition; Related Parts and Accessories	84	0	0	0
杂项制品	**Miscellaneous Products**	14290	543	15990	776
家具；寝具、褥垫、弹簧床垫、软坐垫及类似的填充制品；	Furniture,Bedding,Mattess and other Lighting Equipment,Luminous Sign and Portakabin	8603	439	10517	668
玩具、游戏品、运动用品及其零件、附件	Toy,game,Sports products	4093	46	3876	49
杂项制品	Miscellaneous Products	1593	58	1597	59
艺术品、收藏品及古物	**Works of Art, Collectibles and Antiques**	19	1	59	244
特殊交易品及未分类商品	**Special Transactions Goods and Products Not Otherwise Classified**	18	6	20	89

16-4 按企业性质分海关进出口商品总额（2018年）

Import and Export Value of Commodities by Ownership（2018）

单位：万美元 (10 000 USD)

指 标	Indicator	合 计 Total	国有企业 State-owned Enterprises	外商投资企业 Foreign Funded nterprises 小计 Total	中外合作 Cooperation Enterprises	中外合资 Joint-venture Enterprises	外商独资 Wholly Foreign-owned	集体企业 Collective-owned Enterprises	其他 Others
进口商品总额	**Total Value of Imports**	463118	207847	87785	46	30524	57214	913	166574
一般贸易	General Trade	422956	201844	66822	46	12491	54285	913	153378
来料加工装配贸易	Processing and Assembling Trade with Sent Materials	980	0	495	0	422	73	0	485
进料加工贸易	Processing Trade with Imported Materials	14622	5300	3647	0	1614	2033	0	5675
租赁贸易	Leasing Trate	0	0	0	0	0	0	0	0
海关特殊监管区域进口设备	Import of Equipment in Special Customs Supervision Area	95	0	1	0	0	1	0	94
海关特殊监管区域物流货物	Logistics Freight of Equipment in Special Customs Supervision Area	6380	100	364	0	0	364	0	5915
投资设备	Investment Goods	603	0	603	0	312	291	0	0
保税监管场所进出境货物	Bonded Supervision Entry and Exit Goods	16910	574	15419	0	15419	0	0	917
国际无偿援助和捐赠物资	International Aid and Material Donations	0	0	0	0	0	0	0	0
其他贸易	Others	573	29	433	0	265	168	1	110
出口商品总值	**Total Value of Exports**	855089	61894	218474	551	75603	142320	21906	552815
一般贸易	General Trade	740339	39274	187327	551	56040	130736	21705	492034
国际无偿援助和捐赠物资	International Aid and Material Donations	1130	1039	0	0	0	0	92	0
来料加工装配贸易	Processing and Assembling Trade with Sent Materials	1770	0	921	0	706	215	0	849
进料加工贸易	Processing Trade with Imported Materials	48804	14315	19500	0	8661	10838	0	14989
对外承包工程出口货物	Export of Contracted projects	50279	6481	59	0	59	0	104	43635
保税监管场所进出境货物	Bonded Supervision Entry and Exit Goods	10030	0	10030	0	10030	0	0	0
海关特殊监管区域物流货物	Logistics Freight of Equipment in Special Customs Supervision Area	2473	770	449	0	0	449	0	1254
其他贸易	Others	264	15	189	0	106	83	5	54

16-5 历年海关进出口总额

Total Value of Imports and Exports by Category of Commodities

单位：万美元 (10 000 USD)

年份 Year	进出口总额 Total Value of Imports and Exports	进口总额 Total Value of Imports	出口总额 Total Value of Exports
1993	27446	21371	6075
1994	41746	23579	18167
1995	66587	29812	36775
1996	91347	48193	43154
1997	104230	52862	51368
1998	79943	45096	34847
1999	96125	60199	35926
2000	143935	86827	57108
2001	150143	90746	59397
2002	149264	79755	69509
2003	201554	117980	83545
2004	304678	167373	137305
2005	376213	198370	177843
2006	438930	194981	243949
2007	621804	278277	343527
2008	802699	342979	459720
2009	565704	260998	304706
2010	743776	338888	404888
2011	1041422	436966	604456
2012	913286	341844	571442
2013	957442	409126	548316
2014	1048867	442950	605917
2015	911424	311763	599661
2016	1086259	352229	734030
2017	1130449	379887	750562
2018	1318209	463119	855090

16-6 利用外资情况

Utilization of Foreign Capital

指　　标	Indicator	2013 年	2014 年	2015 年	2016 年	2017 年	2018 年
利用外资合同数(个)	Use of Foreign Contracts(unit)	86	78	104	104	110	239
外商直接投资	Foreign Direct Investments	86	78	104	104	110	239
合同外资金额(万美元)	Total Amount of Contracted Foreign Capita(10 000 USD)	165341	187974	303100	179479	218692	556119
外商直接投资	Foreign Direct Investments	165341	187974	303100	179479	218692	556119
实际使用外资(万美元)	Total Amount of Foreign Capital Actually Utilized(10 000 USD)	132054	143497	157851	171625	187623	272847
外商直接投资	Foreign Direct Investments	132054	143497	157851	171625	187623	272847

16-7 对外经济技术合作

Technological Cooperation with Foreign Countries or Territories

指　　标	Indicator	单　位 Unit	2013 年	2014 年	2015 年	2016 年	2017 年	2018 年
对外承包和劳务合作合同金额	Foreign Contracted Projects and Service Contrate	万美元 (10 000 USD)	190515	519758	530383	539589	539598	565706
对外承包	Contracted Projects with Foreign Countries or Regions	万美元 (10 000 USD)	190515	519758	530383	539589	539598	565706
对外承包和劳务合作营业额	Foreign Contracted Projects and Service Contrate	万美元 (10 000 USD)	197113	215461	308737	350099	373739	408427
对外承包	Contracted Projects with Foreign Countries or Regions	万美元 (10 000 USD)	197113	215461	308737	350099	373739	408427
外派劳务人数	Number of Persons Sent out	人 (person)	8339	6833	6886	6976	7037	6586
境外投资企业数	Numberof Overseas Investment Enterprises	个 (unit)	48	48	50	55	42	50
中方实际投资额	China Actual Investment	万美元 (10 000 USD)	54231	60174	70052	70175	83760	102434

注“中方实际投资额”，2016 年以前为“中方协议投资额”口径。

Note: "China's actual investment" was the caliber of "agreed investment amount of China" before 2016.

16-8 出口1000万美元以上企业一览（2018年）

Summary of Enterprises with Annual Exports Value Above 10 Million Dollar（2018）

单位名称 Name of Enterprises	单位名称 Name of Enterprises
中国重汽集团进出口有限公司	济南市冶金科学研究所有限责任公司
山东一达通企业服务有限公司	山东中天重工有限公司
山东浪潮进出口有限公司	福士汽车零部件（济南）有限公司
山东鲁电国际贸易有限公司	济南秦工国际贸易有限公司
济南玫德铸造有限公司	中能华辰集团有限公司
济南裕兴化工有限责任公司	济南轻骑铃木摩托车有限公司
山东齐鲁医药进出口有限公司	济南邦和工贸有限公司
济南澳海炭素有限公司	济南轻骑对外贸易有限责任公司
山东太古飞机工程有限公司	济南博意达商贸有限公司
济南万方炭素进出口有限公司	山东电力基本建设总公司
济南迈克管道科技股份有限公司	山东电力建设第一工程公司
齐鲁天和惠世制药有限公司	斯凯孚（济南）轴承与精密技术产品有限公司
山东中农联合生物科技股份有限公司	山东大鲁阁织染工业有限公司
山东绿霸化工股份有限公司	山东科兴生物制品有限公司
山东伊莱特重工有限公司	山东华民钢球股份有限公司
山东齐发药业有限公司	济南汉锦源电子有限公司
济南金麒麟刹车系统有限公司	山东银丰纳米新材料有限公司
济南圣泉集团股份有限公司	山东冠世针织有限公司
济南邦德数控设备有限公司	济南派克线缆有限公司
济南鲁东耐火材料有限公司	济南乐邦贸易有限公司
齐鲁安替制药有限公司	济南东烨国际贸易有限公司
费斯托气动有限公司	济南瑞泰克制冷设备有限公司
济南二机床集团有限公司	山东威明汽车产品有限公司
山东临沃重机有限公司	济南鸿天国际贸易有限公司
济南西门子变压器有限公司	济南宏创博展汽车销售有限公司
九阳股份有限公司	山东科赛怡锐化工有限公司
浪潮集团有限公司	瀚瑞森（中国）汽车悬挂系统有限公司
济南轨道交通装备有限责任公司	山东凯莱(国际)贸易有限公司
山东集鑫汽车销售有限公司	山东东铁铸锻有限公司
济南沃德汽车零部件有限公司	济南尼克焊接技术有限公司
山东冠世时装加工有限公司	济南创凯科技有限公司
山东省冶金设计院股份有限公司	济南赛恩经贸有限公司
济南轻骑标致摩托车有限公司	济南艾伯特商贸有限公司
济南大自然新材料有限公司	济南森峰科技有限公司
济南弘正科技有限公司	济南浩丰进出口有限公司
山东电力建设第二工程公司	中铁十四局集团有限公司
山东电力设备有限公司	济南嘉亚经贸发展有限公司
山东润科国际贸易有限公司	济南亚国经贸有限公司
济南台有玻璃制品有限公司	海湾电子（山东）有限公司
济南金威刻科技发展有限公司	章丘重诺锻铸有限公司
山东商龙经贸有限公司	章丘振宇锻造有限公司
山东希诺金属材料有限公司	济南海航化工有限公司
济南实达紧固件有限公司	济南拓迪电子商务有限公司
山东省永信非织造材料有限公司	济南东进皮草有限公司
山东三禾农业开发有限公司	济南九鼎中泰国际贸易有限公司
山东力诺特种玻璃股份有限公司	济南华尔重型汽车销售有限公司
华熙生物科技股份有限公司	济南天马泰山石材有限公司
卧龙电气章丘海尔电机有限公司	山东博世磨具实业有限公司
济南诚信通铝业有限公司	济南星辉数控机械科技有限公司
山东圣泉新材料股份有限公司	济南思迈迩制衣有限公司
山东钢铁集团国际贸易有限公司	济南易安达保税物流有限公司
济南华辰实业有限责任公司	济南雅洁地毯有限公司
山东立达进出口公司	济南圣泉唐和唐生物科技有限公司

16-9 旅游住宿单位接待入境游客

Received Inbound Tourists by Hotels

指 标	Indicator	2013 年	2014 年	2015 年	2016 年	2017 年	2018 年
入境游客人数(人次)	**Number of Inbound Tourists(person-time)**	307244	314536	332942	351526	375469	398721
外国人	Foreigners	194003	194567	205477	216899	232260	247086
#日 本	Japan	24457	22336	22154	21972	21967	23123
菲律宾	Philippines	2231	2237	2215	2357	2622	2901
新加坡	Singapore	13525	13840	14837	15586	16588	17503
韩 国	Republic of Korea	32026	33839	34238	36137	34695	37432
加拿大	Canada	5283	5361	5697	5558	6445	6970
英 国	United Kingdom	8978	9164	9693	10286	10918	11602
德 国	Germany	13245	13722	14688	15608	16543	17706
法 国	France	5873	6207	6694	7041	7532	8000
意大利	Italy	3752	3825	4086	4330	5190	5524
瑞 士	Switzerland	895	931	986	1051	1119	1216
澳大利亚	Australia	8250	8411	8934	9456	10089	10762
新西兰	New Zealand	1448	1519	1625	1825	1958	2078
美 国	United States	19243	19844	21396	23187	24797	26325
港澳和台湾同胞	Compatriots from Hong Kong, Macao and Taiwan	113241	119969	127465	134627	143209	151635
#台湾同胞	Compatriots from Taiwan	54031	57586	61726	65050	68839	72667
入境游客人天数(人天)	**Number of Days on Inbound Tourists(person-day)**	725144	739926	786451	829300	878238	1086701
外国人	Foreigners	453894	443823	460937	483753	513621	683730
港澳和台湾同胞	Compatriots from Hong Kong, Macao and Taiwan	271250	296061	325514	345547	364617	402971
#台湾同胞	Compatriots from Taiwan	124750	138269	172776	178839	187351	265047
旅游外汇收入(亿美元)	**Foreign Exchange Income of Tourism (100 million USD)**	1.51	1.71	1.84	1.96	2.08	2.23
#商品性收入	Commecial Income	0.32	0.58	0.53	0.51	0.54	0.6
附：平均每天来济国际旅游人数(人次)	Number of Tourists Per Day(person-time)	842	862	912	963	1029	1092
星级宾馆客房出租率(%)	Star Hotel Room Rate(%)	61.0	62.55	61.0	64.5	64.56	63.4

注：2018 年接待入境游客包含了过夜游客和一日游游客。

Note: Entry visitors received in 2018 included overnight visitors and excursionists.

16-10 济南与国外结成友好城市一览表（2018年末）

Foreign Friendly Cities of Jinan（End of 2018）

国 别	Country	城 市	City	缔结日期 Day
日本	Japan	和歌山市（和歌山县首府）	Wakayama	1983.01.14
英国	United Kingdom	考文垂市（英国汽车工业故乡，制造业中心之一）	Coventry	1983.10.03
日本	Japan	山口市（山口县首府）	Yamaguchi	1985.09.20
美国	United States	萨克拉门托市（加利福尼亚州首府）	Sacramento	1985.05.29
加拿大	Canada	里贾纳市（萨斯喀彻温省省会）	Regina	1987.08.10
巴布亚新几内亚	Papua New Guinea	莫尔斯比港（巴布亚新几内亚首都）	Port Moresby	1988.09.28
韩国	Republic of Korea	水原市（京畿道首府）	Suwon	1993.10.27
俄罗斯	Russia	下诺夫哥罗德市（下诺夫哥罗德州首府）	Nizhny novgorod	1994.09.25
芬兰	Finland	万达市（欧洲机场城市、芬兰第四大城市）	Vantaa	2001.08.27
法国	France	雷恩市（布列塔尼大区首府）	Renne	2002.07.17
澳大利亚	Australia	郡德勒普市（西澳洲新兴教育科技中心）	Draper	2004.09.04
德国	Germany	奥格斯堡市（施瓦本地区首府）	Augsburg	2004.10.10
乌克兰	Ukraine	哈尔科夫市（哈尔科夫州首府）	Kharkov	2007.05.23
以色列	Israel	卡法萨巴市（沙龙地区中心城市）	Kafassaba	2009.05.11
白俄罗斯	Belorussia	维捷布斯克市（ 维捷布斯克州首府）	Vitebsk	2009.09.20
佛得角	Cape Verde	普拉亚市（佛得角首都）	Praia	2009.09.22
巴西	Brazil	波多韦柳市（朗多尼亚州首府）	Bothoweri	2011.10.13
土耳其	Turkey	马尔马里斯市（地中海沿岸港口城市和旅游胜地）	Marmaris	2011.10.21
印度尼西亚	Indonesia	徐图利祖市（东爪哇省泗水市机场城市、新兴经济城市）	Xu Tzu Chi City	2012.09.21
保加利亚	Bulgaria	卡赞勒格市（保加利亚玫瑰精油生产中心）	Kazanlak	2013.08.29
墨西哥	Mexico	萨博潘市（哈利斯科州经济首府）	Saab Pan	2014.05.20
意大利	Italy	奇维塔韦基亚市（欧洲第三大客运港）	Civitavecchia	2016.6.20
印度	India	那格浦尔市（印度地理中心城市、马哈拉施特拉邦第二首府）	Nagpur	2017.12.08
埃塞俄比亚	Ethiopia	阿尔巴门奇市(埃塞俄比亚西南部重要城镇，格穆戈法州首府)	Arba Minch	2018.09.06

16-11 济南市与各友好城市交流

Basic Statistics of Transmission Between Foreign Friendly Cities and Jinan

单位：批数、人次 (batch.person-time)

指 标	Indicator	2013年	2014年	2015年	2016年	2017年	2018年
出访交流考察	Exchange Visits						
批 数	Batch	257	430	583	780	747	781
人 次	Number	866	994	1444	1907	1906	2107
接待来访团组	Receive Visitors						
批 数	Batch	140	128	123	204	207	206
人 次	Number	1786	1296	1107	1352	1829	1730

主要统计指标解释

海关进出口商品总额 指实际进出我国国境的货物总金额。包括对外贸易实际进出口货物，来料加工装配进出口货物，国家间、联合国及国际组织无偿援助物资和赠送品，华侨、港澳台同胞和外籍华人捐赠品，租赁期满归承租人所有的租赁货物，进料加工进出口货物，边境地方贸易及边境地区小额贸易进出口货物（边民互市贸易除外），中外合资企业、中外合作经营企业、外商独资经营企业进出口货物和公用物品，到、离岸价格在规定限额以上的进出口货样和广告品（无商业价值、无使用价值和免费提供出口的除外），从保税仓库提取在中国境内销售的进口货物，以及其他进出口货物。进出口总额用以观察一个国家在对外贸易方面的总规模。我国规定出口货物按离岸价格统计，进口货物按到岸价格统计。

利用外资 指我国各级政府、部门、企业和其他经济组织通过对外借款、吸收外商直接投资以及用其他方式筹措的境外现汇、设备、技术等。

外商直接投资 指外国企业和经济组织或个人（包括华侨、港澳台胞以及我国在境外注册的企业）按我国有关政策、法规，用现汇、实物、技术等在我国境内开办外商独资企业、与我国境内的企业或经济组织共同举办中外合资经营企业、合作经营企业或合作开发资源的投资（包括外商投资收益的再投资）。即“外方投资者的投资股本”和总投资与注册资本差额部分的“外方股东对企业的直接贷款”。

对外承包工程 指各对外承包公司以招标议标承包方式承揽的下列业务：（1）承包国外工程建设项目，（2）承包我国对外经援项目，（3）承包我国驻外机构的工程建设项目，（4）承包我国境内利用外资进行建设的工程项目，（5）与外国承包公司合营或联合承包工程项目时我国公司分包部分，（6）对外承包兼营的房屋开发业务。对外承包工程的营业额是以货币表现的本期内完成的对外承包工程的工作量，包括以前年度签订的合同和本年度新签订的合同在报告期内完成的工作量。

对外劳务合作 指以收取工资的形式向业主或承包商提供技术和劳动服务的活动。我国对外承包公司在境外开办的合营企业，中国公司同时又提供劳务的，其劳务部分也纳入劳务合作统计。劳务合作营业额按报告期内向雇主提交的结算数（包括工资、加班费和奖金等）统计。

入境游客 指报告期内来中国(大陆)观光、度假、探亲访友、就医疗养、购物、参加会议或从事经济、文化、体育、宗教活动的外国人、港澳台同胞等游客(即入境旅游人数)。

外国人 指属外国国籍的人，加入外国国籍的中国血统华人也计入外国人。

旅游外汇收入 入境游客在中国(大陆)境内旅行、游览过程中用于交通、参观游览、住宿、餐饮、购物、娱乐等全部花费。

Explanatory Notes on Main Statistical Indicators

Total Value of Customs Export–import Commodities refers to the total value of cargoes actually importing from and exported to China. It includes cargoes actually imported and exported in the foreign trade; cargoes imported and exported of processing and assembly of supplied materials; free aid and gift between countries, from The United Nations and international organizations; donation of overseas Chinese, Hong Kong, Macao and Taiwan compatriots and Chinese of foreign nationality; lease cargoes belonging to the tenant when the lease term expires; cargoes imported and exported of processing with imported materials; cargoes imported and exported of local border trade and small trade in border areas (except for fair among the inhabitants of border areas); cargoes imported and exported and public objects of Sino–foreign joint venture, Chinese–foreign co–operative enterprise and wholly foreign–owned enterprises; sample goods and advertising samples imported and exported based on cost insurance and freight and FOB above the specified limit (except for export without commercial value or use value and freely provided); import goods extracted from bonded warehouse which are sold in China and other cargoes imported and exported. Total export–import volume is used to observe the total scale of a country in the aspect of foreign trade. China specifies exported goods are subject to statistics as per FOB and import goods are subject to statistics pursuant to cost insurance and freight.

Utilization of Foreign Capital refers to remittance, equipment and technology financed from abroad, by foreign loans, attracting foreign direct investment and other forms undertaken by the Chinese governments at all levels, by various departments, enterprises and other economic organizations.

Foreign Direct Investment refers to investments by exclusively foreign–owned enterprises established by foreign enterprise and economic organization or individual (including overseas Chinese, Hong Kong, Macao and Taiwan compatriots and China's enterprise registered abroad) in China according to related policies and regulations of China based on spot exchange, material object and technology, joint venture with Chinese and foreign investment, cooperative enterprise or cooperative development resources jointly organized by enterprises or economic organizations in China, (including reinvestment of foreign direct investment income), namely "direct loan from foreign shareholders to enterprises" of the balance between "investment capital of foreign investors" and total investment as well as registered capital.

Contract Foreign Projects refer to the following business undertaken by all foreign contract companies based on the method of contract through bidding negotiation: (1) Contracting foreign construction projects, (2) Contracting China's foreign economic assistance projects, (3) Contracting construction projects of China's institution functioning abroad, (4) Contracting projects constructed based on foreign capital in China, (5) Subcontracting part of China's company at the time of joint operation with foreign contracting company or united contracting of the project, and (6) Contracting the housing development business operated concurrently. Turnover of contract foreign projects is the workload of contract foreign projects completed in the current period embodied with currency, including workload of the contract signed in previous year and the contract newly signed in this year which is completed in the reporting period.

Foreign Labor Cooperation refers to the activities of providing technology and labor services for owners or contractors in the forms of receiving salaries and wages. China's foreign contract companies refer to cooperative enterprises established outside the border with labor service provided by Chinese company at the same time whose labor service is included into labor service cooperation statistics as well. The business volume of labor service cooperation shall be counted in accordance with the settlement amount (wages and salaries, overtime pay, bonuses and other remuneration) submitted to the employers during the reporting period.

Entry Visitors refer to foreigners and compatriots from Hong Kong, Macao and Taiwan coming to China (Chinese Mainland) for sightseeing, vacation, visiting relatives and friends, medical treatment, shopping, attending the meeting or engaging in economic, cultural, sports and religious activities in the reporting period (namely the number of inbound travelers). The entry visitors of year 2018 including tourists staying overnight and one–day tour tourists.

Foreigners refer to persons with foreign nationality and ethnic Chinese with Chinese descent and foreign nationality is also included into foreigners.

Income from Tourism Foreign Exchange refers to total cost spent by entry visitors on transportation, sightseeing, accommodation, catering, shopping and entertainment, etc. in the process of travelling and sightseeing in China (Chinese Mainland).

科　技

SCIENCE AND TECHNOLOGY

17－1 科技综合情况

Basic Statistics on Science and Technology

指 标	Indicator	单位 Unit	2011 年	2012 年	2013 年	2014 年	2015 年	2016 年	2017 年
R&D 活动单位	R&D Activity Units	个(Unit)	401	446	573	660	803	890	964
R&D 活动全时人员	Full-time R&D Personnel	人年(man-years)	37048	37824	41643	46796	51297	52395	57506
R&D 活动经费内部支出	Internal Expenditure on R&D	万元(10 000 yuan)	955341	989528	1111522	1205441.6	1330543.8	1567365	1851538.7
#基础研究	Basic Research	万元(10 000 yuan)	53609	72717	77918	81092.8	106229	128504.7	152909.2
#应用研究	Applied Research	万元(10 000 yuan)	126146	135575	127176	142847.5	136507.2	151841.2	208526.4
#试验发展	Experimental Development	万元(10 000 yuan)	775586	781236	906428	981501.4	1087807.6	1287019.1	1490103.1
#日常性支出	Daily Expenditure	万元(10 000 yuan)	852242	859567	967345	1068380.6	1161517.8	1376837.7	1636821.4
人员劳务费	Staff Service Fee	万元(10 000 yuan)	266312	277486	320273	376372.8	470989.9	522676.7	616187.2
#资产性支出	Capital Expenditure	万元(10 000 yuan)	103101	129961	144177	137061	169026	190527.3	214717.4
仪器设备	Instrument and Equipment	万元(10 000 yuan)	96654	123932	135607	126101.9	160989.5	185967.8	188836.8
R&D 活动经费外部支出	External expenditure on R&D	万元(10 000 yuan)	40140	38990	46679	57993	42612	62140.8	70569.2
科技成果情况	Scientific Achievements								
专利申请数	Patent Applications	件(pieces)	6301	8699	10221	12196	14178	15490	19645
#发明专利申请数	Inventions	件(pieces)	2678	3903	4755	6234	8454	9138	12027
拥有发明专利数	Number of Invention Patents	件(pieces)	5624	4973	6087	7712	10007	13808	20059
科技项目（课题）情况	Scientific Projects								
项目（课题）数	Number of Projects	项(item)	11174	15899	17683	18811	21177	22570	27666
项目参加人员折合全时当年	Number of Participants	人年(man-years)	35518	36702	39557	43828.2	46715	44188	46457.1

17－2 科技投入情况（2017 年）

Basic Statistics on Scientific and Technological Funds（2017）

指　标	Indicator	单位 Unit	合计 Total	科研机构 Research Institutions	高等院校 colleges and universities	规模以上工业企业 Industrial Enterprises above Designated Size	其他 Others
有 R&D 活动单位数	Number of Enterprises with R&D Activities	个(unit)	964	69	58	718	119
R&D 人员	R&D Personnel	人(Person)	84762	5911	16439	41189	21223
#研究人员	Research Personnel	人(Person)	45752	4545	14308	17761	9138
博士生	Doctor	人(Person)	7936	1100	6230	460	146
硕士生	Master	人(Person)	16072	1976	5943	6796	1357
本科生	Undergraduate	人(Person)	42660	2191	3888	30947	5634
其他	Others	人(Person)	18094	644	378	2986	14086
R&D 人员折合全时人员	Full-time Equivalent of R&D Personnel	人年(man-years)	50170	5363	7681	27349	9776
基础研究	Basic Research	人年(man-years)	7050	1998	3816	36	1200
应用研究	Applied Research	人年(man-years)	7497	2025	3467	448	1557
试验发展	Experimental Development	人年(man-years)	35624	1340	399	26864	7021
R&D 经费内部支出	Internal Expenditure on R&D	万元(10 000 yuan)	1851539	131545	193598.1	1165629	360767
基础研究	Basic Research	万元(10 000 yuan)	152909	31876.3	96758.8	1157	23117
应用研究	Applied Research	万元(10 000 yuan)	208526	49974.7	81912.3	15931	60708
试验发展	Experimental Development	万元(10 000 yuan)	1490103	49694.4	14927	1148540	276942
日常性支出	Routine Expenses	万元(10 000 yuan)	1636821	107085.4	155164.5	1055723	318848
#人员劳务费	Labor Cost	万元(10 000 yuan)	616187	60868.1	28431.4	389725	137163
资产性支出	Assets Expenditure	万元(10 000 yuan)	214717	24460	38433.7	109906	41918
#仪器和设备	Instrument and Equipment	万元(10 000 yuan)	188837	22698.9	22546.4	1783	141809

17-3 规模以上工业企业科技活动情况（2017年）

Main Indicators of Industrial Enterprises Above Designated Size（2017）

单位：个 (unit)

指标	Indicator	企业数 Number of Industial Enterprises	#有R&D活动的单位数 Number of Units with Research and Development Activities	企业办科技机构数 Number of Technology Institutions Run By Enterprises
总计	**Total**	2050	716	254
按登记注册类型分	**by Status of Registration**			
国有企业	State-owned Enterprises	10	4	2
集体企业	Collective-owned Enterprises	14	2	
股份合作企业	Cooperative Enterprises	3		
有限责任公司	Private Limited Liability Corporations	777	271	113
国有独资公司	State Sole funded Corporations	28	19	9
其他有限责任公司	Other Limited Liability Corporations	749	252	104
股份有限公司	Share-holding Corporations Limited	89	58	28
私营独资企业	Private-funded Enterprises	54	3	
私营合伙企业	Private Partnership Enterprises			
私营有限责任公司	Private Limited Liability Corporations	894	299	84
私营股份有限公司	Private Share-holding Corporations Ltd.	57	23	9
其他企业	Other Enterprises	6		
合资经营企业(港或澳、台资)	Joint-ventures Enterprises	21	7	1
合作经营企业(港或澳、台资)	Cooperative Enterprises	2	1	
港、澳、台商独资经营企业	Enterprises with Sole Investment	25	6	2
港、澳、台商投资股份有限公司	Share-holding Corporations Ltd. With Funds from	1	1	1
中外合资经营企业	Joint-venture Enterprises	54	21	9
中外合作经营企业	Cooperation Enterprises	2		
外资企业	Enterprises with Sole Foreign Funds	40	20	5
外商投资股份有限公司	Share-holding Corporations Ltd. With Foreign Investment	1		
按工业行业大类分	**by Sector**			
煤炭开采和洗选业	Mining and Washing of Coal	1	1	
石油和天然气开采业	Extraction of Petroleum and Natural Gas	3		
黑色金属矿采选业	Mining of Ferrous Metal Ores	1		
非金属矿采选业	Mining and Processing of Nonmetal Ores	9	1	1
农副食品加工业	Processing of Food from Agricultural Products	72	32	9
食品制造业	Manufacture of Foods	70	26	12

指标	Indicator	企业数 Number of Industial Enterprises	#有 R&D 活动的单位数 Number of Units with Research and Development Activities	企业办科技机构数 Number of Technology Institutions Run By Enterprises
酒、饮料和精制茶制造业	Manufacture of Wine, Drinks and Refined Tea	25	7	3
烟草制品业	Manufacture of Tobacco	1	1	1
纺织业	Manufacture of Textile	50	16	3
纺织服装、服饰业	Manufacture of Textile Wearing Apparel and Finery	31	3	
皮革、毛皮、羽毛及其制品和制鞋业	Manufacture of Leather, Fur, Feather & Its Products and Footwear	9	1	1
木材加工和木、竹、藤、棕、草制品业	Processing of Timbers, Manufacture of Wood, Bamboo, Rattan, Palm, and Straw Products	18	4	1
家具制造业	Manufacture of Furniture	17	3	
造纸和纸制品业	Manufacture of Paper and Paper Products	25	4	
印刷和记录媒介复制业	Printing, Reproduction of Recording Media	47	12	5
文教、工美、体育和娱乐用品制造业	Manufacture of Culture, Education,Arts and crafts，Sport and Entertainment Goods	30	9	1
石油加工、炼焦和核燃料加工业	Processing of Petroleum, Coking and Nucleus Fuel	10	4	2
化学原料和化学制品制造业	Manufacture of Chemical Raw Material and Chemical Products	125	55	22
医药制造业	Manufacture of Medicines	65	43	23
化学纤维制造业	Manufacture of Chemical Fiber	5	2	1
橡胶和塑料制品业	Manufacture of Rubber and Plastic	74	17	5
非金属矿物制品业	Manufacture of Non-metallic Mineral Products	189	43	16
黑色金属冶炼和压延加工业	Manufacture and Processing of Ferrous Metals	37	9	3
有色金属冶炼和压延加工业	Manufacture & Processing of Non-ferrous Metals	19	1	1
金属制品业	Manufacture of Metal Products	233	50	12
通用设备制造业	Manufacture of General Purpose Machinery	291	104	39
专用设备制造业	Manufacture of Special Purpose Machinery	190	90	25
汽车制造业	Manufacture of Automotive	105	28	9
铁路、船舶、航空航天和其他运输设备制造业	Manufacture of Railroad,Marine,Aerospace and Other Transportation Equipment	31	9	4
电气机械和器材制造业	Manufacture of Electrical Machinery & Equipment	100	49	21
计算机、通信和其他电子设备制造业	Manufacture of Computer, Communications and Other Electronic Equipment	50	38	16
仪器仪表制造业	Manufacture of Measuring Instrument	63	43	15
其他制造业	Other Manufacture	4	1	
废弃资源综合利用业	Comprehensive Utilization of Waste	4		
金属制品、机械和设备修理业	Metal Products, Machinery and Equipment Repair Industry	3	2	2
电力、热力生产和供应业	Production and Supply of Electric Power and Heat Power	20	3	
燃气生产和供应业	Production and Supply of Gas	14	1	
水的生产和供应业	Production and Supply of Water	9	4	1

17－4 规模以上工业企业技术改造及引进吸收（2017年）

Innovation and Resorb of Industrial Enterprises Above Designated Size（2017）

单位：万元 (10 000 yuan)

指标	Indicator	技术改造经费支出 Technical Reform Expenditure	引进国外技术经费支出 Acquisition of Foreign Technology Expenditure	引进技术的消化吸收经费支出 Expenditure for Assimilation Technology	购买国内技术经费支出 Expenditurefor Purchase Domestic Technology
总计	**Total**	470719	10627	2837	84474
按登记注册类型分	**by Status of Registration**				
国有企业	State-owned Enterprises	1798	12	13	11
集体企业	Collective-owned Enterprises				
股份合作企业	Cooperative Enterprises				
有限责任公司	Private Limited Liability Corporations	294586	6499	880	83516
国有独资公司	State Sole funded Corporations	54435	1189	16	15
其他有限责任公司	Other Limited Liability Corporations	240150	5310	865	83502
股份有限公司	Share-holding Corporations Limited	143571	819	1800	309
私营独资企业	Private-funded Enterprises				
私营合伙企业	Private Partnership Enterprises				
私营有限责任公司	Private Limited Liability Corporations	4435	106	106	609
私营股份有限公司	Private Share-holding Corporations Ltd.	24243	79		10
其他企业	Other Enterprises				
合资经营企业(港或澳、台资)	Joint-ventures Enterprises				
合作经营企业(港或澳、台资)	Cooperative Enterprises				
港、澳、台商独资经营企业	Enterprises with Sole Investment	489			
港、澳、台商投资股份有限公司	Share-holding Corporations Ltd. With Funds from				
中外合资经营企业	Joint-venture Enterprises	1425	2343		18
中外合作经营企业	Cooperation Enterprises				
外资企业	Enterprises with Sole Foreign Funds	173	769	38	
外商投资股份有限公司	Share-holding Corporations Ltd. With Foreign Investment				
按工业行业大类分	**by Sector**				
煤炭开采和洗选业	Mining and Washing of Coal				
石油和天然气开采业	Extraction of Petroleum and Natural Gas				
黑色金属矿采选业	Mining of Ferrous Metal Ores				
非金属矿采选业	Mining and Processing of Nonmetal Ores	5			
农副食品加工业	Processing of Food from Agricultural Products	73			13
食品制造业	Manufacture of Foods	376			145

指标	Indicator	技术改造经费支出 Technical Reform Expenditure	引进国外技术经费支出 Acquisition of Foreign Technology Expenditure	引进技术的消化吸收经费支出 Expenditure for Assimilation Technology	购买国内技术经费支出 Expenditurefor Purchase Domestic Technology
酒、饮料和精制茶制造业	Manufacture of Wine, Drinks and Refined Tea	53			
烟草制品业	Manufacture of Tobacco				
纺织业	Manufacture of Textile	834			1
纺织服装、服饰业	Manufacture of Textile Wearing Apparel and Finery				
皮革、毛皮、羽毛及其制品和制鞋业	Manufacture of Leather, Fur, Feather & Its Products and Footwear	81			
木材加工和木、竹、藤、棕、草制品业	Processing of Timbers, Manufacture of Wood, Bamboo, Rattan, Palm, and Straw Products				
家具制造业	Manufacture of Furniture				
造纸和纸制品业	Manufacture of Paper and Paper Products				
印刷和记录媒介复制业	Printing, Reproduction of Recording Media	120			
文教、工美、体育和娱乐用品制造业	Manufacture of Culture, Education,Arts and crafts, Sport and Entertainment Goods				
石油加工、炼焦和核燃料加工业	Processing of Petroleum, Coking and Nucleus Fuel	119830	101	1901	201
化学原料和化学制品制造业	Manufacture of Chemical Raw Material and Chemical Products	30591	800		120
医药制造业	Manufacture of Medicines	51539	4985	13	82913
化学纤维制造业	Manufacture of Chemical Fiber				
橡胶和塑料制品业	Manufacture of Rubber and Plastic				
非金属矿物制品业	Manufacture of Non-metallic Mineral Products	19291			
黑色金属冶炼和压延加工业	Manufacture and Processing of Ferrous Metals	21230			
有色金属冶炼和压延加工业	Manufacture & Processing of Non-ferrous Metals	300			
金属制品业	Manufacture of Metal Products	20937			
通用设备制造业	Manufacture of General Purpose Machinery	10827	1586	5	276
专用设备制造业	Manufacture of Special Purpose Machinery	1880	19		97
汽车制造业	Manufacture of Automotive	44121	45	38	18
铁路、船舶、航空航天和其他运输设备制造业	Manufacture of Railroad,Marine,Aerospace and Other Transportation Equipment	515	2578	400	377
电气机械和器材制造业	Manufacture of Electrical Machinery & Equipment	4161	434	480	286
计算机、通信和其他电子设备制造业	Manufacture of Computer, Communications And Other Electronic Equipment	140215	79		27
仪器仪表制造业	Manufacture of Measuring Instrument	862			
其他制造业	Other Manufacture				
废弃资源综合利用业	Comprehensive Utilization of Waste				
金属制品、机械和设备修理业	Metal Products, Machinery and Equipment Repair Industry	896			
电力、热力生产和供应业	Production and Supply of Electric Power and Heat Power	1815			
燃气生产和供应业	Production and Supply of Gas				
水的生产和供应业	Production and Supply of Water	169			

17－5 规模以上工业企业技术资源（2017年）

Technical Resources of Industrial Enterprises Above Desitnated Size（2017）

指　　标	Indicator	R&D经费内部支出合计（万元）Internal Expenditure on R&D (10 000 yuan)	新产品产值（万元）Output Value of New Products (10 000 yuan)	研究与试验发展(R&D)人员（人）R&D sonnel (Person)	R&D人员折合全时当量（人年）R&D rsonnelEquivalent in Full Time (man-years)
总计	**Total**	1154806	17175422	40711	27049
按登记注册类型分	**by Status of Registration**				
国有企业	State-owned Enterprises	15711	131856	362	286
集体企业	Collective-owned Enterprises	1966	5827	121	49
股份合作企业	Cooperative Enterprises				
有限责任公司	Private Limited Liability Corporations	837251	13982463	27585	18464
国有独资公司	State Sole funded Corporations	212675	6020998	6511	5067
其他有限责任公司	Other Limited Liability Corporations	624577	7961465	21074	13398
股份有限公司	Share-holding Corporations Limited	99836	1251329	4460	2832
私营独资企业	Private-funded Enterprises	393		28	15
私营合伙企业	Private Partnership Enterprises				
私营有限责任公司	Private Limited Liability Corporations	98785	768541	4647	2753
私营股份有限公司	Private Share-holding Corporations Ltd.	36742	503777	1198	775
其他企业	Other Enterprises				
合资经营企业(港或澳、台资)	Joint-ventures Enterprises	7409	55164	278	207
合作经营企业(港或澳、台资)	Cooperative Enterprises	904		34	34
港、澳、台商独资经营企业	Enterprises with Sole Investment	10266	81784	233	219
港、澳、台商投资股份有限公司	Share-holding Corporations Ltd. With Funds from	3460	48237	188	188
中外合资经营企业	Joint-venture Enterprises	30945	217729	1071	879
中外合作经营企业	Cooperation Enterprises				
外资企业	Enterprises with Sole Foreign Funds	11138	128715	506	347
外商投资股份有限公司	Share-holding Corporations Ltd. With Foreign Investment				
按工业行业大类分	**by Sector**				
煤炭开采和洗选业	Mining and Washing of Coal	2831		336	324
石油和天然气开采业	Extraction of Petroleum and Natural Gas				
黑色金属矿采选业	Mining of Ferrous Metal Ores				
非金属矿采选业	Mining and Processing of Nonmetal Ores	80	1053	14	6
农副食品加工业	Processing of Food from Agricultural Products	13109	64192	455	232
食品制造业	Manufacture of Foods	8033	38625	463	263
酒、饮料和精制茶制造业	Manufacture of Wine, Drinks and Refined Tea	1891	16283	171	82

指　　标	Indicator	R&D 经费内部支出合计（万元）Internal Expenditure on R&D (10 000 yuan)	新产品产值（万元）Output Value of New Products (10 000 yuan)	研究与试验发展(R&D)人员（人）R&D sonnel (Person)	R&D 人员折合全时当量（人年）R&D rsonnelEquivalent in Full Time (man-years)
烟草制品业	Manufacture of Tobacco	55	2114	3	1
纺织业	Manufacture of Textile	6995	124236	464	304
纺织服装、服饰业	Manufacture of Textile Wearing Apparel and Finery	445	500	20	6
皮革、毛皮、羽毛及其制品和制鞋业	Manufacture of Leather, Fur, Feather & Its Products and Footwear	433	4027	17	17
木材加工和木、竹、藤、棕、草制品业	Processing of Timbers, Manufacture of Wood, Bamboo, Rattan, Palm, and Straw Products	264	1000	24	11
家具制造业	Manufacture of Furniture	225	2753	29	19
造纸和纸制品业	Manufacture of Paper and Paper Products	1641	34722	61	54
印刷和记录媒介复制业	Printing, Reproduction of Recording Media	7482	90621	405	321
文教、工美、体育和娱乐用品制造业	Manufacture of Culture, Education,Arts and crafts， Sport and Entertainment Goods	1669	7181	116	84
石油加工、炼焦和核燃料加工业	Processing of Petroleum, Coking and Nucleus Fuel	5327	80851	373	118
化学原料和化学制品制造业	Manufacture of Chemical Raw Material and Chemical Products	99266	914332	1842	1220
医药制造业	Manufacture of Medicines	124407	1594765	2956	2324
化学纤维制造业	Manufacture of Chemical Fiber	5515	17829	25	14
橡胶和塑料制品业	Manufacture of Rubber and Plastic	3996	21942	131	81
非金属矿物制品业	Manufacture of Non-metallic Mineral Products	38107	570991	1217	617
黑色金属冶炼和压延加工业	Manufacture and Processing of Ferrous Metals	4802	14242	252	152
有色金属冶炼和压延加工业	Manufacture & Processing of Non-ferrous Metals	923	22794	107	92
金属制品业	Manufacture of Metal Products	42989	461579	1661	904
通用设备制造业	Manufacture of General Purpose Machinery	75103	606349	4531	3020
专用设备制造业	Manufacture of Special Purpose Machinery	46056	417107	2094	1399
汽车制造业	Manufacture of Automotive	183024	6057871	4950	3800
铁路、船舶、航空航天和其他运输设备制造业	Manufacture of Railroad,Marine,Aerospace and Other Transportation Equipment	25978	343088	680	423
电气机械和器材制造业	Manufacture of Electrical Machinery & Equipment	77958	955607	2072	1445
计算机、通信和其他电子设备制造业	Manufacture of Computer, Communications And Other Electronic Equipment	341920	4495810	12905	8068
仪器仪表制造业	Manufacture of Measuring Instrument	22992	138263	1765	1203
其他制造业	Other Manufacture	100	1580	14	4
废弃资源综合利用业	Comprehensive Utilization of Waste				
金属制品、机械和设备修理业	Metal Products, Machinery and Equipment Repair Industry	4278	45059	354	317
电力、热力生产和供应业	Production and Supply of Electric Power and Heat Power	4485	28058	120	87
燃气生产和供应业	Production and Supply of Gas	1150		7	2
水的生产和供应业	Production and Supply of Water	1278		77	38

17－6 规模以上工业企业科技活动项目（2017）

Technology Projict Activities of Industrial Enterprises Above Designated Size（2017）

指　　标	Indicator	R&D 活动项目经费内部支出（万元）Internal Expenditure on R&D (10 000 yuan)	新产品开发项目数（项）Number of on new products evelopment (unit)	新产品开发经费支出（万元）Expenditure on new Products evelopment (10 000 yuan)
总计	**Total**	1154806	4407	1121249
按登记注册类型分	**by Status of Registration**			
国有企业	State-owned Enterprises	15711	59	11567
集体企业	Collective-owned Enterprises	1966	7	1203
股份合作企业	Cooperative Enterprises			
有限责任公司	Private Limited Liability Corporations	837251	2179	814684
国有独资公司	State Sole funded Corporations	212675	500	207617
其他有限责任公司	Other Limited Liability Corporations	624577	1679	607066
股份有限公司	Share-holding Corporations Limited	99836	691	94403
私营独资企业	Private-funded Enterprises	393	2	200
私营合伙企业	Private Partnership Enterprises			
私营有限责任公司	Private Limited Liability Corporations	98785	910	97461
私营股份有限公司	Private Share-holding Corporations Ltd.	36742	166	38426
其他企业	Other Enterprises			
合资经营企业(港或澳、台资)	Joint-ventures Enterprises	7409	53	7576
合作经营企业(港或澳、台资)	Cooperative Enterprises	904	3	954
港、澳、台商独资经营企业	Enterprises with Sole Investment	10266	59	10077
港、澳、台商投资股份有限公司	Share-holding Corporations Ltd. With Funds from	3460	12	3461
中外合资经营企业	Joint-venture Enterprises	30945	165	31761
中外合作经营企业	Cooperation Enterprises			
外资企业	Enterprises with Sole Foreign Funds	11138	101	9477
外商投资股份有限公司	Share-holding Corporations Ltd. With Foreign Investment			
按工业行业大类分	**by Sector**			
煤炭开采和洗选业	Mining and Washing of Coal	2831		
石油和天然气开采业	Extraction of Petroleum and Natural Gas			
黑色金属矿采选业	Mining of Ferrous Metal Ores			
非金属矿采选业	Mining and Processing of Nonmetal Ores	80	3	177
农副食品加工业	Processing of Food from Agricultural Products	13109	66	13406
食品制造业	Manufacture of Foods	8033	80	6269
酒、饮料和精制茶制造业	Manufacture of Wine, Drinks and Refined Tea	1891	16	2013

指　　标	Indicator	R&D 活动项目经费内部支出（万元）Internal Expenditure on R&D (10 000 yuan)	新产品开发项目数（项）Number of on new products evelopment (unit)	新产品开发经费支出（万元）Expenditure on new Products evelopment (10 000 yuan)
烟草制品业	Manufacture of Tobacco	55	1	55
纺织业	Manufacture of Textile	6995	38	6840
纺织服装、服饰业	Manufacture of Textile Wearing Apparel and Finery	445	2	10
皮革、毛皮、羽毛及其制品和制鞋业	Manufacture of Leather, Fur, Feather & Its Products and ootwear	433	7	327
木材加工和木、竹、藤、棕、草制品业	Processing of Timbers, Manufacture of Wood, Bamboo, Rattan, Palm, and Straw Products	264	3	668
家具制造业	Manufacture of Furniture	225	6	566
造纸和纸制品业	Manufacture of Paper and Paper Products	1641	3	442
印刷和记录媒介复制业	Printing, Reproduction of Recording Media	7482	36	4718
文教、工美、体育和娱乐用品制造业	Manufacture of Culture, Education,Arts and crafts, Sport and Entertainment Goods	1669	12	1687
石油加工、炼焦和核燃料加工业	Processing of Petroleum, Coking and Nucleus Fuel	5327	11	3173
化学原料和化学制品制造业	Manufacture of Chemical Raw Material and Chemical Products	99266	316	83479
医药制造业	Manufacture of Medicines	124407	521	115473
化学纤维制造业	Manufacture of Chemical Fiber	5515	14	5526
橡胶和塑料制品业	Manufacture of Rubber and Plastic	3996	30	3619
非金属矿物制品业	Manufacture of Non-metallic Mineral Products	38107	152	30222
黑色金属冶炼和压延加工业	Manufacture and Processing of Ferrous Metals	4802	23	3056
有色金属冶炼和压延加工业	Manufacture & Processing of Non-ferrous Metals	923	7	965
金属制品业	Manufacture of Metal Products	42989	195	35673
通用设备制造业	Manufacture of General Purpose Machinery	75103	613	68169
专用设备制造业	Manufacture of Special Purpose Machinery	46056	424	45463
汽车制造业	Manufacture of Automotive	183024	340	188587
铁路、船舶、航空航天和其他运输设备制造业	Manufacture of Railroad,Marine,Aerospace and Other ransportation quipment	25978	142	25536
电气机械和器材制造业	Manufacture of Electrical Machinery & Equipment	77958	383	77274
计算机、通信和其他电子设备制造业	Manufacture of Computer, Communications and Other Electronic Equipment	341920	618	367207
仪器仪表制造业	Manufacture of Measuring Instrument	22992	289	25260
其他制造业	Other Manufacture	100	5	73
废弃资源综合利用业	Comprehensive Utilization of Waste			
金属制品、机械和设备修理业	Metal Products, Machinery and Equipment Repair Industry	4278	44	4412
电力、热力生产和供应业	Production and Supply of Electric Power and Heat Power	4485	1	362
燃气生产和供应业	Production and Supply of Gas	1150		
水的生产和供应业	Production and Supply of Water	1278	6	542

17－7 规模以上工业企业

R&D Funds of Industrial Enterprises

单位：万元

指　　标	Indicator	合计 Total	按活动类型分组 By Activity Type		
			基础研究 Basic Research	应用研究支出 Applied Research	试验发展支出 Experimental Development
总计	**Total**	1154806	1157	14409	1139240
按登记注册类型分	**by Status of Registration**				
国有企业	State-owned Enterprises	15711	904	2843	11964
集体企业	Collective-owned Enterprises	1966		289	1677
股份合作企业	Cooperative Enterprises				
有限责任公司	Private Limited Liability Corporations	837251	238	5307	831706
国有独资公司	State Sole funded Corporations	212675	238	1974	210463
其他有限责任公司	Other Limited Liability Corporations	624577		3333	621243
股份有限公司	Share-holding Corporations Limited	99836		2337	97498
私营独资企业	Private-funded Enterprises	393			393
私营合伙企业	Private Partnership Enterprises				
私营有限责任公司	Private Limited Liability Corporations	98785	15	3429	95341
私营股份有限公司	Private Share-holding Corporations Ltd.	36742			36742
其他企业	Other Enterprises				
合资经营企业(港或澳、台资)	Joint-ventures Enterprises	7409		86	7323
合作经营企业(港或澳、台资)	Cooperative Enterprises	904			904
港、澳、台商独资经营企业	Enterprises with Sole Investment	10266			10266
港、澳、台商投资股份有限公司	Share-holding Corporations Ltd. With Funds from	3460			3460
中外合资经营企业	Joint-venture Enterprises	30945		24	30921
中外合作经营企业	Cooperation Enterprises				
外资企业	Enterprises with Sole Foreign Funds	11138		94	11044
外商投资股份有限公司	Share-holding Corporations Ltd. With Foreign Investment				
按工业行业大类分	**by Sector**				
煤炭开采和洗选业	Mining and Washing of Coal	2831			2831
石油和天然气开采业	Extraction of Petroleum and Natural Gas				
黑色金属矿采选业	Mining of Ferrous Metal Ores				
非金属矿采选业	Mining and Processing of Nonmetal Ores	80			80
农副食品加工业	Processing of Food from Agricultural Products	13109		11	13098
食品制造业	Manufacture of Foods	8033		827	7206
酒、饮料和精制茶制造业	Manufacture of Wine, Drinks and Refined Tea	1891			1891

R&D 经费情况（2017 年）

Above Designated Size（2017）

（10 000 yuan）

R&D 经费内部支出 Internal Expenditure on R&D						R&D 经费外部支出 External expenditure on R&D
按支出用途分组 By Object of Expenditure		按资金来源分组 By Capital Source				
经常费支出 Daily Expenditure	资产性支出 Capital Expenditure	政府资金 Government Appropriation Funds	企业资金 Self-raised Funds by Enterprises	境外资金 Foreign funds	其他资金 Other Funds	
1044928	109878	35674	1061155	11482	46495	35635
12800	2911	3046	12665			239
1966		40	1926			
756391	80860	22797	758692	10958	44804	27936
198964	13711	2490	210107	78		16158
557427	67149	20307	548585	10880	44804	11777
91943	7893	3479	95846	488	23	2356
383	11		301		92	49
86366	12420	3943	94060		783	3024
35337	1404	2018	34724			752
7252	157	200	7209			96
843	61		904			
10040	227		10125		141	44
2286	1175		3460			40
28712	2233	152	30788	5		292
10610	528		10454	32	653	809
2831			2831			
73	7		80			8
12315	794	57	12911		141	311
7045	988	274	7700		60	207
1741	151	4	1887			216

17–7 续 1

指　　标	Indicator	合计 Total	按活动类型分组 By Activity Type		
			基础研究 Basic Research	应用研究支出 Applied Research	试验发展支出 Experimental Development
烟草制品业	Manufacture of Tobacco	55			55
纺织业	Manufacture of Textile	6995		106	6890
纺织服装、服饰业	Manufacture of Textile Wearing Apparel and Finery	445			445
皮革、毛皮、羽毛及其制品和制鞋业	Manufacture of Leather, Fur, Feather & Its Products and Footwear	433			433
木材加工和木、竹、藤、棕、草制品业	Processing of Timbers, Manufacture of Wood, Bamboo, Rattan, Palm, and Straw Products	264			264
家具制造业	Manufacture of Furniture	225			225
造纸和纸制品业	Manufacture of Paper and Paper Products	1641		1197	443
印刷和记录媒介复制业	Printing, Reproduction of Recording Media	7482		647	6835
文教、工美、体育和娱乐用品制造业	Manufacture of Culture, Education,Arts and crafts, Sport and Entertainment Goods	1669			1669
石油加工、炼焦和核燃料加工业	Processing of Petroleum, Coking and Nucleus Fuel	5327		2290	3037
化学原料和化学制品制造业	Manufacture of Chemical Raw Material and Chemical Products	99266		1439	97827
医药制造业	Manufacture of Medicines	124407	904	2868	120635
化学纤维制造业	Manufacture of Chemical Fiber	5515			5515
橡胶和塑料制品业	Manufacture of Rubber and Plastic	3996			3996
非金属矿物制品业	Manufacture of Non–metallic Mineral Products	38107		639	37468
黑色金属冶炼和压延加工业	Manufacture and Processing of Ferrous Metals	4802			4802
有色金属冶炼和压延加工业	Manufacture & Processing of Non–ferrous Metals	923			923
金属制品业	Manufacture of Metal Products	42989		293	42696
通用设备制造业	Manufacture of General Purpose Machinery	75103		2011	73092
专用设备制造业	Manufacture of Special Purpose Machinery	46056	15	655	45386
汽车制造业	Manufacture of Automotive	183024		313	182712
铁路、船舶、航空航天和其他运输设备制造业	Manufacture of Railroad,Marine,Aerospace and Other Transportation Equipment	25978			25978
电气机械和器材制造业	Manufacture of Electrical Machinery & Equipment	77958	238	410	77310
计算机、通信和其他电子设备制造业	Manufacture of Computer, Communications and Other Electronic Equipment	341920		525	341396
仪器仪表制造业	Manufacture of Measuring Instrument	22992		49	22943
其他制造业	Other Manufacture	100			100
废弃资源综合利用业	Comprehensive Utilization of Waste				
金属制品、机械和设备修理业	Metal Products, Machinery and Equipment Repair Industry	4278		130	4148
电力、热力生产和供应业	Production and Supply of Electric Power and Heat Power	4485			4485
燃气生产和供应业	Production and Supply of Gas	1150			1150
水的生产和供应业	Production and Supply of Water	1278			1278

R&D 经费内部支出 Internal Expenditure on R&D						R&D 经费外部支出 External expenditure on R&D
按支出用途分组 By Object of Expenditure		按资金来源分组 By Capital Source				
经常费支出 Daily Expenditure	资产性支出 Capital Expenditure	政府资金 Government Appropriation Funds	企业资金 Self-raised Funds by Enterprises	境外资金 Foreign funds	其他资金 Other Funds	
44	10		27		27	44
6033	962		6995			6033
445		150	295			445
413	20		433			413
215	49	0	264			215
225			213		13	225
1625	15		1641			1625
5678	1804	85	7103	293	1	5678
1417	253	42	1481		146	1417
4994	333	913	4415			4994
84883	14383	879	97691	32	664	84883
110149	14258	6039	118348	21		110149
5394	121		5515			5394
3450	546	39	3958			3450
35181	2927	557	35385	467	1698	35181
4331	471		4802			4331
798	125		923			798
38370	4619	405	42358		226	38370
71518	3585	2919	71770	83	332	71518
42888	3168	3410	42544	101	1	42888
170737	12288	443	182529		52	170737
25579	399	20	25958			25579
72588	5370	1416	76426		116	72588
303021	38900	16248	272168	10486	43018	303021
22164	828	1336	21656			22164
84	16		100			84
3634	644		4278			3634
2707	1778	440	4045			2707
1150			1150			1150
1211	67		1278			1211

17－8　规模以上工业企业办科技机构情况（2017年）

Science and Technology Institutions of Industrial Enterprises Above Designated Size（2017）

指　标	Indicator	机构数（个）Number (unit)	机构人员（人）Research Personnel(Person)			机构经费支出（万元）Agency Expenditure (10 000 yuan)	仪器和设备原价（万元）Original price of Equipment (10 000 yuan)
			合计 Total	博士毕业 Doctor	硕士毕业 Master		
总计	**Total**	366	30427	454	6768	716575	833687
按登记注册类型分	**by Status of Registration**						
国有企业	State-owned Enterprises	8	376	18	160	546	13380
集体企业	Collective-owned Enterprises						
股份合作企业	Cooperative Enterprises						
有限责任公司	Private Limited Liability Corporations	174	23607	275	5686	603547	683560
国有独资公司	State Sole funded Corporations	20	3199	22	646	93551	78199
其他有限责任公司	Other Limited Liability Corporations	154	20408	253	5040	509997	605361
股份有限公司	Share-holding Corporations Limited	42	2195	68	466	38120	38668
私营独资企业	Private-funded Enterprises						
私营合伙企业	Private Partnership Enterprises						
私营有限责任公司	Private Limited Liability Corporations	99	1787	44	228	24750	27273
私营股份有限公司	Private Share-holding Corporations Ltd.	21	1055	20	147	30496	18110
其他企业	Other Enterprises						
合资经营企业(港或澳、台资)	Joint-ventures Enterprises	4	82	22	2	3462	211
合作经营企业(港或澳、台资)	Cooperative Enterprises						
港、澳、台商独资经营企业	Enterprises with Sole Investment	2	92		1	1925	2332
港、澳、台商投资股份有限公司	Share-holding Corporations Ltd. With Funds from	1	272		9	3460	16197
中外合资经营企业	Joint-venture Enterprises	10	813	1	30	7799	8691
中外合作经营企业	Cooperation Enterprises						
外资企业	Enterprises with Sole Foreign Funds	5	148	6	39	2470	25266
外商投资股份有限公司	Share-holding Corporations Ltd. With Foreign Investment						
按工业行业大类分	**by Sector**						
煤炭开采和洗选业	Mining and Washing of Coal						
石油和天然气开采业	Extraction of Petroleum and Natural Gas						
黑色金属矿采选业	Mining of Ferrous Metal Ores						
非金属矿采选业	Mining and Processing of Nonmetal Ores	1	4		2	80	182
农副食品加工业	Processing of Food from Agricultural Products	11	320	20	120	8324	3164
食品制造业	Manufacture of Foods	14	401	10	50	3550	6892
酒、饮料和精制茶制造业	Manufacture of Wine, Drinks and Refined Tea	4	121	3	5	1846	2304

17-8 续 1

指　标	Indicator	机构数（个）Number (unit)	机构人员（人）Research Personnel(Person) 合计 Total	博士毕业 Doctor	硕士毕业 Master	机构经费支出（万元）Agency Expenditure (10 000 yuan)	仪器和设备原价（万元）Original price of Equipment (10 000 yuan)
烟草制品业	Manufacture of Tobacco	1	8		3	54	134
纺织业	Manufacture of Textile	4	30		1	371	454
纺织服装、服饰业	Manufacture of Textile Wearing Apparel and Finery						
皮革、毛皮、羽毛及其制品和制鞋业	Manufacture of Leather, Fur, Feather & Its Products and Footwear	1	28			490	604
木材加工和木、竹、藤、棕、草制品业	Processing of Timbers, Manufacture of Wood, Bamboo, Rattan, Palm, and Straw Products	1	18			25	30
家具制造业	Manufacture of Furniture						
造纸和纸制品业	Manufacture of Paper and Paper Products						
印刷和记录媒介复制业	Printing, Reproduction of Recording Media	8	346	1	10	3952	18942
文教、工美、体育和娱乐用品制造业	Manufacture of Culture, Education,Arts and crafts，Sport and Entertainment Goods	1	21			379	133
石油加工、炼焦和核燃料加工业	Processing of Petroleum, Coking and Nucleus Fuel	2	12		3	114	986
化学原料和化学制品制造业	Manufacture of Chemical Raw Material and Chemical Products	35	1459	45	254	58940	27043
医药制造业	Manufacture of Medicines	34	2637	92	893	101067	89746
化学纤维制造业	Manufacture of Chemical Fiber	1	22		1	13	1100
橡胶和塑料制品业	Manufacture of Rubber and Plastic	5	72	2	2	699	298
非金属矿物制品业	Manufacture of Non-metallic Mineral Products	24	781	28	61	21242	28659
黑色金属冶炼和压延加工业	Manufacture and Processing of Ferrous Metals	3	96	2	18	1422	1138
有色金属冶炼和压延加工业	Manufacture & Processing of Non-ferrous Metals	1	150		5	923	1500
金属制品业	Manufacture of Metal Products	16	422	2	30	6468	7804
通用设备制造业	Manufacture of General Purpose Machinery	55	2725	21	367	49515	59864
专用设备制造业	Manufacture of Special Purpose Machinery	33	938	16	96	6909	15002
汽车制造业	Manufacture of Automotive	12	2000	22	400	62250	44863
铁路、船舶、航空航天和其他运输设备制造业	Manufacture of Railroad,Marine,Aerospace and Other Transportation Equipment	9	541	4	161	13182	14153
电气机械和器材制造业	Manufacture of Electrical Machinery & Equipment	30	1768	49	369	56455	63008
计算机、通信和其他电子设备制造业	Manufacture of Computer, Communications And Other Electronic Equipment	32	13940	120	3758	303077	431245
仪器仪表制造业	Manufacture of Measuring Instrument	24	1117	17	138	11811	10106
其他制造业	Other Manufacture						
废弃资源综合利用业	Comprehensive Utilization of Waste						
金属制品、机械和设备修理业	Metal Products, Machinery and Equipment Repair Industry	3	436		18	3393	4111
电力、热力生产和供应业	Production and Supply of Electric Power and Heat Power						
燃气生产和供应业	Production and Supply of Gas						
水的生产和供应业	Production and Supply of Water	1	14		3	24	225

17－9 规模以上工业企业自主

Independent Intellectual Property Rights of

指　　标	Indicator	专利申请数（件）Patent Applications (piece)	#发明专利（件）Inventions (piece)
总计	**Total**	11537	7235
按登记注册类型分	**by Status of Registration**		
国有企业	State-owned Enterprises	49	35
集体企业	Collective-owned Enterprises	15	2
股份合作企业	Cooperative Enterprises		
有限责任公司	Private Limited Liability Corporations	8514	6333
国有独资公司	State Sole funded Corporations	389	99
其他有限责任公司	Other Limited Liability Corporations	8125	6234
股份有限公司	Share-holding Corporations Limited	1536	328
私营独资企业	Private-funded Enterprises		
私营合伙企业	Private Partnership Enterprises		
私营有限责任公司	Private Limited Liability Corporations	972	305
私营股份有限公司	Private Share-holding Corporations Ltd.	265	166
其他企业	Other Enterprises		
合资经营企业(港或澳、台资)	Joint-ventures Enterprises	13	5
合作经营企业(港或澳、台资)	Cooperative Enterprises		
港、澳、台商独资经营企业	Enterprises with Sole Investment	32	16
港、澳、台商投资股份有限公司	Share-holding Corporations Ltd. With Funds from	3	1
中外合资经营企业	Joint-venture Enterprises	83	36
中外合作经营企业	Cooperation Enterprises		
外资企业	Enterprises with Sole Foreign Funds	55	8
外商投资股份有限公司	Share-holding Corporations Ltd. With Foreign Investment		
按工业行业大类分	**by Sector**		
煤炭开采和洗选业	Mining and Washing of Coal	5	1
石油和天然气开采业	Extraction of Petroleum and Natural Gas		
黑色金属矿采选业	Mining of Ferrous Metal Ores		
非金属矿采选业	Mining and Processing of Nonmetal Ores		
农副食品加工业	Processing of Food from Agricultural Products	12	12
食品制造业	Manufacture of Foods	78	48
酒、饮料和精制茶制造业	Manufacture of Wine, Drinks and Refined Tea	3	1

知识产权及相关情况（2017年）

Industrial Enterprises Above Designated Size（2017）

有效发明专利数 （件） Effective Invention Patent (piece)	发表科技论文 （篇） Science Paper (piece)	拥有注册商标数 （件） Registered Trademarks (piece)	#境外注册 （件） Overseas Registered (piece)	形成国家或行业标准数 （项） Industry or National Standards (unit)
8393	1055	6000	888	383
211	63	388	2	4
7				
4565	472	2936	577	214
615	79	612	58	51
3950	393	2324	519	163
1053	77	984	205	56
1529	360	942	18	42
561	32	184	15	32
201	3	376	60	1
23	6	83	7	
11		16		1
179	26	73	1	33
53	16	18	3	
7	6			
4		4		1
108		75	1	
146	9	96	1	3
5	1	52		1

17-9 续 1

指　　标	Indicator	专利申请数（件）Patent Applications (piece)	#发明专利（件）Inventions (piece)
烟草制品业	Manufacture of Tobacco	15	3
纺织业	Manufacture of Textile	97	49
纺织服装、服饰业	Manufacture of Textile Wearing Apparel and Finery		
皮革、毛皮、羽毛及其制品和制鞋业	Manufacture of Leather, Fur, Feather & Its Products and Footwear	4	4
木材加工和木、竹、藤、棕、草制品业	Processing of Timbers, Manufacture of Wood,Bamboo, Rattan, Palm, and Straw Products	9	
家具制造业	Manufacture of Furniture	2	
造纸和纸制品业	Manufacture of Paper and Paper Products	8	1
印刷和记录媒介复制业	Printing, Reproduction of Recording Media	27	9
文教、工美、体育和娱乐用品制造业	Manufacture of Culture, Education,Arts and crafts，Sport and Entertainment Goods	9	8
石油加工、炼焦和核燃料加工业	Processing of Petroleum, Coking and Nucleus Fuel	21	3
化学原料和化学制品制造业	Manufacture of Chemical Raw Material and Chemical Products	343	226
医药制造业	Manufacture of Medicines	224	164
化学纤维制造业	Manufacture of Chemical Fiber	7	
橡胶和塑料制品业	Manufacture of Rubber and Plastic	27	14
非金属矿物制品业	Manufacture of Non-metallic Mineral Products	129	42
黑色金属冶炼和压延加工业	Manufacture and Processing of Ferrous Metals	45	12
有色金属冶炼和压延加工业	Manufacture & Processing of Non-ferrous Metals	8	1
金属制品业	Manufacture of Metal Products	179	49
通用设备制造业	Manufacture of General Purpose Machinery	491	148
专用设备制造业	Manufacture of Special Purpose Machinery	457	134
汽车制造业	Manufacture of Automotive	334	74
铁路、船舶、航空航天和其他运输设备制造业	Manufacture of Railroad,Marine,Aerospace and Other Transportation Equipment	132	59
电气机械和器材制造业	Manufacture of Electrical Machinery & Equipment	1379	227
计算机、通信和其他电子设备制造业	Manufacture of Computer, Communications and Other Electronic Equipment	7211	5865
仪器仪表制造业	Manufacture of Measuring Instrument	228	64
其他制造业	Other Manufacture	8	
废弃资源综合利用业	Comprehensive Utilization of Waste		
金属制品、机械和设备修理业	Metal Products, Machinery and Equipment Repair Industry	27	12
电力、热力生产和供应业	Production and Supply of Electric Power and Heat Power	11	5
燃气生产和供应业	Production and Supply of Gas		
水的生产和供应业	Production and Supply of Water	7	

有效发明专利数（件）Effective Invention Patent (piece)	发表科技论文（篇）Science Paper (piece)	拥有注册商标数（件）Registered Trademarks (piece)	#境外注册（件）Overseas Registered (piece)	形成国家或行业标准数（项）Industry or National Standards (unit)
15	3			
72		24	15	6
		1		
		7		1
9				
1				1
35		18		1
21		2		
25	27	15		5
992	110	1488	27	67
611	209	1587	77	34
2		3	2	
17	1	13		1
509	15	139	77	9
185	18	96	19	2
12	3	1		
214	18	192	78	20
687	102	387	137	77
837	93	164	14	32
518	7	536	17	10
536	35	17		3
897	102	100	2	21
1624	7	835	418	32
259	259	146	3	24
35	14	1		32
10		1		
	16			

主要统计指标解释

科技活动 是指在自然科学、农业科学、医药科学、工程与技术科学、人文与社会科学领域（简称科学技术领域）中，与科技知识的产生、发展、传播和应用密切相关的有组织的活动。在企（事）业中只有列入单位工作计划的科技活动才予以统计，而独立发明人等在企（事）业外或计划外进行的科技活动不在统计范围之内。科研活动可分为研究与试验发展（简称R&D，包括基础研究、应用研究和试验发展）、研究与试验发展（R&D）成果应用及相关的科技服务三类活动。

基础研究 是指为了获得关于现象和可观察事实的基本原理的新知识（揭示客观事物的本质、运动规律，获得新发现、新学说）而进行的实验性或理论性研究。基础研究属于科学研究范畴。从研究目的看，基础研究不以任何专门或特定的应用或使用为目的，它只是通过试验分析或理论性研究对事物的特性、结构和各种关系进行分析，加深对客观事物的认识，解释现象的本质，揭示物质运动的规律或提出和验证各种设想、理论和定律。从研究结果看，基础研究的结果具有一般的或普遍的正确性，通常表现为一般的原则、理论和规律，其成果以科学论文和科学著作为主要形式。

应用研究 是指为获得新知识而进行的创造性研究，主要针对某一特定的目的或目标。应用研究也属于科学研究范畴。从研究目的看，应用研究是探索基础研究成果的可能用途，或是为达到预定的目标探索应采取的新方法（原理性）或新途径，为解决实际问题提供科学依据。从研究结果看，应用研究的成果一般只影响科学技术的某些领域和有限范围，并具有专门的性质，针对具体的领域、问题或情况，其成果形式以科学论文、专著、原理性模型或发明专利等为主。

试验发展 是指利用从基础研究、应用研究和实际经验所获得的现有知识，为产生新的产品、材料和装置，建立新的工艺、系统和服务，以及对已产生和建立的上述各项做实质性的改进而进行的系统性工作。在社会科学领域，试验发展是指通过把基础研究、应用研究获得的知识转变成可以实施的计划（包括为检验和评估实施示范项目）的过程。

专利申请数 指企业在报告期内向国内外知识产权行政部门提出专利申请并被受理的件数。

专利申请数中发明专利 指企业在报告期内向国内外知识产权行政部门提出发明专利申请并被受理的件数。

新产品产值 指报告期企业生产的新产品的产值。新产品是指采用新技术原理、新设计构思研制、生产的全新产品，或在结构、材质、工艺等某一方面比原有产品有明显改进，从而显著提高了产品性能或扩大了使用功能的产品。新产品产值、新产品销售收入既包括经政府有关部门认定并在有效期内的新产品，也包括企业自行研制开发，未经政府有关部门认定，从投产之日起一年之内的新产品。

拥有注册商标 指企业在报告期末拥有的注册商标件数。包括在境内和境外注册的商标件数，一件商标在境内外同时注册时只统计一件。

技术改造经费支出 指企业在报告期进行技术改造而发生的费用支出。技术改造指企业在坚持科技进步的前提下，将科技成果应用于生产的各个领域（产品、设备、工艺等），用先进工艺、设备代替落后工艺、设备，实现以内涵为主的扩大再生产，从而提高产品质量、促进产品更新换代、节约能源、降低消耗，全面提高综合经济效益。

Explanatory Notes on Main Statistical Indicators

Scientific and Technological Activities refer to organized activities closely related to generation, development, dissemination and application of knowledge of science and technology in natural science, agricultural science, pharmaceutical science, engineering and technical science, humanities and social sciences field (called as science and technology field for short). Only scientific and technological activities listed into the work plan of the enterprise (institution) will be included, while scientific and technological activities by independent inventors outside the enterprise (institution) or the plan are out of the statistics scope. Scientific research activities can be divided into three categories -- research and experimental development (called as R&D for short, including fundamental research, application research and experimental development), application of results of research and experimental development (R&D) and related science and technology services.

Fundamental Research refers to empirical or theoretical research aiming at obtaining new knowledge on the fundamental principles of phenomena of observable facts to reveal the nature and law of movement of objects and to acquire new discoveries or new theories. Fundamental research falls into scientific research. From the perspective of research purpose, fundamental research takes no specific or designated application as the aim of the research which only involves analysis on features, structures and various relationships of things by experimental analysis or theoretical research to deepen the understanding of objective things, explain the nature of the phenomenon and reveal the laws of the motion of matter or put forward and verify various assumptions, theories and laws. From the perspective of research result, the result of fundamental research is of general or universal correctness, usually presented as general principle, theory and law. Results of fundamental research are mainly released or disseminated in the form of scientific papers or monographs.

Applied Research refers to creative research aiming at obtaining new knowledge on a specific objective or target. Applied research also falls into scientific research. From the perspective of research purpose, purpose of the applied research is to identify the possible use of results from basic research, or to explore new (fundamental) methods or new approaches as well as provide scientific basis for solving practical problems. From the perspective of research result, achievements of application research only influence some fields and limited scope of science and technology generally and are of a specialized nature and expressed in the form of scientific papers, monographs, fundamental models or invention patents on the basis of specific field, problem or situation.

Experiments and Development refer to systematic activities aiming at using the knowledge from fundamental and applied researches or from practical experience to develop new products, materials and equipment, to establish new production process, systems and services, or to make substantial improvement on the existing products, process or services. In social sciences, experiment and development activities refer to the process of converting the knowledge from or applied researches into feasible programs (including conduct of demonstration projects for assessment and evaluation).

Quantity of Patents Applied refers to the quantity of patents accepted with application for a patent filed by the enterprise to intellectual property administrative departments at the home and abroad in the reporting period.

Quantity of Invention Patent in the Patents Applied refers to the quantity of patents for invention accepted with application for an invention patent filed by the enterprise to intellectual property administrative departments at the home and abroad in the reporting period.

Output Value of New Products refers to output value of new products produced by enterprises in the reporting period. New products refer to new products developed or produced by new know-why and design concept and products with properties of products obviously improved or use function expanded due to the obvious improvement in structure, texture or technology in comparison to those of original products. Output value of new products and sales revenue from new products include new products approved by relevant government departments whose valid term fails to expire and new products developed independently by the enterprise and not approved by relevant government departments which exist for less than one year as of the date of going into operation.

Possession of Registered Trademark refers to the quantity of registered trademarks owned by the enterprise at the end of the reporting period, including quantity of trademark registered at home and abroad. Statistics of a trademark are only conducted once at the moment of being registered at the home and abroad at the same time.

Expenditure on Technological Transformation refers to the expenditure incurred by technological transformation by the enterprise in the reporting period. Technological transformation refers to the enterprise applying scientific and technological achievements to all fields of production (product, equipment and technology, etc.) and replacing backward technology and equipment with advance technology and equipment to realize intention-based expanded reproduction, thus to improve product quality, promote product upgrading, save energy, lower consumption and comprehensively enhance composite economic results in the premise of insisting on scientific and technological progress.

18

教育与文化

EDUCATION AND CULTURE

18-1 教育事业

Basic Statistics

指　　标	Indicator	1952年	1957年	1962年	1965年	1970年
学校数(所)	Number of Schools(nuit)	2679	3106	3731	4318	5359
#高等教育	Higher Education	5	4	12	8	2
中等教育	Secondary Education	37	67	112	410	1204
#中等职业学校	Vocational Secondary Education	16	16	15	15	17
普通中学	Regular Junior Secondary Schools	21	51	93	159	1024
小　学	Primary Schools	2636	3034	3606	3899	4152
专任教师(人)	Full-time Teachers(person)	8555	13452	19606	26760	32508
#高等教育	Higher Education	671	1325	2598	2451	922
中等教育	Secondary Education	1108	2569	3418	5321	9607
#中等职业学校	Vocational Secondary Education	311	787	765	685	914
普通中学	Regular Junior Secondary Schools	797	1782	2629	3502	8445
小　学	Primary Schools	6773	9550	13571	18971	21954
在校学生（万人）	Total Enrollment(10 000 persons)	26.87	31.95	49.82	68.27	80.20
#高等教育	Higher Education	0.43	0.82	1.65	1.40	0.30
中等教育	Secondary Education	2.73	5.14	5.80	10.43	18.97
#中等职业学校	Vocational Secondary Education	0.69	0.93	0.51	0.65	0.12
普通中学	Regular Junior Secondary Schools	2.04	4.21	5.22	7.50	17.81
小　学	Primary Schools	23.70	25.98	42.35	56.42	60.91
各类学校毕业生数(万人)	Graduates(10 000 persons)	4.38	8.58	10.60	10.45	12.09
#高等教育	Higher Education	0.14	0.11	0.31	0.43	—
中等教育	Secondary Education	0.60	1.14	1.72	1.90	1.02
#中等职业学校	Vocational Secondary Education	0.13	0.14	0.32	0.03	—
普通中学	Regular Junior Secondary Schools	0.46	1.00	1.40	1.80	0.38
小　学	Primary Schools					
每一教师负担学生数(人)	Each Teacher Burden Number of Students(person)	31.41	23.75	25.41	23.27	24.67
#高等教育	Higher Education	6.41	6.19	6.35	5.71	3.25
中等教育	Secondary Education	24.64	20.01	16.97	19.60	19.75
#中等职业学校	Vocational Secondary Education	22.33	11.84	6.64	9.51	1.36
普通中学	Regular Junior Secondary Schools	25.63	23.64	19.84	21.41	21.09
小　学	Primary Schools	34.99	27.20	31.21	29.74	27.74
平均每万人口在校学生(人)	Number of Enrollment Per 10000 Population(person)	843	922	1418	1829	1968
#大学生	Undergraduate	14	24	47	38	7
中专生	Secondary Students	22	27	14	17	3
中学生	Middle School Students	64	122	150	256	463
小学生	Elementary School Students	743	750	1206	1513	1494

注：2017年高等教育在校生、毕业生均包含网络教育学生。

Notes: In 2017, students and graduates of higher education include online education students.

基 本 情 况

on Education

1975 年	1980 年	1985 年	1990 年	1995 年	2000 年	2005 年	2010 年	2015 年	2017 年	2018 年
5412	5066	4511	3924	3360	1725	1251	1025	946	953	930
4	11	16	16	16	16	59	66	72	69	51
922	759	593	529	440	423	348	302	280	293	304
21	30	40	39	41	40	91	73	41	35	34
783	710	491	417	312	297	247	209	214	238	251
4485	4295	3899	3368	2890	1273	832	645	582	580	575
42432	49608	46806	55978	58779	62869	77334	83106	88487	95704	101305
2468	3744	4614	7245	7500	8269	24341	29526	31693	33282	37539
15274	19062	17530	21618	23946	26817	27435	28370	30589	32892	33161
985	1338	2367	2890	2941	2916	4738	4511	4068	3978	3711
13571	17294	13572	16065	17621	20585	21915	21943	23643	25676	26588
24654	26775	24579	26922	27417	27417	25201	24801	25795	29109	30605
90.28	83.56	78.38	79.48	91.69	95.79	129.28	144.60	153.71	163.59	168.97
0.61	1.58	3.02	3.73	5.66	9.30	48.71	64.25	71.40	79.21	79.63
25.43	20.24	25.34	28.08	36.64	44.99	42.50	41.76	40.77	39.62	42.68
0.58	0.31	1.92	2.51	4.79	5.75	9.88	8.10	5.93	5.52	5.16
23.86	19.63	21.49	22.45	27.15	33.82	30.91	30.18	30.16	30.56	31.18
64.22	61.47	49.98	47.57	49.23	41.40	37.88	38.40	41.44	44.66	46.66
22.66	18.07	17.31	17.12	20.88	23.65	33.58	38.10	39.83	47.24	50.65
0.20	0.03	0.45	1.03	1.68	1.55	13.49	17.57	19.48	27.37	26.29
11.83	8.41	7.36	8.24	10.39	10.80	14.03	13.55	14.22	12.73	12.28
0.20	0.46	0.52	0.62	1.16	1.84	3.29	3.13	2.75	1.68	2.43
11.58	7.89	6.39	6.66	7.78	8.16	10.40	9.20	10.23	10.03	9.65
21.28	16.84	16.75	14.20	15.60	15.24	16.72	17.40	17.37	17.09	16.68
2.47	4.22	6.55	5.15	7.54	11.25	20.01	21.76	22.53	23.79	21.21
16.65	10.62	14.46	12.99	15.30	16.78	15.49	14.72	13.33	12.04	12.87
5.95	2.29	8.12	8.69	16.30	18.84	20.86	17.96	14.58	13.80	13.90
17.58	11.35	15.83	13.98	15.41	16.43	14.10	13.75	12.76	11.89	11.73
26.05	22.96	20.33	17.67	18.20	15.10	15.03	15.48	16.07	15.35	15.25
2062	1822	1605	1518	1691	1702	2177	2395	2465	2563	2600
14	34	62	71	104	165	820	1064	1145	1241	1226
13	7	39	48	88	102	195	192	170	142	177
566	429	473	473	553	601	521	500	484	479	480
1466	1339	1024	908	908	736	638	636	664	700	718

18－2　普通高等院校一览（2018年）

Basic Statistics on Institutions of Higher Education（2018）

单位：人　　(person)

指　　标	普通本专科在校学生数 Total Enrollment	普通本专科毕业生数 Graduates	普通本专科招生数 New Enrollment	教职工人数 Teachers and Staff	#专任教师 Full-time Teachers		
					合计 Total	#正高级 Senior	#副高级 Sub-Senior
总计	638564	174191	189845	54382	37420	5066	11843
综合性大学							
山东大学	40784	9774	9977	7642	4261	1307	1596
济南大学	34394	8177	8429	2850	2117	304	761
山东青年政治学院	12930	3342	3448	801	592	46	167
山东女子学院	12083	3431	4083	738	549	43	179
理工院校							
山东建筑大学	25868	5738	6725	1957	1502	201	612
山东科技大学	36162	8221	8945	3020	2081	287	609
齐鲁工业大学	27996	7302	7209	3119	2016	270	748
山东交通学院	25775	5946	7500	1570	1199	100	387
山东电力高等专科学校	2136	561	853	297	136	32	27
医药院校							
山东第一医科大学	22448	5516	5743	3688	1578	337	653
山东中医药大学	18308	4118	4627	1290	1067	267	368
山东医学高等专科学校	22190	7021	9457	1122	897	53	200
济南护理职业学院	5431	2004	1865	396	237	18	97
师范院校							
山东师范大学	31275	7564	7346	2473	2026	361	557
齐鲁师范学院	12866	3840	4459	857	635	80	146
济南幼儿师范专科学校	4008	1583	1702	542	264	0	76
财经院校							
山东财经大学	30360	7207	7145	2421	1940	300	731
山东财经大学燕山学院	7115	1839	2055	450	396	48	152
政法院校							
山东警察学院	4507	1192	1150	548	279	21	129
山东司法警官职业学院	5807	1959	1823	242	141	3	26
山东政法学院	12445	3530	2856	827	601	59	151

指　　标	普通本专科在校学生数 Total Enrollment	普通本专科毕业生数 Graduates	普通本专科招生数 New Enrollment	教职工人数 Teachers and Staff	#专任教师 Full-time Teachers		
					合计 Total	#正高级 Senior	#副高级 Sub-Senior
体育院校							
山东体育学院	8269	1834	2105	691	558	47	185
艺术院校							
山东艺术学院	10112	2662	2632	931	769	87	233
山东工艺美术学院	6921	1794	1834	706	507	60	149
职业技术学院							
山东协和学院	19145	2472	6192	1210	938	60	251
山东商业职业技术学院	14130	5221	5002	1049	720	32	220
山东劳动职业技术学院	10831	4060	4097	771	597	28	158
山东职业学院	15034	5304	5277	859	646	31	171
山东圣翰财贸职业学院	7220	3678	2358	725	398	13	86
山东艺术设计职业学院	2205	662	904	223	170	6	17
山东英才学院	19479	4573	6232	1554	1011	99	335
山东旅游职业学院	7379	2305	2651	470	373	14	77
济南工程职业技术学院	10717	4193	3772	664	531	16	144
山东电子职业技术学校	8771	3344	3062	534	409	9	111
济南职业学院	12500	4675	4747	814	622	37	119
山东现代职业学院	15609	3984	5769	964	759	82	209
山东凯文科技职业学院	6182	3278	3022	623	428	83	139
山东城市建设职业学院	11685	4473	4293	708	562	10	182
山东管理学院	11543	3331	3522	692	564	48	130
齐鲁理工学院	15112	2897	4908	1286	778	115	194
山东农业工程学院	12651	3564	3696	704	540	33	129
山东特殊教育职业学院	897	184	434	177	123	2	19
山东传媒职业学院	7260	1966	2456	438	368	2	61

注：本表仅包括普通高等院校本专科在校学生，不包括成人高等院校、培养研究生科研机构、技师学院及没有在校生的普通高校。

Notes:This table only includes students in general colleges and universities, excluding adult colleges and universities, training postgraduate research institutions, technicians college and universities without students.

18－3　中等专业学校一览（2018 年）

Basic Statistics on Specialized Secondary Schools（2018）

单位：人 (person)

指　　标	在校学生数 Total Enrollment	毕业生数 Graduates	招生数 New Enrollment	教职工人数 Teachers and Staff	#专任教师 Full-time Teachers		
					合　计 Total	#副高级 Sub-Senior	#中级 Middle
总计							
工科学校							
济南信息工程学校	2734	864	922	192	140	39	88
山东省特殊教育职业学院	459	252	158				
济南电子机械工程学校	1806	884	548	197	156	47	80
医药学校							
济南护理职业学院	587	216	195				
师范学校							
济南幼儿师范高等专科学校	994	612	195				
财经学校							
山东省济南商贸学校	1834	1401	581	251	185	57	97
体育学校							
济南市体育运动学校	772	276	233	119	43	11	16
艺术学校							
山东省文化艺术学校	716	96	148	138	88	11	48
济南艺术学校	641	245	174	166	140	38	79
山东省艺术设计职业学院	326	87	109				

18－4　分区县儿童学前教育基本情况（2018 年）

Student Enrollment in Pre-school Education（2018）

单位：人 (person)

指　　标	Indicator	幼儿园数（所） Number of Kindergartens (unit)	在园人数 Enrolment	入园人数 Entrants	教职工数 Teachers and Staff	#专任教师 Full-timeTeachers
全市	total	1461	221440	69813	29748	16116
历下区	Li xia	100	28319	9028	4395	2224
市中区	Shi zhong	150	26875	8205	4243	2291
槐荫区	Huai yin	106	22987	6683	3271	1678
天桥区	Tian qiao	117	23201	6577	3578	1703
历城区	Li cheng	147	27267	10639	4057	2165
长清区	Chang qing	138	14228	5181	1497	1011
章丘区	Zhang qiu	199	22857	5975	2580	1562
济阳区	Ji yang	129	11773	3387	1132	581
高新区	Gao xin	81	13278	3959	1908	1026
南部山区	Nan Shan	48	5564	2599	617	338
平阴县	Ping yin	52	8598	2753	783	529
商河县	Shang he	194	16493	4827	1687	1008

18－5　文化事业机构和人员

Number of Institutions and Persons in Culture

指　　标	Indicator	2013 年	2014 年	2015 年	2016 年	2017 年	2018 年
机构数(个)	Number(unit)						
电影业	Movies	25	30	38	44	52	54
艺术业	Arts	28	27	27	27	27	27
文物业	Cultural Relics	37	40	42	48	48	48
图书馆业	Libraries	12	12	12	12	12	12
群众文化业	Mass Culture	153	153	152	155	153	153
艺术教育业	Art Education	1	1	1	1	1	1
文艺科研业	Culture Research	1	1	1	1	1	1
从业人员数(人)	Personnel(person)						
电影业	Movies	631	637	705	913	936	1380
艺术业	Arts	1693	1608	1569	1557	1569	1537
文物业	Cultural Relics	1057	1083	1119	1173	1158	1068
图书馆业	Libraries	454	447	431	447	462	472
群众文化业	Mass Culture	693	908	699	710	719	695
艺术教育业	Art Education	114	112	123	164	167	170
文艺科研业	Culture Research	57	46	49	51	49	47

注：电影业机构、从业人员数据为城市电影院线数据，不含农村。

Notes: The data of the film industry institutions and employees are urban cinema line data, excluding rural.

主要统计指标解释

Explanatory Notes on Main Statistical Indicators

普通高等学校　指按照国家规定的设置标准和审批程序批准举办，通过国家统一招生考试，招收高中毕业生为主要培养对象，实施高等教育的全日制大学、独立设置的学院和高等专科学校、短期职业大学。

文化事业机构　指从事专业文化工作和为专业文化工作服务的独立建制的单位。不包括这些单位另外举办独立核算的其他机构和各部门的业余文化组织。

Explanatory Notes on Main Statistical Indicators

Regular Institutions of Higher Education refer to educational establishments that set up according to the government evaluation and approval procedures, enrolling graduates from senior secondary schools and providing higher education courses and training for senior professionals. They include full time universities, colleges and high professional schools which set up independently as well as short-term vocational colleges.

Cultural Institutions refer to units which have their own organizational system, work on professional culture work and serve the professional culture work, excluding other institutions for independent accounting established by such units separately and amateur cultural organizations of all departments.

19

体育与卫生

SPORTS AND PUBLIC HEALTH

19－1 体 育 事 业

Statistics of Sports Instituons

指　　标	Indicator	2011 年	2012 年	2013 年	2014 年	2015 年	2016 年	2017 年	2018 年
体育部门职工人数（人）	**Number of Persons of Physical System(person)**	660	632	650	671	656	724	720	591
#业余体育学校	Spare-time Sports School	234	148	156	166	219	221	9	423
总计中：教练员	Referees	208	216	235	241	232	151	231	191
等级裁判员（人）	**Number of Referees in Grades(person)**								
一级裁判员	First Grade Referees							7	
二级裁判员	Second Grade Referees	175	292	216	184	246	122	153	268
三级裁判员	Third Grade Referees	263						55	
二级运动员发展人数（人）	**Number of Second Grade Sportsmen(person)**	372	351	397	376	359	401	465	279
少年儿童业余体校在校学生（人）	Enrollment Spare-time Sports School(person)		692	647	898	973	1036	845	1140
业余体校（所）	Spare-time Sports School(unit)	12	3	3	3	3	5	7	5
运动员获奖牌数（枚）	**Number of Medals Wonby Athletes(unit)**	633	507	617	594.5	585	1110	1188.5	1186
#世界级　金　牌	World　Gold Medals	18	10	20	6	5	12	1	3
银　牌	Silver Medals	8	3	7	4	3	4	2	1
铜　牌	Copper Medal	5	2	1	6	0	4	1	2
#洲　际　金　牌	Intercontinental　Gold Medals	0	2	4	5	5	7	3	3
银　牌	Silver Medals	0	7	3	1	1	4	3	2
铜　牌	Copper Medal	0	0	2	0	2	4	0	1
#全　国　金　牌	Country　Gold Medals	19	42	72	75	48	43	85	50
银　牌	Silver Medals	19	32	31	32	23	29	61	36
铜　牌	Copper Medal	30	32	34	43	29	16	100	41
#全　省　金　牌	Province　Gold Medals	172	132	177	201.5	215	402	395.5	430
银　牌	Silver Medals	190	145	141.5	93.5	119	292	273	319
铜　牌	Copper Medal	172	100	124.5	127.5	135	293	264	288
体育设施（个）	**Sports Facility(unit)**								
体育场	Stadium	12	12	12	12	12	12	6	12
体育馆	Gymnasium	9	9	9	9	9	9	17	9
游泳馆	Natatorium	5	5	5	5	5	5	11	5
室内外游泳池	Indoor Swimming Pool	2	2	2	2	2	2	5	4
有固定看台的灯光球场	Light Count With Fixed Stand	2	2	2	2	2	2	7	2

注：1. 等级裁判员为当年新评定的人数。
2. 2017 年体育设施统计口径为市、区县体育部门主管的设施数量
3. 2017 年写作体育学校统计口径只指学位，不包括业训网点

Note: 1. The number of referees is the number of new assessments in the current year.
2. The number of sports facilities in 2017 is the number of facilities in charge of the sports department of the city, district and county.
3. In 2017, the statistical caliber of writing sports schools only refers to degrees, excluding industry training outlets.

19－2　各时期卫生事业情况

Statistics of Health Institutions in Major Years

年份 Year	卫生机构(个) Number of Health Institutions (unit)		卫生工作人员(人) Medical Technical Personnel (person)		卫生机构床位(张) Number of Beds (set)	
	小　计 Total	#医院及卫生院 Hospitals and Township Hospitals	小　计 Total	#卫生技术人员 Medical Technical Personnel	小　计 Total	#医院及卫生院 Hospitals and Township Hospitals
1952	208	22	6277	4778	3160	1906
1957	708	45	10740	7991	5972	3401
1962	1191	98	13705	9648	7917	5662
1965	1144	114	18885	14881	9035	6438
1970	682	130	13273	10341	7878	6462
1975	934	137	20021	14956	9066	8050
1978	1017	148	24949	19198	11496	9856
1979	1078	152	26385	20110	11902	10781
1980	1091	151	27843	21295	12301	11052
"六五"时期						
1981	1188	152	29597	22559	12428	11436
1982	1159	151	30636	22814	12379	11383
1983	1177	156	31924	23948	12966	11674
1984	1160	157	32967	24502	13728	12960
1985	1175	165	34232	26185	14356	13791
"七五"时期						
1986	1184	167	35803	27360	14757	14165
1987	1137	166	37129	28159	15457	14721
1988	1103	171	38384	29167	16165	15580
1989	1137	180	39926	29878	16698	16176
1990	1300	178	41444	31130	18214	17216
"八五"时期						
1991	1233	177	40957	30815	18439	17538
1992	1331	180	41996	31541	18818	18178
1993	1285	193	43274	32871	20243	19320
1994	1228	213	43630	33007	20001	19064
1995	1185	216	43648	32848	20747	19534

19–2 续 1

年份 Year	卫生机构(个) Number of Health Institutions (unit)		卫生工作人员(人) Medical Technical Personnel (person)		卫生机构床位(张) Number of Beds (set)	
	小 计 Total	#医院及卫生院 Hospitals and Township Hospitals	小 计 Total	#卫生技术人员 Medical Technical Personnel	小 计 Total	#医院及卫生院 Hospitals and Township Hospitals
"九五"时期						
1996	1674	214	45765	35219	20428	19716
1997	1567	220	44664	34188	21422	20706
1998	1574	227	45110	34596	21965	21130
1999	1570	226	45121	34000	21735	21086
2000	1414	231	45166	35669	21698	20830
"十五"时期						
2001	1414	231	45296	35790	21906	21033
2002	1708	243	39386	31945	21576	21042
2003	1868	246	41925	33803	22674	22262
2004	1917	243	41625	33998	24044	22588
2005	2138	246	41499	34129	24695	23524
"十一五"时期						
2006	2285	240	43023	35124	27695	26101
2007	2265	243	42513	34579	26055	25328
2008	5092	286	44416	36143	28939	27555
2009	5163	281	46311	37648	30920	28749
2010	5086	277	54711	39366	31947	29844
"十二五"时期						
2011	5159	262	58590	42116	34920	31545
2012	5239	243	60426	44331	38834	35194
2013	5368	255	76955	57700	45465	41287
2014	5784	265	84515	63604	48280	44058
2015	5947	269	89117	71778	49311	45195
"十三五"时期						
2016	6188	270	92060	76447	52191	47524
2017	5770	289	97663	76273	54855	50142
2018	6030	293	104347	82834	57460	51207

备注：2015 年及 2016 年的卫生技术人员为注册卫生技术人员，其他年份为在岗卫生技术人员。

Notes: Health technicians in 2015 and 2016 are registered health technicians, and other years are on-the-job health technicians.

19－3　卫生事业机构及床位

Number of Health Institutions and Beds

指　　标	Indicator	2013 年	2014 年	2015 年	2016 年	2017 年	2018 年
各类卫生机构数(个)	**Number of Institutions(unit)**	5368	5784	5947	6188	5770	6030
医院	Hospital	197	207	213	217	238	246
社区卫生服务中心(站)	Health Service Center for Community	270	268	275	286	283	314
卫生院	Health Centers	58	58	56	53	51	47
门诊部	Outpatient Department	68	66	72	89	115	135
急救中心（站）	First–Aid Center	2	2	2	2	1	1
采血供应机构	Pick and Supply Blood Institution	4	4	4	4	2	2
妇幼保健院（所、站）	Women and Children Care Agencies	12	12	12	12	12	12
专科疾病防治院（所、站）	Specialized Disease Prevention &Treatment Institution	10	10	10	10	10	11
疾病预防控制中心（防疫站）	Center for Disease Control and Prevention	12	12	12	12	12	12
医学科学研究机构	Medical Science Research Institutes	0	2	2	2	2	2
其他卫生机构	Other Medical Institutions	11	15	17	18	27	29
各类卫生机构病床数（张）	**Number of Institutions Beds(set)**	45465	48280	49311	52191	54855	57460
医院	Hospital	38001	40874	42204	44526	47575	48843
社区卫生服务中心(站)	Health Service Center for Community	2774	2857	2792	2946	3195	3361
卫生院	Health Centers	3286	3184	2991	2998	2567	2364
门诊部	Outpatient Department	175	133	127	112	46	65
妇幼保健院（所、站）	Women and Children Care Agencies	782	777	834	1243	1126	1158
专科疾病防治院（所、站）	Specialized Disease Prevention	447	455	360	366	346	1669
千人拥有量(张、人）	**Number Per 1000 Population(set.person)**						
平均每千人拥有病床	Number Of Beds Per 1000 Population	7.41	6.83	6.91	7.22	7.49	7.70
每千人拥有卫生技术人员	Number Of Medical Technical Personnel Per 1000 Population	9.41	9.00	10.06	10.57	10.42	11.10
每千人拥有医生	Number Of Doctors Per 1000 Population	3.71	3.50	4.60	4.75	3.97	4.31
每千人拥有护士	Number Of Nurses Per 1000 Population	3.94	3.89	5.32	5.82	4.62	5.03

注：2011 年以前“医院”包含卫生院。

Notes: Before 2011,“hospitals” included health centers.

19－4　分地区卫生事业机构及床位（2018 年）

Number of Health Institutions and Beds by District（2018）

指　　标	Indicator	全　市 Total	市　区 Urban	平阴县 Pingyin	商河县 Shanghe
各类卫生机构数(个)	**Number of Institutions(unit)**	6030	5296	273	461
医院	Hospital	246	237	4	5
疗养院	Health Service Center for Community	0	0	0	0
社区卫生服务中心(站)	Health Centers	314	300	6	8
卫生院	Outpatient Department	47	29	7	11
门诊部	Outpatient Department	135	129	2	4
诊所、卫生所、医务室	Infirmaries and Clinics	2398	2234	80	84
急救中心（站）	First-Aid Center	1	1	0	0
采血供应机构	Pick and Supply Blood Institution	2	2	0	0
妇幼保健院（所、站）	Women and Children Care Agencies	12	10	1	1
专科疾病防治院（所、站）	Specialized Disease Prevention &Treatment Institution	11	9	2	0
疾病预防控制中心（防疫站）	Center for Disease Control and Prevention	12	10	1	1
卫生监督所	Medical Supervision Institution	12	10	1	1
医学科学研究机构	Medical Science Research Institutes	2	2	0	0
其他卫生构	Other Medical Institutions	29	29	0	0
各类卫生机构病床数（张）	**Number of Institutions Beds(bed)**	57460	53209	2111	2140
医院	Hospital	48843	45776	1439	1628
疗养院	Sanatorium	0	0	0	0
社区卫生服务中心(站)	Health Service Center for Community	3361	3319	0	42
卫生院	Health Centers	2364	1348	546	470
门诊部	Outpatient Department	65	65	0	0
妇幼保健院（所、站）	Women and Children Care Agencies	1158	1152	6	0
专科疾病防治院（所、站）	Specialized Disease Prevention&Treatment Institution	1669	1549	120	0
千人拥有量(张、人）	**Number Per 1000 Population(set.person)**				
平均每千人拥有病床	Number Of Beds Per 1000 Population	7.70	8.16	5.90	3.69
每千人拥有卫生技术人员	Number Of Medical Technical Personnel Per 1000 Population	11.10	12.01	6.39	3.86
每千人拥有医生	Number Of Doctors Per 1000 Population	4.31	4.66	2.30	1.61
每千人拥有护士	Number Of Nurses Per 1000 Population	5.03	5.46	2.87	1.52

19－5 医疗机构年收入与支出（2018年）

Revenue and Expenditure in Health Insititutions（2018）

单位：万元 (10 000 yuan)

机构分类	Institutions	总收入 Total Income			
		合计 Total	财政补助收入 Financial Subsidy Income	上级补助收入 Grant From Higher Authority	业务收入/事业收入 Business Income
合计	Total	4353399.4	541480.5	13702.0	3602096.1
医院	Hospital	3689343.7	307745.2	0.0	3275116.8
社区卫生服务中心(站)	Health Service Center for Community	139071.1	41136.0	2917.3	87864.3
卫生院	Health Centers	63263.4	35039.2	395.5	26458.8
门诊部	Outpatient Department	18046.8	0.0	0.0	12100.0
诊所.卫生所.医务室	Infirmaries and Clinics	42706.6	0.0	0.0	33528.2
急救中心(站)	First-Aid Center	2563.9	2496.9	0.0	67.0
妇幼保健院(所、站)	Women and Children Care Agencies	130655.5	23496.0	0.0	102910.3
专科疾病防治院(所、站)	Specialized Disease revention&Treatment Institution	47043.5	10542.0	0.0	35367.8

19-5 续

机构分类	Institutions	总支出 Total Expenditure			总支出中：人员支出 Staff Expenditure
		合计 Total	财政专项支出 Financial Expenditure	业务收入/事业收入 Business Income	
合计	Total	4130446.9	303771.5	3171172.0	1347202.3
医院	Hospital	3496979.2	164085.4	2800458.9	1105777.7
社区卫生服务中心(站)	Health Service Center for Community	150614.8	10696.0	137822.7	55919.3
卫生院	Health Centers	60809.3	557.3	59683.5	30540.2
门诊部	Outpatient Department	15655.1	0.0	0.0	5962.1
诊所.卫生所.医务室	Infirmaries and Clinics	33190.3	0.0	0.0	18477.5
急救中心(站)	First-Aid Center	2643.3	2546.6	96.7	1295.7
妇幼保健院(所、站)	Women and Children Care Agencies	120264.9	12658.8	83786.2	50978.1
专科疾病防治院(所、站)	Specialized Disease revention&Treatment Institution	47920.4	6486.7	33944.1	19096.7

备注：门诊部及诊所.卫生所.医务室不填报财政补助收入、上级补助收入、财政专项支出、业务支出/事业支出四项指标。

Notes: Outpatient department and clinic. Health clinic. The medical office does not report four indicators: financial subsidy income, superior subsidy income, fiscal special expenditure, business expenditure/business expenditure.

19－6 医院、卫生院工作情况

Basic Statistics on Hospitals and Health Institutions in Rural Areas

指　　标	Indicator	2011 年	2012 年	2013 年	2014 年	2015 年	2016 年	2017 年	2018 年
医院	**Hospital**								
单位数（个）	Unit Number(unit)	200	167	197	207	213	217	238	246
诊疗人次数（万人次）	Visits (10 000 person-times)	1809	2097	2293	2594	2716	2865	3157	3309
#门诊人次数	OutPatients	1652	1907	2077	2352	2446	2570	2779	2960
急诊人次数	Emergency Patients	81	97	107	126	150	165	207	228
健康检查人数（万人次）	check-up(10 000 person-times)	94	97	108	132	131	154	166	201
入院人数（万人）	Inpatients(10 000 person-times)	65.8	80.1	94.5	106.3	112.5	127.9	140.4	150.0
出院人数（万人）	Discharged(10 000 person-times)	65.9	80.2	91.8	106.1	112.1	127.3	139.7	149.4
平均开放病床数（张）	Average Bed Opened(bed)	26090	29890	34550	37218	39632	41402	44400	45132
病床使用率（%）	Utilization Rate of Beds(%)	84.18	86.33	83.93	84.14	82.37	86.12	87.52	87.28
病床周转次数（次）	Turnover of Beds(time)	25.30	26.80	26.50	28.52	28.30	30.70	31.50	33.10
出院者平均住院日（日）	Average Stay Days in Hospital(day)	12.30	11.70	11.40	10.74	10.60	10.10	9.90	9.40
卫生院	**Health Centers**								
单位数（个）	Unit Number(unit)	62	76	58	58	56	53	51	47
诊疗人次数（万人次）	Visits (10 000 person-times)	261.0	256.0	269.0	280.5	211.7	233.4	208.1	195.2
#门诊人次数	OutPatients	240.0	238.0	255.0	271.4	205.7	224.6	197.6	190.3
急诊人次数	Emergency Patients	4.7	8.3	5.1	4.6	3.0	3.4	6.5	3.3
健康检查人数（万人次）	check-up(10 000 person-times)	36.6	34.5	34.0	30.3	23.9	23.0	20.2	20.4
入院人数（万人）	Inpatients(10 000 person-times)	7.1	8.9	8.4	6.4	4.7	6.6	5.3	4.4
出院人数（万人）	Discharged(10 000 person-times)	7.1	8.9	8.4	6.4	4.7	6.5	5.3	4.4
平均开放病床数（张）	Average Bed Opened(bed)	3309	3086	3136	3062	2930	2907	2479	2277
病床使用率（%）	Utilization Rate of Beds(%)	43.48	52.36	55.02	46.60	38.62	54.54	52.00	54.85
病床周转次数（次）	Turnover of Beds(time)	21.40	28.80	26.70	20.87	15.90	22.40	21.40	19.40
出院者平均住院日（日）	Average Stay Days in Hospital(day)	6.40	6.10	7.60	8.33	8.20	8.40	8.30	9.70

注：2011 年以前“医院”包含卫生院。

Notes: Before 2011, “hospitals” included health centers.

19－7　分地区卫生技术人员分类情况（2018年）

Medical Technical Personnel by Region（2018）

单位：人

指　　标	Indicator	全市 Total	市区 Urban	平阴县 Pingyin	商河县 Shanghe
各类卫生机构工作人员合计	Medical TechnicalPersonnel	104347	97776	3029	3542
#卫生技术人员小计	Medical TechnicalPersonnel	82834	78306	2286	2242
医　生	Licensed Doctors	32131	30372	825	934
注册护士	Registered Nurse	37492	35582	1026	884
其　他	Others	13211	12352	435	424

主要统计指标解释

等级裁判员人数　指经考核正式批准授予等级裁判员称号的人数。裁判员等级分为国际裁判、国家级裁判、一级裁判、二级裁判、三级裁判。

体育场　指有400 米跑道（中心含足球场），有固定道牙，跑道6 条以上，并有固定看台的室外田径场地。体育场按看台容纳观众人数分为：甲级25000 人以上，乙级15000-25000人，丙级5000-15000 人，丁级5000 人以下。

体育馆　指有固定看台，可供篮球、排球、羽毛球、乒乓球、体操等项目训练比赛活动用的室内运动场地。体育馆按看台容纳观众人数分为：甲级6000 人以上，乙级4000-6000人，丙级2000-4000 人，丁级2000 人以下。

医院　包括综合医院、中医医院、中西医结合医院、民族医医院、各类专科医院和护理院，不包括专科疾病防治院、妇幼保健院和疗养院，包括医学院校附属医院。

卫生技术人员　包括执业医师、执业助理医师、注册护士、药师(士)、检验及影像技师(士)、卫生监督员和见习医(药、护、技)师(士)等卫生专业人员。

医生　指取得医师执业证书且实际从事临床工作的人。

卫生机构　指从卫生（卫生健康）行政部门取得《医疗机构执业许可证》、《中医诊所备案证》、《计划生育技术服务许可证》或从民政、工商行政、机构编制管理部门取得法人单位登记证书，为社会提供医疗服务、公共卫生服务或从事医学科研和学在职培训等工作的单位。

Explanatory Notes on Main Statistical Indicators

Number of Grade Referees refers to the number of referees formally approved upon evaluation to be granted with the title of grade referee. Referees are divided into international referee, national referee, Level I referee, Level II referee and Level III referee.

Stadium refers to outdoor athletic field with 400m track (football field in the center), fixed kerbs, more than 6 tracks and fixed stands. Stadiums can be divided as follows as per the quantity of spectators contained by the standard: Class A stadium for above 25,000 persons, Class B stadium for 15,000–25,000 persons, Class C stadium for 5,000–15,000 persons and Class D stadium for less than 5,000 persons.

Gymnasium refers to indoor sports ground with fixed stands which can be used for training and competition of basketball, volleyball, badminton, table tennis and gymnastics. Gymnasium can be divided as follows as per the quantity of spectators contained by the standard: Class A gymnasium for above 6,000 persons, Class B gymnasium for 4,000–6,000 persons, Class C gymnasium for 2,000–4,000 persons and Class D gymnasium for less than 2,000 persons.

Hospital includes general hospital, traditional Chinese medicine hospital, hospital of traditional Chinese and Western medicine, ethnic medical hospital, various specialized hospital and nursing home and affiliated hospital of medical college other than specialized disease prevention and maternity and child care center and nursing home.

Medical Technical Personnel refers to health professionals such as medical practitioner, assistant medical practitioner, registered nurse, pharmacist, senior pharmacist (assistant pharmacist), inspection and imaging technician (assistant technician), health supervisor and medical intern (trainee medical assistant), pharmacy intern (probationary pharmacist), trainee nurse (practice nurse) or medical trainee (apprentice technician).

Doctors refer to persons getting the medical practitioner certificate and actually engaging in clinical work.

Health Care Institution refers to units getting *Practicing License of Medical Institution*, *Registration Certificate of TCM Clinic* and *Family Planning Technical Service License* from the administrative department of health (hygiene and health) or getting the registration certificate of legal entity from civil affairs, industrial and commercial administration, institutional establishment management departments, providing the society with medical service and public health service or engaging in medical scientific research and studying on–the–job training.

20

民政、司法和其它

SOCIAL WELFARE CIVIL ADMINISTRATION AND JUSTICE

20－1 社会治安主要指标

Main Indicators of Social Offense

指　　标	Indicator	2011 年	2012 年	2013 年	2014 年	2015 年	2016 年	2017 年	2018 年
刑事案件（件）	**Criminal Cases(case)**								
当年全部立案数	Put on Record	53770	50680	47721	45118	35047	21142	19648	18594
破获当年刑事案件数	Cracked the Number of Criminal Cases	29560	25306	27252	26939	20806	7610	8571	7103
治安案件（件）	**Public Security Cases(case)**								
受理数	Cases Accepted	177322	139252	113246	91877	86217	71868	66375	75393
查处数	Cases Punished	168373	136769	110288	87656	81754	68439	63734	73700
城市交通事故	**Traffic Accidents**								
交通事故（起）	Number of Traffic Accidents(case)	762	1453	1801	2948	2946	2944	3075	3071
伤亡人数（人）	Number of Injuries and Deaths(person)	838	1713	2249	3708	3885	3573	3219	3618
#死亡人数（人）	Number of Deathsa(person)	259	272	286	440	439	403	421	419
损失折款（万元）	Direct Losses(10 000 yuan)	247	632	443	737	840	875.2	1020.3	947.4
火灾事故	**Fires**								
火灾起数（起）	Number of Fire Accidents(case)	571	246	2751	2848	2609	1825	1752	1539
伤亡人数（人）	Number of Injuries and Deaths(person)	1	2	12	7	12	15	11	12
#死亡人数（人）	Number of Deaths(person)	1	2	9	6	12	13	10	10
损失折款（万元）	Direct Losses(10 000 yuan)	773	395	1471	1104	1571	1903	599	827

注：“破获当年刑事案件数”2015 年以前为当年全部破案数口径

Note: "The number of uncovering criminal cases in the year" was the total quantity before 2015.

20－2 分地区社会治安主要指标（2018 年）

Main Indicators of Social Offense by District（2018）

指 标	Indicator	全市 Total	市区 Urban	平阴县 Pingyin	商河县 Shanghe
刑事案件（件）	**Criminal Cases(case)**				
当年全部立案数	Put on Record	18594	17601	542	451
破获当年刑事案件数	Cracked the Number of Criminal Cases	7103	6541	294	268
治安案件（件）	**Public Security Cases(case)**				
受理数	Cases Accepted	75393	70659	2455	2279
查处数	Cases Punished	73700	69194	2459	2047
城市交通事故	**Traffic Accidents**				
交通事故（起）	Number of Traffic Accidents(case)	3071	2986	46	39
伤亡人数（人）	Number of Injuries and Deaths(person)	3618	3518	62	38
#死亡人数（人）	Number of Deathsa(person)	419	382	28	9
损失折款（万元）	Direct Losses(10 000 yuan)	947.4	935	7	5
火灾事故	**Fires**				
火灾起数（起）	Number of Fire Accidents(case)	1539	1502	19	18
伤亡人数（人）	Number of Injuries and Deaths(person)	12	12	0	0
#死亡人数（人）	Number of Deaths(person)	10	10	0	0
损失折款（万元）	Direct Losses(10 000 yuan)	827	785	22	20

20－3 社会保障和救济

Basic Statistics on Social Security and Receiving Relief Flinds

指　　标	Indicator	2011 年	2012 年	2013 年	2014 年	2015 年	2016 年	2017 年	2018 年
优抚情况（人）	**Veteran Benefit and Placement(person)**								
享受定期抚恤金人数	Number of Receiving Periodic Pensions	2360	2058	1428	1169	939	907	831	784
在乡复员军人	Demobilized Soldiers in Countryside	11020	8254	4512	3708	2725	2319	1892	1486
参战退役人员	Veterans	5091	4962	4765	4524	4454	4741	4705	4630
社会救济情况（人）	**Social Relief(person)**								
城镇居民最低生活保障人数	Number of Urban Residents for Minimum Livelihood Guarantee	55868	40070	32947	24925	22303	19742	16742	13364
农村居民最低生活保障人数	Number of Rural residents for Minimum Livelihood Guarantee	82562	75978	76223	80535	81215	80147	77121	64271
民政经费（万元）	**Civil Affairs Expenditures(10 000 yuan)**								
退役安置费	Decommissioning Costs	48089	54566	64014	71530	89415	96164	134557	12656.3
城市居民最低生活保障费	Urban Residents for Minimum Livelihood Guarantee	18828	17126	16064	12882	8585	11573	10966	9562.8
农村最低生活保障费	Rural residents for Minimum Livelihood Guarantee	10876	12973	14709	16376	13343	24938	26929	26438.8
其它社会救助费	Other Social Assistance Expenses	7903	7303	6670	7397	11446	6614	5757	3087.9
社会福利费	Social Welfare Funds	11588	19928	18975	28987	33569	35898	32194	47653.8
自然灾害生活救助费	Natural Disaster Assistance Expenses	840	1529	1295	570	1646	654	259	没有
医疗救助费	Medical Assistance Expenses	4987	5579	5564	6788	4581	7245	8396	131.3
社会保障及扶贫（个、元）	**Social Security and Poverty Alleviation(unit.yuan)**								
建立社会保障服务网络的乡镇数	Number of Towns With Social Security Service Network	55	55	53	53	48	39	29	29
城市市区居民最低生活保障金标准	Minimum Living Standards for Urban Residents	400	480	480	550	550	580	596	616

20－4 分地区社会

Basic Statistics on Social Security and

指　　标	Indicator	济南市(汇总) Total	济南市(市本级) Urban	历下区 Li xia	市中区 Shi zhong	槐荫区 Huai yin
优抚情况（人）	**Veteran Benefit and Placement(person)**					
享受定期抚恤金人数	Number of Receiving Periodic Pensions	784	0	39	66	31
在乡复员军人	Demobilized Soldiers in Countryside	1486	0	25	60	30
参战退役人员	Veterans	4630	0	71	204	141
社会救济情况（人）	**Social Relief(person)**					
城镇居民最低生活保障人数	Number of Urban Residents for Minimum Livelihood Guarantee	13346	0	1881	2284	1420
农村居民最低生活保障人数	Number of Rural residents for Minimum Livelihood Guarantee	64271	0	0	1095	396
民政经费（万元）	**Civil Affairs Expenditures(10 000 yuan)**					
退役安置费	Decommissioning Costs	12656.3	9337.7	260.0	427.7	319.4
城市居民最低生活保障费	Urban Residents for Minimum Livelihood Guarantee	9562.8	0.0	1495.4	1614.2	1045.5
农村最低生活保障费	Rural residents for Minimum Livelihood Guarantee	26438.8	0.0	0.0	625.8	202.1
其它社会救助费	Other Social Assistance Expenses	3087.9	1090	1069.9	265.8	51.3
社会福利费	Social Welfare Funds	47653.8	17298.4	5180.3	968.5	2126.6
医疗救助费	Medical Assistance Expenses	131.3		13.0	13.8	8.0
社会保障及扶贫（个、元）	**Social Security and Poverty Alleviation(unit.yuan)**					
建立社会保障服务网络的乡镇数	Number of Towns With Social Security Service Network	29				
城市市区居民最低生活保障金标准	Minimum Living Standards for Urban Residents	616.0		616.0	616.0	616.0

保 障 和 救 济（2018年）

Receiving Relief Flinds by Region（2018）

天桥区 Tian qiao	历城区 Li cheng	长清区 Chang qing	章丘区 Zhang qiu	济阳区 Ji yang	平阴县 Ping yin	商河县 Shang he	高新区 Gao xin	南部山区 Nan shan
35	69	111	140	69	57	104	27	36
78	214	134	281	268	84	93	78	141
280	328	799	903	620	297	597	193	197
4151	438.0	523	1662	198	175	542	21	51
1131	1314.0	9833	18188	9452	4028	14336	821	3677
517.3	307.0	184.5	368.1	192.4	208.9	320.1	123.27	90
2950.3	362.9	320.5	1140.1	103.8	117.0	256.7	117.6	38.8
639.1	680.5	3582.6	8384.4	3476.3	1736.5	4858.3	573.1	1680.1
0.0	0.0	0.0	350.0	18.9	0.0	0.0	242.0	0.0
2186.9	2512.5	2159.5	5796.9	1686.4	2568.4	2817.0	1853.6	498.8
18.1	28.0	20.0	10.0	3.9	9.5	5.0	0.0	2
	1	3	3	4	6	11		1
616.0	616.0	616.0	616.0	616.0	616.0	616.0	616.0	616.0

20－5 律师、公证、司法基本情况（2018年）

Basic Statistics on Law、Notarizations and Mendiation（2018）

指　　标	Indicator	单　位 Unit	全　市 Total	市　区 Urban	平阴县 Pingyin	商河县 Shanghe
律师工作	Lawyers					
律师事务所	Number of Law Offices	个(unit)	397	376	5	16
执业律师	Number of Lawyers	人(person)	6663	6389	27	247
#专职律师	Full-time Lawyers	人(person)	5958	5771	27	160
担任常年法律顾问	Permanent Legal Advisor	家(unit)	6784	5920	104	760
民事诉讼代理	Civil Agent	件(case)	58742	55970	772	2000
刑事诉讼辩护及代理	Criminal Defense and Agent	件(case)	8265	7799	66	400
行政诉讼代理	Administrative Agent	件(case)	2665	2618	7	40
非诉讼法律事务	Non-litigation Legal Matters	件(case)	10929	7929	0	3000
公证工作	Notarization					
公证处	Number of Notary Offices	个(unit)	12	8	1	3
公证处人员	Personnel of Notary Offices	人(person)	295	224	10	61
#公证员	Notaries	人(person)	111	82	4	25
办理公证总数	Number of Notarized Affair	件(case)	130462	112428	2418	15616
#国内民事公证	Domestic Civil Notarization	件(case)	43753	35822	675	7256
国内经济公证	Domestic Commerce Notarization	件(case)	72033	61930	1743	8360
涉外公证	Foreign-related Notarization	件(case)	13982	12192	0	1790
办理经济公证涉及金额	Money ofCommerce Notarization	亿元(100 million yuan)	4.50	0.19	0.11	4.20
基层司法行政工作	Basic Judicical Administration					
人民调解委员会	People's Mediation Committee	个(unit)	5453	3965	363	1125
人民调解员	People's Mediators	人(person)	19630	13769	1338	4523
调解纠纷总数	Number of Mediation Disputes	件(case)	19492	10262	1189	8041
#调解成功	Success Mediation	件(case)	18956	9777	1172	8007
法律服务所	Legal Service Office	个(unit)	124	88	9	27
基层法律工作者	Grassroots Legal Workers	人(person)	806	755	37	14
担任法律顾问	Legal Advisor	家(unit)	796	723	65	8
民事诉讼代理	Civil Agent	件(case)	8230	7172	540	518
非诉讼代理	Non-litigation Agent	件(case)	5499	5346	90	63
法律援助工作	Legal Aid					
法律援助机构	Legal Aid Institution	个(unit)	11	9	1	1
执业人员	Practitioners	人(person)	97	97	0	0
办理法律援助案件	Legal Aid Cases	件(case)	9278	8209	425	644

主要统计指标解释

律师　指受聘参加法律顾问处工作，担任法律顾问、刑（民）事代理人、刑事辩护人，办理非诉讼事件、解答法律询问，代写法律事务文书等主要从事律师业务的专职法律工作者和兼职律师。

公证人员　指在国家公证机关依法办理公证事务的司法人员，包括公证员、助理公证员和在公证处工作的其他人员。

调解人员　指在人民调解委员会担负调解民间一般民事纠纷和轻微违法行为引起纠纷的工作人员，包括调解委员会的委员和调解小组的调解员。

立案　指检察机关对犯罪线索进行初步调查后，认为存在职务犯罪事实并需要追究刑事责任时，依法决定作为刑事案件进行侦查的诉讼活动，是追究犯罪的开始。

Explanatory Notes on Main Statistical Indicators

Lawyers refer to full-time legal workers and part-time lawyers hired to work in the legal advisory office, serving as legal adviser, criminal (civil) agent and criminal advocate and mainly engaging in law practice (such as handling non-contentious matter, answering legal questions and ghostwriting legal papers).

Notary Personnel refers to judicial personnel legally handling notarial affairs at the state notary organ, including notary, assistant notary and other personnel working in the notary office.

Mediation Personnel refers to staff taking charge of mediating ordinary civil disputes among the people and disputes arising from minor infraction at the people's mediation committee, including the member of the mediation committee and the mediator of the mediation team.

Case Filing refers to the litigious activity involving investigation of criminal case according to law when existence of duty-related crimes is deemed and it is necessary to investigate the criminal responsibility after preliminary investigation of crime clues by the investigating and prosecuting apparatus. It is the start of the investigation of crime.

21

原莱芜市主要经济指标

MAIN ECONOMIC INDICATORS OF THE ORIGINAL LAIWU CITY

国民经济和社会发展主要指标

Principal Aggregate Indicators on National Economic and Social Development

指　标	Indicators	单位 Unit	2018
面积	**Area**		
土地面积	Land Area	平方公里(sq.km)	2246
#建成区面积	Built-up Area of Seven Districts in the City	平方公里(sq.km)	120
人口	**Population**		
年末总户数（户籍人口）	Total year-end Households（Household Population）	万户(10 000 households)	47.12
年末总人口	Total year-end Population	万人(10 000 persons)	129.4
#男性	Male	万人(10 000 persons)	65.32
年末常住总人口	Total Resident Population at the Year-end	万人(10 000 persons)	137.9
申报出生率	Birth Rate	‰	11.03
申报死亡率	Death Rate	‰	7.3
自然增长率	Natural Growth Rate	‰	3.73
就业	**Employment**		
城镇登记失业率	Registered Urban Unemployment Rate	%	2.72
国民经济核算	**National Accounting**		
地区生产总值	Gross Domestic Product	亿元(100 million yuan)	1005.65
#非公有制经济	Non-ppublic Economy	亿元(100 million yuan)	468.56
第一产业	Primary Industry	亿元(100 million yuan)	60.31
第二产业	Secondary Industry	亿元(100 million yuan)	566.08
第三产业	Tertiary Industry	亿元(100 million yuan)	379.26
人均地区生产总值	Per Capita GDP	元(yuan)	73005
固定资产投资	**Investment in Fixed Assets**		
固定资产投资增速	Investment in Fixed Assets	‰	7.2
第一产业增速	Primary Industry	‰	-42.4
第二产业增速	Secondary Industry	‰	4.8
第三产业增速	Tertiary Industry	‰	13.8
#房地产投资增速	Real Estate Investment	‰	27.6
财政税收	**Fiscal Tax Revenue**		
一般公共预算收入	General Pubilic Budget Revenue	亿元(100 million yuan)	62.57
一般公共预算支出	General Pubilic Budget Expenditure	亿元(100 million yuan)	100.35
地域税收收入	Regional Tax Revenue	亿元(100 million yuan)	90.03
一般公共预算收入占生产总值比重	Proportion of General Public Budget Revenue in GDP	%	6.22
一般公共预算支出占生产总值比重	Proportion of General Public Budget Expenditure in GDP	%	9.98
金融保险	**Fiancial and Insurance**		
金融机构人民币存款余额	RMB Deposits Balance of Financial Institutions	亿元(100 million yuan)	1028.23
#住户存款	Deposits of Households	亿元(100 million yuan)	630.25
金融机构人民币贷款余额	RMB Loans Balance of Financial Institutions	亿元(100 million yuan)	815.25
#短期贷款	Short-term Loans	亿元(100 million yuan)	472.49
保险承保额	Insurance Premium	万元(10 000 yuan)	9722.54
保险业务收入	Premium	万元(10 000 yuan)	305246

续 1

指 标	Indicators	单位 Unit	2018
赔付支出	Compensation Expenses	万元(10 000 yuan)	93403
农业	Agriculture		
农林牧渔业总产值	Gross Output Value of Farming Forestry,Animal Husbandry and Fishery	亿元(100 million yuan)	108.86
农用机械总动力	total power of agricultural machinery	万千瓦(10 000kw)	88.48
机耕率	Machine-cultivated Rate	%	82.6
粮食总产量	Total Output of Grain	万吨(10 000 tons)	25.52
蔬菜总产量	Total Output of Vegetable	万吨(10 000 tons)	131.76
肉类总产量	Total Output of meat	万吨(10 000 tons)	7.94
奶类总产量	Total Output of Milk	万吨(10 000 tons)	0.34
棉花总产量	Total Output of Cotton	万吨(10 000 tons)	0.15
规模以上工业	Industry Enterprises above Designated Size		
单位数	Number of Enterprises	个(unit)	552
工业总产值	Gross Industrial Output Value	亿元(100 million yuan)	1873.01
主营业务收入	Revenue from Principal Business	亿元(100 million yuan)	2102.19
利税总额	Total Profits and Taxes	亿元(100 million yuan)	148.26
利润总额	Total Profits	亿元(100 million yuan)	101.34
资产总计	Total Assets	亿元(100 million yuan)	1396.61
所有者权益	Owner's Equities	亿元(100 million yuan)	518.61
建筑业	Construction		
资质以上企业个数	Number of Qualification Enterprises	个(unit)	145
建筑业总产值	Gross Output Value of Construction Enterprises	亿元(100 million yuan)	97.31
施工面积	Floor Space under Construction	万平方米(10 000 sq.m)	502
竣工面积	Floor Space of Completed	万平方米(10 000 sq.m)	292
其中：住宅	Residential	万平方米(10 000 sq.m)	139
交通运输	Transport		
货运量	Freight Traffic		
公路	Highways	万吨(10 000 tons)	7929
客运量	Passenger Traffic		
公路	Highways	万人(10 000 persons)	149
民用汽车拥有量	Possession of Private Vehicles	辆(unit)	241566
邮电通信	Post and Telecommunication Services		
固定电话	Fixed Telephone	万户(10 000 households)	29.62
移动电话	Mobile Telephone	万户(10 000 households)	223.10
互联网用户	Internet Broad Band	万户(10 000 households)	75.69
国内贸易	Domestic Trade		
社会消费品零售总额	Total Retail Sales of Consumer Goods	亿元(100 million yuan)	373.16
#批发零售业	Wholesale and Retail Trade	亿元(100 million yuan)	351.20
#餐饮业	Catering Services	亿元(100 million yuan)	21.96
对外经济和国际旅游	Foreign Economy and Trade,Tourism		
全年货物进出口总额	Total Value of Imports and Exports	亿元(100 million yuan)	111.39

续 2

指　标	Indicators	单位 Unit	2018
进口	Exports	亿元(100 million yuan)	38.99
出口	Imports	亿元(100 million yuan)	72.40
教育	**Education**		
普通高等学校在校生	Total Enrollment of Regular Institutions of Higher Education	万人(10 000 persons)	1
普通高等学校专任教师	Full-time Teachers of Regular Institutions of Higher Education	人(person)	535
中等专业学校在校生	Total Enrollment of Secondary Professional Schools	万人(10 000 persons)	0.75
中等专业学校专任教师	Full-time Teachers of Secondary Professional Schools	人(person)	515
普通中学在校生	Total Enrollment of Regular Senior Secondary Schools	万人(10 000 persons)	7.62
普通中学专任教师	Full-time Teachers of Regular Senior Secondary Schools	人(person)	6234
小学在校生	Total Enrollment of Regular Primary Schools	万人(10 000 persons)	5.53
小学专任教师	Full-time Teachers of Regular Primary Schools	人(person)	4099
文化	**Culture**		
图书馆藏书量	Number of Books in Library	万册(10 000 copies)	31.78
卫生	**Public Health**		
卫生机构数	Number of Health Institutions	个(unit)	1313
#医院及卫生院	Hospitals and Township Hospitals	个(unit)	50
卫生机构床位数	Number of Beds	张(bed)	7351
#医院及卫生院	Hospitals and Township Hospitals	张(bed)	6600
卫生工作人员	Medical Personnel	人(person)	11777
# 卫生技术人员	Medical Technical Personnel	人(person)	8832
每万人拥有医院卫生院数	Number of Health Institutes per 10000 Population	个(unit)	0.36
每万人拥有医生数	Number of Doctors per 10000 Population	人(person)	25.45
每万人拥有医院床位数	Number of Hospitals Beds per 10000 Population	张(bed)	53.31
人民生活	**People's Livelihood**		
城镇居民人均可支配收入	Per Capita Disposable Income of Urban Residents	元(yuan)	37401
城镇居民人均生活消费支出	Per Capita Life Consumption Expenditure of Urban Residents	元(yuan)	21304
城镇人均住宅居住面积	Urban Per Capita Living Space	平方米(sq.m)	38.7
城镇居民恩格尔系数	Engel's Coefficient of Urban Residents	%	25
农村居民人均可支配收入	Per Capita Disposable Income of Rural Residents	元(yuan)	17468
农村居民人均生活消费支出	Per Capita Life Consumption Expenditure of Rural Residents	元(yuan)	12263
农民人均住宅居住面积	Rural Residential Area Per Capita	平方米(sq.m)	47.5
农村居民恩格尔系数	Engel's Coefficient of Rural Residents	%	30.4
社会治安	**Public security**		
交通事故起数	Number of Traffic Accidents	起(case)	258
交通事故死伤人数	Deaths and Injuries from Traffic Accidents	人(person)	241
交通事故损失折款	Property Losses from Traffic Accidents	万元(10 000 yuan)	62.31
火灾事故起数	Number of Fire Accidents	起(case)	76
火灾事故死伤人数	Deaths and Injuries from Fire Accidents	人(person)	0
火灾事故损失折款	Property Losses from Fire Accidents	万元(10 000 yuan)	177

县区所辖镇、街道办事处（2018 年末）

Town and Street Communities Under the Jurisdiction（End of 2018）

县区	Region	镇、街道办事处数量（个） Number of Towns and Street Communities (unit)	镇、街道办事处名称 Name of Towns and Street Communities
莱芜区	Lai wu	15	凤城街道、张家洼街道、高庄街道、鹏泉街道、口镇、羊里镇、方下镇 牛泉镇、苗山镇、雪野镇、大王庄镇、寨里镇、杨庄镇、茶业口镇 和庄镇
钢城区	Gang cheng	5	艾山街道、里辛街道、汶源街道、颜庄镇、辛庄镇

年末总户数、总人口（户籍人口）

Total Household and Population in Years-end（registered population）

年　份 Year	年末总户数 (万户) Total year-end Households (10 000 households)	年末总人口 (万人) Total year-end Population (10 000 persons)	按性别分（万人） Grouped by Sex (10 000 persons)		性别比(女＝100) Sex Ratio (Femal=100)	人口密度 (人/平方公里) Density of Population (Person/sq.km)
			男性 Male	女性 Femal		
2018	47.12	129.40	65.32	64.09	101.92	576

年末人口自然变动情况

Natural Change of Population in Years-end

年份 Year	申报出生人口(人) Population ofBirth (person)	申报出生率（‰） Birth Rate（‰）	申报死亡人口(人) Population of Death (person)	申报死亡率（‰） Death Rate（‰）	人口自然增长(人) Population of Natural Growth (person)	人口自然增长率 （‰） Natural Growth Rate （‰）
2018	14363	11.03	9455	7.30	4908	3.73

结 婚 情 况

Number of　Marriages

单位：对　(couple)

地　区	Region	2018 年
总计	Total	5782
市直	Departments Directiy Under the Municipal Government	10
莱芜区	Lai wu	4551
钢城区	gang cheng	1221

离 婚 情 况

Number of　Divorces

单位：对　(couple)

地　区	Region	2018 年
总　计	Total	2914
法院数	Divorce Case Handled	1284
民政数	Divorces Handled through Civil	1630
市　直	Departments Directiy Under the Municipal Government	1
莱芜区	Lai wu	1209
钢城区	Gang cheng	420

生产总值（2018 年）（分行业，按当年价格计算）

Value of Gross Domestic Product（2018）(Sub Industry、Calculated at Current Prices)

单位：亿元 (100 million yuan)

指　标	Indicator	原莱芜市 Total City
地区生产总值	**Gross Domestic Product**	1005.65
农、林、牧、渔业	Agriculture, Forestry, Animal Husbandry and Fishery	61.89
#农、林、牧、渔服务业	Services of Agriculture,Forestry,Animal Husbandry and Fishing	1.58
工业	Industry	525.12
#开采辅助活动	Mining Support Activities	
#金属制品、机械和设备修理业	Metal Products, Machinery and Equipment Repair Industry	1.44
建筑业	Construction	42.4
批发和零售业	Wholesale and Retail Trade	92.25
批发业	Wholesale	58.6
零售业	Retail Trade	33.65
交通运输、仓储和邮政业	Transport, Storage and Post	43.6
住宿和餐饮业	Accommodations and Catering Services	11.86
住宿业	Accommodations	3.04
餐饮业	Catering Services	8.82
金融业	Financial Intermediation	42.05
房地产业	Real Estate	40.13
房地产业(K 门类)	Real estate industry (K category)	24.07
自有房地产经营活动	Own Real Estate Operating Activities	16.06
其他服务业	Other Services	146.35
营利性服务业	Profit service industry	76.9
非营利性服务业	Non-profit service industry	69.45
第一产业	Primary Industry	60.31
第二产业	Secondary Industry	566.08
第三产业	Tertiary Industry	379.26

规模以上服务业企业分行业

Main Economic Indicators of Service Enterprise

指标	Indicator	单位 Unit	合计 Total	交通运输、仓储和邮政业 Transport, Storage and Postal Services	信息传输、软件和信息技术服务业 Information Transmission, Software and Information Technology	房地产业 Real Estate
单位数	Number of Enterprises	个(unit)	155	62	9	17
固定资产原价	Original Value of Fixed Assets	万元(10 000 yuan)	608985.8	156441.1	248450.5	69312.0
本年折旧	Depreciation in the Year	万元(10 000 yuan)	35630.6	15059.5	12767.6	1469.2
折旧率	Depreciation Rate	%	5.9	9.6	5.1	2.1
营业收入	Operating Income	万元(10 000 yuan)	772034.0	323731.7	80221.0	66726.2
税金及附加	Taxes and Other Surcharges	万元(10 000 yuan)	4598.7	1812.4	404.7	1173.1
营业利润	Profits from Business	万元(10 000 yuan)	60326.8	14567.7	5768.9	26679.0
利润总额	004-2	万元(10 000 yuan)	64476.5	15315.1	5997.2	28885.8
应付职工薪酬（本年贷方累计发生额）	Total Wages Payable	万元(10 000 yuan)	139025.5	45061.9	8393.8	13843.2
从业人员平均人数	Average Number of Employees	人(person)	23518	7103	1148	2860
人均工资	Per Capita Wages	元(yuan)	59115	63441	73117	48403
应交增值税	Value Added Tax Payable	万元(10 000 yuan)	12974.6	4581.5	2098.2	3057.0

主要经济指标（2018 年）

Above Designated Size by Sector（2018）

租赁和商务服务业 Leasing and Business Services	科学研究和技术服务业 Scientific Research, Technical Services	水利、环境和公共设施管理业 Management of Water Conservancy, Environment and Public Facilities	居民服务、修理和其他服务业 services to Households, Repair and Other Services	教育 Education	卫生和社会工作 Health and Social Work	文化、体育和娱乐业 Culture, Sports and Recreation
21	13	14	8	5	3	3
16889.1	3795.9	20971.2	30814.0	4397.1	51637.0	6277.9
980.1	234.5	729.7	884.0	484.1	2661.9	360.0
5.8	6.2	3.5	2.9	11.0	5.2	5.7
143989.7	21807.2	15971.8	31685.4	2426.9	81091.4	4382.7
313.9	314.5	160.1	367.6	29.3	5.1	18.0
2669.6	2134.9	1969.1	5566.6	-753.2	2066.2	-342.0
2731.7	2079.6	1931.3	5622.8	-747.7	2348.7	312.0
17502.3	4231.1	2275.9	17876.9	1298.9	26893.2	1648.3
3373	601	719	5205	362	1948	199
51889	70401	31654	34346	35881	138055	82829
1352.3	773.0	235.1	674.0	66.9		136.6

社会保障基本情况

Basic Statistics on Social Security

指　标	Indicator	单位 Unit	2018 年
职工基本养老保险参保人数	Urban Basic Pension Insurance	万人(10 000 persons)	45.85
# 企业	Enterpris	万人(10 000 persons)	41.43
事业机关	Institution and Government Agency	万人(10 000 persons)	4.42
参加失业保险人数	Unemployment Insurance	万人(10 000 persons)	21.86
工伤保险参保人数	Work Injury Insurance	万人(10 000 persons)	26.92
职工基本医疗保险参保人数	Medcial Care Insurance	万人(10 000 persons)	27.92
生育保险参保人数	Maternity Insurance	万人(10 000 persons)	19.28
城镇登记失业率	Registered Urban Unemployment Rate	%	2.72

固定资产投资分类（2018 年）

Investment in Fixed Assets（2018）

指　　标	Indicator	固定资产投资增长速度（%）
本年完成投资	**Investment Completed This Year**	7.2
按构成分	**Investment by Structure**	
建筑安装工程		3.8
设备工器具购置	Purchase of Equipment and Instruments	8.8
#购置旧设备	Purchase of Second-hand Equipment	66.6
其他费用	Others	54.6
按产业分	**Grouped by Three Strata of Industry**	
第一产业	Primary Industry	-42.4
第二产业	Secondary Industry	4.8
第三产业	Tertiary Industry	13.8
按单位登记注册类型分	**Registration Status**	
内资	**Domestic Fund**	7.0
国有	State-owned	-3.9
集体	Collective-owned	-20.6
股份合作	Cooperative	7.5
私营个体		26.9
港澳台投资	**Fund from Hong Kong,Macao and Taiwan**	-68.2
#港澳台股份有限公司	Share-holding	-34.9
外商投资	**Fund from Overseas**	118.8
#外商合资经营	Joint Venture	38.3
#外商独资	Foreign Funded	125.2
其他	Others	-12.4
按建设性质分	**Investment by Type of Construction**	
新建	New Construction	1.7
扩建	Expansion	-23.6
改建和技术改造	Reconstruction and Technical Transformation	16.2
其他	Others	29.0

续 1

指　　标	Indicator	固定资产投资增长速度（%）
按国民经济行业分	**Investments in Fixed Assets by Sector**	
农、林、牧、渔业	Farming, Forestry, Animal Husbandry and Fishery	-43.5
采矿业	Mining	107.1
制造业	Manufacture	9.1
电力、热力、燃气及水生产和供应业	Production and Supply of Electric, Heat, Gas and Water	-16.2
建筑业	Construction	-18.6
批发和零售业	Wholesale and Retail Trade	-52.6
交通运输、仓储和邮政业	Transport, Storage and Postal Services	224.1
住宿和餐饮业	Accommodations and Catering Services	-33.6
信息传输、软件和信息技术服务业	Information Transmission, Computer Services and Software	-100.0
金融业	Finance	-91.1
房地产业	Real Estate	37.7
租赁和商务服务业	Leasing and Business Services	57.0
科学研究和技术服务业	Scientific Research and Technical Services	11.3
水利、环境和公共设施管理业	Management of Water Conservancy,Environment and Public Facilities	12.4
居民服务、修理和其他服务业	Households services, Repair and Other Service	66.8
教育	Education	-28.1
卫生和社会工作	Health and Social Work	26.0
文化、体育和娱乐业	Culture, Sports and Recreation	86.7
公共管理、社会保障和社会组织	Public Management,Social Security and Social Organizations	-79.6
新增固定资产	**Newly Increased Fixed Assets**	-47.3
施工项目个数(个)	**Number of Project under Construction(unit)**	776
#新开工	Started This Year	328
竣工项目个数(个)	**Number of Buildings Completed(unit)**	338
施工房屋面积（万平方米）	**Project under Construction(10 000 sq.m)**	59.3
#住 宅	Residential Buildings	20.0
竣工房屋面积（万平方米）	**Project Completed and Put into Use(10 000 sq.m)**	9.1
#住宅	Residential Buildings	2.4

房地产开发投资分类（2018 年）

Investment in Fixed Assets（2018）

单位：万元　　　　　　　　　　　　　　　　　　　　（10000 yuan）

指　　标	Indicator	房地产开发投资 Real Estate Investment
本年完成投资额(万元)	**Investment Completed This Year(10 000 yuan)**	682127
按构成分	**Investment by Structure**	
建筑工程	Construction	410279
安装工程	Installation	163895
设备、工器具购置	Purchase of Equipment and Instruments	20484
其他费用	Others	87469
按单位登记注册类型分	**Registration Status**	
内资	**Domestic Fund**	682127
有限责任公司	Limited Liability	244531
国有独资公司	Solely State-owned Company	15020
其他有限责任公司	other Limited Liability Company	229511
股份有限公司	Share-holding Corporations Ltd.	60500
私营	Private	377096
新增固定资产（万元）	**Newly Increased Fixed Assets (10 000 yuan)**	348524
施工项目个数(个)	**Number of Project under Construction(unit)**	66
施工房屋面积（万平方米）	**Project under Construction(10 000 sq.m)**	557.96
#住 宅	Residential Buildings	421.82
竣工房屋面积（万平方米）	**Project Completed and Put into Use(10 000 sq.m)**	100.24
#住宅	Residential Buildings	76.71

房地产开发公司经营情况

Real Estate Development and Managment in Major Years

指　　标	Indicator	单　位 Unit	2018 年
开发公司家数	**Number of Real Estate Enterprises**	家(unit)	67
企业资本金	**Enterprises Funds**	万元(10 000 yuan)	168369
资产与负债	**Property debt**		
资产总计	Assets	万元(10 000 yuan)	2805736
负债总计	Liabilities	万元(10 000 yuan)	2543182
所有者权益	Owners' Equity	万元(10 000 yuan)	262554
损益情况	**Net Income or Loss**		
经营收入	Revenues from Business	万元(10 000 yuan)	550821
土地转让收入	Revenues from Land Transfer	万元(10 000 yuan)	1000
商品房销售收入	Revenues from Commercial Housing Sale	万元(10 000 yuan)	542361
房屋出租收入	Housing Rental Income	万元(10 000 yuan)	312
其他收入	Others	万元(10 000 yuan)	4732
经营成本	Business Cost	万元(10 000 yuan)	438520
经营税金及附加	Business Tax and Extra Charges	万元(10 000 yuan)	18803
利润总额	Total Profits	万元(10 000 yuan)	37486
房屋销售与出租			
本年实际销售房屋面积	Floor Space of Buildings to Lease	平方米(sq.m)	1128179
#住　宅	Residential Buildings	平方米(sq.m)	1051276
本年房屋实际销售额	Total Sales of Buildings	万元(10 000 yuan)	721805
#住　　宅	Residential Buildings	万元(10 000 yuan)	662830
待售房屋面积	Floor Space of Waiting For Sale	平方米(sq.m)	317818
#住　宅	Residential Buildings	平方米(sq.m)	248231
出租房屋面积	Floor Space of Buildings to Lease	平方米(sq.m)	0

农林牧渔业增加值(2018 年）(按当年价格计算)

Added Value of Agriculture, Forestry, Animal Husbandry and Fishery(2018)(Calculated at Current Prices)

单位：亿元 (100 million yuan)

年 份 Year	合计 Total	农业 Farming	林业 Forestry	牧业 Animal Husbandry	渔业 Fishery	农林牧渔服务业 Services of Agriculture,Forestry,Animal Husbandry and Fishing
2018	61.89	44.43	2.31	12.62	0.95	1.58

农林牧渔业总产值（2018 年）（按当年价格计算）

Gross Output Value of Agriculture, Forestry, Animal Husbandry and Fishery(2018)(Calculated at Current Prices)

单位:亿元 (100 million yuan)

年 份 Year	合计 Total	农业 Farming	林业 Forestry	牧业 Animal Husbandry	渔业 Fishery	农林牧渔服务业 Services of Agriculture,Forestry,Animal Husbandry and Fishing
2018	108.86	72.91	3.45	27.52	1.63	3.35

主要农作物播种面积及产量

Sown Areas and Output of Main Farm Crops

指　　标	Indicator	2018 年
农作物总播种面积(万公顷)	Total Sown Area of Crops(10 000 ha)	
粮食作物	Grain	39.66
谷物	Cereals	37.11
小麦	Wheat	6.66
稻谷	Rice	0.00
玉米	Corn	29.17
谷子	Millet	1.27
高粱	Chinese Sorghum	0.02
其他	Others	0.00
豆类	Beans	0.37
薯类	Tubers	2.19
油料作物	Oil-bearing Crops	1.11
#花生	Peanuts	1.10
棉花	Cotton	0.13
蔬菜	Vegetable	2.38
果用瓜	Melon	0.02
其他作物	Other Farm Crops	0.06
果园种植面积(万公顷)	Orchard Area(10 000 ha)	0.87
#苹果	Apple	0.20
梨	Pear	0.03

续 1

指　　标	Indicator	2018 年
葡萄	Grape	0.01
桃	Peach	0.31
农作物总产量(万吨)	**Total Output of Farm Crops(10 000 tons)**	
粮食作物产量	Output of Grain Crops	25.52
谷物	Cereals	23.25
小麦	Wheat	3.59
稻谷	Rice	0.00
玉米	Corn	19.33
谷子	Millet	0.32
高粱	Chinese Sorghum	0.00
其他	Other Cereals	0.00
豆类	Beans	0.09
薯类	Tubers	2.18
油料作物	Oil-bearing Crops	2.84
#花生	Peanuts	2.83
棉花	Cotton	0.15
蔬菜	Vegetable	131.76
果用瓜	Melon	0.88
水果总产量(万吨)	**Output of Fruits(10 000 tons)**	21.10
#苹果	Apple	5.71
梨	Pear	0.68
葡萄	Grape	0.18
桃	Peach	9.86
杏	Apricot	0.38

续2

指　　标	Indicator	2018年
枣(鲜)	Jujube	0.15
柿子(鲜)	Persimmon	1.79
山楂	Hawthorn	1.85
樱桃	Cherry	0.32
其他	Others	0.09
农作物单位面积产量(公斤/公顷)	**Output per Hectare of Farm Crops(kg/ha)**	
粮食作物单位面积产量	Output per Hectare of Grain Crops	6433.95
谷物	Cereals	0.00
小麦	Wheat	5399.25
稻谷	Rice	0.00
玉米	Corn	6626.40
谷子	Millet	2545.80
高粱	Chinese Sorghum	2621.85
其他	Others	0.00
豆类	Beans	2429.85
薯类	Tubers	9977.55
油料作物	Oil-bearing Crops	2563
#花生	Peanuts	2580
棉花	Cotton	1145
蔬菜	Vegetable	55389
果用瓜	Melon	56210

林、牧、渔业生产情况

Basic Statistics on Forestry、Animal Husbandry and Fishery

指　　标	Indicator	单 位 Unit	2018 年
牧业生产	Production of Animal Husbandry		
大牲畜存栏	Stocked Large Livestock	万头(10 000 heads)	1.79
#役畜	Draught Animal	万头(10 000 heads)	
#牛	Cattle	万头(10 000 heads)	1.79
猪存栏	Stocked Pigs	万头(10 000 heads)	38.88
羊存栏	Stocked Sheep	万只(10 000 heads)	22.57
家禽存栏	Stocked Poultry	万只(10 000 heads)	953.10
猪出栏数	Slaughtered Pigs	万头(10 000 heads)	62.06
羊出栏数	Slaughtered Sheep and Goats	万只(10 000 heads)	30.05
肉类总产量	Output of Meat	吨(tons)	79401.11
#猪牛羊肉	Meat	吨(tons)	45375.97
猪肉	Pork	吨(tons)	38929.97
牛肉	Beef	吨(tons)	2539
羊肉	Mutton	吨(tons)	3907
禽肉	Poultry Meat	吨(tons)	32856.37
奶类	Milk	吨(tons)	3402
#牛奶	Cow Milk	吨(tons)	3402
禽蛋	Poultry Eggs	吨(tons)	48030
#鸡蛋	Hen's Eggs	吨(tons)	47473

指　标	Indicator	企业单位数（个）Number of Industial Enterprises(unit)
总计	**Total**	551
按登记注册类型分组	**by Status of Registration**	
内资企业	Domestically-invested Enterprises	533
国有企业	State-owned Enterprises	1
地方企业	Local Enterprises	1
集体企业	Collectively-owned Enterprises	1
联营企业	Joint Ownership Enterprises	1
集体联营企业	Collective Joint Ownership Enterprises	1
有限责任公司	Limited Liability Corporations	185
国有独资公司	State Sole Funded Corporations	4
其他有限责任公司	Other Limited Liability Corporations	181
股份有限公司	Share-holding Corporations Ltd.	26
私营企业	Private Enterprises	319
私营独资企业	Private-funded Enterprises	8
私营有限责任公司	Private Limited Liability Corporations	294
私营股份有限公司	Private Share-holding Corporations Ltd.	17
港、澳、台商投资企业	Enterprises with Funds from Hong Kong,Macao and Taiwan	12
合资经营企业(港或澳、台资)	Joint-venture Enterprises	4
港澳台商独资经营企业	Enterprises with Sole Fund	7
港澳台商投资股份有限公司	Share-holding Corporations Ltd. with Investment	1
外商投资企业	Foreign Funded Enterprises	6
中外合资经营企业	Joint-venture Enterprises	3
中外合作经营企业	Cooperation Enterprises	1
外资企业	Enterprises with Sole Fund	2
按轻重工业分	**by Light & Heavy Industry**	
轻工业	Light Industry	171
重工业	Heavy Industry	380
按企业规模分	**by Enterprise Size**	
大型企业	Large-sized Enterprises	8
中型企业	Medium-sized Enterprises	38
小型企业	Small-sized Enterprises	421
微型企业	Micro-sized Enterprises	84

经济指标（2018 年）

Enterprises Above Designated Size（2018）

亏损企业数（个）Loss Enterprises (unit)	工业总产值（现价）（亿元）Gross Industrial Output Value(Calculated at Current Prices) (100 million yuan)	工业销售产值（现价）（亿元）IndustrialOutput Value of Products Sold(Calculated at Current Prices) (100 million yuan)	全部从业人员年平均人数（万人）Annual Average of Empolyed Persons(10 000 persons)
110	1873.01	1863.32	12.19
106	1842.49	1831.96	11.97
0	0.34	0.34	0.03
0	0.34	0.34	0.03
0	0.17	0.16	0.01
0	0.23	0.23	0.02
0	0.23	0.23	0.02
40	1133.88	1125.31	6.85
0	629.52	630.56	2.84
40	504.36	494.76	4.01
2	93.00	92.31	1.94
64	614.87	613.61	3.11
3	4.82	4.81	0.03
55	599.40	598.36	2.93
6	10.65	10.43	0.15
3	24.25	25.20	0.12
2	6.82	6.78	0.02
1	9.74	9.61	0.05
0	7.69	8.81	0.05
1	6.26	6.16	0.10
1	1.93	1.91	0.05
0	1.26	1.27	0.00
0	3.08	2.98	0.05
30	158.86	154.01	1.64
80	1714.15	1709.31	10.55
1	1339.52	1342.21	6.73
4	187.22	183.99	2.10
80	327.76	317.91	3.22
25	18.51	19.21	0.13

续 1

指 标	Indicator	企业单位数（个）Number of Industial Enterprises(unit)
按工业行业分	by Sector	
煤炭开采和洗选业	Mining and Washing of Coal	10
黑色金属矿采选业	Mining of Ferrous Metal Ores	13
农副食品加工业	Processing of Food from Agricultural Products	56
食品制造业	Manufacture of Foods	5
酒、饮料和精制茶制造业	Manufacture of Wine, Drinks and Refined Tea	6
纺织业	Manufacture of Textile	28
纺织服装、服饰业	Manufacture of Textile Wearing Apparel and Finery	6
木材加工和木、竹、藤、棕、草制品业	Manufacture of Leather, Fur, Feather & Its Products and Footwear	3
造纸和纸制品业	Manufacture of Paper and Paper Products	8
印刷和记录媒介复制业	Printing, Reproduction of Recording Media	8
文教、工美、体育和娱乐用品制造业	Manufacture of Culture, Education,Arts and crafts，Sport and Entertainment Goods	11
石油、煤炭及其他燃料加工业	Processing of Petroleum, Coking and Nucleus Fuel	2
化学原料和化学制品制造业	Manufacture of Chemical Raw Material and Chemical Products	34
医药制造业	Manufacture of Medicines	2
化学纤维制造业	Manufacture of Chemical Fiber	4
橡胶和塑料制品业	Manufacture of Rubber and Plastic	30
非金属矿物制品业	Manufacture of Non-metallic Mineral Products	61
黑色金属冶炼和压延加工业	Manufacture and Processing of Ferrous Metals	28
有色金属冶炼和压延加工业	Manufacture & Processing of Non-ferrous Metals	3
金属制品业	Manufacture of Metal Products	40
通用设备制造业	Manufacture of General Purpose Machinery	53
专用设备制造业	Manufacture of Special Purpose Machinery	46
汽车制造业	Manufacture of Automotive	25
铁路、船舶、航空航天和其他运输设备制造业	Manufacture of Railroad,Marine,Aerospace and Other Transportation Equipment	2
电气机械和器材制造业	Manufacture of Electrical Machinery & Equipment	30
计算机、通信和其他电子设备制造业	Manufacture of Computer, Communications and Other Electronic Equipment	12
仪器仪表制造业	Manufacture of Measuring Instrument	3
其他制造业	Other Manufacture	1
废弃资源综合利用业	Waste Rrecycling and Recovery	3
电力、热力生产和供应业	Production and Supply of Electric Power and Heat Power	12
燃气生产和供应业	Production and Supply of Gas	4
水的生产和供应业	Production and Supply of Water	2

亏损企业数（个） Loss Enterprises (unit)	工业总产值（现价）（亿元） Gross Industrial Output Value(Calculated at Current Prices) (100 million yuan)	工业销售产值（现价)（亿元） IndustrialOutput Value of Products Sold(Calculated at Current Prices) (100 million yuan)	全部从业人员年平均人数（万人） Annual Average of Empolyed Persons(10 000 persons)
5	12.18	13.05	0.41
3	44.01	44.19	1.00
10	70.02	69.14	0.54
1	11.25	10.82	0.10
1	11.56	7.44	0.04
4	15.31	15.26	0.19
0	1.54	1.51	0.04
1	0.64	0.64	0.03
0	13.96	15.12	0.18
3	7.33	7.29	0.06
2	6.11	6.10	0.16
1	2.35	2.35	0.01
4	33.47	33.18	0.20
0	1.02	1.02	0.01
1	1.99	1.97	0.05
7	13.56	13.49	0.26
12	60.19	59.28	0.89
10	1319.52	1321.24	5.56
1	1.51	1.50	0.03
8	42.58	40.45	0.47
11	42.68	40.51	0.46
9	31.69	31.20	0.47
3	22.44	22.18	0.36
0	0.37	0.37	0.01
3	32.27	30.59	0.29
3	5.82	5.69	0.12
0	0.53	0.53	0.01
0	0.13	0.13	0.00
2	0.06	0.06	0.00
4	53.16	52.92	0.13
1	13.21	13.51	0.07
0	0.54	0.55	0.04

规模以上工业损益及分配（2018 年）

Profit、Loss and Distribution of Industrial Enterprises Above Designated Size（2018）

单位：亿元 (100 million yuan)

指标	Indicator	主营业务收入 Revenue from Principal Business	利润总额 Total Profits	利税总额 Total Profits and Taxes
总计	**Total**	2102.19	101.34	157.14
按登记注册类型分	**by Status of Registration**			
内资企业	Domestically-invested Enterprises	2079.28	99.02	154.34
国有企业	State-owned Enterprises	60.99	9.01	4.62
地方企业	Local Enterprises	0.34	0.13	0.18
集体企业	Collectively-owned Enterprises	0.16	0.00	0.01
联营企业	Joint Ownership Enterprises	0.23	0.00	0.01
集体联营企业	Collective Joint Ownership Enterprises	0.23	0.00	0.01
有限责任公司	Limited Liability Corporations	889.49	43.13	104.02
国有独资公司	State Sole Funded Corporations	262.39	19.98	61.98
其他有限责任公司	Other Limited Liability Corporations	627.10	23.15	42.03
股份有限公司	Share-holding Corporations Ltd.	512.58	24.98	14.26
私营企业	Private Enterprises	615.82	21.89	31.42
私营独资企业	Private-funded Enterprises	4.34	0.13	0.21
私营有限责任公司	Private Limited Liability Corporations	603.83	21.64	30.92
私营股份有限公司	Private Share-holding Corporations Ltd.	7.65	0.12	0.29
港、澳、台商投资企业	Enterprises with Funds from Hong Kong,Macao and Taiwan	17.78	1.88	2.29
合资经营企业(港或澳、台资)	Joint-venture Enterprises	1.54	0.00	0.12
港澳台商独资经营企业	Enterprises with Sole Fund	7.52	1.39	1.62
港澳台商投资股份有限公司	Share-holding Corporations Ltd. with Investment	8.72	0.49	0.55
外商投资企业	Foreign Funded Enterprises	5.13	0.43	0.51
中外合资经营企业	Joint-venture Enterprises	2.06	0.11	0.11

续 1

指标	Indicator	主营业务收入 Revenue from Principal Business	利润总额 Total Profits	利税总额 Total Profits and Taxes
中外合作经营企业	Cooperation Enterprises	0.19	0.02	0.07
外资企业	Enterprises with Sole Fund	2.88	0.31	0.32
按轻重工业分	**by Light & Heavy Industry**			
轻工业	Light Industry	150.83	3.64	5.60
重工业	Heavy Industry	1951.36	97.70	151.54
按企业规模分	**by Enterprise Size**			
大型企业	Large-sized Enterprises	1580.36	80.44	112.99
中型企业	Medium-sized Enterprises	181.16	12.27	28.53
小型企业	Small-sized Enterprises	322.39	7.83	14.67
微型企业	Micro-sized Enterprises	18.29	0.80	0.95
按工业行业分	**by Sector**			
煤炭开采和洗选业	Mining and Washing of Coal	17.51	0.76	2.42
黑色金属矿采选业	Mining of Ferrous Metal Ores	44.59	-0.69	3.76
农副食品加工业	Processing of Food from Agricultural Products	60.74	0.90	1.93
食品制造业	Manufacture of Foods	9.52	0.95	0.97
酒、饮料和精制茶制造业	Manufacture of Wine, Drinks and Refined Tea	7.56	0.05	0.21
纺织业	Manufacture of Textile	16.25	0.32	0.53
纺织服装、服饰业	Manufacture of Textile Wearing Apparel and Finery	1.67	0.05	0.09
木材加工和木、竹、藤、棕、草制品业	Manufacture of Leather, Fur, Feather & Its Products and Footwear	0.66	0.02	0.04
造纸和纸制品业	Manufacture of Paper and Paper Products	15.02	0.55	0.62
印刷和记录媒介复制业	Printing, Reproduction of Recording Media	6.66	0.02	0.05
文教、工美、体育和娱乐用品制造业	Manufacture of Culture, Education,Arts and crafts, Sport and Entertainment Goods	6.38	0.19	0.32
石油、煤炭及其他燃料加工业	Processing of Petroleum, Coking and Nucleus Fuel	1.96	-0.06	-0.04

续 2

指标	Indicator	主营业务收入 Revenue from Principal Business	利润总额 Total Profits	利税总额 Total Profits and Taxes
化学原料和化学制品制造业	Manufacture of Chemical Raw Material and Chemical Products	30.95	2.25	3.45
医药制造业	Manufacture of Medicines	1.15	0.03	0.04
化学纤维制造业	Manufacture of Chemical Fiber	2.01	0.10	0.11
橡胶和塑料制品业	Manufacture of Rubber and Plastic	23.87	0.04	0.30
非金属矿物制品业	Manufacture of Non-metallic Mineral Products	62.23	7.01	10.35
黑色金属冶炼和压延加工业	Manufacture and Processing of Ferrous Metals	1501.95	68.18	103.65
有色金属冶炼和压延加工业	Manufacture & Processing of Non-ferrous Metals	1.48	0.07	0.09
金属制品业	Manufacture of Metal Products	43.86	3.01	4.40
通用设备制造业	Manufacture of General Purpose Machinery	36.85	1.52	2.58
专用设备制造业	Manufacture of Special Purpose Machinery	24.93	0.81	1.40
汽车制造业	Manufacture of Automotive	20.85	1.09	1.45
铁路、船舶、航空航天和其他运输设备制造业	Manufacture of Railroad,Marine,Aerospace and Other Transportation Equipment	0.37	0.00	0.03
电气机械和器材制造业	Manufacture of Electrical Machinery & Equipment	27.95	0.91	1.80
计算机、通信和其他电子设备制造业	Manufacture of Computer, Communications and Other Electronic Equipment	5.80	-0.18	-0.10
仪器仪表制造业	Manufacture of Measuring Instrument	0.48	0.00	0.01
其他制造业	Other Manufacture	1.12	0.00	0.00
废弃资源综合利用业	Waste Rrecycling and Recovery	0.06	-0.01	-0.01
电力、热力生产和供应业	Production and Supply of Electric Power and Heat Power	113.62	11.83	14.51
燃气生产和供应业	Production and Supply of Gas	13.57	1.45	1.99
水的生产和供应业	Production and Supply of Water	0.55	0.15	0.20

工业企业能源购进、消费及库存（2018 年）

Purchases、Consumption and Invetory of Main Energy Source in Industrial Enterprises(2018)

能源名称	Energy	计量单位 Unit	年初库存量 Beginning Stock	本年购进量 Purchases This Year	本年消费 Consumption of This Year			年末库存量 Year-end Stock
					合计 Total	工业生产消费 Industrial Consumption	非工业生产消费 Non-Industrial Consumption	
能源合计	Total Energy	吨标准煤 (tons of SCE)			28894361	28500995	393367	
原煤	Raw Coal	吨	393392	8685511	8682514	8548911	133602	677269
洗精煤（用于炼焦）	Cleaned Coal	吨	495007	7905939	8006052	8006052	0	394895
其它洗煤	Other Cleaned Coal	吨	56	25901	25907	25907	0	309
煤制品	Coal Product	吨	59953	144092	191449	191449	0	12676
焦炭	Coke	吨	117293	2603383	8666949	8666831	118	91358
焦炉煤气		万立方米	0	12014	108002	102228	5773	0
高炉煤气		万立方米	0	239	2270007	2237243	32764	0
转炉煤气		万立方米	0	0	72176	51429	20747	0
天然气	Natural Gas	万立方米	8	6596	6448	6421	27	0
液化天然气	Liquefied Nutural Gas	吨	30	11622	11603	11574	29	49
汽油	Gasoline	吨	55	643	657	336	320	42
煤油	Kerosene	吨	0	48	48	48	0	0
柴油	Diesel Oil	吨	1501	15009	15515	12624	2891	789
燃料油	Fuel Oil	吨	0	43	43	43	0	0
液化石油气	Liquefied Petroleum	吨	0	25	25	24	1	0
热力	Heating	百万千焦	0	209974	824572	824572	0	0
电力	Electricity	万千瓦时	0	807750	1097478	1085516	11962	0
煤矸石（用于燃料）		吨	17543	252661	241924	241924	0	28279
余热余压		百万千焦	0	0	22298296	17835953	4462343	0
其他燃料	Other Fuel	吨标准煤	0	110	110	110	0	0

注：按照经济普查要求，免填能源合计中，年初库存、购进量、年末库存。

Note: According to the requirements of economic census, the total amount of spare energy is included in the inventory at the beginning of the year, the purchase amount, and the year–end inventory.

指 标	Indicator	原煤(吨) Coal (ton)
总计	**Total**	8682514
采矿业	**Mining**	
煤炭开采和洗选业	Mining and Washing of Coal	496114
石油和天然气开采业	Extraction of Petroleum and Natural Gas	0
黑色金属矿采选业	Mining of Ferrous Metal Ores	22977
制造业	**Manufacture**	
农副食品加工业	Processing of Food from Agricultural Products	7201
食品制造业	Manufacture of Foods	60141
酒、饮料及精制茶制造业	Manufacture of Wine, Drinks and Refined Tea	0
烟草制品业	Manufacture of Cigarettes and Tobacco	0
纺织业	Manufacture of Textile	32
纺织服装、服饰业	Manufacture of Textile Wearing Apparel and Finery	0
皮革、毛皮、羽毛及其制品和制鞋业	Manufacture of Leather, Fur, Feather & Its Products and Footwear	0
木材加工和木、竹、藤、棕、草制品业	Processing of Timbers, Manufacture of Wood, Bamboo, Rattan, Palm, and Straw Products	0
家具制造业	Manufacture of Furniture	0
造纸和纸制品业	Manufacture of Paper and Paper Products	79065
印刷和记录媒介复制业	Printing, Reproduction of Recording Media	0
文教、工美、体育和娱乐用品制造业	Manufacture of Culture, Education,Arts and crafts, Sport and Entertainment Goods	0
石油、煤炭及其他燃料加工业	Processing of Petroleum, Coking and Nucleus Fuel	0
化学原料和化学制品制造业	Manufacture of Chemical Raw Material and Chemical Products	3938
医药制造业	Manufacture of Medicines	0
化学纤维制造业	Manufacture of Chemical Fiber	0
橡胶和塑料制品业	Manufacture of Rubber and Plastic	0
非金属矿物制品业	Manufacture of Non-metallic Mineral Products	449713
黑色金属冶炼和压延加工业	Manufacture and Processing of Ferrous Metals	2594133
有色金属冶炼和压延加工业	Manufacture & Processing of Non-ferrous Metals	0
金属制品业	Manufacture of Metal Products	440
通用设备制造业	Manufacture of General Purpose Machinery	0
专用设备制造业	Manufacture of Special Purpose Machinery	160
汽车制造业	Manufacture of Automotive	0
铁路、船舶、航空航天和其他运输设备制造业	Manufacture of Railroad,Marine,Aerospace and Other Transportation Equipment	0
电气机械和器材制造业	Manufacture of Electrical Machinery & Equipment	0
计算机、通信和其他电子设备制造业	Manufacture of Computer, Communications and Other Electronic Equipment	0
仪器仪表制造业	Manufacture of Measuring Instrument	0
其他制造业	Other Manufacture	0
废弃资源综合利用业	Waste Rrecycling and Recovery	0
电力、热力、燃气及水生产和供应业	**Production and Supply of Electric Power and Heat Power**	
电力、热力生产和供应业	Production and Supply of Electric Power and Heat Power	4968600
燃气生产和供应业	Production and Supply of Gas	0
水的生产和供应业	Production and Supply of Water	0

能源消费量（2018年）

Industrial Enterprises by Sector（2018）

汽油(吨) Gasoline (ton)	煤油（吨）Kerosene (ton)	柴油（吨）Diesel Oil (ton)	燃料油（吨）Fuel Oil (ton)	热力（百万千焦）Heating (mkj)	电力（万千瓦时）Electricity (10 000 kwh)
657	48	15515	43	824572	1097478
6	0	50	0	0	13083
0	0	0	0	0	0
125	0	1831	0	0	44977
66	0	5	0	38108	7768
0	0	0	0	0	2599
0	0	0	0	0	1723
0	0	0	0	0	0
0	0	0	0	0	7786
0	0	0	0	0	919
0	0	0	0	0	0
0	0	0	0	0	107
0	0	0	0	0	0
0	0	0	0	313658	13595
0	0	0	0	0	1910
4	0	0	0	0	1834
0	0	0	0	0	237
11	0	0	0	153116	27402
0	0	0	0	0	21
0	0	0	30	18750	2799
3	0	16	0	0	7894
10	0	6244	0	0	41388
56	0	6791	0	300940	769682
0	0	0	0	0	276
82	48	113	13	0	34001
184	0	0	0	0	16133
42	0	24	0	0	9908
35	0	143	0	0	11813
0	0	0	0	0	223
2	0	0	0	0	1992
15	0	0	0	0	1394
0	0	0	0	0	104
0	0	0	0	0	119
0	0	0	0	0	96
16	0	298	0	0	74754
0	0	0	0	0	508
0	0	0	0	0	434

建筑业主要指标

Main Indicators of Construction Enterprises

指 标	Indicator	单 位 Unit	2018 年
汇总单位数	Number of Enterprises	个(unit)	145
建筑业增加值	Construction Inscreased	万元(10 000 yuan)	250318
建筑业总产值	Gross Output Value	万元(10 000 yuan)	973090
按隶属关系分	by Ownership		
省 属	Provincial	万元(10 000 yuan)	34128
市 属	Region	万元(10 000 yuan)	173205
县及县以下	County	万元(10 000 yuan)	19850
其 他	Others	万元(10 000 yuan)	745907
按工程性质分	by Sector		
建筑工程	Building and Civil Engineering Construction	万元(10 000 yuan)	797776
安装工程	Construction Installation	万元(10 000 yuan)	133297
其他产值	Others	万元(10 000 yuan)	42018
竣工产值	Value of Construction Completed	万元(10 000 yuan)	647093
房屋施工面积	Floor Space Completed	万平方米(10 000 sq.cm)	502
#本年新开工	Startde This year	万平方米(10 000 sq.cm)	337
房屋竣工面积	Floor Space Completed	万平方米(10 000 sq.cm)	292
#住 宅	Residential	万平方米(10 000 sq.cm)	139
所有者权益	Creditors'Equity	万元(10 000 yuan)	481684
利润总额	Total Profits	万元(10 000 yuan)	37173
工资总额	Total wages	万元(10 000 yuan)	167611

建筑企业损益及分配（2018年）

Output Value of Construction by Structure（2018）

单位：万元 (10 000yuan)

指标（总承包与专业承包）	Indicator	营业收入 Business Revenue	利税总额 Total Profits and Taxes	营业利润 Profits from Business	利润总额 Total Profits	应付职工薪酬（本年贷方累计发生额） Total Wages Payable
总计	**Total**	795764	61337	37373	37173	167611
其中：国有及国有控股企业	State-owned and State-controlled Enterprises	109644	5802	4910	4971	8694
一、按登记注册类型分组	**Grouped by Registration Status**					
内资企业	Domestic Funded	795764	61337	37373	37173	167611
国有企业	State-owned	4468	24	15	15	193
集体企业	Collective-owned	6026	413	203	203	1643
有限责任公司	Company with Limited Liabilition	428175	29786	18384	18260	93411
国有独资公司	State-owned	31372	67	-110	-26	261
其他有限责任公司	Others	396803	29719	18494	18286	93150
股份有限公司	Stock-holding Company limited	6825	302	-45	-45	484
私营企业	Private-owned	350270	30812	18817	18740	71880
私营有限责任公司	Company with Limited Liabilition	347573	30304	18316	18239	70790
私营股份有限公司	Stock-holding Company limited	2697	508	501	501	1090
二、按国民经济行业分组	**by Sector**					
房屋建筑业	Building Construction	458408	35631	19439	19422	106781
土木工程建筑业	Civil Engineering Construction	195440	15933	13195	13011	31235
建筑安装业	Construction Installation	106926	7673	3589	3578	21638
建筑装饰和其他建筑业	Construction Decoration and Others	34990	2100	1151	1163	7958
三、按隶属关系分组	**by Ownership**					
省(自治区、直辖市)	Provincial	127494	8105	6917	7002	12498
地区(州、盟、省辖市)及以下、其他	Region	668270	53233	30457	30171	155113
四、按企业资质等级分组	**by Qualification Criteria**					
施工总承包	Construction Contract	711918	55826	34126	33965	139615
一级	First Grade	137182	8831	7379	7468	15910
二级	Second Grade	316193	24506	13260	13285	75003
三级以下	Third Grade and below	258542	22489	13486	13212	48702
专业承包	Professional Contract	83846	5511	3248	3208	27996
一级	First Grade	3290	76	18	18	426
二级	Second Grade	30953	2360	1335	1334	7900
三级以下	Third Grade and below	49603	3075	1895	1856	19671

限额以上批发零售贸易企业损益及分配（2018 年）

Profit Loss and Distribution of Wholesales and Retail Sales Trade Above Designated Size （2018）

单位：万元 (10 000yuan)

指标名称	Indicator	法人企业数（个）Number of Corporation Enterprises (unit)	主营业务收入 Revenue from Principal Business	营业利润 Profits from Business	利润总额 Total Profits
总计	Total	359	8486928.2	33142.3	36341.1
一、批发业	Wholesalel Trade	250	7810325.4	25386.6	28081.6
农、林、牧产品批发	Wholesale of Farm Produce and Livestock Products	2	11836.6	680.9	653.4
食品、饮料及烟草制品批发	Wholesale of Food, Beverages and Tobaccos	6	111112.8	2757.2	2998.4
纺织、服装及家庭用品批发	Wholesale of Textiles, Garments and Daily Consumer Articles	8	31723.4	702.3	702.3
医药及医疗器材批发	Wholesale of Medicines and Medical Appliances	2	25898.2	1928.4	1933.4
矿产品、建材及化工产品批发	Wholesale of Mineral Products, Building Materials and Chemical Products	228	7602996.9	19606.9	22083.2
机械设备、五金产品及电子产品批发	Wholesale of Machinery, Hardware and Electronic Equipment	3	21220.5	-399.5	-399.5
其他批发业	Other Wholesale not Classified Elsewhere	1	5537.0	110.4	110.4
内资企业	Domestic Funded Enterprises	248	7797263.2	25118.7	27795.8
有限责任公司	Limited Liability Corporations	53	3646931.9	9875.4	10535.8
股份有限公司	Share-holding Corporations Limited	5	1174693.7	12237.9	14375.9
私营企业	Private Enterprises	190	2975637.6	3005.4	2884.1
外商投资企业	Foreign Funded Enterprises	2	13062.2	267.9	285.8
二、零售业	Retail Trade	109	676602.8	7755.7	8259.5
综合零售	Integrated Retail	19	181520.7	7797.6	7734.0

续 1

指标名称	Indicator	法人企业数（个）Number of Corporation Enterprises (unit)	主营业务收入 Revenue from Principal Business	营业利润 Profits from Business	利润总额 Total Profits
食品、饮料及烟草制品专门零售	Retail of Food, Beverages and Tobaccos	20	28834.9	881.5	888.7
纺织、服装及日用品专门零售	Special Retail of Textiles, Garments and Daily Consumer Articles	5	21424.4	1677.2	1677.2
文化、体育用品及器材专门零售	Retail of Culture, Sports Appliances and Equipments	5	14160.6	1686.8	1923.8
医药及医疗器材专门零售	Retail of Medicines and Medical Appliances	4	35195.8	24.7	594.6
汽车、摩托车、零配件和燃料及其他动力销售	Cars,motorcycles,spare part and fuel and other power sales	39	344437.5	–5868.7	–6129.3
家用电器及电子产品专门零售	Special Retail of Household Electric Appliances and Electronic Products	9	28775.3	298.7	310.1
五金、家具及室内装饰材料专门零售	Special Retail of Hardware, Furniture and Decoration Materials	5	11738.6	300.4	300.4
货摊、无店铺及其他零售业	Non–shop and Other Retails	3	10515.0	957.5	960.0
内资企业	Domestic Funded Enterprises	108	655681.8	6851.1	7342.9
国有企业	State–owned	1	26956.5	–64.6	507.4
集体企业	Collective–owned	1	9850.8	8.9	5.1
股份合作企业	Cooperative	1	6934.6	–32.8	–32.8
有限责任公司	Limited Liability Corporations	30	212194.6	147.1	496.4
股份有限公司	Share–holding Corporations Limited	7	172164.4	–2438.7	–2897.4
私营企业	Private Enterprises	68	227580.9	9231.2	9264.2
港、澳、台商投资企业	Enterprises with Funds from Hong Kong, Macao and Taiwan	1	20921.0	904.6	916.6

限额以上住宿业和餐饮业

Main Economic Indicators of Enterprises in Quartering

单位：万元

指标名称	Indicator	法人企业数(个) Number of Corporation Enterprises (unit)	营业额 Business Revenue (10 000yuan)	客房收入 From Hotel Rooms	餐费收入 From Meals
总计	Total	34	25005.2	7703.7	13895.1
一、住宿业	Hotels	11	12957.4	6071.2	4832.6
旅游饭店	Tourist Hotels	8	12392.3	5515.0	4827.0
一般旅馆	General Hotels	3	565.1	556.2	5.6
内资企业	Domestic Funded Enterprises	11	12957.4	6071.2	4832.6
国有企业	State-owned	1	5131.8	1439.5	2094.6
有限责任公司	Limited Liability Corporations	8	7454.8	4269.8	2732.4
私营企业	Private Enterprises	2	370.8	361.9	5.6
二、餐饮业	Catering Services	23	12047.8	1632.5	9062.5
正餐服务	Dinner service	22	11429.8	1632.5	8444.5
快餐服务	Fast Food Service	1	618.0	0.0	618.0
内资企业	Domestic Funded Enterprises	23	12047.8	1632.5	9062.5
国有企业	State-owned	1	717.6	104.5	389.2
有限责任公司	Limited Liability Corporations	13	7051.6	1035.1	5261.4
股份有限公司	Share-holding Corporations Limited	2	1715.4	0.0	1567.0
私营企业	Private Enterprises	7	2563.2	492.9	1844.9

法人企业经营情况（2018年）

Trades and Cataring Trades Above Designated Size（2018）

(10 000yuan)

商品销售收入 Revenue from Commodities	其他收入 Other Revenue	客房数（间） Number of Room(room)	床位数（个） Number of Beds(bed)	餐位数（位） Number of dining-seats(seat)	年末餐饮营业面积(平方米) Business Area of Catering Services at Year-end(sq.m)
2919.8	486.6	1890	3124	11894	52368
1750.3	303.3	1307	2054	2676	15623
1747.0	303.3	1078	1707	2616	11523
3.3	0.0	229	347	60	4100
1750.3	303.3	1307	2054	2676	15623
1597.7	0.0	245	366	236	269
149.3	303.3	920	1480	2380	14554
3.3	0.0	142	208	60	800
1169.5	183.3	583	1070	9218	36745
1169.5	183.3	583	1070	9160	36300
0.0	0.0	0	0	58	445
1169.5	183.3	583	1070	9218	36745
223.9	0.0	51	102	998	3000
591.8	163.3	430	758	5724	22745
148.4	0.0	0	0	315	3700
205.4	20.0	102	210	2181	7300

卫生事业机构及床位

Number of Health Institutions and Beds

指　标	Indicator	2018 年
各类卫生机构数(个)	**Number of Institutions(unit)**	1313
医院	Hospital	33
社区卫生服务中心(站)	Health Centers	26
卫生院	Outpatient Department	17
门诊部	Outpatient Department	10
采血供应机构	Pick and Supply Blood Institution	1
妇幼保健院（所、站）	Women and Children Care Agencies	3
专科疾病防治院（所、站）	Specialized Disease Prevention &Treatment Institution	1
疾病预防控制中心（防疫站）	Center for Disease Control and Prevention	3
其他卫生机构	Other Medical Institutions	7
各类卫生机构病床数（张）	**Number of Institutions Beds(bed)**	7351
医院	Hospital	5598
社区卫生服务中心(站)	Health Service Center for Community	411
卫生院	Health Centers	1002
妇幼保健院（所、站）	Women and Children Care Agencies	310
专科疾病防治院（所、站）	Specialized Disease Prevention&Treatment Institution	30
千人拥有量(张、人）	**Number Per 1000 Population(set.person)**	
平均每千人拥有病床	Number Of Beds Per 1000 Population	5.33
每千人拥有卫生技术人员	Number Of Medical Technical Personnel Per 1000 Population	6.40
每千人拥有医生	Number Of Doctors Per 1000 Population	2.54
每千人拥有护士	Number Of Nurses Per 1000 Population	2.69
各类卫生机构工作人员合计	**Medical TechnicalPersonnel**	11777
#卫生技术人员小计	Medical TechnicalPersonnel(person)	8832
医　生	Licensed Doctors	3509
注册护士	Registered Nurse	3706
其　他	Others	663

社会治安主要指标

Main Indicators of Social Offense

指　　标	Indicator	2018 年
刑事案件（件）	Criminal Cases(case)	
当年全部立案数	Put on Record	2465
破获当年刑事案件数	Cracked the Number of Criminal Cases	1425
治安案件（件）	Public Security Cases(case)	
受理数	Cases Accepted	8451
查处数	Cases Punished	4373
城市交通事故	Traffic Accidents	
交通事故（起）	Number of Traffic Accidents(case)	258
伤亡人数（人）	Number of Injuries and Deaths(person)	241
#死亡人数（人）	Number of Deathsa(person)	54
损失折款（万元）	Direct Losses(10 000 yuan)	62.31
火灾事故	Fires	
火灾起数（起）	Number of Fire Accidents(case)	76
伤亡人数（人）	Number of Injuries and Deaths(person)	0
#死亡人数（人）	Number of Deaths(person)	0
损失折款（万元）	Direct Losses(10 000 yuan)	177

社会保障和救济

Basic Statistics on Social Security and Receiving Relief Flinds

指　　标	Indicator	2018 年
社会救济情况（人）	Social Relief(person)	
城镇居民最低生活保障人数	Number of Urban Residents for Minimum Livelihood Guarantee	4816
农村居民最低生活保障人数	Number of Rural residents for Minimum Livelihood Guarantee	8616
民政经费（万元）	Civil Affairs Expenditures(10 000 yuan)	
城市居民最低生活保障费	Urban Residents for Minimum Livelihood Guarantee	2131.3
农村最低生活保障费	Rural residents for Minimum Livelihood Guarantee	3536.3
社会福利费	Social Welfare Funds	7087.5
社会保障及扶贫（个、元）	Social Security and Poverty Alleviation(unit.yuan)	
建立社会保障服务网络的乡镇数	Number of Towns With Social Security Service Network	13
城市市区居民最低生活保障金标准	Minimum Living Standards for Urban Residents	510

各时期人口状况（户籍人口）

Total Household and Population in Major Years（registered population）

年份 Year	总户数 （万户） Total Households (10 000households)	总人口（万人） Total Population (10 000 persons)			总人口中农业人口 （万人） Rural Numbers (10 000 persons)	人口自然增长率 (‰) Natural Growth Rate (‰)	总人口中从业人员 （万人） Total Employed Persons (10 000 persons)
		合计 Total	男 Male	女 Femal			
1949	12.15	53.72	23.47	30.25	52.25	51.65	20.78
1950	12.16	54.11	23.58	30.53	52.64	7.36	20.98
1951	13.16	55.89	26.55	29.34	54.29	32.89	21.14
1952	12.76	56.20	29.41	26.79	54.39	5.58	22.03
1953	12.81	58.74	29.27	29.47	56.15	28.93	22.44
1954	12.93	59.87	29.65	30.22	57.19	24.79	22.72
1955	13.16	61.73	30.21	31.52	59.06	25.43	22.91
1956	13.49	62.79	31.21	31.58	59.37	20.25	23.41
1957	13.95	64.43	31.79	32.64	61.76	24.01	23.63
1958	13.97	67.06	32.74	34.32	63.24	15.26	24.56
1959	14.34	67.78	35.27	32.51	64.08	9.85	23.24
1960	14.75	69.53	36.69	32.84	64.22	10.77	23.09
1961	15.12	71.09	36.67	34.42	67.03	11.22	23.08
1962	16.07	72.19	36.75	35.44	70.06	23.12	23.20
1963	16.38	74.19	37.67	36.52	72.31	28.87	24.13
1964	16.47	75.51	38.57	36.94	73.59	25.27	24.16
1965	16.74	77.42	39.62	34.11	75.41	26.05	24.28
1966	17.04	79.94	41.07	38.87	77.52	27.62	24.61
1967	17.09	81.17	41.21	39.96	78.75	25.74	24.72
1968	17.47	84.00	42.56	41.44	81.59	28.68	25.11
1969	18.24	86.30	44.20	42.10	84.67	24.20	24.79
1970	18.68	90.44	46.80	43.64	85.77	23.68	25.92
1971	19.20	92.96	48.31	44.65	86.46	20.28	27.27
1972	19.75	96.03	50.05	45.98	88.92	23.76	30.49
1973	20.48	98.16	51.14	47.02	90.68	18.60	33.50
1974	20.95	99.46	51.92	47.54	91.69	11.01	33.71
1975	21.18	100.92	52.78	48.14	92.49	10.50	34.56
1976	21.80	102.11	53.45	48.66	93.11	9.20	35.56
1977	22.42	103.28	53.99	49.29	94.05	9.50	37.04
1978	22.91	104.01	54.28	49.74	94.45	9.40	36.35
1979	23.52	104.87	54.71	50.16	94.92	8.70	37.42
1980	24.24	105.43	54.84	50.59	95.26	6.10	38.20
1981	25.47	106.41	55.27	51.14	95.91	8.40	37.22
1982	26.42	107.38	55.80	51.58	96.64	10.68	38.14

年份 Year	总户数 （万户） Total Households (10 000households)	总人口（万人） Total Population (10 000 persons)			总人口中 农业人口 （万人） Rural Numbers (10 000 persons)	人口自然增长率 (‰) Natural Growth Rate (‰)	总人口中 从业人员 （万人） Total Employed Persons (10 000 persons)
		合计 Total	男 Male	女 Femal			
1983	26.97	108.11	56.14	51.97	97.03	7.13	40.34
1984	27.11	108.76	56.42	52.34	96.07	7.04	43.41
1985	27.76	109.39	56.71	52.68	95.56	6.61	45.38
1986	28.54	111.59	57.37	54.22	96.84	10.41	46.59
1987	30.44	113.53	58.28	55.25	97.43	11.14	48.88
1988	31.59	114.86	59.02	55.84	93.17	10.48	49.91
1989	32.86	116.11	59.56	56.55	96.93	9.27	51.39
1990	33.51	117.78	60.34	57.44	98.22	13.05	53.10
1991	34.61	118.44	60.62	57.82	98.48	7.22	60.93
1992	35.17	118.64	60.73	57.91	98.14	3.14	64.56
1993	29.05	118.85	60.89	57.96	95.98	1.71	64.20
1994	37.07	118.75	60.89	57.86	92.50	2.92	62.80
1995	37.30	119.17	61.19	57.98	91.27	4.22	61.86
1996	37.17	119.79	61.37	58.42	82.55	6.54	67.00
1997	37.34	121.01	61.96	59.05	83.29	8.12	67.37
1998	37.51	121.88	62.36	59.52	83.60	9.57	67.79
1999	36.96	122.51	62.62	59.89	83.66	6.09	69.14
2000	39.02	123.19	62.88	60.31	83.80	5.49	69.67
2001	39.56	123.62	63.08	60.54	83.46	4.27	71.53
2002	40.01	123.88	63.10	60.78	82.21	3.53	72.80
2003	40.11	123.88	63.06	60.83	81.52	2.87	74.47
2004	41.00	124.29	63.24	61.05	81.27	5.53	75.85
2005	40.51	124.38	63.23	61.14	74.91	2.31	77.77
2006	42.95	124.86	63.46	61.40	74.68	2.10	77.97
2007	43.71	125.35	63.71	61.64	76.82	1.54	78.21
2008	43.94	125.96	64.01	61.96	76.34	1.16	77.16
2009	45.16	126.38	64.19	62.19	75.97	0.69	78.13
2010	45.94	126.69	64.32	62.38	68.47	0.63	76.16
2011	47.11	126.95	64.41	62.54	68.80	1.02	79.71
2012	47.54	126.30	64.00	62.30	61.65	0.39	80.35
2013	46.64	126.52				1.38	85.70
2014		127.82				5.45	86.48
2015	47.27	128.32	64.93	63.39		5.29	
2016	47.39	129.05	65.26	63.79		8.38	
2017	47.25	129.47	65.37	64.10		6.93	
2018	47.12	129.40	65.32	64.09		3.73	

各时期地区生产总值

Gross Domestic Product in Each Period

年份 Year	地区生产总值（亿元）Gross Domestic Product (100 million yuan)	第一产业 Primary Industry	第二产业 Secondary Industry			第三产业 Tertiary Industry	人均生产总值(元) Per Capita GDP (yuan)
			合计 Total	工业 Industry	建筑业 Construction		
1949	0.27	0.22	0.02	0.02	–	0.03	53
1950	0.30	0.25	0.02	0.02	–	0.03	58
1951	0.31	0.25	0.02	0.02	–	0.04	59
1952	0.38	0.31	0.03	0.03	–	0.04	70
1953	0.35	0.28	0.02	0.02	–	0.05	63
1954	0.39	0.32	0.02	0.02	–	0.05	69
1955	0.44	0.36	0.03	0.03	–	0.05	76
1956	0.52	0.43	0.03	0.03	–	0.06	88
1957	0.49	0.39	0.03	0.03	–	0.07	81
1958	0.70	0.51	0.10	0.10	–	0.09	112
1959	0.85	0.45	0.28	0.28	–	0.12	132
1960	0.80	0.36	0.32	0.32	–	0.12	122
1961	0.55	0.34	0.12	0.12	–	0.09	83
1962	0.61	0.38	0.13	0.12	0.01	0.10	89
1963	0.68	0.46	0.12	0.11	0.01	0.10	99
1964	0.68	0.46	0.11	0.10	0.01	0.11	95
1965	0.83	0.56	0.15	0.14	0.01	0.12	114
1966	0.93	0.61	0.18	0.17	0.01	0.14	124
1967	1.10	0.70	0.26	0.24	0.02	0.14	146
1968	1.00	0.60	0.26	0.23	0.03	0.14	129
1969	1.06	0.65	0.26	0.21	0.04	0.15	130
1970	1.07	0.67	0.22	0.18	0.04	0.18	128
1971	1.28	0.66	0.40	0.35	0.05	0.22	146
1972	1.82	0.74	0.84	0.78	0.06	0.24	202
1973	2.03	0.74	1.04	0.97	0.07	0.25	219
1974	1.59	0.69	0.67	0.60	0.07	0.23	169
1975	2.61	1.15	1.18	1.07	0.11	0.28	274
1976	3.17	1.33	1.52	1.40	0.12	0.32	328
1977	3.38	1.35	1.68	1.54	0.14	0.35	346
1978	3.63	1.46	1.80	1.65	0.15	0.37	368
1979	4.08	1.55	2.10	1.93	0.17	0.43	410
1980	4.34	1.67	2.13	1.95	0.18	0.54	434
1981	4.74	1.75	2.38	2.15	0.23	0.61	470
1982	4.83	2.05	2.14	1.87	0.27	0.64	474

续1

年份 Year	地区生产总值（亿元） Gross Domestic Product (100 million yuan)	第一产业 Primary Industry	第二产业 Secondary Industry			第三产业 Tertiary Industry	人均生产总值（元） Per Capita GDP (yuan)
			合计 Total	工业 Industry	建筑业 Construction		
1983	5.21	2.00	2.45	2.19	0.26	0.76	507
1984	6.50	2.20	3.31	2.93	0.38	0.99	630
1985	7.35	2.63	3.68	3.25	0.43	1.04	708
1986	7.81	2.86	3.80	3.38	0.42	1.15	746
1987	10.08	3.43	5.05	4.55	0.50	1.60	947
1988	13.48	4.62	6.51	5.87	0.64	2.35	1248
1989	16.12	4.76	8.21	7.58	0.63	3.15	1476
1990	18.02	6.46	8.80	7.96	0.84	2.76	1629
1991	16.59	6.23	5.70	5.55	0.15	4.66	1476
1992	21.65	6.53	9.36	8.29	1.07	5.76	1826
1993	39.36	7.32	22.04	20.31	1.73	10.00	3315
1994	53.32	9.20	28.90	26.08	2.81	15.22	4488
1995	63.47	10.07	34.30	29.82	4.47	19.10	5335
1996	73.60	11.51	37.30	32.30	5.00	24.79	6161
1997	81.28	12.12	40.41	34.18	6.23	28.75	6751
1998	89.35	12.36	44.08	37.19	6.89	32.91	7356
1999	94.23	12.41	47.53	40.42	7.10	34.29	7711
2000	104.72	13.25	53.50	47.10	6.40	37.97	8523
2001	118.07	14.26	61.53	54.29	7.24	42.28	9568
2002	132.94	14.74	70.91	63.50	7.40	47.29	10743
2003	159.71	15.52	92.76	84.85	7.91	51.43	12892
2004	212.13	17.42	137.93	128.93	9.00	56.78	17096
2005	262.95	18.42	171.74	160.98	10.76	72.79	21148
2006	298.98	19.55	190.24	177.06	13.18	89.19	23992
2007	372.22	22.62	238.00	221.95	16.05	111.60	29401
2008	466.01	27.98	306.60	286.12	20.48	131.43	36648
2009	471.30	30.35	292.41	268.08	24.33	148.54	36907
2010	555.37	38.61	339.22	311.57	27.65	177.54	43100
2011	622.83	41.18	381.31	351.01	30.30	200.30	47831
2012	642.63	44.20	376.37	343.64	32.73	222.06	49069
2013	664.63	48.97	374.67	341.64	33.94	240.98	50232
2014	699.40	52.74	385.34	349.85	36.43	261.32	52233
2015	677.71	52.72	355.97	318.55	38.28	269.02	50258
2016	715.36	54.75	364.60	325.44	40.01	296.01	52457
2017	894.97	55.53	499.26	459.40	39.86	340.18	65046
2018	1005.65	60.31	566.08	525.12	42.40	379.26	73005

各时期生产总值环比指数（以上年为 100）

Circle Indices of Gross Domestic Product (preceding year=100)

年份 Year	地区生产总值 Gross Domestic Product	第一产业 Primary Industry	第二产业 Secondary Industry	工业 Industry	建筑业 Construction	第三产业 Tertiary Industry	人均生产总值 Per Capita GDP
1949	100	100	100	100		100	100
1950	111.6	111.8	104.1	104.1		115.9	111.2
1951	102.5	101	106.8	106.8		111	100.4
1952	121.3	123.9	107.8	107.8		111.5	119.4
1953	90.2	88.6	88.5	88.5		103.5	87.8
1954	99.2	98.2	98.4	98.4		106.3	96.2
1955	102.9	103.8	103.6	103.6		97	100.5
1956	106.1	108.3	83.9	83.9		103.3	103.7
1957	96.9	93.8	108.1	108.1		113.3	94.7
1958	121.1	110.8	313.8	313.8		105.8	117.7
1959	116.3	82.5	276.9	276.9		134.9	113.7
1960	106.6	91.4	126.8	126.8		114.8	104.8
1961	89.2	122	50.9	50.9	100	92.7	86.8
1962	112.1	114.3	108.5	108.3	111.1	108.9	110.2
1963	100.5	109.2	82.6	82.3	105	91.1	98.4
1964	89.6	90.2	81.3	81.1	102	97.1	87.6
1965	100.5	98.9	109.6	110	103	97.9	98.5
1966	96.1	94.1	105.7	105.7	101	94.1	93.3
1967	116.6	112.7	139.6	139.2	140	103	114.2
1968	91.6	86.4	100.2	100.1	110.5	101.2	89
1969	97.9	100.9	91.6	91.3	106	96.4	94.8
1970	87.9	89	76.3	75.7	110	102.5	84.1
1971	102.9	84.7	155.6	156.4	120.5	105.1	99.2
1972	131.5	104.1	191.6	192.9	120.1	102.6	128.4
1973	105.7	94.1	117.4	118.3	116.7	100.6	102.9
1974	93.2	111.5	77.2	75.8	102.5	105.8	91.5
1975	127.1	128.2	135.9	131.3	147.1	97	125.7
1976	115.3	110.4	122.2	122.8	109.1	106.3	114
1977	95.9	91.4	99.1	99.1	105.2	99.4	94.8
1978	97.5	97.9	97.4	97.2	101.5	96.6	96.6
1979	105.4	99.8	109.5	109.2	113.3	107.9	104.7
1980	94.8	96.2	90.3	90.1	105.9	112	94.1
1981	104.3	102.8	105.8	104.3	127.8	107.4	103.6
1982	94.9	113.5	80.3	80	107.4	101.5	94.2

年份 Year	地区生产总值 Gross Domestic Product	第一产业 Primary Industry	第二产业 Secondary Industry	工业 Industry	建筑业 Construction	第三产业 Tertiary Industry	人均生产总值 Per Capita GDP
1983	103.6	95.9	109.8	110.7	96.3	114.3	102.8
1984	124.9	127.7	125.1	127	112.7	100.1	124.2
1985	102.5	104.5	99.8	98.2	114	106.9	101.9
1986	106.3	108.8	103.2	106.2	97.6	108.9	105.2
1987	130.5	119.6	130.1	131.1	124.5	137.2	128.6
1988	114.2	99.5	117.3	121.3	111.9	131.3	112.8
1989	116.3	98.5	121	121.6	116.2	126.9	115.1
1990	109.5	135.5	107.3	105.6	117.9	87.3	108.2
1991	115	116	103.7	102.6	110.7	136.3	114
1992	124	100.9	141.6	148	106.4	132.2	123.6
1993	149.4	103.5	170.5	170.3	170.6	168.3	149.2
1994	136.8	104.4	151.4	152.2	146.6	135.6	136.8
1995	116.7	102.1	116.4	113.1	142.3	125.3	116.6
1996	113.4	107	110.4	110.3	110.9	121.4	112.9
1997	110.4	104.9	108.4	107.6	114.1	115.6	109.6
1998	114.3	105.7	114.1	112.9	121.4	117.6	113.4
1999	111	105.3	112.3	112.3	112.1	111	110.4
2000	112	106.5	112.8	113.9	106.6	112.5	111.5
2001	112	105.4	113.4	114.2	107.1	112.3	111.5
2002	113	103	114.8	115.3	110.1	113.8	112.7
2003	116.9	106.4	124.2	126	107	109.2	116.8
2004	117.2	105.5	123.9	125.5	106.7	109.3	117
2005	118.5	104.9	123.7	124.3	108.6	112.2	118.3
2006	116.9	105.2	118.1	118.2	116.2	117.3	116.7
2007	117.1	103	117.7	118	113.1	119	115.3
2008	112.7	103.1	111.6	111.3	115.3	117.4	112.2
2009	112.5	102.3	113.2	112.6	122.4	112.9	112.1
2010	112	103.1	112.2	112.6	107.4	113	110.9
2011	110.5	102.7	111.6	112.4	102.4	110	109.3
2012	111.2	105.9	112.5	112.4	114.8	109.7	110.6
2013	110	103.1	111.2	111.4	109	108.8	108.8
2014	108.8	103.6	109.8	110	107.2	107.8	107.5
2015	106.7	103.4	106.8	106.6	108.8	107.1	105.9
2016	107.1	104.1	108.2	108.6	105.5	106.2	105.9
2017	108.1	104.8	107.1	108.6	94.5	109.9	107.1
2018	107.2	103.9	107.0	108.2	94.9	108.1	107.1

各时期职工人数与工资情况

Employed Persons and Wage of Staff in Major Years

年份 Year	职工人数(万人) Employed Persons (10 000 persons)	国有经济单位 State-owned Units	职工工资总额(万元) Total Wages of Staff and Workers (10 000yuan)	国有经济单位 State-owned Units	职工平均工资(元) Average Wage of Staff and Workers (yuan)	国有经济单位 State-owned Units
1949	0.05	0.05				
1950	0.09	0.09				
1951	0.13	0.13				
1952	0.2	0.2				
1953	0.26	0.26				
1954	0.32	0.32				
1955	0.41	0.41				
1956	0.49	0.49		210		439
1957	0.72	0.72		297		464
1958	2.83	2.83		532		407
1959	3.08	3.08		1234		437
1960	3.44	3.44		1535		478
1961	2.62	2.57	1410	1389	482	483
1962	1.48	1.28	920	834	532	545
1963	1.39	1.17	842	726	576	582
1964	1.3	1.1	773	666	583	590
1965	1.3	1.12	749	654	583	592
1966	1.53	1.33	789	685	560	564
1967	1.61	1.39	864	753	548	551
1968	1.69	1.46	895	779	546	550
1969	1.86	1.61	993	865	555	557
1970	1.98	1.72	938	799	488	480
1971	2.69	2.39	1356	1212	576	560
1972	5.59	5.26	3058	2907	567	573
1973	5.7	5.23	3170	2951	557	564
1974	5.76	5.29	3247	3016	569	574
1975	6.07	5.53	3314	3087	567	578
1976	6.53	5.84	3457	3212	555	564
1977	8.4	5.88	3704	3411	572	582
1978	7.6	6.83	4535	4172	602	617
1979	7.51	6.83	5137	4771	687	702
1980	7.5	6.9	5924	5538	791	803
1981	5.89	5.22	4454	4034	760	777
1982	5.93	5.21	4565	4091	766	781

年份 Year	职工人数(万人) Employed Persons (10 000 persons)	国有经济单位 State-owned Units	职工工资总额(万元) Total Wages of Staff and Workers (10 000yuan)	国有经济单位 State-owned Units	职工平均工资(元) Average Wage of Staff and Workers (yuan)	国有经济单位 State-owned Units
1983	5.97	5.24	4733	4234	785	800
1984	6.08	5.12	6186	5361	1048	1086
1985	6.38	5.41	6952	6071	1128	1160
1986	6.78	5.72	8457	7397	1292	1341
1987	6.98	5.83	9571	8427	1410	1476
1988	7.71	6.29	13252	11663	1797	1906
1989	7.75	6.3	16406	14426	2139	2319
1990	7.74	6.3	19291	17137	2426	2773
1991	8.82	7.04	22745	19628	2645	2857
1992	9.56	7.78	27446	24083	2989	3241
1993	14.02	9.43	45072	34826	3438	3844
1994	14.14	9.98	59956	48140	4298	4859
1995	14.56	10.61	71187	58923	5046	5725
1996	14.83	11.01	88171	71270	6091	6610
1997	15.25	11.2	97593	78064	6459	7052
1998	15.93	12.12	111640	93671	7114	7843
1999	15.83	11.99	121455	103602	7686	8664
2000	15.52	7.67	132137	59316	8643	7983
2001	13.76	6.23	136252	59196	9944	9493
2002	13.25	5.41	149501	80824	11309	11253
2003	13.13	5.29	174284	66969	13245	12669
2004	12.97	4.95	204450	76872	15619	15569
2005	13.96	4.6	255674	88634	18282	19216
2006	14.32	5.1	293602	105269	20999	21411
2007	13.61	4.57	348496	123494	25929	27238
2008	13.87	4.98	401675	149656	28774	30097
2009	13.27	5.05	429083	157095	31603	31645
2010	13.94	5.12	512247	176508	36605	34762
2011	16.67	4.86	652328	196392	37747	40632
2012	16.99	5.19	694145	218922	41100	42832
2013	18.37	4.27	864600	241935	47482	54408
2014	18.67	4.39	892384	237478	48716	55568
2015	17.39	3.2	864338	220983	49713	68546
2016	16.31	3.11	901637	228786	55014	73885
2017	14.62	2.76	891708	210869	59740	81335

注：本表 2001 年及以后年度数据为在岗职工口径。职工工资是城镇非私营单位的口径。

Note: In this table, the data for 2001 and subsequent years are the caliber of on–the–job workers. Wages of staff and workers are the caliber of and Urban non–private units,

各时期城乡居民收入支出情况

Per Capital Annual Income and Per Capital Annual Expenditure in Each Period

年 份 Year	农村居民人均可支配收入(元) Per Capita Disposable Income of Rural Inhabitant (yuan)	指数 (以上年为 100) Indices（Preceding Last Year=100）	指数 (以 1978 年为 100) Indices（Preceding 1978=100）	农村居民人均生活消费支出（元） Per Capita onsumer Expenditure of Rural Inhabitant (yuan)	城镇居民人均可支配收入（元） Per Capita Disposable Income of Urban Inhabitant (yuan)	指数 (以上年为 100) Indices（Preceding Last Year=100）	城镇居民人均生活消费支出（元） Per Capita Consumer Expenditure of Urban Inhabitant (yuan)
1978	94	100	100	75			
1979	109	116	116	101			
1980	139	128	148	126			
1981	228	164	243	183			
1982	247	108	263	205			
1983	274	111	291	246			
1984	379	138	403	219			
1985	427	113	454	363			
1986	480	112	511	408			
1987	573	119	610	348			
1988	727	127	773	496			
1989	735	101	782	579			
1990	822	112	874	608			
1991	865	105	920	699			
1992	955	110	1016	727			
1993	1206	126	1283	728			
1994	1640	136	1745	1191			
1995	2009	123	2137	1372			
1996	2475	123	2633	1759	4439		3624
1997	2690	108.7	2862	2330	4541	102.3	3847
1998	2930	108.9	3117	1769	5198	114.5	3949
1999	3071	104.8	3267	1793	5570	107.2	4335
2000	3246	105.7	3453	1552	6532	117.3	4826
2001	3452	106.3	3672	1742	7176	109.9	5165
2002	3622	104.9	3853	2052	7425	103.5	5483
2003	3844	106.1	4089	2145	8469	114.1	6068
2004	4232	110.1	4502	2277	10132	119.6	6462
2005	4684	110.7	4983	2719	10786	106.5	7099
2006	5201	111.4	5532	3410	11588	107.4	7638
2007	5913	113.7	6290	3431	14906	128.6	9200
2008	6646	112.4	7070	3773	17224	115.5	10789
2009	7317	110.1	7784	4116	18943	110.0	12598
2010	8311	113.6	8843	4620	20988	110.8	13645
2011	9626	115.8	10240	5194	23509	112.0	14219
2012	10887	113.1	11582	6093	26589	113.1	15664
2013	12161	111.7	12937	6737	29179	109.7	16977
2014	13540	111.3	14404	7478	31728	108.7	18381
2015	13714	108.9	14589	9615	30219	106.8	17311
2016	14852	108.3	15800	10413	32364	107.1	18523
2017	16144	108.7	17174	11309	34889	107.8	19912
2018	17468	108.2	18583	12263	37401	107.0	21304

注：“农村居民人均可支配收入”2014 年以前为“农民人均纯收入”口径。

Note: "Per capita disposable income of rural residents" was the caliber of "rural per capita net income" before 2014.

各时期固定资产投资、社会消费品零售额及进出口情况

Each Period Investment in Fixed Assets and Retail Sales of Consumer Goods and Value of Imports and Exports

年份 Year	固定资产投资总额 （万元） Investment in Fixed Assets (10 000 yuan)	社会消费品零售总额 （亿元） Retail Sales of Consumer Goods (100 million yuan)	进出口总额 (万美元） Value of Imports and Exports (10 000 USD)	出口总额 （万美元） Exports (10 000 USD)
1949	0.2	0.07		
1950		0.11		
1951	10	0.12		
1952	13	0.14		
1953	37	0.14		
1954	32	0.17		
1955	38	0.18		
1956	72	0.21		
1957	97	0.23		
1958	730	0.29		
1959	2501	0.41		
1960	3438	0.41		
1961	1314	0.30		
1962	316	0.32		
1963	232	0.32		
1964	248	0.35		
1965	301	0.41		
1966	1105	0.45		
1967	584	0.48		
1968	756	0.48		
1969	953	0.50		
1970	2288	0.59		
1971	4184	0.72		
1972	13581	0.80		
1973	10293	0.84		
1974	5588	0.75		
1975	8568	0.94		
1976	5503	1.05		
1977	3608	1.17		
1978	4288	1.24		
1979	3386	1.43		
1980	2983	1.66		
1981	790	1.78		
1982	1987	1.94		
1983	3241	2.13		

续 1

年份 Year	固定资产投资总额 （万元） Investment in Fixed Assets (10 000 yuan)	社会消费品零售总额 （亿元） Retail Sales of Consumer Goods (100 million yuan)	进出口总额 （万美元） Value of Imports and Exports (10 000 USD)	出口总额 （万美元） Exports (10 000 USD)
1984	3085	2.59		
1985	5237	2.89		
1986	8503	3.51		
1987	8917	4.01		
1988	13731	5.18		
1989	29894	5.93		
1990	27146	6.74		
1991	43375	8.30		
1992	107498	10.52		
1993	186314	12.26		
1994	224666	17.26		
1995	233403	22.28	3445	3445
1996	185640	29.78	12636	8308
1997	228633	34.66	21520	12273
1998	459852	39.60	11719	8446
1999	393531	41.78	13830	10122
2000	372997	45.97	21483	16868
2001	406913	50.88	22968	15408
2002	514637	56.60	25373	16672
2003	766671	55.69	30001	19533
2004	1035971	67.10	71870	43478
2005	1293498	81.75	105280	66029
2006	1404211	95.34	122326	97379
2007	1653221	113.31	164837	121507
2008	2074578	137.94	276283	136619
2009	2605500	160.60	157400	59144
2010	3213597	182.06	264980	103288
2011	3501011	198.39	358142	114095
2012	4410577	228.05	212778	73855
2013	4726266	257.75	250403	75095
2014	5454332	290.36	221884	92056
2015	6190739	320.88	189713	98413
2016	6356731	347.80	1125735	647963
2017	6681406	380.00	1071089	703575
2018		373.16	1113903	724017

注：2006 年以前固定资产投资统计口径为全社会固定资产投资，2006 年统计口径为规模以上固定资产投资。2016 年及以后进出口数据单位为人民币万元。

Note：Before 2006, the statistical standard of investment in fixed assets was the whole society's investment in fixed assets,After 2006, the statistical standard is fixed asset investment above scale.The unit of import and export data for 2016 and thereafter is RMB (ten thousand yuan).

各时期农业基本情况

Major Economic Indicators of Agriculture in Each Period

年份 year	农林牧渔业总产值（亿元） Gross Output Value of Farming, Forestry,Animal Husbandry and Fishery (100 million yuan)	农业机械总动力 (万千瓦) Total power of agricultural machinery(10 000 kw)	农村用电量 (万千瓦时） Rural Electricity Consumption (10 000 kwh)	有效灌溉面积 (千公顷) Effective Irrigated rea (1000 hectares)	乡村从业人员 (万人) Rural Labor (10 000 persons)
1949				8.00	20.73
1950				8.15	20.89
1951				8.37	21.01
1952				9.06	21.83
1953				9.56	22.18
1954				10.82	22.40
1955				12.85	22.50
1956		0.01		15.75	22.92
1957		0.02		18.32	21.91
1958		0.05		18.61	21.73
1959		0.13	3	19.98	20.16
1960		0.28	3	19.59	19.66
1961		0.40	20	20.21	20.46
1962		0.39	32	21.00	21.72
1963		0.36	40	21.63	22.74
1964		0.39	110	22.69	22.86
1965		0.52	220	23.51	22.98
1966		0.66	290	23.38	23.08
1967		0.84	340	22.30	23.11
1968		1.10	375	20.43	23.42
1969		1.29	410	21.84	22.93
1970		1.86	452	22.54	23.94
1971		2.47	540	23.60	24.58
1972		3.25	626	25.20	24.90
1973		5.60	822	27.14	27.80
1974		6.69	985	28.21	27.95
1975		7.64	1516	30.20	28.45
1976		8.11	2606	32.00	29.03
1977		9.87	2601	37.87	28.64
1978	2.27	13.28	3699	42.12	28.75
1979	2.32	14.64	3387	38.00	29.91
1980	2.43	16.11	5963	41.33	30.70
1981	2.53	19.05	7321	41.51	31.33
1982	2.70	20.58	5922	41.60	32.21

续 1

年份 year	农林牧渔业总产值（亿元） Gross Output Value of Farming, Forestry,Animal Husbandry and Fishery (100 million yuan)	农业机械总动力 (万千瓦) Total power of agricultural machinery(10 000 kw)	农村用电量 (万千瓦时) Rural Electricity Consumption (10 000 kwh)	有效灌溉面积 (千公顷) Effective Irrigated rea (1000 hectares)	乡村从业人员 (万人) Rural Labor (10 000 persons)
1983	2.79	25.77	5625	41.10	34.37
1984	2.77	22.83	5523	41.25	37.33
1985	3.12	23.93	7630	41.44	39.00
1986	3.94	29.03	11014	41.49	39.82
1987	4.64	28.73	12657	41.61	41.90
1988	5.47	33.60	14681	41.65	42.20
1989	5.32	38.94	16259	39.19	43.64
1990	7.56	33.91	14190	39.96	45.36
1991	8.83	31.36	14900	41.27	49.57
1992	9.45	31.28	20067	41.89	51.02
1993	11.16	39.98	19621	42.11	51.36
1994	15.61	46.74	23184	41.78	50.80
1995	18.86	45.41	23692	41.95	50.32
1996	21.02	47.28	18517	42.34	50.69
1997	21.13	57.75	26121	42.64	51.76
1998	20.81	60.98	22692	42.71	52.14
1999	21.52	65.83	23697	43.47	52.32
2000	22.86	68.10	26609	43.80	48.33
2001	24.51	70.29	31477	44.89	51.84
2002	25.42	70.65	37882	42.87	52.09
2003	27.89	74.19	38561	41.54	52.15
2004	30.68	76.48	54000	41.40	52.78
2005	33.23	79.70	65736	41.59	52.81
2006	35.37	82.47	57084	41.59	54.57
2007	40.95	87.91	66400	40.64	54.60
2008	55.39	87.91	68630	36.98	52.04
2009	58.84	97.90	99750	38.11	50.95
2010	72.51	99.35	99608	37.95	51.47
2011	78.28	102.26	97740	39.60	51.65
2012	82.40	105.04	98613	39.42	51.82
2013	89.52	106.80	76660	37.34	52.35
2014	95.97	109.64	78607	36.66	52.27
2015	96.95	113.18	78989	36.70	52.32
2016	102.16	101.33	80462	36.70	52.45
2017	104.59	87.40	76070	37.40	48.60
2018	108.86	88.50	75973	40.20	

各时期农作物播种面积和产量（一）

Sown Areas and Output of Main Farm Crops in Each Period(firstly)

年份 year	农作物总播种面积 (千公顷) Total Sown Area of Farm Crops (1000 ha)	农作物复种指数(%) Crop Multiple Cropping Index (%)	粮食作物播种面积 (千公顷) Total Sown Area of Grain Crops (1000 ha)	粮食产量 (万吨) Output of Grain Crops (10 000 tons)	花生产量 (万吨) Output of Peanuts (10 000 tons)	蔬菜产量 (万吨) Output of Vegetable (10 000 tons)
1949	100.17	166	88.72	7.06	0.41	4.43
1950	98.89	164	88.69	8.71	0.42	4.67
1951	110.26	150	100.78	9.05	0.36	5.02
1952	110.31	149	100.52	10.94	0.5	8.14
1953	110.77	149	100.23	8.89	0.58	7.92
1954	110.11	148	98.89	10.78	0.56	8.9
1955	110.34	147	99.03	12.47	0.41	8.59
1956	114.87	150	100.51	14.9	0.76	11.71
1957	114.88	150	102.15	12.18	0.32	11.6
1958	111.49	153	111.49	16.76	0.29	12.28
1959	104.82	149	104.82	14.52	0.27	13.95
1960	106.07	154	106.07	11.64	0.03	12.91
1961	103.77	151	103.77	10.86	0.07	9.83
1962	102.1	148	102.1	11.91	0.14	7.34
1963	100.26	148	100.26	12.78	0.24	6.94
1964	102.05	151	102.05	14.98	0.33	6.42
1965	102.43	153	102.43	16.35	0.38	10.02
1966	102.33	153	102.33	15.62	0.41	9.2
1967	101.27	152	101.27	18.48	0.38	8.35
1968	100.2	152	100.2	15.01	0.27	8.73
1969	100.58	155	89.67	18.15	0.16	7.81
1970	99.81	154	89.1	17.27	0.37	3.04
1971	98.89	154	87.04	18.87	0.62	9.79
1972	98.15	154	87.77	19.53	0.38	6.39
1973	96.97	154	86.93	22.73	0.43	6.5
1974	97.14	155	86.98	20.79	0.45	5.51
1975	95.69	154	84.97	28.43	0.61	6.24
1976	95.99	156	82.67	30.19	0.72	8.9
1977	94.63	155	80.16	27.78	0.57	9.99
1978	94.77	157	80.88	30.94	0.81	9.9
1979	94.93	158	80.97	34.33	0.55	11.2
1980	94.68	158	79.86	34.1	0.91	12.4
1981	94.27	158	79.09	34.55	0.73	13
1982	93.46	157	77.15	37.43	1.35	15.9

续 1

年份 year	农作物总播种面积(千公顷) Total Sown Area of Farm Crops (1000 ha)	农作物复种指数(%) Crop Multiple Cropping Index (%)	粮食作物播种面积(千公顷) Total Sown Area of Grain Crops (1000 ha)	粮食产量(万吨) Output of Grain Crops (10 000 tons)	花生产量(万吨) Output of Peanuts (10 000 tons)	蔬菜产量(万吨) Output of Vegetable (10 000 tons)
1983	93.77	156	77.33	36.85	1.10	17.8
1984	92.77	157	77.47	39.03	1.16	24.7
1985	91.79	157	75.19	39.64	1	25.7
1986	91.29	157	75.19	40.2	0.56	39.2
1987	93.33	156	75.16	41.67	1.01	41.1
1988	91.03	158	75.47	42.55	0.58	33.3
1989	94.31	165	74.95	34.17	0.22	37.7
1990	92.47	161	74.65	44.41	1.27	42.1
1991	99.15	164	79.62	50.89	1.26	47.76
1992	99.12	165	78.7	47.99	0.46	50.23
1993	99.54	167	74.95	45.39	1.36	55.88
1994	99.5	168	74.05	44.01	1.39	67.73
1995	99.45	167	75	45.46	1.48	69.89
1996	99.23	166	75.35	45.26	1.42	73.78
1997	97.45	164	71.31	42.97	1.24	83.77
1998	96.15	158	68.11	42.42	1.47	94.47
1999	97.91	163	67.85	41.02	1.05	101.87
2000	98.67	164	61.49	35.77	1.24	130.6
2001	94.58	156	51.55	28.98	1.35	139.87
2002	92.48	155	45.6	21.33	1.17	150.88
2003	92.21	155	44.89	23.79	1.56	154.23
2004	92.43	155	45.21	23.8	1.66	134.23
2005	93.73	163	47.07	25.17	1.74	145.67
2006	94.68	180	50.26	26.69	1.62	136.4
2007	91.57	179	51.55	26.67	1.61	118.4
2008	92.78	135	51.12	27.38	1.76	114.78
2009	90.41	160	51.95	27.31	1.65	103.12
2010	91.25	126	52.79	27.78	1.87	98.27
2011	90.95	166	52.33	26.98	1.73	102.1
2012	91.16	168	50	30.34	1.72	98.99
2013	91.26	170	48.06	28.24	1.72	98.04
2014	89.47	168	41.97	24.7	1.95	104.72
2015	90.77		43.27	25.95	1.96	110.58
2016	87.49		37.85	22.99	2.36	103.94
2017			39.51	25.47	2.41	115.51
2018			39.66	25.52	2.83	131.76

各时期农作物播种面积和产量（二）

Sown Areas and Output of Main Farm Crops in Each Period(second)

年份 year	水果产量 (万吨) Output of Fruits (10 000 tons)	棉花产量（吨）Output of Cotton (ton)	粮食单产 (千克/公顷) Output per Hectare of Grain Crops (kg/ha)	花生单产 (千克/公顷) Output per Hectare of Peanuts (kg/ha)	水产品产量 (万吨) Output of Aquatic Products (10 000 tons)	农业人口人均粮食产量 (千克) Per Capita Grain Crops of Rural Numbers (kg)	肉类总产（万吨）Output of Meat (10 000 tons)	禽蛋总产 (万吨) Output of Poultry Eggs (10 000 tons)	水产品产量（吨）Output of Aquatic Products (ton)	平均每一农业劳动者提供粮食(千克) Per Grain Crops of Rural Labor Force (kg)
1949	0.26		795	825		137.8				376.6
1950	0.34		982	1050		168.9				464
1951	0.39		898	1110		170.3				479.7
1952	0.49		1088	1380		205.6				559.7
1953	0.86		887	1455		162				448.7
1954	0.67		1090	1200		192.9				541.4
1955	1.33		1259	855		216.3				628.6
1956	0.68		1482	1530		253				737.5
1957	0.72		1192	660		202.4				597.6
1958	0.64		1672	735		280.8				1023.8
1959	0.81		1555	900		240.1				974.5
1960	0.36		1230	480		192.1				637
1961	0.32		1140	1095		171.7				570.9
1962	0.34		1290	825		180.2				589.8
1963	0.37		1395	1065		187.2				604.1
1964	0.47		1620	975	0.01	215.6				694.4
1965	0.61		1770	1125	0.01	229.7				758.4
1966	0.84		1725	870	0.01	213.5				739.4
1967	0.93		2055	930	0.01	252.2				851.7
1968	1.07		1680	780	0.02	195				702.2
1969	1.58		2025	510	0.01	230.1				879.4
1970	1.15		1938	1230	0.01	212.1				801.4
1971	1.00		2168	1635	0.02	231.3				854.8
1972	1.19		2235	1005	0.03	232.7				881.3
1973	1.35		2621	1245	0.02	266.2				909.9
1974	1.58		2390	1305	0.02	240.2				828.8
1975	1.7		3345	1485	0.02	325.6				1120.9
1976	1.81		3652	1485	0.03	343.6				1168.8
1977	1.76		3466	1155	0.02	313				1090.9
1978	1.74		3825	1680	0.02	347.1				1207.2
1979	1.75		4240	1140	0.02	383.2				1294.4
1980	1.45		4270	1710	0.03	379.2				1272.8
1981	1.73		4368	1275	0.03	381.6				1279
1982	2.17		4852	2355	0.02	410.4				1427.6

续 1

年份 year	水果产量(万吨) Output of Fruits (10 000 tons)	棉花产量(吨) Output of Cotton (ton)	粮食单产(千克/公顷) Output per Hectare of Grain Crops (kg/ha)	花生单产(千克/公顷) Output per Hectare of Peanuts (kg/ha)	水产品产量(万吨) Output of Aquatic Products (10 000 tons)	农业人口人均粮食产量(千克) Per Capita Grain Crops of Rural Numbers (kg)	肉类总产(万吨) Output of Meat (10 000 tons)	禽蛋总产(万吨) Output of Poultry Eggs (10 000 tons)	水产品产量(吨) Output of Aquatic Products (ton)	平均每一农业劳动者提供粮食(千克) Per Grain Crops of Rural Labor Force (kg)
1983	2.46		4765	1965	0.02	402.4				1403.7
1984	2.38		5038	2205	0.03	408				1488.1
1985	2.82		5271	1815	0.04	441.2				1556.2
1986	2.36		5346	1065	0.05	440				1626.7
1987	2.75		5545	2025	0.05	453.2				1643.3
1988	2.75		5638	1185	0.07	485.8				1743.1
1989	2.73		4559	449	0.08	374.2				1301.6
1990	3.85		5949	2625	0.07	480.2				1594.6
1991	4.73		6392	2386	0.08	516.8				1596.8
1992	4.03	157	6099	879	0.11	489			1090	1500.7
1993	5.46	213	6056	2614	0.16	472.9	6.45	2.74	1559	1451.1
1994	7.15	135	5943	2699	0.36	445.8	6.64	3.7	3568	1486.3
1995	7.67	150	6061	2857	0.55	498.1	8.48	4.11	5511	1546.3
1996	7.43	125	6007	2773	0.67	548.3	9.37	4.54	6700	1502.7
1997	6.79	128	6026	2416	0.75	515.9	11.08	4.66	7500	1353.8
1998	7.22	140	6228	2856	0.85	507.4	11.51	6.48	8510	1336.5
1999	7.3	153	6046	2020	0.77	490.3	3.69	2.8	7649	1286.8
2000	8.24	122	5818	2466	0.77	427.2	3.86	2.73	7716	1198.7
2001	9.49	131	5621	2609	0.8	346.5	3.97	2.83	8025	1079.1
2002	7.97	164	4678	3003	0.8	257.5	4.59	2.82	8012	770.7
2003	9.96	240	5306	2488	0.8	291.8	5.02	3.11	8046	762.7
2004	9.89	305	5262	2425	0.8	260.9	5.62	3.63	8236	979.8
2005	9.81	519	5347	2473	0.86	336	6.58	3.69	8272	1159.8
2006	11.54	976	5309	2489	0.8	357.4	5.86	3.23	8036	1151.8
2007	10.2	1005	5174	2523	0.5	347.2	5.09	2.32	5026	1192.4
2008	9.87	1158	5355	2394	0.34	358.6	5.6	2.68	3353	1298.1
2009	9.15	957	5256	2516	0.32	359.5	5.6	2.68	3216	1296.8
2010	9.14	1075	5264	2565	0.33	405.8	6.45	3.11	3300	1319.4
2011	8.99	1187	5154	2568	0.34	392.1	6.3	3.07	3418	1292.4
2012	9.27	1323	6068	2576	0.35	492.1	6.55	3.09	3462	1455.2
2013	10.48	1381	5877	2733	0.35	472.8	6.58	3.04	3536	1330.1
2014	10.07	1400	5887	2825	0.36		6.41	3.14	3580	
2015	11.4	1559	6000	2808	0.35		6.27	3.15	3523	
2016	10.94	3076	6075	2880	0.36		6.33	3.26	3577	
2017	10.47	2954	6450	2211	0.35		6.81	3.3	3539	
2018	21.1		6434				7.94	4.8		

各时期独立核算工业企业主要指标

Main Economic Indicators of Independent Accounting of Industrial Enterprises in Each Period

单位：万元 (10 000 yuan)

年份 year	企业个数（个）Number of Industial Enterprises(unit)	#亏损 Loss Enterprises	产品销售 Product sales 收入 Revenue	产品销售 Product sales 税金 Taxes	盈利企业利润总额 Total Profits of Profitable Enterprise	亏损企业亏损总额 Total Loss of Loss Enterprises	固定资产净值平均余额 Average Balance of Net Fixed Assets	流动资产年平均余额 Annual Average Balance of Current Assets
1978	124	21	33274	1487	1153	3965	54451	17937
1979	131	15	30476	1362	1163	4216	52964	16427
1980	125	14	36727	1364	1179	2504	51629	17048
1981	125	19	28054	1051	909	1251	47704	15543
1982	137	13	31622	1307	1205	674	47052	13769
1983	142	3	31363	1617	1706	30	48173	12118
1984	157	9	39016	2004	2846	22	51371	12722
1985	165	18	49270	2734	4277	164	55268	16102
1986	219	20	72982	5660	8319	297	60768	18271
1987	243	30	90804	6427	8685	188	66595	2224
1988	270	16	117276	6639	10380	47	76928	26352
1989	303	34	146443	9197	10695	470	87351	35719
1990	303	44	165325	11955	8009	1746	148590	45080
1991	306	36	206415	13436	9156	991	152702	53064
1992	307	15	292744	15714	21944	532	165770	133032
1993	304	15	530475	25769	39143	3786	275031	189929
1994	298	20	636300	12920	28757	2452	318680	328081
1995	289	106	686043	7964	23284	7351	471086	37441
1996	253	28	703463	6871	27934	3002	549607	427876
1997	257	65	821773	6219	27507	5377	743826	499111
1998	123	23	904984	7099	30028	2535	807450	552362
1999	130	22	923840	7781	30335	2016	827086	569533
2000	126	18	1086125	11701	41804	2133	991831	604345
2001	129	16	1273684	14525	47511	3373	1020723	650424
2002	131	27	1462095	16608	49061	4948	992897	898306
2003	145	31	2312550	27885	81113	3665	1086391	1093844
2004	155	38	4075426	27940	224150	6948	1275818	1656526
2005	187	55	6055900	35383	265771	11344	2125572	2180694
2006	238	64	7168517	48016	360564	10322	2839706	2385450
2007	318	75	10051910	107249	775995	41215	3443935	3179213
2008	414	109	12630693	112378	374922	30365	3725891	5005360
2009	449	91	12258214	90338	588209	24973	4361092	5125217
2010	466	69	15062911	77655	573658	23760	5061332	4852606
2011	254	42	15130965	40443	414845	46083	2983702	3997253
2012	339	51	16034618	46387	342702	276726	6057317	4363296
2013	486	79	17701241	30759	410690	62050	4364082	5397098
2014	609	87	19341252	37432	480545	176241	5222041	4899603
2015	635	90	18545712	42932	460423	295731	5716921	5498613
2016	548	78	19349504	45367	696252	143798	7574200	5578557
2017	578	89	20539797	487525	817557	53153	7945332	6741513
2018	552	110	21021893	469152	1084001	70600	7337480	7061123

注：1997年以前统计范围为乡及乡以上独立核算工业企业，1998年以后为全部国有及年销售收入500万元以上非国有工业企业,从2011年开始为年主营业务收入2000万元及以上的工业企业。

Note: Industrial statistical indicators In 1997 and before, the statistical caliber was industrial enterprises at or above the township level. In 1998 and after, they were all state-owned and with an annual sales income of more than 5 million yuan. In 2011 and beyond,the annual main business income was 20 million yuan and above industrial enterprises legal entities.

各时期财政金融、税收情况

Financial and Tax Situation in Each Period

单位：万元 (10 000 yuan)

年份 year	公共财政预算收入 Pubilic Budget Revenue	公共财政预算支出 Pubilic Budget Revenue	金融机构人民币各项存款 The Balance of RMB Deposits in Financial Institutions	金融机构人民币各项贷款 The Balance of RMB Loans in Financial Institutions	#城乡储蓄存款 Household Deposits	税收总收入 Regional Tax Revenue	国税收入 National Tax Revenue	地税收入 Land Tax Revenue
1949			10	4				
1950			10	5				
1951			12	6	2			
1952			55	16	13			
1953	32	159	55	60	14			
1954	87	304	77	91	13			
1955	115	348	224	447	12			
1956	167	395	146	611	24			
1957	192	424	184	564	41			
1958	385	974	494	2178	79			
1959	417	760	1179	3078	147			
1960	1058	1426	1708	4335	220			
1961	730	1058	1414	3073	122			
1962	637	688	793	2041	83			
1963	733	864	699	1679	92			
1964	636	868	701	1251	125			
1965	674	952	939	1646	146			
1966	638	743	1190	1719	170			
1967	649	911	1570	1996	176			
1968	659	889	1457	1982	190			
1969	653	1027	1803	2340	197			
1970	850	1103	2973	3789	249			
1971	1369	1245	4454	4797	346			
1972	1664	1659	3215	5483	450			
1973	1936	1957	3899	5783	515			
1974	1916	2034	4364	7149	593			
1975	2738	2857	5520	9104	181			
1976	3233	3276	6392	9777	721			
1977	3716	3668	5400	10681	786			
1978	3689	3765	5868	11770	874			
1979	3421	3431	6410	12896	1035			
1980	649	1761	11670	14656	3170			
1981	3524	4727	12399	16800	3701			
1982	4133	4727	16388	13187	5324			

续 1

年份 year	公共财政预算收入 Pubilic Budget Revenue	公共财政预算支出 Pubilic Budget Revenue	金融机构人民币各项存款 The Balance of RMB Deposits in Financial Institutions	金融机构人民币各项贷款 The Balance of RMB Loans in Financial Institutions	#城乡储蓄存款 Household Deposits	税收总收入 Regional Tax Revenue	国税收入 National Tax Revenue	地税收入 Land Tax Revenue
1983	4743	5283	19846	10966	7067			
1984	5496	5703	26778	18124	9355			
1985	4682	5632	36349	24902	12811			
1986	5139	7144	34449	37546	18124			
1987	6448	840	44478	51384	25211			
1988	8269	9569	53314	65409	34770			
1989	10016	9220	63266	74708	43073			
1990	11061	10437	79358	94977	60722			
1991	12191	10750	99352	118581	78093			
1992	14174	12355	129494	143868	99551			
1993	21673	19614	172040	182108	126880			
1994	12908	25656	254094	221749	181823	32223		
1995	17562	30330	330144	279195	259278	37796		
1996	22461	36955	467873	358908	361478	48174	33385	14789
1997	28079	44816	560755	467899	423862	65128	39628	25500
1998	32727	50420	648582	564362	493800	74005	46162	27843
1999	37329	56254	694581	672064	527055	90501	53016	37485
2000	42006	60841	770192	741296	558511	107501	60649	46852
2001	50836	68879	958993	906686	629951	137000	79449	57551
2002	63471	82435	1188246	1091065	713095	145406	92680	52726
2003	75827	114230	1500660	1283534	847742	172544	109296	63248
2004	102950	144815	1886698	1660555	1014981	251271	167686	83585
2005	145624	220310	2501752	2167041	1302778	365265	253665	111600
2006	192572	282419	3186034	2875137	1570485	492639	354516	138123
2007	260688	345318	3651196	3134473	1721919	681234	491215	190019
2008	302488	393815	4448052	3501433	2164091	801219	582448	218771
2009	327009	446068	5624396	4268906	2619492	618756	398738	220018
2010	353207	519371	5857834	4647035	2994407	658535	437823	220712
2011	392316	592276	6049739	4900461	3229688	783564	505798	277766
2012	420178	667256	7192407	5480663	3779019	827286	491773	335513
2013	467616	758101	7517493	5737779	4178637	843481	499388	344093
2014	496017	801172	7882468	6035272	4586224	839144	484514	354630
2015	501717	838437	8293481	6196001	4894442	777324	437881	339443
2016	530005	865777	9076722	6612483	5386568	734004	438229	295775
2017	560078	887679	9481654	7256990	5678664	852935	593235	259715
2018	625687	1003535	10282253	8152542	6302452	900345		

注：1994 年财税体制改革后财政收入统计口径与 1993 年以前不一致。

Note: After the reform of the fiscal and taxation system in 1994, the statistical caliber of fiscal revenue is different from that before 1994

各时期公路交通、邮电情况

Basic situation of Transportation Postal and Telecommunications in Each Period

年份 year	公路客运量（万人）Highways Passenger Traffic (10 000 persons)	公路客运周转量（万人公里）Highways Passenger Turnover (10 000 passengers-km)	公路货运量（万吨）Highways Freight Traffic (10 000 tons)	公路货运周转量（万吨公里）Highways Freight Turnover (10 000 ton-km)	公路通车里程（公里）Length of Highways in Operation (km)	邮电业务总量（1990年不变价格）（万元）Total Postal and Telecommunications Services (Preceding 1990=100) (10 000 yuan)
1949						0.76
1950						0.75
1951						0.93
1952						1.09
1953						3.42
1954						4.86
1955						5.31
1956						7.17
1957						8.1
1958			62.1			21
1959			89.46			51.9
1960			117.43			58.5
1961			13.77			55.1
1962			12.38			39.8
1963			39.62			33.5
1964			39.13			36.5
1965			7.82			38.6
1966			7.63			25
1967			5.94			26
1968			3.97			27
1969			3.62			27
1970			21.72			37
1971			47.5			46
1972			74.45			55
1973			92.42			61
1974			68.3			48
1975			105.1			57
1976			123.9			64
1977			163			67
1978			178	1669	370	72
1979			158	1314	408	74
1980			105	752	417	73
1981			92	1639	432	104
1982			94	2646	443	106
1983			96	3550	463	114
1984			115	3727	470	134

续 1

年份 year	公路客运量 （万人） Highways Passenger Traffic (10 000 persons)	公路客运周转量 （万人公里） Highways Passenger Turnover (10 000 passengers-km)	公路货运量 （万吨） Highways Freight Traffic (10 000 tons)	公路货运周转量 （万吨公里） Highways Freight Turnover (10 000 ton-km)	公路通车里程 （公里） Length of Highways in Operation (km)	邮电业务总量 （1990 年不变价格） （万元） Total Postal and Telecommunications Services (Preceding 1990=100) (10 000 yuan)
1985			133	4081	487	159
1986			197	7306	509	177
1987			197	7795	537	205
1988			463	15047	551	268
1989			413	13582	563	321
1990			371	14246	573	341
1991			355	13302	585	849
1992	679		372	14121	598	1333
1993	1279		537	14297	637	2402
1994	1300		651	18679	658	4075
1995	1310		621	20423	788	6388
1996	541	19539	645	24331	816	8704
1997	563	23341	603	28332	842	11709
1998	685	18131	539	31041	870	17038
1999	841	38321	741	36107	936	20279
2000	917	38597	821	40951	1023	28312
2001	931	43727	1053	47797	1010	26300
2002	1002	46352	1069	49009	1089	28818
2003	962	45221	1048	51440	1108	33131
2004	1080	51558	1086	57405	1125	35386
2005	1236	58396	1504	79091	1125	41595
2006	1391	65824	2116	112088	3187	51118
2007	1467	66917	3772	164887	3334	56091
2008	1484	71008	4645	237040	3458	63315
2009	2774	105267	5715	457836	3522	64366
2010	2923	108247	6202	519854	3557	67102
2011	3603	123473	6231	519664	3600	73722
2012	3899	127915	6438	548589	3893	79594
2013	4055	130344	6519	586746	4161	85732
2014	155	18784	6518	885243	4239	84354
2015	130	18018	6160	866703	4325	82119
2016	137	18676	6742	895349	4405	84987
2017	149	18950	7526	981934	4597	92370
2018	149		7929			

注：1. 公路通车里程自 2006 年起调整统计口径，增加了村道公路统计。

2. 2000 年以前邮电业务总量为按 1990 年不变价格计算邮电业务总量,2001 年以后为邮电业务收入。

Note: 1. The mileage in highway open to traffic was adjusted to be statistical caliber as of 2006, increasing statistics of village road highway.

2.Before 2000, the total amount of postal and telecommunications business is calculated at the same price as in 1990. After 2001, it is the income of postal and telecommunications business.

各时期教育卫生情况

Basic Statistics on Education and Public Health in Each Period

年份 year	各类学校（所）Number of Schools (nuit)	各类学校专任教师（人）Full-time Teachers (person)	各类学校在校学生（万人）Total Enrollment (10 000 persons)	卫生机构数（个）Number of Health Institutions (unit)	卫生机构床位数（张）Number of Health Institutions Beds (set)	卫生机构从业人员数（人）Medical Technical Personnel (person)
1978				93	1783	3105
1979				96	1773	3104
1980				95	1604	2590
1981				100	1622	2891
1982				92	1499	2704
1983				86	1518	2664
1984				86	1558	2759
1985				87	1686	3017
1986				122	1872	3339
1987				101	1758	3267
1988				91	1741	3359
1989				95	1797	3401
1990				92	1790	3614
1991				110	1796	3910
1992				113	2297	4972
1993	816	9952	16.47	169	3018	5361
1994	689	10502	16.91	165	3275	5724
1995	608	10860	17.87	170	3011	6146
1996	652	10788	18.36	168	3090	6398
1997	628	11479	18.51	177	3142	6548
1998	578	11463	18.65	173	3147	6762
1999	516	11453	17.99	176	3336	7106
2000	438	11277	17.26	217	3444	6989
2001	416	11104	16.69	207	3479	7145
2002	406	12258	16.63	225	3521	7223
2003	363	11864	16.52	281	4099	7401
2004	349	12753	17.24	295	4018	7297
2005	325	12893	17.53	320	4084	6885
2006	287	12703	17.47	327	4465	6763
2007	279	13005	17.78	292	4101	6801
2008	270	13217	17.72	314	4474	7016
2009	246	13274	17.61	243	4958	7057
2010	240	13235	17.34	287	5162	7083
2011	236	12966	17.35	284	5588	7831
2012	227	12868	17.1	294	6151	7845
2013	219	12090	16.96	282	6440	8398
2014	197	11515	16.52	315	6486	8908
2015	188	11415	16.19	312	6509	8913
2016	188	11583	15.64	326	6737	9189
2017	182	11527	15.07	345	7219	9299
2018	179	11444	14.91	1313	7351	11777

注：2018 年卫生机构、卫生机构从业人员数据包含村卫生室。

Note: Data of employees in health institutions and health institutions in 2018 include village clinics.

附　录

APPENDIX

山东省十七城市

Main Statistical Indicators

单位：亿元

城市名称	Region	地区生产总值 Gross National Product	第一产业 Primary Industry	第二产业 Secondary Industry	第三产业 Tertiary Industry	固定资产投资比上年增长(%) Growth rate Investment in Fixed Assets (%)	房地产开发投资额 Estate Development Investment	一般公共预算收入 General Pubilic Budget Revenue	一般公共预算支出 General Pubilic Budget Expenditure	金融机构本外币存款余额 The Balance of RMB and Foreign Currencies Deposits in Financial Institutions	#住户存款 Household Deposits
全省	Total	76469.7	4950.5	33641.7	37877.4	4.1	7553.0	6485.4	10099.0	96412.7	48800.0
济南市	Ji'nan	7856.6	272.4	2829.3	4754.8	9.6	1369.3	752.8	1018.3	17060.1	5067.3
青岛市	Qingdao	12001.5	386.9	4850.6	6764.0	7.9	1485.2	1231.9	1561.2	16121.0	6036.7
淄博市	Zibo	5068.4	145.9	2639.9	2282.6	6.6	269.5	385.2	474.6	4617.3	2793.4
枣庄市	Zaozhuang	2402.4	156.9	1219.7	1025.8	-19.8	243.8	146.7	259.6	2037.7	1302.7
东营市	Dongying	4152.5	146.5	2583.2	1422.7	-10.0	167.2	244.6	306.3	3721.4	1624.7
烟台市	Yantai	7832.6	510.0	3844.0	3478.5	6.0	586.7	636.6	756.0	8211.9	4492.2
潍坊市	Weifang	6156.8	511.6	2742.4	2902.8	4.4	650.2	569.8	733.5	7929.8	4694.7
济宁市	Jining	4930.6	491.2	2234.2	2205.1	7.1	401.3	400.0	619.7	5486.8	3366.2
泰安市	Taian	3651.5	285.4	1615.2	1751.0	5.8	177.7	219.5	381.1	3672.3	2363.2
威海市	Weiha	3641.5	281.2	1601.2	1759.1	7.5	345.3	284.4	363.8	3682.0	2060.6
日照市	Rizhao	2202.2	166.5	1064.2	971.5	6.3	186.6	159.8	259.6	2530.6	1397.5
莱芜市	Laiwu	1005.7	60.3	566.1	379.3	7.2	68.2	62.6	100.4	1033.7	632.9
临沂市	Linyi	4717.8	369.7	2028.8	2319.4	7.8	535.6	311.8	639.1	6371.6	3954.5
德州市	Dezhou	3380.3	320.1	1612.8	1447.4	7.3	299.3	202.5	414.2	3456.0	2275.6
聊城市	Liaocheng	3152.2	310.9	1547.5	1293.7	-4.3	314.3	194.3	409.2	3505.8	2343.9
滨州市	Binzhou	2640.5	233.8	1185.2	1221.5	-16.8	165.9	240.5	345.3	2875.1	1521.5
菏泽市	Heze	3078.8	301.1	1570.3	1207.4	8.0	286.9	206.0	551.5	3905.3	2870.4
济南位次	Position	2	11	3	2	1	2	2	2	1	2

注：本表内其他城市数据根据内部资料整理，不做正式发布，仅供参考。各项指标最终数据，敬请关注各城市官方发布机构。

Note: The data regarding other cities in this table is sorted out according to internal data which is for reference only instead of being released officially. As for final data regarding various indicators, refer to official release mechanism in each city.

主要经济指标（2018年）

Indicators of 17 Cities in Shandong（2018）

(100 million yuan)

金融机构本外币贷款余额 The Balance of RMB and Foreign Currencies Loans in Financial Institutions	社会消费品零售总额 Total Retail Sales of Consumer Goods	进出口总额 Total Import & Export	#出口总额 Total Export	实际使用外资 Actual Use of Foreign Capital	城镇居民人均可支配收入（元）Disposable Income of Urban Households (yuan)	城市镇居民人均消费支出(元) Urban Consumption Expenditure (yuan)	农村居民人均可支配收入（元）Disposable Income of rural Households (yuan)	农村居民人均消费支出（元）Consumption Expenditure of rural Households (yuan)	居民消费价格指数(%) Consumer Price Indices (%)
77810.5	–	19302.5	10569.6	1362.8	39549	24798	16297	11270	102.5
16059.9	4404.5	825.0	519.3	178.2	50146	32977	17924	11172	102.6
16098.0	4842.5	5321.3	3172.2	577.4	50817	32890	20820	13885	102.1
3199.9	–	952.4	418.5	59.2	42277	26973	18273	13035	102.9
1344.3	950.3	106.1	99.0	7.1	32001	18549	15345	10073	101.7
3553.1	867.0	1627.9	369.0	10.6	47912	28900	17485	13258	102.8
5550.0	3079.4	3053.6	1773.1	176.3	44875	29495	19425	13899	102.1
5803.1	2702.7	1630.9	1043.7	89.4	39042	24417	18719	12126	102.6
3516.1	2288.1	426.6	221.4	50.2	34796	20825	16055	10452	102.7
2357.9	1593.8	160.8	127.6	46.0	35196	20862	16959	10942	102.9
2518.7	–	1392.0	913.8	93.7	45896	29975	20423	12704	102.4
2355.7	774.1	895.4	406.1	14.0	33280	20573	15785	8538	102.4
825.3	373.2	111.4	72.4	0.7	37401	21304	17468	12263	101.7
5099.4	2482.2	680.7	539.2	15.5	35727	17090	13638	8698	102.6
1955.5	1525.5	294.4	189.3	13.8	26562	16272	14564	11681	102.3
2464.2	1334.4	489.6	245.8	5.2	27276	15828	13492	9853	102.4
2615.6	993.7	820.0	305.5	13.4	35049	23097	16061	11224	101.3
2267.4	1811.4	514.6	153.6	12.1	26176	16787	12848	10241	101.5
2	2	8	6	2	2	1	6	10	5

十五副省级城市

Main Statistical Indicators

单位：亿元

城市名称	Region	地区生产总值 Gross National Product	第一产业 Primary Industry	第二产业 Secondary Industry	第三产业 Tertiary Industry	固定资产投资比上年增长(%) Growth rate Investment in Fixed Assets (%)	房地产开发投资比上年增长(%) Growth rate Estate Development Investment (%)	一般公共预算收入 General Pubilic Budget Revenue	一般公共预算支出 General Pubilic Budget Expenditure	金融机构人民币存款余额 The Balance of RMB Deposits in Financial Institutions	#住户存款 Household Deposits
济南	Ji'nan	7856.6	272.4	2829.3	4754.8	9.6	11.1	752.8	1018.3	16571.9	5008.1
沈阳	Shenyang	6292.4	260.1	2376.6	3655.7	15.3	22.4	720.6	964.9	17553.6	7288.1
大连	Dalian	7668.5	442.7	3241.6	3984.2	10.1	21.5	704.0	1001.4	13485.1	6040.0
长春	Changchun	7175.7	301.4	3508.9	3365.4	6.7	35.7	478.0	894.3	11475.7	4993.2
哈尔滨	Harbin	6300.5	525.5	1689.3	4085.7	−7.2	17.6	384.4	962.2	11504.0	5394.3
南京	Nanjing	12820.4	273.4	4721.6	7825.4	9.4	8.5	1470.0	1532.7	33740.6	6914.8
杭州	Hangzhou	13509.0	306.0	4572.0	8632.0	10.8	12.2	1825.1	1717.1	38810.1	10198.5
宁波	Ningbo	10745.5	306.0	5507.5	4932.0	3.6	15.5	1379.7	1594.1	18532.5	6561.3
厦门	Xiamen	4791.4	24.4	1980.2	2786.9	10.1	0.5	754.5	892.5	10446.8	2150.8
青岛	Qingdao	12001.5	386.9	4850.6	6764.0	7.9	11.6	1231.9	1561.2	15532.0	5914.0
武汉	Wuhan	14847.3	362.0	6377.8	8107.5	10.6	3.5	1528.7	1929.3	25720.5	–
广州	Guangzhou	22859.4	223.4	6234.1	16401.8	8.2	0.0	1632.3	2505.8	52647.5	16042.1
深圳	Shenzhen	24222.0	22.1	9962.0	14237.9	20.6	23.6	3538.4	4282.5	68697.6	13478.9
成都	Chengdu	15342.8	522.6	6516.2	8304.0	10.0	−8.8	1424.2	1837.5	36656.0	13141.0
西安	Xi'an	8349.9	258.8	2925.6	5165.4	8.5	7.9	684.7	1151.6	20948.2	8360.3
济南位次	Position	10	10	12	10	8	9	10	10	10	12

注：1. 为便于排序，济南、厦门实际使用外资数据根据人民币口径和年均汇率推算。
2. 本表内其他城市数据根据内部资料整理，不做正式发布，仅供参考。各项指标最终数据，敬请关注各城市官方发布机构。

Note: 1. To facilitate ranking, the data regarding foreign investment actually used by Jinan and Xiamen is calculated as per RMB caliber and average annual rate.
2. The data regarding other cities in this table is sorted out according to internal data which is for reference only instead of being released officially. As for final data regarding various indicators, refer to official release mechanism

主要经济指标（2018年）

of 15 Vice-provincial Cities（2018）

(100 million yuan)

金融机构人民币贷款余额 The Balance of RMB Loans in Financial Institutions	社会消费品零售总额 Total Retail Sales of Consumer Goods	进出口总额 Total Import & Export	#出口总额 Total Export	实际使用外资（亿美元） Actual Use of Foreign Capital (100 million USD)	城镇居民人均可支配收入（元） Disposable Income of Urban Households (yuan)	农村居民人均可支配收入（元） Disposable Income of rural Households (yuan)	居民消费价格指数(%) Consumer Price Indices (%)
14700.1	4404.5	825.0	519.3	26.7	50146	17924	102.6
14726.8	4051.2	984.3	342.1	14.3	44054	16530	103.0
11346.0	3880.1	4701.4	1889.6	26.8	43550	18103	103.0
11463.1	3003.6	1054.6	152.5	3.3	35332	14237	102.0
10921.2	4125.1	209.7	103.5	36.5	37828	16934	102.5
28402.3	5832.5	4317.2	2500.7	38.5	59308	25263	102.4
35877.6	5715.0	5245.3	3417.1	68.3	61172	33193	102.3
19341.1	4154.9	8576.3	5550.6	43.2	60134	33633	102.2
9759.6	1542.4	6002.1	3338.5	16.3	54401	18842	101.8
15194.0	4842.5	5321.2	3172.2	86.9	50817	20820	102.1
26839.4	6843.9	2146.0	1272.7	109.3	47359	22652	101.9
39764.4	9256.2	9810.2	5607.6	66.1	59982	26020	102.4
48282.4	6168.9	29983.7	16274.7	82.0	57543	–	102.8
31423.0	6801.8	4983.2	2746.9	76.3	42128	22135	101.4
19729.8	4658.7	3303.9	1957.5	63.5	38729	13286	101.9
11	9	14	12	12	8	10	4

二十六省会城市

Main Statistical

单位：亿元

城市名称	Region	地区生产总值 Gross National Product	第一产业 Primary Industry	第二产业 Secondary Industry	第三产业 Tertiary Industry	固定资产投资比上年增长(%) Growth rate Investment in Fixed Assets (%)	房地产开发投资比上年增长(%) Growth rate Estate Development Investment (%)	一般公共预算收入 General Pubilic Budget Revenue	一般公共预算支出 General Pubilic Budget Expenditure	金融机构本外币存款余额 The Balance of RMB and Foreign Currencies Deposits in Financial Institutions
济南	Ji'nan	7856.6	272.4	2829.3	4754.8	9.6	11.1	752.8	1018.3	17060.1
石家庄	Shijiazhuang	6082.6	420.5	2285.5	3376.7	6.4	-16.8	519.7	994.7	13315.8
太原	Taiyuan	3884.5	41.1	1439.1	2404.3	26.2	11.2	373.2	542.5	12317.3
呼和浩特	Hohehot	2903.5	108.4	801.4	1993.7	-26.5	-26.9	204.7	357.0	5803.8
沈阳	Shenyang	6292.4	260.1	2376.6	3655.7	15.3	22.4	720.6	964.9	17746.2
长春	Changchun	7175.7	301.4	3508.9	3365.4	6.7	35.7	478.0	894.3	11551.2
哈尔滨	Harbin	6300.5	525.5	1689.3	4085.7	-7.2	17.6	384.4	962.2	11616.0
南京	Nanjing	12820.4	273.4	4721.6	7825.4	9.4	8.5	1470.0	1532.7	34524.9
杭州	Hangzhou	13509.0	306.0	4572.0	8632.0	10.8	12.2	1825.1	1717.1	39810.5
合肥	Hefei	7822.9	277.6	3612.3	3933.1	7.1	-1.9	712.5	1004.9	15677.3
福州	Fuzhou	7856.8	494.7	3204.9	4157.3	11.7	-15.0	680.4	923.4	14204.3
南昌	Nanchang	5274.7	190.7	2660.9	2423.1	10.9	12.6	461.8	752.1	10733.1
郑州	Zhengzhou	10143.3	147.1	4450.7	5545.5	10.9	-3.0	1152.1	1763.3	22710.6
武汉	Wuhan	14847.3	362.0	6377.8	8107.5	10.6	3.5	1528.7	1929.3	26331.6
长沙	Changsha	11003.4	318.7	4660.2	6024.5	11.5	0.7	879.7	1329.5	18633.6
广州	Guangzhou	22859.4	223.4	6234.1	16401.8	8.2	0.0	1632.3	2505.8	54788.1
南宁	Nanning	-	-	-	-	11.8	15.5	359.0	697.9	-
海口	Haikou	1510.5	64.0	276.0	1170.6	-6.2	1.0	169.9	237.4	4899.3
成都	Chengdu	15342.8	522.6	6516.2	8304.0	10.0	-8.8	1424.2	1837.5	37826.0
贵阳	Guiyang	3798.5	153.1	1413.7	2231.7	15.0	-3.9	411.3	627.5	11418.5
昆明	Kunming	5206.9	222.2	2038.0	2946.7	5.5	9.3	595.6	756.8	-
西安	Xi'an	8349.9	258.8	2925.6	5165.4	8.5	7.9	684.7	1151.6	21266.7
兰州	Lanzhou	2732.9	43.0	938.0	1752.0	12.1	35.7	253.3	465.7	8814.3
西宁	Xining	1286.4	46.1	468.0	772.3	9.0	-16.8	92.9	297.5	3802.2
银川	Yinchuan	1901.5	67.3	867.3	966.8	-21.9	-26.7	181.2	370.8	3718.6
乌鲁木齐	Urumqi	3060.1	26.3	950.2	2083.7	10.0	56.7	458.3	659.8	8477.9
济南位次	Position	10	10	11	9	14	10	8	9	10

注：1、为便于排序，贵阳、昆明进出口总额、出口总额数据根据美元口径和年均汇率推算；济南、福州实际使用外资数据根据人民币口径和年均汇率推算。

2、本表内其他城市数据根据内部资料整理，不做正式发布，仅供参考。各项指标最终数据，敬请关注各城市官方发布机构。

Note: 1. To facilitate ranking, total export-import volume and total export of Guiyang and Kunming are calculated pursuant to USD caliber and average annual exchange rate; The data regarding foreign investment actually used by Jinan and Fuzhou is calculated in terms of RMB caliber and average annual exchange rate.

2. The data regarding other cities in this table is sorted out according to internal data which is for reference only instead of being released officially. As for final data regarding various indicators, refer to official release mechanism in each city.

主要经济指标（2018年）

Indicators of 26 Provincial Capitals（2018）

(100 million yuan)

金融机构本外币贷款余额 The Balance of RMB and Foreign Currencies Loans in Financial Institutions	社会消费品零售总额 Total Retail Sales of Consumer Goods	进出口总额 Total Import & Export	#出口总额 Total Export	实际使用外资（亿美元） Actual Use of Foreign Capital (USD 100 million)	城镇居民人均可支配收入（元） Disposable Income of Urban Households (yuan)	农村居民人均可支配收入（元） Disposable Income of rural Households (yuan)	居民消费价格指数(%) Consumer Price Indices (%)
16059.9	4404.5	825.0	519.3	26.7	50146	17924	102.6
10171.8	2934.1	915.5	571.6	14.5	35563	14518	102.3
12684.2	1811.9	1086.3	663.3	0.1	33672	16860	101.8
8057.0	1603.2	116.7	55.9	–	46565	17190	102.1
14911.6	4051.2	984.3	342.1	14.3	44054	16530	103.0
11488.3	3003.6	1054.6	152.5	3.3	35332	14237	102.0
11079.8	4125.1	209.7	103.5	36.5	37828	16934	102.5
29065.7	5832.5	4317.2	2500.7	38.5	59308	25263	102.4
36598.3	5715.0	5245.3	3417.1	68.3	61172	33193	102.3
14196.5	2976.7	2030.6	1203.5	32.3	41484	20389	102.0
15364.3	4666.5	2452.8	1654.8	8.4	44457	19419	101.5
12124.6	2131.6	787.6	451.7	34.9	40844	17866	102.3
22055.7	4268.1	4105.0	2577.1	42.1	39042	21652	102.4
28270.8	6843.9	2146.0	1272.7	109.3	47359	22652	101.9
18360.9	4765.0	1283.3	823.2	57.8	50792	29714	102.0
40749.3	9256.2	9810.2	5607.6	66.1	59982	26020	102.4
–	–	738.8	355.1	13.7	35276	13654	102.5
5700.7	757.6	341.2	67.2	2.5	36137	14886	102.4
32637.0	6801.8	4983.2	2746.9	76.3	42128	22135	101.4
12508.7	1299.5	231.1	150.0	15.9	35115	15648	101.6
–	2787.4	867.7	248.9	8.5	42988	14895	101.7
19891.6	4658.7	3303.9	1957.5	63.5	38729	13286	101.9
11269.2	1352.1	133.2	75.6	–	35014	12368	101.7
5468.4	564.4	31.3	11.0	–	32500	11504	102.7
5028.5	552.7	168.8	127.8	0.7	35586	14160	102.2
7001.8	1383.0	513.5	361.4		40101	19623	102.2
9	9	16	13	12	5	11	3

附录四

中华人民共和国统计法

Statistical Law of The People's Republic of China

（1983年12月8日第六届全国人民代表大会常务委员会第三次会议通过　根据1996年5月15日第八届全国人民代表大会常务委员会第十九次会议《关于修改〈中华人民共和国统计法〉的决定》修正　2009年6月27日第十一届全国人民代表大会常务委员会第九次会议修订）

第一章　总　则

第一条　为了科学、有效地组织统计工作，保障统计资料的真实性、准确性、完整性和及时性，发挥统计在了解国情国力、服务经济社会发展中的重要作用，促进社会主义现代化建设事业发展，制定本法。

第二条　本法适用于各级人民政府、县级以上人民政府统计机构和有关部门组织实施的统计活动。

统计的基本任务是对经济社会发展情况进行统计调查、统计分析，提供统计资料和统计咨询意见，实行统计监督。

第三条　国家建立集中统一的统计系统，实行统一领导、分级负责的统计管理体制。

第四条　国务院和地方各级人民政府、各有关部门应当加强对统计工作的组织领导，为统计工作提供必要的保障。

第五条　国家加强统计科学研究，健全科学的统计指标体系，不断改进统计调查方法，提高统计的科学性。

国家有计划地加强统计信息化建设，推进统计信息搜集、处理、传输、共享、存储技术和统计数据库体系的现代化。

第六条　统计机构和统计人员依照本法规定独立行使统计调查、统计报告、统计监督的职权，不受侵犯。

地方各级人民政府、政府统计机构和有关部门以及各单位的负责人，不得自行修改统计机构和统计人员依法搜集、整理的统计资料，不得以任何方式要求统计机构、统计人员及其他机构、人员伪造、篡改统计资料，不得对依法履行职责或者拒绝、抵制统计违法行为的统计人员打击报复。

第七条　国家机关、企业事业单位和其他组织以及个体工商户和个人等统计调查对象，必须依照本法和国家有关规定，真实、准确、完整、及时地提供统计调查所需的资料，不得提供不真实或者不完整的统计资料，不得迟报、拒报统计资料。

第八条　统计工作应当接受社会公众的监督。任何单位和个人有权检举统计中弄虚作假等违法行为。对检举有功的单位和个人应当给予表彰和奖励。

第九条　统计机构和统计人员对在统计工作中知悉的国家秘密、商业秘密和个人信息，应当予以保密。

第十条　任何单位和个人不得利用虚假统计资料骗取荣誉称号、物质利益或者职务晋升。

第二章　统计调查管理

第十一条　统计调查项目包括国家统计调查项目、部门统计调查项目和地方统计调查项目。

国家统计调查项目是指全国性基本情况的统计调查项目。部门统计调查项目是指国务院有关部门的专业性统计调查项目。地方统计调查项目是指县级以上地方人民政府及其部门的地方性统计调查项目。

国家统计调查项目、部门统计调查项目、地方统计调查项目应当明确分工，互相衔接，不得重复。

第十二条　国家统计调查项目由国家统计局制定，或者由国家统计局和国务院有关部门共同制定，报国务院备案；重大的国家统计调查项目报国务院审批。

部门统计调查项目由国务院有关部门制定。统计调查对象属于本部门管辖系统的，报国家统计局备案；统计调查对象超出本部门管辖系统的，报国家统计局审批。

地方统计调查项目由县级以上地方人民政府统计机构和有关部门分别制定或者共同制定。其中，由省级人民政府统计机构单独制定或者和有关部门共同制定的，报国家统计局审批；由省级以下人民政府统计机构单独制定或者和有关部门共同制定的，报省级人民政府统计机构审批；由县级以上地方人民政府有关部门制定的，报本级人民政府统计机构审批。

第十三条　统计调查项目的审批机关应当对调查项目的必要性、可行性、科学性进行审查，对符合法定条件的，作出予以批准的书面决定，并公布；对不符合法定条件的，作出不予批准的书面决定，并说明理由。

第十四条　制定统计调查项目，应当同时制定该项目的统计调查制度，并依照本法第十二条的规定一并报经审批或者备案。

统计调查制度应当对调查目的、调查内容、调查方法、调查对象、调查组织方式、调查表式、统计资料的报送和公布等作出规定。

统计调查应当按照统计调查制度组织实施。变更统计调查制度的内容，应当报经原审批机关批准或者原备案机关备案。

第十五条 统计调查表应当标明表号、制定机关、批准或者备案文号、有效期限等标志。

对未标明前款规定的标志或者超过有效期限的统计调查表，统计调查对象有权拒绝填报；县级以上人民政府统计机构应当依法责令停止有关统计调查活动。

第十六条 搜集、整理统计资料，应当以周期性普查为基础，以经常性抽样调查为主体，综合运用全面调查、重点调查等方法，并充分利用行政记录等资料。

重大国情国力普查由国务院统一领导，国务院和地方人民政府组织统计机构和有关部门共同实施。

第十七条 国家制定统一的统计标准，保障统计调查采用的指标涵义、计算方法、分类目录、调查表式和统计编码等的标准化。

国家统计标准由国家统计局制定，或者由国家统计局和国务院标准化主管部门共同制定。

国务院有关部门可以制定补充性的部门统计标准，报国家统计局审批。部门统计标准不得与国家统计标准相抵触。

第十八条 县级以上人民政府统计机构根据统计任务的需要，可以在统计调查对象中推广使用计算机网络报送统计资料。

第十九条 县级以上人民政府应当将统计工作所需经费列入财政预算。

重大国情国力普查所需经费，由国务院和地方人民政府共同负担，列入相应年度的财政预算，按时拨付，确保到位。

第三章 统计资料的管理和公布

第二十条 县级以上人民政府统计机构和有关部门以及乡、镇人民政府，应当按照国家有关规定建立统计资料的保存、管理制度，建立健全统计信息共享机制。

第二十一条 国家机关、企业事业单位和其他组织等统计调查对象，应当按照国家有关规定设置原始记录、统计台账，建立健全统计资料的审核、签署、交接、归档等管理制度。

统计资料的审核、签署人员应当对其审核、签署的统计资料的真实性、准确性和完整性负责。

第二十二条 县级以上人民政府有关部门应当及时向本级人民政府统计机构提供统计所需的行政记录资料和国民经济核算所需的财务资料、财政资料及其他资料，并按照统计调查制度的规定及时向本级人民政府统计机构报送其组织实施统计调查取得的有关资料。

县级以上人民政府统计机构应当及时向本级人民政府有关部门提供有关统计资料。

第二十三条 县级以上人民政府统计机构按照国家有关规定，定期公布统计资料。

国家统计数据以国家统计局公布的数据为准。

第二十四条 县级以上人民政府有关部门统计调查取得的统计资料，由本部门按照国家有关规定公布。

第二十五条 统计调查中获得的能够识别或者推断单个统计调查对象身份的资料，任何单位和个人不得对外提供、泄露，不得用于统计以外的目的。

第二十六条 县级以上人民政府统计机构和有关部门统计调查取得的统计资料，除依法应当保密的外，应当及时公开，供社会公众查询。

第四章 统计机构和统计人员

第二十七条 国务院设立国家统计局，依法组织领导和协调全国的统计工作。

国家统计局根据工作需要设立的派出调查机构，承担国家统计局布置的统计调查等任务。

县级以上地方人民政府设立独立的统计机构，乡、镇人民政府设置统计工作岗位，配备专职或者兼职统计人员，依法管理、开展统计工作，实施统计调查。

第二十八条 县级以上人民政府有关部门根据统计任务的需要设立统计机构，或者在有关机构中设置统计人员，并指定统计负责人，依法组织、管理本部门职责范围内的统计工作，实施统计调查，在统计业务上受本级人民政府统计机构的指导。

第二十九条 统计机构、统计人员应当依法履行职责，如实搜集、报送统计资料，不得伪造、篡改统计资料，不得以任何方式要求任何单位和个人提供不真实的统计资料，不得有其他违反本法规定的行为。

统计人员应当坚持实事求是，恪守职业道德，对其负责搜集、审核、录入的统计资料与统计调查对象报送的统计资料的一致性负责。

第三十条 统计人员进行统计调查时，有权就与统计有关的问题询问有关人员，要求其如实提供有关情况、资料并改正不真实、不准确的资料。

统计人员进行统计调查时，应当出示县级以上人民政府统计机构或者有关部门颁发的工作证件；未出示的，统计调查对象有权拒绝调查。

第三十一条 国家实行统计专业技术职务资格考试、评聘制度，提高统计人员的专业素质，保障统计队伍的稳定性。

统计人员应当具备与其从事的统计工作相适应的专业知识和业务能力。

县级以上人民政府统计机构和有关部门应当加强对统计人员的专业培训和职业道德教育。

第五章 监督检查

第三十二条 县级以上人民政府及其监察机关对下级人民政府、本级人民政府统计机构和有关部门执行本法的情况，实施监督。

第三十三条 国家统计局组织管理全国统计工作的监督检查，查处重大统计违法行为。

县级以上地方人民政府统计机构依法查处本行政区域内发

生的统计违法行为。但是，国家统计局派出的调查机构组织实施的统计调查活动中发生的统计违法行为，由组织实施该项统计调查的调查机构负责查处。

法律、行政法规对有关部门查处统计违法行为另有规定的，从其规定。

第三十四条 县级以上人民政府有关部门应当积极协助本级人民政府统计机构查处统计违法行为，及时向本级人民政府统计机构移送有关统计违法案件材料。

第三十五条 县级以上人民政府统计机构在调查统计违法行为或者核查统计数据时，有权采取下列措施：

（一）发出统计检查查询书，向检查对象查询有关事项；

（二）要求检查对象提供有关原始记录和凭证、统计台账、统计调查表、会计资料及其他相关证明和资料；

（三）就与检查有关的事项询问有关人员；

（四）进入检查对象的业务场所和统计数据处理信息系统进行检查、核对；

（五）经本机构负责人批准，登记保存检查对象的有关原始记录和凭证、统计台账、统计调查表、会计资料及其他相关证明和资料；

（六）对与检查事项有关的情况和资料进行记录、录音、录像、照相和复制。

县级以上人民政府统计机构进行监督检查时，监督检查人员不得少于二人，并应当出示执法证件；未出示的，有关单位和个人有权拒绝检查。

第三十六条 县级以上人民政府统计机构履行监督检查职责时，有关单位和个人应当如实反映情况，提供相关证明和资料，不得拒绝、阻碍检查，不得转移、隐匿、篡改、毁弃原始记录和凭证、统计台账、统计调查表、会计资料及其他相关证明和资料。

第六章 法律责任

第三十七条 地方人民政府、政府统计机构或者有关部门、单位的负责人有下列行为之一的，由任免机关或者监察机关依法给予处分，并由县级以上人民政府统计机构予以通报：

（一）自行修改统计资料、编造虚假统计数据的；

（二）要求统计机构、统计人员或者其他机构、人员伪造、篡改统计资料的；

（三）对依法履行职责或者拒绝、抵制统计违法行为的统计人员打击报复的；

（四）对本地方、本部门、本单位发生的严重统计违法行为失察的。

第三十八条 县级以上人民政府统计机构或者有关部门在组织实施统计调查活动中有下列行为之一的，由本级人民政府、上级人民政府统计机构或者本级人民政府统计机构责令改正，予以通报；对直接负责的主管人员和其他直接责任人员，由任免机关或者监察机关依法给予处分：

（一）未经批准擅自组织实施统计调查的；

（二）未经批准擅自变更统计调查制度的内容的；

（三）伪造、篡改统计资料的；

（四）要求统计调查对象或者其他机构、人员提供不真实的统计资料的；

（五）未按照统计调查制度的规定报送有关资料的。

统计人员有前款第三项至第五项所列行为之一的，责令改正，依法给予处分。

第三十九条 县级以上人民政府统计机构或者有关部门有下列行为之一的，对直接负责的主管人员和其他直接责任人员由任免机关或者监察机关依法给予处分：

（一）违法公布统计资料的；

（二）泄露统计调查对象的商业秘密、个人信息或者提供、泄露在统计调查中获得的能够识别或者推断单个统计调查对象身份的资料的；

（三）违反国家有关规定，造成统计资料毁损、灭失的。

统计人员有前款所列行为之一的，依法给予处分。

第四十条 统计机构、统计人员泄露国家秘密的，依法追究法律责任。

第四十一条 作为统计调查对象的国家机关、企业事业单位或者其他组织有下列行为之一的，由县级以上人民政府统计机构责令改正，给予警告，可以予以通报；其直接负责的主管人员和其他直接责任人员属于国家工作人员的，由任免机关或者监察机关依法给予处分：

（一）拒绝提供统计资料或者经催报后仍未按时提供统计资料的；

（二）提供不真实或者不完整的统计资料的；

（三）拒绝答复或者不如实答复统计检查查询书的；

（四）拒绝、阻碍统计调查、统计检查的；

（五）转移、隐匿、篡改、毁弃或者拒绝提供原始记录和凭证、统计台账、统计调查表及其他相关证明和资料的。

企业事业单位或者其他组织有前款所列行为之一的，可以并处五万元以下的罚款；情节严重的，并处五万元以上二十万元以下的罚款。

个体工商户有本条第一款所列行为之一的，由县级以上人民政府统计机构责令改正，给予警告，可以并处一万元以下的罚款。

第四十二条 作为统计调查对象的国家机关、企业事业单位或者其他组织迟报统计资料，或者未按照国家有关规定设置原始记录、统计台账的，由县级以上人民政府统计机构责令改正，给予警告。

企业事业单位或者其他组织有前款所列行为之一的，可以并处一万元以下的罚款。

个体工商户迟报统计资料的，由县级以上人民政府统计机构责令改正，给予警告，可以并处一千元以下的罚款。

第四十三条 县级以上人民政府统计机构查处统计违法行为时，认为对有关国家工作人员依法应当给予处分的，应当提出给予处分的建议；该国家工作人员的任免机关或者监察机关应当依法及时作出决定，并将结果书面通知县级以上人民政府统计机构。

第四十四条 作为统计调查对象的个人在重大国情国力普查活动中拒绝、阻碍统计调查，或者提供不真实或者不完整的普查资料的，由县级以上人民政府统计机构责令改正，予以批评教育。

第四十五条 违反本法规定，利用虚假统计资料骗取荣誉称号、物质利益或者职务晋升的，除对其编造虚假统计资料或者要求他人编造虚假统计资料的行为依法追究法律责任外，由作出有关决定的单位或者其上级单位、监察机关取消其荣誉称号，追缴获得的物质利益，撤销晋升的职务。

第四十六条 当事人对县级以上人民政府统计机构作出的行政处罚决定不服的，可以依法申请行政复议或者提起行政诉讼。其中，对国家统计局在省、自治区、直辖市派出的调查机构作出的行政处罚决定不服的，向国家统计局申请行政复议；对国家统计局派出的其他调查机构作出的行政处罚决定不服的，向国家统计局在该派出机构所在的省、自治区、直辖市派出的调查机构申请行政复议。

第四十七条 违反本法规定，构成犯罪的，依法追究刑事责任。

第七章 附 则

第四十八条 本法所称县级以上人民政府统计机构，是指国家统计局及其派出的调查机构、县级以上地方人民政府统计机构。

第四十九条 民间统计调查活动的管理办法，由国务院制定。

中华人民共和国境外的组织、个人需要在中华人民共和国境内进行统计调查活动的，应当按照国务院的规定报请审批。

利用统计调查危害国家安全、损害社会公共利益或者进行欺诈活动的，依法追究法律责任。

第五十条 本法自2010年1月1日起施行。

附录五

中华人民共和国统计法实施条例

Regulations for the Implementation of the Statistics Law
of the People's Republic of China

中华人民共和国国务院令

第 681 号

《中华人民共和国统计法实施条例》已经 2017 年 4 月 12 日国务院第 168 次常务会议通过，现予公布，自 2017 年 8 月 1 日起施行。

总理　李克强

2017 年 5 月 28 日

中华人民共和国统计法实施条例

第一章　总　则

第一条　根据《中华人民共和国统计法》（以下简称统计法），制定本条例。

第二条　统计资料能够通过行政记录取得的，不得组织实施调查。通过抽样调查、重点调查能够满足统计需要的，不得组织实施全面调查。

第三条　县级以上人民政府统计机构和有关部门应当加强统计规律研究，健全新兴产业等统计，完善经济、社会、科技、资源和环境统计，推进互联网、大数据、云计算等现代信息技术在统计工作中的应用，满足经济社会发展需要。

第四条　地方人民政府、县级以上人民政府统计机构和有关部门应当根据国家有关规定，明确本单位防范和惩治统计造假、弄虚作假的责任主体，严格执行统计法和本条例的规定。

地方人民政府、县级以上人民政府统计机构和有关部门及其负责人应当保障统计活动依法进行，不得侵犯统计机构、统计人员独立行使统计调查、统计报告、统计监督职权，不得非法干预统计调查对象提供统计资料，不得统计造假、弄虚作假。

统计调查对象应当依照统计法和国家有关规定，真实、准确、完整、及时地提供统计资料，拒绝、抵制弄虚作假等违法行为。

第五条　县级以上人民政府统计机构和有关部门不得组织实施营利性统计调查。

国家有计划地推进县级以上人民政府统计机构和有关部门通过向社会购买服务组织实施统计调查和资料开发。

第二章　统计调查项目

第六条　部门统计调查项目、地方统计调查项目的主要内容不得与国家统计调查项目的内容重复、矛盾。

第七条　统计调查项目的制定机关（以下简称制定机关）应当就项目的必要性、可行性、科学性进行论证，征求有关地方、部门、统计调查对象和专家的意见，并由制定机关按照会议制度集体讨论决定。

重要统计调查项目应当进行试点。

第八条　制定机关申请审批统计调查项目，应当以公文形式向审批机关提交统计调查项目审批申请表、项目的统计调查制度和工作经费来源说明。

申请材料不齐全或者不符合法定形式的，审批机关应当一次性告知需要补正的全部内容，制定机关应当按照审批机关的要求予以补正。

申请材料齐全、符合法定形式的，审批机关应当受理。

第九条　统计调查项目符合下列条件的，审批机关应当作出予以批准的书面决定：

（一）具有法定依据或者确为公共管理和服务所必需；

（二）与已批准或者备案的统计调查项目的主要内容不重复、不矛盾；

（三）主要统计指标无法通过行政记录或者已有统计调查资料加工整理取得；

（四）统计调查制度符合统计法律法规规定，科学、合理、可行；

（五）采用的统计标准符合国家有关规定；

（六）制定机关具备项目执行能力。

不符合前款规定条件的，审批机关应当向制定机关提出修改意见；修改后仍不符合前款规定条件的，审批机关应当作出不予批准的书面决定并说明理由。

第十条 统计调查项目涉及其他部门职责的，审批机关应当在作出审批决定前，征求相关部门的意见。

第十一条 审批机关应当自受理统计调查项目审批申请之日起 20 日内作出决定。20 日内不能作出决定的，经审批机关负责人批准可以延长 10 日，并应当将延长审批期限的理由告知制定机关。

制定机关修改统计调查项目的时间，不计算在审批期限内。

第十二条 制定机关申请备案统计调查项目，应当以公文形式向备案机关提交统计调查项目备案申请表和项目的统计调查制度。

统计调查项目的调查对象属于制定机关管辖系统，且主要内容与已批准、备案的统计调查项目不重复、不矛盾的，备案机关应当依法给予备案文号。

第十三条 统计调查项目经批准或者备案的，审批机关或者备案机关应当及时公布统计调查项目及其统计调查制度的主要内容。涉及国家秘密的统计调查项目除外。

第十四条 统计调查项目有下列情形之一的，审批机关或者备案机关应当简化审批或者备案程序，缩短期限：

（一）发生突发事件需要迅速实施统计调查；

（二）统计调查制度内容未作变动，统计调查项目有效期届满需要延长期限。

第十五条 统计法第十七条第二款规定的国家统计标准是强制执行标准。各级人民政府、县级以上人民政府统计机构和有关部门组织实施的统计调查活动，应当执行国家统计标准。

制定国家统计标准，应当征求国务院有关部门的意见。

第三章 统计调查的组织实施

第十六条 统计机构、统计人员组织实施统计调查，应当就统计调查对象的法定填报义务、主要指标涵义和有关填报要求等，向统计调查对象作出说明。

第十七条 国家机关、企业事业单位或者其他组织等统计调查对象提供统计资料，应当由填报人员和单位负责人签字，并加盖公章。个人作为统计调查对象提供统计资料，应当由本人签字。统计调查制度规定不需要签字、加盖公章的除外。

统计调查对象使用网络提供统计资料的，按照国家有关规定执行。

第十八条 县级以上人民政府统计机构、有关部门推广使用网络报送统计资料，应当采取有效的网络安全保障措施。

第十九条 县级以上人民政府统计机构、有关部门和乡、镇统计人员，应当对统计调查对象提供的统计资料进行审核。统计资料不完整或者存在明显错误的，应当由统计调查对象依法予以补充或者改正。

第二十条 国家统计局应当建立健全统计数据质量监控和评估制度，加强对各省、自治区、直辖市重要统计数据的监控和评估。

第四章 统计资料的管理和公布

第二十一条 县级以上人民政府统计机构、有关部门和乡、镇人民政府应当妥善保管统计调查中取得的统计资料。

国家建立统计资料灾难备份系统。

第二十二条 统计调查中取得的统计调查对象的原始资料，应当至少保存 2 年。

汇总性统计资料应当至少保存 10 年，重要的汇总性统计资料应当永久保存。法律法规另有规定的，从其规定。

第二十三条 统计调查对象按照国家有关规定设置的原始记录和统计台账，应当至少保存 2 年。

第二十四条 国家统计局统计调查取得的全国性统计数据和分省、自治区、直辖市统计数据，由国家统计局公布或者由国家统计局授权其派出的调查机构或者省级人民政府统计机构公布。

第二十五条 国务院有关部门统计调查取得的统计数据，由国务院有关部门按照国家有关规定和已批准或者备案的统计调查制度公布。

县级以上地方人民政府有关部门公布其统计调查取得的统计数据，比照前款规定执行。

第二十六条 已公布的统计数据按照国家有关规定需要进行修订的，县级以上人民政府统计机构和有关部门应当及时公布修订后的数据，并就修订依据和情况作出说明。

第二十七条 县级以上人民政府统计机构和有关部门应当及时公布主要统计指标涵义、调查范围、调查方法、计算方法、抽样调查样本量等信息，对统计数据进行解释说明。

第二十八条 公布统计资料应当按照国家有关规定进行。公布前，任何单位和个人不得违反国家有关规定对外提供，不得利用尚未公布的统计资料谋取不正当利益。

第二十九条 统计法第二十五条规定的能够识别或者推断单个统计调查对象身份的资料包括：

（一）直接标明单个统计调查对象身份的资料；

（二）虽未直接标明单个统计调查对象身份，但是通过已标明的地址、编码等相关信息可以识别或者推断单个统计调查对象身份的资料；

（三）可以推断单个统计调查对象身份的汇总资料。

第三十条 统计调查中获得的能够识别或者推断单个统计调查对象身份的资料应当依法严格管理，除作为统计执法依据外，不得直接作为对统计调查对象实施行政许可、行政处罚等具体行政行为的依据，不得用于完成统计任务以外的目的。

第三十一条 国家建立健全统计信息共享机制，实现县级以上人民政府统计机构和有关部门统计调查取得的资料共享。制定机关共同制定的统计调查项目，可以共同使用获取的统计资料。

统计调查制度应当对统计信息共享的内容、方式、时限、渠道和责任等作出规定。

第五章　统计机构和统计人员

第三十二条 县级以上地方人民政府统计机构受本级人民政府和上级人民政府统计机构的双重领导，在统计业务上以上级人民政府统计机构的领导为主。

乡、镇人民政府应当设置统计工作岗位，配备专职或者兼职统计人员，履行统计职责，在统计业务上受上级人民政府统计机构领导。乡、镇统计人员的调动，应当征得县级人民政府统计机构的同意。

县级以上人民政府有关部门在统计业务上受本级人民政府统计机构指导。

第三十三条 县级以上人民政府统计机构和有关部门应当完成国家统计调查任务，执行国家统计调查项目的统计调查制度，组织实施本地方、本部门的统计调查活动。

第三十四条 国家机关、企业事业单位和其他组织应当加强统计基础工作，为履行法定的统计资料报送义务提供组织、人员和工作条件保障。

第三十五条 对在统计工作中做出突出贡献、取得显著成绩的单位和个人，按照国家有关规定给予表彰和奖励。

第六章　监督检查

第三十六条 县级以上人民政府统计机构从事统计执法工作的人员，应当具备必要的法律知识和统计业务知识，参加统计执法培训，并取得由国家统计局统一印制的统计执法证。

第三十七条 任何单位和个人不得拒绝、阻碍对统计工作的监督检查和对统计违法行为的查处工作，不得包庇、纵容统计违法行为。

第三十八条 任何单位和个人有权向县级以上人民政府统计机构举报统计违法行为。

县级以上人民政府统计机构应当公布举报统计违法行为的方式和途径，依法受理、核实、处理举报，并为举报人保密。

第三十九条 县级以上人民政府统计机构负责查处统计违法行为；法律、行政法规对有关部门查处统计违法行为另有规定的，从其规定。

第七章　法律责任

第四十条 下列情形属于统计法第三十七条第四项规定的对严重统计违法行为失察，对地方人民政府、政府统计机构或者有关部门、单位的负责人，由任免机关或者监察机关依法给予处分，并由县级以上人民政府统计机构予以通报：

（一）本地方、本部门、本单位大面积发生或者连续发生统计造假、弄虚作假；

（二）本地方、本部门、本单位统计数据严重失实，应当发现而未发现；

（三）发现本地方、本部门、本单位统计数据严重失实不予纠正。

第四十一条 县级以上人民政府统计机构或者有关部门组织实施营利性统计调查的，由本级人民政府、上级人民政府统计机构或者本级人民政府统计机构责令改正，予以通报；有违法所得的，没收违法所得。

第四十二条 地方各级人民政府、县级以上人民政府统计机构或者有关部门及其负责人，侵犯统计机构、统计人员独立行使统计调查、统计报告、统计监督职权，或者采用下发文件、会议布置以及其他方式授意、指使、强令统计调查对象或者其他单位、人员编造虚假统计资料的，由上级人民政府、本级人民政府、上级人民政府统计机构或者本级人民政府统计机构责令改正，予以通报。

第四十三条 县级以上人民政府统计机构或者有关部门在组织实施统计调查活动中有下列行为之一的，由本级人民政府、上级人民政府统计机构或者本级人民政府统计机构责令改正，予以通报：

（一）违法制定、审批或者备案统计调查项目；

（二）未按照规定公布经批准或者备案的统计调查项目及其统计调查制度的主要内容；

（三）未执行国家统计标准；

（四）未执行统计调查制度；

（五）自行修改单个统计调查对象的统计资料。

乡、镇统计人员有前款第三项至第五项所列行为的，责令改正，依法给予处分。

第四十四条 县级以上人民政府统计机构或者有关部门违反本条例第二十四条、第二十五条规定公布统计数据的，由本级人民政府、上级人民政府统计机构或者本级人民政府统计机构责令改正，予以通报。

第四十五条 违反国家有关规定对外提供尚未公布的统计资料或者利用尚未公布的统计资料谋取不正当利益的，由任免机关或者监察机关依法给予处分，并由县级以上人民政府统计机构予以通报。

第四十六条 统计机构及其工作人员有下列行为之一的，由本级人民政府或者上级人民政府统计机构责令改正，予以通报：

（一）拒绝、阻碍对统计工作的监督检查和对统计违法行为的查处工作；

（二）包庇、纵容统计违法行为；

（三）向有统计违法行为的单位或者个人通风报信，帮助其逃避查处；

（四）未依法受理、核实、处理对统计违法行为的举报；

（五）泄露对统计违法行为的举报情况。

第四十七条 地方各级人民政府、县级以上人民政府有关部门拒绝、阻碍统计监督检查或者转移、隐匿、篡改、毁弃原始记录和凭证、统计台账、统计调查表及其他相关证明和资料的，由上级人民政府、上级人民政府统计机构或者本级人民政府统计机构责令改正，予以通报。

第四十八条 地方各级人民政府、县级以上人民政府统计机构和有关部门有本条例第四十一条至第四十七条所列违法行为之一的，对直接负责的主管人员和其他直接责任人员，由任免机关或者监察机关依法给予处分。

第四十九条 乡、镇人民政府有统计法第三十八条第一款、第三十九条第一款所列行为之一的，依照统计法第三十八条、第三十九条的规定追究法律责任。

第五十条 下列情形属于统计法第四十一条第二款规定的情节严重行为：

（一）使用暴力或者威胁方法拒绝、阻碍统计调查、统计监督检查；

（二）拒绝、阻碍统计调查、统计监督检查，严重影响相关工作正常开展；

（三）提供不真实、不完整的统计资料，造成严重后果或者恶劣影响；

（四）有统计法第四十一条第一款所列违法行为之一，1年内被责令改正3次以上。

第五十一条 统计违法行为涉嫌犯罪的，县级以上人民政府统计机构应当将案件移送司法机关处理。

第八章 附 则

第五十二条 中华人民共和国境外的组织、个人需要在中华人民共和国境内进行统计调查活动的，应当委托中华人民共和国境内具有涉外统计调查资格的机构进行。涉外统计调查资格应当依法报经批准。统计调查范围限于省、自治区、直辖市行政区域内的，由省级人民政府统计机构审批；统计调查范围跨省、自治区、直辖市行政区域的，由国家统计局审批。

涉外社会调查项目应当依法报经批准。统计调查范围限于省、自治区、直辖市行政区域内的，由省级人民政府统计机构审批；统计调查范围跨省、自治区、直辖市行政区域的，由国家统计局审批。

第五十三条 国家统计局或者省级人民政府统计机构对涉外统计违法行为进行调查，有权采取统计法第三十五条规定的措施。

第五十四条 对违法从事涉外统计调查活动的单位、个人，由国家统计局或者省级人民政府统计机构责令改正或者责令停止调查，有违法所得的，没收违法所得；违法所得50万元以上的，并处违法所得1倍以上3倍以下的罚款；违法所得不足50万元或者没有违法所得的，处200万元以下的罚款；情节严重的，暂停或者取消涉外统计调查资格，撤销涉外社会调查项目批准决定；构成犯罪的，依法追究刑事责任。

第五十五条 本条例自2017年8月1日起施行。1987年1月19日国务院批准、1987年2月15日国家统计局公布，2000年6月2日国务院批准修订、2000年6月15日国家统计局公布，2005年12月16日国务院修订的《中华人民共和国统计法实施细则》同时废止。

附录六

统计违法违纪行为处分规定

Statistics Regulation Violations of Law

中华人民共和国监察部
中华人民共和国人力资源和社会保障部　令
国家统计局

第 18 号

《统计违法违纪行为处分规定》已经监察部2009年2月9日第一次部长办公会议、人力资源社会保障部2008年12月30日第十六次部务会议、国家统计局2008年11月6日第十八次局务会议审议通过。现予公布，自2009年5月1日起施行。

监察部部长 马馼
人力资源社会保障部部长 尹蔚民
国家统计局局长 马建堂
二〇〇九年三月二十五日

统计违法违纪行为处分规定

第一条 为了加强统计工作，提高统计数据的准确性和及时性，惩处和预防统计违法违纪行为，促进统计法律法规的贯彻实施，根据《中华人民共和国统计法》、《中华人民共和国行政监察法》、《中华人民共和国公务员法》、《行政机关公务员处分条例》及其他有关法律、行政法规，制定本规定。

第二条 有统计违法违纪行为的单位中负有责任的领导人员和直接责任人员，以及有统计违法违纪行为的个人，应当承担纪律责任。属于下列人员的（以下统称有关责任人员），由任免机关或者监察机关按照管理权限依法给予处分：

（一）行政机关公务员；

（二）法律、法规授权的具有公共事务管理职能的事业单位中经批准参照《中华人民共和国公务员法》管理的工作人员；

（三）行政机关依法委托的组织中除工勤人员以外的工作人员；

（四）企业、事业单位、社会团体中由行政机关任命的人员。

法律、行政法规、国务院决定和国务院监察机关、国务院人力资源社会保障部门制定的处分规章对统计违法违纪行为的处分另有规定的，从其规定。

第三条 地方、部门以及企业、事业单位、社会团体的领导人员有下列行为之一的，给予记过或者记大过处分；情节较重的，给予降级或者撤职处分；情节严重的，给予开除处分：

（一）自行修改统计资料、编造虚假数据的；

（二）强令、授意本地区、本部门、本单位统计机构、统计人员或者其他有关机构、人员拒报、虚报、瞒报或者篡改统计资料、编造虚假数据的；

（三）对拒绝、抵制篡改统计资料或者对拒绝、抵制编造虚假数据的人员进行打击报复的；

（四）对揭发、检举统计违法违纪行为的人员进行打击报复的。

有前款第（三）项、第（四）项规定行为的，应当从重处分。

第四条 地方、部门以及企业、事业单位、社会团体的领导人员，对本地区、本部门、本单位严重失实的统计数据，应当发现而未发现或者发现后不予纠正，造成不良后果的，给予警告或者记过处分；造成严重后果的，给予记大过或者降级处分；造成特别严重后果的，给予撤职或者开除处分。

第五条 各级人民政府统计机构、有关部门及其工作人员在实施统计调查活动中，有下列行为之一的，对有关责任人员，给予记过或者记大过处分；情节较重的，给予降级或者撤职处分；情节严重的，给予开除处分：

（一）强令、授意统计调查对象虚报、瞒报或者伪造、篡改统计资料的；

（二）参与篡改统计资料、编造虚假数据的。

第六条 各级人民政府统计机构、有关部门及其工作人员在实施统计调查活动中，有下列行为之一的，对有关责任人员，给予警告、记过或者记大过处分；情节较重的，给予降级处分；情节严重的，给予撤职处分：

（一）故意拖延或者拒报统计资料的；

（二）明知统计数据不实，不履行职责调查核实，造成不良后果的。

第七条 统计调查对象中的单位有下列行为之一，情节较重的，对有关责任人员，给予警告、记过或者记大过处分；情节严重的，给予降级或者撤职处分；情节特别严重的，给予开除处分：

（一）虚报、瞒报统计资料的；

（二）伪造、篡改统计资料的；

（三）拒报或者屡次迟报统计资料的；

（四）拒绝提供情况、提供虚假情况或者转移、隐匿、毁弃原始统计记录、统计台账、统计报表以及与统计有关的其他资料的。

第八条 违反国家规定的权限和程序公布统计资料，造成不良后果的，对有关责任人员，给予警告或者记过处分；情节较重的，给予记大过或者降级处分；情节严重的，给予撤职处分。

第九条 有下列行为之一，造成不良后果的，对有关责任人员，给予警告、记过或者记大过处分；情节较重的，给予降级或者撤职处分；情节严重的，给予开除处分：

（一）泄露属于国家秘密的统计资料的；

（二）未经本人同意，泄露统计调查对象个人、家庭资料的；

（三）泄露统计调查中知悉的统计调查对象商业秘密的。

第十条 包庇、纵容统计违法违纪行为的，对有关责任人员，给予记过或者记大过处分；情节较重的，给予降级或者撤职处分；情节严重的，给予开除处分。

第十一条 受到处分的人员对处分决定不服的，依照《中华人民共和国行政监察法》、《中华人民共和国公务员法》、《行政机关公务员处分条例》等有关规定，可以申请复核或者申诉。

第十二条 任免机关、监察机关和人民政府统计机构建立案件移送制度。

任免机关、监察机关查处统计违法违纪案件，认为应当由人民政府统计机构给予行政处罚的，应当将有关案件材料移送人民政府统计机构。人民政府统计机构应当依法及时查处，并将处理结果书面告知任免机关、监察机关。

人民政府统计机构查处统计行政违法案件，认为应当由任免机关或者监察机关给予处分的，应当及时将有关案件材料移送任免机关或者监察机关。任免机关或者监察机关应当依法及时查处，并将处理结果书面告知人民政府统计机构。

第十三条 有统计违法违纪行为，应当给予党纪处分的，移送党的纪律检查机关处理。涉嫌犯罪的，移送司法机关依法追究刑事责任。

第十四条 本规定由监察部、人力资源社会保障部、国家统计局负责解释。

第十五条 本规定自2009年5月1日起施行。

附录七

济南市统计局二〇一八年统计工作大事记

Chronicle of Events of Jinan Statistical Undertaking

1 月初，济南市统计局荣获全市妇女儿童工作先进集体荣誉称号。

1 月初，济南统计局被授予“创建全国文明城市工作先进单位”荣誉称号。

1 月初，济南市统计局社情民意调查中心开展了“户外广告和牌匾标识整治提升行动”民意调查，撰写《合民心顺民意 市民点赞—济南市户外广告和牌匾标识整治提升行动民意调查报告》，山东省委副书记、济南市市委书记王文涛，市委副书记、市长王忠林，市委常委、宣传部部长杨峰等领导同志先后对调查报告作出批示。

1 月 3 日，济南市纪委派驻第六纪检组到市统计局就党风廉政建设工作与局党组全体成员及人事处、机关党委的负责人进行座谈，党组书记、局长苑子建向纪检六组介绍了党风廉政建设及统计工作情况。

1 月 16 日，济南统计局党组成员、副局长张谨国与市商务局一行赴槐荫区进行企业调研。

1 月中旬，王忠林市长就济南市统计局呈报的《关于 2017 年全年法人企业“上规入库”情况汇报》做出重要批示：“这项工作 2017 年做得很有成效，呈报文涛书记阅示。”

1 月 17 日，济南市委常委、副市长卢江到市统计局进行工作调研，与市统计局领导班子成员、部分业务处室负责人座谈交流。市政府办公厅副主任张蓉陪同调研。市统计局党组书记、局长苑子建汇报工作开展情况及下步工作要点。

1 月 22 日，国家统计局服务业统计司副司长刘富江一行到济南开展专题调研。省统计局副巡视员陆万明、服务业统计综合处处长彭丽芳，市统计局局长苑子健、副局长张谨国，历下区副区长刘佳等陪同调研。

1 月 23 日，济南市统计局召开党组（扩大）会议，专题传达学习全国、全省统计工作会议精神，安排部署下步工作。党组副书记、市社会经济调查局局长唐军主持会议。市统计局局级领导、各处室主要负责人参加会议。

2 月初，济南市委办公厅对 2017 年度全市党委信息工作考核进行了通报，济南局被评为信息工作先进单位。

2 月初，济南市政府办公厅通报了 2017 年政务信息采用情况，济南局以累计 1135 分的成绩在政府部门中排第 8 名，进入前十，为近十年来的最好成绩。

2 月 1 日，济南局领导班子成员，区县统计局局长，处室、执法监察支队、社情民意调查中心负责人参加《作风监督面对面》行风政风评议电视问政节目录制。

2 月 7 日，济南统计局党组组织召开了 2017 年度民主生活会。市统计局党组书记、局长苑子建主持会议并代表班子作对照检查，局全体党组成员参加会议。市委第七督导组到会指导，督导组组长韩新友代表市委作点评讲话。市纪委派驻第六纪检组组长郭尚兰、副组长程虎、市统计局组织人事处处长和机关党委专职副书记列席会议。

2 月 8 日，济南市召开全市统计系统局长座谈会，学习贯彻党的十九大、全国统计工作会议和全省统计工作会议精神、交流县区统计工作情况、筹备召开全市统计工作会议，安排部署 2018 年重点工作，市统计局领导班子和县区统计局长参加会议。

2 月 9 日，济南市局到平阴县东阿镇西南坝村、贾庄村、魏院村，对结对困难家庭开展帮扶和春节慰问，党组书记、局长苑子建，党组成员、副局长吕历源及副处级以上党员干部参加慰问活动。

3 月 12 日，市统计局党组召开党组（扩大）会议，认真组织传达学习习近平总书记在参加十三届全国人大一次会议山东代表团审议时的重要讲话精神。党组书记、局长苑子建主持会议并安排部署下一步工作。市统计局局领导班子和各处室（单位）负责人参加了学习，市纪委派驻第六纪检组邱鲁军到会指导。

3 月 12 日，市统计局党组书记、局长苑子建代表局党组与局属事业单位市统计执法监察支队、市社情民意调查中心 7 名新提任处级干部进行任前集体谈话。组织人事处处长张德军陪同谈话。

3 月 15 日，济南市统计学会第五次会员代表大会召开。全市政府统计系统，中央、省驻济单位，市直各相关部门，大专院校、科研院所，企事业单位等 120 余名会员代表出席了本次会议。

3 月 21 日，济南市委常委、副市长卢江同志带领市政府办公厅副主任张蓉同志、市统计局局长苑子建同志等相关人员组成调研组，对我市 8 家重点企业开展集中服务活动。历下区、天桥区分管负责同志、相关部门和所在办事处的同志陪同调研。

3 月 22 日下午，济南市委常委、副市长徐群同志率市发改委、市统计局等相关人员，山东高速集团有限公司、山东出版传媒股份有限公司两家服务业企业进行实地走访调研。

3 月 23 日，济南市政府召开第 26 次常务会议，审议通过了市统计局起草的《关于深化统计管理体制改革提高统计数据真实性的实施意见》。市统计局党组书记、局长苑子建进行了汇报并提出了下一步工作建议。济南市委副书记、市长王忠林对全市统计工作给予充分肯定。市发改委、经信委、财政局、人力资源社会保障局、城乡建设委、城乡交通运输委、农业局、商务局、工商局等部门列席会议。同时邀请市监察委、市委组织部、市编办、市信访局列席。

3月28日，济南局召开2018年全市统计工作会议。深入学习贯彻党的十九大和中央、省经济工作会议精神，山东省全面展开新旧动能转换重大工程动员大会和全国、全省统计工作会议精神，传达学习市委副书记、市长王忠林同志和市委常委、副市长卢江同志对统计工作提出的要求，总结2017年统计工作，安排部署2018年工作重点任务。

3月28日，济南局召开2018年度全市统计系统党风廉政建设工作会议。市纪委纪检监察派驻六组组长郭尚兰到会指导并讲话，各县区统计局、高新区科技经济运行局负责人，市统计局各处室副处级以上干部参加会议。

3月30日，省统计局总统计师李坤道一行四人来济调研“5+5”十强产业发展情况。济南局副局长吕历源陪同调研。

3月30日，济南局召开“大学习、大调研、大改进”动员大会，会议由统计局党组副书记、市社会经济调查局局长唐军主持，党组书记苑子建传达全市“大学习、大调研、大改进”会议精神并讲话。

4月1日，济南市副市长李自军会同相关部门对重点商贸企业开展“大学习、大调研、大改进”服务活动，市政府办公厅副秘书长杨永斌同志，市商务局、市统计局主要负责同志和分管负责同志，历下区、市中区、天桥区、历城区主要负责同志和分管负责同志及相关部门负责人陪同调研。

4月12日，省统计局执法监督局局长官照华、投资处处长刘毅一行到济南四建（集团）有限责任公司、山东黄河工程集团有限公司进行调研，济南市局巡视员刘东涛陪同调研。

4月19日，济南市委第八巡察组巡察市统计局（市社会经济调查局）党组工作动员会召开。市委第八巡察组组长董悦华就开展巡察工作作动员讲话。市纪委常委、市委巡察工作领导小组成员、巡察办主任魏莉萍就配合做好巡察工作提出要求。市统计局党组书记、局长苑子建主持会议并作表态发言。

5月10日，济南市政府召开加强统计基层基础建设工作专题会议，市委常委、副市长卢江，市统计局党组成员，各区县政府、高新区管委会、南部山区管委会分管负责同志及统计部门主要负责同志参加会议，市政府办公厅副主任张蓉主持会议。

5月18日，济南市政府组织收看全省第四经济普查电视会议，副市长王桂英，市统计局班子成员，市有关部门分管负责同志在济南市分会场参加会议。

5月20日—26日，济南市局举办第一期全市统计干部学习党的十九大精神暨综合能力提升培训班，各县区统计局、市局各处室、省、市有关部门统计业务骨干参加培训。

5月22日，济南市局召开局长办公会议，专门听取第四次经济普查前期工作情况汇报，并对下步工作进行部署。

5月23日，济南市局启动“精准扶贫慈善捐款”仪式，局领导班子成员争当表率，带头捐款，各处室负责人与全局党员干部职工踊跃参与，慷慨捐款。

6月6日，济南市委常委、副市长卢江会同有关部门对对口企业开展服务帮扶活动。市政府办公厅、市发改委有关领导，济南市局党组书记、局长苑子建陪同调研。

6月12日，济南市局召开局长办公会专题审议深入贯彻落实深化统计管理体制改革，提高统计数据真实性实施意见的相关文件。

6月15日，省统计局党组成员、副局长马金栋一行到济南高新区调研。济南市副市长孙斌，市统计局局长苑子建、副局长张谨国，高新区管委会副主任白秋生、科技经济运行局局长刘宪宝等陪同调研。

6月19日，济南市第四次经济普查专项试点动员暨业务培训会议在济南市长清区举行。济南市局党组成员、副局长、市经普办常务副主任谈友军出席会议并做动员讲话。

6月21日，国家发改委副主任、国家统计局局长、党组书记宁吉喆一行来济南调研，省委常委、市委书记王忠林，省统计局局长陈迪桂，市委常委、秘书长蒋晓光，市委常委、副市长卢江，市统计局局长苑子建等陪同调研。

6月25日，济南市局召开警示教育会议，党组书记、局长苑子建上廉政党课，党组成员、副局长崔瑞宁传达全市“汲取教训 严守规矩 强化担当”警示教育会议精神，全体干部职工参加会议。

6月28日，国家统计局人口和就业统计司专项调查处处长崔红艳一行在省统计局城镇化和人口就业统计处处长孙明清陪同下，到济南调研1％人口抽样调查手册的编写工作，市统计局局长苑子建、副局长崔瑞宁参加调研。

7月3日，济南市局贯彻落实《中共济南市委办公厅印发〈关于在“大学习、大调研、大改进”中开展“三照三转三改三推”活动的实施方案〉的通知》要求，召开全体人员大会，对全局开展“三照三转三改三推”活动作动员部署。

7月上旬，济南市局服务业处何宇晖同志撰写的《改善营商环境，济南等不起！——济南市营商环境调查报告》获市委副书记、市长孙述涛批示。调查报告中企业集中反映的问题得到相关部门的高度重视。

7月12日，国家统计局人口和就业统计司普查处处长武超一行，到济南调研全国第七次人口普查试点工作，省统计局副局长周尊考、省统计局城镇化和人口就业统计处处长孙明清陪同调研，济南市委常委、副市长卢江、市统计局局长苑子建、副局长崔瑞宁参加调研。

7月31日，省统计局二级巡视员、省经普办常务副主任陆万明一行，到济南市督导检查四经普“五落实”情况。副市长孙斌，市统计局党组书记、局长、市经济普查领导小组副组长苑子建，市统计局党组成员、副局长、市经普办常务副主任谈友军陪同检查。

8月13日，济南市政府召开全市第四次经济普查工作会议，市委常委、副市长、市第四次经济普查领导小组组长卢江到会并讲话，副组长、市统计局局长苑子建通报了全市经济普查进展情况及下一步工作安排。各县区、高新区、南部山区管委会、有关部门分管负责同志参加会议。

8月20日，济南市局党组理论学习中心组围绕《习近平谈治国理政》第二卷第六个专题“坚定不移贯彻新发展理念”进行集中学习研讨，局党组书记、局长、中心组组长苑子建主持学习，各中心组成员参加会议并交流，市纪委派驻第六纪检组副组长李强到会指导，市统计局有关处室负责人列席会议。

8月21日—23日，济南市局认真学习贯彻全省统计系统党组中心组（扩大）理论学习读书会精神，举办全市统计系统党组中心组（扩大）理论学习读书会暨统计业务骨干培训班，市局党组中心组成员，副处级以上干部，调研课题主要执笔人，各县区统计局、高新区科技经济运行局党组（党支部）书记、局长参加会议。市纪委派驻第六纪检监察组组长郭尚兰、正科级纪检员郑尔贤到会指导。

9月1日，李自军副市长利用周六就餐的高峰期，对舜和餐饮集团所属的三家企业的经营情况进行实地“暗访”，与企业负责人进行交流，听取了企业今年以来的经营情况、发展趋势以及在经营中碰到的困难和问题。市商务局、市统计局相关部门负责人陪同调研。

9月初，国家统计局人口和就业统计司一级调研员刘勇利一行来济南与省、市、区统计局共同对全国第七次人口普查住房试点工作开展座谈。刘勇利对当前的试点工作给予了充分肯定。希望下一步继续克服困难，不断探索新的经验做法，发现更多新问题，确保全面完成试点工作。

9月10日，国家统计局人口和就业统计司普查处处长武超和住建部房地产司陈勇处长一行9人，在山东省统计局副局长周尊考和人口处处长孙明清的陪同下，到济南市槐荫区就全国第七次人口普查住房试点工作进行调研座谈。汇报会前，槐荫区委书记国承彦、区长朱玉明会见了调研组一行。市统计局局长苑子建主持了汇报会。会后，调研组实地查看了我市普查试点各项部门行政资料获取及利用情况。

9月10日至12日，国家统计局人口和就业统计司普查处处长武超一行在济南进行第七次人口普查住房试点调查工作督导。调研组实地调研了6个试点村居的建筑物分布绘制、现场登记等工作，详细了解了试点村居各类住房情况及工作中的问题及建议。

9月13日−14日，省统计局社会经济调查中心主任李玉国、副主任袁晓勇一行3人，对济南市商河县、济阳区开展统计基层基础建设工作专项督查。督查组分别听取了济南市统计局、商河县统计局、济阳区统计局《关于鲁政办字〔2018〕43号和鲁统字〔2018〕63号》文件的贯彻落实情况，以及前期工作开展情况汇报。市统计局巡视员刘东涛、商河县常务副县长陈晓东、济阳区常务副区长高继锋陪同督查。

9月20日，由山东省第四次经济普查领导小组、山东省统计局、国家统计局山东调查总队、济南市人民政府主办，济南市第四次经济普查领导小组、济南市统计局、国家统计局济南调查队、济南日报报业集团承办的第九届“中国统计开放日”活动在泉城广场举行。

9月25日，济南市局召开第四次经济普查清查督查动员暨培训会议，结合全市第四次经济普查单位清查工作进展情况，就第四次经济普查清查督查工作进行了部署。市统计局局长、经普办主任苑子建出席会议并讲话。

9月27日，省经普办常务副主任、省统计局二级巡视员陆万明带工作组前往济南市历城区，对第四次经济普查清查工作情况进行了督导检查，济南市经普办常务副主任、市统计局副局长谈友军带工作组陪同督查。

9月27日−28日，张谨国副局长带领第五督导组赴天桥区、济阳区开展第四次经济普查单位清查阶段督导工作。

9月28日，第七次全国人口普查住房试点调查总结座谈会在我市举行。国家统计局副局长贾楠，国家统计局人口和就业统计司司长李希如，济南市委常委、副市长卢江，省统计局局长陈迪桂，省统计局副局长陈汉臻，市统计局局长苑子建、副局长崔瑞宁，槐荫区区长朱玉明等出席会议，陈汉臻主持会议。

9月28日，国家统计局副局长贾楠一行深入济南市槐荫区普查试点社区，检查指导第七次全国人口普查住房试点工作。进社区看望慰问了调查员，对调查员的辛勤工作表示慰问和感谢。省统计局副局长陈汉臻，市统计局局长苑子建和市、区试点单位相关人员陪同检查。

9月29日，济南市局党组书记、局长苑子建带领第四次经济普查督导小组，到南部山区管委会现场督导单位清查工作。南部山区管委会副主任曲永伦陪同督导。

9月27和29日，由济南市局副局长吕历源带队，第四督查组分别对平阴县和槐荫区进行了督导检查。

10月8日，根据市委巡察工作领导小组安排，市委第八巡察组向市统计局（市社会经济调查局）党组反馈巡察情况。市纪委常委、市委巡察工作领导小组成员、市委巡察办主任魏莉萍向市统计局（市社会经济调查局）党组书记、局长苑子建传达了省委常委、市委书记王忠林在市委书记专题会议上的讲话精神，市委第八巡察组组长董悦华向苑子建反馈了巡察情况。随后，董悦华代表市委巡察组向市统计局党组进行了反馈，魏莉萍对巡察整改工作提出要求。苑子建主持会议并作表态发言。

10月8日，国家统计局副局长鲜祖德一行到济南市调研工业企业运行情况和第四次经济普查单位清查工作。市委常委、副市长卢江，省统计局二级巡视员陆万明，市统计局局长苑子建，副局长谈友军，历下区区委副书记、区长谢兆村等陪同调研。

10月12日，济南市召开全市第四次经济普查工作会议。会议通报了全市单位清查督查情况，安排部署了单位清查省级督查迎查工作、全市上规入库和行业编码工作。市统计局局长、市经普办主任苑子建出席会议并讲话，市统计局副局长、市经普办常务副主任谈友军主持会议。

10月12日，为进一步推进机关党组织联系社区工作，全面深入准确了解掌握社区实际情况，积极引导在职党员发挥先锋模范作用,持续推进“两学一做”学习教育常态化制度化，结合“不忘初心、牢记使命”主题教育以及“大学习、大调研、大改进”活动，在了解到洪北社区在全国第四次经济普查工作中遇到困难的情况，市统计局迅速反应，党组书记、局长苑子建亲自带领一行人深入社区，开展社区共建及统计服务进社区活动。历城区区委书记吴承丙、副区长张庆国，区政协副主席、统计局局长吕大海、党组书记谷艳等人一同来到洪北社区参加了此次活动。

10月15日，在九九重阳节来临之际，为进一步弘扬中华民族"尊老、敬老、爱老、助老"的传统美德，以及丰富老年人的精神文化生活，我局在帮扶的平阴县西南坝村开展了宣传党十九大精神、扫黑除恶等文艺节目。

10月18日，济南市召开全市第四次经济普查领导小组第一次（扩大）会议。市委常委、副市长、市第四次经济普查领导小组组长卢江出席会议并讲话，市统计局局长、市第四次经济普查领导小组副组长苑子建汇报了全市经济普查工作进展情况。会议由市政府办公厅副主任张蓉主持。

10月18日，市委常委、副市长、市第四次经济普查领导小组组长卢江，在市统计局局长、市第四次经济普查领导小组副组长苑子建的陪同下，于龙奥大厦北大厅参观“经济大普查助力新动能——济南市第四次经济普查单位清查宣传展示”。

10月24日，省经普办常务副主任、省统计局二级巡视员陆万明率督查组对我市单位清查工作进行督导检查。济南市经普办常务副主任、市统计局副局长谈友军，市中区副区长付华陪同督查。

10月30日，市统计局党组书记、局长苑子建带队走进直播间参加济南人民广播电台《作风监督热线》节目，现场解答统计工作和经济普查等方面的问题。局、队相关处室参加了直播。

10月31日，济南市委常委、副市长卢江同志赴省统计局，拜会了新到任省统计局局长郭训成同志，济南市统计局局长苑子建参加了相关活动。

近期，市统计局召开共青团济南市统计局支部委员会换届选举工作会议。机关党委组织委员张德军同志以及局团员青年参加了会议。会后，召开新一届的共青团济南市统计局委员会第一次全体会议，选举支部书记、宣传委员、文艺委员、组织委员和学习委员。

11月15日，我市召开全市第四次经济普查工作推进会议。市委常委、副市长、市第四次经济普查领导小组组长卢江出席会议并讲话，市统计局局长、市第四次经济普查领导小组办公室主任苑子建通报了全市单位清查情况，市工商局、税务局以及各区县政府负责同志发言。

11月16日，为促进我市经济发展，打造“金牌环境”，建立“亲清”政商关系，济南市统计局党组书记、局长苑子建一行到高新区迪亚实业有限公司调研座谈，开展对接服务。

12月10日，为贯彻落实中央、省、市关于“把统计法纳入各级党校、行政学院、干部学院、社会主义学院领导干部教育培训的必修课”工作要求，突出普法重点，拓展宣传渠道，推进我市统计普法向纵深发展，济南市统计局党组书记、局长苑子建同志应邀为济南市委党校优秀年轻干部递进式培训班（中青班）学员作了题为“深化统计改革，坚持依法统计，为推动经济实现更高质量发展提供统计保障”的专题辅导报告。

12月10日，济南市统计局会同市委组织部、财政局、市人力资源和社会保障局联合发文印发《济南市基层统计人才培育工程实施办法》的通知（济统字〔2018〕51号），通知要求建立健全基层统计人才培养机制，加快培育一支高素质、专业化，适应统计工作转型变革需要的基层统计人才队伍。

12月16日，市统计局党组副书记、调查局局长唐军主持召开了我市第三次农业普查课题结项评审会议，邀请省社科院、省委党校和市委党校等科研单位的专家组成评审委员会，对中标课题研究成果进行了认真审阅和评审。

12月27日，由省统计局二级巡视员、省经普办常务副主任陆万明带队，省经普调研组一行六人来我市指导调研四经普工作。市人大副主任孙积港、市政府办公厅副主任张蓉出席座谈会，市统计局局长、市第四次经济普查领导小组副组长兼办公室主任苑子建向调研组汇报了我市第四次经济普查开展情况。市统计局领导班子成员、相关业务处室负责人参加座谈。

12月28日，济南市政府新闻办召开第四次经济普查新闻发布会。市统计局新闻发言人、副局长崔瑞宁向媒体通报了全市第四次经济普查工作有关情况，市第四次经济普查领导小组办公室常务副主任、副局长谈友军出席发布会。发布会由市新闻办副主任石舒波主持。

中国统计出版社有限公司最新图书简目

(仅供参考,以实际出版为准)

统计资料

中国统计年鉴　中国统计摘要　中国第三产业统计年鉴
中国第三次全国农业普查综合资料　国际统计年鉴　金砖国家联合统计手册
中国-东盟国家统计手册　中国农村统计年鉴　中国县域统计年鉴
中国农产品价格调查年鉴　中国城市统计年鉴　中国价格统计年鉴
中国贸易外经统计年鉴　中国零售和餐饮连锁企业统计年鉴　中国商品交易市场统计年鉴
大中型批发零售和住宿餐饮企业统计年鉴　中国住户调查年鉴　中国工业统计年鉴
中国环境统计年鉴　中国能源统计年鉴　中国建筑业统计年鉴
中国房地产统计年鉴　中国固定资产投资统计年鉴　中国对外直接投资统计公报
中国人口和就业统计年鉴　中国劳动统计年鉴　中国社会统计年鉴
中国科技统计年鉴　中国高技术产业统计年鉴　全国企业创新调查年鉴
中国文化及相关产业统计年鉴　2018年时间利用调查资料　中国妇女儿童状况统计资料
中国基本单位统计年鉴　中国教育统计年鉴　中国教育经费统计年鉴
中国民族统计年鉴　中国残疾人事业统计年鉴　长江经济带发展统计年鉴

省级综合统计年鉴系列

北京 天津 河北 山西 内蒙古 辽宁 吉林 黑龙江 上海 江苏 浙江 安徽 福建 江西 山东 河南 湖北 湖南
广东 广西 海南 重庆 四川 贵州 云南 西藏 陕西 甘肃 青海 宁夏 新疆 新疆生产建设兵团

市(县)级综合统计年鉴系列

滨海新区 石家庄 唐山 邯郸 保定 沧州 邢台 廊坊 承德 衡水 秦皇岛 张家口 太原 大同 阳泉 长治 晋城
朔州 晋中 运城 忻州 临汾 吕梁 呼和浩特 鄂尔多斯 包头 沈阳 大连 长春 延吉 四平 白山 通化 哈尔滨
齐齐哈尔 黑龙江垦区 上海浦东新区 南京 无锡 徐州 常州 苏州 南通 连云港 淮安 盐城 扬州 镇江 泰州
宿迁 江阴 丹阳 海门 张家港 杭州 宁波 温州 嘉兴 湖州 绍兴 金华 衢州 舟山 台州 丽水 合肥 安庆 福州
厦门 宁德 漳州 龙岩 莆田 泉州 三明 南平 南昌 九江 上饶 新余 抚州 赣州 景德镇 济南 青岛 潍坊 枣庄
潍坊 聊城 郑州 洛阳 平顶山 三门峡 南阳 商丘 信阳 济源 汝州 武汉 十堰 荆州 宜昌 荆门 咸宁 黄冈
长沙 鹰潭 广州 深圳 惠州 东莞 汕尾 湛江 肇庆 南宁 柳州 桂林 贵港 梧州 来宾 河池 防城港 海口 三亚
儋州 成都 内江 贵阳 黔南 毕节 昆明 文山 德宏 西安 延安 安康 铜川 汉中 商洛 银川 兰州 庆阳 乌鲁木齐
昌吉 阿勒泰 兵团一师、二师、三师、四师、六师、七师、八师、十师、十三师、十四师

调查年鉴系列

天津 内蒙古 上海 河南 湖北 湖南 广东 广西 重庆 四川 云南 甘肃 宁夏 南宁 贵港 昆明

统计方法应用/实用手册

Python数据分析基础（第二版）　医用多元统计分析（第三版）　中华生物统计用表
中国国民经济核算体系（2016）基础知识　国民经济核算初级教程　医学统计学手册
全国统计专业技术资格考试系列考试用书：统计业务知识（第四版修订版）　统计业务知识学习指导与习题
全国统计专业技术资格考试系列考试用书：统计相关知识（第四版）　统计相关知识学习指导与习题

统计通俗读物/统计科普图书

领导干部统计知识问答　《防范和惩治统计造假、弄虚作假督察工作规定》辅导读本
统计新媒体运营指南　统计公文知识问答　理解国民账户　中国古代统计史简编

重点图书

新中国70年　第三次全国农业普查农作物面积遥感测量图集　中国第四次经济普查年鉴
新编英汉汉英统计大词典　中国国民经济核算体系2016　国民经济行业分类注释
挑大学选专业2019—考研择校指南　挑大学选专业2019—高考志愿填报指南　中华医学统计百科全书

发行部电话：（010）63376907　63376908　63376909　同棋行书店电话：68783171　68783172
地址：北京市丰台区西三环南路甲6号　邮政编码：100073　网址：http://www.zgtjcbs.com